THE
ARMED CONFLICT SURVEY

2024

The worldwide review of
political, military and humanitarian
trends in current conflicts

published by

for

The International Institute for Strategic Studies

The International Institute for Strategic Studies
Arundel House | 6 Temple Place | London | WC2R 2PG | UK

THE ARMED CONFLICT SURVEY 2024

First published December 2024 by **Routledge**
4 Park Square, Milton Park, Abingdon, Oxon, OX14 4RN

for **The International Institute for Strategic Studies**
Arundel House, 6 Temple Place, London, WC2R 2PG, UK

Simultaneously published in the USA and Canada by **Routledge**
52 Vanderbilt Avenue, New York, NY 10017

Routledge is an imprint of Taylor & Francis, an Informa business

© 2024 The International Institute for Strategic Studies

DIRECTOR-GENERAL AND CHIEF EXECUTIVE Dr Bastian Giegerich
EDITOR Dr Irene Mia
CONSULTING EDITOR Dr Benjamin Petrini
ASSOCIATE EDITOR Jana Phillips
GRAPHICS COORDINATOR Adam Walters
EDITORIAL Christopher Harder, Lauren Whelan
DESIGN AND PRODUCTION Alessandra Beluffi, Ravi Gopar, Charlotte Gurr, James Lemon, Jade Panganiban, James Parker, Kelly Verity, Jillian Williams
COUNTRY PROFILES Adam Weinstein (Afghanistan and Pakistan), Dr Ryan Berg (Brazil), Grace Ellis and Mathijs Cazemier (Burkina Faso, Mali and Niger), Dr Carlo Palleschi (Cameroon, Central African Republic and Mozambique), Constantin Gouvy (Chad), Juan Pablo Medina Bickel (Colombia), Dr Umberto Profazio (Egypt and Libya), Tiziano Breda (El Salvador and Honduras), Dr Dan Watson (Ethiopia, Nigeria, Somalia, South Sudan and Sudan), Sandra Pellegrini (Haiti), Dr Alex Waterman (India and Kashmir), Deka Anwar (Indonesia), Dr Haid Haid (Iraq and Syria), Rym Momtaz (Lebanon and Israel–Palestinian Territories), Kathryn Babineau (Mexico), Hein Htet (Myanmar), Maximilian Hess (Nagorno-Karabakh and Russia–Ukraine), Michael Hart (Philippines), Don Pathan (Thailand), Dr Federico Donelli (Turkiye), Wolf-Christian Paes (Yemen)
REGIONAL ANALYSES Dr Irene Mia, Juan Pablo Medina Bickel and Callum Fraser (Americas), Adam Weinstein (Asia), Maximilian Hess (Europe and Eurasia), Dr Neda Bolourchi, Sascha Bruchmann and Dr Benjamin Petrini (Middle East and North Africa), Dr Benjamin Petrini (Sub-Saharan Africa)
REGIONAL SPOTLIGHTS John Raine and Erica Pepe (The Centrality of Non-state Armed Groups in Iran's Foreign Policy and Strategic Thinking), Dr Federico Donelli (The Ethiopia–Somaliland MoU: A Driver of Regional Instability?), Douglas Farah (The Expansion and Diversification of Mexican Cartels: Dynamic New Actors and Markets), Dr Dimitar Bechev (The Western Balkans: Controlled Instability?), Rahul Roy-Chaudhury (Towards the Reintegration of Afghanistan into the International Community)
THE CHART OF ARMED CONFLICT Erica Pepe, Birna Gudmundsdottir, Juan Pablo Medina Bickel
RESEARCH CONTRIBUTIONS Dr Hasan Alhasan, Matthew Bamber, Edward Beales, Henry Boyd, Karl Dewey, Dr Nigel Gould-Davies, James Hackett, Emile Hokayem, Jumpei Ishimaru, Gauthier Lefèvre, Antoine Levesques, Iris Madeline, Morgan Michaels, Munya Yusuf, Christopher Zoromski

COVER IMAGES Getty Images

All rights reserved. No part of this book may be reprinted or reproduced or utilised in any form or by any electronic, mechanical, or other means, now known or hereafter invented, including photocopying and recording, or in any information storage or retrieval system, without permission in writing from the publisher.

British Library Cataloguing in Publication Data
A catalogue record for this book is available from the British Library

Library of Congress Cataloguing in Publication Data

ISBN: 978-1-041-00457-8 (Paperback)
ISBN: 978-1-003-60993-3 (eBook)
ISSN 2374-0973

Hizbullah militants and supporters attend the funeral of Ali al-Debs, one of the group's commanders, in Nabatieh, Lebanon, 16 February 2024

Contents

Editor's Introduction 5

Notes on Methodology 13

Regional Sections 19

1 Americas 20
   Regional Analysis 20
   Regional Spotlight
     The Expansion and Diversification of Mexican
     Cartels: Dynamic New Actors and Markets 34
   Country Profiles
     Mexico 40
     Colombia 48
     Brazil 54
     Haiti 60
     El Salvador 66
     Honduras 72

2 Europe and Eurasia 78
   Regional Analysis 78
   Regional Spotlight
     The Western Balkans: Controlled Instability? 90
   Country Profiles
     Russia–Ukraine 96
     Nagorno-Karabakh 102

3 Middle East and North Africa 108
   Regional Analysis 108
   Regional Spotlight
     The Centrality of Non-state Armed Groups in
     Iran's Foreign Policy and Strategic Thinking 120
   Country Profiles
     Syria 126
     Iraq 132
     Israel–Palestinian Territories 138
     Lebanon 144
     Yemen 150
     Libya 156
     Egypt 162
     Turkiye 166

Sudanese refugee families arrive at a transit centre in Renk, South Sudan, 13 February 2024

4 Sub-Saharan Africa	170
Regional Analysis	170
Regional Spotlight	
The Ethiopia–Somaliland MoU: A Driver of Regional Instability?	182
Country Profiles	
Mali	186
Burkina Faso	192
Niger	198
Nigeria	204
Cameroon	212
Chad	220
Central African Republic	226
Sudan	232
South Sudan	238
Ethiopia	244
Somalia	252
Democratic Republic of the Congo	258
Uganda	266
Mozambique	270
5 Asia	274
Regional Analysis	274
Regional Spotlight	
Towards the Reintegration of Afghanistan into the International Community	286
Country Profiles	
Afghanistan	292
Pakistan	298
Kashmir	304
Myanmar	310
India	318
Thailand	324
Philippines	328
Indonesia	334
Data Appendix	339
Index	361

Editor's Introduction

As we approach the final quarter of 2024, the global outlook for peace remains bleak. The world is experiencing an unprecedented number of conflicts, which appear increasingly intractable due to the growing involvement of both domestic and external actors, a complex array of underlying drivers, and escalating geopolitical tensions.[1] The conflicts in Gaza, Sudan and Ukraine – arguably the most consequential of 2023–24 due to their geopolitical significance and human impact – are amplified examples of these broader trends. Meanwhile, the intensity and human cost of armed conflicts continue to surge (see Figure 1). Fatalities from violent events rose by 37% year-on-year during the reporting period (1 July 2023–30 June 2024) of *The Armed Conflict Survey 2024*, reaching nearly 200,000 globally. Although fatalities slightly declined in the Americas (-9%) and Asia (-3%), they skyrocketed by 315% in the Middle East and North Africa (MENA) region. This was primarily driven by spiralling violence in the Palestinian Territories, where deaths related to violent events soared to nearly 40,000 compared to 321 in the previous year. Significant year-on-year increases in fatalities were also recorded (in descending order) in Israel, Lebanon, Azerbaijan, Sudan and Niger. Additionally, the overall ratio of fatalities per event increased by approximately 17%, underscoring the growing intensity and lethality of armed violence.[2]

This disheartening state of affairs is unfolding at the same time that the resources available to affected governments and international actors to address the unprecedented reconstruction and humanitarian needs created by ongoing armed violence are becoming increasingly strained. The United Nations Office for the Coordination of Humanitarian Affairs' (UNOCHA) latest Global Humanitarian Overview report calculates that over 290 million people are in need of assistance in 2024. Of the US$48.3 billion required to support the 182.2m people targeted for relief, only US$7.3bn in humanitarian funding had been raised by the end of April 2024, reflecting a 36% decrease year-on-year.[3] Financial gaps have been compounded by successive external shocks in recent years including the coronavirus pandemic and the impact of the Russia–Ukraine war on food and energy security. These factors, combined with the accelerating climate crisis, have also intensified the root causes of conflict. The financial resources needed for the reconstruction of Ukraine and Gaza are stark examples of these challenges. The World Bank estimates that Ukraine's reconstruction and recovery will cost nearly US$486bn over the next decade, while the direct damage to Gaza's infrastructure exceeds US$18.5bn, amounting to 97% of the Palestinian Territories' total GDP in 2022.[4]

The above underscores the urgent need to thoroughly understand conflict drivers, actors and external influences, and repercussions in order to develop innovative policies and solutions aimed at reducing armed violence globally. *The Armed Conflict Survey* series has long contributed to this endeavour by unpacking the complexities of conflicts as well as offering strategic analyses of the factors that must be considered by policymakers and peacebuilding operators to design effective policies and strategies to address armed conflicts.

The resurgence of inter-state conflicts

The reporting period saw a further acceleration of a crucial trend that *The Armed Conflict Survey* series has highlighted since its inception in 2015: the growing internationalisation of internal conflicts. Civil wars, which remain the dominant form of conflict globally, are increasingly shaped by the intervention of regional and global powers pursuing their strategic interests. As noted in last year's report, this trend is driven by heightened great-power competition and the more assertive foreign-policy stances of many emerging powers, set against a backdrop of increasing geopolitical fragmentation.

While Russia's invasion of Ukraine in February 2022 had already marked an inflection point in this dynamic, developments in the reporting period have further underscored the growing risk of inter-state wars. Beyond the continuation of the Russia–Ukraine war, now in its third year, the outbreak of the

Editor's Introduction

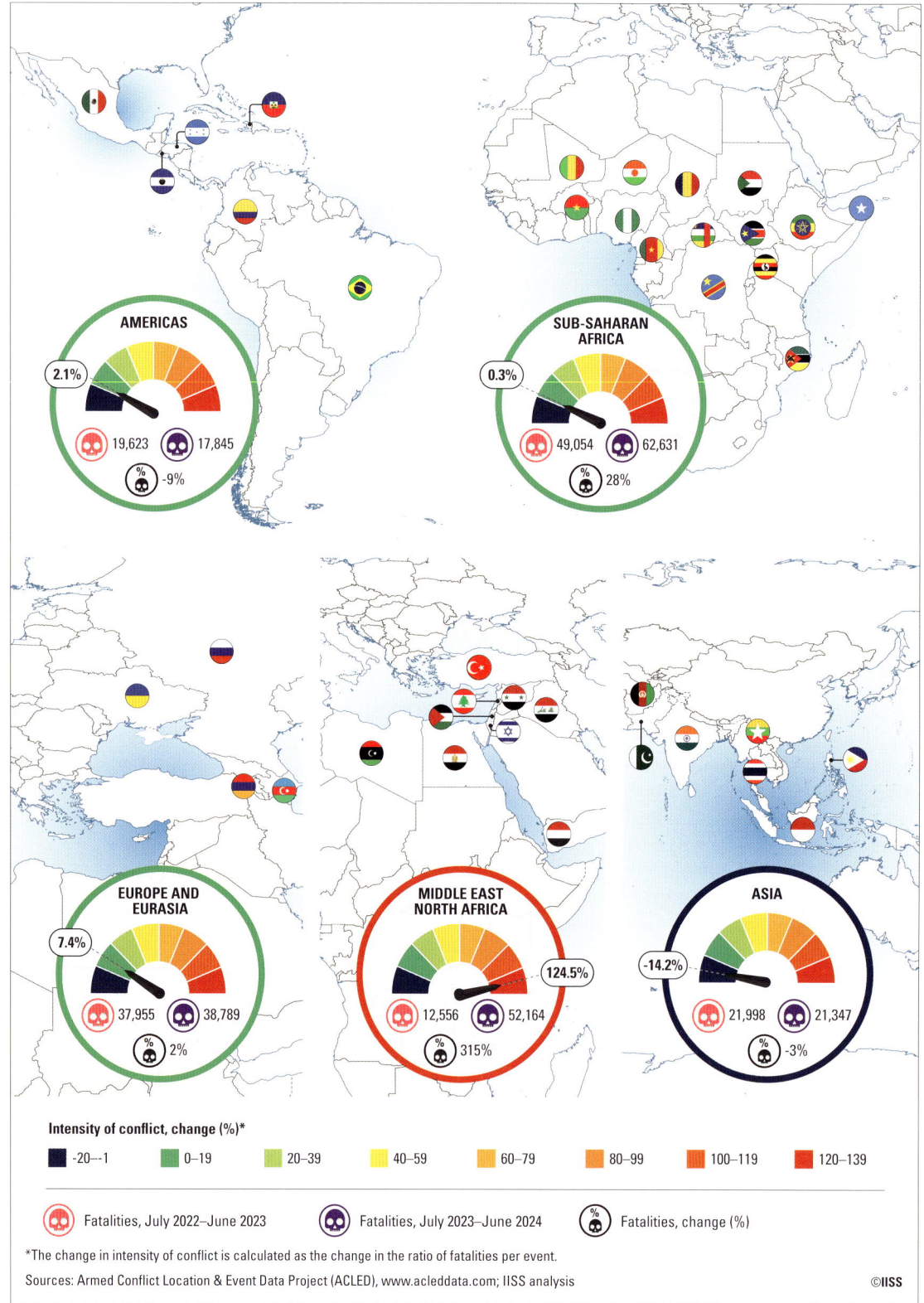

Figure 1: Human impact and intensity of conflict

Israel–Hamas war has destabilised the Middle East and beyond, threatening the start of various inter-state conflicts, most notably a full-scale war between Iran and Israel, after decades of low-intensity proxy conflict between the two. In Asia, tensions between the United States and China over the Taiwan Strait, between Pakistan and India along the Line of Control (LoC), and between China and India along the Line of Actual Control (LAC) retained the potential to turn into major conventional wars, with nuclear implications. In Sub-Saharan Africa, frictions between the Democratic Republic of the Congo (DRC) and Rwanda and between Ethiopia and Somalia, as well as the stand-off between Niger (alongside Mali and Burkina Faso) and the Economic Community of West African States, particularly Nigeria, all posed significant risks of escalating into inter-state conflicts. Even in the Americas, a region that has not experienced a major inter-state conflict since the 1930s, bilateral tensions flared up after a referendum in Venezuela in December 2023 reaffirmed its claim over the oil-rich Essequibo region, a long-disputed territory of Guyana. While the crisis was de-escalated through international mediation, it heightened the risk of the first inter-state confrontation occurring in the region in nearly a century.

The turmoil in the Middle East following Hamas's unprecedented attack on Israel on 7 October 2023 has likely been the most visible and concerning development in this trend. Hamas's close ties with the Iran-led 'Axis of Resistance' – which includes various non-state armed groups (NSAGs) in Iraq, Lebanon, Syria and Yemen – prompted retaliatory attacks on Israel and its allies in response to Israel's offensive in Gaza. In Lebanon, Hizbullah re-engaged in conflict with Israel, with violence escalating throughout the reporting period and Israel decapitating the group's leadership and invading southern Lebanon in September–October 2024.

In Iraq and Syria, Iran's proxies launched repeated assaults on US and Western military forces, while in Yemen, Ansarullah (the Houthis) repeatedly targeted Western commercial vessels in the Red Sea and Gulf of Aden using missiles, uninhabited aerial vehicles and uninhabited surface vessels. More alarmingly, the events in Gaza inflamed the Iran–Israel low-intensity conflict, culminating in Iran's first direct attack on Israel since the establishment of the Islamic Republic in 1979 in April 2024 – in response to a deadly Israeli strike on an Iranian embassy complex in Syria. Given the United States' and Western Europe's unwavering support for Israel, this regional crisis has escalated into an international one.

The repercussions of growing geopolitical fragmentation

The foreign-policy assertiveness of non-Western powers intensified during the reporting period, with Russia serving as a prime example. Beyond its ongoing war in Ukraine in violation of international law, Russia has remained active in crucial theatres in the MENA region. More notably, following the collapse of the Wagner Group after the death of its chief, Yevgeny Prigozhin, in August 2023, Russia has increased its direct involvement in Sub-Saharan Africa through the Africa Corps, controlled by Russia's Ministry of Defence. This move has solidified Moscow's security and diplomatic influence in the region and reinforced its anti-Western agenda, especially in the Sahel. Russia has deepened ties with the military regimes in Burkina Faso, Mali and Niger, formalising security partnerships with these countries.

Russia's efforts to secure allies, coupled with the rise of other emerging powers and growing resentment from many countries in the Global South towards the West's perceived disengagement and double standards (particularly regarding Israel's actions in Gaza), have continued to fuel geopolitical fragmentation. This has notably undermined the legitimacy and effectiveness of established conflict-resolution mechanisms and international law more broadly.

The UN Security Council has continued to struggle to fulfil its primary role of maintaining global peace and security due to internal divisions fuelled by geopolitical fragmentation. The inability of the international system and Western powers (such as the US) to broker ceasefires in conflicts like those in Gaza and Sudan, or mediate domestic and international conflicts, including those between Russia and Ukraine, Ethiopia and Somalia, and the DRC and Rwanda, and in Venezuela after its contested elections in July 2024, has been a constant feature of the reporting period. Meanwhile, emerging geopolitical powers, such as the Gulf countries, Brazil, China and Turkiye, have also failed to demonstrate greater effectiveness in their mediation efforts.

In addition, international humanitarian law has come under increasing attack. The conflicts in

Sudan and Gaza have been marred by widespread violations and alleged war crimes perpetrated by all parties involved. Both state actors and NSAGs have shown a blatant disregard for civilian lives, resulting in alarming levels of displacement, including 90% of Gazans and 7.7m internally displaced Sudanese.[5] These violations have included the use of lethal violence in proximity to or against civilians, the obstruction of humanitarian-aid deliveries, the reported use of food insecurity as a weapon of war, and the destruction of civilian infrastructure, particularly in Gaza's urban areas.

NSAGs as political and geopolitical actors

The Armed Conflict Survey series has consistently highlighted the central role of NSAGs as a driving force behind the increasing complexity and intractability of most contemporary wars. It has also documented their growing importance as political actors and providers of governance to the population under their control, often filling the void left by the state's inability to meet basic socio-economic, political and security needs. According to the International Committee of the Red Cross (ICRC), 455 armed groups of humanitarian concern were active globally as of July 2024, with approximately 210m people living under their full or contested control. Of these groups, 80% provide some form of public service (including security, healthcare, education and social support) and/or extract taxes from the population under their control.[6] This phenomenon is of notable concern for Sub-Saharan Africa and the MENA region, where a total of 284 groups operate, but it is also an issue in the rest of the world, with 84, 76 and 11 such groups active in the Americas, Asia, and Europe and Eurasia respectively.

The rise of NSAGs as domestic political actors has often coincided with their increasing internationalisation, as many have been developing transnational networks and receiving support from third-party states. Their geopolitical significance was particularly evident during the reporting period in the MENA region, where groups like Hamas, Hizbullah and the Houthis played pivotal roles in shaping the conflict landscape. These groups illustrate the growing international and geopolitical influence of NSAGs, as they engage with or challenge state actors to further their strategic aims. The ICRC notes that at least 15% of armed groups globally provide support to states, while 25% receive backing from states. Moreover, around 50% of these actors give and receive support from other armed groups, pointing to their extensive networks of alliances and strategic interests.

To enhance understanding of the varying types and characteristics of NSAGs, *The Armed Conflict Survey* series provides detailed, standardised information on these groups in each country it covers. This includes data on their strength, areas of operation, organisational structure, leadership, resources, and domestic and international allies and adversaries. The Regional Analysis chapters in *The Armed Conflict Survey 2024* also focus on the most important NSAGs per region, shedding light on their main characteristics, dynamics, and regional and global interlinkages.

The increasingly pressing need to unpack the climate–conflict nexus

The Armed Conflict Survey 2024 continues to reflect the disproportionate impact of the accelerating climate crisis on fragile countries, which are especially vulnerable to its manifestations. This aggravates underlying causes of conflict, leading to forced displacement and instability across borders while amplifying humanitarian needs globally.

Moreover, the growing competition for scarce natural resources, such as water and land, has increasingly become a significant driver of both internal and inter-state conflicts, with NSAGs notably leveraging control over these resources as a weapon of war and a means of gaining political power. In turn, armed violence and conflict weaken states' capacities to adapt to climate change and build resilience. Additionally, conflicts often hinder climate-mitigation efforts, as seen in narco-deforestation in Latin America and the pollution from illegal mining in many regions of the world.

Visualising conflict dynamics

The data-rich analysis of *The Armed Conflict Survey 2024* is enhanced by multiple visual elements, including regional and conflict-specific maps, charts and tables. These visual aids help illustrate key conflict trends from the reporting period, covering data on violent events, fatalities, military interventions, humanitarian impacts and forced displacement, among others. They also highlight regional and global connections and spillovers, offering a comprehensive understanding of the conflict landscape. An exhaustive categorisation and analysis of conflict parties, together with regional timelines of key military/violent and political events for the reporting period, provide essential context for the conflicts analysed.

Additionally, the accompanying Chart of Armed Conflict presents a visual overview of the global conflict environment, with a particular focus on the economics of conflict. It highlights the key economic factors driving, enabling or exacerbating conflicts, as well as selected economic aspects of governance structures established by NSAGs over populations under their control, categorised by region.

Regional interlinkages and trends

The Armed Conflict Survey 2024 adopts a regional approach to analysing active conflicts, aiming to better capture their growing regional and international interlinkages as well as the broader geopolitical influences at play. Each regional section includes an extended Regional Analysis chapter, offering an overview of conflict trends, drivers and main actors such as NSAGs and third-party involvements. These analyses explore the regional and international dimensions of conflicts, assessing their potential future trajectories, prospects for peace or escalation, political risks, and possible flashpoints to monitor. This 'horizon-scanning' exercise provides forward-looking insights for policymakers, practitioners and corporate actors operating in or near conflict-affected areas.

Complementing the Regional Analyses are Regional Spotlight chapters, which focus on trends of strategic importance for the regional or global conflict landscape. Trends highlighted and discussed include the expansion and diversification of Mexican drug-trafficking organisations in the Americas section; instability trends in the Western Balkans in the Europe and Eurasia section; Iran and its network of NSAGs in the MENA section; the impact of the Ethiopia–Somaliland memorandum of understanding on regional stability in the Sub-Saharan Africa section; and paths towards the reintegration of Afghanistan into the international community in the Asia section.

Americas
Armed violence tied to illicit economies in the Americas remains widespread, with homicide rates at nearly three times the global average. Organised crime is heavily involved in diverse criminal activities, including human trafficking, environmental crimes and synthetic-drugs trafficking. The convergence of environmental crimes with narco-trafficking, especially in regions like the Amazon, exacerbates climate vulnerabilities and challenges climate-mitigation efforts. NSAGs' growing determination to influence politics and national decision-making in the pursuit of their strategic interests has driven political violence and intimidation across the region. Notably, at least 15 candidates for office were assassinated in Mexico during the run-up to the June 2024 general elections.[7]

Conflict over newly critical trafficking routes and ports has led to surges in violence in countries that had previously been largely spared from armed violence, including Ecuador (where an internal armed conflict was declared by the government in January 2024) as well as Argentina, Chile and Uruguay. These emerging dynamics have led to an increasing internationalisation of most criminal groups' networks and operations, with the international expansion of the Mexican Sinaloa Cartel and Cartel Jalisco New Generation (CJNG) being a case in point.

A new transitional government and the deployment of a Kenya-led Multinational Security Support Mission are important steps towards stabilising the current critical political and security situation in Haiti. However, risks abound given the country's extremely fragile state institutions, all-powerful gangs, and escalating economic and humanitarian crisis.

In Colombia, simultaneous negotiations with most criminal groups under the 'total peace' initiative have had mixed results. In Venezuela, hopes for a democratic transition following the general elections on 28 July 2024 were dashed when President Nicolás Maduro declared himself the winner despite evidence to the contrary and aggressively suppressed dissent. Maduro's continued grip on power, despite growing internal isolation, will solidify Venezuela's role as a hub of regional instability and influence from external powers like Russia and Iran.

Europe and Eurasia
The dissolution of the Soviet Union in 1991 and the resulting political upheavals are key factors driving conflicts in Europe and Eurasia, alongside Russia's revanchist policies under President Vladimir Putin. During the reporting period, various conflicts continued to destabilise the region, with Russia either playing a central role, as in its war in Ukraine, or heavily influencing events, as seen in the Nagorno-Karabakh conflict and the related tensions between

Armenia and Azerbaijan. In 2023, the decades-old conflict in the breakaway region of Nagorno-Karabakh came to a close after Azerbaijan launched a full-scale attack. Azerbaijani forces quickly overpowered the Nagorno-Karabakh Defence Army (NKDA) following a major assault on 19 September, leading to the ethnic Armenian authorities in the region surrendering the next day. An agreement was reached for the disbandment of the NKDA and other Artsakh (Nagorno-Karabakh) institutions, prompting the majority of the 120,000 ethnic Armenians to flee the territory.[8] Despite Western-mediated peace talks, tensions between Armenia and Azerbaijan persist, with clashes along their shared border continuing as recently as late June 2024.

In the Balkans, several unsettled governance and security arrangements as well as disputed borders also remain an issue, primarily as a result of the break-up of Yugoslavia in the 1990s, in particular in Bosnia-Herzegovina and between Serbia and Kosovo.

Armed violence from Islamist movements in both Central Asia and Russia also remains a major threat, as evidenced by the uptick in attacks by such groups, including the bloody attack claimed by the Islamic State Khorasan Province (ISKP), an Asian affiliate of the Islamic State (ISIS), at the Crocus City Hall concert venue outside Moscow on 22 March 2024.

An end to Russia's war against Ukraine, now in its third year, appears unlikely in the foreseeable future. The two sides remain far apart on any possible peace terms, while a durable settlement would require a host of wider political, legal, economic and security issues to be resolved. These include questions around territorial control and recognition thereof under any ceasefire, the terms under which sanctions imposed on Russia by Ukraine's allies might be lifted, the potential for reparation payments to Ukraine, the future of frozen Russian assets, accountability for war crimes, the return of Ukrainian citizens deported to Russia, and the structure of future security guarantees.

Middle East and North Africa
The reporting period was marked by a significant escalation in armed conflict in the MENA region, with the Hamas-led 7 October attacks against Israel and consequent Israeli offensive in the Gaza Strip serving as the most consequential events in the reporting period. The war has witnessed horrific violence in Gaza with the Israel Defense Forces' (IDF) military campaign causing massive destruction of infrastructure (including residential buildings, health facilities, energy and water facilities, and schools, among others) and the internal displacement of the entire Palestinian population, in addition to an estimated death toll of over 40,000 individuals.[9] Increasing levels of violence by the IDF and Israeli settlers have also taken place in the West Bank. Regionally, the war has had dramatic ramifications, notably resulting in an increase in direct confrontations between Israel and Iran (and its allies), as discussed above.

These developments have considerably heightened the risk of a regional war, although regional states, which have recently pursued de-escalation mechanisms, have not abandoned diplomatic tools for conflict resolution after 7 October. Several regional governments, including Bahrain, Egypt, Jordan, Oman and Qatar, among others, have sought a ceasefire and mechanisms to prevent the expansion of the Israel–Hamas war. Nonetheless, the evolution of the war and tensions between Israel and Iran will continue to influence the escalation of violence in other conflict theatres in the region, as notably has been the case in Lebanon. Internationally, the immediate red line for global powers is any regional spillover that threatens global oil supplies.

Sub-Saharan Africa
Sub-Saharan Africa remained the most conflict-affected region globally during the reporting period, with 14 out of 49 countries engulfed in war. In 2023, the region recorded 28 internal conflicts (either with or without external intervention) – its highest number since 1991. Armed violence intensified particularly in the Sahel, where Niger experienced a coup in July 2023 that brought an anti-Western military junta to power. The junta formed the Alliance of Sahel States with the military regimes in Burkina Faso and Mali. In East Africa, Sudan's civil war between the Sudan Armed Forces (SAF) and the paramilitary Rapid Support Forces (RSF) expanded to Darfur, resulting in mass displacement and a humanitarian crisis as state institutions collapsed. In the eastern DRC, the Rwanda-backed rebel group M23 escalated its offensive, heightening tensions between the two countries. The outlook for these conflict zones remains bleak due to entrenched violence, domestic power struggles and foreign interference.

Notably, countries such as Russia, Turkiye and the Gulf states have sought to project their influence and offer alternative visions of stability, often undermining Western rivals. In the Sahel, Burkina Faso, Mali and Niger cut political and security ties with the West (primarily France and the US) in favour of forming closer ties with Russia. Meanwhile, efforts to resolve Sudan's civil war are complicated by external powers backing different sides, with Egypt supporting the SAF and the United Arab Emirates backing the RSF. Inter-state disputes, such as those between the DRC and Rwanda and between Ethiopia and Somalia, also pose significant risks to regional security.

The end of the UN Multidimensional Integrated Stabilization Mission in Mali (MINUSMA) and the request by Kinshasa to terminate the UN Organization Stabilization Mission in the DRC (MONUSCO) reflect the ongoing decline in UN relevance and legitimacy on the continent. At the end of 2023, MONUSCO and MINUSMA combined consumed 35% of the annual UN peacekeeping budget and one-third of the UN's global uniformed peacekeeping personnel. Simultaneously, African-led peace-support operations expanded, with ten active regional missions operating across 17 countries in 2023.[10] However, these regional initiatives face several challenges, including weak or unclear mandates, concerns over legitimacy and impartiality due to national interests, and dependency on external funding, primarily from the UN and international donors. These issues raise questions about the long-term sustainability and effectiveness of regional peace operations as they increasingly supplant UN missions.

Asia

The intensity of two of the three most consequential conflicts in Asia, namely the dispute over Kashmir and especially the war in Afghanistan, has significantly reduced in terms of violence over the reporting period. This is due to the continued ceasefire between India and Pakistan, brokered in February 2021, and the consolidation of power by the Afghan Taliban. Conversely, in Myanmar, the military junta has lost substantial ground in its conflict with a coalition of pro-democracy forces and ethnic armed groups – a struggle that has been ongoing since the military coup by the State Administration Council in February 2021.

Despite the above, the risk of major conventional inter-state war remains high, particularly in regions involving nuclear powers. The tensions between the US and China in the Taiwan Strait, between Pakistan and India along the LoC, and between China and India along the LAC continue to pose significant risks, with the Taiwan Strait and Kashmir being the most likely flashpoints. China's stance on Taiwan, like India's and Pakistan's on Kashmir, is central to its strategic national interests.

Meanwhile, the security threat posed by transnational terrorist groups in Afghanistan and Pakistan, particularly ISKP, may acquire greater strategic implications if these groups continue to target locations outside of the region. The ISKP attack on the concert hall in Moscow and foiled plots in Europe underscore the seriousness of this risk.

Notes

[1] The total number of conflicts as captured by the Uppsala Conflict Data Program (UCDP)/Peace Research Institute Oslo (PRIO) Armed Conflict Dataset has been rising since 2007, totalling 134 in 2023, among the highest in three decades. UCDP disaggregates between state-based (i.e., at least one conflict party is a state) and non-state-based armed conflicts (i.e., conflict parties are exclusively NSAGs), and defines an armed conflict as the 'use of armed force between two parties' that 'results in at least 25 battle-related deaths in one calendar year'. Conflict 'parties' can be either state- or non-state-based depending on the type of conflict under consideration. According to this definition, each country can have several different ongoing conflicts per year. This methodology explains the larger number of conflicts accounted for by UCDP compared to those identified in *The Armed Conflict Survey 2024*, which adopts the country as the primary unit of analysis. See UCDP/PRIO Armed Conflict Dataset Version 24.1 and UCDP Non-State Conflict Dataset Version 24.1. Nils Petter Gleditsch et al., 'Armed Conflict 1946–2001: A New Dataset', *Journal of Peace Research*, vol. 39, no. 5, 2002, pp. 615–37; Shawn Davies et al., 'Organized Violence 1989–2023, and the Prevalence of Organized Crime Groups', *Journal of Peace Research*, vol. 61, no. 4, 2024; and Ralph Sundberg, Kristine Eck and Joakim Kreutz, 'Introducing the UCDP Non-state Conflict Dataset', *Journal of Peace Research*, vol. 49, no. 2, 2012.

[2] IISS calculations based on data from the Armed Conflict Location & Event Data Project (ACLED), www.acleddata.com.

[3] UNOCHA, 'Global Humanitarian Overview 2024, March–April Update (Snapshot as of 30 April 2024)', 9 May 2024.

[4] World Bank et al., 'Ukraine: Third Rapid Damage and Needs Assessment (RDNA3)', February 2024, p. 9; and World

Bank, European Union and UN, 'Gaza Strip Interim Damage Assessment', 2024, p. 6. Estimates for Ukraine and Gaza are as of 31 December 2023 and 31 January 2024 respectively.

5   UNRWA, 'UNRWA Situation Report #119 on the Situation in the Gaza Strip and the West Bank, Including East Jerusalem', 9 July 2024; and UNHCR, 'Operational Data Portal: Sudan Situation'.

6   This data is drawn from the annual ICRC survey on armed groups completed in July 2024. The ICRC uses the generic term 'armed group' for a group that is not a state but has the capacity to cause violence that is of humanitarian concern. Armed groups also include those groups that qualify as conflict parties to a non-international armed conflict according to the Geneva Conventions, which the ICRC define as 'non-state armed groups'. See Matthew Bamber-Zryd, 'ICRC Engagement with Armed Groups in 2024', ICRC Humanitarian Law & Policy, 31 October 2024.

7   'Violencia Electoral en México: el Gobierno Reconoce el Asesinato de 15 Aspirantes' [Electoral violence in Mexico: government acknowledges the murder of 15 candidates], Agencia EFE, 3 April 2024.

8   UN High Commissioner for Refugees, 'Inter-agency Rapid Needs Assessment Report', November 2023; and Claire Mills, 'What Is Happening in Nagorno-Karabakh', no. 9862, United Kingdom Parliament, House of Commons Library, 28 September 2023.

9   UNOCHA, 'Reported Impact Snapshot | Gaza Strip', 11 September 2024.

10 Benjamin Petrini and Erica Pepe, 'Peacekeeping in Africa: From UN to Regional Peace Support Operations', IISS, 18 March 2024.

Notes on Methodology

The Armed Conflict Survey 2024 reviews and analyses developments, dynamics, trends and outlooks related to active armed conflicts around the world. We define an armed conflict as a sustained military confrontation between two or more organised actors making purposive use of armed violence. The inclusion of a conflict in the book is based on this definition and the methodology detailed below.

Armed conflicts in 2023–24

The Armed Conflict Survey 2024 covers armed conflicts that were active between 1 July 2023 and 30 June 2024 (the 'reporting period') globally.[1] These are organised into 38 Country Profiles across five regional sections: the Americas, Europe and Eurasia, the Middle East and North Africa, Sub-Saharan Africa, and Asia. Each section is introduced by an in-depth Regional Analysis, which discusses the main regional trends, how different armed conflicts relate to and influence one another, the outlook of the conflicts in the region and potential flashpoints to monitor. Each Regional Analysis is complemented by a Regional Spotlight, which offers a deep dive into a region-specific dynamic or trend. Country Profiles (which come in a shorter or longer form, depending on any given conflict's global relevance as assessed by IISS analysis) cover all active conflicts in each region and capture specific domestic dynamics as well as developments in the reporting period.

Except for inter-state conflicts, *The Armed Conflict Survey 2024* uses the country as the unit of analysis – including for conflicts in Sub-Saharan Africa, some of which were bundled together in previous editions of *The Armed Conflict Survey* under the regional categories of the Sahel, the Lake Chad Basin and the Great Lakes Region. For Sub-Saharan Africa, this approach ensures a comprehensive coverage of domestic dynamics and developments, while retaining the regional focus through the Regional Analysis chapter. More generally, this approach allows for a more granular assessment and systematisation of the different conflicts active simultaneously in specific countries, for instance in India, Nigeria, Pakistan and Syria.

To reflect changes in the relative global relevance of conflicts in the reporting period, we have expanded the Haiti Country Profile. We have also introduced new Country Profiles for Indonesia and Lebanon to reflect heightened armed-conflict dynamics in these countries during the reporting period. Finally, we removed the stand-alone Country Profile for Rwanda, as the country's involvement in the eastern Congo is now covered in the Country Profile for the Democratic Republic of the Congo.

Criteria for inclusion and removal

Defining armed conflict as a military or violent phenomenon means *The Armed Conflict Survey 2024* does not aim to determine the applicability of international humanitarian law to different conflict situations (as in the Geneva Conventions or the Rome Statute).

The Armed Conflict Survey 2024 covers armed confrontations that meet our criteria for inclusion in terms of **duration**, **intensity** and **organisation** of the conflict parties.

We require an armed conflict to run for three months at a minimum and feature violent incidents on a weekly or at least fortnightly basis.[2] The definition of armed conflict in *The Armed Conflict Survey 2024* does not involve a numerical threshold of battle-related deaths, contrary to conflict datasets such as the Uppsala Conflict Data Program. For wars between states – which feature substantial levels of military mobilisation, simultaneous and numerous armed clashes, or significant fatalities – the duration threshold may be relaxed.

The organisation of the conflict parties refers to their ability to plan and execute military operations or violent attacks. The scale of such attacks is not a factor in this determination – for the purpose of inclusion in *The Armed Conflict Survey 2024*, planting improvised explosive devices, for example, is equivalent to battlefield clashes. For armed conflicts that involve state parties, the deployment of armed forces or militarised (not regular) police is required. Non-state armed groups (NSAGs) must demonstrate some logistical and operational capacity, such as access to weapons and other military equipment, or an ability to devise strategies and carry out operations, coordinate activities, establish communication between members, and recruit and train personnel. Territorial control or a permanent base in an area is not necessary, nor is a specific type of organisational structure. Not all NSAGs have a distinct and effective chain of command; for example, many of those operating in Sub-Saharan Africa do not. Instead, they can be highly decentralised, maintain an amorphous structure, rely on a transnational network or have a global reach. A hierarchical military structure is therefore not an inclusion criterion. In each Country Profile, the Conflict Parties section lists the main organisational capabilities of the actors involved.[3]

The Armed Conflict Survey 2024 excludes cases of protests and riots if they happen in isolation. Instances of government repression, ethnic cleansing or genocide that occur outside of a conflict situation are also not included, regardless of their scale, unless the population develops a capacity to fight back through an armed, organised resistance or another state intervenes – as in the case of the Saddam Hussein regime's repression of the Kurds in Iraq before the United States invaded in 2003.

Due to the increasingly complex interplay of factors fuelling contemporary conflicts, we also are agnostic with respect to the nature of their drivers. *The Armed Conflict Survey 2024* includes conflicts motivated by political, socio-economic, ideological, religious and criminal reasons – or a combination of these elements. This approach allows us to cover conflicts in the Americas, which are mostly driven by criminal contestation over the control of illicit economies and involve actors with elusive political or ideological motives.

Finally, armed conflicts that have lost the above-defined characteristics for inclusion are removed after two years. An armed conflict terminated through a peace agreement also ceases to be included if it is followed by military demobilisation of all conflict parties.

Classification and categorisation of armed conflicts: scope and actors

The unit of analysis in *The Armed Conflict Survey 2024* is the country where the military or violent confrontation(s) that can be defined as armed conflict under our criteria take place. In most cases, conflicts occur within the boundaries of a state and are therefore listed under that country's name. This applies to single conflicts but also to instances of overlapping distinct insurgencies occurring within the boundaries of a single country. Concomitant insurgencies ongoing in India, Iraq, Niger, Pakistan and the Philippines, to mention a few, are combined in one single Country Profile for the purpose of our analysis. Country Profiles identify and analyse the different conflicts within a country (and provide respective names, start dates and typologies) in instances of multiple confrontations. Conflicts that have elements of inter-state confrontation take the name of either the disputed region (i.e., Nagorno-Karabakh and Kashmir) or the parties involved (i.e., Russia–Ukraine and Israel–Palestinian Territories).

Conflicts may involve state or non-state actors. According to the types of actors involved and the interactions between them, armed conflicts have been grouped into one (or more) of the following four categories: inter-state conflicts, internal conflicts, transnational conflicts and internationalised-internal conflicts. However, these categories are not necessarily mutually exclusive, as conflicts often retain features of more than one of these types.

An **inter-state** conflict involves two or more states (or a group of states) and takes place on the territory of one or several states, as well as in the global commons. This is the least common modality of conflict in the current landscape. However, inter-state conflicts are often among the most globally significant, as exemplified by the Russia–Ukraine war.

An **internal** conflict takes place in the territory of one state and is either fought by a government (and possibly allied armed groups) against one or more NSAGs, or between two or more NSAGs without the direct participation of state forces. Within this category, we include the sub-categories of localised insurgencies (such as the one ongoing in southern Thailand), intercommunal conflicts (such as the several in South Sudan) and organised crime (which applies to most of the conflicts in the Americas). Many internal conflicts feature characteristics of two or more of these sub-categories.

Transnational conflicts take place across different countries or have important regional dimensions, such as many confrontations in Sub-Saharan Africa (including in the Sahel or in the Lake Chad Basin) and in the Middle East and North Africa. In this type of conflict, armed actors may be active across countries that share borders, or national armed forces may join together to create a regional coalition.

Finally, **internationalised-internal** conflicts are confrontations in which the kernel of the dispute remains domestic, but which feature the military intervention of one or more external states. Such involvement may include training, equipping or providing military intelligence to a conflict party or participating in the hostilities, either directly or through local proxies and sponsored actors. This modality has shown a marked increase in the last decade.

The Armed Conflict Global Relevance Indicator (ACGRI)

The Armed Conflict Survey 2024 features the fourth edition of our Armed Conflict Global Relevance Indicator (ACGRI) as an additional tool of analysis and prioritisation to complement IISS qualitative expertise. The ACGRI assesses and benchmarks the global significance of conflicts across the world based on three pillars – or drivers – of significance, covering the following dimensions:

- The **human impact** of conflicts, in terms of human losses and hardship. The rationale for including this dimension stems from the nexus between conflict-related fatalities, forced displacement and further domestic social, economic and political instability with spillover effects on regional and global stability.
- The **incidence** of conflicts, as a measure of the intensity of armed violence and the potential for related instability to spill over into neighbouring countries and beyond.
- The **geopolitical impact** of conflicts, measured by several variables we created to capture the involvement of third parties and interventions by the international community, based on IISS proprietary data and other international sources. The pillar also includes humanitarian funding, which captures the financial support provided by governments and multilateral organisations to address domestic humanitarian needs, including those resulting from armed conflicts.

The ACGRI uses the country in which a conflict occurs as the unit of analysis. This methodological choice is justified by the fact that most of the armed conflicts covered are internal (internationalised or not), meaning the conflict can be assimilated to the country in which it takes place. For cases in which multiple insurgencies are happening at once in a country, the country score encompasses all of them. However, the ACGRI is not able to assess the global significance of each domestic insurgency in isolation. Likewise, transnational conflicts are not given a regional score; global relevance is instead assessed at the level of each country involved.

In contrast, for the Nagorno-Karabakh and Israel–Palestinian Territories conflicts, the unit of analysis is the conflict itself. India and Pakistan are treated separately in the case of the conflict in Kashmir due to the presence of other localised insurgencies ongoing in both countries. For the Russia–Ukraine conflict, the indicator is calculated based on Ukraine data only, as the latter has been the main theatre of fighting during the reporting period. Geopolitical indicators specific to Kashmir, such as the number of United Nations Security Council (UNSC) resolutions, are attributed to both India and Pakistan to ensure that the final score for the two countries reflects the geopolitical impact of the inter-state conflict, if applicable.

The indicator is composed of a total of nine variables (see Table 1), which are good proxies for the dimensions of global relevance we seek to cover, considering the availability of reliable data.

As a preliminary step to combine variable scores into pillar and ACGRI scores, data for each variable is normalised on a 0–10 scale, through the following approach:

Eq.1 $(\text{indicator data} - 0)/(y - 0) \times 10 = \text{variable score}$

where the indicator data refers to continuous data, y refers to the maximum value from the target countries and 0 is used as the minimum value.[4]

Each pillar score is the arithmetic mean of the composing variable, multiplied by 10, giving a pillar score between 0 and 100.

The scores of the ACGRI composing pillars are displayed throughout the book in a continuous colour progression (using conditional formatting) in order to respect the cardinal (instead of ordinal) distance between countries and to reflect more precisely the differentiation of conflicts' global relevance based on the continuum of the ACGRI scores for the full sample.

Table 1: ACGRI pillars and variables

Pillar	Variable	Description	Source
Human impact	Fatalities	Number of fatalities due to violent events, by country, 1 July 2023–30 June 2024[5]	Armed Conflict Location & Event Data Project (ACLED), www.acleddata.com
	Refugees	Number of refugees (total), counted by country of origin, as of 31 December 2023	UN High Commissioner for Refugees; UN Relief and Works Agency for Palestine Refugees in the Near East
	Internally displaced persons (IDPs)	Number of IDPs (total), by country, as of 31 December 2023[6]	Internal Displacement Monitoring Centre
Incidence	Violent events	Number of violent events, by country, 1 July 2023–30 June 2024[7]	Armed Conflict Location & Event Data Project (ACLED), www.acleddata.com
Geopolitical impact	Foreign countries' involvement[8]	Number of foreign countries 'involved' in the conflict, by country, as of 30 June 2024[9]	IISS calculation based on data from the Military Balance+, milbalplus.iiss.org; Christoph Trebesch et al., 'The Ukraine Support Tracker: Which Countries Help Ukraine and How?', Kiel *Working Paper*, no. 2218, 2024, pp. 1–75
	Deployments by major geopolitical powers	Number of personnel deployed by major geopolitical powers in conflict-affected countries, by country, as of 30 June 2024[10]	Military Balance+
	UNSC resolutions	Number of UNSC resolutions concerning conflicts under review, by country, 1 July 2023–30 June 2024	UNSC
	Peacekeeping and other multilateral missions	Number of operational peacekeeping, special political and military missions and other multilateral missions concerning conflicts in countries under review, as of 30 June 2024[11]	Military Balance+; Stockholm International Peace Research Institute (SIPRI);[12] UN;[13] regional organisations; ad hoc coalitions
	Humanitarian funding	Total reported incoming funding from governments and multilateral organisations, by recipient country, as of 31 December 2023[14]	UN Office for the Coordination of Humanitarian Affairs (OCHA) Financial Tracking Service (FTS)

Data for all the variables included in the ACGRI is listed in the Data Appendix, along with detailed source information, definitions and the underlying calculation methodology for each variable.

Selected data from the ACGRI is also featured in the Key Conflict Statistics boxes in the Country Profiles, as well as other background variables relevant to the context under analysis, such as the Gini index, GDP per capita (based on purchasing power parity in constant prices–international dollars), the 'functioning of government' pillar of the Economist Intelligence Unit's Democracy Index and the Notre Dame Global Adaptation Initiative's climate-change 'vulnerability' score. Full data for all these background variables is also contained in the Data Appendix.

The Chart of Armed Conflict

The Chart of Armed Conflict depicts relevant data and information for all active conflicts included in *The*

Armed Conflict Survey 2024. Besides providing a visual overview of the conflict landscape, this year's Chart has a special focus on the economics of conflict, including the main economic factors that can drive, enable or exacerbate conflicts. Visualised variables include total minerals production (as a percentage of GDP), ecological threats, criminal markets, climate-change vulnerability and functioning of government. The Chart also illustrates important economic dimensions that are part of the governance structure offered by armed groups of humanitarian concern to the population under their full or contested control at the regional level, notably their provision of public services or social support and their ability to extract taxes. Key humanitarian data, such as conflict-related fatalities and violent events (incidence), is included for conflict-affected countries.

Data is from ACLED, the IMF, the Institute for Economics and Peace, the Global Initiative Against Transnational Organized Crime, the World Bank, the International Committee of the Red Cross and other organisations.

Notes

1. Although the reporting period for the conflicts included in *The Armed Conflict Survey 2024* ends on 30 June 2024, we have covered important developments that happened after this date to make the publication as timely as possible. Such developments include major events related to the conflicts in Ukraine and Israel–Palestinian Territories. For all other cases, events after the end of June 2024 will be covered in *The Armed Conflict Survey 2025*.
2. These numerical criteria are always complemented by an IISS qualitative assessment, which may in exceptional cases overrule the former.
3. Unless otherwise stated, all figures related to military strength and capability, defence economics and arms equipment in the Conflict Parties tables are taken from the Military Balance+.
4. The normalisation formula is partially adjusted for the presence of outliers under the assumption of a normal distribution in the sample. An observation is treated as an outlier if it is three (3) standard deviations larger than the mean of the sample's distribution. The formula is as follows: $x_i > X + z_a S$, where x_i is the observation, X is the mean, z_a equals three (3) and S is the standard deviation of the sample.
5. Conflict fatalities include those resulting from battles, explosions/remote violence and violence against civilians.
6. Most recent available data for Egypt was from 2020.
7. Violent events include battles, explosions/remote violence and violence against civilians.
8. Our methodology includes the following definition of 'involvement' for third parties in conflict. For internal conflicts, foreign countries are considered 'involved' if they are either present through the deployment of military capabilities (outside of a multilateral mission as defined in the ACGRI) or if they meet all the following criteria: presence of intelligence assets; provision of military financial support; role in an advisory or operational command-and-control capacity; and sale or transfer of military equipment. For inter-state conflicts, foreign countries are considered 'involved' if they are either present through the deployment of military capabilities (outside of a multilateral mission as defined in the ACGRI) or if they meet two or more of the following criteria: presence of intelligence assets; provision of military financial support; role in an advisory or operational command-and-control capacity; and sale or transfer of military equipment.
9. Military aid to Ukraine only refers to aid worth more than US$1 billion in funding provided by over 30 countries between 24 January 2022 and 30 April 2024.
10. This is calculated based on the number of military personnel deployed into conflict-affected countries by major geopolitical powers within the G20 (including unilaterally, as part of a combat coalition or as part of a mission under the aegis of an international organisation, but excluding deployments that are not conflict related).
11. These include missions undertaken by the UN, regional organisations or ad hoc groups related to UN sanctions/UNSC resolutions or endorsed by the UN and other international organisations. Data refers to active missions as of 30 June 2024 that fulfil the following two criteria: objective (relating to multidimensional peace and conflict resolution) and geographical scope (relating to the analysed conflicts in the countries under review).
12. SIPRI, 'SIPRI Map of Multilateral Peace Operations, 2024', May 2024.
13. UN, 'UN Special Political Missions and Other Political Presences 2024', April 2024.
14. This includes financial funding received by local governments, multilateral organisations, non-governmental organisations, pooled funds, private organisations, and Red Cross and Red Crescent organisations operating in the country under review. The data was retrieved from FTS in July 2024. Figures are continuously updated, and later reports may differ from the data retrieved at any given point. FTS is a voluntary reporting mechanism in which the donor declares the value of the funding to FTS, which then oversees its curation, validation and processing in a centralised manner.

REGIONAL SECTIONS

Rescuers remove rubble from a residential building destroyed by a Russian uninhabited-aerial-vehicle attack on Odesa, Ukraine, 2 March 2024

1 Americas

Regional Analysis	20	Mexico	40	Haiti	60
Regional Spotlight	34	Colombia	48	El Salvador	66
Country Profiles		Brazil	54	Honduras	72

A policeman points a gun at protesters during a demonstration calling for the resignation of Prime Minister Ariel Henry, Haiti, 7 February 2024

Overview

While the Americas has not experienced a major inter-state conflict since the Chaco War between Bolivia and Paraguay in the 1930s, armed violence derived from internal conflicts in the region remains extensive. The homicide rate in 2021, at 15 per 100,000, was almost three times the global average (5.8 per 100,000), with half of total homicides recorded related to organised crime (compared to 22% globally).[1] Criminal dynamics around lucrative illicit economies are at the heart of armed-conflict trends in the Americas, with multiple non-state armed groups (NSAGs) fighting against each other and the state for control over territory, trafficking routes, and domestic, regional and international markets. These actors have expanded their transnational reach and networks over time and proven capable of reconfiguring their strategies and portfolios to maintain profit margins and respond to trends in demand, accumulating enormous wealth and economic clout in the process. They have also acquired a quasi-political status, despite their largely criminal nature, by alternatively challenging and infiltrating (or capturing) state institutions in pursuit of their strategic goals. This crucially involves trying to influence the outcome of electoral processes through corruption, intimidation and political violence, as well as by leveraging the votes they control to support or extract concessions from certain candidates. In Mexico alone, almost 1,400 crimes against political actors were recorded in 2018–23 (particularly around the 2018 and 2021 electoral seasons), resulting in over 1,600 victims. The

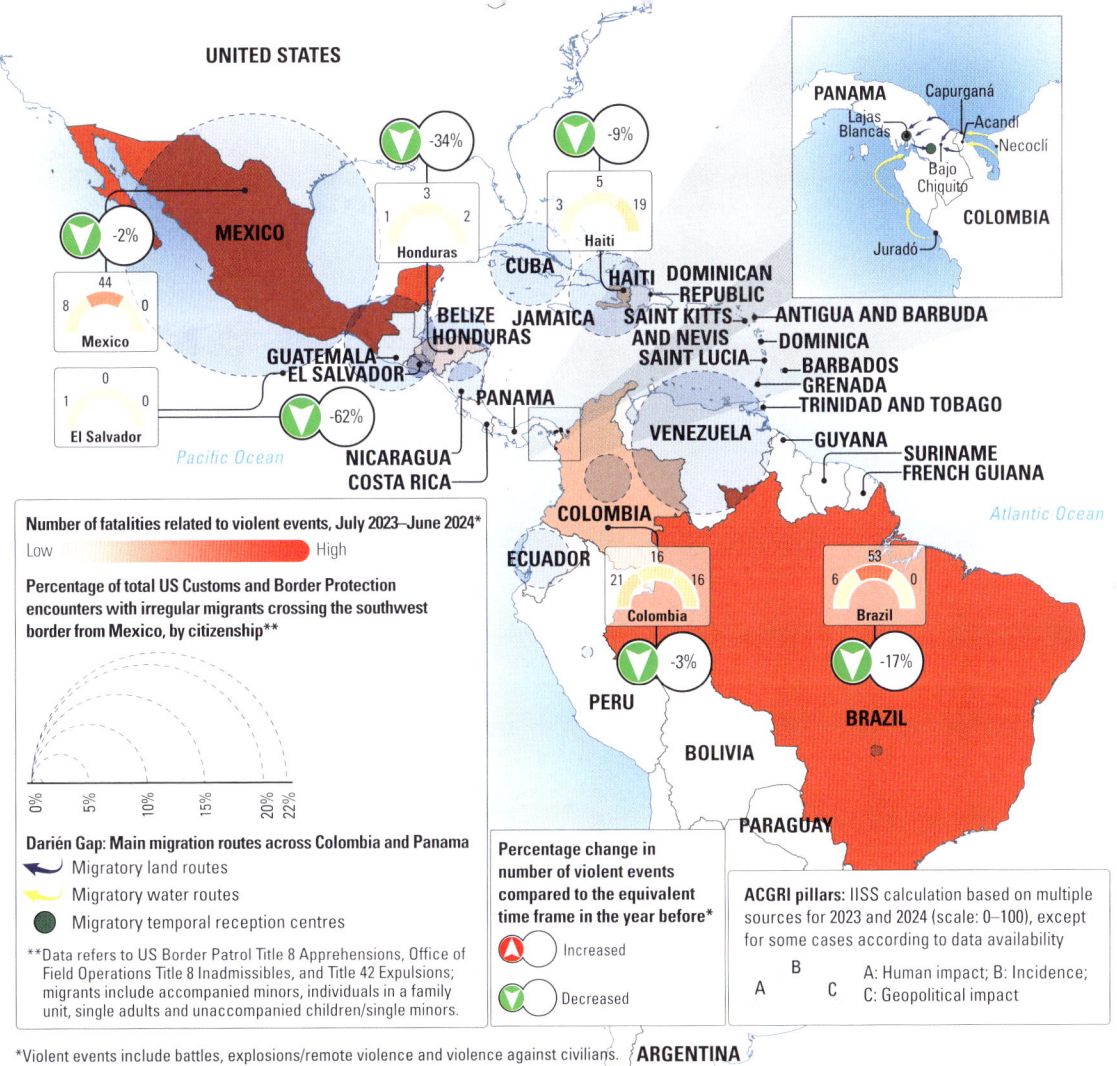

data also shows a marked uptick in 2022–23.[2] Some NSAGs increasingly function like de facto states within the state, imposing taxation and providing basic services in their areas of control, essentially taking over or doubling the state's function as a provider of governance.[3]

NSAGs operate across the region along drug supply chains that stretch from production to final markets in the Americas (mostly the United States and Brazil, which are the largest and second-largest cocaine consumers globally). Recently, especially following the coronavirus pandemic, NSAGs have partially restructured these supply chains to adapt to significant changes in the drug markets. These changes include increased cocaine demand in Europe and South America, as well as the rise of synthetic drugs as a lucrative business with low barriers to entry. Criminal contestation for control over newly critical trafficking routes and ports has led to surges in violence in countries that had previously been largely spared from armed conflict, including Ecuador, which has been especially affected, as well as Argentina (notably its Rosario region), Chile and Uruguay. These emerging dynamics have led to the increasing internationalisation of most criminal groups' networks and operations, which has bolstered their economic power and enhanced their capacity and interest in influencing global policies. The international expansion of the Mexican Sinaloa Cartel and Cartel Jalisco New Generation (CJNG), discussed in detail in the Americas Regional Spotlight chapter, is a case in point.

Internationalisation has also been accompanied by the increasing diversification of criminal portfolios, with most criminal groups now involved in enterprises such as human trafficking, environmental crime, counterfeit trade, agriculture and money laundering, alongside drug trafficking and extortion. The growing convergence between environmental crimes and narco-trafficking, notably in the Amazon, Central America and Mexico, further exacerbates these regions' already high climate vulnerability while also posing a major challenge to national and multilateral climate-mitigation efforts.

Though conflicts in the Americas are not typically viewed as having a significant geopolitical impact, their increasing spillover effects (e.g., in relation to criminal activities and human displacement) elevate their importance for global security and stability. Regional and global security dynamics are crucially shaped by conflict trends in Mexico, Colombia and Venezuela. Mexico's powerful drug-trafficking organisations (DTOs), for instance, have become the primary orchestrators of drug supply chains, fuelling armed violence across the Americas and beyond. Their growing involvement in the synthetic-drugs trade positions them as among the main culprits behind the ongoing fentanyl health emergency in the US. Mexico's shared border with the US also makes it of special relevance in addressing mutual security challenges stemming from criminal groups, irregular migration and arms trafficking.

Colombia, meanwhile, plays a key role in regional conflict dynamics due to its position as the largest coca producer worldwide, representing approximately 60% of global cocaine supply.[4] Venezuela, despite not qualifying for inclusion in *The Armed Conflict Survey 2024*, has also long driven insecurity in the region by harbouring Colombian armed groups, participating in criminal economies, and providing revisionist powers such as Russia and Iran with a platform to infiltrate the Americas. Deteriorating political and economic conditions under the administration of President Nicolás Maduro have caused an unprecedented migration crisis in recent years, with far-reaching implications for regional stability.

The global relevance of armed conflict in Brazil and Haiti is also on the rise. Not only have Brazil's NSAGs, whose activities were once limited to urban areas and the domestic market, been expanding internationally, but thriving criminal economies in the Amazon are also undermining climate-mitigation efforts there, with negative repercussions for global climate security. The severe challenges posed by increasingly emboldened gangs to Haiti's failing state represent another significant flashpoint. Although violence dynamics have largely remained confined to the country, their repercussions – including uncontrolled migration flows and the criminal erosion of institutions – will have global impacts.

The reporting period was largely characterised by a continued reconfiguration of the supply chains, markets and trafficking routes controlled by NSAGs. Notably, a marked escalation in drug-related violence, murders and organised-crime activities in Ecuador prompted President Daniel Noboa to declare in January 2024 that the state was engaged in an internal conflict against organised criminal groups. He designated 22 such groups as terrorist organisations and non-state conflict parties and authorised the military to lead a crackdown.[5] Violence and institutional collapse in Haiti also reached a point of no return, with criminal gangs strengthening their control of key infrastructure, openly confronting the state and demanding a role in negotiations regarding the country's political future.

On a related note, criminal groups' increased determination to influence politics and national decision-making drove political violence and intimidation across the region. The most glaring example of this trend was the assassination of Ecuadorian presidential candidate Fernando Villavicencio in August 2023, allegedly ordered by the Los Lobos gang, just days before the election. Likewise, in Mexico, at least 15 candidates for office were assassinated during the run-up to the June 2024 general elections.[6]

Throughout the reporting period, simultaneous negotiations with most active criminal groups continued in Colombia under President Gustavo Petro's flagship 'total peace' initiatives, yielding mixed results. Meanwhile, the long-standing territorial dispute between Venezuela and Guyana over the oil-rich Essequibo region flared up again following Maduro's December 2023 referendum asserting Venezuela's claim. The crisis was de-escalated through international mediation, but it raised concerns about a potential first inter-state confrontation in the region in decades. In Venezuela, general elections on 28 July 2024 were won by Maduro despite polls and early counting suggesting a large advantage for the opposition candidate. The opposition contested the results, amid widespread international concern regarding the validity of the election outcomes and rising social unrest.

Regional Analysis: Americas

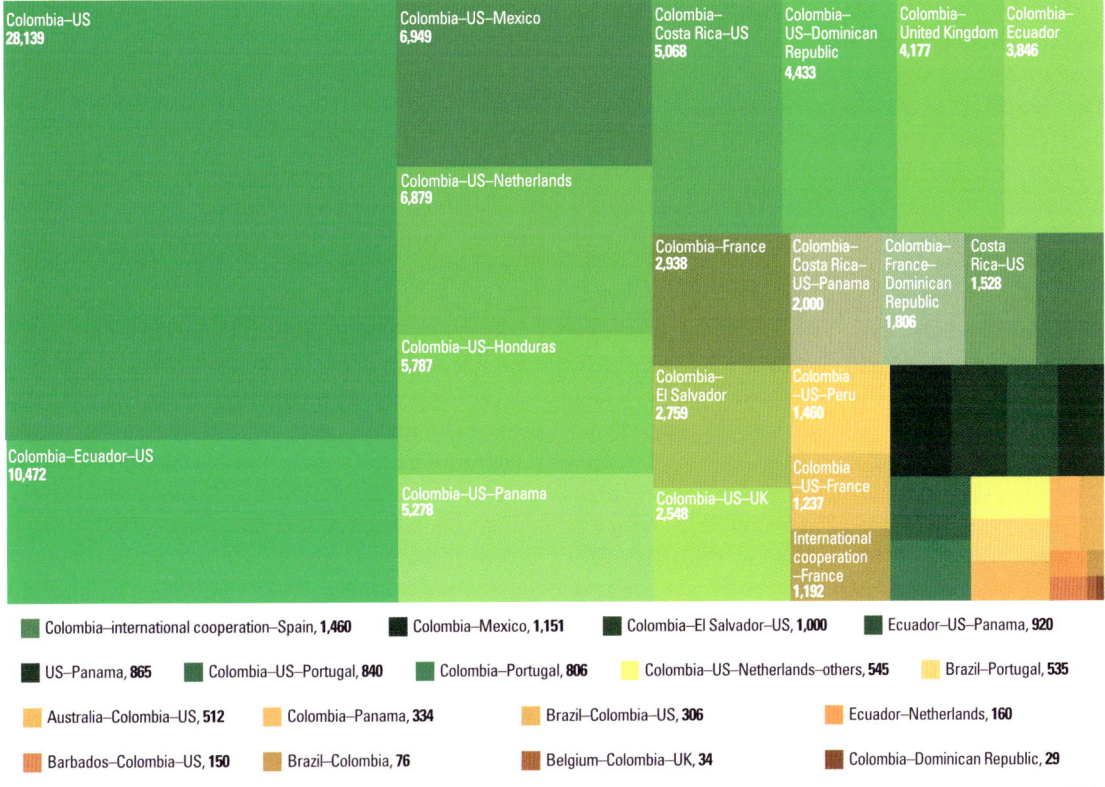

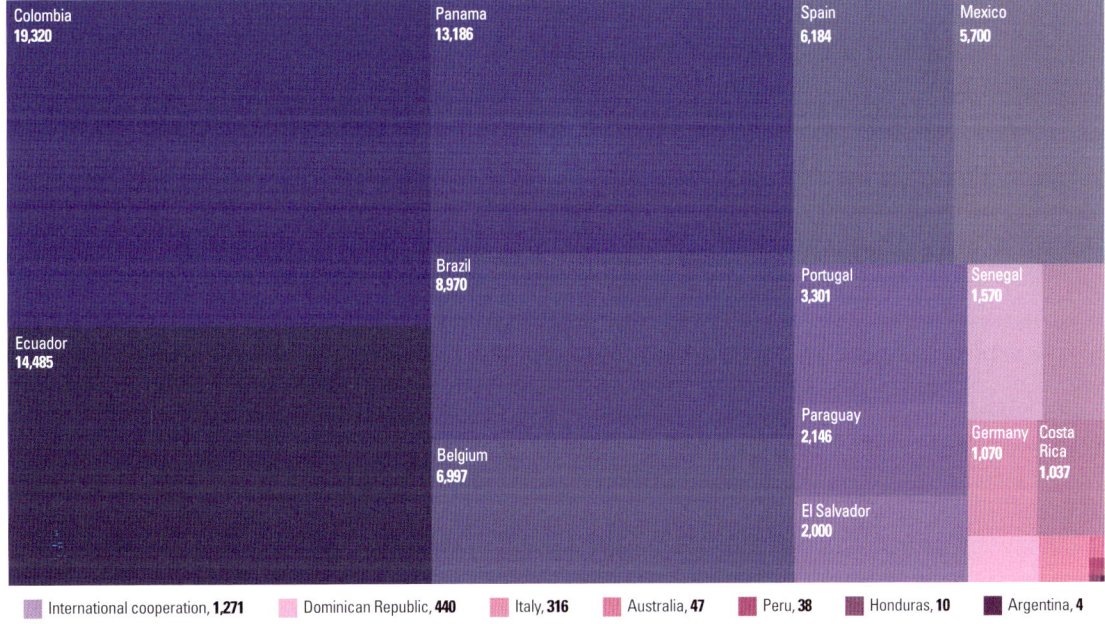

Figure 1: XIII Multinational *Orión* Naval Campaign (2023–24) cocaine seizures (kilograms) by partnership and country

Conflict Drivers

Political and institutional

Institutional weaknesses

The weak rule of law across rural territories in Colombia, marginalised neighbourhoods in Central America and Brazil, and both rural and urban territories in Mexico has opened the way for criminal-governance dynamics and illicit economies to thrive.

Deeply flawed criminal systems promote a culture of impunity which fails to deter criminal activity and further undermines institutional strength. In Mexico, the estimated rate of impunity for violent crimes stands at almost 95%.[7] Inefficient penitentiary systems, overcrowding and a lack of rehabilitation efforts perpetuate violent trends, with extremely high levels of incarceration. El Salvador and Cuba have the highest incarceration rates in the world.[8] The *mano dura* (iron-fist) approach followed by the government of President Nayib Bukele in El Salvador, involving a crackdown on gangs amid a continued state of exception, has exacerbated the situation, with almost 80,000 people imprisoned since March 2022.[9]

The largest criminal groups in Brazil, El Salvador and Honduras all use prisons as their headquarters. High levels of incarceration and overcrowding therefore provide fertile ground for recruitment and indoctrination.

Socio-economic

Structurally unequal societies

Entrenched inequality and widespread poverty have been a hallmark of Latin America's troubled development history, sustaining socio-economic instability and insecurity. The region remains the slowest growing globally, at just 1.6% growth in 2024, and one of the most unequal.[10] The highest 10% of earners make on average 12 times more than the poorest 10%, with 25% of the population living in poor households and 10% of the population controlling 77% of the household wealth.[11] These factors raise the appeal of illicit economies and criminal groups especially for young people, whose lack of economic opportunities is particularly severe, with youth unemployment standing at 14% in 2023.[12]

Violence, including that caused by organised crime, is the leading cause of death of people aged 10–24 in Latin America.[13] The Latin America and Caribbean region accounts for 37% of global homicides, despite making up just 8% of the world population.[14]

Security and military

Drug trafficking and legacies of the 'war on drugs'

Since the 1990s, drug trafficking has been at the core of criminal violence and illicit economies. Proceeds from narco-trafficking, mostly from cocaine, underpin criminal groups' economic wealth and military capabilities (often gained through weapons smuggled from the US – a result of liberal firearms policies there).

The adoption of hardline security policies – spearheaded by the US and centred around increased militarisation, the eradication of illicit crops and drugs interdiction – has further fuelled conflict in the region. Despite important successes in the form of increased drug seizures (mostly of cocaine) and the capture of a few major drug lords, the global supply of cocaine is at record levels and coca-bush cultivation has risen sharply since 2021. Meanwhile, such policies have also had the unintended consequences of increasing criminal actors' fragmentation and reinforcing the military power of criminal groups by prompting them to develop a higher retaliatory capacity to confront the state. The former, in turn, has resulted in increased criminal contestation and the establishment of new trafficking routes within and across countries. Hardline policies have also led to multiple instances of human-rights violations by state forces, including massacres in Brazil and Colombia.

The 'war on drugs' approach is embedded in the international drug-control regime of the United Nations, which prioritises the reduction of the drug supply through security efforts. By abiding by the global legal system, governments have historically been constrained in adopting alternative responses to the ever-expanding drug business, including approaches focused on drug demand and root causes of violence.

Geopolitical

Venezuela's instability

Continuing political and economic insecurity in Venezuela has created a conducive environment for criminal groups and illicit economies to thrive. The involvement of the Maduro regime in regional drug trafficking and its cooperation with Colombian NSAGs have made Venezuela a key node for cocaine trafficking from Colombia to Central America, Mexico, Brazil and Europe. These dynamics have notably strengthened Colombia's NSAGs, undermining that country's domestic security and peacemaking efforts.

Conflict Parties

Coalitions and multilateral responses

Regional security cooperation revolves around combatting illegal economies, especially transnational airborne and seaborne cocaine trafficking. Despite not being directly involved as a conflict party, the US has traditionally played a leading role due to its strategic interest in the region's stability and in curbing illegal drug flows from the region into its territory. Over the past two decades, the US has cemented key security agreements with Mexico and Colombia. While the US–Mexico Mérida Initiative (2008–21) and Plan Colombia (2000–16) focused primarily on military capabilities and training, cooperation has expanded over time to include intelligence sharing (to dismantle criminal networks and finances) and whole-of-government multidimensional initiatives to tackle the socio-economic root causes of violence.

In October 2021, Mexico and the US adopted the Bicentennial Framework for Security, Public Health, and Safe Communities with a particular emphasis on tackling fentanyl trafficking from Mexico. Fentanyl seizures at the Mexico–US border have been growing exponentially in recent years, increasing by 164% from 2020–22.[15] This bilateral agreement has recently been complemented by the US-led Global Coalition to Address Synthetic Drug Threats launched in 2023 with over 150 participatory countries, including Mexico.[16] The coalition aims to curb criminal groups' capabilities to manufacture and traffic fentanyl, as well as monitor and promote health interventions related to its consumption. In a similar vein, Colombia and the US signed a new bilateral cooperation framework in 2024, the Vida Colombia Strategy, which adopts a multidimensional human-security approach prioritising exacerbators of violence such as rural poverty, climate-change vulnerability, migration and human-rights violations, among others.

The US also bolstered its cooperation with Ecuador during the reporting period amid the deteriorating security situation in the latter country. A new bilateral security framework provides for the transfer of US military and financial aid to Ecuador, specialised technical training to fight criminal groups and drug trafficking, and the deployment of US security personnel for joint anti-narcotic operations.[17]

The above-mentioned strategies historically have been complemented by the operations of the US Southern Command and its partnership with over 20 regional armed forces. These operations include regional security exercises such as *Tradewinds*, *Fuerzas Comando*, SOUTHDEC and UNITAS.

Partly due to long-lasting financial and technical support from the US in domestic anti-narcotics efforts, Colombia has become a key player in regional security cooperation. The country leads the largest anti-narcotics operation worldwide, *Operation Orión*, with over 62 partner nations, 125 institutions and nine multilateral organisations across the Americas, Asia and Europe (see Figure 1).[18] It also partners with other regional states to provide technical training to fight drug trafficking. The US–Colombia Action Plan on Regional Security Cooperation, a bilateral cooperation agreement signed in 2012, is an essential component of Colombia's leadership in security partnerships and training in the region.

Curbing human smuggling and trafficking has increasingly taken centre stage in regional security-cooperation efforts. The migration emergency at the Colombia–Panama Darién Gap, which in 2023 saw over 520,000 people cross the border illegally, mostly headed to the US, has prompted new security-cooperation arrangements.[19] Building on its trilateral statement with Panama and Colombia in 2023, the US has included the two countries in its Joint Task Force Alpha designated area, along with El Salvador, Guatemala, Honduras and Mexico. The move provides Panama and Colombia with US law-enforcement support to prosecute criminal groups involved in human trafficking.

Cooperation with European countries has also strengthened against a backdrop of record cocaine consumption in Europe in 2023. This has involved an extension of existing police-cooperation mechanisms to fight transatlantic organised crime. The European Union notably revamped its security-cooperation framework with Latin America – the Europe Latin America

Programme of Assistance against Transnational Organised Crime (EL PAcCTO, now EL PAcCTO 2.0) – in November 2023 by including new Caribbean partners to boost regional and transnational efforts to fight drug trafficking between the Americas and Europe.

Non-state armed groups

The presence and activities of NSAGs in the region are shaped by drug-supply and -trafficking dynamics. In Colombia, the most powerful NSAGs – the Gulf Clan, the National Liberation Army (ELN) and the Central General Staff (EMC) – either directly engage in or oversee coca-leaf cultivation and cocaine-production laboratories, especially in border areas with Ecuador, Peru and Venezuela. They alternatively fight (or ally with) other NSAGs to retain (or expand) their cocaine-trafficking operations while also clashing with state security forces. Colombian criminal groups comprise numerous regional fronts and local units connected by national leadership. Their largest source of income is selling cocaine to Mexican and Brazilian DTOs and more recently to Italian and Balkan mafia-type organisations. Other significant NSAGs operate along key airborne and seaborne cocaine-trafficking routes connecting Colombia with final markets. Urban gangs, notably the Mara Salvatrucha (MS-13), often oversee and protect international drug loads from South America to Mexico, especially in Honduras and Guatemala. They do so while controlling the domestic retail of drugs, including marijuana and cocaine, and imposing illegal taxes on local populations and businesses.

In Mexico, the powerful Sinaloa Cartel and CJNG smuggle South American cocaine into the US. They also control the manufacturing (with precursors produced in China) and trafficking of synthetic drugs across the US southern border, especially fentanyl. Mexican DTOs are characterised by internal departments in charge of military, financial (including money-laundering) and trafficking operations. They increasingly outsource trafficking operations to smaller, local criminal organisations. Their outreach across the region, especially in Colombia, often takes place through investing in local cocaine-production supply chains or providing military financial aid to local NSAGs that sell them cocaine.

Brazil's First Capital Command (PCC) and Red Command have continued to expand their national and international operations as Brazil becomes an increasingly important transit country for South American cocaine trafficking to Europe, Africa and Asia. Brazilian criminal organisations have business ties with Colombian NSAGs, especially the ELN and Revolutionary Armed Forces of Colombia (FARC) dissidents, to buy cocaine and marijuana and transport them through the Amazon rainforest. They have also nurtured connections with European mafia-type organisations.

Across the Americas, extortion, robbery and kidnapping provide additional revenue streams for NSAGs; this is especially relevant for Haitian gangs. Moreover, environmental crimes (including illegal mining and logging) and human trafficking are becoming increasingly important business lines for the largest criminal groups in the region.

Third-party involvement

The deployment of a UN- and US-backed multinational security force led by Kenya in Haiti marked the return of third-party security forces' involvement in domestic armed conflicts in the Americas. The first contingent of 400 Kenyan police officers arrived in Port-au-Prince in June–July 2024. The mission has a target strength of 2,500 foreign troops, mostly from Kenya as well as the Bahamas, Bangladesh, Barbados, Belize, Benin, Chad and Jamaica.[20] It is tasked with protecting key infrastructure and securing safe elections scheduled for 2025.

During the reporting period, the UN Verification Mission in Colombia continued to support conflict-resolution and peacebuilding efforts in the country, as per the 2016 peace deal signed by the Colombian government and the former FARC. In August 2023, the mission extended its operations to verify the compliance of the Temporary National Bilateral Ceasefire between the Colombian government and the ELN, solidifying its role in the current peace process held by Petro's government.

Regional Humanitarian Trends

The human impact of conflict in the Americas remained high in the reporting period, with 17,845 fatalities associated with violent events for the countries covered in *The Armed Conflict Survey 2024*. While fatalities and violent events fell by 9% and 11% on average year-on-year (with significant drops in El Salvador and Honduras), security conditions remained dire in the region.[21] Violence spiked across areas of heightened criminal contestation, including in countries such as Ecuador that do not qualify for inclusion in *The Armed Conflict Survey 2024*.

Armed-violence dynamics, aggravated by the region's extreme climate vulnerability and enduring socio-economic and political fragilities, continued to drive human displacement from and across Latin America, with the number of refugees and internally displaced persons (IDPs) rising by 47% and 3% in the reporting period.[22] More generally, migration flows have continued unabated, often through new routes, including the treacherous Darién Gap, driving bilateral tensions and regional instability. Migration from Venezuela persisted, with approximately 328,000 Venezuelans (over 60% of a record 521,000 total migrants) crossing the Darién jungle in 2023 on their journey northward.[23] Almost eight million Venezuelans have left the country since 2015, mainly to neighbouring states (most notably Colombia) – one of the largest displacement crises in the world.[24]

Almost 190m people experienced severe or moderate food insecurity in Latin America and the Caribbean in 2023, around 28% of its total population. The prevalence of food insecurity was particularly high in the food-import-dependent and climate-vulnerable Caribbean region at 58.8%. Haiti appeared to be in a markedly drastic situation, with nearly 5m people, or half of its total population, experiencing severe food insecurity, one of the worst such situations globally.[25]

As a result of the above-referenced trends, in 2023 over 29m people were considered in need in Latin America and the Caribbean, with a required US$2.3 billion in humanitarian funding. As of December 2023, total funding had reached around US$620m, which ensured only a limited 28% coverage of humanitarian needs.[26]

Outlook

Prospects for peace

The outlook for durable peace in the Americas remains relatively bleak due to the intractable nature of conflict drivers and criminal groups' growing economic and political clout amid weakening state institutions. However, a number of ongoing initiatives and developments provide some reason for optimism regarding violence reduction in the region.

The success of the 'total peace' process in Colombia would arguably have the largest positive implications for the region as a whole, given the crucial role played by the country in global drugs supply chains. The initiative, launched by Petro in August 2022, made some significant progress during the reporting period, with ceasefires and road maps agreed with the ELN and FARC dissidents: the EMC and Second Marquetalia. However, the process remains fragile amid risks of broken ceasefires and the complexities of engaging in simultaneous peace negotiations with all active criminal groups in the country. The failure to date to start formal negotiations and agree on a ceasefire with the Gulf Clan, currently the most powerful NSAG in Colombia, is a case in point. Little international buy-in, notably from the US, for Petro's drug-policy-reform agenda, involving decriminalising coca leaf, is also challenging the initiative's success. Maduro's disputed victory in Venezuela's general elections in July 2024, if confirmed, would perpetuate the status quo, in which the government protects certain Colombian NSAGs and engages directly in criminal economies. This could undermine the 'total peace' process. On the other hand, if international and internal pressure forces Maduro out of office or to negotiate a democratic transition, Colombian NSAGs would likely lose their sponsor in Venezuela, providing them with a strong incentive to make 'total peace' a success.

The iron-fist approach followed by the Bukele government in El Salvador since March 2022 seems to have achieved a fragile pacification of the country, with violence levels decreasing to record lows and the state regaining control of most of its territory from an increasingly weak MS-13. The approach has won many supporters in Central America and beyond and has notably been partially replicated in Ecuador during the reporting period. However, doubts linger over its ability to curb violence in a durable way, amid insufficient fiscal resources to sustain its high costs, the additional strains it imposes on already overcrowded jails, and its debilitating impact on democratic institutions and human rights.

Finally, the appointment of a transitional government in Haiti tasked with organising elections by the end of 2025 along with the long-delayed deployment of a Kenya-led Multinational Security Support Mission are important steps towards stabilising the current critical political and security situation in the country. However, risks abound given the country's extremely fragile state institutions, all-powerful gangs, and escalating economic and humanitarian crises.

Escalation potential and regional spillovers

Criminal actors' reconfiguration of supply chains, networks of alliances and business portfolios will continue to drive conflict in the Americas, creating hotspots of armed violence and insecurity around new routes and market opportunities. Growing drug demand in Europe and South America will notably sustain criminal contestation over crucial drug-trafficking and -smuggling routes (including ports), with continued violence spikes in countries previously considered relatively peaceful. These include Ecuador and Argentina, but also Bolivia, Chile, Costa Rica, Paraguay and Uruguay. The Amazon region will remain another significant flashpoint due to its strategic position for trafficking routes, weak state presence, and under-guarded and porous national borders. The trend of increasing convergence between drug trafficking and various environmental crimes observed in recent years in the Amazon region, as well as in Central America and Mexico, is likely to persist, undermining climate resilience and mitigation efforts while exacerbating conflict drivers.

The rise of human trafficking and smuggling as a major revenue stream for criminal organisations will likely intensify, driven by restrictive immigration policies in the US and increasing migration flows due to instability in Venezuela, Central America and the Caribbean, including Haiti and Cuba. This presents a significant low-risk, high-profit opportunity for criminal groups, ranging from established Mexican DTOs to emerging groups like the Venezuelan Tren de Aragua gang, which has been expanding across the region by capitalising on its successful human-trafficking operations.

In North America, without major changes in current anti-narcotics approaches on both sides of the Mexico–US border and an improvement in the United States' relations with China, the fentanyl business will continue to flourish, driving increased overdose deaths, violence in Mexico and bilateral tensions.

Strategic prospects

The recent trend of heightened great-power competition in a region where the geopolitical order has traditionally been unipolar will likely intensify and continue to influence security dynamics. Specifically, the economic and geopolitical rivalry between China and the US is likely to worsen under a potential second Donald Trump presidency, should he win the November 2024 US elections. This will impact efforts to control the fentanyl health crisis in the US and the trafficking of synthetic drugs from Mexico, given China's key role in supplying precursors to Mexican DTOs. Considering China's growing importance to Latin America as a major importer, investor and provider of critical infrastructure (including for 5G deployment and safe-cities projects), US pressure to fully sever economic ties with China would face resistance from Latin American countries. It could lead to diplomatic frictions within the region and it might incentivise China to bolster its backing to authoritarian governments and engage in malicious activities, negatively impacting regional stability. Additionally, such a decoupling would strain the already limited resources of cash-strapped governments, hampering their ability to address underlying causes of conflict and potentially worsening trends in armed violence.

While less extensive than China's influence, the presence established in the region by revisionist powers like Russia and Iran, especially through their engagement with Venezuela, remains a significant concern. This is especially true given the likely continuation of high geopolitical tensions surrounding the Russia–Ukraine and Israel–Hamas wars.

Growing cocaine consumption and criminal infiltration in Europe will elevate Latin America's importance on the EU's foreign-policy agenda. This will likely prompt the EU to take a more active role in security cooperation with the region. The EU could also lend support to the growing calls from regional leaders, including Petro in Colombia, to explore alternatives to the current 'war on drugs' approach, addressing also the demand side and the root causes of drug trafficking.

A Trump presidency would likely result in a more confrontational stance towards Mexico on drug trafficking, particularly concerning fentanyl. However, the necessity for Mexico's cooperation in implementing US migration policies could help contain bilateral tensions and maintain cooperation on security and migration issues. This might preserve the cautious progress made by the Bicentennial Framework for Security, Public Health, and Safe Communities in addressing public-health issues related to drug consumption. Nonetheless, given Trump's support for liberal firearms policies in the US, the outlook for reducing the free movement of firearms across the border would remain bleak, perpetuating a persistent source of bilateral tension.

Regional Key Events

POLITICAL EVENTS

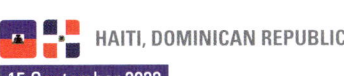
HAITI, DOMINICAN REPUBLIC

15 September 2023

Dominican President Luis Abinader closes the border with Haiti and deploys military and police forces to secure it.

MILITARY/VIOLENT EVENTS

 BRAZIL

2 August 2023

A military-police raid in the north of Rio de Janeiro State kills ten presumed members of local gangs.

 COLOMBIA

3 August

The Colombian government begins a six-month ceasefire with the ELN.

 **BOLIVIA, BRAZIL, COLOMBIA, ECUADOR, GUYANA, PERU, SURINAME, VENEZUELA**

8 August

Amazon Cooperation Treaty Organization member countries Bolivia, Brazil, Colombia, Ecuador, Guyana, Peru, Suriname and Venezuela sign the Belém Declaration to revamp multilateral initiatives against transnational crime in the Amazon.

 ECUADOR

9 August

Leading Ecuadorian presidential candidate Villavicencio is assassinated.

 HAITI

14–18 September

The Haitian police kill at least 30 civilians and gang members during clashes with the Baz Gran Grif de Saviengang in Artibonite.

VENEZUELA
17 October

Venezuela's Maduro government and the political opposition sign an agreement to ensure free and competitive presidential elections in 2024.

VENEZUELA
3 December

The Maduro government in Venezuela wins a non-binding referendum on annexing the disputed Essequibo region (Guyana), although the turnout appears lower than officially claimed.

HAITI
13–16 November

Clashes between the G9 and G-Pèp gang alliances in Cité Soleil, Port-au-Prince, result in 166 casualties.

BRAZIL
24 December

The Brazilian police arrest Luís Antônio da Silva Braga (alias 'Zinho'), the leader of the largest militia group in Rio de Janeiro known as the Gang of Zinho.

MEXICO
30 December

Armed groups kidnap 32 migrants in Tamaulipas, Mexico, for extortion.

MEXICO
4 January 2024

The Michoacán Family criminal group carries out a drone attack in Buenavista de los Hurtado, Guerrero, Mexico, killing six and injuring 13 civilians.

ECUADOR
9 January 2024

Ecuador's President Noboa declares an 'internal armed conflict' amid a spike in criminal violence.

EL SALVADOR
4 February

Bukele is re-elected for a second term in controversial Salvadoran presidential elections in a landslide victory.

BRAZIL
8 February

The Brazilian police carry out search warrants against four ministers who served in former president Jair Bolsonaro's administration for their attempts to overturn the results of the 2022 presidential elections.

CHILE, VENEZUELA
21 February

Unidentified men dressed as Chilean police officers kill a former Venezuelan military officer in Santiago in an attack attributed by Chilean authorities to the Venezuelan criminal group Tren de Aragua.

HAITI
29 February

A gang coalition launches a series of attacks against Haiti's government institutions in Port-au-Prince, including the National Palace, main penitentiary centres and police stations.

COLOMBIA
17 March

The Colombian government announces the suspension of its ceasefire deal with the EMC in three provinces after violence breaks out in Cauca.

Regional Analysis: Americas 31

HAITI
2 March
Gangs attack Haiti's National Penitentiary, prompting the escape of nearly 4,000 prisoners, including notable gang leaders and the 17 Colombians involved in the assassination of president Jovenel Moïse.

EL SALVADOR
25 March
Bukele deploys 5,000 troops and 1,000 police officers to Chalatenango, El Salvador, in response to two gang-related deaths.

COLOMBIA
16 April
Colombia's government confirms that the EMC's leader, alias 'Ivan Mordisco', is no longer participating in the 'total peace' process and is resuming military operations.

ECUADOR
22 April
Ecuadorian security forces capture Los Lobos gang leader Fabricio Colón Pico after his escape from prison in January.

PARAGUAY
24 April
The Rotela Clan and Brazil's PCC clash in Pedro Juan Caballero jail in Paraguay, leaving four inmates dead.

VENEZUELA
18 April
The US reimposes sanctions on Venezuelan oil in response to the Maduro administration's non-compliance with the commitments it made to facilitate an inclusive 2024 election.

HAITI
25 April
Haitian prime minister Ariel Henry resigns from office as a transitional council is sworn in to form a new interim government.

COLOMBIA
1 May
The Colombian government announces a break in diplomatic ties with Israel in protest against Israeli military operations in Gaza.

MEXICO
2 June
Claudia Sheinbaum, from the ruling Morena party, is elected as the first female president of Mexico amid the deadliest political campaign cycle in recent years.

HONDURAS
26 June
A US court sentences former president of Honduras Juan Orlando Hernández (2014–22) to 45 years in prison for drug trafficking.

HAITI
25 June
The first contingent of Kenyan police officers land in Haiti as part of an international task force to contain gang violence.

VENEZUELA
28 July
Both Maduro and his political opponent claim victory in Venezuelan general elections marred by widespread irregularities and fraud.

Notes

1. UN Office on Drugs and Crime (UNODC), 'Global Study on Homicide 2023', 2023.
2. Votar Entre Balas [Voting Amid Bullets], 'Democracia vulnerada: el crimen organizado en las elecciones y la administración pública en México' [Democracy undermined: organised crime in elections and public administration in Mexico], April 2024; and Céline González and Sandra Ley, '¿Cómo vulnera el crimen organizado las elecciones y los gobiernos municipales?' [How does organised crime undermine elections and municipal governments?], Animal Politico, 19 April 2024.
3. The International Committee of the Red Cross (ICRC) counts 84 armed groups of humanitarian concern in the Americas, with over 40m people living under their full or contested control. See Matthew Bamber-Zryd, 'ICRC Engagement with Armed Groups in 2024', ICRC Humanitarian Law & Policy, 31 October 2024.
4. UNODC, 'Global Report on Cocaine 2023: Local Dynamics, Global Challenges', March 2023.
5. David Ehl, 'Understanding Ecuador's "Internal Armed Conflict"', Deutsche Welle, 14 January 2024.
6. 'Violencia Electoral en México: el Gobierno Reconoce el Asesinato de 15 Aspirantes' [Electoral violence in Mexico: government acknowledges the murder of 15 candidates], Agencia EFE, 3 April 2024.
7. Corbin Aron Lee, 'The Institutional Deficiencies Which Cause Mexico's 95% Impunity Rate', *Mexican Law Review*, vol. 15, no. 2, December 2022.
8. Data available from World Prison Brief, 'Highest to Lowest – Prison Population Rate'.
9. Pan Ho Liu, 'Central America Rights Organization Reports Almost 80,000 Arrests and Over 250 Deaths in El Salvador Since 2022 State of Emergency', Jurist News, 11 July 2024.
10. William Maloney et al., *Competition: The Missing Ingredient for Growth?* (Washington DC: World Bank Publications, 2024).
11. IDB, 'The Complexities of Inequality in Latin America and the Caribbean', 6 March 2024; Carlos Rodríguez Castelán et al., 'Nine Key Facts About Poverty and Inequality in Latin America and the Caribbean', World Bank Blogs, 2 July 2024; and Lucas Chancel et al., 'World Inequality Report 2022', World Inequality Lab, 2022, p. 12.
12. Aaron O'Neill, 'Youth Unemployment Rate in Selected World Regions in 2000 to 2023', Statista, 12 July 2024.
13. Pan American Health Organization, 'Half of All Deaths of Young People in the Americas Can Be Prevented', 5 March 2019.
14. American Institutes for Research, 'Latin America and the Caribbean – Youth Violence Prevention'.
15. Aldrin Ballesteros, 'Fentanyl Seizures at the Southwest Border: A Breakdown by CBP Areas of Responsibility', Wilson Center, 29 August 2023.
16. Office of the Spokesperson, 'Global Coalition to Address Synthetic Drug Threats', US Department of State, 15 March 2024.
17. In June 2023, the inaugural US–Ecuador Defense Bilateral Working Group agreed on a shared national road map. This was followed by a memorandum of understanding including an agreement to allow the presence of US military personnel, later ratified in September 2023. As part of the bilateral agreements, in January 2024 the first lot of US military equipment was delivered to Ecuador and in March 2024 the first US–Ecuador High-Level Dialogue was held.
18. The latest *Orión* campaign (2023–24), *Orión* XIII, achieved record-high levels of cocaine seizures (196,000 kilograms). Centro Internacional de Investigación y Análisis contra el Narcotráfico Marítimo [International Centre for Research and Analysis against Maritime Drug Trafficking], Colombian Navy, 2024.
19. Defensoría del Pueblo [Ombudsman's Office], 'Más de 520.000 personas migrantes atravesaron la selva del Darién en el 2023' [More than 520,000 migrants crossed the Darién jungle in 2023], 26 January 2024.
20. Marina Daras, Gloria Aradi and Pascal Fletcher, 'Haiti Vows to Restore Order With Kenya-led Force's Help', BBC News, 26 June 2024; and White House, 'Statement by President Joe Biden on the Deployment of the Multinational Security Support Mission to Haiti', 25 June 2024.
21. IISS analysis based on data from the Armed Conflict Location & Event Data Project (ACLED), www.acleddata.com.
22. The IDP figure includes only displacement as a result of conflict and violence.
23. Manuel Rueda, 'A Record 400k Migrants Have Crossed the Treacherous Darién Jungle to Reach the U.S.', WUNC, 5 October 23; and Daniela Mohor, 'The Darién Gap Migration Crisis in Six Graphs, and One Map', *New Humanitarian*, 15 January 2024.
24. Betilde Muñoz-Pogossian and Alexandra Winkler, 'The Persistence of the Venezuelan Migrant and Refugee Crisis', Center for Strategic and International Studies, 27 November 23; and UN High Commissioner for Refugees, 'Venezuela Situation'.
25. Food and Agriculture Organization of the United Nations (FAO), International Fund for Agricultural Development (IFAD), United Nations Children's Fund (UNICEF), World Food Programme (WFP) and World Health Organization (WHO), *The State of Food Security and Nutrition in the World 2024 – Financing to End Hunger, Food Insecurity and Malnutrition in All Its Forms* (Rome: FAO, IFAD, UNICEF, WFP and WHO, 2024).
26. Humanitarian Action, 'Global Humanitarian Overview 2024: Latin America and the Caribbean', 8 December 2023, p. 86.

The Expansion and Diversification of Mexican Cartels: Dynamic New Actors and Markets

The Latin American transnational criminal landscape is undergoing a profound, violent evolution. As it transforms, the organisations able to adapt, diversify and exercise territorial control are imposing new operational paradigms across the hemisphere. Traditionally, cartels controlled limited geographic areas and moved a single product, usually cocaine. The new transnational criminal elite, however, move multiple products far beyond the geographic and market confines of the recent past (see Figure 1).

The CJNG now leading the way

The Cartel Jalisco New Generation (CJNG), based in Jalisco, Mexico, leads these paradigm shifts. The CJNG is known for its violence and military skills in combating both rival cocaine cartels and the Mexican state. Beyond moving tonnes of cocaine to the United States and European markets and laundering billions of dollars in illicit proceeds, the CJNG has grown into a multifaceted, transnational criminal structure. As the US Drug Enforcement Administration (DEA) noted, 'internationally, the Jalisco Cartel has a presence and influence through associates, facilitators, and brokers on every continent except Antarctica'.[1]

The CJNG's current documented activities comprise, among other things, supplying methamphetamine and fentanyl to the growing market in the US; sourcing precursors from China, India and Turkiye; controlling illicit gold-mining operations in Ecuador and Venezuela in alliance with Colombian and Venezuelan criminal groups; gaining access to and partial control of key ports in Mexico, Central America and the Southern Cone; expanding cocaine-distribution networks and money-laundering operations into Europe with the Italian 'Ndrangheta; controlling new operational centres in Argentina, Brazil and Paraguay; controlling key human-smuggling and human-trafficking routes through Central America and Mexico; and driving the multibillion-dollar counterfeit-pharmaceutical trade by disguising its synthetic-drug products as pharmaceuticals. These myriad activities have diversified the CJNG's revenue streams and allowed it to enhance its military capacities, which are evident in the countless videos the group posts on social media featuring its members armed with machine guns, tanks, body armour and armoured vehicles. The organisation has formed new alliances from a position of strength as it has expanded its global reach. Among others, it has forged new partnerships with Brazil's First Capital Command (PCC) for port access and weapons; emerging Ecuadorian gangs due to their control of prime real estate in illicit pathways in that country; and the Italian 'Ndrangheta and other European organised-crime groups to expand illicit markets and diversify money-laundering operations.

The CJNG's main rival in the contest for diversification and territorial control is the more traditional and older Sinaloa Cartel. The CJNG is widely viewed as more aggressive, ruthless and less willing to negotiate with rival power centres when moving into new territory than the Sinaloa organisation. Though it has been pushed out of many territories in its heightened struggle for routes and dominance with the CJNG, the Sinaloa Cartel remains formidable in the cocaine, methamphetamine and fentanyl trades. The CJNG began as an offshoot of a Sinaloa Cartel ally, the Milenio Cartel, more than a decade ago. A series of further divisions and arrests led to the CJNG's formation. It fought several bloody wars with the Sinaloa Cartel, the Los Zetas cartel and other rival groups in Mexico as well as the Mexican state.

Both the CJNG and the Sinaloa Cartel began as cocaine- and marijuana-trafficking organisations, and both traditionally confined their criminal economies to moving cocaine from Central America across Mexico and into the US market. They remain among the top cocaine-trafficking organisations in the world. Over the past five years, the Sinaloa Cartel has established close ties with the Colombian-based National Liberation Army (ELN) guerrilla group, currently mostly operating in Venezuela under the protection of the Maduro regime, which gave it access to border jungle areas in exchange for military

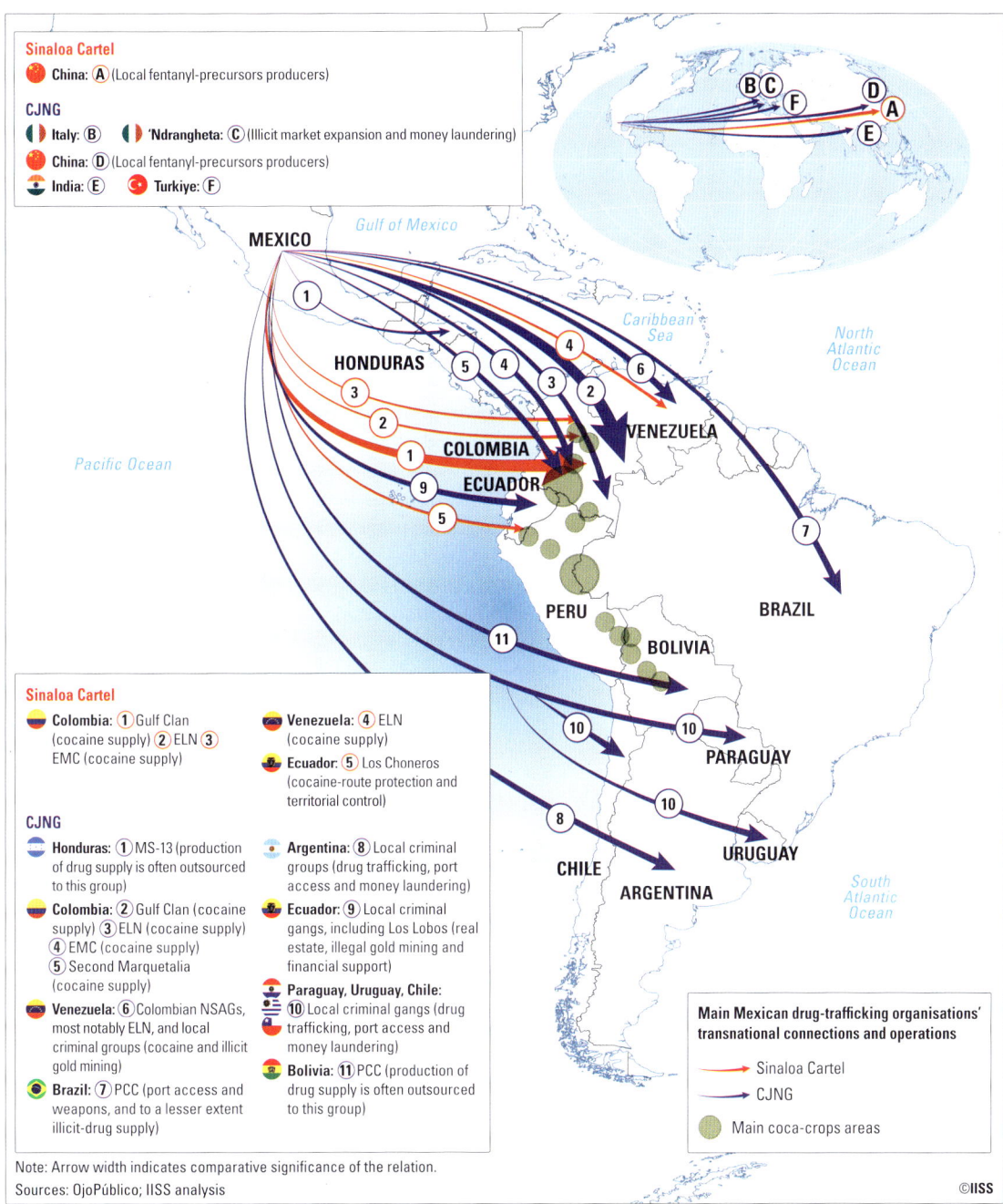

Figure 1: Main Mexican drug-trafficking organisations' transnational connections and operations

and economic support. As the ELN pushed into the cocaine trade, the Sinaloa Cartel became its primary international ally to move product to market.

However, global markets have shifted and expanded beyond cocaine, as described in *The Armed Conflict Survey 2023* Americas Regional Spotlight essay, 'Shifting Dynamics and New Conflict Zones in Latin America', introducing new extra-regional actors and economic prospects. As an opportunistic enterprise, the CJNG added additional products to its global portfolio. Although there is little hard data to quantify the values of the surging global synthetic-drug market, the United Nations and the US DEA believe that the sheer volume of users and ease of production have expanded the market so much that it now rivals the global cocaine market in importance. The Sinaloa Cartel is engaged in some of these new markets, but it does not command the market share, global reach or sophistication of its rival. One recent study of synthetic-drug trafficking in Latin America found that the CJNG and the Sinaloa Cartel buy and move synthetic drugs in bulk, getting paid a premium for their services, but, once the drugs are sold wholesale, retail of the drugs falls largely to local criminal networks. This keeps the high-profit part of the supply chain in the hands of the cartels but leaves the labour-intensive, lower-profit side of sales to local groups looking for ways to move up in the drug-trafficking structural pyramid.

Ecuador: the violent-rivalry epicentre

The two Mexican cartels' power and their conflict are most visible in Ecuador, which for decades had been one of the least violent countries in the hemisphere. The CJNG and the Sinaloa Cartel now compete there for territory, allies and routes; access to ports and the Panama Canal; control of cocaine-production centres on the Colombia–Ecuador border and cocaine warehouses in Ecuador; and control of the poorly regulated banking system operating in US dollars that has made Ecuador a money-laundering hub.

Violence is driven by the contest between the two largest local gangs in Ecuador – Los Lobos and Los Choneros, allied with the CJNG and the Sinaloa Cartel respectively – as well as the CJNG's aggressive push into new areas controlled by local gangs, cocaine-trafficking groups linked to the former Revolutionary Armed Forces of Colombia guerrillas, and an assortment of criminal bands. In 2023, for the first time ever, Ecuador claimed the title of the most violent country in Latin America, with the national homicide rate rising by 74.5% year-on-year from 22.5 per 100,000 inhabitants in 2022 to 44.5 in 2023. The homicide rate rose by 800% over the past five years.[2]

Both the older and more established Los Choneros – which takes its name from its original hometown of Chone – and Los Lobos provide route protection and territorial control for their respective Mexican allies. The Mexican cartels supplied weapons, military training and financing to the Ecuadorian groups to fight for vital illicit pathways along the coast, primarily centred on the main port of Guayaquil. This allowed the once-local street gangs to evolve into powerful non-state armed groups (NSAGs) that raise tens of millions of dollars a year, extorting protection money from thousands of small businesses that operate in territories controlled by the groups. The groups' territorial control also allows them to raise millions of dollars through the local retail sale of cocaine and synthetic drugs in their areas of dominance, provided by the Mexican groups, who often pay the gangs in product rather than cash.[3] The groups' diversification goes beyond drugs to other commodities. Los Lobos, for instance, also directly controls at least 20 centres of illegal gold mining, using CJNG muscle and support to push out smaller local groups. The group reportedly collects protection money, known as *vacuna*, from another 30 mines. In each place, 'the criminal structure has established ties to the police, military, state agents and the justice system to guarantee its protection and impunity'.[4] This trade is particularly valuable to Mexican cartels because gold can easily be used to launder illicit proceeds into an economy that is dollarised.

These groups and their Mexican allies showed their power in the 9 August 2023 assassination of leading presidential candidate Fernando Villavicencio, gunned down in the capital of Quito following a campaign event. Ecuadorian investigators say the assassination of Villavicencio, an outspoken anti-corruption candidate, was planned in the Cotopaxi prison by Los Lobos with the CJNG's backing and carried out by Colombian hitmen hired by the Mexican cartel. In January 2024, a series of bloody events led President Daniel Noboa to declare a 60-day 'state of exception' followed by an indefinite and unprecedented declaration of a 'state of internal conflict', allowing the military to deploy to the streets and take over the nation's prisons.[5]

Synthetic drugs in diversification plans

The expansion of both the CJNG and the Sinaloa Cartel pushed illicit markets toward the synthetic-drug trade, which now rivals cocaine as a bedrock of cartels' business models. Synthetic-drug consumption is on the rise, is highly addictive and is often lethal. It is now considered by the US and much of Latin America to pose a greater health danger and conflict risk than cocaine. The director of the US DEA said the agency's 'top operational priority is to relentlessly pursue and defeat … the Sinaloa Cartel and the Jalisco Cartel[,] … [which] are primarily responsible for driving the current illicit fentanyl and drug poisoning epidemic in the United States'.[6]

Synthetic drugs, primarily methamphetamine and fentanyl, offer several advantages in comparison to cocaine and heroin for cartels. As the UN Office on Drugs and Crime (UNODC) found, synthetic drugs incur lower operational costs, face fewer production impediments, have a lower risk of interdiction, are not tied to a fixed geographic location or climate conditions, and have shorter production times. These are significant advantages to trafficking structures with global reach and alliances, and the premier group of that nature is the CJNG. The Mexican cartels import precursor chemicals and produce their own synthetic drugs, usually in the form of pills that cost ten cents to make and are sold for US$5–U$25 each.[7] While the Mexican groups function as the CEOs in these drugs supply chains, much of the actual production is farmed out to smaller criminal groups such as the Mara Salvatrucha (MS-13) gang in Honduras and the PCC in Brazil and Bolivia.[8]

A study of the precursor flow into Mexico identified two provinces in China as producing and exporting most precursors reaching Latin America largely via cargo ships. The products arrive in Mexico camouflaged through mislabelled bills of lading, front companies and false invoices, and are protected by webs of corruption. The chemicals are marketed and sold on the internet and dark net through networks of fixers who keep the CJNG and other groups' production facilities supplied.

More diversification on the horizon

The expanding illicit economies and the weak state responses to these challenges make it likely that the CJNG and the Sinaloa Cartel will continue increasing their territorial control and product placement, with the accompanying violence their rivalry brings. With the CJNG now visible on the ground in Argentina, Chile, Paraguay and Uruguay in drug-trafficking, port-access and money-laundering activities, these countries risk following Ecuador's path toward rising violence and empowered local gangs.[9] None of these countries are prepared for NSAGs' rapid emergence as significant forces in the near term, as they lack the necessary law-enforcement training, banking regulations, anti-money-laundering and other legal frameworks, and overall situational awareness of the dynamics of the evolving criminal economies.

Beyond the growing synthetic-drug trade, other illicit economies are expanding, both through criminal hydras like the CJNG and through local and regional groups that control specific territories that make these economies viable. These include wildlife trafficking; the swelling human-smuggling and human-trafficking business; the unregistered movement of strategic minerals such as lithium, cobalt and rare-earth minerals; and counterfeit pharmaceuticals. All these markets have enormous growth potential where the model of territorial control, coupled with alliances between super groups like the CJNG and local groups, is likely to succeed. At the same time, states under siege have struggled to successfully challenge the Mexican cartels and their seemingly endless financial resources, willingness to resort to extreme violence and almost blanket impunity. Given its proven ability to embrace new economies far from the traditional cocaine-based model, the CJNG will likely be the dominant illicit actor in the hemisphere for the foreseeable future.

Notes

[1] US Department of Justice, 'Statement of Anne Milgram, Administrator, Drug Enforcement Administration, U.S. Department of Justice, Before the Senate Committee on Foreign Relations, for a Hearing Entitled "Countering Illicit Fentanyl Trafficking"', 15 February 2023.

[2] Juliana Manjarrés and Christopher Newton, 'InSight Crime's 2023 Homicide Round-up', InSight Crime, 21 February 2024.

[3] This summary is drawn from author interviews with police intelligence officials and transnational-organised-crime experts in Quito, Ecuador, March 2024.

[4] 'Narcomafias del oro: grupo criminal Los Lobos opera más de 20 minas en Ecuador' [Gold narcomafias: the Los Lobos criminal group operates more than 20 mines in Ecuador], Ojo Público, 7 January 2024.

[5] The immediate cause of the January wave of violence was the discovery that José Adolfo Macías Villamar, alias 'Fito', the leader of Los Choneros, had escaped from a prison he had turned into a luxury resort. According to Ecuadorian police intelligence officials, Macías probably escaped before Christmas, at least two weeks before he was declared a

fugitive. The ensuing prison raids set off coordinated riots in six prisons, the takeover of a major television station in Guayaquil by a group of armed men threatening to kill the employees on live television, and the kidnapping of several policemen. Cristina J. Orgaz, 'Quien es Adolfo Macías, "Fito", cuya fuga de una prisión en Ecuador llevó al presidente Noboa a declarar el estado de excepción en el país' [Who is Adolfo Macias, 'Fito', whose escape from a prison in Ecuador led President Noboa to declare a national state of exception], BBC News, 9 January 2024; 'Los rehenes contaron como fue la toma del canal de TV en Ecuador: "Hemos vivido el terror en vivo"' [The hostages tell how the TV station in Ecuador was taken: 'We lived the terror live'], Infobae, 9 January 2024; Vanessa Buschschlüter, 'Ecuador Prisoners Take Guards Hostage After Drug Lord's Escape', BBC News, 9 January; and author interviews in Quito, Ecuador, March 2024.

[6] US Department of Justice, 'Statement of Anne Milgram, Administrator, Drug Enforcement Administration, U.S. Department of Justice, Before the Senate Committee on Foreign Relations, for a Hearing Entitled "Countering Illicit Fentanyl Trafficking"'.

[7] *Ibid.*

[8] The author visited an MS-13 methamphetamine laboratory in San Pedro Sula, Honduras, in August 2023, controlled by the CJNG, which bought the product for resale on the local market, in Mexico and in the US. In author interviews with Brazilian police intelligence in November 2023, the officials possessed documentation of PCC methamphetamine and fentanyl production.

[9] Author interviews in each country, June–November 2023.

Regional Spotlight: Americas

MEXICO

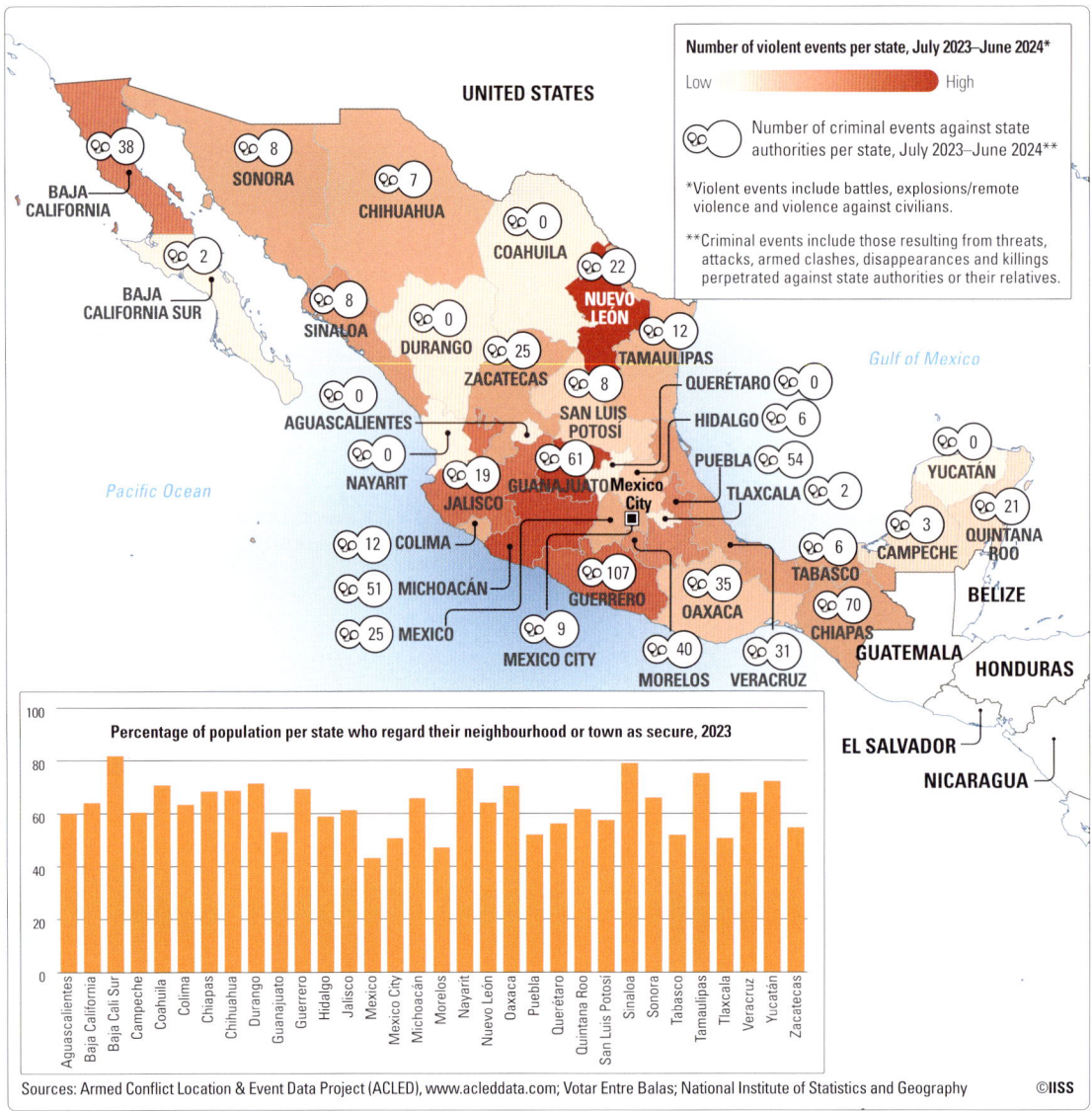

Conflict Overview

Mexico has contended with large and powerful drug-trafficking organisations (DTOs) since the 1970s. The current phase of armed conflict began in 2006, after the breakdown of numerous unofficial agreements at the state and local levels (following the end of the Institutional Revolutionary Party's 70-year rule in 2000) resulted in a surge in cartel violence. This, in turn, led then-president Felipe Calderón (2006–12) to launch the 'war on drugs'. By confronting Mexico's DTOs directly, Calderón aimed to break their power, which is derived from a diversified set of revenue and money-laundering streams. He received significant support from the United States in this effort, notably through the Mérida Initiative in 2008.

Country Profile: Mexico

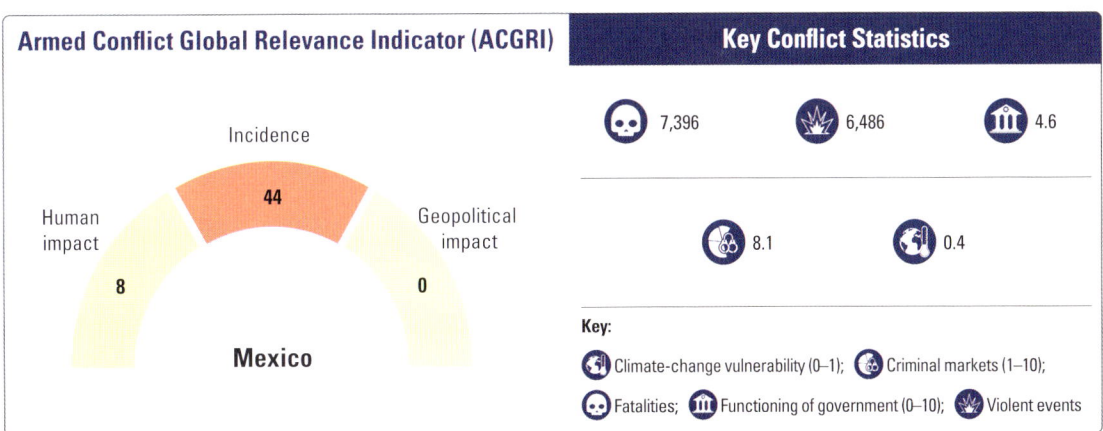

ACGRI pillars: IISS calculation based on multiple sources for 2023 and 2024 (scale: 0–100), except for some cases according to data availability. See Notes on Methodology and Data Appendix for all variables and further details on Key Conflict Statistics.

Conflict(s)	Type	Start date
Armed violence driven by DTOs	I OC	2006

Key: I OC Internal: organised crime

Since then, the conflict has evolved through multiple phases and presidential administrations. The DTO landscape has repeatedly splintered over time, initially due to the Calderón administration's 'decapitation strategy' targeting DTO leadership. The Sinaloa Cartel and Cartel Jalisco New Generation (CJNG) have become the most powerful groups, with large international networks (see the Americas Regional Spotlight chapter). DTOs have continued to diversify their revenue streams beyond illicit drugs, while accessing increasingly powerful weapons and ammunition primarily from the US. These developments have expanded the geographical reach and intensity of cartel violence, particularly in the southern Mexican states, including Chiapas, Guerrero and Michoacán.

Mexican authorities have been successful in making some high-profile arrests of DTO leaders, particularly among those in the Sinaloa Cartel.[1] Nevertheless, these organisations have leveraged their almost endless economic resources to infiltrate state institutions, as was made abundantly clear by the 2023 conviction in the US of Calderón's secretary of public security, Genaro García Luna, for using his position to protect the Sinaloa Cartel in exchange for bribes. Instances of corruption and collaboration with DTOs are reported at all levels of the Mexican government and continue to exacerbate conflict. Despite these concerns, the US, Mexico's most important ally in the fight against DTOs, signed a new security-cooperation agreement with Mexico in 2021 (the Mexico–US Bicentennial Framework for Security, Public Health, and Safe Communities), which remains in force.[2]

Conflict Update

During the reporting period, DTOs continued to expand their activities in the production and distribution of illicit drugs, while also diversifying into new products and markets. They notably increased their production of methamphetamine, synthetic opioids and heroin for international sale, using Chinese mafia-type organisations that launder money via major investments in the marijuana industry in the US. While the US remains the main market for such drugs, DTOs' reach has expanded to Asia, Australia and Europe.

Revenue-stream diversification beyond illicit drugs also accelerated over the last year. This potentially signals a new era of DTO activity that includes control of human-smuggling routes, as well as recruitment networks for migrants looking to travel abroad, often through collaboration with smaller criminal groups. Migrant smuggling is likely to become an increasingly important revenue stream in the coming years. By late 2023, its profitability had sparked violent disputes within the ranks of the Sinaloa Cartel, as rival factions fought for control of key routes. New groups are now struggling for control of this lucrative industry, including the CJNG. Some groups are also increasing activity in Mexico's growing export agriculture industry. DTOs' ties to the avocado industry in Michoacán, for example, go back decades. Their involvement includes both extortion rackets, run by groups like Los Zetas and the Michoacán Family, and arrangements with avocado producers to illegally displace local communities and clear forest land (including in protected areas) to plant avocado trees.

After spending his first four years in office advocating a 'hugs, not bullets' approach to anti-DTO operations, outgoing President Andrés Manuel López Obrador largely abandoned that position over the reporting period and intensified military involvement in public-security operations. The president has increasingly placed more responsibilities for security and transport infrastructure under military (rather than civilian) control, including customs operations as well as the construction and operation of airports and railways. As a result, total military budgets have more than doubled since the year before he took office, although growth in core defence spending has been more modest, averaging 4.2% in real terms once spending on infrastructure is excluded. As a result of both López Obrador's decision to escalate Mexico's direct confrontation with DTOs and increasing rates of violence, instances of armed interaction between criminal groups and police and military forces grew in key hotspots by 24% from 2022–23, even as López Obrador and his Morena party attempted to downplay this trend.[3] There is also active debate over the accuracy of the federal government's homicide and violent-crimes statistics, which many victims and human-rights organisations claim are artificially low.

Throughout the reporting period, the Sinaloa Cartel and the CJNG continued to fight over territorial control of key trafficking routes from Central America to Chiapas and Guerrero. At the same time, the Sinaloa Cartel engaged in turf wars in Nuevo León and Guanajuato with the CJNG and other criminal groups, including the Cártel del Noreste (a Los Zetas splinter group). While violent struggles in the north and centre of the country are long-standing, increasing violence in the southern Mexican states is relatively new and suggests an intensifying level of conflict with major potential impacts on tourism and other industries. Persistently high rates of political violence in the run-up to the June 2024 general elections were particularly concerning, with at least 15 candidates for office assassinated and at least 100 candidates requesting additional protection due to threats of violence.[4] (Non-governmental expert monitoring organisations claim that even more candidates – at least 29 – have been killed since the start of 2024).[5] The wave of violence against candidates demonstrates the close relationship between DTO power struggles and Mexico's major political parties.

Mexico's incoming president, Claudia Sheinbaum, is the former mayor of Mexico City and a member of the Morena party. Unlike López Obrador, Sheinbaum has spent extended time in the US and demonstrated a greater willingness for bilateral cooperation as Mexico City's mayor. She has recently announced the appointment of Omar García Harfuch, a former federal police officer, as security minister; in his first public comments, García indicated that Sheinbaum will continue the close coordination between federal police and military forces on security policy that has been a hallmark of López Obrador's security strategy.

Conflict Parties

Secretariat of National Defence (SEDENA) – army and air force

Strength: 216,000 active military personnel (186,000 army and 30,000 air force); additional 75,500 military personnel assigned to the National Guard (GN).[6]

Areas of operation: Nationwide but concentrated in the north and west Pacific states: Baja California, Chihuahua, Coahuila, Guerrero, Jalisco, Michoacán, Sonora and Tamaulipas.

Secretariat of National Defence (SEDENA) – army and air force

Leadership: Maj.-Gen. Luis Crecencio Sandoval (head of SEDENA), Maj.-Gen. Ricardo Trevilla Trejo (head of the joint chiefs of staff), Maj.-Gen. Celestino Ávila Astudillo (head of the army) and Maj.-Gen. Bertín Hernández Mercado (head of the air force).

Structure: Mexico's defence ministry has two sections: SEDENA and the Secretariat of the Navy (SEMAR). SEDENA comprises the army and the air force. The army is split into 12 military divisions and 46 zones. The air force has four divisions. The General Staff of National Defence is made up of eight divisions, of which the second and seventh divisions focus on DTOs.

History: The Ministry of War and the Navy was created in 1821 to supervise the army and the navy. In 1939, it was divided to create SEDENA and SEMAR.

Objectives: Provide internal security and fight drug trafficking.

Opponents: DTOs.

Affiliates/allies: SEMAR, GN and special-forces combat group GAIN (Drug Trafficking Information Analysis Group), which is in charge of capturing DTO leaders. SEDENA is also supported by the National Intelligence Centre (CNI) and the Attorney General's Office, as well as foreign governments, through cooperation programmes (e.g., the Bicentennial Framework for Security, Public Health, and Safe Communities with the US and, previously, the Mérida Initiative).

Resources/capabilities: Infantry, light armoured vehicles and helicopters. 2023 budget: US$6.3 billion (MXN 111.9bn); 2024 budget: US$15.2bn (MXN 259.4bn).[7]

Secretariat of the Navy (SEMAR)

Strength: 71,000 active military personnel; 14,500 additional military personnel assigned to the GN.[8]

Areas of operation: Mexico's coasts, divided into the Pacific and the Gulf of Mexico–Caribbean zones.

Leadership: Adm. José Rafael Ojeda Durán (head of SEMAR) and Adm. Alfredo Hernández Suárez (chief of the naval staff).

Structure: Divided into General (70%) and Naval Infantry Corps (marines; 30%), which operate in eight naval regions and 18 naval zones (12 in the Pacific and six in the Gulf and Caribbean). The marines' special forces also combat criminal groups in Mexico's interior.

History: Created in 1821. SEMAR separated from SEDENA in 1939.

Objectives: Defend Mexico's coasts, strategic infrastructure (mainly oil platforms in the Gulf of Mexico) and the environment at sea, and fight piracy.

Opponents: DTOs, especially those that traffic people along the coasts, from South America and Central America, and those that transport drugs via the sea from Colombia and Venezuela.

Affiliates/allies: SEDENA, GN and CNI. SEMAR also cooperates with the US Coast Guard at the border.

Resources/capabilities: Fast vessels for interception, exploration and intelligence; supported by naval aviation. 2023 budget: US$2.4bn (MXN 41.9bn); 2024 budget: US$4.2bn (MXN 71.9bn).[9]

National Guard (GN)

Strength: 115,000 active personnel (including 90,000 personnel assigned from SEDENA and SEMAR).[10]

Areas of operation: Across the whole country. The states of Guanajuato, Guerrero, Jalisco, México, Michoacán, Oaxaca and Veracruz had the highest number of GN units (referred to as 'operational control regions') at the end of 2022.

Leadership: Gen. (retd) David Córdova Campos (commissioner).

Structure: Organised in 266 coordination regions across the country. In September 2022, SEDENA took full management control of the GN. However, in April 2023, Mexico's Supreme Court ruled that this move was unconstitutional.

History: After the creation of the Secretariat of Public Security (SSP) and the formation of the Federal Police under the Calderón administration, both president Enrique Peña Nieto (2012–18) and President López Obrador (2018–24) dissolved, then dramatically reorganised, functions of the SSP. The GN began operating in May 2019 by presidential order. The law gave GN personnel the authority to stop suspected criminals on the streets. López Obrador has increasingly moved anti-DTO operations under military control; by 2022, the Federal Police, along with military and naval police, were incorporated into a newly created GN unit under SEDENA.

Objectives: Reduce the level of violence in the country and combat DTOs.

Opponents: DTOs and medium-sized criminal organisations.

Affiliates/allies: SEDENA, SEMAR, and local and municipal police.

Resources/capabilities: Acquired resources from the defunct Federal Police, including helicopter teams and equipment such as assault rifles. The GN relies on intelligence from SEDENA, SEMAR and the CNI. The 2023 citizen-protection operational budget for the GN was US$1.9bn (MXN 34.5bn); the budget for 2024 is US$2.2bn (MXN 37.8bn).[11]

Cartel Jalisco New Generation (CJNG)

Strength: Unclear.

Areas of operation: Headquartered in the state of Jalisco, with a presence in most states, particularly Colima, Guanajuato, Guerrero, Jalisco, Michoacán and Nayarit. It also controls the Pacific ports of Manzanillo and Lázaro Cárdenas, where chemicals from China enter Mexico. It has rapidly expanded

Cartel Jalisco New Generation (CJNG)

in the US, where it is thought to have a presence in 35 states and Puerto Rico, and in South America, including Argentina, Colombia and Ecuador.

Leadership: The main leader is Nemesio Oseguera Cervantes, commonly known as 'El Mencho'.

Structure: El Mencho successfully co-opted all regional leaders of the Michoacán Family and the Knights Templar to control the laboratories in the Michoacán mountains.

History: Formed in 2011 in Guadalajara, Jalisco, the CJNG initially produced methamphetamine in rural laboratories in Jalisco and Michoacán. In 2012–13, it expanded to Veracruz. Since 2015–16, its influence has grown throughout the country, thanks in part to gaps left after the government successfully targeted other DTOs (such as the Michoacán Family, the Knights Templar, Los Zetas and the Sinaloa Cartel). It has also shifted to producing and trafficking synthetic drugs such as fentanyl and counterfeit pharmaceuticals, using precursor chemicals sourced from Asia.

Objectives: Maintain supremacy among Mexico's criminal networks.

Opponents: Other DTOs, particularly Sinaloa Cartel; SEMAR, SEDENA's intelligence section and SEDENA's special forces; and US Drug Enforcement Administration (DEA) and Defense Intelligence Agency (DIA).

Affiliates/allies: Demobilised members of the Michoacán Family and the Knights Templar, as well as large numbers of collaborating communities.

Resources/capabilities: Estimated capital of US$1bn from the sale of methamphetamine and fentanyl as well as the extortion of merchants and money-laundering activities in Guadalajara. The group is known to possess high-powered weapons including military-grade equipment and has used drones to attack government forces.

Sinaloa Cartel

Strength: Unclear.

Areas of operation: Headquartered in Culiacán, Sinaloa, but with a presence in all 32 states of Mexico and particularly in the Pacific (the cartel is also known as the Cártel del Pacífico or Cártel del Pacífico–Sinaloa). Outside Mexico, it is active in Asia, Canada, Central America and Europe. In the US, it has an important presence in California, Colorado, New York and Texas.

Leadership: Historical leader since the mid-1990s, Joaquín 'El Chapo' Guzman, was captured in 2016 and imprisoned for life in the US in 2019. His number two, Ismael 'El Mayo' Zambada García, is in a leadership struggle with El Chapo's son, Iván Archibaldo Guzmán Salazar. Ovidio Guzmán López, El Chapo's other powerful son, was arrested on 5 January 2023.

Structure: Hierarchical organisation, with three subdivisions: finance/business, logistics for drug transportation and military structures. In recent years, the cartel has associated with numerous smaller DTOs such as Los Salazar and Los Talibanes.

History: Preceded by the Guadalajara Cartel, co-founded in the late 1970s by leader Rafael Caro Quintero. In the 1990s, following the peace processes in Central America, the large-scale ground transit of cocaine began. In the mid-1990s, El Chapo became leader of the Sinaloa Cartel, opened routes from Guatemala to Mexico and the Tijuana route, and forged alliances with the Medellín Cartel in Colombia. The cartel focused on cocaine for 20 years, but is now diversifying into heroin, methamphetamine and fentanyl.

Objectives: Control all drug markets (for cocaine and methamphetamine, in particular), including production networks in Colombia, distribution in Central America and Mexico, and consumption in the US; and recover its position as the dominant DTO in Mexico.

Opponents: Other DTOs, particularly CJNG; SEMAR, SEDENA's intelligence section and SEDENA's special forces; and US DEA and DIA.

Affiliates/allies: Many subordinate medium-sized and small criminal organisations at the regional level, including cocaine-producing partners in Colombia. The cartel also partners with many corrupt Mexican government officials, particularly in its home state of Sinaloa and other regions where it operates.

Resources/capabilities: High-powered weapons, such as the Barrett M107 sniper rifle and anti-aircraft missiles, and a large fleet of drug-transport planes.

Los Zetas

Strength: Unclear; the group was hit hard by the government between 2012 and 2016.

Areas of operation: Tamaulipas State, mainly along the border with Texas, as well as Coahuila, Nuevo León, Tabasco, Veracruz and the area along the border with Guatemala.

Leadership: Founded by Heriberto Lazcano, former member of the Mexican army. Since 2013, at least 33 of its main leaders (including Lazcano) have been arrested or killed in combat by military forces. Its Cártel del Noreste splinter group is believed to be led by Juan Gerardo Treviño-Chávez 'El Huevo'.

Structure: Originally a horizontal, decentralised structure that worked as a large business with multiple criminal activities. Less successful at drug trafficking, its cells were involved in extortion, kidnapping, the collection of criminal taxes from businesses and migrant trafficking from Central America to Texas. Los Zetas is currently split into two main groups, Zetas Vieja Escuela and the Cártel del Noreste. Another group known as Los Talibanes operates in north-central Mexico in association with the Sinaloa Cartel.

Los Zetas

History: Began as the armed wing of the Gulf Cartel, drawing most of its members from the Mexican and Guatemalan armies. The group is notorious for perpetrating mass violence against the civilian population and migrants. Between 2010 and 2012, a major SEMAR offensive to dismantle the 'Gulf Corridor' weakened the group significantly. It is the DTO against which the Mexican government has been most successful.

Objectives: Control criminal activity in the Gulf of Mexico states.

Opponents: CJNG, Gulf Cartel and special forces of SEMAR.

Affiliates/allies: Criminal networks in Tamaulipas State.

Resources/capabilities: Migrant smuggling and criminal taxes on merchants.

Gulf Cartel

Strength: Unclear.

Areas of operation: Operates and controls territory in Tamaulipas State, particularly the border area with Texas, including strategic border cities, such as Matamoros, Nuevo Laredo and Reynosa.

Leadership: The Gulf Cartel was led by Osiel Cárdenas Guillén at the peak of its power in the early 2000s but has suffered from high turnover of leadership since his capture in 2003. Numerous Gulf Cartel leaders have been arrested or killed by government forces in recent years.

Structure: Unstable, with fragmented leadership. Splinter groups include Los Ciclones, Los Metros, Panteras and Grupo Sombra.

History: The second-oldest DTO in the country, smuggling alcohol, weapons and drugs across the US border since the 1940s. After forging a partnership with the Colombian Cali Cartel in the 1990s, the group focused on introducing cocaine to the US market. Los Zetas violently separated from the group in 2010.

Objectives: Smuggle drugs on the Texas–Tamaulipas border and control drug trafficking in northeast US.

Opponents: Los Zetas, CJNG and special forces of SEMAR and SEDENA.

Affiliates/allies: Closely linked to Tamaulipas State's governors (three former governors have been charged in Texas) and criminal networks.

Resources/capabilities: Many Tamaulipas businessmen help the cartel to launder money.

Beltrán Leyva Organisation (BLO)

Strength: Unclear.

Areas of operation: Mainly in the states of Guerrero and Morelos, and the México City–Acapulco highway. The group controls poppy production and the export of heroin from Iguala, Guerrero, to Chicago, IL.

Leadership: Founded by brothers Arturo, Alfredo, Carlos and Héctor Leyva. Arturo was killed in 2009 and the other three were imprisoned, with Héctor dying in 2018. The organisation is now split into various groups.

Structure: Based around vertically organised cells. After the death or imprisonment of the four brothers, it fragmented into different groups which primarily operate in the state of Guerrero. The two largest are Los Rojos and Guerreros Unidos, the latter of which also traces its origins to splinter cells of the Knights Templar cartel. Both groups have been identified as being responsible for the 2014 Ayotzinapa massacre and are also believed to be in conflict with each other.

History: A breakaway group of the Sinaloa Cartel formed in 2008 in Sinaloa before moving to the South Pacific–Acapulco (Guerrero State), Morelos State and México State. The groups are among the most important DTOs operating in the highly violent region known as 'Tierra Caliente', which covers parts of the states of Guerrero, México and Michoacán.

Objectives: Control heroin trafficking in the South Pacific and from Mexico to Chicago.

Opponents: Sinaloa Cartel, CJNG and special forces of SEDENA.

Affiliates/allies: An estimated 100,000 peasants who grow poppies in Guerrero.

Resources/capabilities: Profits from the sale of heroin in the US and from criminal activities such as extortion and kidnapping in Mexico.

Michoacán Family/Knights Templar (Cárteles Unidos)

Strength: Unclear.

Areas of operation: The surviving criminal cells moved to the states of Guanajuato, Guerrero and México.

Leadership: Fragmented following the 2015 arrest of Servando Gómez Martínez. The current organisation, known as Cárteles Unidos, is led by Juan José Farías Álvarez 'El Abuelo'.

Structure: Organised into independent groups – including the Cártel del Abuelo and Los Viagras – that in recent years banded together under the name Cárteles Unidos. Many of these groups are notable for having begun as vigilante-style *autodefensa* (self-defence) groups but later branched out into criminal activities.

History: Gained power by producing methamphetamine, importing chemical precursors from China. Founded by Nazario Moreno Gonzalez in 2005, the organisation's initial recruitment was based on a religious discourse. Between 2006

Michoacán Family/Knights Templar (Cárteles Unidos)

and 2012, the group built a broad network of collaborators among the population, bribed many local politicians on the Pacific coast of Michoacán and ran methamphetamine laboratories in the mountains. However, the group was practically dismantled by Mexican government forces between 2013 and 2016. Following the capture of its first leaders, the Michoacán Family became the Knights Templar in 2013–14, under the leadership of Servando Gómez. The organisation known as Cárteles Unidos was created in 2019 as a response to CJNG activity in Michoacán.

Objectives: Control mining and agricultural production (of avocados for export to the US) in Michoacán State; control the port of Lázaro Cárdenas (for smuggling the chemical base for producing methamphetamine); and steal fuel in Guanajuato State.

Opponents: Sinaloa Cartel, CJNG and special forces of SEDENA.

Affiliates/allies: A large number of collaborating peasants.

Resources/capabilities: Revenue from criminal taxes on many economic activities.

Tijuana Cartel (also known as Arellano Felix Family Organisation)

Strength: Exact numbers unclear, but thought to have regained some strength since 2018.

Areas of operation: A binational, cross-border organisation operating between Tijuana, Baja California and San Diego, CA, as well as in Los Angeles, CA.

Leadership: Its original leaders, Benjamín Arellano Félix and his brothers Ramón, Eduardo, Luis Fernando, Francisco, Carlos and Javier, are all imprisoned in jails in California. The cartel is currently led by their sister, Enedina Arellano Félix.

Structure: Groups of young people become either gunmen or cocaine exporters (middle-class youth who have visas to cross the border). Their leaders are family members. A splinter group associated with the CJNG is known as the Cartel Tijuana New Generation.

History: During the 1980s and 1990s, the Arellano Félix brothers controlled the north of the country and transported drugs across the border using tunnels and people crossing the border, as well as migrants. The arrest of the Arellano Félix brothers led to the cartel's decline amid the Sinaloa Cartel's dominance in the region. However, the latter's troubles in recent years have led to a resurgence of the Tijuana Cartel.

Objectives: Control drug trafficking from Baja California to California, US.

Opponents: Sinaloa Cartel, special forces of SEDENA, and US intelligence services cooperating with Mexican authorities at the border.

Affiliates/allies: Many people crossing the border daily with small amounts of drugs.

Resources/capabilities: Revenue from the cross-border cocaine trade.

Other relevant parties

There are several other significant DTOs operating in Mexico, including Cártel del Noreste, La Unión Tepito, the Santa Rosa de Lima Cartel and the Juárez Cartel.

Notes

[1] For example, Ovidio Guzmán López, son of the famed Sinaloa Cartel leader Joaquín 'El Chapo' Guzman, was arrested by Mexican authorities in a violent operation in January 2023.

[2] The agreement is designed to address a number of issues, but as of 2023, the main focuses of the partnership were the prevention of cross-border crime, especially arms trafficking from the US to Mexico and illicit-drugs trafficking from Mexico to the US; the pursuit of DTO criminal networks; and the improvement of Mexico's public-security apparatus, including addressing the extremely high rates of feminicide throughout the country. For more information, see Office of the Spokesperson, 'Joint Statement: U.S.–Mexico High Level Security Dialogue 2023', US Department of State, 23 October 2023.

[3] Tiziano Breda, 'Mexico: Confronting Deadly Political and Criminal Power Struggles in an Election Year', Armed Conflict Location & Event Data Project (ACLED), 17 January 2024.

[4] 'Violencia Electoral en México: el Gobierno Reconoce el Asesinato de 15 Aspirantes' [Electoral violence in Mexico: government acknowledges the murder of 15 candidates], Agencia EFE, 3 April 2024.

[5] Data as of July 2024. Votar Entre Balas [Voting Amid Bullets], 'Los Datos' [The data].

[6] Gobierno de México [Government of Mexico], 'Proyecto de Presupuesto de Egresos de la Federación 2024: Analítico de Plazas y Remuneraciones' [Federal expenditure budget project 2024: analysis of positions and remunerations], September 2023.

[7] Estados Unidos Mexicanos, Presidencia de la República [United Mexican States, Presidency of the Republic], 'Proyecto de

Presupuesto de Egresos de la Federación Para el Ejercicio Fiscal 2024' [Draft expenditure budget of the federation for fiscal year 2024]; and Estados Unidos Mexicanos, Presidencia de la República [United Mexican States, Presidency of the Republic], 'Proyecto de Presupuesto de Egresos de la Federación Para el Ejercicio Fiscal 2023' [Draft expenditure budget of the federation for fiscal year 2023].
8   Gobierno de México, 'Proyecto de Presupuesto de Egresos de la Federación 2024: Analítico de Plazas y Remuneraciones'.
9   Estados Unidos Mexicanos, Presidencia de la República, 'Proyecto de Presupuesto de Egresos de la Federación Para el Ejercicio Fiscal 2024'; and Estados Unidos Mexicanos, Presidencia de la República, 'Proyecto de Presupuesto de Egresos de la Federación Para el Ejercicio Fiscal 2023'.
10 Estimate based on various sources. See, for example, Gobierno de México, 'Proyecto de Presupuesto de Egresos de la Federación 2024: Analítico de Plazas y Remuneraciones'.
11 Estados Unidos Mexicanos, Presidencia de la República, 'Proyecto de Presupuesto de Egresos de la Federación Para el Ejercicio Fiscal 2024'; and Estados Unidos Mexicanos, Presidencia de la República, 'Proyecto de Presupuesto de Egresos de la Federación Para el Ejercicio Fiscal 2023'.

COLOMBIA

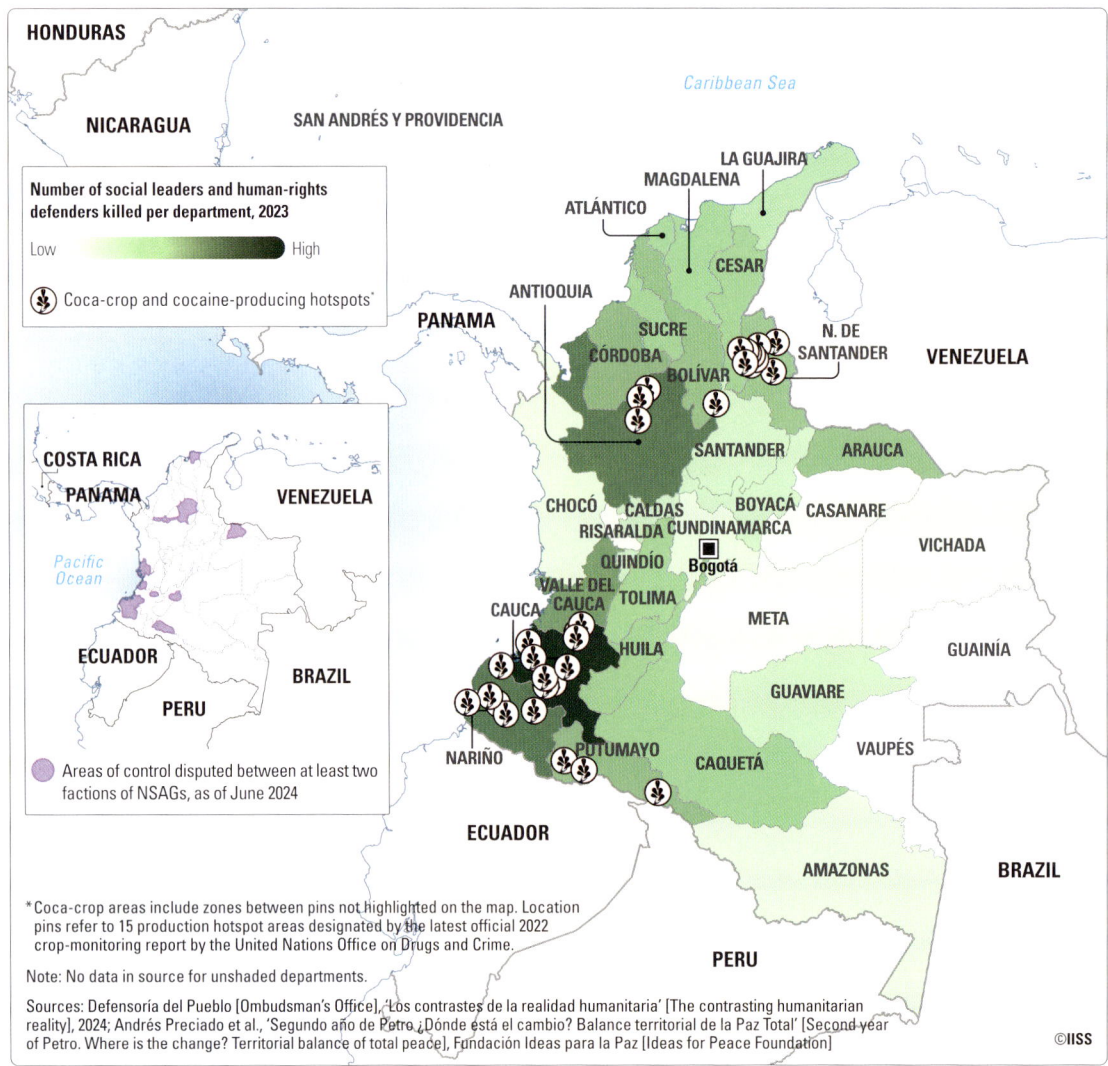

Conflict Overview

Armed conflict in Colombia has been ongoing for six decades, featuring an evolving constellation of actors and violence dynamics. Between 1964 and 1966, left-wing guerrilla groups took up arms against the state, driven by a desire to reduce entrenched rural poverty and political-power concentration. The emergence two decades later of right-wing paramilitary groups (supported by segments of the agrarian elite) to counter the guerrilla groups' expansion further complicated the conflict landscape. At the same time, cocaine trafficking rapidly became the main source of income for all non-state armed groups (NSAGs). Contestation over control of the cocaine business continues to drive conflict amid widespread corruption and institutional fragility, especially in rural areas. In recent years, NSAGs have diversified into other illicit economies, with gold mining, logging, cattle ranching and human trafficking providing groups with additional revenue streams.

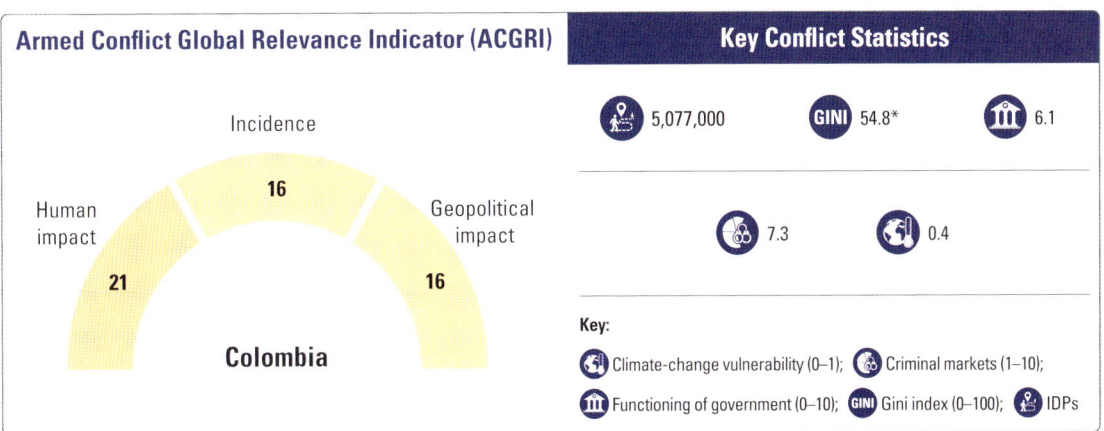

Conflict(s)	Type	Start date
Political insurgency	Internal: localised insurgency	Mid-1960s
Armed violence driven by DTOs	Internal: organised crime	Mid-2000s

Over the last two decades, several military and political developments have also altered the conflict landscape. Between 2000 and 2016, the Colombian armed forces steadily expanded their capabilities and anti-narcotics operations through a US$9.6 billion assistance package backed by the United States government under the bilateral cooperation framework Plan Colombia. Revamped military operations quickly reduced coca-crop extension by half by 2006, with violent events involving NSAGs dropping by two-thirds by the end of Plan Colombia.[1] Alongside these military wins, the government pushed major NSAGs to engage in political negotiations. From 2002–06, the United Self-Defense Forces of Colombia (AUC) paramilitaries demobilised. In 2016, the strongest guerrilla group at the time, the Revolutionary Armed Forces of Colombia (FARC), signed a peace agreement with the government and became a political party. However, flaws in the designs of those processes and a lack of political consensus among ruling parties to effectively implement them resulted in significant security setbacks. Since 2020, coca-crop extension and coca-leaf production have steadily increased, reaching a record level in 2022, and splinter groups linked to demobilised paramilitaries and FARC dissidents have resumed armed conflict against the state, reigniting violence.[2]

Conflict Update

By the end of the reporting period, President Gustavo Petro's 'total peace' flagship policy, which aims to strike simultaneous deals with all NSAGs and reduce violence, encompassed eight processes. Three of these involve political negotiations with the National Liberation Army (ELN) and FARC dissidents: Central General Staff (EMC) and Second Marquetalia. The remaining processes focus on judicial settlements for the mass demobilisation of criminal groups.[3]

The political negotiations have yielded important progress. In October 2023, the EMC officially joined the 'total peace' initiative, having agreed to a bilateral ceasefire and road map, which has been followed by four regional dialogue cycles to date. In February 2024, the Second Marquetalia also formally entered peace talks with the government, agreeing on a road map and unilateral ceasefire in June 2024. Meanwhile, in May 2024, the ELN signed the first point of a six-point peace agenda, making its process the most advanced in the 'total peace' initiative, with the longest bilateral and binational ceasefire (including ELN combatants in Venezuela).[4]

However, these negotiation efforts have also faced substantial obstacles. In February 2024, the ELN froze its peace talks after the government launched an exploratory regional process with the ELN's Comuneros del Sur Front in the department of Nariño, despite the ELN national leadership's stiff opposition. Then, in early May 2024, the ELN resumed kidnappings nationwide, breaching the negotiation conditions agreed with the government.[5] Moreover, in March 2024, the government indefinitely suspended the ceasefire with the EMC in the departments of Cauca, Nariño and Valle del Cauca in response to an attack by the EMC's Joint Western Command against an indigenous community. This decision prompted the EMC's leader, Néstor Gregorio Vera Fernández (alias 'Ivan Mordisco'), to exit the 'total peace' process and resume clashes with the armed forces. Yet two EMC fronts (out of six), comprising almost 40% of the group's total members, contravened Mordisco's decision and remained in the negotiations.[6] This resulted in (what can be deemed as) the formation of the first dissenting group of a FARC dissident group after the 2016 peace agreement.[7]

By June 2024, the absence of a formal negotiation process and ceasefire with the Gulf Clan, currently the most powerful NSAG in Colombia, further strained the progress of the 'total peace' initiative. The Colombian government regards the Gulf Clan as a criminal group without political goals and, therefore, as only eligible to demobilise under a judicial settlement, not a political agreement.

Against this backdrop, all NSAGs took steps to increase their strength. The number of Gulf Clan members, for instance, rose by around 55% to 14,000 from 2022–23; and National ELN and FARC dissidents also boosted their ranks, although by a lower increment.[8] Moreover, from 2022–24, the Gulf Clan's territorial presence expanded by 54% to 392 of Colombia's 1,101 municipalities, while the presence of FARC dissidents and the National ELN increased by 28% and 22% to 299 and 232, respectively.[9] While the augmented military strength of NSAGs did not seem to translate into a higher humanitarian impact between 2022 and 2023, as the number of internally displaced persons and killings of social leaders and human-rights defenders dropped by 25% and 11% respectively, the confinement of communities and clashes among NSAGs increased by 11% and 54%.[10] All these dynamics suggest a revamped criminal-governance strategy that tries to contain human impact while striving for greater territorial and social control – in an effort to increase NSAGs' leverage in negotiations with the government.

Lastly, a number of international factors challenged the 'total peace' initiative. While the new bilateral Vida Colombia Strategy signed with the US in May 2024 adopted a more holistic approach to the two countries' security partnership compared to Plan Colombia and its successor Peace Colombia, it failed to include decriminalisation of the coca leaf, one of Petro's flagship initiatives to reduce cocaine-trafficking proceeds financing NSAGs. Additionally, the Colombian army's capabilities to tackle drug-trafficking operations by NSAGs that oppose 'total peace' negotiations may be weakened after the break in diplomatic ties between Colombia and Israel in May 2024. Petro followed his condemnation of Israeli military operations in Gaza with the suspension of all of Colombia's new defence contracts with the country. Israel is the provider of some of the equipment and technology that the Colombian army uses in operations against NSAGs, including its only fighter-jet fleet and related maintenance services; helicopter intelligence and communication technology; radar systems; and components for assault rifles produced internally.[11]

Conflict Parties

Colombian armed forces

Strength: Army: 187,400; navy: 27,750; air force: 9,350; supported by the National Police (PONAL): 165,050.

Areas of operation: Across the country, but limited presence in some rural areas such as the Catatumbo and Urabá, as well as some areas of the Eastern Plains region, the Pacific coast region and border areas.

Colombian armed forces

Leadership: President Gustavo Petro Urrego (president and commander-in-chief), Iván Velásquez Gómez (minister of defence) and Adm. Francisco Hernando Cubides Granados (general commander of the armed forces).[12]

Structure: Army, navy and air force. PONAL oversees public and civil security; it has been controlled and administered by the Ministry of National Defence and has included militarised units since 1953.

History: Originated in the late eighteenth century as the Liberating Army of the independence movement against the Spanish Empire. The military forces were formally created with the 1821 Cúcuta Constitution.

Objectives: Defend national sovereignty; militarily attack and defeat NSAGs; and maintain rule and order.

Opponents: ELN, FARC dissidents, Gulf Clan and other criminal organisations.

Affiliates/allies: PONAL.

Resources/capabilities: Defence budget of US$5.6bn in 2023 and US$7.2bn in 2024. Overall capabilities and professionalisation have improved in recent decades.

Gulf Clan (also known as Gaitanistas Self-Defence Forces of Colombia (AGC) or the Urabeños)

Strength: 5,000–14,000 members.[13]

Areas of operation: Present in at least 15 of Colombia's 32 departments, as well as in Panama and Venezuela. The group is based in the Urabá region, in northwest Colombia, and has an extensive presence in the city of Medellín and departments of Antioquia, Bolívar, Chocó, Córdoba, Magdalena, Sucre and Valle del Cauca.

Leadership: Jobanis de Jesús Ávila Villadiego (alias 'Chiquito Malo'), who consolidated his leadership after previous leader Dairo Antonio Úsuga David (alias 'Otoniel') was extradited to the US in 2022. Second in command is José Gonzalo Sánchez Sánchez (alias 'Gonzalito'), followed by Orozman Orlando Ostén Blanco (alias 'Rodrigo Flechas').

Structure: Organised into five regional structures (Central Urabá, Jairo Durango Restrepo, Roberto Vargas Gutiérrez, Arístides Mesa Páez and Nelsón Hurtado Simaca) and 26 local fronts.[14] Other local criminal organisations are subcontracted and expected to provide services and follow strategic orders when requested.

History: Emerged from the demobilisation of AUC paramilitaries in 2006. Some of its leaders were either former Popular Liberation Army combatants who demobilised in 1991 or former FARC members who demobilised in the 2000s.

Objectives: Drug trafficking. The Gulf Clan uses the name Gaitanistas Self-Defence Forces as a way of legitimising itself as a group with political goals.

Opponents: Colombian armed forces; EMC and ELN in Bajo Cauca region; and ELN in Bolívar, Chocó and Valle del Cauca.

Affiliates/allies: Corrupt elements of the Colombian armed forces and state officials; Jalisco New Generation (CJNG) and Sinaloa Cartel in Mexico; and Italian and Balkan mafia-type organisations.

Resources/capabilities: Financing mainly comes from transnational drug trafficking, providing services for independent drug traffickers and illegal mining. Multiple group members, including leaders, run their own international trafficking routes. The group also runs migrant smuggling in the Darién region on the border with Panama.

National Liberation Army (ELN)

Strength: 6,158 members in arms, though estimates vary.[15]

Areas of operation: Varied presence in at least 19 departments and some cities, including Medellín, Cali, Cúcuta and very limitedly in Bogotá.[16] It retains a particularly strong presence along the border with Venezuela, especially in the departments of Arauca, Casanare, Norte de Santander and Vichada, as well as to a lesser extent in Cesar, Guainía and La Guajira. It also has an extensive presence in Venezuela, including Amazonas and Bolivar states.

Leadership: Eliécer Erlington Chamorro Acosta (alias 'Antonio García'; commander).

Structure: Organised into a federal structure. The Central Command directs the ELN's strategy and is composed of four publicly recognised commanders and a larger 30-person National Direction. The ELN has seven major war fronts.

History: Founded in 1964 by a group of left-wing intellectuals and students embracing liberation theology, who took inspiration from the Cuban Revolution.

Objectives: On paper, overthrow the Colombian government and create a socialist state; operationally, local 'armed resistance'.

Opponents: Gulf Clan in Antioquia, Bolívar, Chocó and Norte de Santander, and EMC in Valle del Cauca, Nariño and Cauca, and in Apure State, Venezuela.

Affiliates/allies: Second Marquetalia in Nariño, Norte de Santander and Valle del Cauca (Buenaventura) departments, and in Apure State, Venezuela; 33rd, 24th, 4th, 36th and 18th EMC fronts in Norte de Santander (Catatumbo) and Bajo Cauca region mainly; some members of the Venezuelan armed forces (Venezuelan National Guard), particularly in Apure State; First Capital Command (PCC) and Red Command (CV) in Brazil; and Sinaloa Cartel and CJNG in Mexico.

Resources/capabilities: Extortion, kidnapping, illegal mining and gasoline trafficking are important sources of income. The group also imposes taxes on and regulates the drug trade in Cauca, Chocó and Norte de Santander.

FARC dissidents: Central General Staff (EMC)[17]

Strength: 3,860, though estimates vary.[18]

Areas of operation: Varied presence in at least 19 departments including Amazonas, Arauca, Bolívar, Caquetá, Casanare, Cauca, Guainía, Guaviare, Huila, Meta, Nariño, Norte de Santander, Putumayo, Valle del Cauca, Vaupes and Vichada, as well as in Amazonas State in Brazil.[19]

Leadership: Néstor Gregorio Vera Fernández (alias 'Iván Mordisco'; top commander and coordinator, and leader of the 1st Front) and Alexander Díaz Mendoza (alias 'Calarca'; second in command).[20]

Structure: Replicates the former FARC operational structure with six fronts (Amazonas, Central Isaías Pardo, Jorge Suárez Briceño, Joint Western Command, Magdalena Medio and Jacobo Arenas Occidental) and at least 34 units.[21] However, the leadership only coordinates individual structures' operations and peace dialogues with the government.

History: The EMC is the name of the former Gentil Duarte FARC dissidents, which they adopted after their historical leader Miguel Botache Santillana (alias 'Gentil Duarte') was killed by the ELN in May 2022 in Venezuela. In March 2023, for the purposes of the 'total peace' negotiations, the group's new leader Mordisco ratified the coordination of actions across the group's FARC units. Other units have emerged between 2018 and 2024. They all claim to be the 'true' FARC.

Objectives: Rebuild the old FARC; recover the areas of the old FARC; and fight the state and 'establishment'.

Opponents: Colombian armed forces; Gulf Clan in Antioquia, Bolívar and Nariño; ELN in Arauca, Bolívar, Cauca and Nariño; Second Marquetalia units in Cauca, Meta, Nariño and Putumayo; and Venezuelan armed forces in Apure State, Venezuela.

Affiliates/allies: ELN in Cauca department, Catatumbo region and Bajo Cauca region; Mexican drug-trafficking organisations, mainly Sinaloa Cartel and CJNG; and PCC and CV in Brazil.

Resources/capabilities: Inherited the FARC's former economic structures and rent-seeking activities (including extortion, drug trafficking and illegal mining). The group generates income through drug-trafficking or tax collection on drug distribution in its areas of influence.

FARC dissidents: Second Marquetalia

Strength: 1,751 members in arms, though figures vary.[22]

Areas of operation: Departments along the border with Venezuela, mainly Guainía, Norte de Santander and Vichada, as well as the Venezuelan states of Amazonas, Bolívar and Zulia; departments along the border with Ecuador, mainly Nariño and Putumayo; the western departments of Cauca and Buenaventura (Valle del Cauca); and the central departments of Meta and Caquetá.

Leadership: The main commanders include Luciano Marín Arango (alias 'Iván Márquez'), José Aldinever Sierra Sabogal (alias 'Zarco Aldinever'), José Vicente Lesmes (alias 'Walter Mendoza') and Géner García Molina (alias 'Jhon 40').[23]

Structure: Has three fronts and 15 units.[24] Its organisational structure includes a 'National Direction'.

History: Created in 2018 when a group of senior FARC commanders abandoned the reincorporation process from the 2016 peace agreement and resumed fighting; its existence was publicly announced in August 2019.

Objectives: Recreate the original FARC, take over the state or initiate a new negotiation process.

Opponents: Colombian armed forces and EMC dissidents in Cauca, Nariño and Putumayo, as well as Apure State, Venezuela.

Affiliates/allies: ELN, especially on a political level, but also on a local level in Cauca, Buenaventura (Valle del Cauca) and Nariño departments, as well as Apure State, Venezuela. It also works with the Mexican CJNG and the Brazilian PCC.

Resources/capabilities: Its sources of financing include former undeclared assets of the FARC, drug trafficking and illegal gold mining. It has also upgraded its weaponry with more modern rifles.

Notes

1. Between 2000 and 2014, Plan Colombia provided professional training and military equipment to the Colombian army, mainly to fight drug-trafficking and terrorist organisations. The Colombian army's strength went from about 23,000 to 80,000 soldiers and from three to 36 mobile battalions. It created eight high-land battalions and 52 mobile troops. The helicopter fleet also increased from 35 to 200, and it procured over 30 new aircraft.

2. Per the latest estimates, there are 230,028 hectares of coca crops and a production capacity of 1.4 million tonnes of coca leaves per hectare in Colombia. Oficina de las Naciones Unidas contra la Droga y el Delito (UNODC)-Sistema Integrado de Monitoreo de Cultivos Ilícitos (SIMCI) [Integrated Illicit Crops Monitoring System (SIMCI)], *Monitoreo de los territorios con presencia de cultivos de coca 2022* [Monitoring territories with coca crops 2022] (Bogotá: UNODC-SIMCI, 2023).

3. These criminal groups include three urban criminal gangs in Buenaventura, Quibdó and Medellín, the Conquering Self-Defense Forces of the Sierra Nevada in the department of Magdalena, and the Gulf Clan nationwide. Processes with the first three groups do not have any agreed road map, the process

with the fourth is in an exploratory phase, and nothing has yet been defined with the fifth group.
4   The first point of the agenda refers to civil-society engagement to transform state policies such as those regarding the economy, defence and democratic participation. The ongoing ceasefire entered into force on 3 August 2023 for six months and was renewed for another six months until 3 August 2024.
5   The ELN cited delays in the implementation of a foreign multi-donor fund, which had been agreed by both parties to offset the guerrillas' financial loss from ceasing kidnapping, as the reason behind this decision.
6   Santiago Rodríguez Álvarez, 'La paz total sin "Mordisco": así se dividió el EMC en la mesa de diálogos' [Total peace without alias 'Mordisco': this is how the EMC was divided at the dialogue table], La Silla Vacía, 17 April 2024.
7   If the EMC fronts that remain at the 'total peace' negotiation table eventually reach an agreement with the government, Ivan Mordisco's fronts would officially become the first dissenting group to a dissident organisation in Colombia.
8   ELN members increased by around 5% to 6,158 while EMC and Second Marquetalia members increased by about 9% and 5% to 3,860 and 1,751 respectively, though estimates vary. Santiago Rodríguez Álvarez, 'Cifras secretas del gobierno confirman que todos los grupos armados crecieron' [Secret government figures confirm that all armed groups expanded], La Silla Vacía, 13 March 2024.
9   Data is from January 2022–March 2024. Territorial presence refers to direct or outsourced (via allied groups) actions, meddling and transit as per the Ombudsman's Office of Colombia (Defensoría del Pueblo). In March 2024, the EMC was present in 234 municipalities and Second Marquetalia was in 65. Defensoría del Pueblo [Ombudsman's Office], 'Los contrastes de la realidad humanitaria' [The contrasting humanitarian reality], 2024.
10 The number of internally displaced persons, homicides and killings of social leaders have been calculated from Internal Displacement Monitoring Centre (IDMC), 'IDMC Data Portal'; Defensoría del Pueblo, 'Los contrastes de la realidad humanitaria'; and María Victoria Llorente, 'Total Peace: Armed Groups Win Head and Shoulders', Fundación Ideas para la Paz [Ideas for Peace Foundation].

11 In February 2024, the Colombian government announced the suspension of Israeli military imports, and in May 2024 it officially broke diplomatic ties with Israel.
12 Cubides's appointment took place shortly after the end of the reporting period in July 2024.
13 Álvarez, 'Cifras secretas del gobierno confirman que todos los grupos armados crecieron'.
14 Alicia Liliana Méndez, 'Así está conformado el "clan del Golfo", la red más grande de tráfico de cocaína' [This is how the 'Gulf Clan' is formed, the largest cocaine trafficking network], El Tiempo, 19 March 2024.
15 Ibid.
16 Indepaz, 'Informe sobre presencia de grupos armados en Colombia 2021–2022 (1)' [Report of presence of armed groups in Colombia 2021–2022 (1)], pp. 90–9.
17 Information is from before Mordisco's leadership fracture in April 2024.
18 Álvarez, 'Cifras secretas del gobierno confirman que todos los grupos armados.
19 Andrés Preciado R. et al, 'El proyecto "Estado Mayor Central" Un intento de unificación disidente' [The Central General Staff project: unifying dissident attempt], Fundación Ideas para la Paz [Ideas for Peace Foundation], no. 38, October 2023.
20 As of October 2023, before Mordisco left the 'total peace' initiative in April 2024 and EMC leadership. The current structure is unclear.
21 After April 2024, Mordisco is believed to have continued as the leader of the Joint Western Command and Jacobo Arenas Occidental fronts while Calarca retained leadership of the Magdalena Medio and Jorge Suarez Briceño fronts, which remained in the 'total peace' talks. See Conflict Responses, '¿En que está el "EMC" actualmente?' [What is the 'EMC' up to?], 25 April 2023.
22 Álvarez, 'Cifras secretas del gobierno confirman que todos los grupos armados crecieron'; and Preciado R. et al, 'El proyecto "Estado Mayor Central" Un intento de unificación disidente'.
23 Márquez's national leadership is weak across certain units.
24 Conflict Responses, 'Disidencias de las FARC-EP: dos caminos de una guerra en construcción – partes 1 y 2' [FARC-EP dissidents: two paths of a war under construction – parts 1 and 2'], 1 March 2024.

BRAZIL

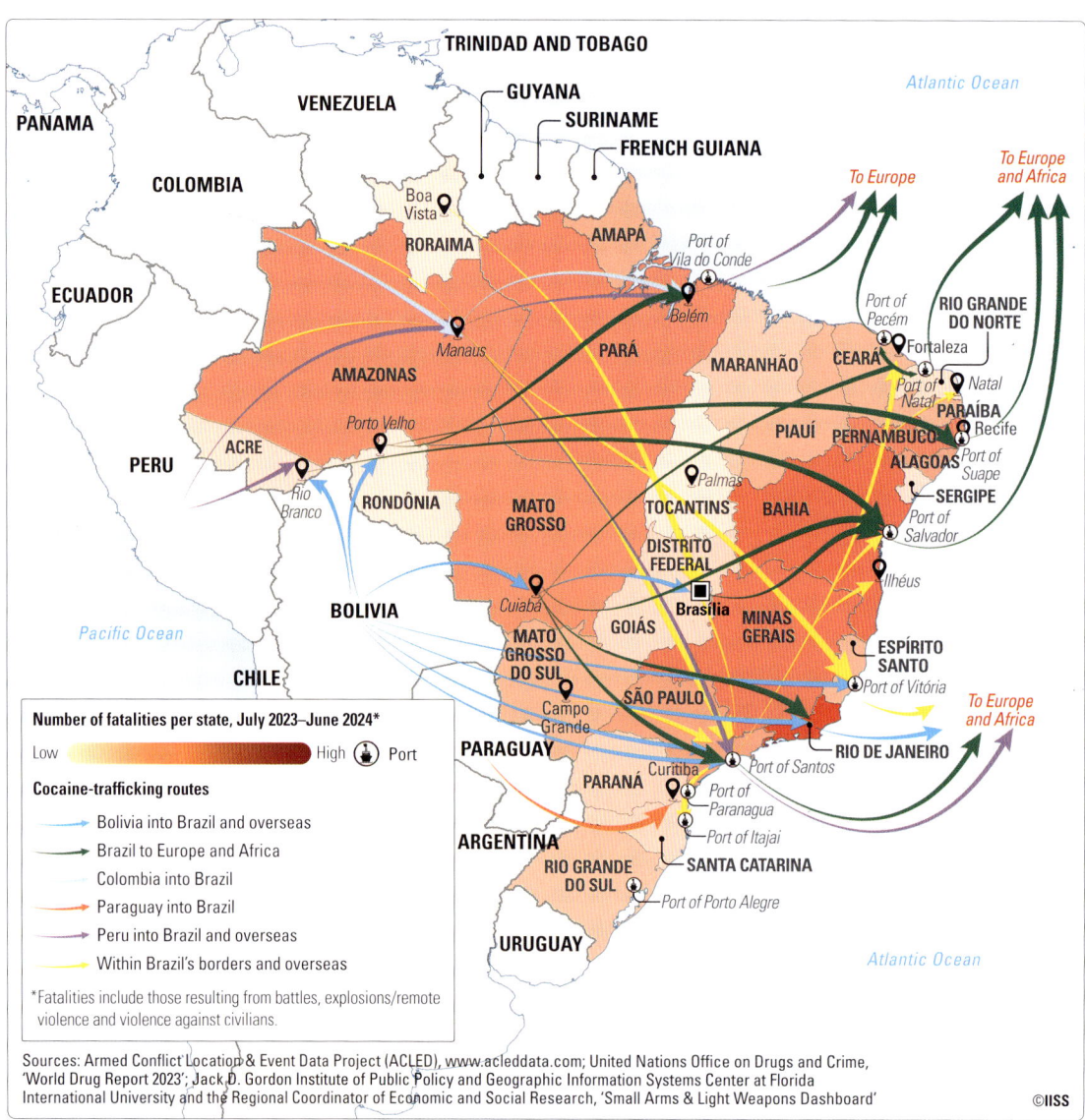

Conflict Overview

Brazil's transnational criminal landscape, although fluid and dynamic, has changed little in terms of its fundamentals over the years. The country remains locked in an armed conflict involving several prominent criminal organisations that use prisons as their base of operations, most notably the São Paulo-based First Capital Command (PCC), the Rio de Janeiro-based Red Command (CV) and the Manaus-based Family of the North (FDN). In recent years, state-based, smaller criminal organisations have emerged and often aligned with these major criminal groups to control territory and drug routes and thereby augment their power. Militia groups have also become increasingly involved, especially in states such as Rio de Janeiro. Such groups recruit former

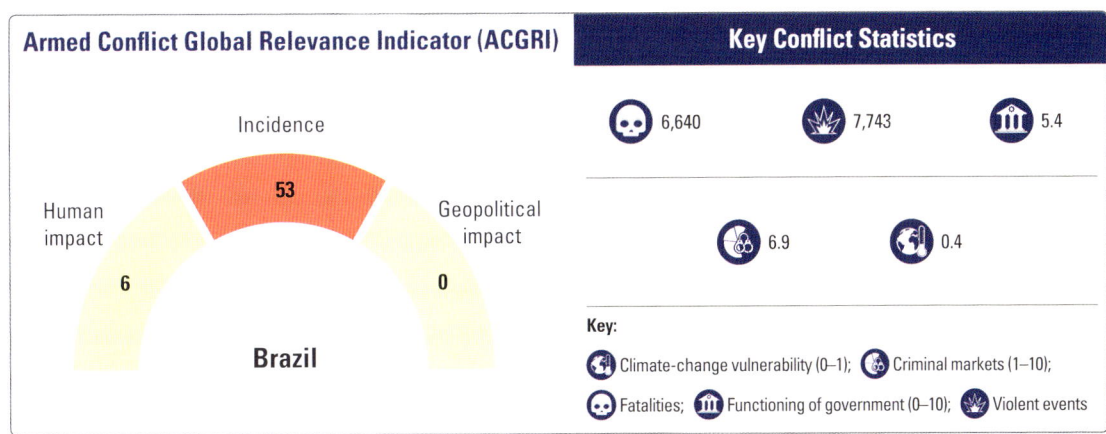

and current police officers, as well as politicians, to compete against criminal organisations for control of illicit economies, and they often have access to state resources. Like other criminal organisations, militias extort businesses and traffic drugs in their areas of control.

Brazil's criminal organisations have also rapidly internationalised in recent years to meet the growing intercontinental demand for drugs – especially cocaine. Groups such as the PCC maintain an international presence with important alliances in Asia, Europe and Latin America. Brazil has excellent transport links to these increasingly important markets, especially to Europe – either directly or oftentimes via lusophone Africa (principally Angola, Cabo Verde and Mozambique). As in other countries in Latin America, the key to criminal organisations' internationalisation strategy has been control of ports and other transport links. The PCC, for instance, has consolidated control of the so-called 'Caipira Route', a key trafficking route in the central and southwest regions of Brazil. Meanwhile, Brazil's dominant factions have continued to seek greater control of port infrastructure in Brazil's northeastern cities, displacing local groups such as the Crime Syndicate (Rio Grande do Norte State) and the Guardians of the State (Ceará State) in the process. Trafficking from the northeast is facilitated by both direct routes to Europe and important routes via Caribbean countries (often overseas territories of European countries). Through such expansion, Brazil's criminal organisations have diversified their international income streams by becoming increasingly commodity agnostic, preferring rent-seeking behaviour of any kind over drug trafficking exclusively. This has brought greater trafficking in illegal minerals, wildlife, logging, counterfeit goods, fertilisers and much more. Domestically, criminal groups continue to generate revenue by serving local drug markets and extorting communities under their control.

While geographically the bulk of Brazil's violence has been concentrated in urban areas since the 1980s, it has spread more recently in Brazil's rural areas, fuelled by landowners and illegal mining and logging groups allying with criminal organisations. The Amazon region, being less consolidated than other spaces in Brazil's criminal landscape, has emerged as a key area for contestation, offering criminal organisations further opportunities to diversify their portfolio to include activities such as illegal gold mining and logging, wildlife trafficking and extortion rackets.

Conflict Update

Brazil continued to experience significant conflict during the reporting period. Despite a slight decrease from over 41,100 homicides in 2022, the number of homicides for 2023 remained very high at 39,500.[1] Significantly, the political change represented by the election of President Luiz Inácio Lula da Silva in 2022 has not translated into the pursuit of a security strategy that differs substantially from those of previous presidents. Lula has preserved a militarised security policy, deploying the military to ports and airports in cities such as Rio de Janeiro and São Paulo – an approach which has not led to any significant progress. Notably, Brazilians rank security, not the economy, as their greatest worry under the Lula government. Furthermore, the modest decline in homicide numbers may be due to the emergence of a 'pax mafiosa', as opposed to policy success. Organisations such as the PCC have emerged as the dominant force in recent years, victorious over many of their rivals and capable of imposing their rule over parts of São Paulo, Mato Grosso, Mato Grosso do Sul and Amazonas states.[2] While the number of homicides in 2023 was far from its peak in 2017 and 2018, when it eclipsed 60,000, some of Brazil's main areas of criminal contestation remain sites of tremendous violence, including the lucrative Solimões River route in the Amazon, which stretches from the tri-border area with Colombia and Peru to the convergence of the Amazon River with the Atlantic Ocean.[3]

Indeed, the Amazon region, comprising nine Brazilian states, witnessed more than 8,000 homicides in 2022, a rate of violent crime higher than most areas in Brazil, and more like rates in Mexico.[4] Meanwhile, Rio de Janeiro State also remained an epicentre of conflict. Police raids on *favelas* in Maré, Vila Cruzeiro and Cidade de Deus resulted in deaths throughout 2023, with one raid leading to nine deaths in Vila Cruzeiro – making it the deadliest since the police operations in the Jacarezinho (2021) and Vila Cruzeiro (2022) *favelas*, which killed 28 and at least 23 people, respectively.[5]

One extremely important development was the emergence of rumours regarding a split in the PCC, a group traditionally guided by a well-defined ethos and a spirit of 'organisation first'. After the February 2024 assassination of a member close to top leader Marcos Willians Herbas Camacho (alias 'Marcola') by several of his lieutenants, reports of divisions within the group and a potential plot on Marcola's life began to circulate. Brazilian authorities even played a tape recording of conversations between PCC senior leaders discussing disciplinary actions against those who killed the member. Rather than heralding a factional split, however, it is more likely that these rumours were part of an effort by the Brazilian authorities to drive a wedge between personalities in the PCC, one of the most hardened and disciplined criminal organisations in the world.

Conflict Parties

Military Police of Rio de Janeiro (PMERJ/PM)

Strength: About 43,000 members (estimate).[6]

Areas of operation: Rio de Janeiro State.

Leadership: Col. Luiz Henrique Marinho Pires (commander-in-chief).

Structure: Accountable to the Rio State government. Its hierarchy resembles that of the army and its members are reserves for the armed forces.

History: Created in May 1809; current structure introduced in July 1975.

Objectives: Fight organised-crime groups.

Opponents: Organised-crime groups and militias.

Affiliates/allies: Unofficially, some militias and Pure Third Command (TCP).

Resources/capabilities: Small arms, including automatic weapons.

Red Command (CV)

Strength: 30,000 members (approximately).[7]

Areas of operation: Rio de Janeiro metropolitan area, with most important bases in Complexo do Alemão, Chapadão and Salgueiro complexes and the *favelas* of Chatuba, Antares and Rocinha. Since the 2000s, the CV has expanded into other states, such as Amazonas, Acre, Ceará, Mato Grosso and Pará.

Red Command (CV)

Leadership: The most prominent leaders are Luiz Fernando da Costa (alias 'Fernandinho Beira-Mar'), Márcio Nepomuceno (alias 'Marcinho VP') and Elias Pereira da Silva (alias 'Elias Maluco'). Gelson Lima Carnaúba (alias 'Gê'), one of the founders of the FDN, switched sides in 2018 and now leads the CV in Amazonas State.

Structure: Decentralised structure with 'area leaders' in charge of neighbourhoods and *favelas*, and 'managers' responsible for drug-dealing spots, which are secured by 'soldiers' who fend off threats by other dealers or the police. 'Scouts' keep watch for potential risks and warn 'soldiers'.

History: The oldest and second-largest criminal faction in the country, the CV emerged in 1979 in a prison on Ilha Grande, off the southern coast of Rio de Janeiro. Its first sources of income were bank and jewellery-store robberies, before it shifted to drug trafficking in the 1980s, importing cocaine from Colombia and exporting it to Europe. Its activity declined after a police pacification programme in the Alemão *favela* complex in November 2010, but the group has since regained prominence and spread throughout Brazil and beyond.

Objectives: Maintain and enlarge its operating area to other neighbourhoods in Rio de Janeiro and other Brazilian states to expand its drug-trafficking market and extortion practices.

Opponents: In Rio de Janeiro: PMERJ, TCP, Friends of Friends (ADA), militia groups and PCC. In the rest of Brazil: 13 Tram (B13), Guardians of the State (GDE), Crime Syndicate, Tocantins Mafia, Class A Command, 30 Tram, Northern Union and PCC.

Affiliates/allies: In Rio de Janeiro: None. In the rest of Brazil: First Group of Santa Catarina and regional CV affiliates in Pará, Amazonas and Mato Grosso states.

Resources/capabilities: Revenue sources include drug trafficking, extortion of small businesses, kidnapping for ransom and weapons smuggling. Members are equipped with large numbers of handguns, AK-47s, bazookas and grenades.

First Capital Command (PCC)

Strength: 20,000–30,000 members.[8]

Areas of operation: Based in São Paulo State but maintains operations throughout much of Brazil, especially in Amazon border regions. Also operates (independently or in cooperation with local gangs and mafia-type organisations) in Argentina, Bolivia, Colombia, Italy, Mozambique, the Netherlands, Paraguay, Peru, Portugal, South Africa and Venezuela.

Leadership: Marcos Willians Herbas Camacho (alias 'Marcola') took over the leadership in 2002, although he has been imprisoned since 1999. Other important leaders are Valdeci Alves dos Santos (alias 'Colorido') and Geraldo dos Santos Filho.

Structure: Highly organised, with a CEO (Marcola) and strategic deliberative council, board of directors, administrative board, legal board, state board, economic board, institutional relations board, human resources and an intelligence branch. These groupings are referred to as *'sintonias'*. The structure on the street is comprised of 'managers', 'soldiers', 'scouts' and 'killers'.

History: Created in the early 1990s by eight inmates in Taubaté Prison, the group became well known after its attacks against state officers and institutions in São Paulo State. In May 2006, on the orders of PCC leaders, the group instigated around 50 prison rebellions and 251 attacks in one week, resulting in 453 dead and 53 wounded.[9] The group has since expanded to other Brazilian states and abroad, trafficking drugs to West Africa and Europe especially.

Objectives: Deepen and entrench its control of illegal economies in Brazil and beyond.

Opponents: CV, FDN and GDE.

Affiliates/allies: In Brazil: First Command of Vitória, B13 and Ifara. Internationally: the Italian 'Ndrangheta and Serbian mafia.

Resources/capabilities: Revenue sources include drug trafficking, bank and cargo robbery, money laundering, illegal gambling and kidnapping for ransom. The gang uses pistols, rifles, bazookas and grenades.

Friends of Friends (ADA)

Strength: Unclear. However, according to PMERJ intelligence, numbers have been waning for several years.

Areas of operation: Rio de Janeiro State.

Leadership: Celso Luis Rodrigues (alias 'Celsinho da Vila Vintém'), one of the gang's founders.

Structure: Decentralised structure with 'area leaders' in charge of neighbourhoods and *favelas*, and 'managers' responsible for drug-dealing spots, which are secured by 'soldiers' who fend off threats by other dealers or the police. 'Scouts' keep watch for potential risks and warn 'soldiers'.

History: Created in the late 1990s in the penitentiary system of Rio de Janeiro State, ADA has in recent years suffered heavy losses in clashes with the CV and, to a lesser extent, the TCP.

Objectives: Maintain its few areas of control in Rio de Janeiro city and expand operations to other neighbourhoods, especially outside the Rio de Janeiro metropolitan area where there is less competition.

Opponents: CV, TCP, militias and PMERJ.

Affiliates/allies: Unofficially, PCC.

Resources/capabilities: Main revenue source is drug trafficking. Weapons include guns, pistols, rifles, bazookas and grenades.

Militias (various)

Strength: Unclear.

Areas of operation: About 256 square kilometres (approximately 50%) of the Rio de Janeiro metropolitan area.[10]

Leadership: Gang of Zinho (formerly the Justice League) is the largest and most organised of the Rio de Janeiro militias; the group's leadership is currently unclear, due to the arrest of its commander Luís Antônio da Silva Braga (alias 'Zinho') in December 2023. Natalino Guimarães, the Justice League's founder, remains influential. The leadership of other smaller militia groups is unclear.

Structure: Similar structure to gangs, with 'area leaders', 'managers' and 'soldiers', although at a different scale. 'Area leaders' control more than one neighbourhood or region, while 'managers' are responsible for a region or neighbourhood. Unlike in drug groups, 'soldiers' operate from privileged positions (such as police stations). 'Killers' are responsible for executions.

History: Militias are comprised of former or current police officers, firefighters and other professionals in the area of public security. The militias claim to provide security but also traffic drugs and extort, abduct and kill locals. During the recent Rio de Janeiro administration of Wilson Witzel and current administration of Cláudio Castro, militias have expanded significantly.

Objectives: Expand control over licit and illicit business and gain political influence, including by directly holding public offices in municipalities.

Opponents: ADA, CV and occasionally the PMERJ.

Affiliates/allies: TCP and corrupted state officials.

Resources/capabilities: Revenue sources include both licit and illicit business, such as drug trafficking, extortion, murder-for-hire operations, oil theft and sale, money laundering, real-estate transactions, and internet and TV services. Since militia members are often law-enforcement agents, they have access to the same weapons as those agencies, especially .40-calibre pistols and various types of rifles.

Family of the North (FDN)

Strength: Approximately 13,000 members, but numbers might be lower after changes in leadership since 2018.[11]

Areas of operation: Amazonas, Acre, Ceará and Pará states.

Leadership: José Roberto Barbosa (alias 'Zé Roberto da Compensa').

Structure: Decentralised structure with 'area leaders' in charge of neighbourhoods and *favelas*, and 'managers' responsible for drug-dealing spots, which are secured by 'soldiers' who fend off threats by other dealers or the police. 'Scouts' keep watch for potential risks and warn 'soldiers'.

History: Created by Carnaúba (now in the CV) and Barbosa between 2006 and 2007, it became widely known after instigating prison massacres in Manaus in 2015. That year, the FDN, together with the CV, carried out murders of PCC leaders; efforts by the state to broker a truce failed. The FDN competes for the treasured Solimões route, used to transport cocaine produced in Colombia and Peru through rivers in the Amazon region towards strategic ports and airports in Bahia, Ceará, Pará and Pernambuco.

Objectives: Expand and consolidate control of drug-trafficking routes in the Amazon region, and survive the onslaught from the CV and PCC in Amazonas State.

Opponents: PCC, CV and B13.

Affiliates/allies: GDE.

Resources/capabilities: Revenue sources include drug trafficking and money laundering. Members use pistols, rifles, bazookas and grenades.

Pure Third Command (TCP)

Strength: Unclear.

Areas of operation: Rio de Janeiro State.

Leadership: Fernando Gomes de Freitas (alias 'Fernandinho Guarabu'), Bruno da Silva Loureiro (alias 'Coronel') and Alvaro Malaquias Santa Rosa (alias 'Peixão').

Structure: Decentralised structure with 'area leaders' in charge of neighbourhoods and *favelas*, and 'managers' responsible for drug-dealing spots, which are secured by 'soldiers' who fend off threats by other dealers or the police. 'Scouts' keep watch for potential risks and warn 'soldiers'.

History: Created from the 2002 union of dissidents from ADA and the now-defunct Third Command (formed in the 1980s) after the death of Ernaldo Pinto de Medeiros (alias 'Uê') and the arrest of Celsinho da Vila Vintém (head of ADA). It has acquired partial control over several *favelas* since 2016, establishing itself as the second-most-powerful criminal organisation in Rio after the CV (excluding the vigilante militias). During 2017 and 2018, the rapid decline of ADA led many of its members to switch their allegiance to the TCP. The TCP's evangelical Christian members have been known to attack and expel followers of Afro-Brazilian religions from their areas.

Objectives: Maintain areas currently under its control and expand its operating area to other neighbourhoods in Rio de Janeiro and other states.

Opponents: CV, ADA and PMERJ.

Affiliates/allies: Militias, in some areas.

Resources/capabilities: Revenue sources include drug trafficking and extortion. Weapons include pistols, rifles, bazookas and grenades.

Other relevant parties

There are many other relevant criminal organisations whose territory is more circumscribed, such as the B13 and Ifara. They remained relevant throughout the reporting period by allying themselves with Brazil's largest criminal organisations and playing an active role in achieving territorial expansion. Like their larger allies, they are mostly prison-based criminal organisations.[12]

Notes

[1] 'Brasil registra 39.5 mil assassinatos em 2023, com queda de 4% em relação no ano anterior, aponta Monitor da Violência' [Brazil records 39,500 murders in 2023, a 4% drop compared to the previous year, points out Violence Monitor], *O Globo*, 12 March 2024.

[2] Ciro Biderman et al., '*Pax Monopolista* and Crime: The Case of the Emergence of the *Primeiro Comando da Capital* in São Paulo', *Journal of Quantitative Criminology*, vol. 35, September 2019, pp. 573–605.

[3] Ryan C. Berg, 'Tussle for the Amazon: New Frontiers in Brazil's Organized Crime Landscape', Florida International University, October 2021.

[4] Tom Phillips and Jonathan Watts, 'Brazilian Amazon at Risk of Being Taken Over by Mafia, Ex-Police Chief Warns', *Guardian*, 1 June 2023.

[5] Carla Bridi, 'Police Raid in Rio Favela Sets Off Gunbattle That Kills 9 People and Wounds 2 Officers', AP News, 2 August 2023; G1 Rio, 'Polícia diz que operação no Jacarezinho teve 28 mortos' [Police say that operation in Jacarezinho resulted in 28 deaths], globo.com, 7 May 2021; 'Vila Cruzeiro: o que se sabe sobre operação policial que deixou mais de 20 mortos no Rio' [Vila Cruzeiro: what is known about the police operation that left more than 20 people dead in Rio], BBC News Brasil, 24 May 2022; and Guilherme Boisson, TV Globo, 'Polícia Civil diz que número de mortos na Vila Cruzeiro é de 23; outros 3 morreram no Juramento em outro confronto' [Civil Police say the number of deaths in Vila Cruzeiro is 23; another 3 died in Juramento in another confrontation], globo.com, 26 May 2022.

[6] See 'Sem Concurso, PMERJ Tem 30 Mil Soldados a Menos que Previsto em Lei' [Without competition, PMERJ has 30 thousand fewer soldiers than provided for by law], Folha Dirigida, 7 October 2019.

[7] Robson Bonin, 'Comando Vermelho vira preocupação do governo Bolsonaro – entenda' [Red Command is a concern in Bolsonaro's administration – understand], *Veja*, 22 August 2020.

[8] Marcos Alan S.V. Ferreira, 'Brazilian Criminal Organizations as Transnational Violent Non-state Actors: A Case Study of the Primeiro Comando da Capital (PCC)', *Trends in Organized Crime*, vol. 22, 2019, pp. 148–65; and 'Crime e poder: PCC movimenta R$ 1 bilhão e tem "batizados" fora do país' [Crime and power: PCC moves R$1 billion and has members outside the country], UOL, 9 January 2023.

[9] Ferreira, 'Brazilian Criminal Organizations as Transnational Violent Non-state Actors: A Case Study of the Primeiro Comando da Capital (PCC)'.

[10] Daniel Hirata and Maria Isabel Couto, 'Mapa Histórico dos Grupos Armados do Rio de Janeiro' [Historical map of armed groups in Rio de Janeiro], Grupo de Estudos dos Novos Ilegalismos/Instituto Fogo Cruzado, September 2022.

[11] 'PCC', *Americas Quarterly*; and InSight Crime and American University's Center for Latin American & Latino Studies, 'The Rise of the PCC: How South America's Most Powerful Prison Gang Is Spreading in Brazil and Beyond', CLALS Working Paper Series No. 30, 6 December 2020, p. 23.

[12] These organisations are (by state): Acre: Bonde dos 13 (13 Tram, B13), Ifara; Amapá: Família Terror do Amapá, Amigos para Sempre, União do Crime do Amapá; Amazonas: Revolucionários do Amazonas, Crias da Tríplice; Bahia: Katiara, Comando da Paz, Caveira, Bonde do Maluco, Mercado do Povo Atitude, Ordem e Progresso, Bonde do Ajeita; Ceará: Guardiões do Estado (Guardians of the State, GDE); Distrito Federal: Comboio do Cão; Espírito Santo: Primeiro Comando de Vitória, Trem Bala; Goiás: Família Monstro; Maranhão: Bonde dos 40, Primeiro Comando do Maranhão; Minas Gerais: Família Monstro; Pará: Comando Classe A (Class A Command), Bonde dos 30, União do Norte (Northern Union), Equipe Rex, Equipe Real; Paraíba: Okaida, Estados Unidos; Paraná: Máfia Paranaense; Pernambuco: Okaida; Rio Grande do Norte: Sindicato do Crime (Crime Syndicate, SDC); Rio Grande do Sul: Abertos, Bala na Cara, Os Manos, Comando Pelo Certo, Farrapos, Unidos pela Paz, Os Tauras, Vândalos, Mata rindo, Grupo K2, Cebolas, Primeiro Comando do Interior; Rondônia: Primeiro Comando do Panda; Santa Catarina: Primeiro Grupo Catarinense (First Group of Santa Catarina), Comando Vermelho de Santa Catarina, Força Revolucionária Catarinense, Primeiro Crime Revolucionário Catarinense; Sergipe: Bonde dos Maluco; Tocantins: Máfia Tocantinense (Tocantins Mafia).

HAITI

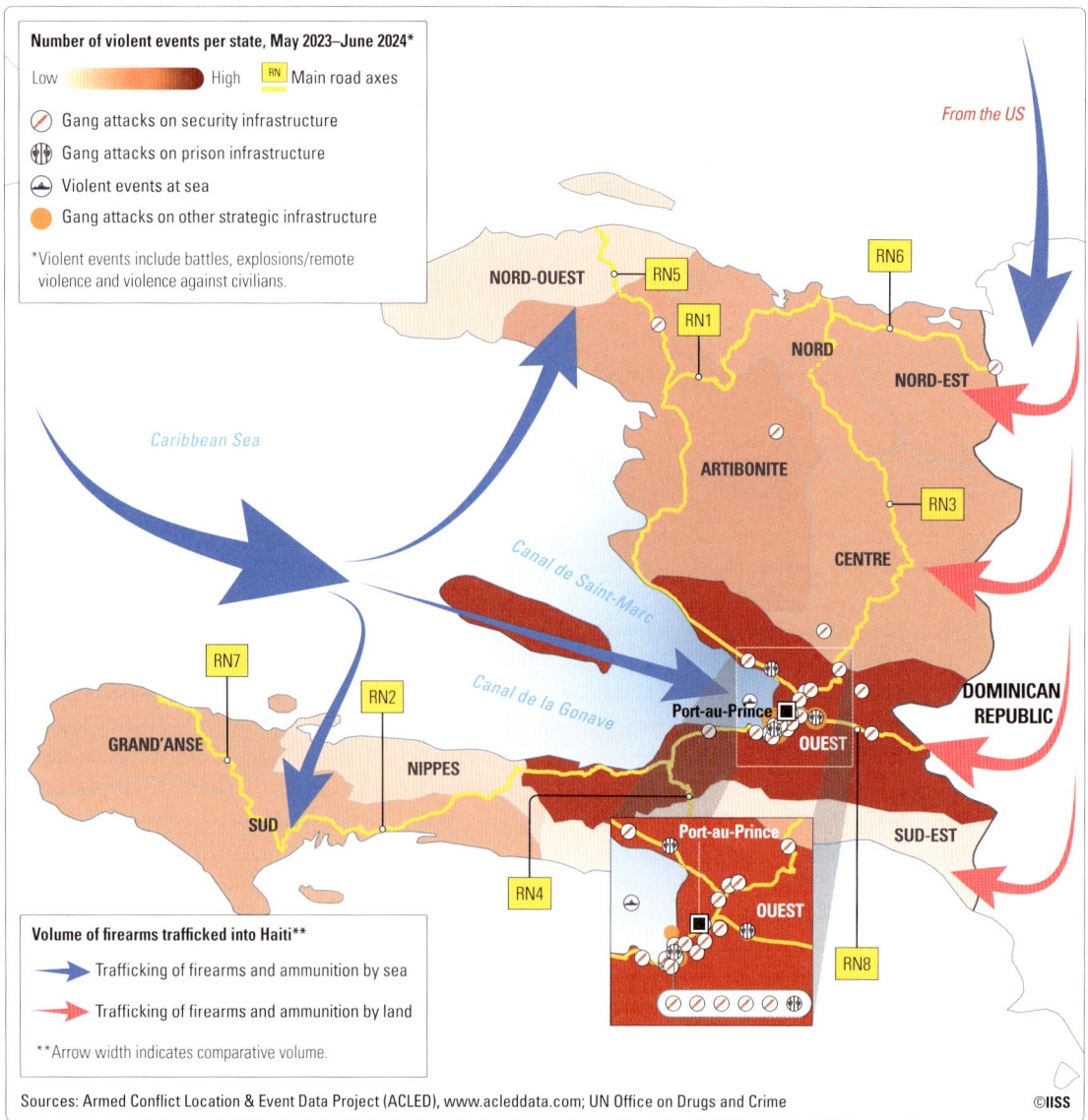

Conflict Overview

Gangs have been used for political ends in Haiti for decades, as exemplified by the Tonton Macoutes during the presidencies of François and Jean-Claude Duvalier (1957–71 and 1971–86, respectively) and the Chimères under Jean-Bertrand Aristide (1991, 1994–96 and 2001–04). Jovenel Moïse's government (2017–21) was accused of using gangs to control voting constituencies and quell dissent, including during the La Saline massacre in 2018. In recent years, the security situation in Haiti has deteriorated as gangs have gained independence from their political backers and become more professional in their operations. This process has taken place

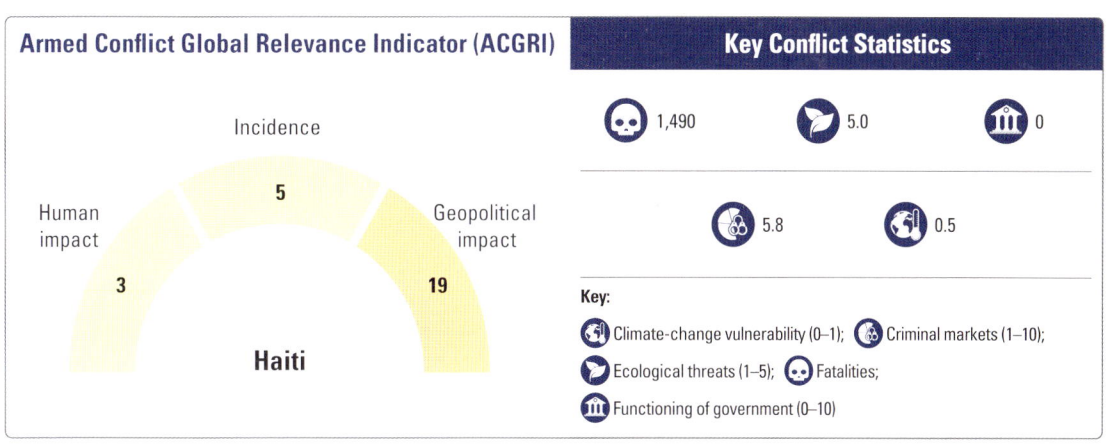

against a backdrop of political instability and the erosion of democratic institutions under Moïse, with the postponement of legislative elections, large-scale anti-government mobilisation and fragmentation of the political landscape. The evolution of gang tactics was evident as early as 2020, with a steady increase in violence – including a rise in kidnappings for ransom – as well as the formation of the G9 gang alliance and the rival G-Pèp counter-alliance. The assassination of Moïse in July 2021 was a pivotal moment: reported fatalities stemming from gang activity more than doubled in 2022 compared to the previous year.

Under the unpopular interim government of prime minister Ariel Henry, gangs took advantage of the increasing weakening of institutions. Challenging negotiations on political transition took place, involving opposition members, civil society and the private sector, including signatories of the Montana Accord – a 2021 agreement that had proposed an interim government and wider plan for solving Haiti's governance crisis – who opposed Henry's leadership. In December 2022, the government and opposition signed the National Consensus Agreement, which included provisions for holding elections and inaugurating a new government in February 2024. Persistent insecurity and gang violence, however, have prevented the organisation of elections. Haiti has therefore been without elected representatives in government since the mandate of its last elected officials expired in January 2023, and the interim government has continued to govern by decree.

Under a climate of impunity and political instability, criminal groups have intensified their campaigns to extend control to new territories with the aim of expanding extortion markets and gaining control of the country's key resources. Criminal contestation has expanded within the Port-au-Prince metropolitan area and other regions, with civilians often caught in the crossfire or deliberately targeted by gangs. Additionally, gangs controlling or targeting key resources and infrastructure, such as health facilities, docks, the Varreux oil terminal and main transport routes connecting the capital with the rest of the country, have constrained the population's access to healthcare and basic commodities, including food. As a result of the inability of police to curb gang expansion – due to a lack of resources and capacity – Henry requested the intervention of an international security force. Meanwhile, the country has seen an increase in vigilantism, with groups of citizens trying to protect their communities with makeshift barricades and collective lynchings.

Conflict Update

The security situation remained critical during the reporting period amid persistent political instability. Gangs continued to vie for control of new territories within the Port-au-Prince metropolitan area and Ouest region, also extending their influence to the Artibonite and Centre departments. Despite the commitment made by some gangs to not target civilians, Haitians remained vulnerable to violence, with more than 6.4 million people exposed to violent incidents between July 2023 and June 2024.[1] Gang control over key roadways and infrastructure continued to have serious humanitarian implications, with at least 245,000 people internally displaced in 2023, and nearly 5m Haitians in need of food assistance as of April 2024.[2] Largely outgunned and outnumbered, the police forces struggled to repel gang incursions amid a growing number of attacks targeting police stations. In a context of persistent impunity, Haitians continued to take justice into their own hands – sometimes in support of police operations – and gangs responded with violent reprisals.

Henry's interim government faced growing criticism for its inability to resolve the political crisis and prevent gang incursions. Following Henry's calls for international assistance, in October 2023 the United Nations backed the deployment of a Kenya-led Multinational Security Support Mission (MSS) tasked with restoring security. Gangs have increasingly confronted the state in response to the potential deployment. Nationwide demonstrations and unrest were further intensified by the return of former police officer and rebel leader Guy Philippe in November 2023. Philippe, who had previously mobilised armed militias and played a role in the 2004 overthrow of Jean-Bertrand Aristide, called for civil disobedience and organised demonstrations across the country demanding Henry's resignation. He received support from the Security Brigade for Protected Areas, an armed police unit affiliated with the Ministry of Environment. Calls for Henry's resignation intensified as the end of his mandate, originally scheduled for 7 February 2024, approached.

In September 2023, G9 gang leader Jimmy Chérizier announced the creation of the Viv Ansanm (Living Together) gang coalition, which brought together gangs from the G9 and G-Pèp alliances, and his intention to overthrow Henry's government. Amid widespread anti-Henry mobilisation, partly coordinated by political contenders and some gang leaders, the coalition launched a series of attacks in February 2024 against institutions, including the National Palace, main penitentiary centres and police stations. The attacks prompted the government to declare a state of emergency and led to Henry stepping down, allowing the establishment of a new transitional body, the Transitional Presidential Council (TPC) – a solution proposed by members of the Caribbean Community and other international partners. The TPC elected Garry Conille as interim prime minister on 3 June, and with a mandate set to expire in February 2026, it will supervise the organisation of the next elections.

Despite Henry's departure, alleged members of the Viv Ansanm coalition continued to pressure the transitional authorities, notably by attacking the National Palace ahead of the TPC's swearing-in ceremony, as a deterrent against the deployment of the MSS. Gangs continued to warn against the deployment, which nevertheless proceeded on 25 June with the arrival of 200 Kenyan officers. The deployment commenced as Kenyan security forces were accused of using excessive force to quell demonstrations against new tax proposals in Kenya, during which at least 13 people died, thus reviving concerns about the Kenyan police force's poor human-rights record and their future conduct within the MSS framework.

Conflict Parties

Haitian National Police (PNH)

Strength: Approximately 14,500 including coastguards and fire service, although the number of police officers on active duty is estimated to be closer to 4,450.[3]

Areas of operation: Nationwide.

Leadership: Rameau Normil (director general).

Structure: The PNH is divided into several branches and special units, including:
- Intervention and Maintenance of Order Corps (CIMO)

Haitian National Police (PNH)

- Departmental Unit for the Maintenance of Order (UDMO)
- Departmental Operation and Intervention Brigade (BOID)
- Controlling of Narcotics Trafficking Brigade (BLTS)
- Temporary Anti-Gang Unit (UTAG; launched in September 2023).

Each of Haiti's ten administrative departments also has its own police force.

History: Created in June 1995 after the Haitian army was demobilised in April that year.

Objectives: The PNH is the main law-enforcement body and the main force fighting gang violence. Its functions include protecting the president and official infrastructure such as the Office of the Prime Minister and the National Palace, anti-narcotics and crowd control.

Opponents: Most gangs, including Kraze Baryè, 400 Mawozo and 5 Segond. The PNH also clashed with members of the Security Brigade for Protected Areas (BSAP) who were backing rebel leader Guy Philippe.

Affiliates/allies: Some elements of the PNH are believed to have ties with gangs, especially within the G9 alliance. Members of the Grand Ravine and 5 Segond have also made alliances with police officers, while other criminal groups include current and former police officers, including Baz Pilate and 400 Mawozo. Self-organised citizens affiliated with the vigilante movement Bwa Kale support police operations and carry out lynchings of criminals, sometimes with tacit police approval.

Resources/capabilities: The PNH is understaffed and lacks equipment and training. In some areas, it is outnumbered and outgunned by gangs.

G9 Family and Allies (G9)

Strength: Over 1,000 members.[4]

Areas of operation: The full extent of the G9's reach is unclear, but it is reportedly heavily concentrated in the Port-au-Prince metropolitan area, with operations in various neighbourhoods, including Delmas, Belekou, Ti Bois, Fontamara, downtown Port-au-Prince, Bas Bel-Air, La Saline, Nan Chabon, Wharf Jérémie, Fort Dimanche, Duvivier, Cité Soleil, Simon Pelé and Cite Eternel. Areas under the control of the G9's allies include Croix-des-Missions and Tabarre.

Leadership: Jimmy Chérizier (alias 'Barbecue'), a former PNH officer with UDMO. He went rogue following a November 2017 PNH raid against a gang in the Grand Ravine slum, in which at least two police officers and nine civilians died.

Structure: The G9 is an alliance of several gangs. While its hierarchy and internal functioning are largely unclear, it is composed of the following criminal groups:
- Delmas 6 Gang, led by Jimmy Chérizier, with control over neighbourhoods in Delmas.
- Belekou Gang, leader unclear following the killing of former leader Iscar Andrice in November 2023, with control over the Belekou neighbourhood.
- Nan Ti Bwa, led by Christ-Roi Chery (alias 'Cristla'), with control over Martissant.
- Baz Krache Dife, led by Jean Gardy (alias 'Pece Pim'), and Baz Nan Chabon, led by Marc, with control over La Saline.
- Wharf Jérémie, led by Micanor Altès (alias 'Monel Felix'), with control over Wharf Jérémie, La Saline and Fort Dimanche.
- Gang de Pierre VI, led by Wilson Pierre (alias 'Sonson'), with control over Duvivier and Cité Soleil.
- Nan Boston, led by Mathias Sainthil, with control over Boston.
- Baz Pilate, led by Ezekiel Alexandre, with control over Cité Eternel.

The G9 coalition also has ties with allied groups such as Chen Mcchan, Fort Dimanche, Gang de Tokyo, Chancerelle, Carrefour Drouillard and Terre Noire.

History: Jimmy Chérizier founded the gang alliance in June 2020.

Objectives: The G9 is thought to have functioned at first as an armed operator of its political sponsor, but Chérizier's discourse has grown increasingly political over time. He publicly positioned the G9 as a revolutionary group against inequalities and the country's elites, opposed the deployment of the MSS and expressed interest in taking part in political negotiations following Henry's departure.

Opponents: G-Pèp and allies, including Kraze Baryè, 5 Segond, Grand Ravine, 400 Mawozo and Canaan, although gangs have reportedly observed a truce since February 2024 as part of the Viv Ansanm coalition.

Affiliates/allies: The G9 is believed to hold ties with some members of the PNH.

Resources/capabilities: Extensive resources stemming from extortion, kidnapping, theft of goods and looting of businesses, as well as the control of key infrastructure such as the Varreux oil terminal, main road axes and docks in the Port-au-Prince metropolitan area.

G-Pèp Federation and allies

Strength: Over 1,500 members.[5]

Areas of operation: G-Pèp operates from Cité Soleil commune. Since its creation, the alliance has incorporated other criminal groups, widening its sphere of influence in downtown Port-au-Prince (Martissant, Bicentenaire, Champs de Mars and Grand Ravine) and the east of the capital (Tabarre, Croix-des-Bouquets and Canaan).

Leadership: Gabriel Jean-Pierre (alias 'Ti Gabriel'), leader of the Nan Brooklyn gang, created the alliance.

Structure: G-Pèp is an alliance of several armed groups. While its hierarchy and internal functioning is largely unclear, it is composed of the following groups:
- Nan Brooklyn Gang, led by Gabriel Jean-Pierre, with control over several neighbourhoods in Cité Soleil commune.

G-Pèp Federation and allies

- Village de Dieu/5 Segond, led by Johnson André (alias 'Izo') and Emmanuel Solomon (alias 'Manno'), with control over neighbourhoods in downtown Port-au-Prince such as Bicentenaire, Champs de Mars, Village de Dieu and Martissant, and communes northwest of Port-au-Prince such as Cabaret, Titanyen and Arcahaie. The group has increasingly sought control over maritime routes, to connect Port-au-Prince with municipalities northwest of the capital.
- Kraze Baryè, led by Vitelhomme Innocent, with control over Tabarre and neighbourhoods in Pétion-Ville and Croix-des-Bouquets.
- 400 Mawozo, led by Joseph Wilson (alias 'Lanmo Sanjou'), with control over downtown Croix-des-Bouquets.
- Grand Ravine Gang, led by Bougoy, Killik and Renel Destina (alias 'Ti Lapli'), with control over Martissant and Grand Ravine neighbourhoods.
- Canaan Gang, currently led by Jeff Larose (alias 'Jeff'), with control over Canaan, Onaville, Bon Repos, Lilavois and Jerusalem.

History: Ti Gabriel founded the alliance in response to the creation of the G9 in June 2020.

Objectives: G-Pèp originally emerged as a counter-alliance to the G9 to repel the latter's violent incursions. Some members such as Kraze Baryè have openly positioned themselves against the country's elites and the alliance has advocated against the deployment of the MSS as part of the Viv Ansanm coalition.

Opponents: G9, although gangs have reportedly observed a truce since February 2024 as part of the Viv Ansanm coalition.

Affiliates/allies: G-Pèp is thought to be sponsored by the political opposition.

Resources/capabilities: G-Pèp has increased cooperation with allied groups such as Kraze Baryè, 400 Mawozo, 5 Segond, Grand Ravine and Canaan, significantly bolstering its manpower and resources.

Multinational Security Support Mission (MSS)

Strength: The MSS has a target strength of 2,500 police officers, including at least 1,000 Kenyan National Police Service personnel.[6] The Bahamas, Bangladesh, Barbados, Belize, Benin, Chad and Jamaica have also all formally committed to contributing to the mission.

Areas of operation: Unclear, likely the Ouest region.

Leadership: Godfrey Otunge (head of operations at the Kenyan Administration Police Service and senior assistant inspector general of police).

Structure: Unclear.

History: In October 2023, following calls made by Ariel Henry, the UN backed the deployment of a Kenya-led international security force to help fight gang violence. Following delays in the deployment of the mission due to political instability and Henry's announcement of his resignation in March 2024, the first 200 Kenyan personnel arrived in Haiti on 25 June.[7]

Objectives: Provide operational support to the PNH and the Haitian armed forces, and run security operations to curb gang violence and allow for the holding of free and fair elections.

Opponents: G9 and G-Pèp, and members of the Viv Ansanm coalition.

Affiliates/allies: PNH.

Resources/capabilities: The United States has pledged US$100m to the mission, including the delivery of armoured vehicles and food rations.[8] The full funding of the mission is estimated by Kenyan officials to be US$600m for one year.[9]

Notes

[1] Armed Conflict Location & Event Data Project (ACLED), 'Conflict Exposure Calculator', www.acleddata.com.

[2] Internal Displacement Monitoring Centre, 'Displacement Data'; and UN Sustainable Development Group, 'Explainer: 5 Things to Know About Food Security in Haiti in Times of Crisis', 1 April 2024.

[3] UN Security Council (UNSC), 'Final Report of the Panel of Experts on Haiti Submitted Pursuant to Resolution 2653 (2022)', S/2023/674, 15 September 2023; and Jean Junior Celestin, '455 nouveaux policiers spécialisés prêts à renforcer la lutte contre les gangs armés [455 new police officers ready to join the ranks of specialized units], *Le Nouvelliste*, 18 June 2024.

[4] UNSC, 'Final Report of the Panel of Experts on Haiti Submitted Pursuant to Resolution 2653 (2022)'.

[5] *Ibid*.

[6] Marina Daras, Gloria Aradi and Pascal Fletcher, 'Haiti Vows to Restore Order With Kenya-led Force's Help', BBC News, 26 June 2024; and White House, 'Statement by President Joe Biden on the Deployment of the Multinational Security Support Mission to Haiti', 25 June 2024.

[7] Daras, Aradi and Fletcher, 'Haiti Vows to Restore Order With Kenya-led Force's Help'.

[8] Nike Ching, 'US Commits $100 Million More to Multinational Force for Haiti Amid Violence', VOA, 11 March 2024.

[9] Global Initiative Against Transnational Organized Crime, 'Who Is in Charge of the Haiti Mission?', 18 June 2024; and Jacqueline Charles, '200 More Kenyan Police Arrive in Haiti to Help Country Tackle Violent Criminal Gangs', *Miami Herald*, 16 July 2024.

EL SALVADOR

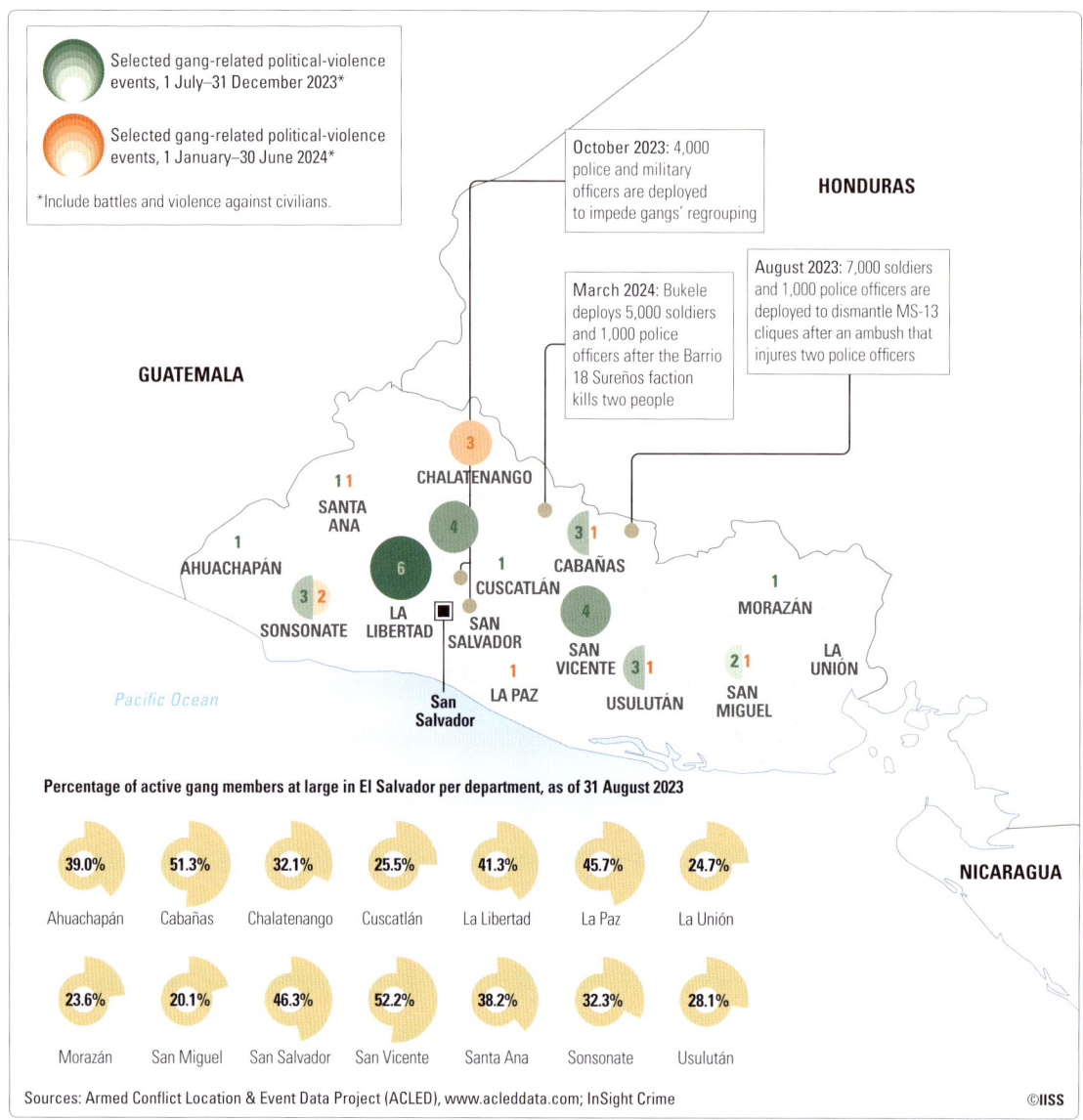

Conflict Overview

Over the last several decades, El Salvador has been ravaged by criminal violence spearheaded by three main gangs: the Mara Salvatrucha (MS-13) and the Barrio 18's Sureños and Revolucionarios factions. The MS-13 and Barrio 18 were established in El Salvador in the mid-1990s by members deported from prisons in Los Angeles, California. Newly recovered from civil war (1979–92), with weak state institutions and high poverty levels, El Salvador contained the perfect conditions for gangs to take root among marginalised young people. In the early 2000s, successive right-wing governments implemented *mano dura* (iron-fist) policies to curb gang expansion. However, mass incarcerations and grouping inmates according to gang membership had the unintended consequences of consolidating

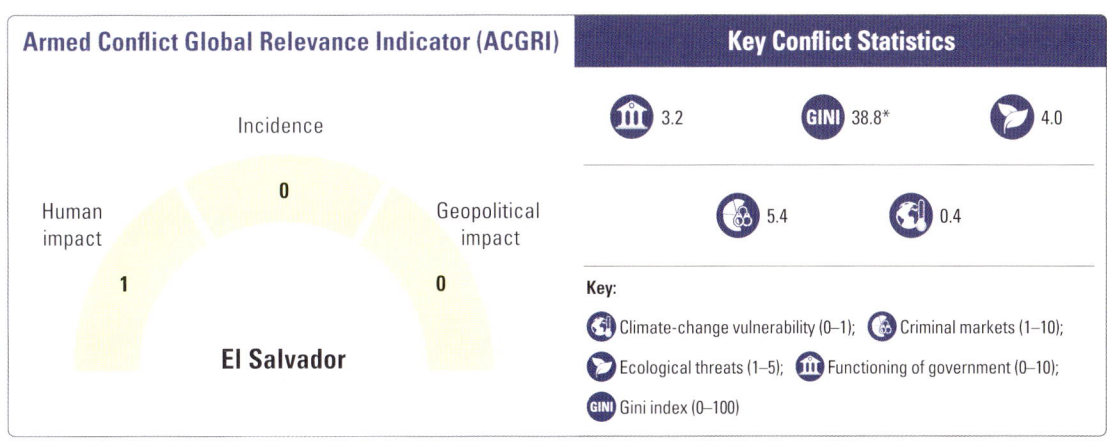

Conflict(s)	Type	Start date
Armed violence driven by gangs	I OC	2003

Key: I OC Internal: organised crime

gangs' leadership in prisons and encouraging increased extortion activities to cover legal expenses and provide for detainees' family members. Divergencies within the Barrio 18 leadership split the gang into two factions in the late 2000s.

Gangs continued to grow and vie for territory until 2012, when the left-wing government of president Mauricio Funes engaged in talks with the MS-13, the Barrio 18 and other minor gangs to facilitate a truce. This temporarily lowered the level of violence, but also contributed to defining and consolidating gangs' areas of territorial control. The process thus faced widespread public disapproval, which prompted the following government of Salvador Sánchez Céren to disavow it, triggering a wave of armed violence that resulted in at least 23,000 homicides during his term.[1] By 2019, when president Nayib Bukele took office, there were at least 65,000 gang members (two-thirds of which belonged to the MS-13) active in over 90% of the country's municipalities, earning hundreds of millions of dollars a year from extortion activities and drug sales.[2]

Conflict Update

March 2022 marked a significant shift in Bukele's security approach. Up to that point, the Bukele administration had primarily addressed gang violence by engaging in secretive talks with gang leaders to negotiate a reduction of homicides, in exchange for certain concessions. However, in response to a killing spree by the MS-13, reportedly prompted by a breakdown of those talks, Bukele launched an unprecedented dragnet on gangs through a state of exception, which has been renewed monthly ever since.[3] By early 2024, authorities claimed to have apprehended around 78,000 gang members and collaborators, transferring thousands to a newly built maximum-security prison known as the Centre for the Confinement of Terrorism (CECOT), and to have effectively dismantled most gang operations, including in the gangs' former strongholds.[4] This brought down homicides to an unprecedented rate of 2.4 murders per 100,000 inhabitants in 2023.[5]

These successes, however, have come at the cost of widespread human-rights abuses. The government has already released around 10,000 people for lack of evidence, and human-rights groups – who have denounced the growing concentration of power in the hands of the executive branch – estimate over 26,000 people have been unjustly detained in the last two years.⁶ Yet national police reports suggest that, as of September 2023, 43,000 gang members and collaborators still remained at large.⁷ While the dragnet has proven effective at curbing gang violence in the short term, Bukele will need to create alternative initiatives for at-risk youth and rebuild communities torn for decades by gang violence if he wants to make lasting progress. The country's public debt and stagnant economy, however, will represent major hurdles to this and to his government's ability to improve services and create jobs.

Conflict Parties

National Civil Police (PNC)

Strength: 27,460.⁸

Areas of operation: Country wide, particularly in urban settings, and jails.

Leadership: Mauricio Antonio Arriaza Chicas (director general).

Structure: The security force tasked with countering the MS-13 comprises three anti-gang units of approximately 600 special-forces troops and 400 PNC officers.⁹ This force is separate from the PNC's counter-narcotics and organised-crime units.

History: Founded by the 1992 Chapultepec Peace Accords to repair civil society's relationship with the security forces. The PNC has faced significant challenges since its formation, most notably organised crime led by the MS-13 and the Barrio 18. In 2022, the government sent into forced retirement around 3,000 officials who were over 60 or had been in office for more than 30 years, with the official motivation to rejuvenate the force.¹⁰ This was, however, widely seen as a move to replace the leadership with more loyal officers.

Objectives: Ensure public safety, including combatting gangs, organised crime and drug trafficking. Anti-gang units are tasked with targeting non-incarcerated leaders of the MS-13 and the Barrio 18 and restricting the communications capabilities of the leadership in prison.

Opponents: MS-13, Barrio 18, cocaine-transport groups and other smaller criminal groups in El Salvador.

Affiliates/allies: El Salvador's armed forces.

Resources/capabilities: The budget for the Ministry of Justice and Public Security is US$604.5m for 2024, up from US$588.1m in 2023.¹¹ The police have been provided with new equipment in recent years, such as drones. A new maximum-security prison called CECOT, designed to host up to 40,000 inmates, was built in record time in 2022–23.¹²

El Salvador armed forces

Strength: 26,000.

Areas of operation: Throughout El Salvador, with a particular presence in rural areas, but increasingly in urban settings too.

Leadership: René Francis Merino Monroy (minister of defence).

Structure: Six brigades across the country; three infantry battalions; one special military-security brigade with two military-police and two border-security battalions; one artillery brigade; one mechanised cavalry regiment; a special-forces command with one special-operations group; and an anti-terrorist command.

History: The armed forces held long-standing control over the government, to the detriment of El Salvador's democracy, which contributed to the outbreak of the 1979–92 civil war. The 1992 Chapultepec Peace Accords introduced key reforms to the relationship between the military and civil society, establishing civilian oversight of the military and creating a civilian police force. The military's involvement in public security has grown over the past decade, and it has accelerated under the Bukele administration, which promised in 2021 to double the force personnel in five years, from 20,000 to 40,000 troops.¹³

Objectives: Responsible for defence against external threats. The armed forces also work with the police for internal-security purposes, including fighting the MS-13 and the Barrio 18. They play a primary role in counter-narcotics operations and continue to play a law-enforcement role alongside the police (despite this being ruled unconstitutional by the Supreme Court in 2020).

Opponents: MS-13, Barrio 18, cocaine-transport groups and other smaller criminal groups.

Affiliates/allies: PNC.

Resources/capabilities: The defence ministry was allocated US$261.4m in 2024, up from US$250.6m in 2023. The armed forces' capabilities include a special-operations command, high-mobility multi-purpose wheeled vehicles, light armoured vehicles, multiple other armoured vehicles, eight UH-1H helicopters, two UH-1M helicopters, eight MD-530F helicopters and assorted other aircrafts, including an uninhabited aerial vehicle.

Mara Salvatrucha (MS-13)

Strength: Approximately 35,000 members and 43,000 collaborators.¹⁴

Areas of operation: Before the state of exception, the MS-13 was estimated to operate in 94% of El Salvador's municipalities.¹⁵ Following the mass arrests of alleged gang members under the state of exception, its current territorial control appears to have been reduced, but it seems to maintain at least some presence in all of the country's departments.

Mara Salvatrucha (MS-13)

Leadership: The most renowned leaders are Borromeo Enrique Henríquez (alias 'Diablito de Hollywood'), Elmer Canales Rivera (alias 'El Crook', detained in Mexico and extradited to the United States in 2023), Efraín Cortéz (alias 'Tigre de Park View'), César Humberto López Larios (alias 'El Greñas de Stoners', detained in Mexico and extradited to the US in 2024), Saul Antonio Turcios (alias 'Trece de Teclas') and Arístides Dionisio Umanzor (alias 'Sirra de Teclas').

Structure: Run by the *ranfla histórica* (national leadership), which sets the overall policies and strategies from prisons in El Salvador. As communication between incarcerated and non-incarcerated leaders has become more difficult, the *ranfla libre* (gang leadership not in prison) has earned greater decisional power. Each *ranflero* leads one or more *programas* (groups of highly compartmentalised street-level units, known as *clicas*), coordinated by a *corredor de programa*. Each *clica* is led by a *palabrero*. Below them are soldiers, *chequeos* (potential gang members on probation) and collaborators.

History: Founded in the 1980s in poor and marginalised neighbourhoods of Los Angeles. In the 1990s, US authorities deported many incarcerated Salvadoran MS-13 members. They arrived in El Salvador with limited community and country ties at a time when El Salvador was emerging from its civil war with experienced combat veterans, weak institutions and widely available weapons.

Objectives: Control territory in which it can exercise its own laws and authority. The group does not aim to overthrow the national government, rather its strategy includes embedding members within the state structure to facilitate the systemic extortion of entire government agencies rather than just targeting individuals. The group seems to have scaled down its extortion activities and focused on running the businesses it owns as a result of the state of exception.

Opponents: Barrio 18 factions and security forces. However, the MS-13's animosity with the Barrio 18 has drastically diminished since the 2012 truce between gangs.

Affiliates/allies: MS-13 structures in Guatemala, Honduras, Mexico and the US.

Resources/capabilities: Financial resources derived mainly from extortion, as well as protecting cocaine loads for other groups in the coastal departments and money laundering. In recent years, the group had started to set up its own businesses, particularly restaurants, car lots and private transport. The MS-13 possesses mostly civil-war-era rifles, but also some Uzis, rocket-propelled grenades and a small number of light anti-tank weapons.

Barrio 18

Strength: The Sureños faction has approximately 11,500 members and 9,500 collaborators; the Revolucionarios faction has approximately 12,000 members and 7,500 collaborators.[16]

Areas of operation: Before the state of exception, it was estimated to operate in 94% of El Salvador's municipalities.[17] Following the mass arrests of alleged gang members under the state of exception, the territorial control of the group's factions appears to have been reduced, but they seem to maintain at least some presence in all the country's departments.

Leadership: The Sureños faction's most renowned leader is Carlos Lechuga Mojica (alias 'El Viejo Lin'). Within the Revolucionarios faction, the most renowned leaders are William David González (alias 'Charly'), César Daniel Renderos Díaz (alias 'el Muerto de Las Palmas') and Marvin Douglas Martínez Panameño (alias 'Duke').

Structure: Most of the leaders of the two factions are currently held in maximum-security jails. However, both factions have a somewhat horizontal organisational structure, with greater decisional power held by leaders of the *canchas* (units of territorial control that may or may not represent municipalities), each of which comprises various *tribus* (tribes, or small social units).[18]

History: Founded in the 1960s in poor and marginalised neighbourhoods of Los Angeles. In the 1990s, US authorities deported many incarcerated Salvadoran Barrio 18 members. They arrived in El Salvador with limited community and country ties at a time when El Salvador was emerging from its civil war with experienced combat veterans, weak institutions and widely available weapons.

Objectives: Control territory in which the Barrio 18 can exercise its own laws and authority. The two Barrio 18 factions do not want to overthrow the national government, but past negotiations prompted them to acknowledge their political weight and shift their political strategies. They actively embedded members within the state structure to facilitate the systemic extortion of all economic activities in the areas they control and negotiated vote-buying with the previous governments, rather than just targeting individuals. The groups seem to have scaled down extortion activities to focus on running the businesses they own, as a result of the state of exception.

Opponents: MS-13 and security forces. However, the Barrio 18's animosity with the MS-13 has drastically diminished since the 2012 truce between the two gangs.

Affiliates/allies: Barrio 18 structures in Honduras, Guatemala, Mexico and the US.

Resources/capabilities: Revenues from extortion. In particular, the Revolucionarios faction has been able to consolidate extortion rackets even in the wealthiest areas of San Salvador, including the Zona Rosa. In recent years, both factions have started to set up their own businesses, particularly restaurants, car lots and private transport.

Notes

1. Héctor Silva Ávalos, 'Ex-president Sánchez Cerén Leaves El Salvador Facing Same Threats', InSight Crime, 3 June 2019.
2. International Crisis Group, 'Life Under Gang Rule in El Salvador', 26 November 2018; and Julia Yansura, 'Extortion in the Northern Triangle of Central America: Following the Money', Global Financial Integrity, 7 September 2022.
3. See Carlos Martínez, 'Collapsed Government Talks with MS-13 Sparked Record Homicides in El Salvador, Audios Reveal', El Faro, 17 May 2022.
4. 'El Salvador suma 78.000 presos en "guerra" contra pandillas' [El Salvador totals 78,000 prisoners in 'war' against gangs], Deutsche Welle, 27 March 2024.
5. Juliana Manjarrés and Christopher Newton, 'InSight Crime's 2023 Homicide Round-up', InSight Crime, 21 February 2024.
6. Williams Sandoval, 'Cifra de liberados ya supera los 10,000, pero no hay reparación' [Number of released persons already exceeds 10,000, but there is no reparation], La Prensa Gráfica, 29 March 2024; and Asier Vera, 'Los "errores" del plan de Bukele contra las pandillas: 26.000 inocentes detenidos y 241 muertos en las cárceles: "Hay torturas y crímenes de lesa humanidad"' [The 'mistakes' of Bukele's anti-gang plan: 26,000 innocent people detained and 241 deaths in prisons: 'there are tortures and crimes against humanity'], El Mundo, 4 April 2024.
7. Roberto Valencia, 'El Salvador Police Reports Contradict Bukele's Triumphalism', InSight Crime, 22 September 2023.
8. David Bernal and Williams Sandoval, 'El Salvador cuenta con el ejército más grande de la región centroamericana' [El Salvador has the largest military in the Central American region], La Prensa Gráfica, 28 November 2023.
9. Jeannette Aguilar, 'Las políticas de seguridad pública en El Salvador 2003–2018' [Public security policies in El Salvador 2003–2018], National Civil Police, 10 March 2021, p. 61.
10. Gabriela Villarroel, 'Gobierno de El Salvador pide nuevo retiro forzoso para el Ministerio de Seguridad' [Government of El Salvador demands new forced retirement for the Ministry of Security], La Prensa Gráfica, 8 December 2022.
11. Susana Peñate, 'Promedio de fondos para Seguridad y Defensa ronda $845.9 millones en cinco años' [Security and defense funding averages are around $845.9 million over five years], elsalvador.com, 2 January 2024.
12. BBC Mundo, World Service, 'El Salvador's Secretive Mega-jail', BBC, 14 July 2023.
13. Bryan Avelar and Nathaniel Janowitz, 'El Salvador Is Trying to Control MS-13 by Doubling Its Army', Vice, 30 July 2021.
14. Valencia, 'El Salvador Police Reports Contradict Bukele's Triumphalism'.
15. International Crisis Group, 'Life Under Gang Rule in El Salvador'.
16. Valencia, 'El Salvador Police Reports Contradict Bukele's Triumphalism'.
17. International Crisis Group, 'Life Under Gang Rule in El Salvador'.
18. See Steven Dudley, 'Barrio 18 in El Salvador: A View from the Inside', InSight Crime, 25 March 2015.

HONDURAS

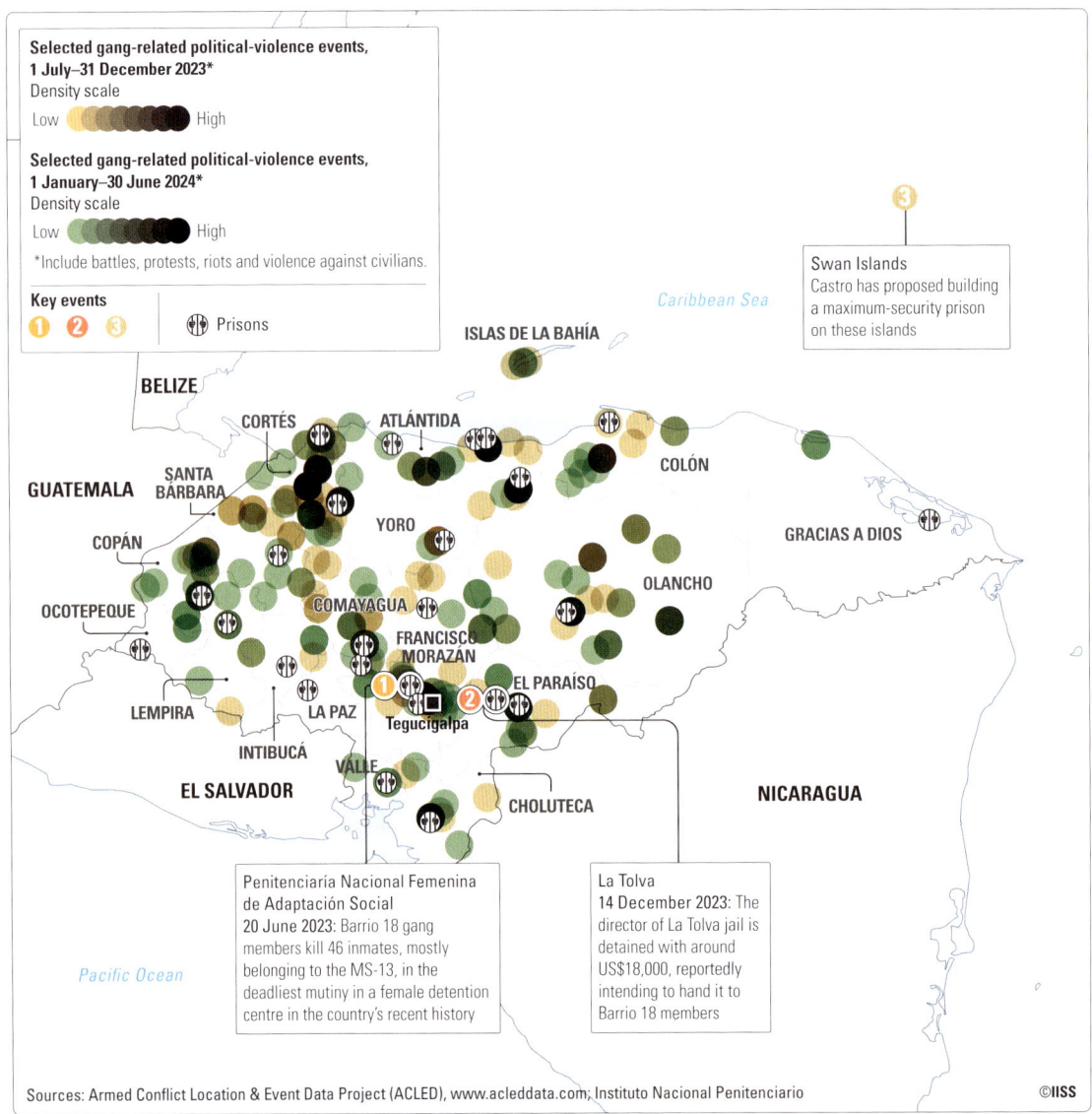

Conflict Overview

The predominant driver of violence in Honduras is competition between gangs for the control of extortion and drug-trafficking markets. The two main gangs, the Mara Salvatrucha (MS-13) and the Barrio 18, originated among Central American migrants in the United States and became active throughout Central America following a wave of deportations in the 1990s. The gangs mostly operate in the suburbs of Tegucigalpa and San Pedro Sula but are reportedly expanding into coastal areas and along Honduras's western borders. Although the Barrio 18 is larger, the MS-13 is the most powerful gang, having diversified into cocaine production and smuggling. Dozens of other smaller organisations alternately work for, ally with or fight against the two main groups. Furthermore, the country's geostrategic position and

Country Profile: Honduras

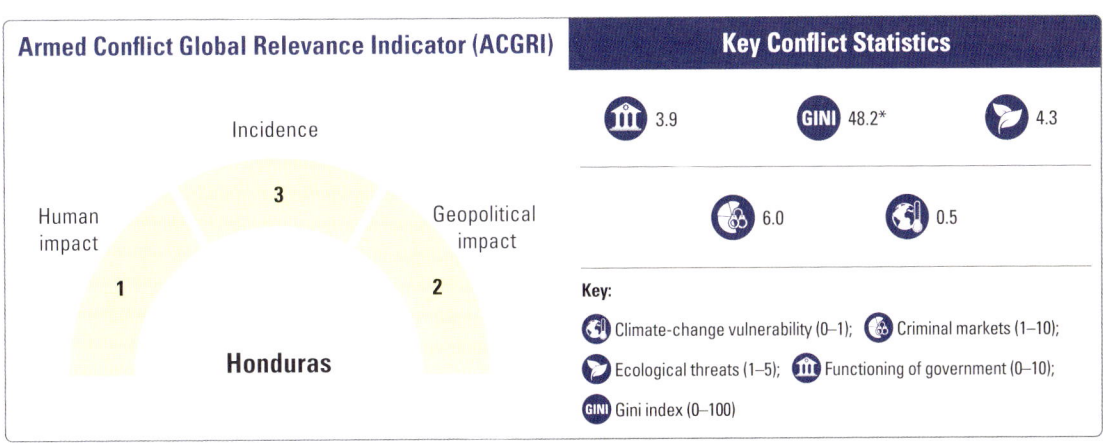

ACGRI pillars: IISS calculation based on multiple sources for 2023 and 2024 (scale: 0–100), except for some cases according to data availability. See Notes on Methodology and Data Appendix for all variables and further details on Key Conflict Statistics. *2019 as latest available data.

Conflict(s)	Type	Start date
Armed violence driven by gangs	I OC	2003

Key: I OC Internal: organised crime

topography have historically attracted drug-trafficking organisations that have used it as a stopover location for cocaine departing from Colombia and Venezuela. This, combined with persistent economic weakness, stagnating growth and high poverty levels, has created fertile ground for corruption.[1]

Since the early 2000s, successive governments have relied on heavy law enforcement and increasing military intervention to deal with gangs and drug-trafficking rings. Though local cartels affected by the capture or flight of their leaders initially scaled down their operations in the 2010s, they eventually regrouped in smaller, atomised groups. Meanwhile, larger gangs have continued to grow and consolidate their control of jails and poor neighbourhoods.[2] Ahead of taking office in January 2022, President Xiomara Castro vowed to de-militarise public security and fight corruption through the creation of a United Nations-backed International Commission against Impunity in Honduras (CICIH). However, she soon reversed this course amid public outcry over a surge in gang-led extortion activities in late 2022, which prompted her to mimic El Salvador's crackdown on gangs by imposing a state of exception and handing the control of prisons and other public-security tasks back to the military.[3]

Conflict Update

The conviction by a US court of former president Juan Orlando Hernández for drug trafficking in March 2024 demonstrated how criminal interests have penetrated state institutions at all levels in Honduras. While the CICIH could help reduce institutional corruption, the government has shown little interest in ensuring its full autonomy. Remnants of the drug-trafficking cartels that wreaked havoc in the country in the late 2000s continue to operate and generate violence, particularly in rural, eastern departments such as Colón, Yoro and Gracias a Dios. The state of exception imposed in late 2022 on 162 neighbourhoods has been expanded to 158 of the country's 298 municipalities, and renewed monthly ever since, leading to the detention of over 32,000 suspected criminals, though only 464 were accused of extortion.[4] In June 2024, Castro announced new measures, including penal-code reforms to prosecute gang members on terrorism charges and the construction of a new prison for 20,000 inmates between the Olancho and Gracias a Dios departments.[5] Although the homicide rate decreased from 38.1 per 100,000 people in

2022 to 31.1 per 100,000 people in 2023, Honduras remained the second most violent country in Latin America that year, and around four million citizens were exposed to a violent event.⁶ Meanwhile, criminal gangs have continued to expand into rural areas and run prisons, as evidenced by the several prison riots that occurred in 2023, and coca cultivation has remained a key concern, with the government eradicating 4.7m coca plants in 2023 – down from 6.5m in 2022 but considerably up from 500,000 in 2021.⁷ It is unlikely, however, that Castro's approach will be successful in curbing violence to the extent seen in El Salvador. This is largely because Honduras possesses a more fragmented gang landscape, with gangs having greater control over jails; employs fewer police and military officers; and has an independent judiciary that is more prone to releasing suspects due to lack of evidence or corruption.⁸

Conflict Parties

National Police

Strength: 17,920.⁹

Areas of operation: Nationwide, particularly in the main cities.

Leadership: Gen. Juan Manuel Aguilar Godoy (director).

Structure: The National Police has 18 departmental offices and two metropolitan headquarters (in Tegucigalpa and San Pedro Sula).¹⁰ It comprises violence-prevention, investigation, counter-narcotics and anti-gang units, among others.

History: Since its creation in 1998, the National Police has suffered from a lack of resources and corruption, which have translated into high levels of public distrust. In 2016–19, it underwent a purge, whereby almost 6,000 officials were dismissed, though only 2,100 for alleged wrongdoings, including collusion with criminal groups.¹¹ The force has not fully recovered from that process and the government is struggling to solidify its plans to reach 28,000 police officers by 2026.¹² The Police Directorate Against Maras, Gangs and Organised Crime (DIPAMPCO) was created in July 2022 to replace the extinct, military-led National Anti-Gang Force.

Objectives: Address violent crimes, especially gang-related ones, with a particular focus on investigating extortion and money-laundering activities.

Opponents: MS-13, Barrio 18, other smaller gangs, and local and transnational drug-trafficking organisations.

Affiliates/allies: Military Police of Public Order (PMOP), though the two entities compete for budget allocations and respond to different chains of command.

Resources/capabilities: The budget for the security ministry in 2024 is US$467.8m, some 53m more than in 2023.¹³ Recently, two of the ten *Black Mamba* armoured vehicles ordered by the government have been provided to the police's special forces, but one of them caught fire.¹⁴

Military Police of Public Order (PMOP)

Strength: 4,000 officers.

Areas of operation: Main cities and, since July 2023, all jails. The PMOP is also tasked with controlling remote rural areas.

Leadership: Col. Ramiro Fernando Muñoz (commander).

Structure: The PMOP has eight combat battalions and one canine battalion and reports to the Ministry of Defence.

History: The PMOP was created by Congress in 2013 to address the increasing presence of organised criminal groups in Honduras. Despite plans to gradually dissolve it, the Castro administration has relied on the PMOP to control jails and operations during the ongoing state of exception.

Objectives: Retake territory from criminal gangs and dismantle their operational structures, as well as combat transnational organised crime and drug trafficking, the latter particularly in rural areas.

Opponents: MS-13, Barrio 18, other smaller gangs, and local and transnational drug-trafficking organisations.

Affiliates/allies: DIPAMPCO, though the two entities compete for budget allocations and respond to different chains of command.

Resources/capabilities: Honduras's total defence budget for 2023 was US$442.4m. The total defence budget for 2024 is US$457.1m.

Mara Salvatrucha (MS-13)

Strength: At least 5,000 members.¹⁵

Areas of operation: Concentrated in Cortés and Francisco Morazán departments, but increasingly present in departments bordering Guatemala (Copán and Santa Bárbara) and El Salvador (Lempira and Intibucá) and in the department of Atlántida.

Leadership: MS-13 leadership is mostly in jail, but the most prominent leader is Yulan Adonay Archaga Carias (alias 'El Porky'), who escaped prison in February 2020.

Structure: The Honduran chapter of the MS-13 appears to have dropped the system of cliques and programmes and has started referring to itself as the 'big family of MS-13', a sort of unified mafia.

Mara Salvatrucha (MS-13)

History: Founded around the 1980s in poor and marginalised neighbourhoods of Los Angeles, CA. In the 1990s, US authorities deported many incarcerated Honduran MS-13 members. Once in Honduras, they started founding new cells and recruiting, and engaged in a still-active fight for territorial control. Unlike in El Salvador, the MS-13 and the Barrio-18 in Honduras were unable to absorb all pre-existing local gangs.

Objectives: The MS-13's core activities have traditionally been extortion (affecting local markets and public-transport companies) and drug peddling. Over time, it has been subcontracted by drug-trafficking groups to provide security for their shipments. The MS-13 has increased its participation not only in security provision, but also in the production of drugs, including krispy (a synthetic version of marijuana) and cocaine. It has become so economically independent that it reportedly suspended most of its extortion activities between 2020 and 2022.

Opponents: Barrio 18; other local gangs such as Vatos Locos, Los Tercereños, Los Olanchanos, El Combo Que No Se Deja and Los Aguacates; and security forces.

Affiliates/allies: MS-13 structures in El Salvador, Guatemala, Mexico and the US.

Resources/capabilities: Proceeds from local drug markets and extortion provide the MS-13 with a yearly income of tens of millions of US dollars. Kidnappings and murder-for-hire also contribute to the group's earnings. Other localised revenue sources include money-laundering operations in motels, restaurants, car lots, private-security firms and public transportation. The group's weaponry remains modest, and it has only just started to invest in surveillance technology (cameras) to better control its strongholds.

Barrio 18

Strength: At least 7,000.[16]

Areas of operation: Concentrated in Cortés and Francisco Morazán departments, but increasingly present in departments bordering Guatemala (Copán and Santa Bárbara) and El Salvador (Lempira and Intibucá) and in the department of Atlántida.

Leadership: Leadership is mostly in jail. Nahum Montes Medina (alias 'Tacoma'), Howen Alexis Romero (alias 'Ratón') and Olvin Reinaldo Arriaga Baca (alias 'Porqui') are often referred to as its central leaders.

Structure: Divided into semi-independent *canchas*, which are units of territorial control that may or may not represent municipalities. The leaders of these *canchas* are often referred to as *toros* (bulls).

History: Founded in the 1960s in poor and marginalised neighbourhoods of Los Angeles. In the 1990s, US authorities deported many incarcerated Honduran Barrio 18 members. Once in Honduras, they started founding new cells and recruiting, and engaged in a still-active fight for territorial control. Unlike in El Salvador, the MS-13 and the Barrio-18 in Honduras were unable to absorb all pre-existing local gangs.

Objectives: Control territory and generate revenue from illicit activities such as extortion and drug trafficking. The group is also sometimes subcontracted by drug-trafficking groups to provide security for their shipments.

Opponents: MS-13; other local gangs such as Vatos Locos, Los Tercereños, Los Olanchanos, El Combo Que No Se Deja and Los Aguacates; and security forces.

Affiliates/allies: Barrio 18 structures in El Salvador, Guatemala, Mexico and the US.

Resources/capabilities: Proceeds from drug trafficking and extortion provide the group with a yearly income of tens of millions of dollars. The Barrio-18 also generates revenue through kidnappings, murder-for-hire and money-laundering. Its weaponry remains modest.

Notes

[1] Honduras is one of the poorest countries in the Western Hemisphere, with over half the population living below the poverty line and with an economy largely sustained by remittances sent by Honduran migrants abroad, accounting for around one-fifth of the country's GDP. See World Bank, 'The World Bank in Honduras: Overview', 10 April 2024; and World Bank, 'Data: Honduras'.

[2] Around seven Honduran drug cartels were believed to operate in the country in the early 2000s, the most important being the Valles, the Atlantic and the Cachiros cartels. 'Carteles de Honduras reacomodan mando' [Honduran cartels reshuffle command], *Proceso Digital*, 1 April 2019.

[3] International Crisis Group, 'New Dawn or Old Habits? Resolving Honduras' Security Dilemmas', 10 July 2023.

[4] Asociación para una Sociedad más Justa [Association for a More Just Society], 'Tras 532 días bajo estado de excepción. ¿Y los resultados?' [After 532 days under a state of emergency. And the results?], 21 May 2024.

[5] Gustavo Palencia, 'Honduras Rolls out Widespread Gang Crackdown', Reuters, 15 June 2024.

[6] Policía Nacional de Honduras [National Police of Honduras], 'Situacion comparativa de casos de homicidios a nivel nacional (datos preliminares)' [Comparative situation of homicide cases at the national level (preliminary data)], December 2023;

and Armed Conflict Location & Event Data Project (ACLED), 'Conflict Exposure Calculator', www.acleddata.com.

7   Sandra Pellegrini and Aleksander Pappalardo, 'Fighting Gangs Under the State of Exception in Honduras', ACLED, 5 December 2023; and Christopher Newton and Juliana Manjarrés, 'InSight Crime's 2023 Cocaine Seizure Round-Up', InSight Crime, 20 March 2024.

8   Tiziano Breda, 'Bukele's "War on Gangs" Model Won't Work for Honduras' Castro', World Politics Review, 25 July 2023.

9   Asociación para una Sociedad más Justa [Association for a More Just Society], 'Estado de País: Seguridad y Justicia' [State of the country: security and justice], March 2024.

10 Washington Office on Latin America, 'La Policía Nacional Hondureña: Evaluando la Profesionalización del Cuerpo Policial Civil' [The Honduran National Police: evaluating the professionalisation of the civilian police corps], August 2020, p. 10.

11 International Crisis Group, 'Fight and Flight: Tackling the Roots of Honduras' Emergency', 25 October 2019.

12 Asociación para una Sociedad más Justa [Association for a More Just Society], 'Estado de País: Seguridad y Justicia' [State of the country: security and justice].

13 Daniel Girón, '¿Es justificable el incremento al presupuesto general de la Secretaría de Seguridad?' [Is the increase in the general budget of the Secretariat of Security justifiable?], Criterio, 25 January 2024.

14 'Se incendia vehículo Black Mamba de la Policía en la CA-5' [Police Black Mamba vehicle catches fire on CA-5], Tiempo, 15 May 2024.

15 Elyssa Pachico, 'The Problem with Counting Gang Members in Honduras', InSight Crime, 17 February 2016.

16 *Ibid*.

Country Profile: Honduras 77

2 Europe and Eurasia

Regional Analysis 78
Regional Spotlight 90
Country Profiles

Russia–Ukraine 96
Nagorno-Karabakh 102

A Ukrainian battle tank fires on Russian troops' position in Donetsk region, Ukraine, 9 January 2024

Overview

The break-up of the Soviet Union in 1991 and the ensuing domestic political aftershocks remain the key drivers of conflict within Europe and Eurasia. Security relations and governance agreements between and within the Soviet Union's 15 successor states have not uniformly stabilised into orderly and mutually secure relationships. This is particularly true for Russia, which has become increasingly revanchist under President Vladimir Putin. A variety of conflicts continue to bring instability and violence to the region, with Russia as the primary actor and, even when not directly involved, heavily shaping dynamics, such as in the Nagorno-Karabakh conflict and related tensions between Armenia and Azerbaijan.

In the Balkans, several unsettled governance and security arrangements as well as disputed borders also remain an issue. These are primarily the result of the break-up of Yugoslavia in the 1990s, in particular in Bosnia-Herzegovina and between Serbia and Kosovo. While these countries have not in the last two decades experienced levels of conflict comparable to those involving former Soviet states, the reporting period saw one of the most notable violent incidents in years. In northern Kosovo in September 2023, a shoot-out erupted between Kosovo police and about 30 Serb militants after the latter attempted to take control of a monastery in Banjska, resulting in at least four deaths.[1] There are also enduring disputes over borders and identity questions between Bulgaria, Greece and North Macedonia, which play a key role in shaping regional relations and the latter's aspirations to join the European Union. While

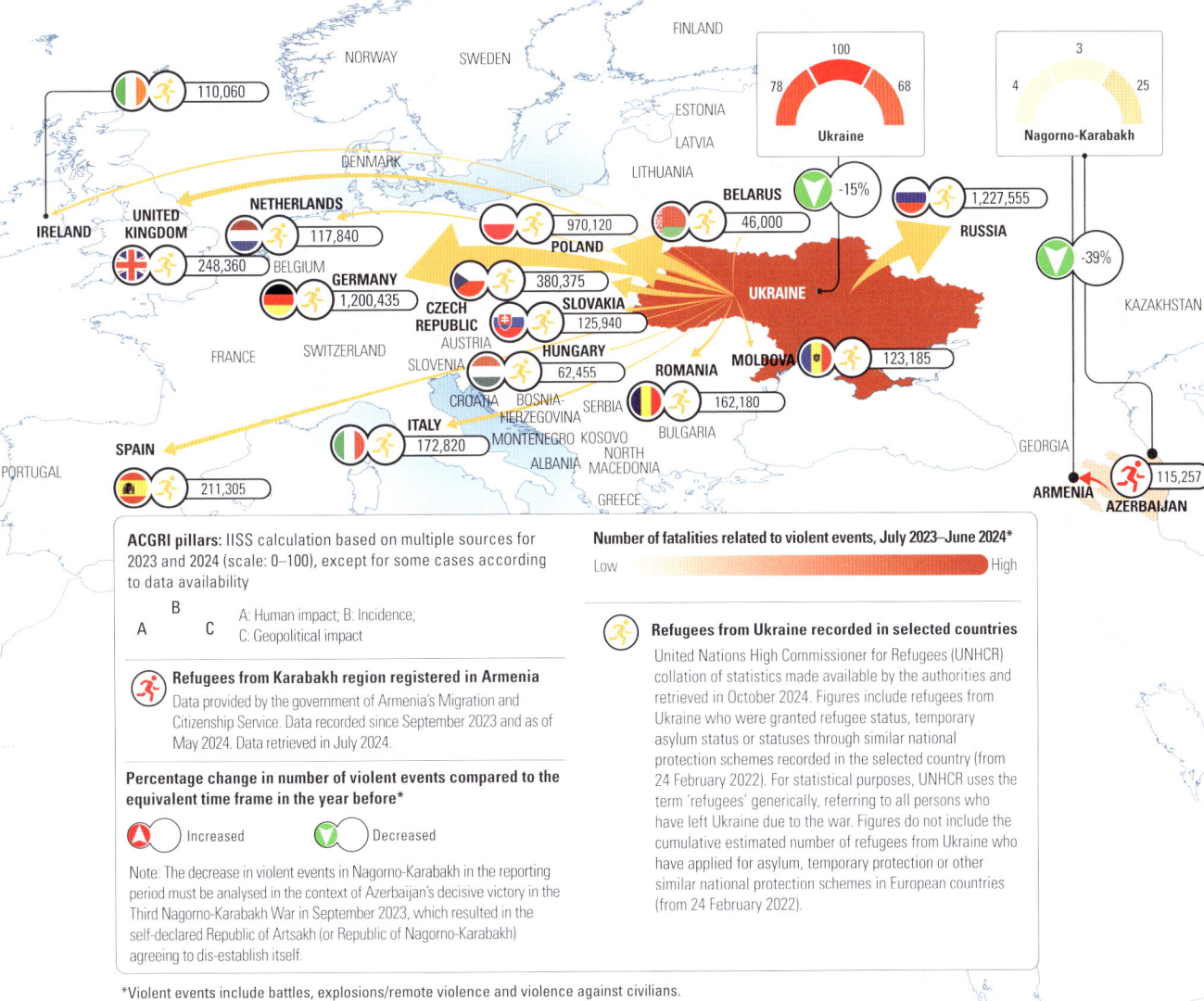

some of the fiercest disputes were settled by the 2018 Prespa Agreement between North Macedonia and Greece, these have come under renewed scrutiny following the May 2024 North Macedonian elections.[2]

During the reporting period, the Russia–Ukraine war and the Armenian–Azerbaijani conflict over Nagorno-Karabakh continued to be the largest active conflicts in the region. Both relate to the delineation of borders – inter-state and internal ones – that are not accepted as legitimate by all parties. However, it would be simplistic to imply that such disputes are purely the legacy of the Soviet Union's break-up, since they involve specific choices by political leaders. This is particularly true of Russia's February 2022 invasion of Ukraine, in which Putin rejected a legitimate, internationally recognised border and sought to annex Ukrainian territory into Russia as well as, in the longer term, dominate the country. Similar dynamics also shape other areas of instability, including ongoing tensions within Georgia in relation to its Russia-backed breakaway states of South Ossetia and Abkhazia, and continued spats between Tajikistan and Kyrgyzstan over their shared border (although there was no notable violence related to the Tajikistan–Kyrgyzstan conflict in July 2023–June 2024, unlike in the previous reporting period).

Moreover, there is an ongoing threat of armed violence from Islamist movements both in Central Asia and in Russia, as evidenced by the uptick in attacks by such groups. The most notable one occurred at the Crocus City Hall concert venue outside Moscow on 22 March 2024 and was claimed by the Islamic State Khorasan Province (ISKP), an

Asian affiliate of the Islamic State (ISIS). It was the deadliest attack in Europe ever claimed by the group, with at least 137 casualties.[3]

Russia's invasion of Ukraine was by far the most significant conflict in the region over the reporting period. It has had profound consequences not only for the region, including by aggravating many of the dynamics underpinning other conflict risks in Europe and Eurasia, but also for the world. It is the largest war in Europe since 1945 and has already led to hundreds of thousands of casualties. It continues to generate severe humanitarian, economic and environmental consequences and could escalate further. By violating state sovereignty, it challenges basic principles of the international order. Furthermore, the impact on commodity prices has pressured fragile economies, and although this has abated somewhat in the last year, the risk of further commodity supply shocks remains high. The invasion therefore continues to be one of the most acute geopolitical crises worldwide.

The war has also begun to spread into Russia itself. While acts of sabotage and arson carried out by Ukrainian partisans and dissident Russians continued during the reporting period, the level of attacks within Russia has been significantly increased by the development of new long-range Ukrainian uninhabited aerial vehicles (UAVs) (see Figure 1). In August 2024, Ukrainian forces also launched direct cross-border raids into Kursk region. Russia, for its part, has adapted its UAV and missile tactics against Ukraine as well. In the second half of 2023, the country launched a sustained campaign of targeting Ukrainian ports in Odesa region, but this was ineffective in limiting Ukrainian shipping, which instead increased. From December 2023, Russia has carried out a sustained campaign of targeting power infrastructure across Ukraine, which has heavily depleted power production there, leading to the worst and widest blackouts to date. These are expected to be sustained through the forthcoming winter due to challenges in repair timelines and continued attacks.

Sources: Armed Conflict Location & Event Data Project (ACLED), www.acleddata.com; IISS analysis ©IISS

Figure 1: Number of Ukrainian air and drone strikes on Russian territory, July 2023–June 2024

Conflict Drivers

Political and institutional
Absence of accepted borders
The lack of accepted, legitimate borders by the countries that share them has been a recurring driver of conflict in the region. In many cases, this is because little progress has been made in border demarcation since the collapse of the Soviet Union, although the current reporting period did see an increase in such efforts, particularly between Kyrgyzstan and Tajikistan. Disputes over access to shared water resources also exacerbate tensions, having played a key role in fomenting border clashes in Central Asia in recent decades. In the case of Uzbekistan, issues related to its internal borders continue to fuel discontent and instability, with simmering tensions over the central government's failures to keep promises regarding granting autonomy to the country's Karakalpakstan region. Tensions also remain over the status of Uzbekistan's exclaves that are surrounded by territory belonging to Kyrgyzstan and Tajikistan and these countries' enclaves within Uzbekistan's primary borders.

In the case of the Russia–Ukraine war, the inter-state border had previously been accepted as legitimate by both countries. Indeed, Russia signed numerous inter-state agreements with Ukraine, including the 1994 Budapest Memorandum with the United States and United Kingdom, in which it committed to respecting Ukraine's territorial integrity. In violation of international law, Russia's first invasion in February 2014 led to its occupation of Crimea and to it gaining effective control, through puppet administrations, over Donbas region in eastern Ukraine. Its second, full-scale invasion in February 2022 sought to occupy almost all the country and to forcibly replace Ukraine's elected government. Russia initially claimed it was merely recognising its puppet statelets in Donetsk and Luhansk regions as 'independent' but then later declared both to have been annexed alongside Ukraine's Kherson, Luhansk and Zaporizhzhia regions in September 2022 (though none have ever been wholly occupied as of June 2024). Russia amended its constitution to incorporate these regions into its territory and has sought to administer them as subjects of the Russian Federation. Almost no other country recognises these annexations, nor the 2014 annexation of Crimea.

Geopolitical
Russia's geopolitical ambitions
Another major cause of instability in the region is Russia's aspirations to reinstate influence and dominance over the former countries of the Soviet Union (a region the Kremlin describes as the 'near abroad') as well as restore its position as a revisionist global power.[4] This led it to occupy Abkhazia and South Ossetia after its war with Georgia in 2008 and then to launch its two invasions of Ukraine in 2014 and 2022. Russia's ambitions to redraw the geopolitical map have also been felt far beyond Europe and Eurasia, driving the Kremlin's willingness to send military contractors and its armed forces abroad, notably to Syria and across Sub-Saharan Africa. The victory that Putin hoped to achieve with the 2022 full-scale invasion of Ukraine was also aimed at projecting Russian power into Europe to press for a major revision of the European security order. This would entail, in particular, a de facto reversal of the post-Cold War enlargement of NATO. Two proposed treaties with the US and NATO, drafted by the Russian Ministry of Foreign Affairs at Putin's behest in December 2021, reflected these ambitions. This effort has so far failed, however, and NATO has continued its expansion, with Finland joining the bloc on 4 April 2023 and Sweden also doing so on 7 March 2024.

Conflict Parties

Coalitions and multilateral responses
Russia and Ukraine are each supported indirectly by a number of countries, albeit to significantly different extents. Ukraine has since 2022 been dependent on military equipment, ammunition and logistical support from Western countries and their partners coordinated through the Ukraine Defense Contact Group – with over US$95 billion in such support to date.[5] This includes the provision of air-defence systems, heavy armour, long-range artillery and missile systems. Some countries also provide military training and

intelligence, notably France, Germany, the UK and the US. Additionally, Western financial support sustains the country's war-ravaged economy.

Russia has a large and vast military-industrial complex and has continued to produce key materiel, including missiles and other high-tech goods, despite sanctions targeting the purchase of Western technology that Russia is dependent on for these production lines. The Kremlin has also received weapons systems and ammunition from Belarus, Iran and North Korea since 2022. At the start of its full-scale invasion, Russia used Belarusian territory to launch ground and air attacks against Ukraine, and it has subsequently deployed tactical nuclear weapons there. Moreover, though China is not known to have provided weapons systems to Russia, it is believed to have increased Russia's supply of militarily useful components and equipment.

In the case of the Nagorno-Karabakh conflict, Israel and Turkiye's military support for Azerbaijan, which includes equipment and training, has been key to Baku's successes in the region. Armenia, meanwhile, is formally allied to Russia through the Collective Security Treaty Organisation (CSTO), but Armenian officials, including Prime Minister Nikol Pashinyan in 2024, have declared their intent to ultimately leave the bloc.

Non-state armed groups
Russia's February 2022 invasion of Ukraine was initially led by its regular armed forces, with other security organisations and militias from the so-called Donetsk People's Republic and Luhansk People's Republic playing a secondary role. Even before the war, such groups had long relied on Russia for arms transfers and the appointment of commanders. Heavy losses suffered by Russian forces resulted in an increased reliance on other sources of personnel, such as mobilised reservists and so-called private military companies (PMCs). While, in practice, PMCs operated as state-linked paramilitary forces, they were at least nominally illegal under Russian law (though the Kremlin increasingly has referred to PMCs as lacking a legal framework rather than being prohibited). Following the 2023 mutiny by Yevgeny Prigozhin and his Wagner Group (Russia's most prominent PMC), however, the Kremlin has begun to bring these groups under the formal control of the Ministry of Defence. Some smaller groups such as Potok, created by state gas company Gazprom, are also used for recruiting combatants.

Both Russia and Ukraine have succeeded in recruiting some foreign fighters. On the Russian side, foreign forces come primarily from the Middle East, Africa, former Soviet countries, and other third countries such as Bosnia-Herzegovina and Serbia. On the Ukrainian side, Kyiv has formed two military units largely staffed by foreign volunteer fighters – the International Legion of the Territorial Defence of Ukraine and the Georgian Legion – while also supporting units principally consisting of Russian and Chechen nationals. Though the Georgian Legion contains other third-country nationals, Georgians are estimated to make up the largest number of foreign nationals killed fighting in the conflict.

Regional Humanitarian Trends

The Russia–Ukraine war has had a devastating impact on the humanitarian situation in Ukraine. At least 23,000 people remain missing and 3.7 million are internally displaced. Meanwhile, 6.2m Ukrainian refugees have been recorded globally, with the overwhelming majority residing within Europe.[6] Russian forces and officials have credibly been accused of severe violations of international humanitarian law, including executions and widespread torture in occupied territory. They have engaged in organised abductions of Ukrainian children from occupied territory and attempted to move citizens the Kremlin deems loyal into these areas as well. Russian attacks on civilian infrastructure, which as already mentioned escalated notably within the second half of the reporting period, also have had a major impact on Ukrainians' access to potable water, electricity and other basic necessities. These issues are at risk of worsening, particularly during the upcoming winter.

The humanitarian situation in Russia has been comparatively little impacted by the war directly, although the Kremlin has resorted to forced conscription to sustain its troop numbers and may do so again. The situation may also further deteriorate. The reporting period has seen a renewed crackdown by the Russian security forces on Central Asian migrant labour, particularly after ISKP's March attack on the Crocus City Hall concert venue. Although Central Asian migrants are necessary for sustaining the Russian economy, they are subjected to poor working conditions, often in irregular environments, and arbitrary responses from the security forces. Migrants have also been pressured to join the Russian military and Russian PMCs.

Internal border disputes in Georgia – aggravated by Russia's effective occupation of Abkhazia and South Ossetia – have left the country with a large number of internally displaced persons (IDPs). These number around 286,000 or 6% of the population, the vast majority of whom hail from Abkhazia and have not been able to return since the 1992–93 war between Georgian and Abkhaz forces.[7]

The reporting period also saw a substantial refugee flow from Nagorno-Karabakh to Armenia, with over 100,000 ethnic Armenians, almost the entirety of the region's remaining population as of August 2023, displaced following Baku's September offensive and the subsequent collapse of the Armenian entity in the region.[8] Though the conflict was brief, Azerbaijan and the former Nagorno-Karabakh de facto Armenian authority both reported notable casualties, with 192 and 190 soldiers killed respectively. The civilian death toll remains unknown due to Baku's restrictions on independent reporting in the region.[9] The subsequent refugee flow and divisions between Nagorno-Karabakh Armenians and the wider Armenian population have strained social environments and helped fuel anti-government protests in Armenia as well. At the same time, the Azerbaijani government has engaged in efforts to return ethnic Azerbaijani IDPs from the First Nagorno-Karabakh War (1988–94), which displaced more than 500,000 people from Nagorno-Karabakh and surrounding regions, to the territories retaken by Baku in recent years.[10]

Arbitrary detention and abuse by the security forces remain areas of concern in numerous countries in the post-Soviet space, albeit to varying extents. The worst abuses are at their most widespread in Azerbaijan, Belarus, Russia, Tajikistan and Turkmenistan, where arbitrary detention and torture of political prisoners are common.

Outlook

Prospects for peace

An end to Russia's war against Ukraine in the foreseeable future appears unlikely. The two sides remain far apart on any possible peace terms. Russia demands that Ukraine accept the 'new territorial reality' of its current occupation as a precondition of peace negotiations.[11] It also insists on the surrender of territory within Donetsk, Kherson, Luhansk and Zaporizhzhia regions that it has previously withdrawn from as well as territory in those areas that its forces never managed to occupy. In addition, there is no indication that Russia has abandoned the initial primary goal of its full-scale invasion, namely the subjugation of Ukraine. There is thus no assurance that a peace agreement recognising Russia's control of the areas it currently occupies would represent a stable outcome, rather than a prelude to further aggression.

Ukraine, for its part, has not publicly changed its position that settlement of the conflict requires the full restoration of its territorial sovereignty, although it was reportedly willing to leave the question of Crimea's sovereignty out of any agreement during brief negotiations held in Belarus in the first weeks after Russia's invasion began. Kyiv has regularly supported international peace conferences but primarily has used these as a vector to try to build support among non-aligned countries.

A sustainable end to the war, rather than a temporary ceasefire, would require a host of wider political, legal, economic and security issues to be resolved. These include questions around territorial control and recognition thereof, the terms under which sanctions imposed on Russia might be lifted, the potential for reparation payments to Ukraine, the future of frozen Russian assets, accountability for war crimes, the return of Ukrainian citizens deported to Russia, and the structure of future security guarantees. A settlement would therefore require a complex diplomatic process.

Escalation potential and regional spillovers

There are at least four ways that Russia's war in Ukraine could still escalate further. Firstly, its intensity could increase if Russia turns more of its human and material potential into a usable military force. Thus far, the regime has balanced its mobilisation of resources with the need to maintain domestic stability, though it has consistently increased the share of its budget and GDP allocated to the war effort. Notably, in June 2024, it began the process of legislating a series of tax hikes to try to sustain this. Ukraine's increasing targeting of industrial infrastructure within Russia in 2024 may strain the Russian economy, and while Kyiv has thus far avoided copying Russia's tactics of purposefully targeting civilian infrastructure, such attacks cannot be ruled out in the future. Ukraine's August 2024 cross-border incursion into Russia's Kursk region also could result in new Russian counter-attacks in northern Ukraine or further such Ukrainian counter-offensives.

Secondly, political opposition within the West to continued support for Ukraine (regarding both sanctions and whether to sustain or even increase existing high levels of materiel and financial aid) is increasingly posing a risk to Ukraine's victory prospects. It took the US Congress six months to respond to the last major request to budget additional aid for Ukraine. Moreover, the future of such support will be a key question in the forthcoming November US general election with the Republican candidate, former president Donald Trump, having declared that he is willing to suspend additional support to Ukraine and has commissioned plans to do so. Without additional aid, Ukrainian forces will lack crucial air defences and hardware to resist further Russian attacks.

Thirdly, Russia may continue to escalate horizontally through attacks on Western assets and within Western countries. These grew increasingly brazen during the reporting period, with British, Czech, German and Spanish authorities all blaming Russian intelligence for carrying out attacks within their territory. There is also increasing concern that Russia may further test NATO's resolve by probing the borders of NATO members. In August 2023, Belarusian helicopters violated Polish airspace, and there have been sustained efforts by Russian and Belarusian authorities to push migrants towards the Finnish and Polish borders, respectively.[12]

Lastly, it cannot be ruled out that Russia may escalate vertically by using weapons of mass destruction, especially tactical nuclear weapons, as it has threatened to do since shortly after the start of its full-scale invasion in 2022. The probability of such deployments is low, but it cannot be fully discounted. Russia might also resort to a smaller, but still very serious, nuclear operation by destroying the Zaporizhzhia Nuclear Power Plant that it currently occupies or by targeting other Ukrainian nuclear infrastructure. On 19 September 2022, Ukrainian officials reported that a Russian missile struck within 300 metres of the South Ukraine Nuclear Power Plant in Mykolaiv region, and on 25 October 2023 they accused Russia of launching kamikaze UAV strikes on the Khmelnytskyi Nuclear Power Plant in Khmelnytskyi region.[13]

Meanwhile, tensions continue between Armenia and Azerbaijan despite Western-mediated peace talks. Additional conflict between the two countries remains a risk, with clashes along their mutual border reported as recently as late June 2024. Russia's ongoing occupation of 20% of Georgia's territory and its creeping expansion of the borders of South Ossetia also serve as an effective threat against Tbilisi that the Kremlin might launch additional military action if Georgia directly supports Ukraine or takes any other action that the Kremlin strongly opposes.

Strategic prospects

The course of the Russia–Ukraine war remains dependent on the wider contest of resolve between Russia and the West and their competition for support from the wider international community, notably in relation to increasing efforts to crack down on Russia's and certain third countries' evasion of trade controls. The war also continues to have potential implications for the future unity of Western security alliances, in particular NATO. Despite its recent expansion, there remain fierce divides over potential future membership for Ukraine, and leading US politicians have openly considered the idea of collapsing the Alliance. Russia, on the other hand, has used the war to try to appeal to the so-called Global South by arguing that it is fighting against Western and, in particular, US hegemony – rhetoric that has had some appeal in Sub-Saharan Africa in particular.

China's policy is another key variable. Direct Chinese materiel support could mitigate the disadvantage Russia faces with respect to the West and thus help sustain its war effort. However, if China decreases its support for Russia or aligns with the West more directly in diplomatic efforts to end the crisis, it could conceivably help pressure Russia to end the war on terms acceptable to Ukraine and its supporters.

Regional Key Events

POLITICAL EVENTS

 **UZBEKISTAN**

9 July 2023

Uzbekistan's incumbent president, Shavkat Mirziyoyev, wins elections by a large margin, earning another seven-year term.

 **BELARUS, LITHUANIA, RUSSIA**

4 August

Lithuania designates over a thousand Russian and Belarusian citizens as national-security threats and revokes their permanent-residency permits.

 **KAZAKHSTAN, KYRGYZSTAN, TAJIKISTAN, TURKMENISTAN, UZBEKISTAN**

19 September

US President Joe Biden holds the first C5+1 summit with Central Asian leaders to discuss security, economic cooperation and critical minerals.

 **NAGORNO-KARABAKH**

28 September

Nagorno-Karabakh's separatist president Samvel Shakhramanyan signs a decree to dismantle the region's state institutions by year end.

MILITARY/VIOLENT EVENTS

 **BELARUS, RUSSIA–UKRAINE**

14 July 2023

Following a failed mutiny in June 2023, the Wagner Group begins training with Belarusian troops.

 **RUSSIA–UKRAINE**

2 August

Russia authorises UAV strikes on a critical Ukrainian port for grain exports following its withdrawal from the Black Sea Grain Initiative.

 **RUSSIA–UKRAINE**

18 August

The US approves the transfer of F-16 *Fighting Falcon* fighter aircraft to Ukraine from Denmark and the Netherlands.

 **RUSSIA–UKRAINE**

23 August

Yevgeny Prigozhin, chief of the Wagner Group, dies in a plane crash alongside other prominent Wagner Group leaders.

 **NAGORNO-KARABAKH**

19–20 September

Azerbaijan launches a major assault in Nagorno-Karabakh, resulting in a decisive victory for Azerbaijan and prompting the mass displacement of over 100,000 ethnic Armenians.

 **SERBIA, KOSOVO**

24 September

Open fire between Kosovar police and around 30 Serb militants results in four deaths.

KYRGYZSTAN, TAJIKISTAN
13 December

Kyrgyz and Tajik officials announce that they have reached an agreement regarding over 90% of their shared border.

  NAGORNO-KARABAKH
1 January 2024

The self-declared Republic of Artsakh (also known as the Republic of Nagorno-Karabakh) formally dissolves.

 RUSSIA–UKRAINE
3 January

230 Ukrainian and 248 Russian prisoners of war return home in the first prisoner exchange in nearly five months.

  RUSSIA–UKRAINE
2–8 February

Ukrainian President Volodymyr Zelenskyy replaces his top military leader Gen. Valery Zaluzhny with the commander of ground forces, Col.-Gen. Oleksandr Syrsky.

 RUSSIA
16 February

Prominent Russian opposition leader Alexei Navalny dies in prison while serving a 19-year sentence on extremism charges.

 BELARUS
25 February

Candidates loyal to incumbent President Alyaksandr Lukashenka win Belarusian parliamentary elections in which opposition parties are banned.

 **RUSSIA–UKRAINE**
6 October

A Russian rocket strikes the village of Hroza in eastern Ukraine, killing at least 51 civilians.

 RUSSIA–UKRAINE
4 November

15 Ukrainian missiles are fired at a shipyard in Crimea, damaging a Russian ship.

 RUSSIA–UKRAINE
25 November

Ukrainian air defences intercept all but one of 75 Iranian-made *Shahed* UAVs launched in an intense Russian attack on Kyiv.

 RUSSIA–UKRAINE
29 December

Russian forces bombard six Ukrainian cities with 122 missiles and 36 UAVs, leaving 18 dead and at least 86 injured.

 RUSSIA–UKRAINE
21 January 2024

Ukrainian shelling kills at least 27 people and injures 25 at a market in Russian-occupied Donetsk city.

 MOLDOVA
28 February

Transnistria, a breakaway region in eastern Moldova, holds its first Congress of Deputies meeting since 2006, appealing for Russian support.

 RUSSIA
15–17 March

Putin wins Russia's presidential election with 87% of the vote.

 MOLDOVA, UKRAINE
17 March

Transnistria's de facto authorities report a UAV attack on its military base in Tiraspol launched from Ukraine.

 RUSSIA
22 March

ISKP attacks the Crocus City Hall concert venue outside Moscow, Russia, killing 137 and injuring 180 civilians.

 UZBEKISTAN, KYRGYZSTAN
15 April

Uzbekistan acquires the village of Barak and Kyrgyzstan receives Andijon province in a historic deal regarding their disputed border.

 RUSSIA–UKRAINE
21 May

The EU declares its intention to allocate around US$3.3bn in profits from frozen Russian sovereign assets to support Ukraine and its military annually.

 RUSSIA–UKRAINE
15–16 June

Zelenskyy hosts a peace summit in Switzerland to garner support from critical non-Western countries for his ten-point 'peace formula'.

 RUSSIA
23 June

Places of worship across two cities in Dagestan, Russia, suffer from coordinated terrorist attacks, leaving 19 dead and 16 injured.

 RUSSIA–UKRAINE
6 August

Ukrainian forces launch a cross-border incursion into Russia's Kursk region, subsequently holding a bridgehead of roughly 1,000 square kilometres.

Notes

1. Marita Moloney, 'Kosovo Monastery Siege Ends After Heavy Gun Battles', BBC News, 24 September 2023.
2. Balkan dynamics are further explored in the Europe and Eurasia Regional Spotlight, 'The Western Balkans: Controlled Instability?'.
3. Jason Burke and Jonathan Yerushalmy, 'Moscow Attack Explainer: Why Would Islamic State Attack Russia and What Will Putin's Response Be?', *Guardian*, 25 March 2024.
4. Gerard Toal, *Near Abroad: Putin, the West, and the Contest Over Ukraine and the Caucasus* (Oxford: Oxford University Press, 2017).
5. C. Todd Lopez, '2-Year Anniversary of Ukraine Defense Contact Group Comes With Billions in New Aid', US Department of Defense, 26 April 2024.
6. International Committee of the Red Cross, 'Russia–Ukraine International Armed Conflict: 23,000 People Reported Missing', 19 February 2024; and UN High Commissioner for Refugees (UNHCR), 'Ukraine'.
7. Giorgi Lomsadze, 'Georgia's Displaced People: A Life in Limbo', Eurasianet, 3 February 2022.
8. UNHCR, 'Inter-agency Rapid Needs Assessment Report', November 2023; and Claire Mills, 'What Is Happening in Nagorno-Karabakh', no. 9862, United Kingdom Parliament, House of Commons Library, 28 September 2023.
9. Avet Demourian, 'Azerbaijan Arrests the Former Head of Separatist Government After Recapturing Nagorno-Karabakh', AP News, 27 September 2023.
10. Amnesty International, 'Armenia/Azerbaijan: Nagorno-Karabakh Conflict Caused Decades of Misery for Older People – New Reports', 17 May 2022.
11. Marita Moloney, 'Ukraine War: Putin Says Russia Does Not Reject Peace Talks', BBC News, 30 July 2023.
12. Svitlana Odynets and Kathryn Cassidy, 'Border and Migration Politics and the Kremlin's Hybrid War', UK in a Changing Europe, 15 January 2024.
13. Karl Ritter and Jon Gambrell, 'Ukraine Warns of "Nuclear Terrorism" After Strike Near Plant', AP News, 20 September 2022.

The Western Balkans: Controlled Instability?

When Russia launched its full-scale invasion of Ukraine in February 2022, there was a great deal of concern that conflict could spread out to former Yugoslavia. The unresolved sovereignty dispute between Kosovo and Serbia and the tense political situation in Bosnia-Herzegovina caused alarm in key European Union capitals, within NATO and in the United States. Russian influence in the region added to fears of spillover. As a result, Western diplomacy shifted into a higher gear in an effort to find a lasting settlement in Kosovo. The EU re-energised its enlargement policy, which many in the region and beyond had hitherto seen as moribund and lacking credibility. Two and a half years later, the Western Balkans appear relatively stable. The worst-case scenario, a return to the wars of the 1990s, failed to materialise. Several states in the region took steps towards EU accession. However, none of the festering security issues have been put to rest. A shoot-out between Serb militants and the Kosovo police in September 2023 highlighted the continued threat of low-intensity violence. Bosnia-Herzegovina remains as divided as ever, with Republika Srpska (RS), the Serb-majority entity, building de facto statehood. Structural ills such as state capture and corruption continue to hamper Western efforts to integrate the region while also facilitating inroads by geopolitical rivals such as Russia and China. The Western Balkans are likely to remain a flashpoint of political risk for the foreseeable future.

Glass half full

The signing of the 1995 Dayton Accords, which ended the war in Bosnia-Herzegovina, and NATO's intervention in Kosovo in 1999 happened at the height of the so-called 'unipolar moment'.[1] US hard power and diplomacy helped stem the violence at a moment in which Western hegemony was at its peak. Russia, under then-president Boris Yeltsin, essentially aligned with NATO, while China was largely absent. Now that the world is moving decisively towards multipolarity and Russia has no qualms about waging a war of territorial aggrandisement and challenging cornerstone norms of international conduct, the risk of nationalism-fuelled conflict over borders may be resurging in the Balkans.

Serbia, a country that benefits from close ties to Russia and where revanchism has never abated, is the usual suspect when it comes to doomsday projections. It sees Kosovo, or at a minimum the four Serb-majority municipalities in the north, as part of its territory. Bosnia-Herzegovina's RS and even NATO member Montenegro, which is viewed by many in Belgrade as a second Serb state, could also be dragged into Serbia's orbit.

Yet recent events show that the EU and NATO are also expanding. Even before Russia's full-scale invasion, NATO had welcomed Montenegro (2017) and North Macedonia (2020) as members. Then, in response to Russia's aggression, the Alliance boosted its troop presence in Kosovo, where it leads the 4,500-strong Kosovo Force (KFOR) peacekeeping operation.[2] Though Serbia's President Aleksandar Vučić has repeatedly threatened to deploy the Serbian army to Kosovo to prevent the alleged ethnic cleansing of local Serbs, it is unlikely that he will risk a confrontation with NATO. Meanwhile, on 21 March 2024, EU leaders agreed to launch accession talks with Bosnia-Herzegovina. The latter has joined the ranks of Albania, Montenegro, North Macedonia and Serbia already involved in negotiations, with only Kosovo excluded for now. While Bosnia-Herzegovina has repeatedly failed to meet all requirements put forward by Brussels, the EU has resolved to continue to engage with the country in the interest of stability. Having already approved membership talks with Ukraine and Moldova, EU leaders felt Bosnia-Herzegovina should not be excluded.

The EU has been increasing its economic offering as well. In November 2023, the European Commission adopted a new Growth Plan which aims to allocate US$2.2 billion in grants and US$4.3bn in concessional loans to the region from 2024–27.[3] The underlying ambition is to double the size of the local economies, the combined GDP of which currently stands at just over US$100bn.[4] The plan foresees the creation of a regional common market as a stepping stone towards inclusion in the EU's single market, even before EU membership. With talk of decoupling from China gaining traction, some experts cast the Western Balkans as a possible 'near-shoring' location, given its proximity to the EU and high level of integration. Furthermore, it is not inconceivable that by 2030 one or more local countries, for instance, Montenegro or North Macedonia, might conclude their accession talks and join the EU.

Thus, for once, geopolitics seems to be working in the region's favour. The dominant trend is speedier inclusion into the West at a time when regional divisions are deepening due to Russia's actions.

Lingering threats

Despite these strides forward regarding the integration of the Western Balkans with the EU and NATO, political dynamics in the region remain a cause for concern.

Volatility in Kosovo

For starters, the so-called 'normalisation talks' between Serbia and Kosovo are deadlocked again. In early 2023, the EU High Representative for Foreign Affairs and Security Policy Josep Borrell and US envoy Gabriel Escobar appeared to be on the cusp of securing a settlement. An agreement negotiated with Serbia's President Vučić and Prime Minister of Kosovo Albin Kurti in Ohrid, North Macedonia,

Figure 1: NATO and EU peacekeepers in the Western Balkans

fleshed out a diplomatic formula involving a de facto recognition of Kosovar sovereignty in exchange for self-rule of the Serb community. However, the March 2023 deal was 'verbally accepted', not signed, and most of it has not been implemented to date. Worse still, in September 2023, Kosovo saw a major escalation in violence when a clash between security forces and Serb militants resulted in four deaths.[5] Several months earlier, over two dozen NATO peacekeepers sustained injuries in a violent Serb protest in the north.[6] Vigorous diplomacy by the US and EU was necessary to defuse the situation on both occasions. Vučić has blamed such episodes on Prishtina authorities' heavy-handed treatment of the Serb community. He has not shied away from putting Serbian troops deployed around Kosovo on alert whenever tensions have risen. The Kosovar government, in turn, has been pointing out Belgrade's malfeasance, with Serbian security operatives and nationalist networks beholden to Vučić carving out a fiefdom in the north. Kurti has pledged to do his utmost to assert Kosovo's sovereignty, lately by banning the circulation of Serbia's national currency, the dinar, in the area.

As Borrell's term comes to an end, the EU appears to be losing momentum in Kosovo. Brussels's energy is spent on managing recurrent crises rather than pushing for a grand bargain. The prospect of Donald Trump's return to the White House in 2025 complicates matters further. During Trump's first term, his Balkan envoy Richard Grennell worked at cross purposes with the EU by championing territorial partition as a solution to the Kosovo issue. A renewed transatlantic rift remains a worrying possibility.

The Bosnian quandary
Bosnia-Herzegovina is likewise facing instability. Milorad Dodik, the leader of the Bosnian Serbs, has repeatedly challenged both central state institutions and the international community's High Representative Christian Schmidt. Over the years, Dodik has threatened to trigger RS's full secession from Bosnia-Herzegovina and, in the process, has succeeded in illegally wresting power from Sarajevo in areas such as taxation and the judiciary. His next target is setting up a separate electoral system. Last year, Dodik banned Schmidt from entering RS, a prohibition Schmidt ignored. The Serb leader is now standing trial for his disruptive activities in violation of the constitution (part of the Dayton peace agreement). If found guilty, he could face a prison sentence of up to five years. However, a judgment against him could trigger a political crisis in the divided country, and it is very unlikely that the EU's peacekeeping force (EUFOR) would arrest the Serb leader (see Figure 1).

Importantly, Dodik has influential allies abroad (alongside Russia, which has always backed him). Though he and his ally Željka Cvijanović, the Serb member of Bosnia-Herzegovina's tripartite presidency, are sanctioned by the US and the United Kingdom governments, the EU has not followed up with sanctions of its own. Hungary's Prime Minister Viktor Orbán supports Dodik, and several other EU member states are against imposing sanctions on him, including Austria and Croatia. The result is disunity within the West, with the US and UK bemoaning the soft approach adopted by the Europeans.[7] Dodik has also built strong ties with the Croatian Democratic Union of Bosnia and Herzegovina (HDZ BiH), the main party representing Bosnia-Herzegovina's Croats. Indeed, his Alliance of Independent Social Democrats and the HDZ BiH are partners in a coalition cabinet at the state level, together with a group of three parties backed primarily by Bosnian Muslims (Bosniaks).

On the positive side, Bosnia-Herzegovina is moving forward on the EU accession track, adopting some legislation requested by Brussels and meeting various benchmarks. Support for EU membership is strong, with even 64% of RS's residents in favour.[8] However, this progress also reflects the fact that the EU has lowered the bar for opening membership negotiations, backtracking on some of its prior conditions such as reforming legislation governing Bosnia-Herzegovina's judiciary. This movement towards the EU does not appear to have changed the Bosnian Serb leadership's preferences either. Dodik maintains that membership of BRICS could be an alternative to joining the EU, a position which aims to add to euroscepticism in RS.

Old woes

For over two decades now, the EU has striven to foster democratic governance and the rule of law in the Western Balkans. Building functioning judiciary systems as well as the passage and enforcement of robust anti-corruption legislation are top priorities, reflecting the lessons learned from Central and Eastern European countries that joined the EU in the 2000s only to begin backsliding thereafter. The Western Balkans' record is not particularly encouraging either when it comes to state capture, authoritarianism and illiberalism. The contested local polls in Belgrade, which took place on 17 December 2023, is a case in point. Faced with protests over electoral fraud, Vučić accused the opposition of executing a Ukraine-style 'colour revolution' in league with unnamed Western powers and aimed at overthrowing a legitimate government. Predictably, Russian officials in Moscow echoed Vučić's rhetoric. All in all, authoritarianism is a palpable trend in Serbia as well as a testament to the West's declining leverage over domestic politics in the Western Balkans. It seems that Vučić is not willing to give up power. The system of governance he has built around himself – based on rampant clientelism, near-complete control of the media and public sector, harassment of civil society, and virulent anti-Western rhetoric in the public sphere – is an alluring model for other countries in the region.

Great-power competition

The shift to a multipolar world order and the challenge posed by rivals to the West like Russia and China raise concerns that the region could become an arena of geopolitical competition. Moscow has cultivated ties with local players such as Serbia, RS, and certain parties, politicians and nationalist activists in Montenegro and North Macedonia in a bid to block NATO and EU enlargement. These efforts have proven ineffective in that Montenegro and North Macedonia have joined the Alliance while the EU has reinvigorated its accession policy. President Vučić has not joined Western sanctions against Russia but has not sided fully with Russia either in order to gain support from the EU and US. Russia's war in Ukraine has also limited the resources Russia can dedicate to the region.

At the same time, however, opinion polls in Serbia and elsewhere suggest that Moscow's anti-Western messages resonate with local audiences due to negative memories of NATO intervention in the 1990s. Waging information warfare in the Balkans is therefore relatively easy, not least because local media and opinion makers are often ideologically aligned with the Kremlin. In addition, over 300,000 Russians have migrated to Serbia since February 2022, strengthening economic ties between the countries, even though many Serbians are opposed to Russia's invasion of Ukraine.[9]

China is likewise influential in the region, particularly in Serbia, thanks to its loan diplomacy in the context of the Belt and Road Initiative (BRI) and foreign direct investment. Beijing's cumulative stock of preferential loans and investment in Serbia is estimated at over US$11bn.[10] Unlike Russia, China does not take strong positions on regional security issues and therefore is acceptable to a wider array of parties. However, the BRI has not delivered a significant amount of funds to countries other than Serbia in the region. At the moment, Chinese contractors tend to bid for infrastructure projects financed by the EU. Pushback from the US on issues such as 5G technology has limited the room for manoeuvre for Beijing as well.

Outlook

The Western Balkans present a chronic political and security challenge to the West. Compared to acute crises such as the ones in Ukraine and Gaza, however, the challenge is neither pressing nor unmanageable. The EU has no choice but to continue pushing for a settlement in Kosovo, ensuring that Bosnia-Herzegovina remains relatively stable, and paving the way for Western Balkan countries to join the bloc. Some countries could take advantage of easing EU membership requirements, implementing some reforms and faking others. Others, like Serbia and Bosnia-Herzegovina, will likely remain in a grey area. If the EU's and NATO's goal is stability rather than a profound transformation of the region, this might be a price worth paying.

Notes

[1] The General Framework Agreement for Peace in Bosnia and Herzegovina, also known as the Dayton Accords, resulted from the mediation efforts of US president Bill Clinton's administration, backed by NATO strikes against Bosnian Serb forces that tipped the military balance on the ground. At the US air-force base in Dayton, Ohio, the then-leaders of Bosnia-Herzegovina, Croatia and Serbia – Alija Izetbegović, Franjo Tudjman and Slobodan Milosevic – agreed on a settlement

2   that included, amongst other things, a constitution for Bosnia-Herzegovina.
2   NATO, 'Additional NATO Reinforcements Arrive in Kosovo', 14 October 2023.
3   European Commission, 'Commission Welcomes Political Agreement on the €6 Billion Reform and Growth Facility for the Western Balkans', 4 April 2024.
4   European Investment Bank, 'The European Investment Bank in the Balkans', June 2021.
5   Marton Dunai, 'Siege of Serb Monastery in Kosovo Ends After Militants Withdraw', *Financial Times*, 24 September 2023.
6   Lili Bayer, 'NATO Soldiers Wounded in Kosovo Clashes', Politico, 29 May 2023.
7   Author interviews in Sarajevo and Banja Luka, 15–18 April 2024.
8   According to a 2022 poll by the National Democratic Institute. National Democratic Institute, 'Bosnia and Herzegovina Poll', 13 May 2022. The International Republican Institute's most recent poll, from February–March 2024, found that 68% of all Bosnians would vote for EU membership in a putative referendum. International Republican Institute, 'Western Balkans Regional Poll: February–March 2024', 16 April 2024.
9   Jovana Georgievski, 'Rusi u Srbiji: "Gledaju nas kao da smo vreće novca", zašto neki stranci plaćaju "ruske cene"' [Russians in Serbia: 'They look at us as if we were walking wallets': why some foreigners are paying 'Russian prices'], BBC News, 10 August 2023.
10 Branislav Staníček and Simona Tarpova, 'China's Strategic Interests in the Western Balkans', European Parliamentary Research Service, June 2022.

RUSSIA–UKRAINE

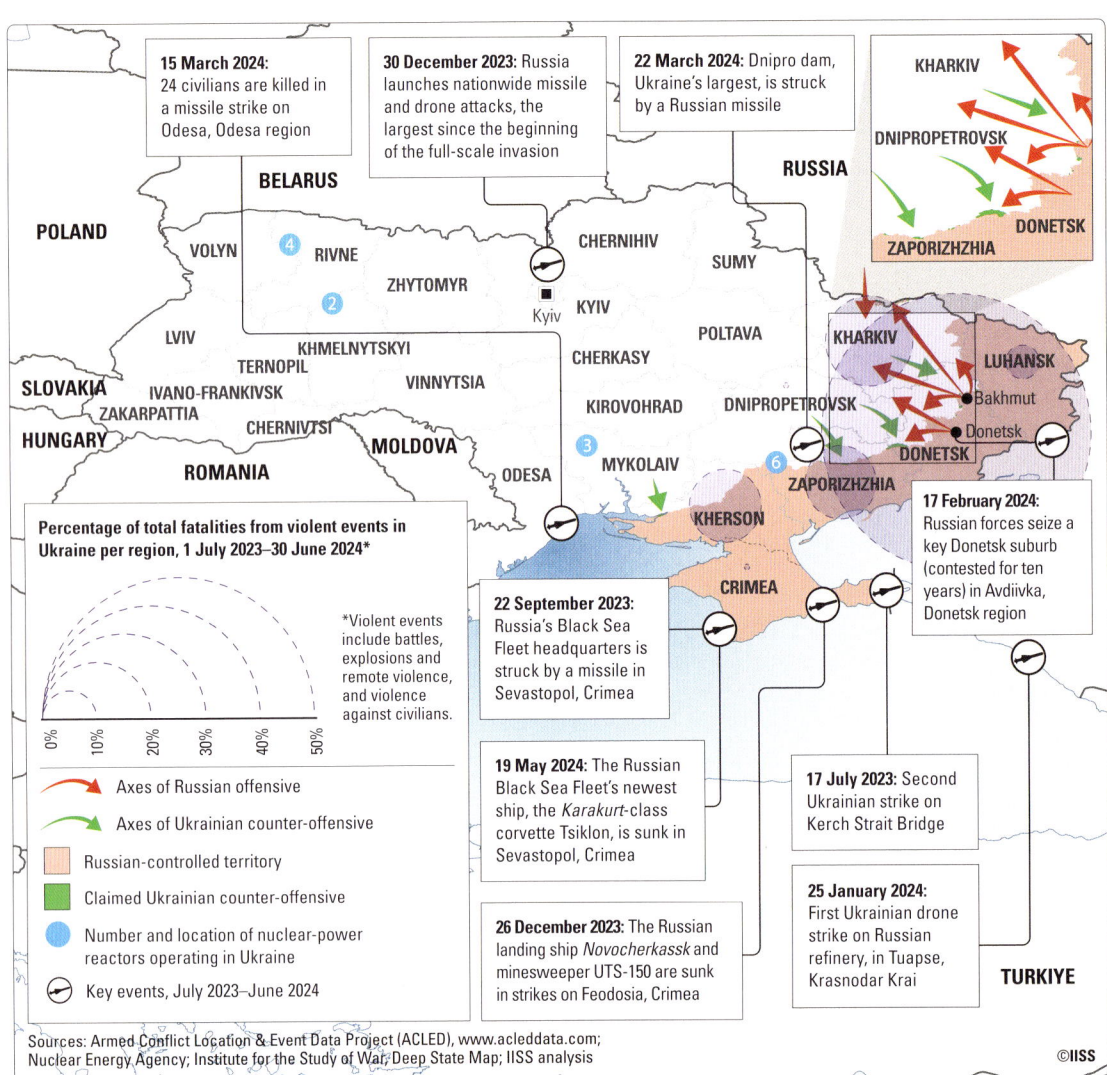

Conflict Overview

Russia's invasion of Ukraine is rooted in historic disputes regarding Russian and Ukrainian identities and the division of the border. While these issues prompted some tensions following the collapse of the Soviet Union, it was during Russian President Vladimir Putin's first two terms in office (2000–08) that the Kremlin increasingly sought to subjugate Kyiv. Putin lashed out at the Western-leaning government that came to power after Ukraine's 2004–05 Orange Revolution and increasingly interfered in Ukraine's politics. The Kremlin then exploited the aftermath of Ukraine's 2014 Revolution of Dignity to annex Crimea and thereafter directly supported separatist movements in Donbas region.

In February 2015, prompted by a major intervention by Russian forces, Ukraine and Russia signed the Minsk II agreement. However, clashes never fully abated. On 24 February 2022, Putin launched a full-scale invasion of Ukraine along the existing lines of control and into the northern regions of Chernihiv,

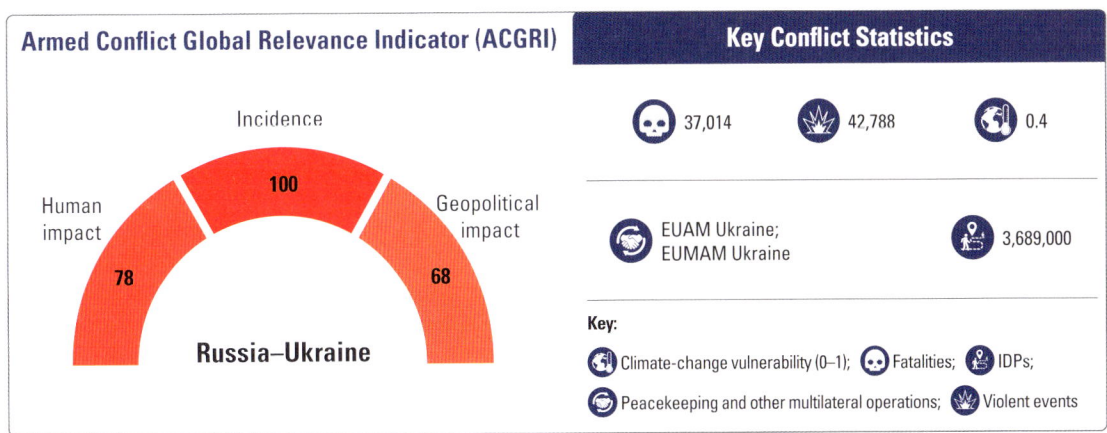

Conflict(s)	Type	Start date
Russian military invasion of Ukraine	I-S	2022

Key: **I-S** Inter-state

Kharkiv, Kyiv, Sumy and Zhytomyr as well as into the southern regions of Kherson, Mykolaiv and Zaporizhzhia, supported by nationwide aerial attacks. By the end of 2022, Ukrainian forces were able to retake Chernihiv, Kyiv, Mykolaiv, Sumy and Zhytomyr regions, most of Kharkiv region, and Kherson region north of the Dnieper River.

A Ukrainian counter-offensive in mid-2023, however, failed to make major gains. With the war now in its third year, Russia has made progress west of the cities of Bakhmut and Donetsk in Donetsk region. In May 2024, it also launched a new cross-border offensive into northern Kharkiv region. Moscow continues to press its advantage in superior airpower and to carry out uninhabited aerial vehicle (UAV) and missile attacks nationwide, though Ukrainian forces have increasingly launched UAV attacks into Russia and constrained the Black Sea Fleet to limit Russia's advantages. Ukraine remains reliant on Western financial support and materiel.

Conflict Update

Russia's war against Ukraine was broadly marked by two phases over the reporting period, the first of which was Ukraine's counter-offensive launched in early June 2023. Although this was not the first time that Ukraine had sought to recapture substantial territory, the counter-offensive was touted as offering Ukraine the potential to push Russian forces back as far as the lines of control that existed prior to the full-scale invasion, or close to them.[1] In the end, however, Ukraine experienced significant losses while only making extremely limited gains around the town of Robotyne in central Zaporizhzhia region and in the Morki Yaly river valley in southwest Donetsk region along the internal border with Zaporizhzhia. These gains came largely in the first two months of the counter-offensive, which subsequently petered out, and by November the then-commander-in-chief of the Ukrainian armed forces, Valeriy Zaluzhnyi, admitted that it had failed. Ukraine's counter-offensive coincided with significant infighting within the Russian military hierarchy, including the June 2023 revolt by Yevgeny Prigozhin and his private military company (and parastatal armed force), the Wagner Group, though this was quickly suppressed. Prigozhin was subsequently killed alongside other key Wagner leaders when his plane crashed en route to St Petersburg.

The second phase saw Russian forces take the initiative, beginning with an assault on the northwestern Donetsk suburb of Avdiivka at the end of January 2024, before it ultimately fell on 17 February. Putin was subsequently re-elected as president on 17 March in elections that were also held in occupied Ukrainian territory, although these were not free or fair there or in Russia. Russian forces then continued to expand their occupation of Donetsk region, occupying the town of Prohres, about 40 kilometres northwest of the city, by late July. The latter half of the offensive was accompanied by escalating attacks both south of Mariinka (the key Ukrainian-held suburb to the southwest of Donetsk city) and from Russian-occupied Bakhmut towards Chasiv Yar in April 2024, as well as by attacks towards Ukrainian-held Pokrovsk the following month. The fall of Pokrovsk or Chasiv Yar could enable further Russian offensives towards Kramatorsk and Slovyansk, the largest cities in Donetsk region still under Ukrainian control. Russia also launched a new cross-border offensive on Kharkiv region on 10 May, but by June it had seized only around 236 square kilometres. Kyiv launched its own cross-border incursions on 6 August from its Sumy region into Russia's Kursk region, ultimately seizing around 1,000 km². Additional cross-border clashes between northern Ukraine and western Russia could follow.

Russian forces responded to Ukraine's air-defence shortages by adopting new glide-bomb tactics enabling the bombing of frontline positions and the city of Kharkiv. This was accompanied by new Russian missile and UAV tactics. These attacks targeted ports throughout the reporting period. However, this did not prevent Kyiv from significantly increasing exports from its Black Sea ports in the ten months after Russia unilaterally abrogated the Black Sea Grain Initiative in July 2023. From December 2023, the Kremlin began increasingly to use such tactics to target power infrastructure across the country, damaging 80% of thermal power generation by mid-April 2024.[2] The city of Odesa was subsequently frequently targeted. Ukraine's lack of sufficient air defences has proven to be a major challenge nationwide and regular attacks on power infrastructure have continued to keep supplies strained.

Ukraine responded by launching a major wave of attacks on Russian energy infrastructure with its own UAVs from mid-January, damaging more than a dozen refineries, even as Western allies warned against the strategy for fear of its impact on global energy markets.[3] There has also been an increase in attacks in Russia's Belgorod, Bryansk and Kursk regions, and in May the United States and Germany agreed to allow some arms they supplied to Ukraine to be used in these areas. Russia's attacks and successes therein were facilitated by a six-month delay in the US Congress passing its key military aid bill for Kyiv, even as major Western European countries increased their support by around 25% year-on-year.[4] On 24 April, US President Joe Biden signed a package providing US$61 billion in military aid to Ukraine over the next three years.[5] However, Russian forces retain advantages in ammunition and troop numbers.

Conflict Parties

Armed Forces of Ukraine

Strength: The active military strength of the Armed Forces of Ukraine was officially stated to be 800,000 personnel in late 2023, although it is unclear if this figure represented a mandated total or an actual headcount. The regular military forces are supplemented by an estimated 200,000–250,000 personnel in other security or paramilitary organisations.

Areas of operation: Ukraine and border areas of Russia used by Moscow to launch attacks on Ukraine. Ukrainian military intelligence also carries out attacks in other areas of Russia, particularly UAV attacks on military and energy-sector infrastructure.

Leadership: President Volodymyr Zelenskyy (supreme commander-in-chief), Col.-Gen. Oleksandr Syrskyi (commander-in-chief), Lt.-Gen. Kyrylo Budanov (chief of the Defence Intelligence of Ukraine, DIU), Lt.-Gen. Vasyl Malyuk (chief of the Security Service of Ukraine, SBU) and Rustem Umarov (defence minister).

Structure: Fights under the command of its General Staff but formally retains divisions between its army, navy and air force. There are also a number of volunteer groups fighting alongside the Armed Forces of Ukraine at varying degrees of integration into the command structure. The DIU and the SBU retain separate command structures, with the former technically under the Ministry of Defence.

Armed Forces of Ukraine

History: The Ukrainian armed forces were formally founded following the Soviet Union's dissolution in 1991 but have been substantially transformed since, first in the aftermath of Russia's initial invasion in February 2014 and again since Russia's full-scale invasion began in February 2022.

Objectives: Defend Ukraine and liberate Russian-occupied territory.

Opponents: Armed Forces of the Russian Federation and Wagner Group.

Affiliates/allies: NATO members have provided Ukraine with military supplies and intelligence support. Since 2020, Ukraine has been a NATO Enhanced Opportunities Partner. Additional aid has come from Australia, Japan and South Korea, amongst others.

Resources/capabilities: Ukraine's ability to fund and equip its military remains largely dependent on Western support, at least to a standard capable of combatting Russia's full-scale invasion. To date, the US has pledged more than US$61bn, with over US$62bn in military and non-military aid previously delivered. Meanwhile, the European Union has provided US$86.3bn in military and non-military aid, with more than US$64.7bn in additional aid committed but not yet delivered.[6] Ukraine has also developed new domestic defence production since the full-scale invasion, in particular with regard to UAV technology.

Armed Forces of the Russian Federation

Strength: Russia formally increased the mandated size of its active military forces to 1.3 million personnel at the end of 2023, with an ambition to further increase this to 1.5m personnel by 2026. In practice, however, actual personnel totals remain short of these targets due to ongoing losses suffered in Ukraine.[7] Russian men aged 18–30 are required to do a year of military service and are thereafter placed in the reserves.[8] Russia has also integrated mobilised and volunteer forces from its former proxy entities in eastern Ukraine, the so-called Luhansk People's Republic and Donetsk People's Republic.

Areas of operation: Occupied areas in Ukraine. Russian forces are also present in Georgia's South Ossetia and Abkhazia regions, Armenia, Kyrgyzstan, Syria, Tajikistan and numerous other countries where operations once assigned to the former Wagner Group have formally become Russian state-backed military operations.

Leadership: President Vladimir Putin (commander-in-chief), Andrei Belousov (defence minister since May 2024) and General of the Army Valery Gerasimov (chief of the general staff).

Structure: Russia's military includes a ground force, navy, airborne force, railway troops and aerospace force. In Ukraine, the armed forces are supported by separate units associated with Russia's security services, from the National Guard to the Federal Security Service.

History: The Russian armed forces were founded in 1991 and took over the majority of the Soviet Army's stock and assets, including bases outside the Russian Federation. Their command and operational structures have been reformed under Putin, but they retain inherited Soviet-era military practices.

Objectives: Annex Ukrainian territory, defend Russia and project power abroad.

Opponents: Armed Forces of Ukraine.

Affiliates/allies: Armed Forces of Belarus (Russia has used Belarusian bases for launching operations against Ukraine) and Wagner Group.

Resources/capabilities: Russia has extensive military capabilities and one of the world's largest defence industries. Western sanctions have targeted Russia's military supply chain and, in particular, computer and microchip technology that Russia does not produce domestically. Russia's defence budget for 2024 is approximately US$116bn, up from US$74.8bn in 2023.

Wagner Group

Strength: There were at least 25,000 troops in the Wagner Group as of late June 2023 according to its leadership, though the actual number was likely higher.[9] Following its subsequent break-up, numbers are difficult to assess; the Africa Corps offshoot set a target of 20,000–40,000 recruits by mid-2024, but it is estimated to have far fewer combatants as of June 2024.[10]

Areas of operation: Belarus, Ukraine and Russia. The Africa Corps offshoot is active in Burkina Faso, Chad (reports disputed), Libya, Mali, Niger and Sudan.

Leadership: Disputed following the deaths of the group's chief, Yevgeny Prigozhin, and commander, Dmitry Utkin, in an aeroplane crash in August 2023. Prigozhin's son, Pavel Prigozhin, has claimed leadership of Wagner, though the group has largely been brought under the control of the Russian Ministry of Defence. Its African operations have been rebranded under the name 'Africa Corps' and are led by Russian Deputy Minister of Defence Col.-Gen. Yunus-bek Yevkurov.

Structure: The company was established by Prigozhin, but its structure has largely been subsumed into the Ministry of Defence following his death.

History: The Wagner Group began as a Kremlin-funded Russian security organisation, with close links to Russian military intelligence and Russia's Ministry of Defence. Wagner was established in 2014 and it and other private military companies proliferated following Russia's involvement in the 2015 war in Syria, where they were often contracted to provide security for extractive operations. The group subsequently took on a similar function in several African countries. It assumed a leading role in the siege of Bakhmut in Donetsk region from August 2022–May 2023, which saw its public profile grow significantly in Russia. However, following the aborted mutiny led by Prigozhin on 23–24 June 2023, Wagner agreed to re-base itself in allied Belarus. The group's contracts for soldiers in Russia and Ukraine were thereafter largely assumed by the Russian

Wagner Group

Ministry of Defence although there have continued to be (contested) claims to Wagner's leadership, including by Pavel Prigozhin. Since late 2023, the African branch of Wagner has been rebranded as the Africa Corps, also in coordination with the Russian Ministry of Defence.

Objectives: Up until 24 June 2023, the group primarily served to provide the Armed Forces of the Russian Federation with a force-multiplication capability and also to recruit prisoners and others seen as undesirable by the formal military leadership, often for use in high-casualty infantry attacks. The group now operates under the Russian Ministry of Defence, participating in its objectives to annex Ukrainian territory, defend Russia and project power abroad.

Opponents: Armed Forces of Ukraine.

Affiliates/allies: Armed Forces of the Russian Federation.

Resources/capabilities: Wagner has been directly armed and supplied by the Armed Forces of the Russian Federation and even received military aircraft during the height of its activity in Ukraine. As it is increasingly brought under the direct control of the Russian Ministry of Defence, it will presumably have access to most of the Russian armed forces' capabilities as well.

Notes

1. Ukraine pushed Russian forces out of Chernihiv, Kyiv, Sumy, Zhytomyr and large parts of Kharkiv region in April 2022 and retook the northern half of Kherson region and almost all of Mykolaiv region in October and November 2022.
2. 'Russia Ramps Up Attacks on Ukraine's Power Plants', BBC News, 8 May 2024.
3. 'Ukrainian Drone Attacks on Russian Oil Refineries and Infrastructure', Reuters, 18 June 2024.
4. Pietro Bomprezzi, Ivan Kharitinov and Christoph Trebesch, 'Ukraine Support Tracker – Methodological Update & New Results on Aid "Allocation" (June 2024)', Kiel Institute for the World Economy, June 2024.
5. Congress.gov, 'H.R.815 – Making Emergency Supplemental Appropriations for the Fiscal Year Ending September 30, 2024, and for Other Purposes', 24 April 2024.
6. Bomprezzi, Kharitinov and Trebesch, 'Ukraine Support Tracker – Methodological Update & New Results on Aid "Allocation" (June 2024)'.
7. Ofitsialnoe opublikovaniye pravovykh atov Официальное опубликование правовых актов [Official publication of legal acts], 'Ukaz Prezidenta Rossiiskoi Federatsii ot 01.12.2023 No.915, "Ob ustanovlenii shtatnoi chislennosti Vooruzhennykh Sil Rossiiskoi Federatsii"' Указ Президента Российской Федерации от 01.12.2023 № 915, 'Об установлении штатной численности Вооруженных Сил Российской Федерации' [Order of the president of the Russian Federation 1 December 2023, No. 915 'On establishing the personnel levels of the Armed Forces of the Russian Federation'], 1 December 2023.
8. 'Russian Defense Minister Calls for Increasing Army to 1.5 Million Troops and Raising Draft Age from 18 to 21', Meduza, 21 December 2022.
9. Torredo, 'Novoe soobshchenie Prigozhina, 25000 idut na Moskvu' Новое сообщение Пригожина, 25000 идут на Москву [Prigozhin's new message, 25,000 go to Moscow], YouTube, 23 June 2023; and Olga Ivshina and Olga Prosvirova, '"Amoralno, no effectivno": kak i kakoi tsenoi ChVK "Wagner" zakhvatyvala Bakhmut' «Аморально, но эффективно»: как и какой ценой ЧВК «Вагнер» захватывала Бахмут ['Amoral, but effective:' how and at what cost 'Wagner' seized Bakhmut], BBC News, 10 June 2024.
10. Filip Bryjka and Jędrzej Czerep, *Africa Corps – A New Iteration of Russia's Old Military Presence in Africa* (Warszawa: Polish Institute of International Affairs, 2024), p. 11.

NAGORNO-KARABAKH

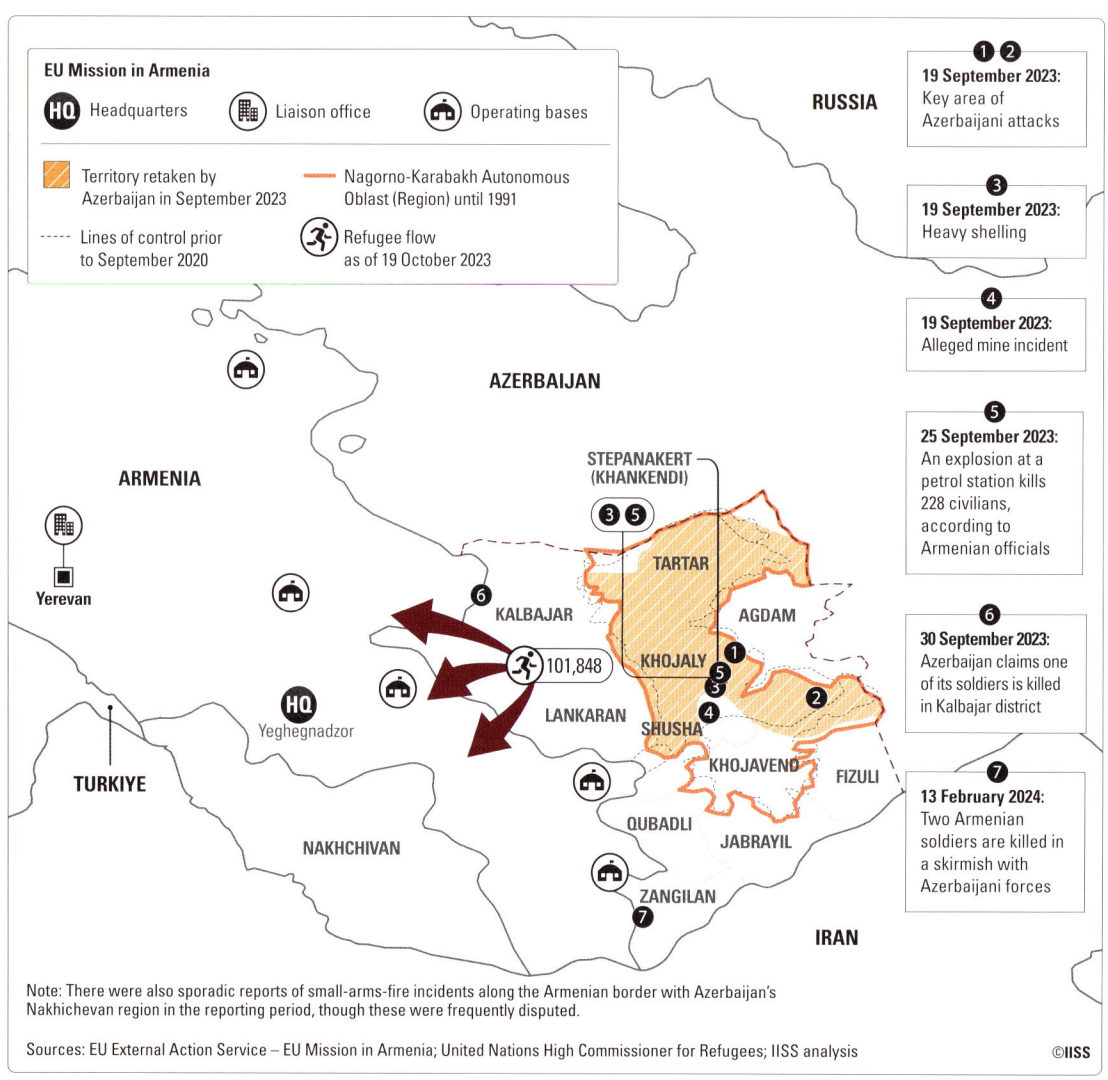

Conflict Overview

Azerbaijan's Nagorno-Karabakh region has been riven by conflict between the country's ethnic-Armenian and ethnic-Azeri populations since 1988, and following the Soviet Union's collapse, the conflict immediately took on an inter-state dimension. Armenian forces effectively won the extended First Nagorno-Karabakh War, with the 1994 Bishkek Protocol leaving Yerevan in control of not only all of the former Nagorno-Karabakh Autonomous Oblast (NKAO) but also significant additional *de jure* Azerbaijani territory. The conflict never fully ended, however, and after years of skirmishes along the lines of control, and increasingly along the *de jure* Armenia–Azerbaijan border, Baku launched the Second Nagorno-Karabakh War in September 2020. The war was settled that November with a Russian-brokered ceasefire, under which Armenia's *de jure* forces withdrew; Baku retook control of nearly 40% of the former NKAO and all of the surrounding

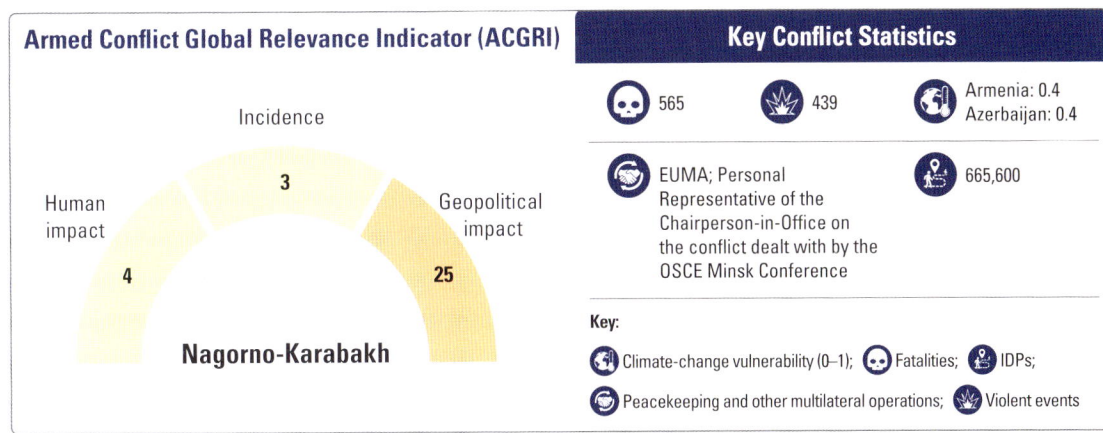

territory; and Russia deployed peacekeeping forces to the region.

The peacekeeping effort failed, however, and the current reporting period saw the brief, but decisive, Third Nagorno-Karabakh War of September 2023. Azerbaijan's victory resulted in the self-declared Republic of Artsakh (or Republic of Nagorno-Karabakh) agreeing to dis-establish itself. The post-war period was dominated by the effectively forced depopulation of the region's Armenian inhabitants.

The Armenian government did not intervene in the latest war, having withdrawn its forces from Nagorno-Karabakh in the preceding years in line with the ceasefire agreement signed in November 2020. However, since 2020, conflict had also spread into *de jure* Armenia, with the Azerbaijani armed forces occupying Armenian territory and slowly expanding their areas of control along the border within Armenia thereafter. Despite renewed peace talks, the risk of additional inter-state conflict remains extremely high.

Conflict Update

Azerbaijani forces swiftly defeated the Nagorno-Karabakh Defence Army (NKDA) after launching a major assault on 19 September 2023, with the ethnic-Armenian authorities in the region suing for peace a day later. An agreement was quickly reached that saw the NKDA and the other institutions of Artsakh agree to disband themselves. Azerbaijan lifted the blockade that it had enforced on Nagorno-Karabakh, separating it from Armenia, since December 2022. According to statistics collated by the Armenian government, within one month of the NKDA's defeat, at least 101,848 out of an estimated population of 120,000 ethnic Armenians had fled the territory, which had already suffered from a large-scale refugee migration after the Second Nagorno-Karabakh War in 2020.[1] Only a handful of ethnic-Armenian residents were identified as still living in the territory in late October, according to investigations by the International Committee of the Red Cross.[2] Azerbaijani officials have not publicly detailed any significant number of ethnic Armenians returning to the territory since then.

The latest war over the region was formally labelled an 'anti-terrorist operation' by Azerbaijan, which reported the deaths of two highway-department employees and four soldiers in landmine explosions along the lines of control shortly before launching its attacks.³ However, tensions had been building for weeks and troop movements within Azerbaijan had indicated that a new conflict was likely.

Despite its brief nature, both sides reported notable casualties: Baku reported that 192 of its soldiers were killed and 511 wounded, while ethnic-Armenian authorities reported that at least 190 of their soldiers were killed and more than 400 wounded.⁴ Much uncertainty remains about the civilian death toll, in part due to the collapse of the ethnic-Armenian de facto governmental institutions in the region. However, one deadly incident at the beginning of the subsequent mass exodus – an explosion at a petrol station outside Stepanakert on 25 September – killed 218 civilians according to Armenian officials, the highest civilian death toll since the First Nagorno-Karabakh War ended in 1994.⁵ Most prisoners of war were released by December 2023, although Azerbaijan has held public trials for a number of the most prominent leaders of the now-defunct ethnic-Armenian government of the territory and they remain in detention.

Following the end of the war, tensions continued along the Armenia–Azerbaijan border, even as European Union member countries and the United States mediated peace talks. While the rate of violent incidents has decreased compared to preceding years, there remain fears that a major conflict could erupt at short notice. The deadliest incident occurred on 13 February 2024, when Armenia reported that four of its soldiers were killed and one wounded around the village of Nerkin Hand in Armenia's Syunik province, near *de jure* Armenian territory that Azerbaijani forces had seized in September 2022.⁶ However, peace talks mediated primarily by the US have since resumed and Yerevan has moved to make concessions to Baku; most notably, Armenian Prime Minister Nikol Pashinyan announced on 19 April that Yerevan would return the territory of four former villages depopulated after the Soviet Union's collapse along the Armenia–Azerbaijan border to Azerbaijan, as Baku had demanded.⁷ The move was accompanied by Russia taking steps to rapidly end its peacekeeping force in Nagorno-Karabakh, but further concessions may risk instability in Armenia, which witnessed major opposition protests in May and June 2024. Additionally, the outcome of the conflict and related peace talks is likely to further shift geopolitical powers' influence over Armenia, which is seeking to break with Russia due to the Kremlin's lack of support in the past two Nagorno-Karabakh wars and to move closer to the West.

Conflict Parties

Azerbaijani armed forces

Strength: 68,200 active military personnel and 300,000 reservists, with conscription mandatory for men aged 18–35. Service is 18 months for conscripts, though a 12-month exception is possible for university graduates. The military is supported by 15,000 active gendarmerie and paramilitary personnel.

Areas of operation: Across Azerbaijan, including all of Nagorno-Karabakh since September 2023. Since 2021, the Azerbaijani armed forces have also occupied territory within Armenia proper along a 200-kilometre stretch of the *de jure* border.

Leadership: President Ilham Aliyev (commander-in-chief), Col.-Gen. Karim Valiyev (chief of the general staff) and Col.-Gen. Zakir Hasanov (defence minister).

Structure: Comprised of three services: the army, air force and naval defence force, the latter of which operates in the Caspian Sea.

History: The Azerbaijani military was initially created in 1991 following the collapse of the Soviet Union but had a difficult beginning amid political infighting and some Soviet-era forces aligning with ethnic-Armenian forces. It was significantly reconstituted following the First Nagorno-Karabakh War and has been a priority for government investment ever since.

Objectives: Defend Azerbaijan and protect Azerbaijan's interests in Armenia. In particular, the armed forces have occupied territory near where the Azerbaijani government has demanded the establishment of a land corridor, which would connect the exclave of Nakhichevan with the rest of Azerbaijan through Armenia's southernmost province of Syunik (a territory referred to as Zangezur by Azerbaijan).

Opponents: NKDA (until it disbanded as of 1 January 2024) and Armenian armed forces.

Affiliates/allies: Turkiye.

Resources/capabilities: Azerbaijan has budgeted US$3.8bn for national security and defence in 2024 (compared to US$3.1bn in 2023). Its annual defence spending significantly exceeds that of Armenia. Azerbaijan has established supply relationships with Israel, Pakistan, Russia and Turkiye. Furthermore, in June 2023, it announced a landmark deal to

Azerbaijani armed forces

purchase Italian-manufactured military transport aircraft, despite a long-standing request from the Organization for Security and Co-operation in Europe that European countries refrain from arms sales to parties in the conflict.

Nagorno-Karabakh Defence Army (NKDA) (disbanded as of 1 January 2024)

Strength: The authorities of the unrecognised Republic of Artsakh (Republic of Nagorno-Karabakh) government did not formally disclose personnel numbers, but the NKDA's strength was estimated at 12,000 until September 2023.

Areas of operation: Until September 2023, personnel were stationed along the lines of control and in major population centres, and they patrolled strategic locations.

Leadership: Arayik Harutyunyan, president of Artsakh (Nagorno-Karabakh) and Lt-Gen. Kamo Vardanyan, defence minister of Artsakh (Nagorno-Karabakh).

Structure: Single branch (ground forces), supported by volunteers and informal fighters.

History: Established in 1992 following the region's unrecognised declaration of independence. Operational control was in part separated from Armenia following the 2020 Second Nagorno-Karabakh War. The NKDA was disbanded in September 2023, with this formally taking effect on 1 January 2024.

Objectives: Self-defence.

Opponents: Azerbaijani armed forces.

Affiliates/allies: Armenian armed forces.

Resources/capabilities: Legacy stock, much of which was sourced from Armenia until 2020 in addition to Soviet-era stock. Azerbaijan has subsequently reported taking possession of large caches.

Armenian armed forces

Strength: 42,900 active military personnel and an additional 210,000 reservists, many of whom have recent combat experience from the 2020 Second Nagorno-Karabakh War. Military service is mandatory for Armenian men aged 18–27 and lasts 24 months. The military is supported by 4,300 active gendarmerie and paramilitary personnel.

Areas of operation: Armenia, mainly deployed along the international border with Azerbaijan.

Leadership: Prime Minister Nikol Pashinyan (commander-in-chief), Lt-Gen. Edvard Asryan (chief of general staff) and Suren Papikyan (defence minister).

Structure: Comprised of four army corps as well as a separate air force.

History: Established in 1991 following the Soviet Union's collapse and subsequently amalgamated with former Soviet and volunteer paramilitary forces, which had participated in the First Nagorno-Karabakh War. Since 2020, Armenian armed forces have no longer formally been stationed in Nagorno-Karabakh.

Objectives: Defence of Armenia.

Opponents: Azerbaijani armed forces.

Affiliates/allies: Armenia is formally allied to Russia through the Collective Security Treaty Organisation (CSTO), but the relationship is highly strained. Moscow retains a base that houses around 3,000 soldiers in Gyumri in northern Armenia.[8] Russia is believed to have drawn down forces in Gyumri and rotated out experienced officers since its full-scale invasion of Ukraine began in February 2022.

Resources/capabilities: Armenia has announced a US$1.3 billion defence budget for 2024, matching its 2023 budget, which was nearly double its budget of US$781 million in 2022. No new contracts with Armenia' historic main supplier, Russia, were announced over the last year, but Armenia did begin to diversify into new contracts with France and India.

Armed Forces of the Russian Federation

Strength: 1,960 peacekeepers, but these began to be withdrawn on 23 April 2024 and their peacekeeping centre was shuttered on 26 April.[9] Russia also has roughly 3,500 soldiers at its leased bases in Gyumri and Erebuni in Armenia.[10]

Areas of operation: The majority of Russian peacekeepers were deployed along the Lachin corridor and outside Stepanakert until April 2024, when they were withdrawn. Russia maintains a military presence in the region, including several bases in Armenia and several outposts in southern Armenia near the border with Azerbaijan.

Leadership: President Vladimir Putin (commander-in-chief), Andrei Belousov (defence minister since May 2024), General of the Army Valery Gerasimov (chief of the general staff), Maj.-Gen. Kirill Kulakov (Nagorno-Karabakh peacekeeping contingent) and Col. Alexei Yakovenko (102nd Military Base).

Structure: Most peacekeeping units stationed in Nagorno-Karabakh belonged to the 15th Separate Motor Rifle Brigade of the Central Military District (Russian Ground Forces). Russia's leased Armenian base in Gyumri (the 102nd Military Base) is formally operated under Russia's Southern Military District and is also the operational parent of the air base at Erebuni outside Yerevan. In March 2024, Armenia abrogated a 1992 agreement for Russian border guards to be stationed at Yerevan's Zvartnots Airport.

History: Russia has formally leased the 102nd Military Base since 1995, and the separate peacekeeping regiment in Nagorno-Karabakh was established as part of the November 2020 ceasefire agreement.

Armed Forces of the Russian Federation

Objectives: Ceasefire monitoring in Nagorno-Karabakh for a minimum of five years, subject to renewal. The 2020 ceasefire agreement also instructs Federal Security Service border guards to guarantee transport links between Azerbaijan and its Nakhichevan exclave, although such transport has not begun.

Opponents: N/A.

Affiliates/allies: Russia's CSTO obligations to Armenia do not extend to Nagorno-Karabakh and the Kremlin has ignored Armenian requests for assistance and support with regard to Azerbaijani occupation of *de jure* Armenian territory. The force does enable Russia to exert influence on the conflict participants, but this is seen as waning.

Resources/capabilities: Russian peacekeepers in Nagorno-Karabakh had light weapons and at least 90 armoured personnel carriers, which have been withdrawn to Armenia. Russia's bases in Gyumri and Erebuni also house various military helicopters and 18 MiG-29 *Fulcrum* fighter aircraft, as well as various rocket-launch and air-defence systems.[11]

Notes

[1] United Nations High Commissioner for Refugees, 'Inter-agency Rapid Needs Assessment Report', November 2023; and Claire Mills, 'What Is Happening in Nagorno-Karabakh', no. 9862, United Kingdom Parliament, House of Commons Library, 28 September 2023.

[2] International Committee of the Red Cross, 'Karabakh – On the Ground With the ICRC One Month On', 19 October 2023.

[3] Associated Press, 'Azerbaijan Announces an "Anti-terrorist Operation" Targeting Armenian Positions in Nagorno-Karabakh', VOA, 19 September 2023.

[4] Avet Demourian, 'Azerbaijan Arrests the Former Head of Separatist Government After Recapturing Nagorno-Karabakh', AP News, 27 September 2023.

[5] Siranush Ghazanchyan, 'Investigative Committee Puts the Death Toll of Stepanakert Fuel Depot Explosion at 218', Public Radio of Armenia, 22 December 2023.

[6] Felix Light and Nailia Bagirova, 'Armenian Soldiers Killed by Azerbaijani Fire in Biggest Skirmish Since Exodus', 13 February 2024.

[7] Jones Hayden, 'Armenia Agrees to Return 4 Villages to Azerbaijan', Politico, 20 April 2024.

[8] 'Armenia Seeks Bigger Russian Military Presence on Its Territory', Reuters, 22 February 2021.

[9] 'Russia Sends Nearly 2,000 Peacekeepers to Nagorno-Karabakh, Defense Ministry Says', TASS, 10 November 2020. The International Crisis Group subsequently reported a total of 'some 4,000 Russian soldiers and emergency services staff'. See International Crisis Group, 'Post-war Prospects for Nagorno-Karabakh', Report no. 264, 9 June 2021, p. i.

[10] Arshaluis Mghdesyan, 'Ukraine Crisis Proves Tense for Armenia', Institute for War & Peace Reporting, 23 February 2022.

[11] 'Vopros vyzhivaniya: 25 let nazad Rossiya sozdala voyennuyo bazu v Armenii' Вопрос выживания: 25 лет назад Россия создала военную базу в Армении [A question of endurance: Russia established its military base in Armenia 25 years ago], Gazeta.ru, 16 March 2020.

Country Profile: Nagorno-Karabakh

3 Middle East and North Africa

Regional Analysis	108	Syria	126	Lebanon	144	Egypt	162
Regional Spotlight	120	Iraq	132	Yemen	150	Turkiye	166
Country Profiles		Israel–Palestinian Territories	138	Libya	156		

Palestinians in Gaza City flee to the southern parts of the Gaza Strip, 13 October 2023

Overview

The reporting period was marked by a significant escalation in armed conflict. The unprecedented Hamas-led attacks against Israel on 7 October 2023 triggered Israel's violent offensive in the Gaza Strip and led to an increase in direct confrontations between Israel and Iran (and its allies), heightening the risk of a regional war.

At the end of the reporting period, the Israel–Hamas war continued unabated with a mounting human toll and regional spillover. A total 97 of the 251 Israeli hostages taken on 7 October remained unaccounted for, while 35,000 Palestinians had been killed and most of Gaza's population had been displaced as of June 2024.[1] Conflict had also spread to the West Bank, with the Israel Defense Forces (IDF) engaging Hamas and Palestinian Islamic Jihad cells, especially around Jenin, and continued settler violence. Other notable spillovers involved Jordan and Lebanon. While the former increasingly became a conduit for Iranian weapons into the West Bank and Syrian drugs into the Gulf, the latter's government appeared impotent in the face of Hizbullah, which had joined the attack against Israel immediately after 7 October. The prompt deployment by the United States of carrier-strike and amphibious ready groups proved effective in deterring further aggression and regional escalation. Iran also appeared to insist on only limited actions by Hizbullah, which remained Tehran's top deterrence tool against Israel. Nonetheless, conflict involving Hizbullah, such as an Israeli invasion of southern Lebanon, remains a distinct possibility in 2024–25.

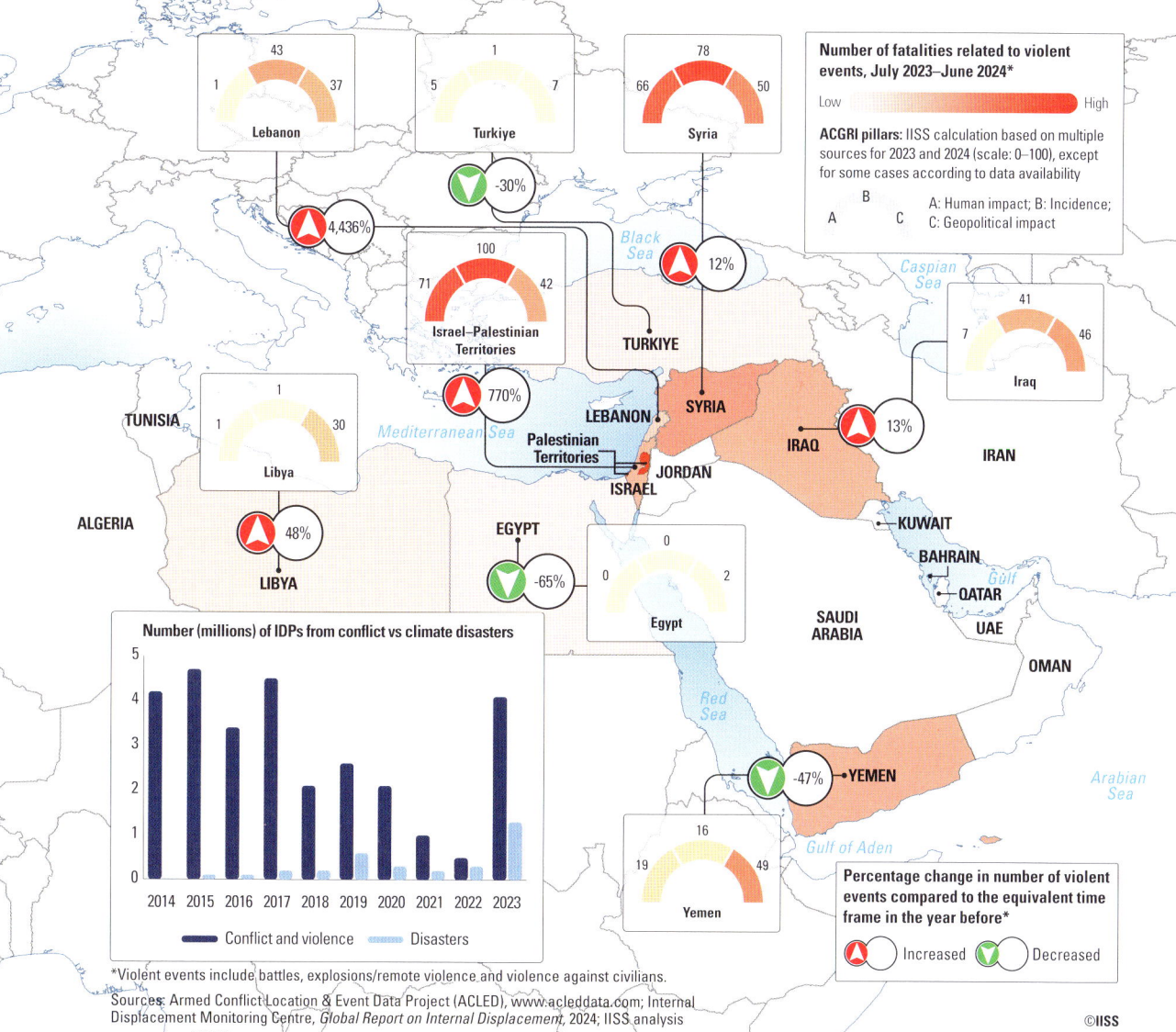

In addition to the Israel–Hamas war, a number of important developments with regional and global repercussions took place during the reporting period. The most salient was in April 2024, when Iran launched a comprehensive attack on Israel with ballistic missiles, cruise missiles and uninhabited aerial vehicles (UAVs) following the latter's assassination of seven high-ranking members of the Islamic Revolutionary Guard Corps (IRGC) in the Iranian embassy complex in Damascus. The unprecedented direct exchange caused almost no damage to Israel thanks to a concerted defensive action with the US, the United Kingdom, France, Jordan and – most likely – Saudi Arabia and the United Arab Emirates (UAE), in a limited way.

The Ansarullah (Houthi) movement in Yemen declared war on Israel, in support of Hamas and the Axis of Resistance. In October 2023, the Houthis significantly increased their attacks on commercial vessels in the Red Sea and Gulf of Aden that they determined – with seemingly broad criteria – to be linked to Israel and its Western allies, using missiles, UAVs and uninhabited surface vessels. The attacks represented a new phenomenon of a non-state armed group (NSAG) using asymmetric warfare to impose geo-economic penalties and financial costs by selectively attacking international shipping. The combination of inexpensive and high-tech weaponry substantively threatening ships as well as control of a strategic territory proved successful, warranting an international intervention to protect freedom of navigation. The US-led *Operation Prosperity Guardian* launched in December 2023 under the coordination of the Combined Maritime

Forces multinational naval partnership, and was followed by the European Union's *Operation Aspides*. Both missions maintained a defensive posture, although the US and the UK attacked Houthi positions in Yemen associated with the movement's anti-ship campaign as part of *Operation Poseidon Archer*, supported by other partners (Bahrain being the only Arab participant).

In Syria, US forces and the Syrian Democratic Forces (SDF) came under sustained attacks from Iran-aligned actors in the northeast while Islamic State (ISIS) attacks increased in the first half of 2024 despite efforts by the SDF, Syrian Armed Forces (SAF) and the US-led Combined Joint Task Force–*Operation Inherent Resolve* (CJTF–OIR) to suppress the group. Increased kinetic conflict between the SDF and Turkiye in Syria further eroded the security landscape. Sinai Province (Wilayat Sinai), the ISIS affiliate in Egypt, attacked the Egyptian National Security Agency headquarters in North Sinai on 30 July 2023. Prior to 7 October, Iraq experienced significant ethnic and political tensions. Clashes occurred between the Iraqi central government and Arab, Turkmen and Kurdish protesters. Divisions deepened between the central government and the Kurdish regional government, and, as in Syria, Turkiye stepped up its military actions against Kurdish groups. ISIS attacks remained limited but Iran-backed NSAGs increasingly targeted US forces.

Despite the regional turmoil, the Abraham Accords – which established diplomatic relations between Israel and Bahrain, Morocco and the UAE (as well as Sudan) – largely held up. Arab signatories de-emphasised the human, cultural and political relationship, but maintained the economic, technological and security dimensions. The normalisation of relations between Saudi Arabia and Israel was paused for the foreseeable future, and Riyadh proved very critical of Israel's conduct of the war, calling the campaign 'genocidal'.[2] The US continued to oversee intelligence and military discussions, including in response to specific threats from Iran or the Houthis. The Chinese-brokered *entente* between Saudi Arabia and Iran also held, reflecting a Saudi desire to avoid being seen as a party to the conflict. The Houthis did not attack Saudi Arabia and vice versa, although Saudi air defence intercepted Houthi missiles. The Houthis did threaten military action against Saudi Arabia if it increased military cooperation with the US, partook in attacks on Iran or sided overtly with Israel. An escalation by the Houthis, contrary to Iranian wishes to maintain detente, remains unlikely, however, unless the regional strategic situation changes drastically. The US, preoccupied with its looming general elections, appeared indecisive and mostly reactive – a stance which might not change, at least until a new administration takes power in January 2025. Iran will continue to exploit this phase by fostering conflict while avoiding direct punishment and escalation. However, the longer the phase of conflict and tit-for-tat strikes last, the higher the chances of miscalculation and errors leading to escalation.

Most regional governments will likely prefer to remain on the sidelines of the conflict between Israel and Hamas and its allies. Support for the Palestinian cause, however, has swelled among ordinary Arabs to unprecedented levels since 7 October. The perception of unquestioning military support from the US and most European nations for Israel means that Western calls for upholding international norms elsewhere in the region increasingly sound hollow to the 'Arab street'.

Conflict Drivers

Political and institutional
Fragility and failed transitions
Fragile institutions characterise conflict-affected countries in the Middle East and North Africa. The 2011 Arab Spring revolutions contested the legitimacy of several autocratic regimes in the region, unleashing protracted armed conflict in Libya, Syria and Yemen (see Figure 1). These states were previously largely autocratic and repressive – lacking democratic representation, accountability and levers of good governance – and have become weak, extremely divided or unable to function or maintain peace.[3]

Socio-economic
Weak social contracts and parallel systems of governance
Several countries in the region suffer from weak social contracts between the rulers and citizens. This has manifested largely through the failure of states

to extend services to marginalised communities generally or in peripheral regions specifically (for example, the Shia community in southern Lebanon or Kurdish minorities in Iraq and Turkiye). Such failure has resulted in the consolidation of parallel informal authorities or NSAG-controlled economies at the local level. The position of Kurds in Iraq today, who were long persecuted and denied access to the resources of their oil-rich region, exemplifies this. In Yemen, communal violence around traditional patterns of competition for scarce resources has long intersected with a chronic lack of state presence. These embedded dynamics provide a basis for insurgencies to form and proliferate.

Sectarian and identity-based divisions
Ethnic and sectarian tensions remain significant drivers of regional conflicts and instability. From an identity-based perspective, the Israel–Palestinian Territories conflict stems from competing claims over land perceived to be sacred by both Israelis and Palestinians. The Jewish and Muslim communities also suffer from internal sectarian and political fractures, which fuel violence. In Iraq, sectarian issues continue to undermine domestic security. In Syria, Shia minorities fight against their more numerous Sunni neighbours, while in Turkiye, Turkish forces fight the Kurdistan Workers' Party (PKK). These are, fundamentally, ethnic conflicts that have proven largely intractable for decades.

Security and military
Fragmentation of security and proliferation of armed actors
NSAG proliferation is one of the main factors behind the protracted and complex nature of conflicts in the region, as highlighted by the actions of Hamas, Hizbullah and the Houthis during the reporting period. NSAGs have multiplied in the security vacuum that followed the Arab Spring and armed sectarianism in Iraq, Libya, Syria and Yemen. In Iraq, for example, where NSAGs divide along religious–political lines, there has been a constant process of accommodation. The mostly Shia Popular Mobilisation Units (PMU) that arose in 2014 to fight ISIS now officially function as part of Iraq's security framework. However, each unit has its own internal leadership and local goals. Thus, some appear to be aligned with Iran while others have a nationalist agenda and work more closely with the central government. Numerically larger than the PMU, the Kurdish Peshmerga remains independent but officially operates as part of Iraqi Kurdistan's military system, and is divided across Kurdish political factions.

Geopolitical
Iran–Israel rivalry
The escalation of the grey war between Israel and Iran, amid Israel's fierce offensive against Hamas in Gaza, has been the most significant geopolitical driver of conflict during the reporting period. Prior to 7 October, Israel bombed locations (mostly in Syria) associated with the IRGC and Iran-aligned NSAGs. Iran, in turn, provided support to these NSAGs to prepare to attack Israel, the US or US allies in Iraq, Lebanon, Syria and Yemen. After 7 October, there was a dramatic escalation of violence and attacks in all regional conflict theatres between Israel and its allies and the Iran-supported NSAGs. This culminated in the direct exchange between the two countries in April 2024.

Syria has also felt reverberations from the Israel–Iran rivalry. Iran-supported groups increased attacks on CJTF–OIR bases in the country after Israeli operations began in Gaza. These groups have also been targeting the Israeli-occupied Golan Heights with mortars and drones. In turn, Israel carried out attacks inside Syria as it doubled efforts to eliminate these NSAGs' assets and commanders.

Great-power competition
Great-power competition has long driven conflict in the region. Prior to 7 October, the US had appeared intent on redefining and reducing its role in the Middle East given its increased focus on the Asia-Pacific. The US had tried to foster Saudi–Israeli normalisation, whereby it would provide security assurances for Saudi Arabia as well as for its nuclear programme, while progressively disengaging from the region. The events of 7 October changed this course of action. Despite ostensible differences on policies, tactics and principles regarding Israel's offensive in Gaza, the US maintained blanket support for the country. It also sent major naval assets to the Eastern Mediterranean and the Gulf, engaged in significant efforts at shuttle diplomacy and sent additional billions of dollars' worth of military equipment and aid to Israel. US military assistance to Israel that proved critical included

precision-guided munitions, Joint Direct Attack Munition conversion kits and heavy bombs that can be used against bunkers and tunnels.

China continued its increased engagement in the Middle East and Gulf region, supporting the prevention of escalation between Iran and Saudi Arabia in Iraq, Lebanon, Syria and Yemen (having brokered the detente between the two in the previous reporting period). On the other hand, Russia's role has been declining in the region, as the country has remained focused on its war on Ukraine. Moscow has expanded relations with Iran to gain military help while boosting political ties with some of Iran's allies, including the Houthis. Russia retained a presence in Syria but seemed unwilling to intervene in domestic matters. While supporting its Iranian and Syrian allies, Russia has tried to maintain regional ties and maximise influence through its military presence and opportunistic diplomacy. Nonetheless, neither China nor Russia has the diplomatic weight to influence the Israel–Hamas war, nor to broker a deal between the two parties.

Conflict Parties

Coalitions and multilateral responses

Prior to 7 October, a number of initiatives had made substantial progress in reducing conflict in the region. In addition to the Iranian–Saudi and Saudi–Houthi detentes, the preceding few years had witnessed a reset in relations between the Gulf states and Turkiye, the end of the Qatar blockade, and the Abraham Accords. The interconnectivity, proximity and significant costs of the region's conflicts pushed de-escalation and negotiation forward.

In parallel, the transnational character of armed conflicts in the region, largely involving jihadist extremist groups as well as US- and Iran-supported groups, often prompted coordinated responses. During the reporting period, the US led two coalitions – *Operation Prosperity Garden* and *Operation Poseidon Archer* – against the Houthis in Yemen, after the movement ramped up its attacks in the Red Sea. Further, the US continued to deploy forces in Iraq and Syria as part of the CJTF–OIR to contain remnants of the Islamic State and train and assist Iraqi forces. Coordinated responses by the US and its allies have also been adopted to support Israel following the 7 October attacks. Notably, the US, the UK, France and Jordan came together to help defend Israel from Iran's aerial attack on 13 April 2024.

Non-state armed groups

At the core of conflict dynamics during the reporting period were the actions of a network of Iran-allied militias carrying out coordinated attacks against Israeli and US assets in the Middle East. Hizbullah, Hamas, the Houthis and the PMU were the most notable actors. Their combined array of missiles facing Israel from all sides was dubbed the 'Ring of Fire'. Iran has continually reorganised this network, introducing interconnections such as Hizbullah training the other groups, the Houthis opening an office in Baghdad and Iran smuggling weapons to Hamas in the West Bank.

Hizbullah and the Houthis have shown increasing capability in using missiles, long-range attack UAVs and Iranian-made munitions. While the Houthis conducted attacks against ships in the Red Sea (and some attacks further out in the Arabian Sea), Hizbullah used Russian-made anti-tank guided missiles to attack IDF bases in northern Israel. This indicates growing capabilities and an accelerated rate of mutual learning within the network of pro-Iranian militias as well as continued military support by Iran and Russia.

Al-Qaeda franchises, such as al-Qaeda in the Arabian Peninsula in Yemen, and the ISIS affiliates in Egypt, Iraq, Libya and Syria showed some degree of resilience, continuing to conduct low-level insurgencies in the reporting period. ISIS-claimed attacks in Syria and Iraq plummeted since their most recent peaks in 2020 and 2021, respectively.[4] Nonetheless, from January–June 2024, the number of attacks claimed by ISIS in both countries increased dramatically, at a pace that – if sustained – would see the number of attacks in both countries double compared to 2023 by the end of 2024.[5] None of the groups, however, appeared capable of controlling and administering territory as they did a decade ago in Iraq, Syria and Yemen. Despite Egypt's successful military campaigns against jihadist groups, the latter launched a few successful attacks in the Sinai during the reporting period. Similarly, ISIS–Libya remained active, largely in peripheral areas of southern and southwestern Libya. It continued its attacks despite the efforts of the central authorities to rein in terrorist and militia groups and the continued presence of Turkish forces deployed to support them. In Syria, ISIS largely targeted the SDF and the SAF.

Third-party involvement
Since the discovery of the region's oil reserves, the Middle East has been subject to external interventions by Russia, the UK, the US and others. Governments in the region – in particular Iraq and Syria – have sought in recent years to reverse this trend, insisting on phased withdrawals of US and international coalition forces. The 7 October attacks and subsequent uptick in strikes on US forces from Iran-backed NSAGs and ISIS have, however, made the prospect of further US withdrawals unlikely in the foreseeable future.

Russia, stretched with its war effort in Ukraine, has limited its activities in Syria and Libya, but remains present through private military contractors, arms sales and, allegedly, technology transfers to Iran. China remained engaged diplomatically and economically. It continued to keep advisers in Syria but refrained from any military or security action. It increased its geo-economic influence in Iraq, winning a majority of the multi-billion-dollar oil and gas projects auctioned in May 2024.

Throughout the reporting period, great and middle powers continued to influence internal conflict dynamics through sales of military equipment. The largest exporters of arms to the Middle East were the US, France, Italy and Germany. Notably, 15% and 8% of all US arms exports went to Saudi Arabia (the largest recipient) and Qatar (the third-largest recipient), respectively.[6]

Regional Humanitarian Trends

In the reporting period, most conflict-affected countries in the region suffered from either a higher number of fatalities or a higher number of violent events, or both, compared to the previous reporting period.[7] Overall, the region has become more violent and more deadly as the war in Gaza has increased fatalities and violent events: while the latter increased by 85% in the reporting period year-on-year, fatalities skyrocketed by 315%.[8]

Conflict continued to have crippling humanitarian consequences. Across the region, 53.8 million people needed humanitarian assistance, including more than 41m food-insecure people.[9] According to the United Nations High Commissioner for Refugees (UNHCR), there were more than 16m forcibly displaced and stateless people in the region facing both protection and socio-economic challenges, as of December 2023.[10]

Prior to 7 October, deteriorating socio-economic conditions, insecurity and conflict had already created a hostile environment for refugees. Several countries experienced heightened anti-refugee rhetoric and there were continued restrictions on access to protection. The refugee crisis arising from over a decade of war in Syria remains the world's largest, with an estimated 14m people displaced. While over 7.2m are internally displaced persons (IDPs), a combined 5m individuals are refugees in neighbouring Jordan, Lebanon and Turkiye.[11]

The Israel–Hamas war has displaced almost the totality of the population, with the UN Relief and Works Agency (UNRWA) listing 1.9m – or nine in ten – people living in Gaza as IDPs by the end of June 2024.[12] The scale of Israeli military operations in Gaza and the limited access granted to aid actors by Israeli authorities have created an unprecedented humanitarian emergency. In Gaza, the UN has been unable to fulfil the most basic needs, including shelter, food, water and sanitation. By the end of the reporting period, the entire population of Gaza was experiencing food insecurity, and 340,000 people were classified as being in 'catastrophe' – a category just below famine – according to a report by the Integrated Food Security Phase Classification (or IPC).[13]

Further, Middle Eastern and North African countries have exhibited extreme vulnerability to climate change over the last two decades. Notably, the multi-year drought that took place in Syria from 2006–10 destroyed rural livelihoods, displaced millions and created socio-economic havoc for the population. This was a catalyst for the start of the civil war in 2011. Natural disasters connected to climate change also create humanitarian emergencies. During the

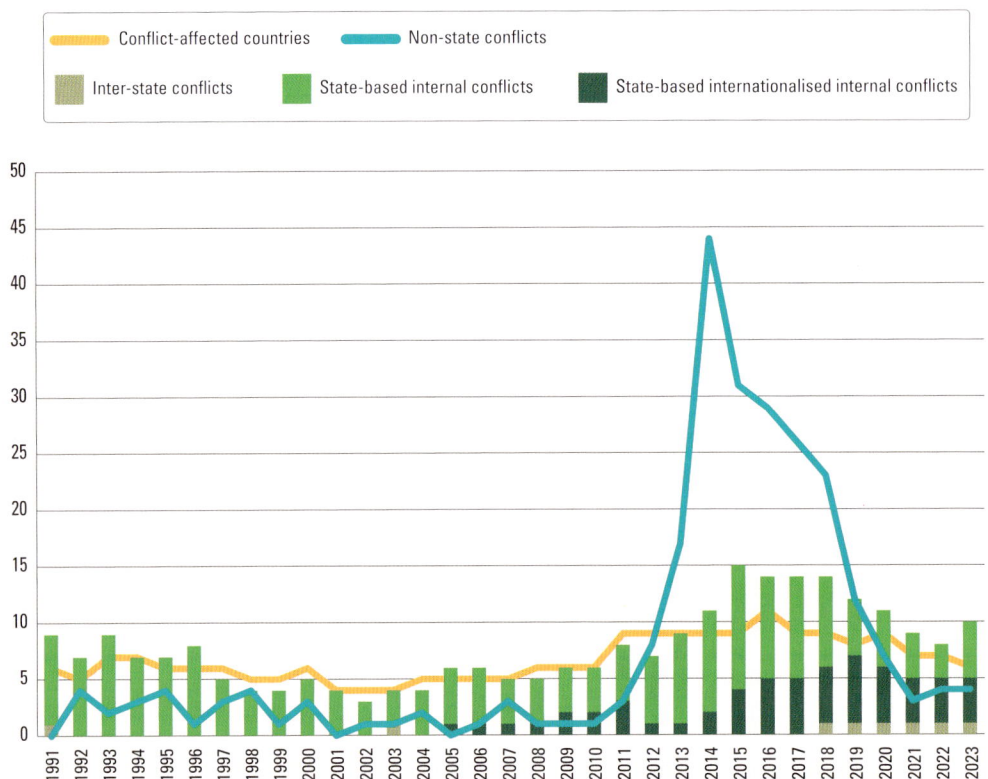

Figure 1: Conflict trends and conflict-affected countries in the Middle East and North Africa, 1991–2023

reporting period, storms in Libya produced record rainfall, causing the collapse of two dams, the deaths of thousands of people and the displacement of some 42,000 people.[14] This situation has aggravated competition over limited resources and led to unrest and possible governance vacuums for NSAGs to exploit.

Outlook

Prospects for peace

The outlook for peace in Gaza remains bleak and has further deteriorated following the killing in an Israeli strike in Beirut of Fuad Shukr, a Hizbullah senior official and close adviser to its secretary-general Hassan Nasrallah, and the alleged assassination of Hamas political leader Ismail Haniyyeh in Tehran at the end of July 2024.

Benjamin Netanyahu's increasingly shaky political coalition does not favour peace, and Israel will likely continue to seek the eradication of Hamas and pursue a strategy of attrition against Hamas forces. Hamas meanwhile will aim to survive and outlive the Israeli offensive, banking on increasing international pressure, while also trying to keep control over the civilian population. Any peace plan that involves replacing Hamas would thus rest on a security provider most likely tied to the Palestinian Authority (PA), whose security forces have historically cooperated with the IDF. A police force under PA and international control has repeatedly been proposed by international mediators.

Iran, for its part, does not want to incur the costs of regional escalation and is refraining from deploying Hizbullah's strategic missile arsenal – which serves as Iran's deterrent to protect its nuclear programme – for now. However, Iran is willing to fuel conflicts in Gaza, the West Bank and the Bab el-Mandeb Strait, and exert pressure on US forces in Syria and Iraq. Hizbullah and Syria's president, Bashar al-Assad, are content with the current level of escalation, enduring the pain but believing they can outlast their enemies and eventually reap the benefits. As a result, the conflict is likely to persist until the military annihilation or political defeat of Hamas, or until the cost–benefit calculation for Hizbullah, Iran or Syria changes drastically.

The US elections will also influence strategic calculations. A victory for Vice President Kamala Harris would likely entail continuity with current policies, but with a more vocal critical stance with respect to Palestinian civilian casualties, whereas a victory for former president Donald Trump would likely mean stronger support for Israel and a heightened anti-Iran stance. These outcomes represent starkly different scenarios for Tel Aviv and Tehran, which may therefore aim to prolong the conflict at least until November to gauge Washington's future direction.

Despite the insecurity created by the Israel–Hamas war, there is little indication that regional states, which have recently pursued de-escalation mechanisms, have abandoned diplomatic tools for conflict resolution after 7 October. Notably, Bahrain has sought to establish new relations with Iran, with both countries announcing formal discussions on the matter in June 2024. Oman has continued to serve as a discreet mediator trusted by Iran, Saudi Arabia and the US. These governments, along with those of Egypt, Jordan and others, have sought a ceasefire and mechanisms to prevent the expansion of the Israel–Hamas war.

Escalation potential and regional spillovers

The evolution of the Israel–Hamas war and tensions between Israel and Iran will continue to influence the escalation of violence in other conflict theatres in the region. The immediate red line for global powers is any regional spillover that threatens global oil supplies, causing a global recession. As it is in the interest of China, the US and most regional actors to secure the flow of oil, this red line will probably be respected, barring mistakes and miscalculations.

In addition to the Gaza front, Israel faces threats of instability from both the West Bank and Lebanon. In the former, violence by both the Israeli military and settlers has skyrocketed since the war in Gaza began. In a context where the PA's legitimacy in the West Bank is increasingly shattered, the prospect of a new Palestinian uprising is real. In Lebanon, by the end of the reporting period, risks of an Israeli invasion had increased, with Hizbullah warning against such action. An Israeli war against Hizbullah in Lebanon may trigger new conflicts and the escalation of several existing ones. Israel would face a full test of its *Iron Dome* as well as a war 'without constraints, rules or limits', according to Hizbullah.[15] In a regional escalation, the Houthis may resume activities against Saudi Arabia, while Iran-supported NSAGs in Iraq and Syria have already increased their attacks since January 2024.

Strategic prospects

From a strategic perspective, the Israel–Hamas war will continue to dominate regional geopolitics. The Biden administration in the US appears focused on containing the war, persuading the right-wing Israeli government to begin ceasefire negotiations, encouraging Arab states to maintain or normalise ties with Tel Aviv, and avoiding any further military confrontation with Iran or its aligned NSAGs. How these issues might develop following the US elections in November 2024 is uncertain. In the meantime, US forces remain in key locations to combat remnants of ISIS and ensure the clear maritime transport of commercial goods.

Beijing, in turn, will continue efforts to steady the detente between Saudi Arabia and Iran. It will also remain a verbal supporter of the Palestinian cause, which has won it support across the Muslim world.

While Iran, Israel and Saudi Arabia have expanded their reach and power across borders in the reporting period, Turkiye's foreign policy has also become more assertive, marked by a growing military and diplomatic presence across the region and beyond. Ankara launched military actions in Azerbaijan, Iraq, Libya and Syria, and supplied drones to a variety of parties, including Ethiopia and Ukraine. As tensions with the West remain, Turkiye continues to expand its relationships with China and Russia, keeping a foot in each camp to manage the power rivalry.

Regional Key Events

POLITICAL EVENTS

 IRAN

4 July 2023

Indian Prime Minister Narendra Modi announces Iran's admission to the Shanghai Cooperation Organisation.

 ISRAEL–PALESTINIAN TERRITORIES

24 July

The Israeli parliament passes a bill abolishing the Supreme Court's power to overrule government decisions.

 SYRIA

3 August

ISIS confirms the death of leader Abu Hussein al-Qurashi and names Abu Hafs al-Hashimi al-Qurashi as his replacement.

 IRAN

10 August

The US reaches a deal with Iran to free detained Americans in exchange for jailed Iranians and access to frozen funds.

MILITARY/VIOLENT EVENTS

 ISRAEL–PALESTINIAN TERRITORIES

3–6 July 2023

Israeli troops and drones strike Jenin in a major West Bank operation; a Palestinian man rams and stabs pedestrians in Tel Aviv; and rockets are fired from Lebanon towards Israel.

 ISRAEL–PALESTINIAN TERRITORIES

7 October

Hamas launches a surprise assault on Israel, which responds within 48 hours and declares a state of war and a 'complete siege' of Gaza.

 ISRAEL–PALESTINIAN TERRITORIES

14 October

The US deploys a second aircraft carrier, the USS *Dwight D. Eisenhower*, to the Eastern Mediterranean to join the USS *Gerald R. Ford* carrier strike group.

 JORDAN

18 October

Jordanian police clash with protesters near the Israeli embassy over the Israeli offensive in Gaza.

 **IRAN, IRAQ, SYRIA**

23 October

Iranian-backed Shiite militias launch an attack on a US base in southeastern Syria, adding to a series of increased attacks across Iraq and Syria.

IRAQ

14 November

Three Iraqi government ministers – allies of ousted parliament speaker Mohammed Halbousi – resign in protest of a court ruling terminating his tenure.

 ISRAEL–PALESTINIAN TERRITORIES

29 December

South Africa opens a case with the International Court of Justice (ICJ) against Israel for its alleged genocide of Palestinians.

 **EGYPT, ISRAEL–PALESTINIAN TERRITORIES, QATAR**

22 November

Egypt, Qatar and the US mediate the first pause in fighting between Hamas and Israel.

 **LEBANON**

2 January 2024

An Israeli drone kills the deputy chief of Hamas in Beirut, marking the first assassination of a Hamas official outside the Palestinian Territories since 7 October.

 **YEMEN**

12 January

The US and Britain conduct extensive airstrikes in Yemen, targeting Houthi forces in response to Red Sea harassment.

 **JORDAN**

28 January

Three US military personnel are killed and 34 more injured in a drone attack on Tower 22, a base in northeastern Jordan.

 **TURKIYE**

22 February

Turkiye pledges maritime security assistance to Somalia to defend its territorial waters as part of a defence and economic cooperation agreement aimed at enhancing ties.

 **ISRAEL**

18 March

A Houthi missile strikes Israeli soil for the first time.

 **IRAQ**

14 March 2024

Iraq's National Security Council bans the PKK, aligning with Turkiye's efforts against the group.

 ISRAEL–PALESTINIAN TERRITORIES

31 March

Tens of thousands protest outside the Israeli parliament building, demanding a ceasefire and calling for an early election.

 **TURKIYE**

1 April

Turkiye's main opposition party claims significant victories in Istanbul and Ankara less than a year after President Recep Tayyip Erdoğan wins his third term as president.

ISRAEL–PALESTINIAN TERRITORIES

1 April

Israeli airstrikes hit a World Central Kitchen aid convoy in central Gaza, killing seven aid workers.

IRAQ
22 April

Erdoğan visits Baghdad in the first Turkish state visit to Iraq since 2011.

 **IRAN, ISRAEL, SYRIA**
1–13 April

Israel conducts airstrikes on the Iranian embassy compound in Damascus, killing 16 people including officers of the IRGC; 12 days later, Iran launches an unprecedented retaliatory strike.

 IRAN
19 May

Iranian president Ebrahim Raisi, foreign minister Hossein Amirabdollahian and others die in a helicopter crash in East Azerbaijan province.

 ISRAEL–PALESTINIAN TERRITORIES
20 May

The chief prosecutor of the International Criminal Court seeks arrest warrants against Israeli and Hamas leaders.

 IRAQ
23 May

Kurdistan's regional elections in Iraq, scheduled for 10 June, are postponed indefinitely.

 ISRAEL–PALESTINIAN TERRITORIES
24 May

The ICJ orders Israel to halt its Rafah offensive.

 **ISRAEL–PALESTINIAN TERRITORIES**
31 May

The IDF ends operations in north Gaza's Jabalia area after more than two weeks of intense engagement and over 200 airstrikes.

 **ISRAEL–PALESTINIAN TERRITORIES**
31 May

US President Joe Biden announces a Gaza ceasefire deal which Hamas accepts with caveats and the Israeli government flatly rejects.

 IRAN
5 July

Reformist Masoud Pezeshkian is elected as Iran's new president, beating hardline conservative Saeed Jalili.

Notes

1. 'Hamas Hostages: Stories of the People Taken from Israel', BBC News, 1 September 2024. As of 30 April, the UN reported 24,686 fully identified deaths (out of 34,622 fatalities) in Gaza, where 7,797 were children, 4,959 were women, 10,006 were men and 1,924 were elderly. An additional estimated 10,000 remain missing and presumed dead under the rubble. See Iain Overton, 'Gaza War: UN Revises Death Toll for Women and Children', Action on Armed Violence, 17 May 2024; Ali Sawafta, '33,360 Palestinians Killed in Israel's Military Offensive on Gaza Since Oct. 7', Reuters, 9 April 2024; and Abeer Salman et al., 'UN Says Total Number of Deaths in Gaza Remains Unchanged After Controversy Over Revised Data', CNN, 14 May 2024.
2. Ahmed Asmar, 'Saudi Arabia Condemns Israel's "Continuous Genocidal Massacres" Against Palestinians in Rafah', Anadolu Agency, 29 May 2024.
3. The World Bank differentiates fragility from conflict. The former is 'characterized by an extremely low level of institutional and governance capacity which significantly impedes the state's ability to function effectively, maintain peace and foster economic and social development'. The latter is 'a situation of acute insecurity driven by the use of deadly force by a group – including state forces, organized non-state groups, or other irregular entities – with a political purpose or motivation. Such force can be two-sided – involving engagement between multiple organized, armed sides, at times resulting in collateral civilian harm – or one-sided, in which a group specifically targets civilians.' See World Bank, 'Classification of Fragility and Conflict Situations (FCS) for World Bank Group Engagement'.
4. Aaron Y. Zelin and Ilana Winter, 'One Year of the Islamic State Worldwide Activity Map', Washington Institute for Near East Policy, 20 March 2024.
5. US Central Command, 'Defeat ISIS Mission in Iraq and Syria for January – June 2024', press release, 16 July 2024.
6. Stockholm International Peace Research Institute (SIPRI), 'Trends in International Arms Transfers, 2023', SIPRI Fact Sheet, March 2024.
7. IISS analysis based on data from the Armed Conflict Location & Event Data Project (ACLED), www.acleddata.com.
8. *Ibid.*
9. Humanitarian Action, 'Global Humanitarian Overview 2024: Middle East and North Africa', 8 December 2023.
10. UNHCR, 'Middle East and North Africa', Global Report 2023.
11. USA for UNHCR, 'Syria Refugee Crisis Explained', 13 March 2024.
12. UNRWA, 'UNRWA Situation Report #119 on the Situation in the Gaza Strip and the West Bank, Including East Jerusalem', 9 July 2024.
13. Aya Batrawy, 'High Risk of Famine Across Gaza as Hunger Spreads, Experts Say', NPR, 25 June 2024; and UNRWA, 'Starvation on Top of Displacement: Palestine Refugees Deprived of Basic Needs as War Rages On in Gaza', 25 June 2024.
14. USA for UNHCR, 'Six Humanitarian Crises that Impacted Refugees and Displaced Communities in 2023', 3 January 2024.
15. Euan Ward, 'Hezbollah's Leader Says It Will Fight Without "Limits" if Israel Attacks', *New York Times*, 19 June 2024.

The Centrality of Non-state Armed Groups in Iran's Foreign Policy and Strategic Thinking

States have commonly instrumentalised non-state armed groups (NSAGs) in pursuit of their foreign and security policies, but Iran has uniquely made its relationship with NSAGs central to its strategic reach and identity. Iran has concentrated its efforts in theatres of critical interest, primarily Gaza, Iraq, Lebanon, Syria and Yemen (see Figure 1). Tehran's regional network of influence, comprised of the wide variety of militias and non-state actors with which it works across the region, is a function of the Iranian Revolution's history, Iran's Shia identity, and a deliberate strategic decision by its leadership to prioritise the capabilities and resources required to instrumentalise NSAGs. This extensive and powerful network of non-state allies is a peculiarity of the Iranian Revolution.

Iran's network has become the means by which Iran projects its power in the MENA region and an outer cordon which is defensive and offensive. Iran's reliance on the network and the capability required to maintain it has resulted in Iran being, as a state, uniquely invested in the perpetuation of the regional and global phenomenon of 'extra-state' power. It has, besides its regional network, supported or worked with NSAGs in distant regions and conflicts (e.g., in Europe, Latin America and East Africa) to bolster their resources and ensure their survival. It has also worked with states engulfed in intra-state conflicts, most notably in Syria and more recently Sudan. A disproportionate amount of its overseas capability, however, is dedicated to supporting actors outside the state-based order and over which it can exercise a measure of control. Through its international isolation and its prioritisation of its NSAG network, Tehran has become more comfortable working with NSAGs than other states.

Recent evolutions of Iran's strategy

Iran's NSAG strategy in the past five years has adapted to a number of dramatic changes. These include the instalment of new leadership at the Islamic Revolutionary Guard Corps (IRGC) Quds Force (QF) after the killing of Qasem Soleimani in Baghdad in January 2020; disturbances in Iran in 2021 and 2022; the suppression of the Islamic State (ISIS) threat in Iraq and Syria; regional detente, in particular with the Gulf states; and most dramatically the Israel–Hamas war. The strategic objectives of the network have remained the same: push the United States out of Iraq and entrench Iranian influence in Baghdad; menace Israel and Saudi Arabia by being present on their borders and enabling their adversaries; maintain the regime's position as global Shia hegemon (although it allows itself to work with Sunni NSAGs too); and buffer hostile-state activity.

The network's operational posture, meanwhile, has been influenced by several events. Iran has, for example, cut deals with the friendly government in Iraq by pushing for the inclusion of the Popular Mobilisation Units in the regular military, but some Iranian-backed groups have remained outside Iraqi government control. Shia NSAGs in Iraq are thus ranged on both sides of the ethnic Shia divide. Iraqi Shia groups with nationalist agendas play a political role distinct from Iranian-backed groups. Iran has no monopoly on NSAGs in the country most vital to it strategically.

Esmail Qaani, Soleimani's successor as the leader of the IRGC QF, has not been as diplomatically active and influential as his predecessor, most notably with Russia and Iraq. However, the group's operational focus has sharpened, with IRGC and related NSAG operations across the region becoming more aggressive and supported by more, and higher-grade, technical assistance. The improved technical support has been manifest in Ansarullah (Houthi) operations, which have benefitted from Iranian transfer of expertise and uninhabited aerial vehicles (UAVs), allowing them to mount sustained and effective operations against shipping lines in the Red Sea starting in November 2023.

The 'Axis of Resistance' strategy

Iran has sought also to promote the concept of a unified umbrella entity called the 'Axis of Resistance' to create the impression of coordinated effort among NSAGs opposing Israel and the US. Promoting this has been a low-cost response to the Israeli offensive in Gaza.

The axis, which has been a feature of Iranian rhetoric for at least two decades, assumed some material form in the IRGC operations room in Lebanon which included groups from Iraq and Syria. The most prominent Iran-backed groups in the region are Hizbullah, the Houthis and Hamas (see box below). Established since the 1979 Iranian Revolution, these long-standing relations have been bolstered by Iran through military support, training and intelligence-sharing. This not only strengthens the capabilities of these groups but also reinforces Iran's geopolitical stance in the Middle East. Tehran also hosted meetings of the 'leadership' of the axis. While this gave the appearance of the axis evolving into more of a standing coalition, in practice many of these groups continued to operate independently and often in pursuit of local agendas.

An Iraqi sub-group of the axis, the 'Islamic Resistance in Iraq', appeared in October 2023 in response to the Israeli offensive in Gaza. There appears to be no enduring structure beneath the moniker. In general, these groups – Iran-backed and others – have found it hard to move from local agendas and identities to a unified effort. They have also increasingly exceeded Tehran's risk appetite. Most strikingly, Hamas launched an operation on 7 October 2023 which was not only unknown to the Iranian leadership but to which they reportedly reacted privately with dismay. Tehran counselled Iraqi Shia groups such as Kataib Hizbullah and Asaib Ahl al-Haq to lie low and avoid US reprisals against their leadership after a dangerous round of escalation that included militia strikes against a US base in Jordan. Like Hamas in Gaza, they have been driven by strong local agendas and vendettas rather than by an overwhelming desire to please Iran.

Iran has thus faced the difficult task of making the axis appear stronger and more united than it is, without assuming ownership or drawing more US and Israeli fire on NSAG leadership and facilities in Syria and Iraq. For their part, the groups have sought to validate themselves against rivals and strengthen their power base by adopting confrontational postures with Israel and the US. The tension is constant between NSAG and Tehran agendas and represents an enduring risk for Tehran, particularly in the super-heated atmosphere after the Hamas-led 7 October attacks against Israel.

The overarching risk for Tehran is that it is dragged into a war which is costly, empowers domestic opposition and divides the regime. It must also manage the risk of not using, or minimally using, its network at a time when the physical threat to Palestinians and the political risk to their aspirations of a homeland are elevated. Iran's credibility and that of the network are at risk. The need to demonstrate material engagement in the fate of Palestine was undoubtedly a factor in the scale and directness of the IRGC-led attack on Israel in April 2024.

'Axis of Resistance': the most prominent NSAGs and Iran's role

Hizbullah

Strategy:
Iran's alliance with Hizbullah is pivotal to its regional security strategy. This close partnership enables Iran to maintain strategic depth and power projection in the Levant, countering the regional influence of Israel, Saudi Arabia and the US as well as supporting training and coordination of other Iran-backed NSAGs. Hizbullah's reserve of battle-hardened forces provides the Iranian regime with additional protection against existential threats.

Support:
Iran significantly boosts Hizbullah's military capabilities with advanced weaponry, including rockets, ballistic missiles, anti-ship and anti-tank guided-missile systems and UAVs. This is supported by extensive training and substantial financial aid estimated at up to US$700 million annually.[1] These activities bolster the group's operational effectiveness and ability to threaten Israeli infrastructure and conduct operations in Syria. Hizbullah has an estimated 50,000 fighters and an arsenal of over 150,000 missiles, drones and rockets.[2]

Ideology:
Hizbullah and Iran share a deep ideological bond rooted in Shia Islam. Hizbullah chief Hassan Nasrallah recognises Iran's Supreme Leader Sayyid Ali Khamenei as his spiritual leader. Iran has significantly influenced Hizbullah's development and leveraged its Arab identity and anti-Israeli stance to counter Arab scepticism towards Tehran. This alliance places Iran and Hizbullah at the forefront of oppo-

sition to Western imperialism and Zionism. Despite its commitment to Iran's strategic goals, the group maintains a degree of operational independence, particularly in Lebanese politics. The Iran–Hizbullah alliance is expected to strengthen, driven by mutual interests in countering Israeli influence and maintaining strategic deterrence.

Houthis
Strategy:
Iran's relatively recent alliance with, and support for, the Houthis in Yemen aligns closely with its broader regional objectives. By backing the group, Iran seeks to undermine Saudi influence, securing a foothold in the strategically critical Bab el-Mandeb Strait. Iran seeks to expand its geopolitical reach and control over critical maritime routes, enhancing its asymmetric warfare capabilities against adversaries, such as being able to disrupt global trade and energy shipping. In turn, the partnership empowers the Houthis to challenge the Yemeni government more effectively and expand the conflict beyond Yemen's borders.

Support:
Iran, with support from Hizbullah, provides the Houthis with sophisticated military capabilities including ballistic missiles, UAVs and anti-ship and anti-tank missile technology, as well as training and intelligence.

With around 150,000–200,000 fighters and additional aligned fighters, the Houthis have conducted significant attacks across the Middle East, targeting Western, Israeli, Saudi and Emirati interests.[3] Iranian financial aid, in cash and fuel, supports the Houthis' governance efforts amid the ongoing conflict in Yemen.

Ideology:
The Houthi–Iranian relationship is more opportunistic than ideologically driven, given the theological differences between Iran's Twelver Shia and the Houthi Zaidi Shia beliefs. Still, a convergence remains of political ideas linked to the Iranian Revolution, and political alignment has strengthened over time. Iran is involved directly and indirectly in political processes to secure the Houthis' long-term survival and regional power projection, and therefore Iran's influence in the region. It is unlikely that Iran's support of the Houthis will decline unless the Saudis and Houthis reach a political settlement which excludes Iran from the area.

Hamas
Strategy:
Iran's support for Hamas as a political and security partner plays a crucial role in Tehran's challenge against Israel and the US and in enhancing its influence in the Arab world. The multifaceted partnership – financial, political and operational – enables Iran to exert pressure on Israel from multiple fronts, undermining Israel's security and diverting Israeli military and political resources from focusing on Iran's nuclear programme and its activities in Syria and Lebanon.

Support:
Iran has significantly bolstered Hamas forces through extensive military aid, training and logistical support, transforming the group into a notable military force capable of sophisticated attacks against Israel. The involvement of the QF and Hizbullah has been crucial, offering hands-on and strategic guidance, military tactics and technical assistance for the production of rockets and drones equipped with advanced guiding systems. Iran's annual military aid to Hamas, reportedly approximately US$70m before the Israel–Hamas war, has been instrumental in strengthening the Izz al-Din al-Qassam Brigades, Hamas's armed wing with an estimated force of 30,000 fighters.[4]

Ideology:
Despite Shia–Sunni sectarian differences, Iran and Hamas have found common ground in opposition to Israel and a shared vision for Palestinian independence. This pragmatic relationship has experienced fluctuations, notably during the Syrian civil war when Hamas supported Sunni rebels against the Bashar al-Assad regime, leading to a temporary rift with Iran. Nonetheless, the alliance was renewed and strengthened in subsequent years. Hamas retained its political and strategic autonomy, as highlighted by the US assessment indicating that Iranian leaders neither orchestrated nor had foreknowledge of the 7 October attacks. The relationship between Iran and Hamas is likely to remain strategically significant for both parties. However, the ongoing conflict in Gaza presents existential challenges to Hamas, potentially depriving Iran of a key ally. More direct involvement from Iran in the conflict could further weaken Iran's future attempts to improve its international stature.

Regional Spotlight: Middle East and North Africa 123

Figure 1: Iran's strategic reach in the Middle East

The challenge of established NSAGs

Iran must also deal with problems arising from NSAGs with established power structures. Corruption and oppressive security mechanisms risk alienating the NSAGs' local support, without which they cannot function. Tehran has the related problem that the regime's support for NSAGs does not attract massive domestic adherence, with Iranians protesting its financial and political cost.

In Iraq, NSAGs receive formal and informal government funding, but groups with strong local control reportedly run extortion rackets and levy taxes at lucrative vehicle checkpoints. This normalisation of criminal activity contrasts with the groups' much-vaunted religious and political idealism and can backfire on their patrons in Tehran. This also may stoke concerns in Tehran over the legitimacy of the groups as local forces, especially where, as in Iraq, there are alternative Shia power centres opposed to Iran. Elsewhere in the region, and more troubling for Tehran, would be the impact corrupt investment in the status quo could have on Hizbullah's willingness to fight.

There are no signs of Tehran abandoning its strategic dependence on the NSAG network despite its risks. The IRGC is dominant in Tehran and deems the network, for all its risks, a more comfortable and less costly vector for confronting Israel than direct state-on-state military action. The fostering of NSAGs remains an instrument of defence and a foreign-policy objective. It exemplifies the regime's deep ideological distrust of state-based order. Iran's interests are best served in a region where power is fractured and NSAGs proliferate. It is more adept at exploiting the requirements, and instrumentalising the capabilities, of groups which lie outside state structures than it is at forming coalitions with states. The regime's commitment to its causes and beliefs supersedes any commitment to state-based order.

Notes

[1] Congressional Research Service, 'Iran's Foreign and Defense Policies', January 2021.

[2] IISS, *The Military Balance 2024* (Abingdon: Routledge for the *IISS*, 2024), p. 369; and John Raine et al., 'Iran and Israel: Everything Short of War', IISS, 17 May 2024.

[3] Justin Salhani, 'Houthis Are Recruiting Record Fighters. How Will This Affect Yemen?', Al-Jazeera, 23 February 2024.

[4] Samia Nakhoul, 'How Hamas Secretly Built a "Mini-army" to Fight Israel', Reuters, 16 October 2023; and IISS, *The Military Balance 2024*, p. 379.

SYRIA

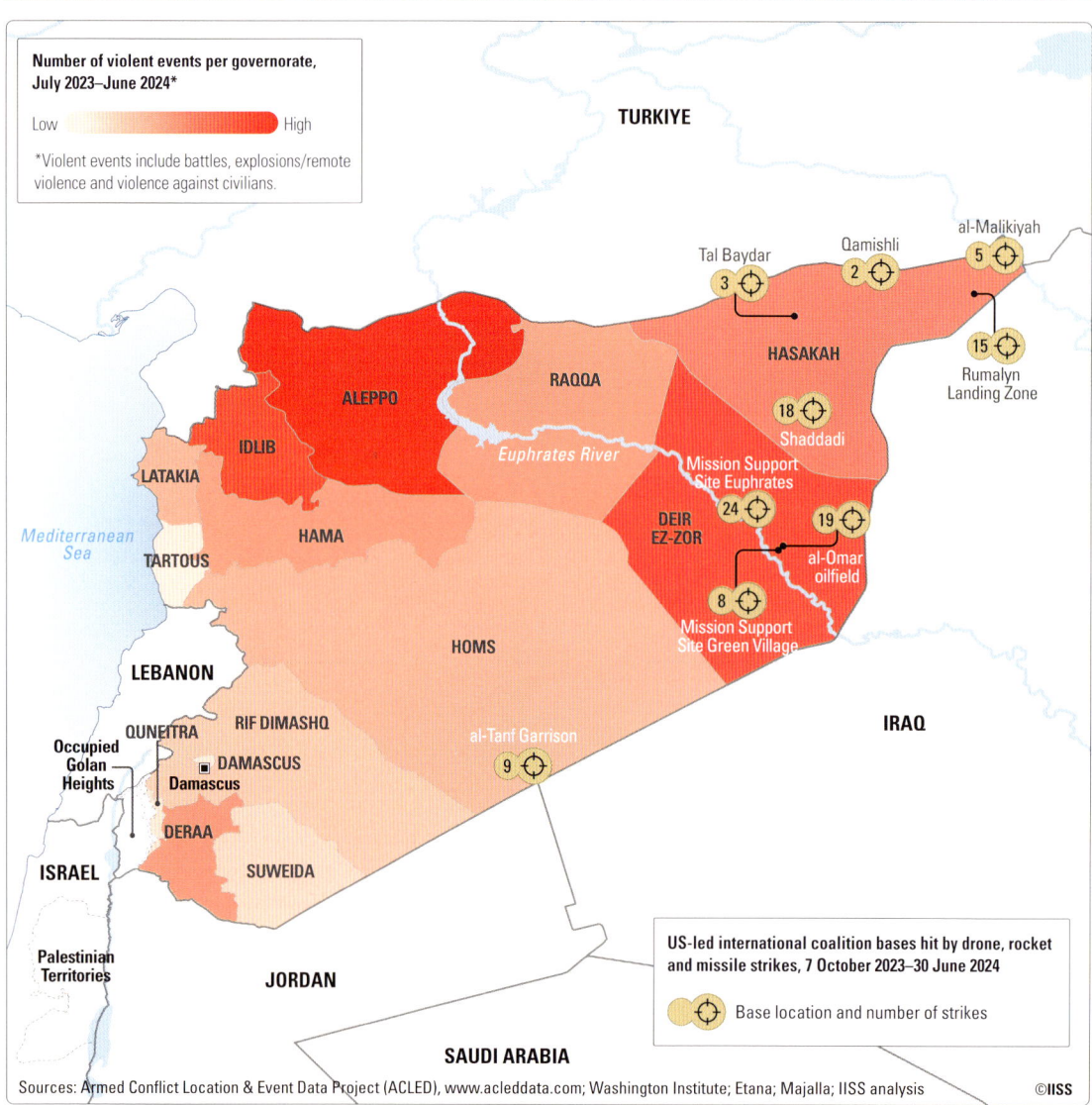

Conflict Overview

The Syrian conflict, originating in 2011, has become one of the most complex and devastating crises of the twenty-first century. Initially sparked by peaceful protests for political reforms, it rapidly escalated into a full-blown civil war, drawing in various actors with divergent interests. Key participants include President Bashar al-Assad's government (Syrian Armed Forces, SAF) and rival armed factions such as Hayat Tahrir al-Sham (HTS), the Syrian Democratic Forces (SDF), the Syrian National Army (SNA) and the Islamic State (ISIS). Direct military engagement or support for different factions by nations such as Iran, Russia, Turkiye, the United States (Combined Joint Task Force–*Operation Inherent Resolve,* CJTF–OIR) and several Gulf states have further complicated matters.

Since Moscow's military intervention in 2015, backed by Iran's armed forces, Russia has significantly bolstered the Assad regime's control over

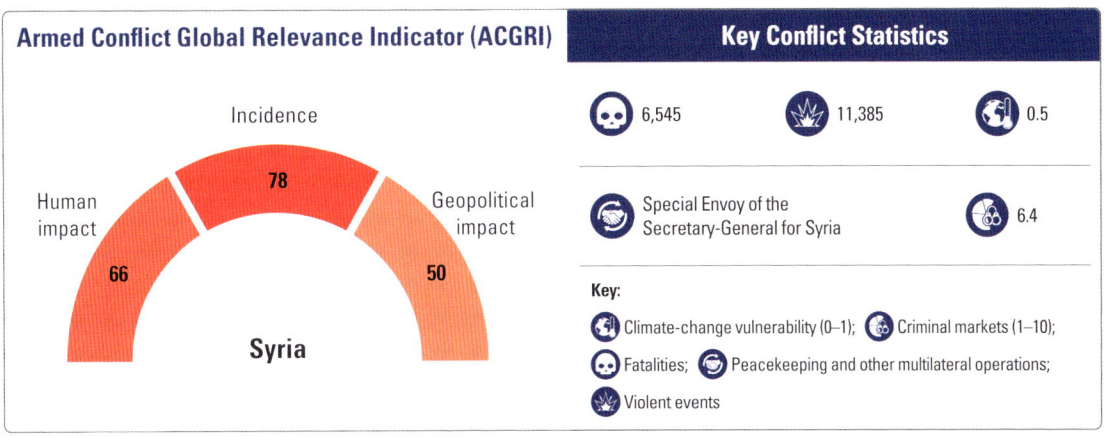

approximately 65% of Syria and around 55% of the pre-war population. Despite benefiting from an illicit war economy, the Syrian government faces persistent challenges, including contested authority, financial constraints and a narrow power base. While ISIS and other non-state armed groups continue to challenge the government's authority, they do not pose an existential threat.

The conflict has resulted in a widespread humanitarian emergency, displacing 6.8 million Syrians internally and creating 6.5m refugees.[1] Despite the immense human suffering and loss of life, efforts to find a political resolution have faced significant hurdles. The Assad-led government has consistently rejected power-sharing arrangements and obstructed United Nations-led mediation efforts in Geneva. Initiatives such as the Astana talks in 2017, facilitated by Iran, Russia and Turkiye, have failed to secure a lasting ceasefire or political settlement. Moreover, the fallout from the Hamas-led 7 October 2023 attacks against Israel has further exacerbated the conflict. Escalating skirmishes between Israeli- and Iranian-backed militias, along with attacks by the latter against US forces in Syria, underscore the continued volatility of the situation.

Conflict Update

Events throughout the reporting period highlighted the fragility of Syria's security landscape and its interconnectedness with regional conflicts. In northeast Syria, hostilities between the Turkish Armed Forces (TSK) and the SDF continued to be a major destabilising factor. Following a Kurdistan Workers' Party (PKK)-claimed attack in Ankara on 1 October 2023, Turkiye significantly increased airstrikes on SDF positions and critical infrastructure, including electricity and water stations and oilfields. In response, SDF attacks on Turkish-backed SNA-held areas in northern Syria intensified.

Worsening ethnic tensions between the Arab-majority communities and the Kurdish-led autonomous administration in northeastern Syria also led to military clashes between the SDF and Arab tribes. The arrest of Abu Khawla, leader of the Arab-led Deir ez-Zor Military Council, by the SDF in August 2023 resulted in a month of heavy clashes, with the SDF ultimately prevailing. However, tribal insurgency against the SDF has continued amid rumours of SAF support.

ISIS attacks persisted across Syria despite efforts by the SDF, SAF and US-led CJTF–OIR to eliminate the group's presence. These attacks primarily targeted the SDF and SAF in northeast and central Syria. While the number of attacks decreased from 2022–23, the first half of 2024 witnessed a surge in incidents.[2] ISIS employed insurgent tactics, including hit-and-run attacks, ambushes and the use of remotely controlled explosive devices, to inflict significant damage on the SAF, leading to the deaths of hundreds of soldiers, while avoiding direct confrontation.

In the last rebel-opposition stronghold in the northwest, daily bombardments between HTS and the SNA on one side and the SAF on the other persisted, with no changes in zones of control. The number of violent incidents surged following a significant attack on the Homs Military Academy on 5 October, resulting in the deaths of over 90 people.[3] In response, the SAF launched an aerial-strike campaign in HTS-held areas targeting civilian infrastructure. This bombardment led to the largest forced displacement of civilians, amounting to approximately 120,000 people, since the March 2020 ceasefire agreement in the northwest between Turkiye and Russia.[4]

Meanwhile, political unrest persisted in Sweida (a government-held area), where protests demanding the overthrow of the regime began in August 2023 and continued throughout the reporting period. Despite the predominantly Druze (an ethnoreligious minority group) composition of the protests and the support lent to them by community leaders, the SAF hesitated to use force. However, the lack of a positive response from the government, coupled with external crises such as the Israel–Hamas war, resulted in decreased participation in the protests.[5]

Government-held areas also continued to play a significant role in the production and smuggling of the amphetamine drug Captagon. Southern Syria witnessed a concerning increase in the scale of smuggling and a shift in tactics, including more frequent smuggling attempts, enhanced coordination and a greater use of violence.[6] Despite diplomatic efforts, the flow of drugs into Jordan has continued, prompting the Jordanian army to intensify anti-narcotics operations on the Syrian border and conduct limited airstrikes on smuggling facilities. Civilian casualties resulting from these airstrikes have sparked public outcry in Damascus and have strained Jordanian–Syrian relations.

The frequency of Iran-backed militia attacks on US-led CJTF–OIR bases in SDF-held areas and al-Tanf significantly increased following the start of the Israel–Hamas war. These attacks initially resulted in very few casualties, until a January 2024 drone attack on a US military outpost northeast of Jordan killed three US soldiers and injured 47 more. Strong US retaliation against the responsible groups in Syria and Iraq led to a halt in Iranian-backed militia attacks against American bases in Syria.[7]

Similarly, the Israel–Hamas war increased tensions and attacks on Syrian soil between Iranian-backed militias and Israel. Iranian-backed militias began sporadically targeting the Israeli-occupied Golan Heights in the south with mortars and drones. In response, Israel increased its attacks against assets and commanders affiliated with those groups, resulting in the highest number of recorded Israeli attacks inside Syria since 2011.[8]

Diplomatically, the Syrian government largely failed to capitalise on the opportunity presented by its readmission to the Arab League in May 2023. The Assad regime did not fulfil the steps proposed by the Arab states, which included fighting drug trafficking and facilitating the return of refugees. Likewise, the Syrian government's efforts to normalise relations with Turkiye stalled following President Recep Tayyip Erdoğan's re-election.

Conflict Parties

Syrian Armed Forces (SAF)

Strength: 169,000 active military personnel and 100,000 gendarmerie and paramilitary personnel.

Areas of operation: Southern, coastal and central Syria and parts of northern Syria.

Syrian Armed Forces (SAF)

Leadership: President Bashar al-Assad (commander-in-chief) and Gen. Abdul Karim Mahmoud Ibrahim (chief of the general staff).

Structure: Consists of the Syrian Arab Army, Syrian Arab Navy, Syrian Arab Air Force, Syrian Arab Air Defence Force and several paramilitary forces, including the National Defence Forces and Local Defence Forces (LDF).

History: Established in 1945 after Syria gained independence from French colonial rule, the armed forces have undergone significant transformations over the years. The military's pivotal role in Syrian politics, marked by coups and power struggles, underscores its significance as a tool for internal stability and regional strategic pursuits.

Objectives: Regain exclusive military control over the entirety of Syrian territory.

Opponents: Israeli forces, Turkish forces, US forces, ISIS, HTS, SNA and SDF.

Affiliates/allies: Iran and Iranian-backed foreign armed factions (including Hizbullah, Iraqi Popular Mobilisation Units, and Zainabiyoun and Fatemiyoun militias), as well as Russia and Russian private military companies.

Resources/capabilities: Possesses a variety of armoured vehicles, air-defence systems, aircraft and naval vessels, and receives support from Russia and Iran.

Hayat Tahrir al-Sham (HTS)

Strength: Approximately 10,000.[9]

Areas of operation: Northwestern Syria.

Leadership: Abu Mohamed al-Golani.

Structure: Operates as a hierarchical organisation with a leadership council overseeing its administrative arm (the Syrian Salvation Government), security apparatus and military bodies.

History: HTS was initially known as Jabhat al-Nusra, which was formed by the Islamic State in Iraq. However, it broke away when the latter declared itself the Islamic State of Iraq and al-Sham (ISIS) in 2013. Subsequently, the group also split from al-Qaeda in 2016 and rebranded itself again to merge with other groups under the name HTS.

Objectives: Topple the Assad-led government and establish Sunni sharia-based rule.

Opponents: SAF, Iranian forces and their affiliates, Russian forces, ISIS, al-Qaeda and SDF.

Affiliates/allies: Turkish forces and SNA.

Resources/capabilities: Significant weaponry including rocket launchers, anti-tank guided missiles, tanks, artillery, makeshift drones and improvised explosive devices (IEDs).

(Turkiye-sponsored) Syrian National Army (SNA)

Strength: Approximately 70,000.[10]

Areas of operation: Northern and northwestern Syria.

Leadership: Brig.-Gen. Hassan al-Hamada (defence minister). SNA units are currently deployed alongside Turkish military forces and therefore operate under Turkish leadership.

Structure: A conglomerate of dozens of different militias, ranging vastly in size, affiliation and ideology, composed of Syrian militants, who are trained and equipped by Turkiye. The SNA is divided into seven main legions, each comprising a wide array of divisions and brigades.

History: Created as a splinter group of the Turkiye-backed Free Syrian Army. The SNA has been trained and equipped by the Turkish government since 2016. In 2019, the Idlib-based and Turkiye-sponsored National Front for Liberation was merged into the SNA.

Objectives: Overthrow the Syrian government and take control of northern Syria.

Opponents: Kurdish forces, PKK, ISIS, and the Syrian government and its allies.

Affiliates/allies: Turkish Armed Forces (TSK).

Resources/capabilities: While a handful of formations have received US-sponsored training and equipment, the SNA has relied entirely on Turkish support since its inception. Turkiye has provided small arms as well as light armoured vehicles, and SNA military operations have benefited from Turkish artillery and air support.

Syrian Democratic Forces/People's Protection Units (SDF/YPG)

Strength: 40,000–60,000.[11]

Areas of operation: Northern Syria.

Leadership: Mazloum Kobani Abdi, also known as Sahin Cilo (military commander), and Mahmoud Berkhadan (general commander). Abdi is a former senior PKK member.

Structure: Organised mainly along ethnic and territorial lines. Syrian Kurds lead the YPG and the Women's Protection Units (YPJ); both include a small component of international volunteers grouped into an international battalion. Other ethnic groups are organised under various military formations within the SDF, mainly as military councils.

History: Created in 2015 as a direct response to the advance of the Islamic State into northern Syria, building on various pre-existing alliances. Since then, it has fought against ISIS and the Turkish military.

Objectives: Establish autonomous control over northeastern Syria.

Opponents: Turkish forces, SNA, ISIS, and al-Qaeda and affiliates.

Affiliates/allies: US and PKK.

Syrian Democratic Forces/People's Protection Units (SDF/YPG)

Resources/capabilities: While it built upon the experience of its militias, since its formal creation the SDF has been equipped, trained and advised by the US. SDF units are equipped with small arms and some light armoured vehicles.

Islamic State (ISIS)

Strength: Unclear.

Areas of operation: Eastern and northern regions of Syria.

Leadership: Abu Hafs al-Hashimi al-Qurashi (calif and leader of ISIS).

Structure: Its structure comprises a core leadership, regional commanders and a decentralised network of smaller cells executing attacks and propaganda campaigns.

History: Emerged in Iraq circa 2003 and sought to establish a caliphate during the Syrian civil war. From 2014–17, it controlled vast territories in Iraq and Syria, governing over eight million people. However, since 2017 in Iraq and 2019 in Syria, ISIS has lost control of all the territories it previously held.

Objectives: Topple the Assad-led government and establish Sunni sharia-based rule.

Opponents: SDF, HTS, SNA, Syrian government and its allies, and Turkish and US armed forces.

Affiliates/allies: ISIS fighters in other countries.

Resources/capabilities: Light weaponry and IEDs.

Armed Forces of the Russian Federation

Strength: 4,000 in Syria.[12]

Areas of operation: Syrian government-held areas and parts of northeastern Syria.

Leadership: President Vladimir Putin (commander-in-chief), General of the Army Valery Gerasimov (chief of the general staff) and Lt.-Gen. Sergei Kisel (commander of Russian forces in Syria).

Structure: The Russian mission in Syria involves ground forces, special forces, attack aircraft and bombers, an air-defence component and military intelligence. Russian private military contractors operate in front-line roles together with conventional units.

History: Since 2015, Russia has shaped the Syrian battlefield, playing a crucial strategic and operational role to shore up and reorganise Syrian government forces and assist the Assad regime in capturing key areas.

Objectives: Protect the Assad-led government.

Opponents: US forces, SNA, HTS, ISIS, and al-Qaeda and affiliates.

Affiliates/allies: SAF, Iran and its affiliates.

Resources/capabilities: Combat aircraft, uninhabited aerial vehicles (UAVs), artillery, air-defence systems and various vehicles.

Iranian armed forces

Strength: 1,500 in Syria.[13]

Areas of operation: Syrian government-held areas and parts of northeastern Syria.

Leadership: Brig.-Gen. Esmail Ghaani (military leader of the Quds Force).

Structure: The Iranian armed forces operate in Syria through a variety of military organisations, proxy militias and elite units like the Quds Force of the Islamic Revolutionary Guard Corps. Iran maintains substantial influence within certain elements of the SAF, particularly militias nominally incorporated within the LDF.

History: Significantly active in Syria since 2012. In the conflict's early stages Tehran provided the Syrian regime with financial aid, arms shipments, communication-jamming equipment and advisory support. Over time, it expanded its presence, deploying troops, militias and advisers; its involvement has been critical in supporting Assad's government and countering rebel factions.

Objectives: Protect the Assad-led government and establish a foothold in Syria to deter Israel.

Opponents: US forces, SNA, HTS, ISIS, and al-Qaeda and affiliates.

Affiliates/allies: SAF and its affiliates, and Russia.

Resources/capabilities: Light weaponry, UAVs, anti-tank guided missiles, and a variety of vehicles are deployed by the Iranian armed forces.

Combined Joint Task Force–*Operation Inherent Resolve* (CJTF–OIR)

Strength: 900 troops in Syria.[14]

Areas of operation: Northeastern Syria and al-Tanf garrison near the Iraqi and Jordanian borders.

Leadership: Maj.-Gen. Joel B. Vowell (commanding officer).

Structure: CJTF–OIR forces in Syria are primarily drawn from the US Army, with support from US and allied special-forces personnel.

History: Created in October 2014 when the US Department of Defense formalised ongoing military operations against ISIS.

Combined Joint Task Force–*Operation Inherent Resolve* (CJTF–OIR)

The first US ground troops entered Syria in late 2015 to recruit, organise and advise Syrian Kurdish and Arab opposition fighters.

Objectives: Defeat ISIS and prevent its re-emergence.

Opponents: ISIS, and al-Qaeda and affiliates.

Affiliates/allies: SDF.

Resources/capabilities: Light weapons, combat aircraft, UAVs, artillery, short-range air- and missile-defence systems, and armoured vehicles.

Turkish Armed Forces (TSK)

Strength: Approximately 3,000 in Syria.[15]

Areas of operation: Northern Syria.

Leadership: President Recep Tayyip Erdoğan (commander-in-chief), Gen. Yaşar Güler (minister of national defence) and Gen. Metin Gürak (chief of general staff).

Structure: The Turkish forces in Syria are organised into several units, including infantry, armoured and special-forces units.

History: Involved in Syria since the conflict began in 2011. For the first five years, it primarily provided training and equipment to the Syrian armed opposition and humanitarian aid. Military operations increased beginning in 2016 with *Operation Euphrates Shield*, aimed at combatting ISIS and Kurdish militia groups near the border. Subsequent operations, such as *Operation Olive Branch* and *Operation Peace Spring*, further expanded Turkish influence in northern Syria, supporting rebel factions and establishing 'safe zones' along the border.

Objectives: Eradicate the PKK and its affiliates; secure Turkiye's border with Syria; and mitigate the influx of refugees into Turkiye.

Opponents: SDF, ISIS, al-Qaeda, SAF and affiliates.

Affiliates/allies: SNA.

Resources/capabilities: Turkiye's defence budget for 2023 was US$8.7 billion. Its military capabilities include combat aircraft; intelligence, surveillance and reconnaissance assets; armoured vehicles; and special-forces units.

Hizbullah

Strength: 7,000–8,000 in Syria.[16]

Areas of operation: Government-held areas of Syria.

Leadership: Hassan Nasrallah (secretary-general).

Structure: Hizbullah forces in Syria typically operate in a hierarchical structure, with centralised command and control. They are organised into units, battalions and brigades, each with defined roles and responsibilities, under the overall leadership of Hizbullah's central command.

History: At Iran's request, Hizbullah became significantly involved in Syria's civil war after 2012, initially providing advisory support to the Syrian government. Over time, the group expanded its presence, deploying troops and advisers alongside other pro-Iranian groups to bolster the Assad regime. Hizbullah's involvement has been key in supporting Assad's government and countering rebel factions.

Objectives: Protect the Assad-led government and establish a foothold in Syria to deter Israel and generate revenues.

Opponents: US forces, SNA, HTS, ISIS, and al-Qaeda and affiliates.

Affiliates/allies: SAF, Iranian-backed forces and Russia.

Resources/capabilities: Light and heavy weaponry, artillery, drones, anti-tank guided missiles, and a variety of military vehicles.

Notes

[1] Word Vision Staff, 'Syrian Refugee Crisis: Facts, FAQs, and How to Help', World Vision, 16 February 2024.

[2] 'ISIS Killed Over 100 in Syria Since Start of Year', *Asharq Al-Awsat*, 25 February 2024.

[3] Haid Haid, 'Culpability Over Homs Drone Attack Shrouded in Mystery', *Al Majalla*, 12 October 2023.

[4] Haid Haid, 'Al-Assad Pounds Idlib as Global Attention on Gaza', *Al Majalla*, 1 January 2024.

[5] Haid Haid, 'Sweida Protests: Al-Assad Clamps Down Elsewhere to Stem Wider Revolt', *Al Majalla*, 9 September 2023.

[6] Haid Haid, 'Jordan Confronts a Fresh Threat in War on Drugs', *Al Majalla*, 25 December 2023.

[7] 'Iraq Says 16 People, Including Civilians, Killed in "New US Aggression"', Al-Jazeera, 3 February 2024.

[8] Haid Haid, 'Is Syria Emerging as a New Front in the Hamas–Israel War?', *Al Majalla*, 19 October 2023.

[9] IISS, *The Military Balance 2024* (Abingdon: Routledge for the IISS, 2023), pp. 387–8.

[10] Ibid.

[11] European Union Agency for Asylum, '1.2. Syrian Democratic Forces and Asayish', September 2020.

[12] Ibid.

[13] Ibid.

[14] Timour Azhari, 'US Forces in Syria Attacked Four Times in Less Than 24 Hours – U.S. Military Official', Reuters, 13 November 2023.

[15] IISS, *The Military Balance 2024*, p. 151.

[16] Ibid., p. 387.

IRAQ

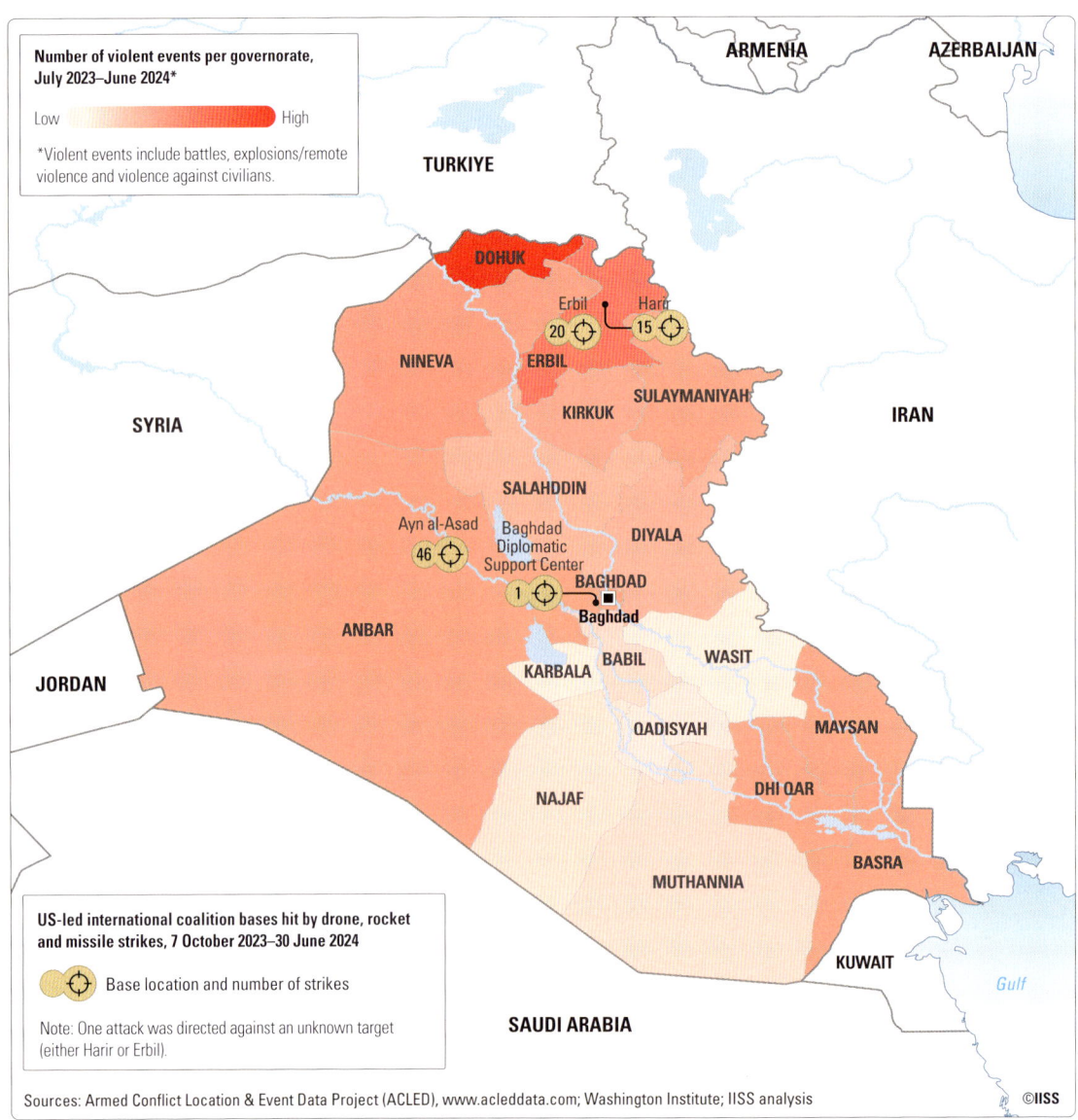

Conflict Overview

Since the United States-led invasion that ousted Saddam Hussein's regime in 2003, Iraq has continued to be plagued by instability and political fragmentation. The social, religious and political discord that resulted from Hussein's repressive Ba'ath Party rule was exacerbated by the US-backed 'de-Ba'athification' process, which left many former party members and the Sunni minority marginalised and discontented.

Sectarian tensions, among other factors, gave rise to various Sunni insurgent groups such as al-Qaeda in Iraq, while Shia insurgencies such as the Mahdi Army and Badr Brigades continued to mobilise fighters, fuelling a protracted conflict. The violence gradually subsided after reaching its peak around 2006–07 due to a combination of factors including a surge in US troop numbers, the Sunni

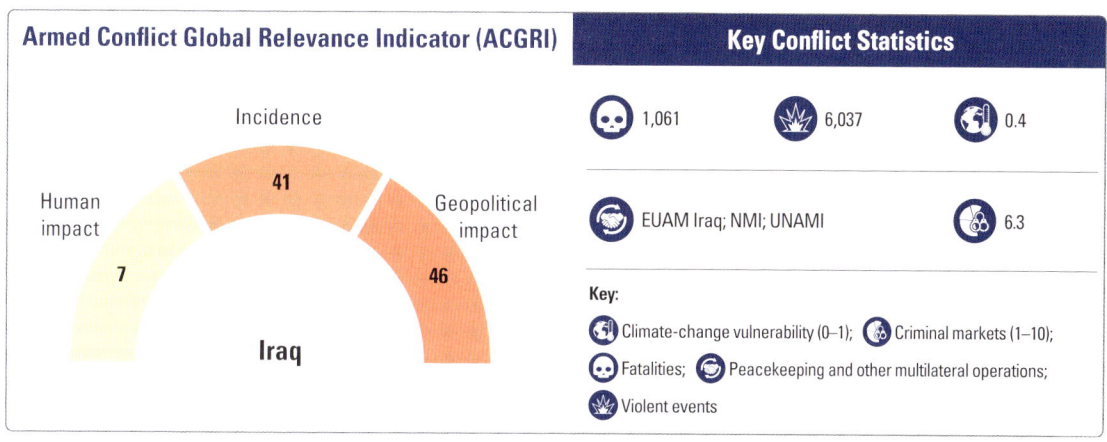

Conflict(s)	Type	Start date
Ethnic (Arab, Turkmen and Kurdish) and sectarian violence	I	2003
Turkiye's conflict with PKK Iraq-based affiliates	T	Pre-2003
Iran-backed groups' conflict with US forces	T	2003

Key: I Internal; T Transnational

Awakening movement and efforts by the Iraqi government to reconcile sectarian differences.

After a period of relative calm, Iraq was destabilised again in 2014 by the rise of the Islamic State (ISIS), which managed to seize large territories, including Mosul. In response, Tehran's religious leaders called for the Shia community to combat ISIS, resulting in the formation of armed militias under the umbrella of the Popular Mobilisation Units (PMU), supported by the West. With the creation of the Shi'ite Coordination Framework (SCF) in late 2019, Iran-backed Shia actors in Iraq (including the PMU) grew in relevance and influence in the country.

Despite military successes against ISIS, Iraq has continued to grapple with political unrest, economic challenges and social divisions. The Sunni–Shia divide and institutional conflicts between the Kurdistan Regional Government (KRG) and Baghdad remain primary sources of tension, exacerbated by divisions within Iraq's main demographic blocs. Efforts to address these challenges have been hampered by corruption, security threats, regional tensions and the legacy of past conflicts. The Kurdistan Workers' Party (PKK) has continued to stoke rivalries among Kurdish parties within the KRG and exacerbate tensions with Turkiye. Meanwhile, the repercussions of the Israel–Hamas war have underscored Iraq's fragility, sparking clashes between Iranian-backed Iraqi factions and US forces, and prompting attacks against Israel.

Conflict Update

Throughout the reporting period, Iraq was plagued by ethnic and political tensions, as well as the spillover of regional rivalries and counter-insurgency activities from neighbouring countries. In August 2023, Turkiye heightened its military operations against the PKK in northern Iraq. A PKK suicide bombing outside a government building in Ankara in October further escalated this trend, leading to retaliatory actions on both sides. After much political pressure from Turkiye, in March 2024, Baghdad finally designated the PKK as a banned organisation.

Iraq's stability deteriorated further following the outbreak of the Israel–Hamas war in October. Iran-backed militias, operating under the banner of the Islamic Resistance in Iraq, increasingly targeted US forces in the western and northern regions of the country. These attacks aimed to pressure the US to halt Israeli attacks in Gaza and expedite the withdrawal of US troops from Iraq. The situation reached its peak in January 2024 when Iran-backed militants carried out a drone attack from Syria on a US base on the Jordanian border, killing three American soldiers. In response, the US conducted a series of retaliatory strikes in Iraq. Fearing further escalation, the Iraqi militias announced the suspension of military actions against US forces, leading to a cessation of tit-for-tat attacks in Iraq. Despite increased risks, the US remains resolute in maintaining its troop presence in Iraq for the foreseeable future, even as ISIS activities in the country have decreased. The number of attacks by the group has seen a significant decline in recent years, dropping from nearly 1,500 in March 2021 to approximately 150 in March 2024.[1]

In a related development, Iran's Islamic Revolutionary Guard Corps (IRGC) claimed responsibility in January 2024 for attacking what it described as Israel's 'spy headquarters' in Iraq's semi-autonomous Kurdistan region. The assault resulted in the deaths of four civilians and injured six others, and it was seen as retaliation for the killing of three IRGC members in Syria in December.[2]

Meanwhile, in the oil-rich city of Kirkuk, ethnic clashes erupted in September 2023 when the central government ordered the Iraqi military's Joint Operations Command to relinquish its headquarters, located in the Kurdish-populated Shoraw neighbourhood, to the Kurdistan Democratic Party (KDP), potentially allowing the KDP to regain control of the city. In response, Arab and Turkmen opponents established a camp outside the building. Tensions escalated when Kurdish protesters approached the camp, resulting in clashes that left four dead and 16 more wounded.[3] The Federal Supreme Court of Iraq subsequently suspended the order for the KDP's return.

Politically, Iraq faced a significant crisis in November 2023 when the Federal Supreme Court terminated speaker Mohammed al-Halbousi's membership in parliament. This followed accusations by another Sunni parliamentarian, Laith al-Dulaimi, that Halbousi had forged Dulaimi's resignation letter. Al-Halbousi's removal triggered disputes among factions over his potential replacement. Despite attempts, no candidate secured the required majority, highlighting both institutional fragility and tensions within the process.

Iraq concluded 2023 by conducting provincial council elections for the first time in a decade. Despite concerns about violence, the voting process unfolded relatively peacefully, with a turnout rate of 41%. The SCF, which consists of various Shia groups backed by Iran and supports the current government led by Iraqi Prime Minister Mohammed Shia' al-Sudani, won a significant 102 of 285 council seats.[4] Its success was aided by a boycott led by opposing Shia leader Muqtada al-Sadr, who aimed to delegitimise the elections and their results.

The KRG continues to wrestle with internal divisions between its two ruling parties, particularly concerning revenue allocation and election reforms. Originally slated for 1 October 2022, parliamentary elections in Iraqi Kurdistan have been repeatedly postponed due to the KDP and the Patriotic Union of Kurdistan (PUK) failing to reach an agreement on the electoral system.[5] In June, the KRG rescheduled the elections for 20 October 2024. Although both parties have consented to this date, they have yet to resolve a months-long dispute over the parliament's controversial minority quota. The failure to conduct elections poses political and governance challenges for the KRG, exacerbating internal rifts and divisions within the region.

Internal struggles in Iraqi Kurdistan have bolstered central-government authority and deepened divisions. This was made evident by the Federal Supreme Court's February rulings, which mandated shifting the responsibility for paying KRG public servants and all revenues to Baghdad, challenging the KRG's authority. Additionally, it deemed all 11 reserved parliamentary seats for ethnic and religious minorities in Iraqi Kurdistan unconstitutional, eliminating them entirely.[6] These decisions fuelled tensions within the region and with Baghdad.

Conflict Parties

Iraqi Armed Forces and Counter Terrorism Service (CTS)

Strength: 193,000 active military personnel.

Areas of operation: All areas of Iraq excluding the Iraqi Kurdistan.

Leadership: Prime Minister Mohammed Shia' al-Sudani (commander-in-chief) and Gen. Abdul Amir Rashid Yarallah (chief of the general staff).

Structure: The Iraqi Armed Forces consists of several branches, including the army, air force, navy and air defence command. Each branch operates under the Ministry of Defence. The CTS is a separate, division-sized, special-forces organisation that reports directly to the prime minister.

History: Established in the early twentieth century following Iraq's independence from British mandate. The armed forces initially focused on maintaining internal security and defending the nation's borders. Over the years, the military saw periods of expansion, modernisation and politicisation under different regimes, including the monarchy, Ba'ath Party rule and post-Hussein governments. The armed forces have been involved in various conflicts, such as the Iran–Iraq War, the Gulf War and the Iraq War.

Objectives: Ensure security across the country and prevent the re-emergence of ISIS.

Opponents: ISIS.

Affiliates/allies: Kurdish Peshmerga, Combined Joint Task Force–*Operation Inherent Resolve* (CJTF–OIR) and PMU.

Resources/capabilities: A range of conventional land, air and naval capabilities, including armoured fighting vehicles, anti-tank missile systems, artillery, and fixed- and rotary-wing aircraft.

Popular Mobilisation Units (PMU)

Strength: Between 200,000 and 240,000 salaried positions. However, effective deployable strength is likely to be lower than these totals would suggest.

Areas of operation: Areas previously held by ISIS.

Leadership: Abdul-Aziz al-Muhammadawi (chief of staff for the PMU Commission), although power is believed to be wielded primarily through a committee comprising senior figures from the key groups operating under the PMU umbrella.

Structure: Roughly 40–60 paramilitary units operate under the collective organisation. Officially, the PMU functions as part of Iraq's security framework. However, each unit is structured around its own internal leadership, prominent individuals and combatants.

History: Emerged in response to Grand Ayatollah Ali al-Sistani's 2014 call to defend Iraq against ISIS. Primarily composed of Shia militias, the PMU also includes some Sunni and Christian factions. However, the lack of rules governing the establishment of PMU units resulted in the formation of groups with diverse goals and ideologies. While some PMU units have been accused of sectarianism and of being proxies for Iran, others advocate a nationalist agenda. These internal differences have persisted even after the formal recognition of these units as part of Iraq's security apparatus in 2016.

Objectives: Combat ISIS and expel US and foreign forces from Iraq.

Opponents: ISIS, US and US-allied forces.

Affiliates/allies: SCF, Iraqi Armed Forces and IRGC.

Resources/capabilities: PMU units possess a diverse array of resources, including weaponry, vehicles and logistical support, enabling them to operate effectively in various environments.

Islamic State (ISIS)

Strength: Approximately 500 fighters in Iraq.[7]

Areas of operation: Active predominantly in Iraq's northern and central provinces in mountainous and desert areas.

Leadership: Abu Hafs al-Hashimi al-Qurashi (calif and leader of ISIS).

Structure: Its structure comprises a core leadership, regional commanders and a decentralised network of smaller cells executing attacks and propaganda campaigns.

History: Emerged in Iraq circa 2003 and sought to establish a caliphate during the Syrian civil war. From 2014–17, it controlled vast territories in Iraq and Syria, governing over eight million people. However, since 2017 in Iraq and 2019 in Syria, ISIS has lost control of all the territories it previously held.

Objectives: Establish Sunni sharia-based rule.

Opponents: Iraqi Armed Forces, CTS, Kurdish Peshmerga, PMU and CJTF–OIR.

Affiliates/allies: ISIS fighters in other countries.

Resources/capabilities: Light weaponry and improvised explosive devices.

Kurdish Peshmerga

Strength: Between 200,000 and 300,000 (estimate).[8]

Areas of operation: KRG.

Leadership: Nechirvan Barzani (commander-in-chief) and Staff Lt-Gen. Issa Ozer (chief of staff of the Ministry of Peshmerga).

Kurdish Peshmerga

Structure: A Kurdish paramilitary force that acts as the military of the KRG and Iraqi Kurdistan. While remaining independent, it operates officially as part of the Kurdish military system. Peshmerga forces are divided between political factions, the most dominant being the KDP and the PUK.

History: Began as a Kurdish nationalist movement in the 1920s and soon developed into a security organisation. Following the ISIS advance, the Peshmerga took disputed territories in June 2014 – including Kirkuk – which were retaken by Iraqi forces in October 2017.

Objectives: Ensure security in the KRG, including by fighting ISIS.

Opponents: ISIS, PKK and PMU.

Affiliates/allies: CJTF–OIR and Iraqi Armed Forces.

Resources/capabilities: Poorly equipped, lacking heavy weapons, armoured vehicles and facilities. The US has provided some financial assistance along with small arms and light weapons.

Kurdistan Workers' Party (PKK)

Strength: 4,000–5,000 (estimate) in Turkiye and Iraq.[9]

Areas of operation: Sinjar, northern Iraq.

Leadership: Abdullah Öcalan (ideological leader, despite his imprisonment since 1999), Murat Karayilan (acting leader on the ground since Öcalan's capture) and Bahoz Erdal (military commander).

Structure: While operating under the same command and leadership, the PKK's armed wing is divided into the People's Defence Forces (HPG) and the Free Women's Unit (YJA-STAR).

History: Founded by Öcalan in 1978. The PKK has been engaged in an insurgency campaign against the Turkish Armed Forces (TSK) since 1984.

Objectives: Preserve its operational autonomy and capacity with a base of operation in Iraq to support its broader agenda in Turkiye.

Opponents: TSK and Kurdish Peshmerga.

Affiliates/allies: Sinjar Alliance in Iraq, PMU and Syrian Democratic Forces/People's Protection Units (SDF/YPG) in Syria.

Resources/capabilities: Generates revenue through money-laundering activities and drug trafficking in addition to donations from the Kurdish community and diaspora and left-wing international supporters. The PKK relies on highly mobile units, using guerrilla tactics against Turkish military targets. It is reported to be equipped with counter-drone technology.

Turkish Armed Forces (TSK)

Strength: 4,000 military personnel in Iraq.[10]

Areas of operation: Northern Iraq, especially Dohuk and Nineva plains.

Leadership: President Recep Tayyip Erdoğan (commander-in-chief), Gen. Yaşar Güler (minister of national defence) and Gen. Metin Gürak (chief of general staff).

Structure: Turkish army units operating under the Turkish Land Forces Command and squadrons carrying out airstrikes operating under the Air Force Command are subordinate to the chief of general staff. Gendarmerie units reporting to the Gendarmerie Command are subordinate to the Ministry of Interior.

History: Rebuilt after the collapse of the Ottoman Empire in 1922. The TSK was significantly restructured after the country joined NATO in 1951 and is currently NATO's second-largest armed force.

Objectives: Defend Turkish territorial integrity; combat the PKK and its allied forces, preventing them from establishing safe havens and mobility corridors in northern Iraq; and prevent the PMU from overrunning Sinjar and establishing a land corridor to Syria for Iran.

Opponents: PKK, Sinjar Alliance and PMU.

Affiliates/allies: KDP and miscellaneous local militias, such as those connected to the Iraqi Turkmen Front, which have received some training from Turkish special forces since 2015.

Resources/capabilities: Turkiye's defence budget for 2023 was US$8.7 billion. Its military capabilities include combat aircraft, intelligence, surveillance and reconnaissance assets, armoured vehicles and special-forces units.

Combined Joint Task Force–*Operation Inherent Resolve* (CJTF–OIR)

Strength: 2,000–2,500 military personnel in Iraq (estimate).

Areas of operation: Works in tandem with the ISF in areas previously held by ISIS, including Anbar, Diyala, Nineva and Salahaddin.

Leadership: Maj.-Gen. Joel B. Vowell (commanding officer).

Structure: The CJTF–OIR is led and primarily staffed by the US military, with smaller contributions from allies and partners.

History: Created in October 2014 when the US Department of Defense formalised ongoing military operations against ISIS.

Objectives: Fight ISIS in Iraq and Syria, through airstrikes in support of Iraqi and Kurdish forces.

Opponents: ISIS and PMU.

Affiliates/allies: Iraqi Armed Forces, CTS and Kurdish Peshmerga.

Resources/capabilities: Light weapons, combat aircraft, uninhabited aerial vehicles, short-range air- and missile-defence systems, and armoured vehicles.

Notes

1. Aaron Y. Zelin and Ilana Winter, 'One Year of the Islamic State Worldwide Activity Map', Washington Institute for Near East Policy, 20 March 2024.
2. Reuters, 'Iran Says Revolutionary Guards Attack Israel's "Spy HQ" in Iraq, Vow More Revenge', VOA, 16 January 2024.
3. Dana Taib Menmy, 'What Is Driving Ethnic Tensions in Iraq's Kirkuk?', New Arab, 13 September 2023.
4. Shimaa Ali, 'Between Power Sharing and Power Consolidation: The Impact of Iraq's Provincial Elections Results', Washington Institute for Near East Policy, 7 March 2024.
5. Bekir Aydoğan, 'Iraqi Kurds Face Legitimacy Issues Amid Election Deadlock and Internal Division', Washington Institute for Near East Policy, 7 August 2023.
6. Ruwayda Mustafah, 'A House Divided: Can Kurdistan Preserve Its Autonomy?', Washington Institute for Near East Policy, 27 March 2024.
7. 'Up to 500 IS Fighters Still Active in Iraq: Military', *Defense Post*, 14 March 2023.
8. Bilal Wahab, 'The Rise and Fall of Kurdish Power in Iraq', Washington Institute for Near East Policy, Spring 2023.
9. Bureau of Counterterrorism, US Department of State, 'Country Reports on Terrorism 2021', 2021, p. 300.
10. 'Irak Savunma Bakanlığı raporu: TSK, Irak sınırının 105 km derinliğine kadar girdi' [Iraqi Ministry of Defense report: TAF penetrated to a depth of 105 km of the Iraqi border], Rûdaw, 23 July 2022.

138 Middle East and North Africa

ISRAEL–PALESTINIAN TERRITORIES

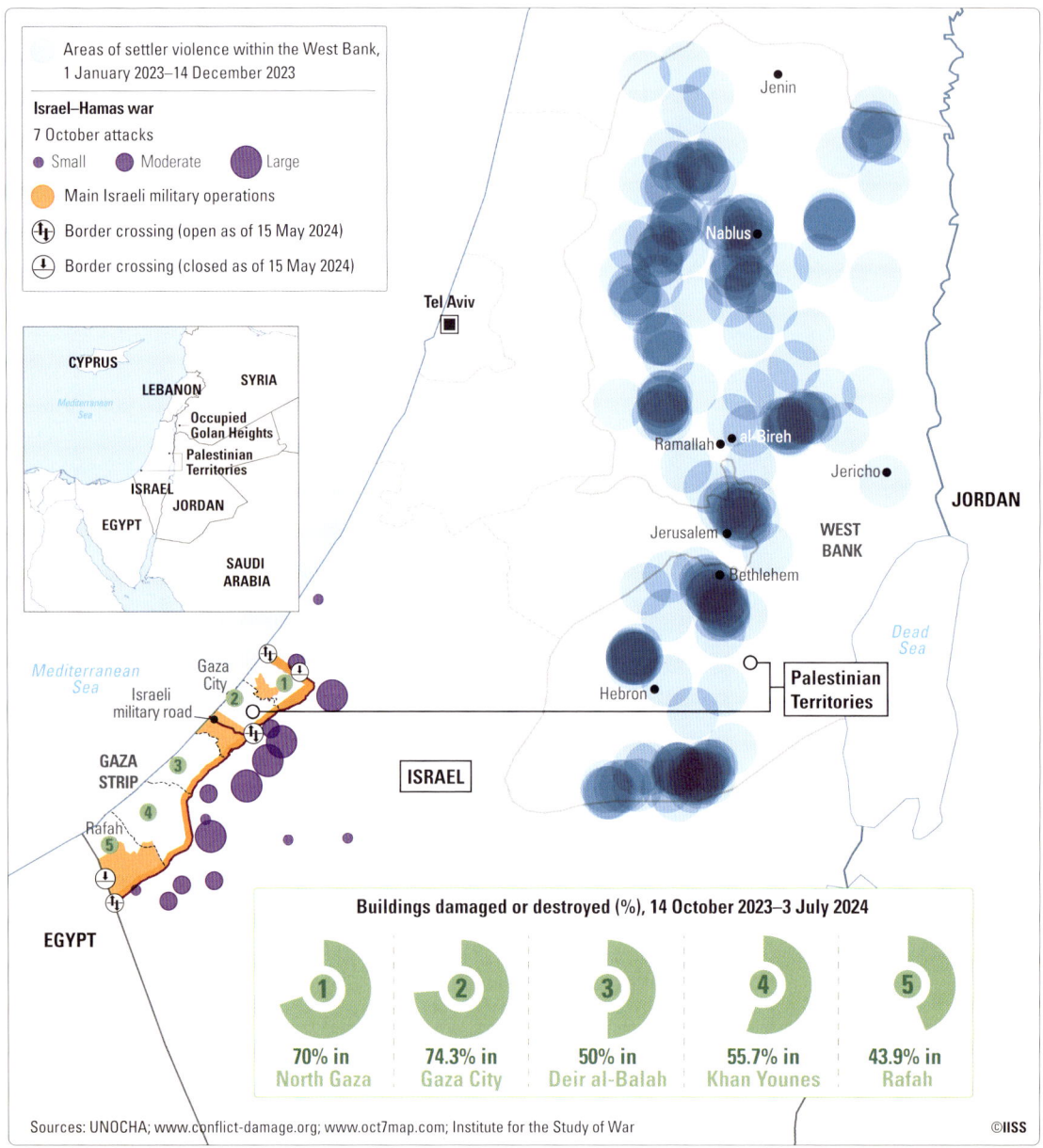

Conflict Overview

The Israel–Palestinian Territories conflict has been ongoing for nearly three-quarters of a century. In November 1947, the United Nations General Assembly adopted Resolution 181, which called for the division of Mandatory Palestine into Jewish and Arab states, inciting conflict between Jewish Zionist and Arab Palestinian groups. By May 1948, the Zionist leadership announced the creation of the state of Israel. An Arab intervention to support the Palestinians, who rejected the partition plan, was defeated. It was followed by the expansion of the Israeli state and the expulsion of approximately 750,000 Palestinians. The

Country Profile: Israel–Palestinian Territories

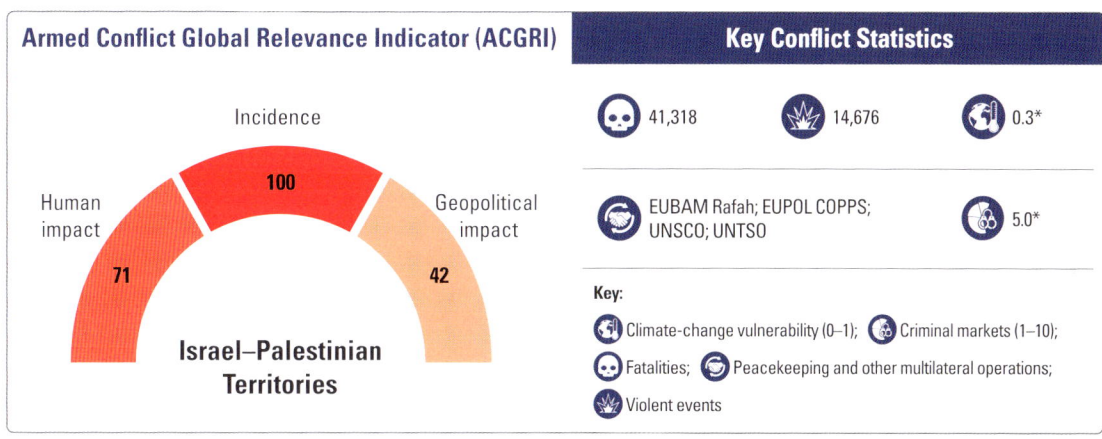

ACGRI pillars: IISS calculation based on multiple sources for 2023 and 2024 (scale: 0–100), except for some cases according to data availability. See Notes on Methodology and Data Appendix for all variables and further details on Key Conflict Statistics. *For Israel only.

Conflict(s)	Type	Start date
War between Hamas and Israel in Gaza	II I-S	2023; recurrent since 2000
Settlers' violence in the West Bank	II I-S	2023; recurrent since 2000
Border conflict and armed attacks between Hizbullah and Israel	T	1982

Key: II Internationalised internal; I-S Inter-state; T Transnational

subsequent 1967 Six-Day War and the 1973 Arab–Israeli War saw Israel triple the size of its territory by capturing East Jerusalem and the West Bank from Jordan; the Gaza Strip and the Sinai Peninsula from Egypt; and the Golan Heights from Syria.

Parts of the West Bank are currently governed by the Palestinian Authority (PA), while the Gaza Strip, which Israel evacuated in 2005, is now ruled by Hamas. The latter group took control of the area in 2006 after a brief civil war with the PA when the Palestinian Territories were de facto split between the two groups. A series of wars between Hamas and Israel then followed in 2008–09, 2012, 2014 and 2021.Israeli occupation, denial of rights and deteriorating socio-economic conditions sparked Palestinian uprisings (intifadas) against Israel in 1987–93 and 2000–05.

Since 2020, armed groups have proliferated in the West Bank in the context of the PA's eroding legitimacy. Subsequent Israeli incursions into the territory led the PA to suspend security coordination with Israel in January 2023, while Israeli authorities have withheld tax revenues collected on behalf of the PA since June 2022, deepening the economic crisis there. The 2020 United States-brokered Abraham Accords – which established diplomatic relations between Israel and Bahrain, Morocco, Sudan and the United Arab Emirates (UAE) – have failed to produce dividends for the Palestinians. Israeli settlement expansion has continued unabated, despite initial reports of a settlement freeze. With peace talks between the parties stalled since the 1993 Oslo Accords, violence has risen in recent years.

Conflict Update

The Hamas-led 7 October 2023 attacks against Israel were unprecedented in scope and destruction, killing the highest number of Jewish people in one day since the Holocaust. Fighters from Hamas and other Palestinian armed groups killed around 1,200 individuals, mostly civilians, injured more than 5,400, and took 253 Israelis and dual nationals hostage as well as dozens of foreigners.[1] By the end of June 2024, 116 hostages had been released, although it is unclear how many of the remaining captives are still alive.[2]

Planned for at least a year, the complex attacks were multi-pronged and simultaneous against villages, *kibbutzim* (communal settlements) and military barracks bordering the Gaza Strip. Israeli security services failed to correctly analyse the warning signs. As a result, the attackers encountered little resistance and it took days for Israeli forces to retake control of Israeli towns.

In response to the attacks, and with the full-throated support of the US and European countries, Israel first carried out intense aerial bombardment followed by a large-scale ground offensive in Gaza (which was ongoing as of June 2024). This resulted in the deaths of more than 35,000 Palestinians, displaced around 1.9 million people (90% of the population of Gaza) and left 1.1m civilians facing catastrophic levels of food insecurity.[3]

Despite the large-scale operation, Israel is struggling to achieve its two main aims of freeing the hostages and destroying Hamas. By the end of June 2024, the Israel Defense Forces (IDF) had struggled to liberate hostages alive. It had degraded Hamas's command and battalion structure, but it had not managed to completely eradicate its ability to launch rockets on Israeli territory.

Israel's military strategy has drawn criticism from within Israel and externally. Israeli Prime Minister Benjamin Netanyahu, who was facing large protests over divisive constitutional changes, has been accused by part of the Israeli populace and political establishment of prioritising his own political survival by prolonging the war. In June, Benny Gantz resigned from the war cabinet and backed holding early elections, while Netanyahu has chosen to pander to his far-right coalition partners. Domestically, the IDF and Israeli settlers have also stepped up their attacks in the West Bank, supported by the governing far-right coalition that wants to make the two-state solution impossible. Since 7 October, an estimated 539 Palestinians have been killed in the West Bank, mostly by the IDF.[4]

Other Iran-backed non-state armed groups (NSAGs) like Ansarullah (the Houthis) in Yemen and Hizbullah in Lebanon have ramped up their attacks against Israel and Israeli interests. The Houthi attacks have primarily served to further legitimise the group in Arab countries. On the Lebanon front, Israel has maintained escalation dominance, but at a significant cost. For the first time in its history, Israel has had to evacuate its northern villages as a result of Hizbullah's attacks and threats. Regionally, a new line was crossed on 14 April 2024 when Iran's Islamic Revolutionary Guard Corps (IRGC) launched an unprecedented attack on Israel in retaliation for an Israeli attack on its consulate in Damascus that killed high-level IRGC commanders on 1 April. Iran launched 170 uninhabited aerial vehicles (UAVs), 30 cruise missiles and 110 ballistic missiles. Israel claims to have intercepted 99% of these thanks to its air-defence system and a regional air-defence coalition coordinated by the US and involving France, Jordan and the United Kingdom.[5]

Despite the indignation of their populations, Arab countries have largely limited their actions to expressions of outrage at the high civilian death toll among Palestinians, and none have exacted a diplomatic or economic price on Israel. Bahrain, Egypt, Jordan, Morocco and the UAE have ring-fenced their diplomatic agreements with Israel – both peace agreements and the Abraham Accords. Of these countries, only Egypt has supported the South African case of genocide against Israel at the International Criminal Court (the second Arab country to do so after Libya), and only after Israel moved into the Philadelphi Corridor at the Egyptian–Gaza border in May. Saudi Arabia has used strong terms to denounce Israel's war conduct but has quietly pressed on with normalisation talks through the US. In contrast, Turkiye has taken a strong diplomatic position against Israel by downgrading diplomatic and commercial relations.

Internationally, even as the US administration and large parts of Congress have provided unconditional and large-scale military, diplomatic and political support for Israel, unprecedented criticism of Israel's war methods has arisen in US public opinion and the political establishment. At the beginning of May, the Biden administration paused the delivery of 1,800 2,000 pound (907 kilogram) bombs and 1,700 500 lb (771 kg) bombs, but remains reluctant to use decisive pressure to end the war.[6] Meanwhile, European Union countries have been split over their positions towards Israel, which has paralysed the bloc's ability to use its leverage – including its trade relationship or association agreement with Tel Aviv – to influence the conduct of the war.

Conflict Parties

Israel Defense Forces (IDF)

Strength: 169,500 active military and 465,000 in reserve.

Areas of operation: Gaza Strip, Lebanon, Syria and the West Bank.

Leadership: Lt-Gen. Herzi Halevi (chief of staff since January 2023).

Structure: Three service branches consisting of the air force, army and navy.

History: The IDF was founded in 1948 from Jewish paramilitary organisations the Haganah and, to a lesser extent, the Etzel (also known as the Irgun) and Lehi, all of which fought during the 1948 Arab–Israeli War.

Objectives: Defend Israel.

Opponents: Hamas, Hizbullah, Houthis, IRGC, Iran-backed groups, Islamic State (ISIS) and Palestinian Islamic Jihad (PIJ).

Affiliates/allies: Israel is a major non-NATO ally of the US and has a mutual defence-assistance agreement with the country.

Resources/capabilities: Possesses sophisticated equipment and training and is one of the principal recipients of US military aid. Israel has a highly capable defence industry, including aerospace; intelligence, surveillance and reconnaissance; and counter-rocket systems. It is also believed to have an operational nuclear-weapons capability, although estimates of the size of this arsenal vary.

Hamas

Strength: Prior to October 2023, Hamas's military wing, the Izz al-Din al-Qassam Brigades (IDQ), was estimated to comprise 30,000 fighters, including 400 naval commandos.[7] Reliable estimates since the start of the war are unavailable.

Areas of operation: Gaza Strip, Israel, Lebanon and the West Bank.

Leadership: Yahya Sinwar (head of Hamas and chief of the Political Bureau). Sinwar's predecessor as chief of the Political Bureau, Ismail Haniyyeh, was assassinated in Tehran on 31 July 2024, allegedly by Israel. Mohamad Deif, who had been head of the IDQ, was also confirmed dead by Israel on 1 August 2024.

Structure: Sinwar has ultimate authority, but he also confers with the group's Shura Council and Political Bureau, as well as the IDQ. He has deepened links to the IRGC and Hizbullah.

History: Founded in 1987 by members of the Muslim Brotherhood in the Palestinian Territories, Hamas is the largest Palestinian militant Islamist group. Australia, Canada, the EU, the UK and the US have designated it a terrorist group. However, many Palestinians view Hamas as a legitimate popular-resistance group.

Objectives: Hamas's original charter called for the destruction of Israel and for the full liberation of Palestine, but Haniyyeh announced in 2008 that Hamas would accept a Palestinian state within the borders of the pre-1967 war. This was confirmed in a new charter in 2017.

Opponents: Fatah-led PA, Israel, PIJ (periodically) and Salafi-jihadist groups.

Affiliates/allies: IRGC and Hizbullah.

Resources/capabilities: The IDQ's capabilities include artillery rockets, mortars and anti-tank systems. Israel's military actions have periodically degraded Hamas's command and physical infrastructure but have seemingly had little effect on the IDQ's long-term ability to import and produce rockets and other weapons.

Palestinian Islamic Jihad (PIJ)

Strength: Prior to October 2023, the PIJ's armed wing, the al-Quds Brigades, was estimated to comprise up to 8,000 fighters.[8] Reliable estimates since the start of the war are unavailable.

Areas of operation: Gaza Strip, Israel, Lebanon and the West Bank.

Leadership: Ziad al-Nakhaleh.

Structure: Governed by a 15-member leadership council. In 2018, the PIJ council elected nine new members to represent its members in the West Bank, the Gaza Strip, Israeli prisons and abroad.

History: Established in 1979 by Fathi Shaqaqi and Abd al-Aziz Awda, who were members of the Egyptian Muslim Brotherhood until the late 1970s. Of the Gaza-based militant groups, the PIJ poses the most significant challenge to Hamas's authority there, having derailed unofficial ceasefire agreements between Hamas and Israel in the past.

Objectives: The destruction of Israel and the establishment of a sovereign, Islamic Palestinian state within the borders of pre-1948 Palestine.

Opponents: Fatah-led PA, Israel and Hamas (periodically).

Affiliates/allies: IRGC, Hizbullah and Syria.

Resources/capabilities: The PIJ has expanded the size of its weapons cache by producing its own rockets. Before the August 2022 hostilities between Israel and the Palestinian factions in Gaza, the PIJ was estimated to have between 6,000 and 7,000 rockets.[9] Reliable estimates since the start of the Israel–Hamas war in October 2023 are unavailable.

Hizbullah

Strength: 40,000–50,000 fighters in Lebanon.[10]

Areas of operation: Iraq, Lebanon, Syria and Yemen.

Hizbullah

Leadership: Hassan Nasrallah (secretary-general since 1992).

Structure: Nasrallah oversees the military, political and social activities of the group. He has an official direct line to Sayyid Ali Khamenei (Iran's supreme leader), Esmail Qaani (leader of the IRGC Quds Force) and Iran's Guardian Council. Hizbullah's overall military structure is unclear, but at least two units have made a public name for themselves: the External Security Organization, which is in charge of Hizbullah's overseas operations and global financial network, and the Redwan Force, a group of special commandos.

History: Formed in the wake of Israel's 1982 invasion of Lebanon, it was inspired by the Iranian Revolution of 1979. Its leadership adheres to the Iranian Islamist Wilayat al-Faqih doctrine and received crucial early support and training from hundreds of military advisers from the IRGC. It built a highly trained and well-equipped fighting force and a vast network of social organisations to cater to the Shia population of Lebanon.

Objectives: Hizbullah is the crown jewel of Iran's forward conventional deterrence, especially against any possible Israeli attacks that would pose an existential threat to the Islamic Republic. The IRGC's crucial involvement in the creation of Hizbullah was done with this goal in mind. Hizbullah also aims to liberate Lebanese land still occupied by Israel, believes in the destruction of Israel and, when it was first created, wanted to increase the power of the marginalised Shia community.

Opponents: Israel and IDF, Syrian revolutionary groups, Jabhat Fatah al-Sham (formerly Jabhat al-Nusra or Al-Nusra Front), ISIS and US.

Affiliates/allies: IRGC, Syrian Armed Forces, Houthis and Iraqi Popular Mobilisation Units (PMU).

Resources/capabilities: Rockets, surface-to-surface ballistic missiles, anti-ship missiles, man-portable anti-tank guided missile systems and armed UAVs.

The Houthi movement (Ansarullah)

Strength: 150,000–200,000 (estimate).[11]

Areas of operation: The group controls much of northern Yemen, parts of the Red Sea coast in and around Hudaydah, and parts of Marib. It has targeted commercial ships it claims are linked to Israel, the UK and the US in the Red Sea and fired missiles and UAVs at Israel since the beginning of the Israel–Hamas war in October 2023.

Leadership: Abdul Malik al-Houthi.

Structure: Abdul Malik al-Houthi is the leader of Ansarullah; however, formally, power in Houthi-controlled areas rests with the Supreme Political Council, headed by President Mahdi al-Mashat. Real political power is held by a group of 'supervisors', mostly *sayyids*, who are appointed by Ansarullah and who shadow the government officials.

History: Beginning as a Zaydi revivalist movement, the Houthis fought a series of insurgencies against the Yemeni government from 2004–10 before taking control of Sanaa and most of northern Yemen in 2014–15.

Objectives: Domestically, the movement aims to hold and govern at least northern Yemen. Internationally, its objective is to play a leading role in the Iran-supported Axis of Resistance by targeting Israel and Western shipping, purportedly in solidarity with the Palestinian resistance.

Opponents: Domestically, the internationally recognised Yemeni government, backed by the Saudi-led coalition. Internationally, Israel and its Western allies, in particular the US and UK.

Affiliates/allies: Iran, Hizbullah and PMU.

Resources/capabilities: Ballistic missiles, cruise missiles and UAVs capable of targeting Israel, neighbouring states such as Saudi Arabia and the UAE, and ships in the Red Sea and the Gulf of Aden. US and UK military operations in Yemen since January 2024 (*Operation Poseidon Archer*) may have degraded the group's capabilities. However, they have not eliminated its ability to manufacture rockets, missiles and UAVs and to fire these at Israel or ships in the Red Sea.

Islamic Revolutionary Guard Corps (IRGC)

Strength: Up to 190,000 active military.

Areas of operation: Iraq, Lebanon, Syria and Yemen.

Leadership: Maj.-Gen. Hossein Salami.

Structure: The IRGC has four main forces: ground, naval, aerospace and Quds. The Quds Force has by far the greatest international reputation and reach. It is the IRGC's unconventional force with a mandate to engage in extraterritorial low-intensity conflicts. The commander of the IRGC is part of the Supreme National Security Council (SNSC) that reports directly to the supreme leader, and the commander of the IRGC's Quds Force is a non-statutory participant in the SNSC.

History: The IRGC was established in April 1979 by the first supreme leader of the Islamic Republic Ayatollah Ruhollah Khomeini to counterbalance the military, which was seen as too Western and suspect, and to gather the hundreds of armed groups associated with the revolutionary committees that dominated Iran in 1979. Its initial focus was on destroying the armed leftist, monarchist, communist and ethnic elements who opposed the new Islamic Republic's ideology. It became Iran's dominant military force. The Quds Force was established in the first years of the Iran–Iraq War from intelligence and special-forces units.

Objectives: The IRGC is in charge of the defence of Iran's territorial integrity and Iran's large network of influence across the region, playing a vital role for groups like Hizbullah, the Houthis and Iraqi armed groups.

Opponents: US, Israel and IDF, Syrian revolutionary groups, Jabhat Fatah al-Sham and ISIS.

Islamic Revolutionary Guard Corps (IRGC)

Affiliates/allies: Syrian Armed Forces, Hizbullah, Houthis and PMU.

Resources/capabilities: Air-defence systems, surface-to-surface missile launchers, fixed-wing aircraft, rotary-wing aircraft, UAVs, loitering and direct-attack munitions, amphibious vessels and coastal-defence systems.

Other relevant parties

Several small armed resistance groups, loosely tied to the PIJ, Hamas and al-Aqsa Martyrs' Brigade, have emerged across the West Bank. These groups are very localised and are generally comprised of young men. The Lion's Den, the Nablus Brigade and the Jenin Brigades are reportedly the largest of such groups. Unaffiliated with the traditional parties of the conflict, their political agendas are unclear. They conduct primarily defensive operations in response to Israeli raids and operations in the West Bank, although they have occasionally attacked Israeli military infrastructure and settlers.

Notes

[1] UN Office for the Coordination of Humanitarian Affairs (UNOCHA), 'Hostilities in the Gaza Strip and Israel – Reported Impact | Day 203', 26 April 2024; and Kathleen Magramo et al., 'January 17, 2024 Israel–Hamas War', CNN, 18 January 2024.

[2] 'Hamas Hostages: Stories of the People Taken from Israel', BBC News, 1 September 2024.

[3] UNOCHA, 'Hostilities in the Gaza Strip and Israel – Reported Impact | Day 202', 15 May 2024; UNOCHA, 'Occupied Palestinian Territory'; UN Relief and Works Agency for Palestine Refugees in the Near East, 'UNRWA Situation Report #119 on the Situation in the Gaza Strip and the West Bank, Including East Jerusalem', 9 July 2024.

[4] UNOCHA, 'Humanitarian Situation Update #186 | West Bank', 3 July 2024.

[5] 'What Was in Wave of Iranian Attacks and How Were They Thwarted?', BBC News, 15 April 2024.

[6] Tara Copp, 'Why the US Paused the Delivery of 2,000-pound Bombs to Israel Ahead of a Possible Rafah Attack', AP News, 8 May 2024.

[7] 'Senior IDF Commander Says Hamas Has 30,000 Men, 7,000 Rockets, Dozens of Drones', *Times of Israel*, 11 February 2021.

[8] Australian National Security, 'Palestinian Islamic Jihad', 17 January 2022.

[9] Shai Levy, '"עלות השחר": מה ההבדל בין מבצע מול הג'יהאד לכזה מול החמאס?' ['Dawn': what is the difference between an operation against jihad and one against Hamas?], Mako, 6 August 2022.

[10] Clayton Thomas and Jim Zanotti, 'Lebanese Hezbollah', IF10703, Congressional Research Service, 10 May 2024.

[11] See Justin Salhani, 'Houthis Are Recruiting Record Fighters. How Will This Affect Yemen?', Al-Jazeera, 23 February 2024.

LEBANON

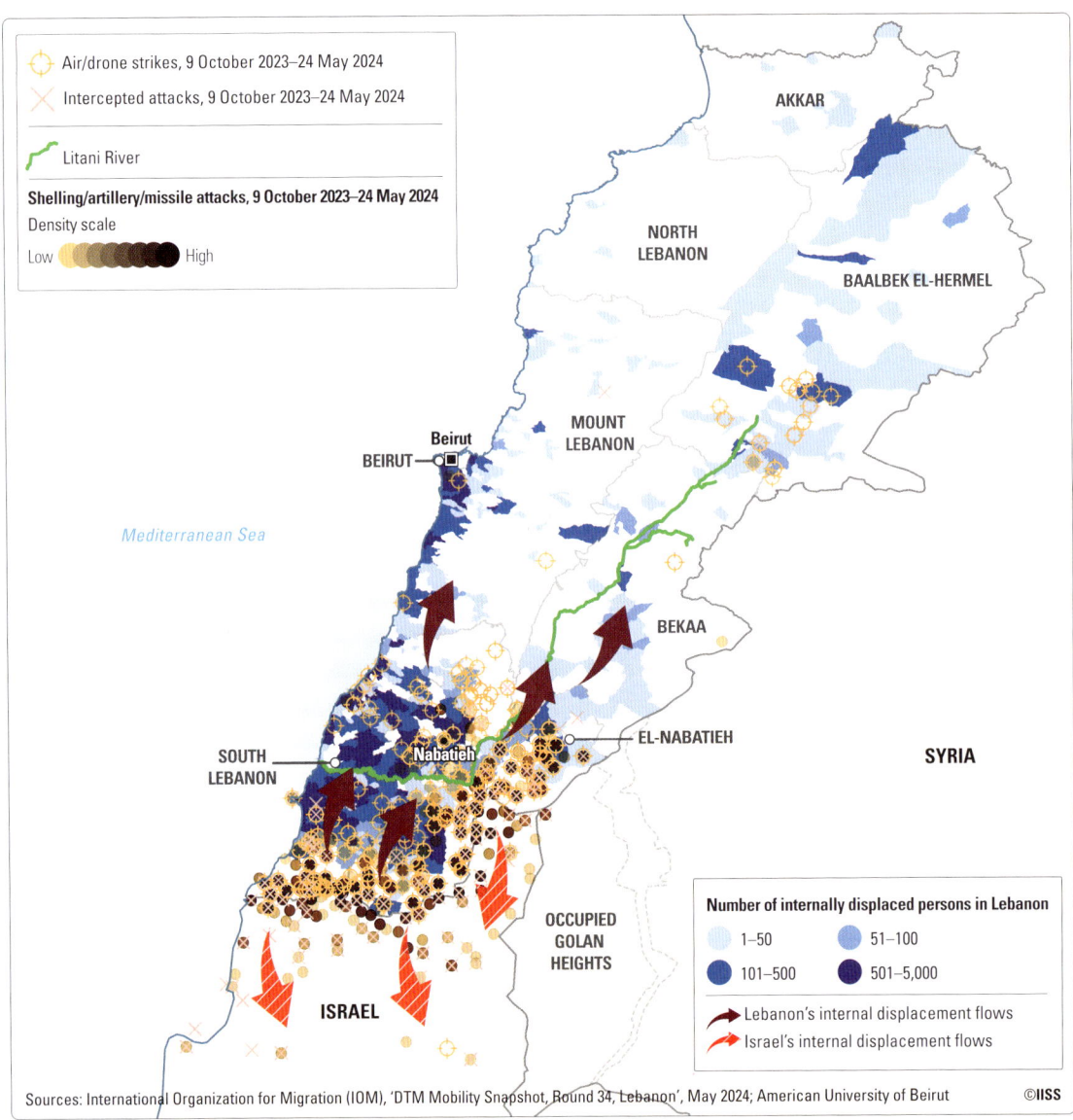

Conflict Overview

Israel and Lebanon have been in conflict since the establishment of the Jewish state in 1948. The conflict has been tied to the Israel–Palestinian Territories conflict and the displacement of Palestinians, 500,000 of whom are still refugees in Lebanon.[1] Lebanon only played a minor role in the 1967 Six-Day War and did not participate in the 1973 Arab–Israeli War. However, in March 1978, Lebanon-based militants attacked Israel, leading to a full-blown military conflict. As violence intensified, Israel launched a new invasion in June 1982.

With Lebanon suffering from a weak central state and fragmented social fabric, Hizbullah emerged in the 1980s from the chronically marginalised Muslim Shia community. It had the direct support of the newly established Islamic Republic of Iran

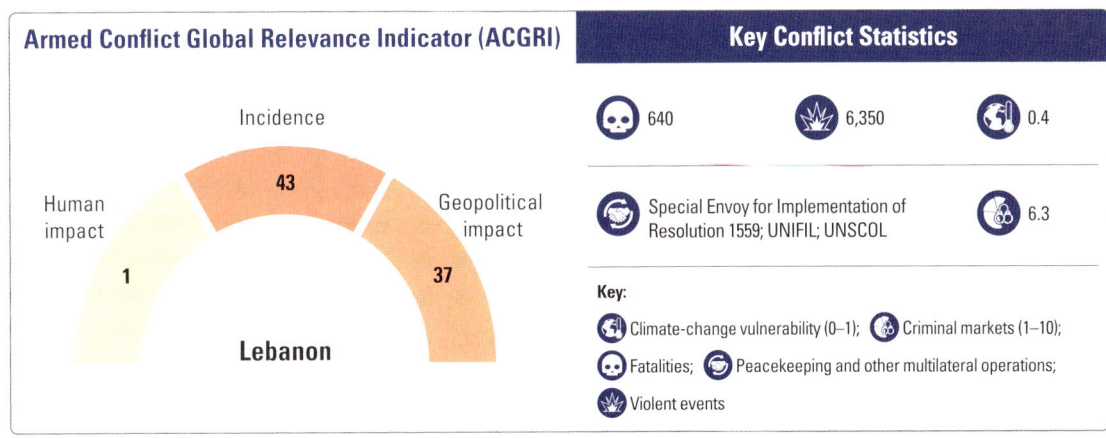

through the Islamic Revolutionary Guard Corps (IRGC), which aimed to project power and build a deterrent force on Israel's border.[2] Progressively, Hizbullah effectively became dominant over the Lebanese state, with an armed wing that is better equipped and financed than the Lebanese Armed Forces (LAF).

Three areas, the Shebaa Farms, Ghajar and the Kfar Chouba hills, situated along the border between Lebanon and Syria's Golan Heights (occupied by Israel since 1967), remain disputed. These comprise the central focus of continuing tensions between Israel and Hizbullah. The status of these areas is further complicated by the lack of border demarcation between Lebanon and Syria.

Hizbullah and Israel fought two major wars in July 1993 and April 1996. In May 2000, Israeli forces withdrew from southern Lebanon under the orders of then-prime minister Ehud Barak. However, cross-border tensions continued between the two sides, and in July 2006, after Hizbullah fighters abducted two Israeli soldiers from across the border, Israel launched a massive war that killed 1,191 Lebanese citizens and displaced over 900,000 people.[3]

The formal end of hostilities was marked by the adoption of United Nations Security Council (UNSC) Resolution 1701, which, among other things, called for the deployment of the LAF to the border with Israel; the disarmament of non-state armed groups (NSAGs) (including Hizbullah) and their withdrawal from border areas; and the respect by Israel of Lebanon's sovereignty. To this day, neither party has implemented the resolution. Instead, since 2006, Israel and Hizbullah have developed implicit rules of engagement that have established a new balance of deterrence between the two sides. As long as their exchanges of fire are contained to the three areas in dispute, no large-scale escalation follows. Israel has regularly gone after Hizbullah commanders in both Lebanon and Syria, while Hizbullah has shelled Israeli border towns. Hamas and the Palestinian Islamic Jihad (PIJ) have also carried out sporadic and limited attacks against Israel from Lebanese territory, ostensibly with the tacit approval of Hizbullah.

Conflict Update

The reporting period was dominated by the fallout of the Hamas-led 7 October 2023 attacks against Israel that killed around 1,200 individuals.[4] In a minimal show of solidarity with

Hamas, Hizbullah carried out limited shelling of a handful of Israeli locations close to the border with Israel in the days following the attacks. Both groups, along with Iran, had announced months prior a new approach to their conflict with Israel that consisted of uniting their fronts, but had not defined the concept in much detail. This triggered an intensification and steady escalation of the tit-for-tat strikes Israel and Hizbullah have been routinely engaging in since 2006.

By the end of the reporting period, the confrontation between the two sides had not yet tipped into an all-out war, but the risks remained elevated. In the absence of a diplomatic solution, the likelihood of a war will increase when Israeli operations in Gaza end and more forces can be diverted north. The forced displacement of tens of thousands of Israelis from towns close to the Lebanese border and the failure of the state to prevent an unprecedented deadly attack within Israel's 1967 borders have made the status quo with Hizbullah no longer acceptable for most Israelis.[5]

In the days following 7 October, Hizbullah's posture was deterred by the swift deployment of United States carrier strike groups into the Eastern Mediterranean along with a US warning not to attack Israel. As Israel's attacks in Gaza have become more intense, despite growing pressure from within Hizbullah ranks and a part of its constituency to escalate its responses to Israeli attacks, the armed group appears to have assessed that it is better off managing the escalation rather than risking consequential losses and large-scale destruction in a full-fledged war. The preservation of its status as Iran's ultimate conventional deterrence tool has prevailed, though the long-term effects on its credibility remain unclear. The dire socio-economic context in Lebanon since the 2019 financial crisis has also played a moderating role.

The Israeli war cabinet, managing two unprecedented blows – one to its security doctrine and the other resulting from the forced displacement of around 60,000 people from its northern towns – has consistently communicated its willingness and preparedness to escalate into a full-blown war with Lebanon.[6] Israel's promise to its people has been, since its inception, that it would be the safest place for Jews in the world, and that it would have the most powerful intelligence services and military in the region in order to prevent a deadly attack within its borders. This security doctrine was built on repressing Palestinians in the occupied territories and regular wars with Hizbullah in Lebanon to keep the fighting outside of Israel. This sense of security was shattered on 7 October.

As a result, Israel has maintained escalation dominance with Hizbullah since Hamas's attacks, dictating the tempo and geographic spread. It created a de facto uninhabitable buffer zone four kilometres within Lebanese territory, including through the prohibited use of white phosphorus and forced displacement of more than 96,829 Lebanese civilians.[7] The Israeli military has claimed that it has killed over 300 Hizbullah operatives, including both rank fighters and middle and senior commanders, while at least 97 civilians have also been killed.[8] In a bid to degrade Hizbullah's fighting capabilities, Tel Aviv targeted its command-and-control centres, missile launchpads, weapons depots, and medium- to high-level commanders.

Israeli offensive activity also extended to Syria, where it targeted Hizbullah as well as the capabilities and commanders of the IRGC. Both Hizbullah and the IRGC have supported the Syrian government against rebel forces, and Hizbullah has used its activities in Syria to extend its presence along Israel's border, operating opposite the Syrian Golan Heights.

As of June 2024, Israeli attacks on Hizbullah and Iranian interests did not seem to have crossed the threshold that warrants an all-out war, despite the unusual direct attack by Iran on Israel on 13 April. This calculus could change in the latter half of the year, depending on how the rest of the Israel–Hamas war unfolds and on the tempo and targets of Israeli attacks in Lebanon and Syria.

Conflict Parties

Lebanese Armed Forces (LAF)

Strength: 60,000 active military.

Areas of operation: Country wide.

Lebanese Armed Forces (LAF)

Leadership: Gen. Joseph Aoun (term expired in January 2024, extended until Lebanese parties agree on the election of a new president).

Structure: Three service branches consisting of the army, air force and navy, with the bulk of the capabilities concentrated in the army.

History: Established in 1943 as a multi-confessional force meant to act as an impartial arbiter among Lebanon's deeply divided social fabric. Its cohesion was severely tested during Lebanon's civil war and the Israeli invasion between 1975 and 1990, and it experienced multiple splits during that time. After the civil war ended, the LAF was rebuilt, and while it has remained a weak fighting force, it consistently ranks as the country's most trusted public institution.

Objectives: Defend Lebanon's national territory, which it did against Islamist militants like Fatah al-Islam in 2007 and the Islamic State (ISIS) and Jabhat Fateh al-Sham (formerly Jabhat al-Nusra or Al-Nusra Front) in 2014. The LAF has not fulfilled this role against Israel. Since the end of the civil war in 1990, the continued Israeli occupation of southern Lebanon until 2000, and Hizbullah's emergence as the dominant armed force in the country, the LAF has mainly been deployed for crowd control during phases of protests against the political class.

Opponents: Israel and Israel Defense Forces (IDF), Jabhat Fateh al-Sham, ISIS and Fatah al-Islam.

Affiliates/allies: No allies or affiliates, but considerable training and financial support from the US and France in addition to Germany, Italy and the United Kingdom.

Resources/capabilities: Limited military capabilities, mainly artillery, infantry and basic anti-tank and air-defence capabilities. It relies heavily on US and French financial and equipment support. Lebanon lacks a defence industry.

Hizbullah

Strength: 40,000–50,000 fighters in Lebanon.[9]

Areas of operation: Country wide in Lebanon; also present in Iraq, Syria and Yemen.

Leadership: Hassan Nasrallah (secretary-general since 1992).

Structure: Nasrallah oversees the military, political and social activities of the group. He has an official direct line to Sayyid Ali Khamenei (Iran's supreme leader), Esmail Qaani (leader of the IRGC Quds Force) and Iran's Guardian Council. Hizbullah's overall military structure is unclear, but at least two units have made a public name for themselves: the External Security Organization, which is in charge of Hizbullah's overseas operations and global financial network, and the Redwan Force, a group of special commandos.

History: Formed in the wake of Israel's 1982 invasion of Lebanon, Hizbullah was inspired by the Iranian Revolution of 1979. Its leadership adheres to the Iranian Islamist Wilayat al-Faqih doctrine and received crucial early support and training from hundreds of military advisers from the IRGC. It built a highly trained and well-equipped fighting force and a vast network of social organisations to cater to the Shia population of Lebanon.

Objectives: Hizbullah is the crown jewel of Iran's forward conventional deterrence, especially against any possible Israeli attacks that would pose an existential threat to the Islamic Republic. The IRGC's crucial involvement in the creation of Hizbullah was done with this goal in mind. Hizbullah also aims to liberate Lebanese land still occupied by Israel, believes in the destruction of Israel and, when it was first created, wanted to increase the power of the marginalised Shia community.

Opponents: Israel and IDF, Syrian revolutionary groups, Jabhat Fateh al-Sham, ISIS and US.

Affiliates/allies: IRGC, Syrian Armed Forces, Ansarullah (the Houthis) and Iraqi Popular Mobilisation Units.

Resources/capabilities: Rockets, surface-to-surface ballistic missiles, anti-ship missiles, man-portable anti-tank guided missile systems and armed uninhabited aerial vehicles.

Israel Defense Forces (IDF)

Strength: 169,500 active military and 465,000 in reserve.

Areas of operation: Gaza Strip, Lebanon, Syria and the West Bank.

Leadership: Lt-Gen. Herzi Halevi (chief of staff since January 2023).

Structure: Three service branches consisting of an air force, army and navy.

History: The IDF was founded in 1948 from Jewish paramilitary organisations the Haganah and, to a lesser extent, the Etzel (also known as the Irgun) and Lehi, all of which fought during the 1948 Arab–Israeli War.

Objectives: Defend Israel.

Opponents: Hamas, Hizbullah, Houthis, IRGC, Iran-backed groups, ISIS and PIJ.

Affiliates/allies: Israel is a major non-NATO ally of the US and has a mutual defence assistance agreement with the country.

Resources/capabilities: Possesses sophisticated equipment and training and is one of the principal recipients of US military aid. Israel has a highly capable defence industry, including aerospace; intelligence, surveillance and reconnaissance; and counter-rocket systems. It is also believed to have an operational nuclear-weapons capability, although estimates of the size of this arsenal vary.

United Nations Interim Force in Lebanon (UNIFIL)

Strength: 10,800, including 10,000 military peacekeepers and 800 civilian peacekeepers.[10]

Areas of operation: Southern Lebanon.

United Nations Interim Force in Lebanon (UNIFIL)

Leadership: Lt-Gen. Aroldo Lázaro Sáenz (head of mission and force commander since February 2022).

Structure: Peacekeepers from 48 contributing countries. It has a Civil Affairs unit and a Civil Military Coordination unit. It is mostly a ground component but also has a Maritime Task Force.

History: UNIFIL was first established in 1978 to confirm the withdrawal of Israeli troops that had invaded southern Lebanon and to help the Lebanese government restore its authority in the region. It has struggled to enforce its mandates since then, due to a lack of appropriate rules of engagement that would empower it to do so.

Objectives: Three UNSC resolutions (425 and 426 of 1978 and 1701 of 2006) define its current mandate. Since the end of the 2006 war between Hizbullah and Israel, its mission has been to monitor the cessation of hostilities; support the deployment of the LAF in southern Lebanon up until the border with Israel; help provide humanitarian assistance to civilian populations; assist the Lebanese government in removing NSAGs from southern Lebanon between the Litani River and the border with Israel; and assist the Lebanese government in securing the border.

Opponents: N/A.

Affiliates/allies: N/A.

Resources/capabilities: Four ships and six helicopters.[11]

Notes

[1] Data as of 2023. UN Relief and Works Agency for Palestine Refugees in the Near East, 'UNRWA Registered Population Dashboard'.

[2] There are 18 officially recognised religious groups in Lebanon, including five Muslim groups, 12 Christian ones and a Jewish group. Throughout the years, many of them have sought the backing of a foreign power. United States Department of State, 'Lebanon 2022 International Religious Freedom Report', May 2023.

[3] International Committee of the Red Cross, 'Israel/Lebanon/Hezbollah Conflict in 2006', How Does Law Protect in War?.

[4] 'Israel Revises Hamas Attack Death Toll to "Around 1,200"', Reuters, 10 November 2023.

[5] 'Gallant: Residents of Northern Border Towns Won't Return Before Hezbollah Pushed Away', *Times of Israel*, 6 December 2023.

[6] Tom Perry, 'Israel, Hezbollah Trade Fire, Israeli Minister Warns of "Hot Summer" at Lebanon Border', Reuters, 9 May 2024.

[7] UN Office for the Coordination of Humanitarian Affairs, 'Lebanon: Flash Update #21: Escalation of Hostilities in South Lebanon as of 27 June 2024', 3 July 2024.

[8] Hizbullah does not provide an overall tally of its losses, but based on its public announcements, which may not be an exhaustive account, more than 270 of its operatives had been killed by 30 April. *Ibid.*; Emanuel Fabian, 'IDF Says Some 4,500 Hezbollah Targets Hit, 300 Operatives Killed Since Start of War', *Times of Israel*, 12 March 2024; and '"We Are With Them": Lebanon Students Rally for Gaza', France 24, 30 April 2024.

[9] Clayton Thomas and Jim Zanotti, 'Lebanese Hezbollah', IF10703, Congressional Research Service, 10 May 2024.

[10] UNIFIL, 'UNIFIL by Numbers'.

[11] *Ibid*.

YEMEN

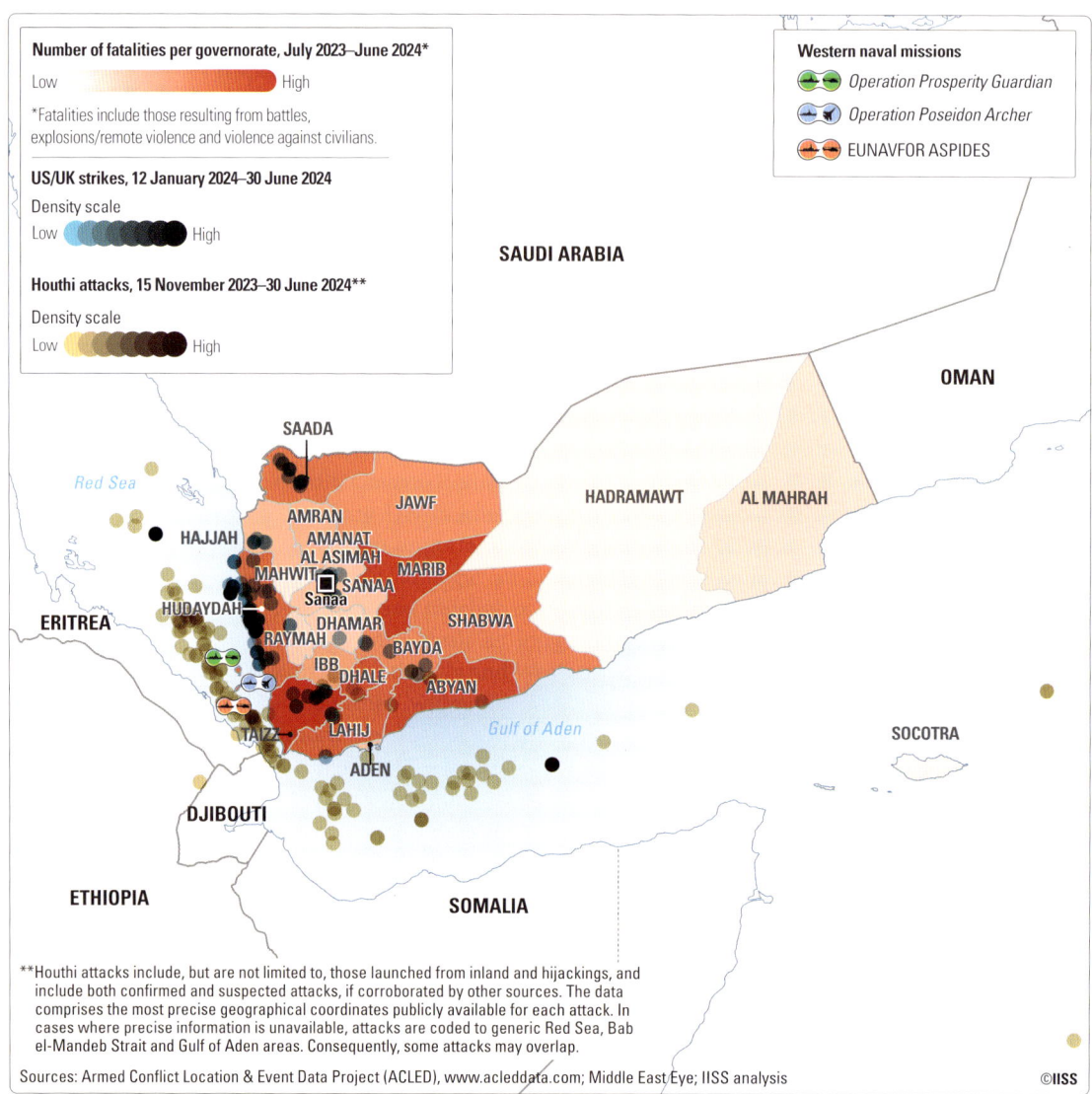

Conflict Overview

The roots of the current conflict in Yemen go back to the fall of the Zaydi Imamate, which was overthrown in a military coup in 1962. Zaydism is a branch of Shia Islam that believes *sayyid*s – the descendants of the Prophet Muhammad – have an elevated role in society.

The Houthis, also known as Ansarullah ('Partisans of God'), grew out of Zaydi dissatisfaction with republican rule and a desire to preserve traditional Zaydi theology. From 2004–10, they fought against Yemen's authoritarian government. Following the Arab Spring, the Houthis began to consolidate control in the north, eventually moving on Yemen's capital, Sanaa, which fell in 2014.

In 2015, Saudi Arabia, concerned that the Houthis could develop into an organisation similar to Hizbullah on its southern border, formed an international coalition to combat the movement.

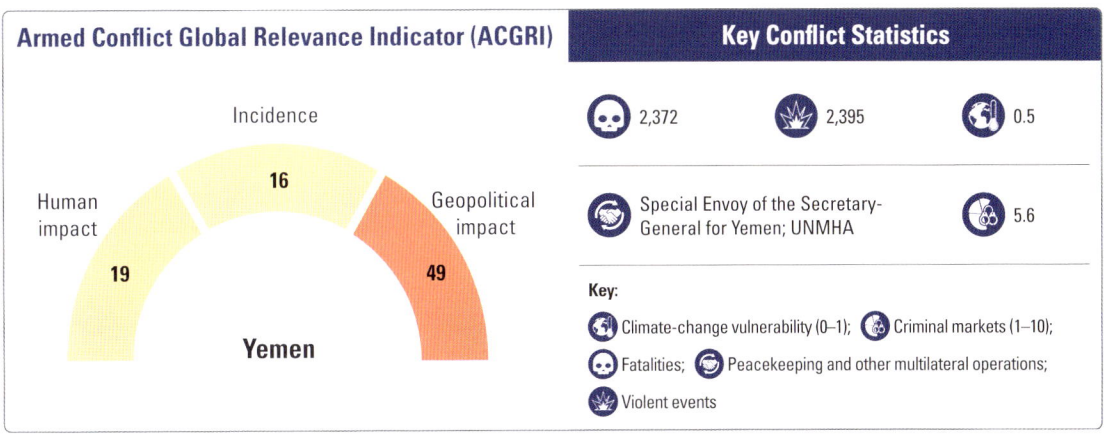

Conflict Update

This coalition relied heavily on local allies in Yemen, including various militias loyal to political parties. Notably, it included the Southern Transitional Council (STC), which advocates for the secession of South Yemen – formerly a socialist state that had been reunified with northern Yemen in 1990.

After some initial military successes, Saudi-led coalition advances mostly halted following the United Nations-brokered Stockholm Agreement in 2018. Meanwhile, the Houthis have benefitted from a growing alliance with Iran, which continues to provide them with weapons, including sophisticated missile systems, in violation of UN Security Council resolutions.[1] The coalition's decision to withdraw its forces and seek a truce with the Houthis created a rift between its local allies as funding for military salaries dried up. This led to clashes in 2019 over the control of strategic assets, such as the Port of Aden, and associated revenue. Though this rift was partially papered over with the creation of the Presidential Leadership Council (PLC) – the executive body of Yemen's internationally recognised government which includes representatives from different parties – the anti-Houthi camp in Yemen remains divided. Meanwhile, the Houthis retain firm political and military control over much of northern Yemen.

Conflict Update

While the UN-mediated ceasefire agreement between the Houthis and Yemen's internationally recognised government lapsed in October 2022, both parties largely continued to honour the terms of the agreement during the reporting period. This resulted in a significant reduction in armed violence and slight improvements in the humanitarian situation in the country. Although the conflict's front lines have largely remained static since the beginning of the truce, the opening of Sanaa airport for limited civilian air services, as well as the lifting of most restrictions on imports through Hudaydah Port, have provided some relief for the population. Against the backdrop of further de-escalation between Saudi Arabia and Iran, which exchanged ambassadors in September 2023 for the first time in seven years, peace negotiations with the Houthis continued as Riyadh attempted to extricate itself from Yemen in exchange for guarantees regarding its southern border. However, despite the shuttle diplomacy, the talks have stalled largely over demands that Saudi Arabia fund the salaries of public servants in northern Yemen, including those of Houthi fighters.[2]

Meanwhile, the internationally recognised government, which has been excluded from most of the peace talks, eyed the rapprochement between Saudi Arabia and the Houthis with suspicion. It fears that the Houthi demand for the withdrawal of the remaining Saudi and Emirati forces would allow Ansarullah to crush the various anti-Houthi forces. As it is both economically and militarily dependent on the Saudi-led coalition, however, the PLC has little political leverage. Though Saudi Arabia continued to bankroll the internationally recognised government to some extent throughout the reporting period, the PLC still struggled to pay salaries and to provide basic services in the areas under its control. Frequent power outages have sparked protests in both Aden and Hadramawt in 2023 and 2024. Despite these challenges, or possibly because of them, the various parties of the anti-Houthi camp in Yemen have continued to cooperate within the PLC.

This period of relative calm ended in October 2023 when the Houthis declared war on Israel, purportedly in solidarity with the Palestinians in the Gaza Strip. This exposed the strong anti-Israel and anti-United States elements in the Houthis' ideology which had previously often been overlooked.[3] Acting in coordination with other Iranian-led 'Axis of Resistance' groups, since the start of the conflict the Houthis have launched more than 220 ballistic and cruise missiles and uninhabited aerial vehicles (UAVs) against targets in Israel, mostly against Eilat in the south.[4] The Houthis have also attacked over 70 commercial ships allegedly linked to Israel and its Western allies in the Red Sea and the Gulf of Aden with missiles, UAVs and uninhabited surface vessels, sinking two and seizing one since November 2023.[5]

The US and the United Kingdom responded by deploying naval assets to the region to protect the freedom of navigation; they were later followed by the European Union, which mandated a similar mission. While the EU's mission is purely defensive, American and British warships and fighter aircraft have attacked Houthi positions in Yemen, destroying launch sites, storage facilities and other locations associated with the movement's anti-ship campaign. Despite these attacks, the Houthis continued their strikes on commercial ships, forcing many shipping lines to take the longer route around the Cape of Good Hope.

While much of regional and international actors' attention has been focused on the Houthis, jihadist violence remains a significant threat in Yemen. Al-Qaeda in the Arabian Peninsula (AQAP) and STC-affiliated forces have continued to clash over the control of territory in Shabwa and Abyan following the signing of the October 2022 peace agreement between the Houthis and the Yemeni government.[6]

Conflict Parties

The Houthi movement (Ansarullah)

Strength: 150,000–200,000 (estimate).[7]

Areas of operation: The group controls much of northern Yemen, parts of the Red Sea coast in and around Hudaydah, and parts of Marib.

Leadership: Abdul Malik al-Houthi.

Structure: Abdul Malik al-Houthi is the leader of Ansarullah, however, formally, power in Houthi-controlled areas rests with the Supreme Political Council, headed by President Mahdi al-Mashat. Real political power is held by a group of 'supervisors', mostly *sayyids*, who are appointed by Ansarullah and who shadow the government officials.

History: Beginning as a Zaydi revivalist movement, the Houthis fought a series of insurgencies against the Yemeni government from 2004–10 before taking control of Sanaa and most of northern Yemen in 2014–15.

Objectives: Domestically, the movement aims to hold and govern at least northern Yemen. Internationally, its objective is to play a leading role in the Iran-supported Axis of Resistance by targeting Israel and Western shipping, purportedly in solidarity with the Palestinian resistance.

Opponents: Domestically, the internationally recognised Yemeni government, backed by the Saudi-led coalition. Internationally, Israel and its Western allies, in particular the US and UK.

The Houthi movement (Ansarullah)

Affiliates/allies: Iran, Hizbullah and Popular Mobilisation Units in Iraq.

Resources/capabilities: Ballistic missiles, cruise missiles and UAVs capable of targeting Israel, neighbouring states such as Saudi Arabia and the United Arab Emirates (UAE), and ships in the Red Sea and the Gulf of Aden. US and UK military operations in Yemen since January 2024 (*Operation Poseidon Archer*) may have degraded the group's capabilities. However, they have not eliminated its ability to manufacture rockets, missiles and UAVs and to fire these at Israel or ships in the Red Sea.

Southern Transitional Council (STC)

Strength: 55,000, integrated into the forces of the internationally recognised government.

Areas of operation: Holds Aden, much of Lahij, Socotra, and parts of Abyan and Shabwa; active in Hadramawt.

Leadership: Aidarous al-Zubaidi (president of the STC, member of the PLC).

Structure: The STC is led by a president and has a leadership council.

History: The STC was formed with UAE support in 2017 following a rift within the anti-Houthi forces over the control of Aden. The organisation is the latest iteration of the Southern Movement, which was comprised of disgruntled military officers from South Yemen who formed the core of the anti-Houthi resistance during the Battle of Aden in 2015.

Objectives: While the STC joined the PLC in 2022, it maintains a long-term goal of establishing an independent South Yemen.

Opponents: Houthis, but also rival elements within the anti-Houthi coalition, in particular the al-Islah party.

Affiliates/allies: UAE.

Resources/capabilities: The STC controls many of the militias formed with the support of the UAE, particularly in Aden and other parts of southern Yemen, such as the Security Belt Forces.

Joint Forces

Strength: 40,000, integrated into the forces of the internationally recognised government.[8]

Areas of operation: Red Sea coast, Taizz and Shabwa.

Leadership: Maj.-Gen. Haytham Qasim Tahir is the commander, but Brig.-Gen. Tareq Saleh, who is a member of the PLC, is the real decision-maker.

Structure: The group is comprised of different military formations but is closely linked to Tareq Saleh's political movement, which controls the strategic city of Mokha on Yemen's west coast.

History: Following the death of his uncle, the late president Ali Abdullah Saleh, at the hands of the Houthis in December 2017, Tareq Saleh together with elements of the Republican Guard joined UAE forces on Yemen's west coast.

Objectives: The group's long-term goal is to free Yemen's west coast and northern governorate. However, its short-term goal is to maintain political and military control, particularly in Mokha.

Opponents: Houthis.

Affiliates/allies: UAE.

Resources/capabilities: Includes the Southern Giants Brigades, which is politically linked to the STC, the National Resistance Forces, led by Tareq Saleh, and the Tihama Resistance, a local militia on the west coast.

Hadrami Elite Forces

Strength: 7,000, integrated into the forces of the internationally recognised government.

Areas of operation: Hadramawt, previously also Shabwa.

Leadership: Maj.-Gen. Faiz Mansur al-Tamimi.

Structure: The Hadrami Elite Forces is a militia recruited by the UAE from local tribes to fight against AQAP in Hadramawt. Like other anti-Houthi militias, it is formally part of the forces of the internationally recognised government but also maintains its own independent formations.

History: Created in 2016 by the UAE to expel AQAP and the Islamic State (ISIS) from Mukalla and other parts of Hadramawt. In recent years, the militia has moved closer to the STC.

Objectives: Strengthen the local autonomy of Hadramawt, particularly regarding the revenue derived from local petroleum resources.

Opponents: Houthis.

Affiliates/allies: UAE and increasingly STC.

Resources/capabilities: Regionally recruited light infantry forces, operating in an anti-insurgency role.

Al-Islah affiliated forces

Strength: 20,000, integrated into the forces of the internationally recognised government.

Areas of operation: Red Sea coast, Taizz, Marib, Shabwa, Abyan and Hadramawt.

Al-Islah affiliated forces

Leadership: Muhammad al-Yadumi is the party's chairman, while Abdullah al-Alimi is a member of the PLC.

Structure: Al-Islah (also known as the Yemeni Congregation for Reform) is a Sunni political party affiliated with the international Muslim Brotherhood. The party has been a key backer of the internationally recognised government and has many members serving within the anti-Houthi forces.

History: Al-Islah was formed in the 1990s. Many of its prominent members were military commanders engaged in fighting the Houthis prior to 2014, which led to reprisals following the Houthi coup. Yemen's internationally recognised government has also relied on al-Islah commanders, but rivalry between the party and the STC has created a rift among the anti-Houthi forces.

Objectives: Maintain the unity of Yemen and retain the party's prominent position in Yemen's government.

Opponents: Houthis, UAE and STC.

Affiliates/allies: Saudi Arabia and increasingly Turkiye.

Resources/capabilities: Many commanders of the armed forces of the internationally recognised government in Marib and Taizz, as well as in the Wadi Hadramawt area, are affiliated with al-Islah.

Saudi Arabian armed forces

Strength: 15,000 (estimate) in Yemen and on the Yemeni border.

Areas of operation: Northern border areas, Marib, Hadramawt and Mahra.

Leadership: Muhammad bin Salman (crown prince and defence minister).

Structure: The Saudi forces in Yemen are drawn from the different branches of Saudi Arabia's military and operate under the command of the joint forces headquarters in Riyadh.

History: Saudi Arabia entered the war in 2015 as the leader of a ten-country coalition. Following the UAE's drawdown in 2019, Saudi Arabia deployed more ground forces, but it is now seeking to extricate itself from the conflict.

Objectives: Exit the war through a negotiated settlement with the Houthis which protects Saudi Arabia's southern border.

Opponents: Houthis.

Affiliates/allies: UAE and internationally recognised government.

Resources/capabilities: Saudi Arabia has access to a modern air force as well as armoured units in Yemen. However, the exact number of deployed assets is unclear and has been steadily reduced since mid-2022.

United Arab Emirates armed forces

Strength: Several hundred.

Areas of operation: Mokha, Shabwa and coastal areas of Hadramawt.

Leadership: Sheikh Muhammad bin Zayed al-Nahyan (president of the UAE).

Structure: Following the drawdown of UAE forces in mid-2019, the remaining Emirati forces are mostly engaged in anti-insurgency and advisory roles, as well as in the protection of critical infrastructure.

History: The UAE joined the Saudi-led coalition as its primary partner in 2015 and deployed as many as 3,500 soldiers to the country.[9] Since 2019, Abu Dhabi has reduced its military presence but continues to support local militias.

Objectives: Maintain a political role in southern Yemen, in particular along the country's coastlines, and limit the influence of al-Islah.

Opponents: Houthis and al-Islah.

Affiliates/allies: Saudi Arabia, STC, Joint Forces and Elite Forces.

Resources/capabilities: The UAE used to have the second-largest modern military presence in Yemen after Saudi Arabia. However, following the 2019 drawdown only a small number of advisers and special forces remain. Nevertheless, the UAE can still provide aerial support if necessary.

Other relevant parties

AQAP and an ISIS affiliate are active in Yemen. AQAP, which comprises roughly 2,000–3,000 fighters, operates in Abyan, Bayda and parts of Shabwa. ISIS, which has 100–150 fighters, is present in southern Yemen.[10] The EU, UK and US are maintaining warships and other military assets in the Red Sea and the Gulf of Aden to protect international shipping from Houthi attacks.

Notes

[1] See UN Security Council (UNSC), 'Final Report of the Panel of Experts on Yemen', S/2018/594, 26 January 2018.

[2] Ahmed Nagi, 'Catching Up on the Back-channel Peace Talks in Yemen', International Crisis Group, 10 October 2023.

3   Hannah Porter, 'Houthi Propaganda Finally Reaches Global Audiences', Italian Institute for International Politial Studies, 15 February 2024.
4   Emanuel Fabian, 'Israel Strikes Houthi-controlled Port in Yemen After Deadly Drone Attack on Tel Aviv', *Times of Israel*, 20 July 2024.
5   Michael Wakin, 'Two Attacks by Yemen's Houthi Rebels Strike Ships in the Red Sea', AP News, 17 July 2024.
6   Armed Conflict Location & Event Data Project (ACLED), 'Violence in Yemen During the UN-mediated Truce: April–October 2022', 14 October 2022.
7   See Justin Salhani, 'Houthis Are Recruiting Record Fighters. How Will This Affect Yemen?', Al-Jazeera, 23 February 2024.
8   ACLED, 'Joint Forces on the West Coast', 31 January 2024.
9   Michael Knights, 'Lessons From the UAE War in Yemen', Lawfare, 18 August 2019.
10 See UNSC, 'Thirty-fourth Report of the Analytical Support and Sanctions Monitoring Team Submitted Pursuant to Resolution 2734 (2024) Concerning ISIL (Da'esh), Al-Qaida and Associated Individuals and Entities', S/2024/556, 19 July 2024, p. 14.

LIBYA

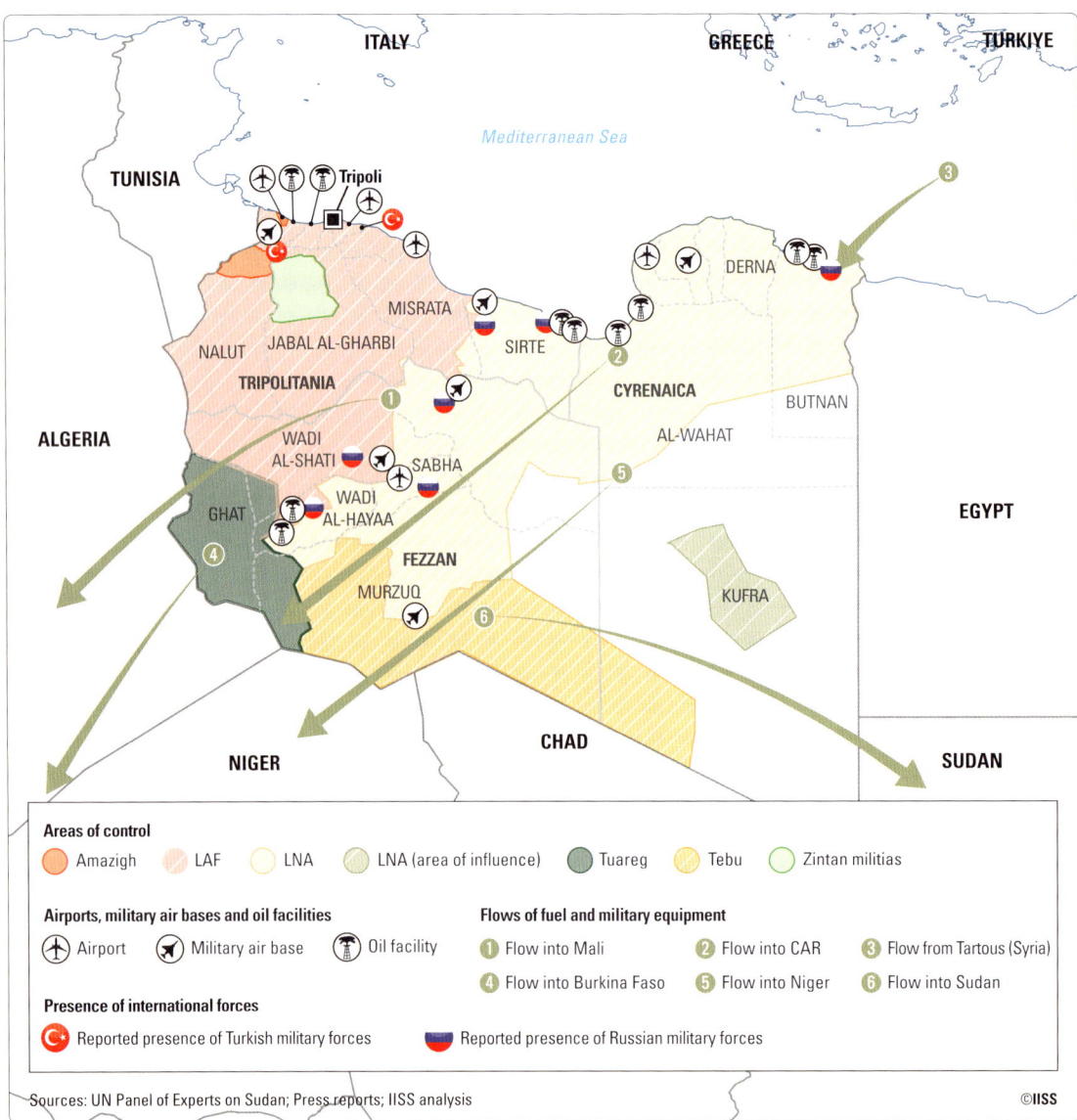

Conflict Overview

Mass protests against the rule of Muammar Gadhafi in 2011 ignited a revolution that plunged Libya into a civil war. The subsequent NATO-led intervention precipitated a regime change, in which the revolutionary forces triumphed, but failed to enact a peaceful transition. A new rift emerged in 2014, mirroring the regional divide between Islamist and secular forces that had become more evident in Egypt following its 2013 military coup. This second phase of the civil war polarised the country, accelerating its fragmentation and creating a breeding ground for terrorist organisations.

A new clash erupted in April 2019 when Field Marshal Khalifa Haftar launched an offensive against the internationally recognised government in Tripoli. Turkiye's direct military intervention tilted the balance,

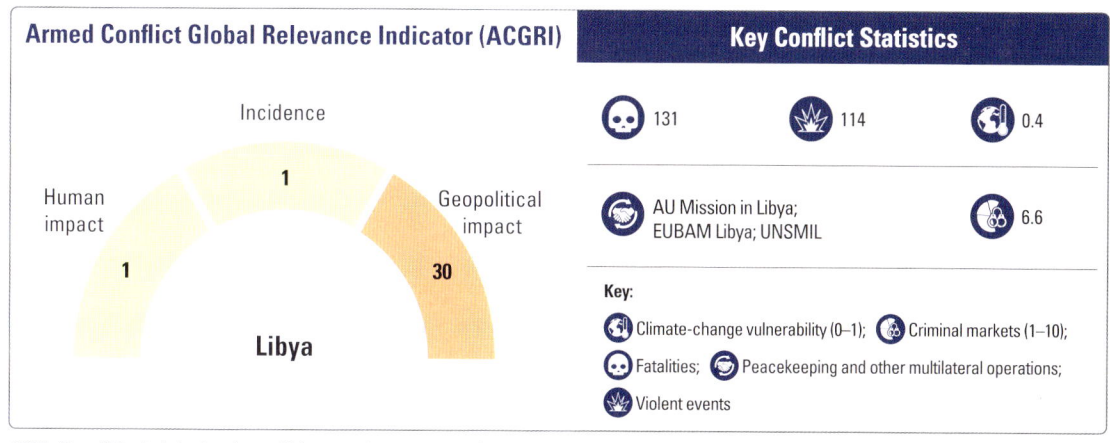

Conflict(s)	Type	Start date
Civil war between competing authorities	II	2011

Key: II Internationalised internal

forcing Haftar to pull his Libyan National Army (LNA) from the capital. The prospect of a rapid collapse of the LNA urged Egypt (which had backed the force) to threaten a direct military intervention. The military stalemate provided a window of opportunity, in which a ceasefire agreement was signed in October 2020.

The failure to hold elections in December 2021 fuelled further political polarisation, leading to the establishment of a Government of National Stability (GNS) challenging the internationally recognised interim Government of National Unity (GNU). Since then, frictions between the two bodies have often resulted in sporadic clashes between rival militias to control Tripoli, but the resilient GNU Prime Minister Abdul Hamid Dbeibah has so far always managed to remain in power.

An implicit arrangement between Dbeibah and Haftar to end the oil blockade in areas under the control of the LNA and share the oil revenues has somewhat defused tensions. At the same time, the GNU is indefinitely delaying elections, protracting the status quo and thwarting attempts by the international community to find a political solution to the frozen conflict.

Conflict Update

Despite several attempts by central authorities to rein in militias in Tripoli, turf wars between rival armed groups have continued, and have been a constant factor since the 2011 revolution. In August 2023, at least 45 people were killed and 146 others were injured after clashes erupted between the Special Deterrence Force (SDF) and the 444 Brigade, both affiliated with the GNU.[1] The release of Mahmoud Hamza, commander of the 444 Brigade, who had been arrested by the SDF at the Mitiga airport, eased tensions between the two groups. An offshoot of the SDF, the 444 Brigade has been increasingly seen as a competitor by the former, a sign of a highly volatile environment in the capital.

Significant developments also occurred in Gharyan where, on 29 October 2023, forces loyal to the GNU repelled an attack by armed groups affiliated with the LNA. In the same month, in Cyrenaica, relations between the LNA and some eastern tribes came under strain. The arrival in Benghazi of Mahdi al-Barghathi (head of the LNA's 204 Tank Brigade before his defection to rival authorities in Tripoli) triggered clashes between the Awaqir tribe to which he belonged and Haftar's forces. At least seven people, including Barghathi, were arrested and then killed by security forces based in eastern Libya.[2]

Having failed to take control of Tripoli several times, GNS prime minister Fathi Bashagha proved useless to Haftar's efforts to impose his rule over the whole of Libya. Mainly for this reason, on 16 May 2023, Bashagha was voted out by the House of Representatives (HoR). His replacement with former finance minister Osama Hammad took place amid widespread reports of a potential power-sharing deal between Dbeibah and Haftar that never materialised. At the same time, the election of the new head of the High Council of State (HCS), Mohamed Takala, in August 2023 did not change the status quo.

Even the major catastrophe produced by the bursting of two dams due to Storm Daniel, which struck eastern Libya in September 2023 (resulting in 4,333 deaths and approximately 8,540 people missing), was not enough to reconcile rival factions.[3] Joint efforts to provide aid to the people of Derna were short-lived and flash protests over mismanagement were immediately stifled. Parallel authorities laid out different reconstruction projects that offered an insight into the race to succeed Haftar in eastern Libya: among his sons, Saddam and Belqasim emerged as important figures, with the latter appointed executive director of the Libya Development and Reconstruction Fund.

Peace initiatives overlapped, protracting the political stalemate. In June 2023, the HCS and the HoR announced an agreement regarding the election laws, voted on by the HoR in October 2023. Nevertheless, key issues remained unresolved and forced the United Nations special representative of the secretary-general for Libya, Abdoulaye Bathily, to announce his resignation. A national reconciliation conference and a meeting of the main stakeholders in the peace process were called off. At the same time, Crown Prince Mohamed Al Senussi launched his own political dialogue to reinstate the monarchy according to the 1951 constitution.

The civil war in Sudan is having important ramifications in Libya, as Haftar has been accused of providing support to the Rapid Support Forces (RSF) in its fight against the Sudan Armed Forces. The shipment of fuel and weapons from military bases in Libya to the RSF has been reportedly overseen by Russia, which, following the demise of Wagner Group leader Yevgeny Prigozhin, is restructuring the group's presence in Africa, bringing it under the control of its Ministry of Defence. Whether this will result in the Russian navy obtaining docking rights in the Libyan deep-water seaport of Tobruk remains to be seen.

While Ankara did not follow up on its plans to establish a naval base in Khoms due to significant local opposition, Turkish forces remain deeply entrenched in Libya, having been authorised by the Turkish parliament to extend their presence there until 2026. At the same time, revelations about a meeting in Rome in August 2023 between the former GNU foreign minister Najla al-Mangoush and her Israeli counterpart Eli Cohen resulted in a significant political quarrel in Libya, where people took to the streets to protest the potential normalisation of diplomatic ties with Tel Aviv. For this reason, as well as due to the ongoing Israel–Hamas war and the political proximity of Tripoli to anti-normalisation stalwart Algeria, the inclusion of Libya in the Abraham Accords remains a distant prospect.

Conflict Parties

Libyan Armed Forces (LAF)

Strength: Unclear. Given the undisclosed number of militias fighting on behalf of the LAF and the undefined relation between these groups and the central command, it is impossible to determine the exact strength.

Areas of operation: After the ceasefire agreement of October 2020, the LAF remained in control of western Libya, including Misrata, Sabratha, Sorman and Tripoli.

Leadership: Mohammed al-Menfi (head of the Presidency Council and supreme commander of the LAF) and Lt-Gen. Mohammed al-Haddad (chief of the general staff).

Structure: Militias in Tripoli represent the backbone of the LAF, which also includes other armed groups from Misrata, Zawiya and Zintan.

History: In the aftermath of Haftar's attack on Tripoli in 2019 armed groups and militias in western Libya rallied in support of the Government of National Accord (GNA, the predecessor to the GNU), which integrated most of these groups into the LAF.

Objectives: Repel any offensive on Tripoli, shore up support for the GNU and foil any attempt to unseat Dbeibah.

Libyan Armed Forces (LAF)

Opponents: The LNA, allies of the LNA, and terrorist groups such as the Islamic State (ISIS) and al-Qaeda in the Islamic Maghreb (AQIM).

Affiliates/allies: Armed groups opposing the LNA's offensive in western and southern Libya. The LAF has received considerable military support from Turkiye.

Resources/capabilities: The LAF has access to various military equipment and weapons of Russian and Soviet origin. It has also benefited from arms transfers made recently by its main external backers and allies.

Libyan National Army (LNA) or the Libyan Arab Armed Forces (LAAF)

Strength: Around 25,000 fighters but the regular army is made up of some 7,000 troops.[4]

Areas of operation: Large swathes of eastern and southern Libya, including Sirte.

Leadership: Agila Saleh (HoR president and supreme commander), Khalifa Haftar (field marshal since 2016 and holds the most power), Lt-Gen. Abdul Razzaq al-Nazhuri (chief of the general staff), Maj.-Gen. Khalid Haftar (Special Units commander and son of Khalifa Haftar), Maj.-Gen. Saddam Haftar (chief of staff of the ground forces and son of Khalifa Haftar), and Oun al-Furjani (chief of staff of Khalifa Haftar's office).

Structure: Includes the Al-Saiqa Special Forces, the 106th Brigade, the 166th Brigade and the 101st Brigade. The LNA also relies on co-opting local armed groups.

History: In 2014, Khalifa Haftar launched *Operation Dignity*, targeting Islamist factions in Benghazi. In 2015, the HoR gave legitimacy to *Operation Dignity*, prompting the LNA's creation.

Objectives: Originally established to fight Islamist and terrorist groups responsible for attacks, the LNA gradually became instrumental in Haftar's project to seek absolute power and avoid civilian oversight.

Opponents: Islamist groups and terrorist organisations; revolutionary groups, such as militias in Misrata, Tripoli and Zintan; and foreign supporters of the GNU, particularly Turkiye.

Affiliates/allies: Tribal militias mainly in Cyrenaica but also in Tripolitania and Fezzan; Sudanese rebel forces and paramilitaries (notably the RSF); mercenaries from Chad and private military companies, such as Russia's rebranded Africa Corps; Egypt and the UAE.

Resources/capabilities: Soviet and Eastern European equipment, including T-54, T-55/62 and a small number of T-72 tanks, BM-21 *Grad* missile launchers and self-propelled Howitzer guns; Toyota pickups with 12.7 millimetre and 14.5mm machine-gun weapons and 106mm recoilless guns; a limited number of fighter jets, including MiG-21s and MiG-23s, and Russian-made helicopters, including Mil Mi-35s and Mi17s, donated by Sudan in 2013; and various patrol vessels.

ISIS–Libya

Strength: 150–400 active militants, including fighters from Chad, Nigeria and Sudan.[5]

Areas of operation: Southern and southwestern areas, such as Murzuq, Sabha and Umm al-Aranib.

Leadership: Former emir Abu Moaz al-Tikrit, also known as Abdul Qader al-Najdi, was killed in September 2020 during clashes with the LNA in Sabha. Another top commander, Mohamed Miloud Ahmed, also known as Abu Omar, was arrested in a raid carried out by the LNA in Obari in March 2021.

Structure: Despite some distinction between regional branches, ISIS has maintained a centralised structure in Libya.

History: ISIS emerged in Libya in 2014–15, when it was able to gain a foothold in Derna and Sirte, threatening Misrata. In 2016, Misrata militias, with the crucial support of the United States Africa Command, took control of Sirte, neutralising the threat.

Objectives: The resumption of hostilities in April 2019 provided ISIS with an opportunity to re-establish its presence. Since then, attacks claimed by ISIS have increased, particularly in remote areas of central and southern Libya.

Opponents: The GNU and affiliated militias, the LNA and its local allies, the Muslim Brotherhood and other moderate Islamist groups (including Sufi followers), and third parties engaged in the fight against terrorism (the US in particular).

Affiliates/allies: The group has always taken a confrontational stance vis-à-vis other terrorist organisations in Libya. However, since its defeat in Sirte, reports suggest that ISIS is collaborating with other jihadist groups, including AQIM.

Resources/capabilities: Human trafficking and gold mining are the main sources of income for ISIS in Libya.

Turkish Armed Forces (TSK)

Strength: Over 700 Turkish military advisers and intelligence officers (on Libyan soil).[6]

Areas of operation: Southern Tripoli, Sabratha, Sorman and Tarhouna, extending to the outskirts of Jufra and Sirte. It has a reported presence at the Mitiga airport in Tripoli and the Watiya air base. Turkish troops have also been based at the Tripoli military port, the Khoms naval base, the Zuwara barracks and several bases in Misrata and Tripoli.

Turkish Armed Forces (TSK)

Leadership: President Recep Tayyip Erdoğan (commander-in-chief), Gen. Yaşar Güler (minister of national defence) and Gen. Metin Gürak (chief of general staff).

Structure: Turkish army units operating under the Turkish Land Forces Command and squadrons carrying out airstrikes operating under the Air Force Command are subordinate to the chief of general staff. Gendarmerie units reporting to the Gendarmerie Command are subordinate to the Ministry of Interior.

History: In 2019, Türkiye signed a memorandum of understanding with the GNA that provided for military assistance and training. In early 2020, Türkiye began to intervene militarily in support of the GNA. Two military cooperation agreements with the GNU followed in 2022.

Objectives: Initially, prevent Haftar's forces from taking control of Tripoli. Following the collapse of the LNA's offensive, its aim has been to consolidate the GNU, while also providing training to the LAF and carrying out demining operations.

Opponents: LNA and its foreign backers.

Affiliates/allies: GNU/LAF and Qatar. The TSK has deployed mercenaries and private military contractors in support of the authorities in Tripoli, including from SADAT, a security firm run by Anrar Tanriverdi, a close associate of Erdoğan.

Resources/capabilities: Türkiye has sent weapons, advisers and military equipment, including *Bayraktar* TB2 and *Anka*-S UAVs, *Kirpi* armoured vehicles, and air-defence systems, such as *Hawk* air-defence missile batteries and 3D *Kalakan* radar, to the Libyan theatre.

Africa Corps/Wagner Group

Strength: At least 1,800 Russian troops and Syrian mercenaries in Libya.[7] There were at least 25,000 troops in the Wagner Group as of late June 2023 according to its leadership, though the actual number was likely higher.[8]

Areas of operation: Russian operatives have been spotted at different air bases (Al Khadim, Al Wigh, Al Jufra, Brak al-Shati, Ghardabiya, Sabha and Waddan), oilfields (El Sharara and El Feel) and oil terminals in Libya. The Wagner Group is also present in Belarus, Ukraine and Russia, while the Africa Corps offshoot is active in Burkina Faso, the Central African Republic, Chad (reports disputed), Mali, Niger and Sudan.

Leadership: Disputed following the deaths of the group's chief, Yevgeny Prigozhin, and commander, Dmitry Utkin, in an aeroplane crash in August 2023. Prigozhin's son, Pavel Prigozhin, has claimed leadership of Wagner, though the group has largely been brought under the control of the Russian Ministry of Defence. Its African operations have been rebranded under the name 'Africa Corps' and are led by Russian Deputy Minister of Defence Col.-Gen. Yunus-bek Yevkurov.

Structure: The company was established by Prigozhin, but its structure has largely been subsumed into the Ministry of Defence following his death.

History: The Wagner Group began as a Kremlin-funded Russian security organisation, with close links to Russian military intelligence and Russia's Ministry of Defence. Wagner was established in 2014 and it and other private military companies proliferated following Russia's involvement in the 2015 war in Syria, where they were often contracted to provide security for extractive operations. The group subsequently took on a similar function in several African countries. It assumed a leading role in the siege of Bakhmut in Ukraine from August 2022–May 2023, which saw its public profile grow significantly in Russia. However, following the aborted mutiny led by Prigozhin on 23–24 June 2023, Wagner agreed to re-base itself in allied Belarus. The group's contracts for soldiers in Russia and Ukraine were thereafter largely assumed by the Russian Ministry of Defence, although there have continued to be (contested) claims to Wagner's leadership, including by Pavel Prigozhin. Since late 2023, the African branch of Wagner has been rebranded as the Africa Corps.

Objectives: Since September 2019, the Wagner Group acted as a force multiplier for the LNA, providing tighter coordination, anti-drone capability, expert snipers and advanced equipment. Recent reports indicate that Russia is interested in obtaining a naval base in eastern Libya to put pressure on NATO's southern flank.

Opponents: GNU, TSK and US.

Affiliates/allies: LNA and its foreign backers. The Wagner Group reportedly recruited several thousand Syrian mercenaries to back the LNA in 2020. Most of them came from pro-Assad militias and paramilitary organisations affiliated with the Syrian Army.

Resources/capabilities: Wagner has been directly armed and supplied by the Armed Forces of the Russian Federation and even received military aircraft during the height of its activity in Ukraine. As it is increasingly brought under the direct control of the Russian Ministry of Defence, it will presumably have access to most of the Russian armed forces' capabilities as well. In 2020, Russian military cargo aircraft, including Il-76s, supplied the Wagner Group with armoured vehicles, *Pantsir* air-defence systems, fuel, ammunition and other supplies. At least 14 MiG-29 and Su-24 aircraft were deployed from Russia to Libya through Syria. The UAE reportedly provided financial assistance to the Wagner Group to deploy its mercenaries to Libya. More recently, there have been reports of Russia moving military equipment (including towed artillery, armoured personnel carriers and multiple-rocket launchers) from its naval base in Tartus, Syria, to Tobruk, eastern Libya. The equipment was transported by two landing ships of the Russian Northern Fleet.[9]

Notes

1. Jack Jeffery, 'Militia Clashes in Libyan Capital Have Killed 45, in City's Most Intense Bout of Violence This Year', AP News, 16 August 2023.
2. UNSMIL (@UNSMILibya), X thread, 21 December 2023.
3. 'Storm Daniel: Urgent Funding Scale-up Needed Four Weeks After Libya Disaster', International Organization for Migration, 7 October 2023.
4. Jason Pack, 'Kingdom of Militias: Libya's Second War of Post-Qadhafi Succession', Italian Institute for International Political Studies, 31 May 2019.
5. UN Security Council, 'Eighteenth Report of the Secretary-General on the Threat Posed by ISIL (Da'esh) to International Peace and Security and the Range of United Nations Efforts in Support of Member States in Countering the Threat', S/2024/117, 31 January 2024, p. 6.
6. Fehim Tastekin, 'Three Challenging Scenarios for Turkey in Libya', Al-Monitor, 14 March 2022.
7. See Andrew McGregor, 'Russian Military Intelligence Takes Over Wagner Operations in Libya', Jamestown Foundation *Eurasia Daily Monitor*, vol. 21, no. 38, 12 March 2024; All Eyes on Wagner, 'Mediterranean Sea Objective for the African Corps', 10 May 2024.
8. Torredo, 'Novoe soobshchenie Prigozhina, 25000 idut na Moskvu' Новое сообщение Пригожина, 25000 идут на Москву [Prigozhin's new message, 25,000 go to Moscow], YouTube, 23 June 2023; and Olga Ivshina and Olga Prosvirova, '"Amoralno, no effectivno". kak i kakoi tsenoi ChVK "Wagner" zakhvatyvala Bakhmut' «Аморально, но эффективно»: как и какой ценой ЧВК «Вагнер» захватывала Бахмут ['Amoral, but effective': how and at what cost 'Wagner' seized Bakhmut], BBC News, 10 June 2024.
9. All Eyes on Wagner, 'Mediterranean Sea Objective for the African Corps'.

EGYPT

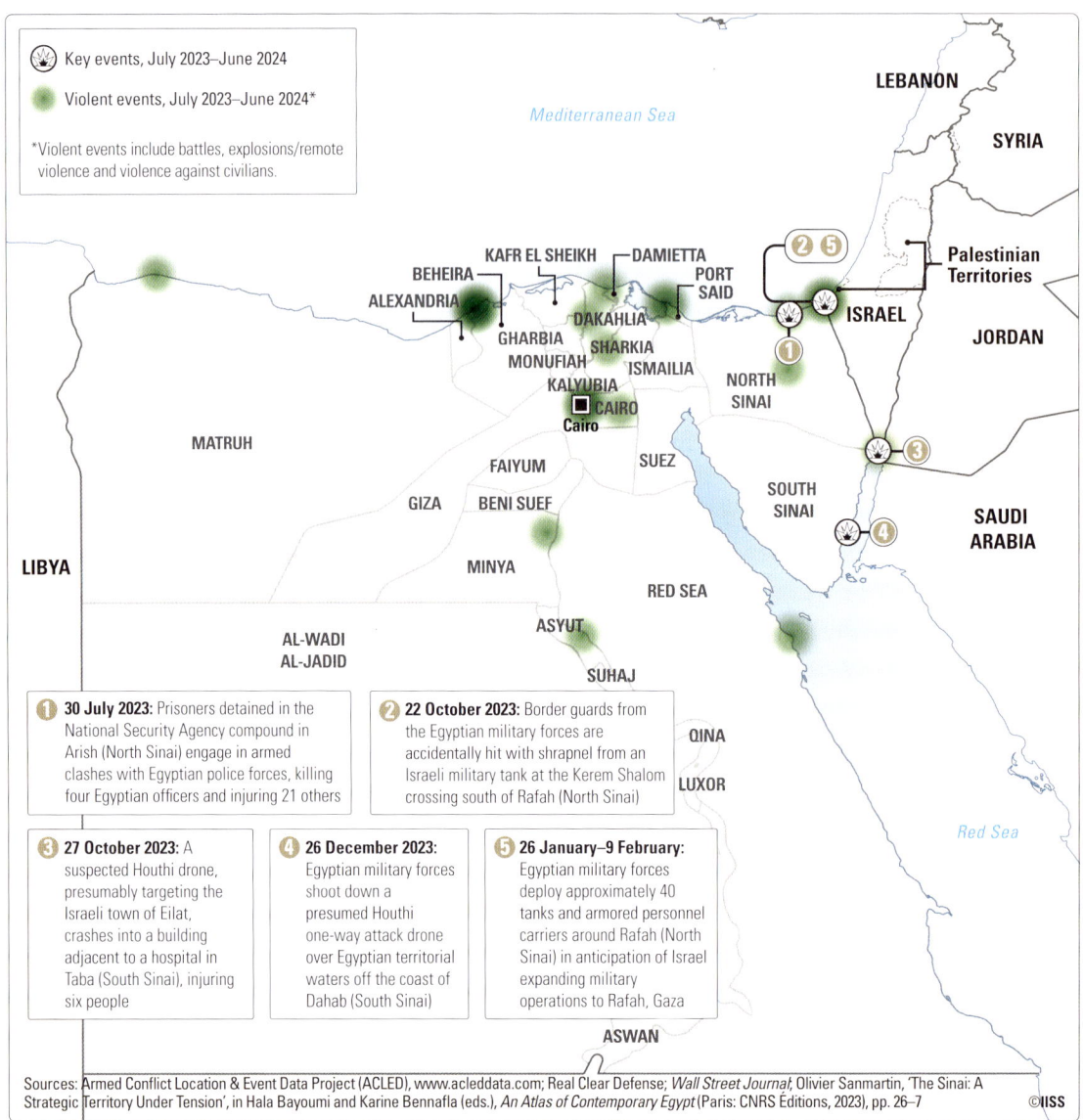

Conflict Overview

Conflicts between Arab states and Israel throughout the twentieth century deeply destabilised the impoverished border region of Sinai in Egypt. As a result of the 1978 Camp David Accords, brokered by the United States between Egypt and Israel, the peninsula became a demilitarised zone. A lack of investment and the visible absence of state institutions allowed tribalism to prosper, leaving Bedouin residents disenfranchised and creating favourable conditions for recruitment by extremist organisations. The rise of Islamist groups after the 2011 revolution that toppled president Hosni Mubarak and the 2013 military coup against his successor Muhammad Morsi exacerbated pre-existing tensions, providing new opportunities for Sinai-based militants.

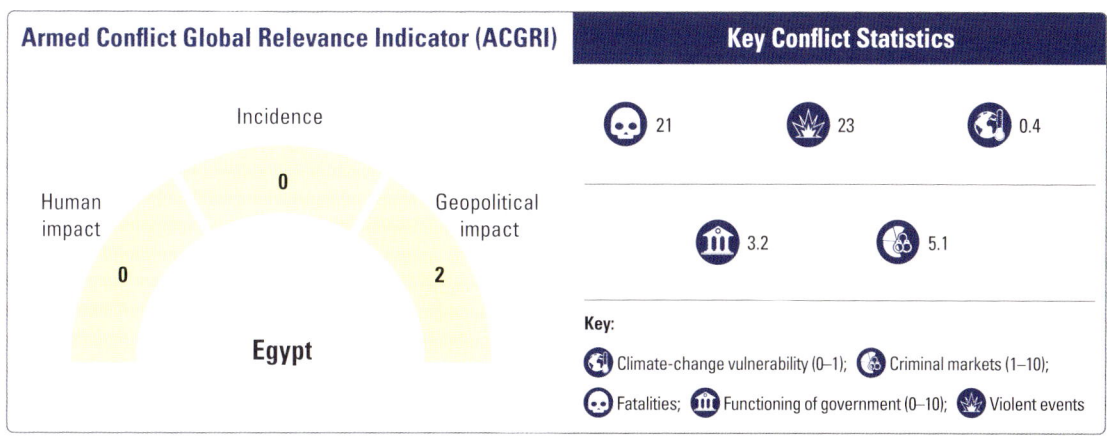

ACGRI pillars: IISS calculation based on multiple sources for 2023 and 2024 (scale: 0–100), except for some cases according to data availability. See Notes on Methodology and Data Appendix for all variables and further details on Key Conflict Statistics.

Conflict(s)	Type	Start date
Islamic State insurgency in the Sinai Peninsula	I LI	2011

Key: I LI Internal: localised insurgency

The most prominent threat has come from Sinai Province (Wilayat Sinai), formed in November 2014 after the jihadist group Ansar Beit al-Maqdis (ABM) switched allegiance from al-Qaeda to the Islamic State (ISIS). The group has conducted frequent terror attacks on security and military outposts and has also targeted civilians. In 2018, the Egyptian Armed Forces (EAF), with the support of its allies, launched a military campaign (codenamed *Operation Sinai*) to retake the area.[1] Israel and the US agreed to a partial re-establishment of Egypt's military presence in Sinai to fight the Islamist insurgency, and Tel Aviv even carried out airstrikes against militants.

Operation Sinai has been largely effective in mitigating the terrorist threat; with help from local tribes within the Sinai Tribes Union, the Egyptian military has successfully degraded Sinai Province's capabilities. However, such counter-terrorism efforts have also drawn criticism from international human-rights groups and non-governmental organisations for their lack of accountability and abuse of civilians.[2]

Conflict Update

Occasional attacks continued in northern Sinai during the reporting period. On 30 July 2023, a shooting inside the National Security headquarters in el-Arish, North Sinai governorate, killed four police officers and injured at least 21 others.[3] Although the circumstances surrounding the shooting were not immediately clear and the authorities did not comment on the incident, it is widely believed that jihadist militants were responsible. Sources suggest that a group of detainees seized weapons and attacked forces stationed there.[4] The incident demonstrated Sinai Province's resilience in the region and its continued ability to conduct a protracted campaign, even though the pace of its attacks has slowed in recent years.

In the aftermath of the Hamas-led 7 October 2023 attacks against Israel and Tel Aviv's retaliation in the Gaza Strip, volatility has also increased in neighbouring Sinai. On 27 October 2023, a drone launched towards Israel by the Iran-backed Houthi movement (Ansarullah) in Yemen crashed into a building in Taba, an Egyptian border crossing with Israel, injuring six people. A second drone was shot down and its debris fell near Nuweiba, approximately 70 kilometres southeast of the Israeli border.[5]

Alongside the regional and global effects of the Israel–Hamas war, adverse post-war prospects for Gaza represent a more immediate concern for Cairo and could complicate its counter-insurgency efforts in Sinai. The risk of a collapse of the Egyptian–Israeli peace treaty still looms large due to Israel's seizure of the Philadelphi Corridor, the 14 km-long border region between Egypt and Gaza, which was demilitarised under the Camp David Accords.[6] Furthermore, Israel's ground offensive in Rafah, where more than one million Palestinians are now sheltering, could result in the displacement of Gazans into Sinai – a prospect officially rejected by Egyptian officials but for which Cairo has been taking precautions.[7]

Conflict Parties

Egyptian Armed Forces (EAF)

Strength: 438,500 active armed personnel, 397,000 active gendarmerie and paramilitary, and 479,000 in reserve.

Areas of operation: North Sinai, South Sinai and Red Sea governorates, militarised triangle (Halayeb/Shalateen), Western Desert and Salloum border (Matrouh governorate – the western border with Libya).

Leadership: Supreme Council of the Armed Forces, led by President Abdel Fattah al-Sisi (supreme commander of the armed forces), Gen. Mohamed Zaki (defence minister) and Lt-Gen. Osama Askar (chief of staff of the armed forces).

Structure: The EAF consists of the army, air defence forces, air force and navy; paramilitary forces are formed under the Ministry of Interior.

History: Military operations to quell the insurgency in the Sinai Peninsula began in 2011 and intensified following the pledge of allegiance to ISIS by militants in the area.

Objectives: Control border security and address all national-security threats originating abroad. Since 2013 it has remilitarised the Sinai Peninsula, notably in North Sinai.

Opponents: Sinai Province, ABM and Muslim Brotherhood.

Affiliates/allies: France, Germany, Israel, Russia, United Arab Emirates, United Kingdom and US.

Resources/capabilities: The EAF does not publicise its defence budget, but estimates place the 2023 budget at US$3.6 billion. Egypt also receives around US$1.3bn in Foreign Military Assistance annually from the US.

Military Intelligence and Reconnaissance Department

Strength: Unclear, although the ascension of Abdel Fattah al-Sisi to Egypt's presidency in 2014 strengthened the department within the armed forces. Sisi was director of the department between 2010 and 2012.

Areas of operation: North Sinai governorate (train and assist programme with local Bedouin militias) and eastern Libya (train and assist programme with the Libyan National Army).

Leadership: Maj.-Gen. Khaled Megawer (director).

Structure: Part of the Ministry of Defense.

History: The department has been the main military actor in the peninsula since December 2018, following a deadly terror attack in November 2017 at Belal Mosque in North Sinai that killed 311 people.[8] The department works in conjunction with the EAF to conduct operations in Sinai against the insurgency.

Objectives: Protect the state, itself and Sisi from any attack; monitor foreign threats towards Egypt (alongside the General Intelligence Services); and lead on local intelligence gathering and community support in the Sinai Peninsula.

Opponents: Sinai Province.

Affiliates/allies: EAF and General Intelligence Services.

Resources/capabilities: Unclear.

Sinai Province (Wilayat Sinai)

Strength: A few hundred fighters.[9]

Areas of operation: North Sinai.

Leadership: In April 2022, the group's senior leader, Abu Omar al-Ansari, was killed in an airstrike reportedly carried out by Israeli aircraft. Past evidence suggested the presence of training camps in Sinai and the Gaza Strip.

Structure: Several jihadists are known to have travelled to Syria for training, suggesting that the ISIS leadership structure periodically plays a role in the Sinai insurgency.

History: First established in November 2014 with a pledge of allegiance by ABM fighters to then-ISIS leader Abu Bakr al-Baghdadi. Its activities reached a peak in 2017 with a series of terror attacks in mainland Egypt and the Sinai Peninsula.

Objectives: Establish an Islamic state and fight the EAF.

Opponents: EAF, wider Egyptian security forces, Israel, non-Sunni Muslims and non-Muslims.

Affiliates/allies: Other terrorist groups affiliated with al-Qaeda and active in Sinai, like Jund al-Islam.

Resources/capabilities: Anecdotal evidence suggests most income is received via economic smuggling between the Sinai Peninsula and Gaza via tunnels. The group also benefits from an active weapons-smuggling war economy bringing weapons from Libya into Sinai.

Sinai Tribes Union (STU)

Strength: Unclear.	**Objectives:** Confront extremist organisations active in the Sinai Peninsula and provide support to the EAF.
Areas of operation: North Sinai.	**Opponents:** Sinai Province.
Leadership: Ibrahim al-Arjani.	**Affiliates/allies:** EAF and DMI.
Structure: The STU includes several Sinai tribes. Among the most prominent are the Armilat, the Sawarka and the Tarabin, the latter being the largest of the Sinai tribes.	**Resources/capabilities:** The EAF has provided the STU with arms and equipment.
History: Formed in 2015.	

Notes

1. See, for example, '"Operation Sinai 2018": What We Know So Far', *Mada Masr*, 9 February 2018.
2. More recently, findings by the UK-based Sinai Foundation for Human Rights showed that the EAF has enlisted children as young as 12 in North Sinai governate, 'with some under 18 directly participating in hostilities' against militants. Dania Akkad, 'Egypt: Children Recruited to Fight Islamic State in North Sinai, Report Finds', Middle East Eye, 8 August 2023.
3. '4 Policemen Dead, 21 Wounded, After Shooting in Egypt', *Le Monde*, 30 July 2023.
4. 'At Least Four Killed in Clash in Egypt's Sinai, Security Sources Say', Reuters, 31 July 2023.
5. Ahmed Mohamed Hassan and Dan Williams, 'Drone Blasts Hit Two Egyptian Red Sea Towns, Israel Points to Houthi', Reuters, 27 October 2023.
6. 'Israel in Effective Control of Entire Gaza Land Border After Taking Philadelphi Corridor in South', *Guardian*, 30 May 2024.
7. There have been multiple reports of a buffer zone or walled enclosure that Egypt is building near the border with the Gaza Strip, alongside the Sheikh Zuweid–Rafah Road. See Margherita Stancati and Abeer Ayyoub, 'Rafah Is Already in a Humanitarian Crisis. Now, an Israeli Offensive Looms', *Wall Street Journal*, 13 February 2024; and Summer Said and Jared Malsin, 'Egypt Builds Walled Enclosure on Border as Israeli Offensive Looms', *Wall Street Journal*, 15 February 2024.
8. The Tahrir Institute for Middle East Policy, 'Attack at Rawda Mosque', 7 December 2017.
9. UN Security Council, 'Eighteenth Report of the Secretary-General on the Threat Posed by ISIL (Da'esh) to International Peace and Security and the Range of United Nations Efforts in Support of Member States in Countering the Threat', S/2024/117, 31 January 2024, p. 6.

TURKIYE

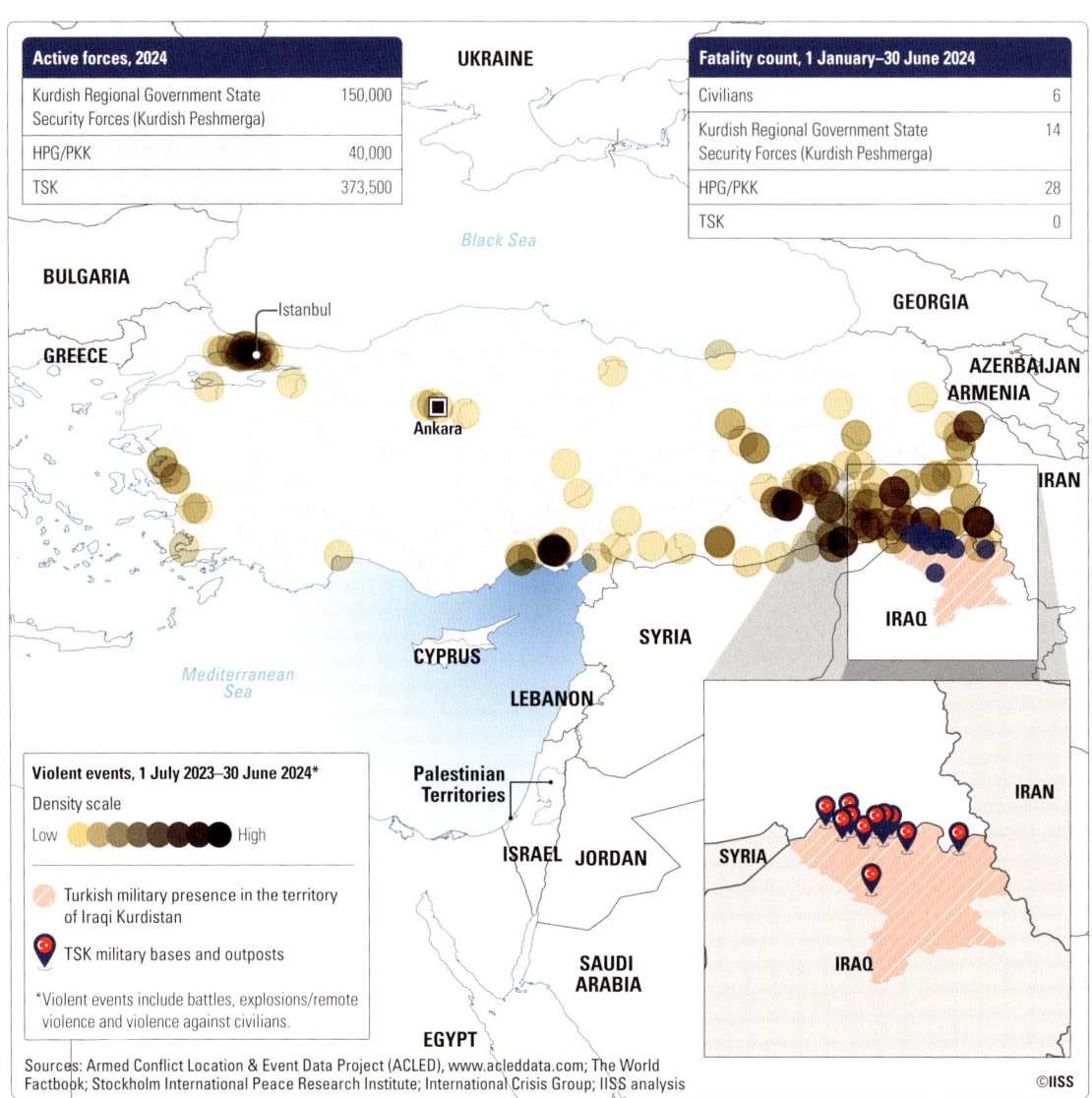

Conflict Overview

The conflict between Turkiye and the Kurdistan Workers' Party (PKK) has been ongoing for almost four decades. Drawing upon a mixture of Marxist ideology and Kurdish nationalism, the group was founded by Abdullah Öcalan in the late 1970s and is listed as a terrorist group by the European Union and the United States. The movement's initial goal was the creation of an independent Kurdish state. Later, the recognition of Kurdish political and cultural autonomy within Turkiye became the focus of the organisation's political agenda.

The Kurdish-majority eastern regions of Turkiye along the borders with Iraq and Syria have historically been most affected by the conflict. There, PKK fighters follow a particularly brutal approach to insurgency. Attacks are usually carried out against representatives of Turkish state authority, such as members of the military, judges, teachers and

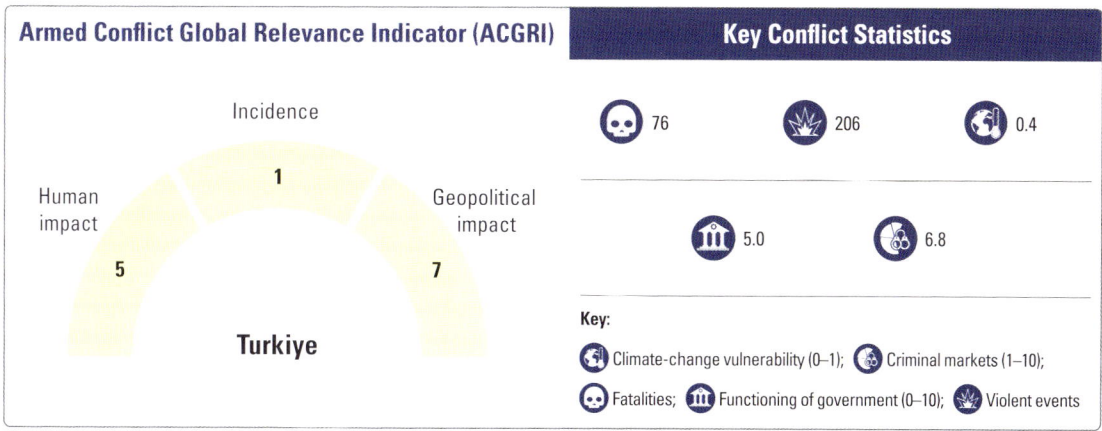

ACGRI pillars: IISS calculation based on multiple sources for 2023 and 2024 (scale: 0–100), except for some cases according to data availability. See Notes on Methodology and Data Appendix for all variables and further details on Key Conflict Statistics.

Conflict(s)	Type	Start date
Conflict with the Kurdish PKK and its offshoot in Iraq	I Li T	1984
Conflict with the Syria-based YPG	T	2012

Key: I Li Internal: localised insurgency; T Transnational

politicians. PKK fighters are able to find a safe haven and support in Iraq and Syria. Therefore, the conflict has always had a transnational dimension.

The PKK's strategy has changed over the past decade due to the failed peace process between its jailed leader Öcalan and the Turkish authorities, as well as the outbreak of the Syrian civil war. The rise of the People's Protection Units (YPG), the Syrian Kurdish affiliate of the PKK, which forms the primary fighting force of the Syrian Democratic Forces (SDF), in northern Syria has increased the perceived threat to Turkiye. As a result, in 2016, Turkiye launched a series of military operations to create a buffer zone between its borders and the Kurdish-controlled Syrian provinces. The conflict with the PKK has thus gradually become focused on cross-border networks in Syria and Iraq.

Conflict Update

During the reporting period, the conflict between the PKK and Turkiye continued at both the domestic and regional levels. Domestically, the Turkish government aimed to dismantle the organisation's recruitment networks, which have shrunk substantially since 2020. The arrest of several figures linked to Kurdish political movements during the Newroz celebrations in March 2024 underlined the close link between the conflict and Kurdish cultural claims in Turkish domestic politics. Overall, excepting two significant attacks in 2022–23, the terrorist threat posed by the PKK in Turkiye has significantly declined.

At the transnational level, since 2022, Turkiye has intensified its military operations against PKK bases in northern Iraq (ongoing since the 1980s). The latest operation, *Operation Claw-Lock*, is scheduled to be completed in the summer of 2024. It aims to establish a safe region in Iraq's border governates and has targeted PKK positions in the mountainous regions of Metina, Avasin-Basyan, Gara, Khakurk, Qandil and Asos. In addition to military gains, Turkiye has achieved major political success with Baghdad's decision to list the PKK as a banned organisation. It already has temporary bases in some regions of northern Iraq and is expected to expand its transnational operations to other parts of the country in 2024. Turkiye has also carried out several targeted uninhabited aerial vehicle (UAV) strikes against prominent PKK figures. However, the PKK is developing the ability to shoot down UAVs, and it is believed to be receiving technology from China and procuring Iranian-made equipment. If such reports are confirmed, the group's possession of anti-drone technology could change the balance on the battlefield.

Meanwhile, the fight against the YPG has reached a stalemate in Syria. The conflict between the Turkish armed forces and the Kurdish militias continues and is increasingly characterised by rapid, localised clashes. In the areas under its control, Turkiye is consolidating governance with the support of the Syrian National Army (SNA).

Conflict Parties

Turkish Armed Forces (TSK)

Strength: 373,500 active military, 378,700 in reserve and 156,800 active gendarmerie and paramilitary.

Areas of operation: Southeastern Turkiye, northern and northwestern Iraq, and northern and northwestern Syria.

Leadership: President Recep Tayyip Erdoğan (commander-in-chief), Gen. Yaşar Güler (minister of national defence) and Gen. Metin Gürak (chief of general staff).

Structure: Turkish army units operating under the Turkish Land Forces Command and squadrons carrying out airstrikes operating under the Air Force Command are subordinate to the chief of general staff. Gendarmerie units reporting to the Gendarmerie Command are subordinate to the Ministry of Interior.

History: Rebuilt after the collapse of the Ottoman Empire in 1922. The TSK was significantly restructured after the country joined NATO in 1951 and is currently NATO's second-largest armed force.

Objectives: Eradicate the PKK and preserve national unity.

Opponents: PKK and its affiliate organisations, particularly those in Iraq and the SDF/YPG in Syria.

Affiliates/allies: Relies extensively on the SNA as a support force in northern Syria.

Resources/capabilities: Turkiye's defence budget for 2023 was US$8.7 billion. Its military capabilities include combat aircraft; intelligence, surveillance and reconnaissance assets; armoured vehicles; and special-forces units.

Kurdistan Workers' Party (PKK)

Strength: 4,000–5,000 (estimate) in Turkiye and Iraq.[1]

Areas of operation: Southeastern Turkiye and northern Iraq.

Leadership: Abdullah Öcalan (ideological leader, despite his imprisonment since 1999), Murat Karayilan (acting leader on the ground since Öcalan's capture) and Bahoz Erdal (military commander).

Structure: While operating under the same command and leadership, the PKK's armed wing is divided into the People's Defence Forces (HPG) and the Free Women's Units (YJA-STAR).

History: Founded by Öcalan in 1978. The PKK has been engaged in an insurgency campaign against the TSK since 1984.

Objectives: Political and cultural recognition of the Kurdish minority in Turkiye, and the adoption of a democratic federalist system of governance.

Opponents: TSK.

Affiliates/allies: SDF/YPG in Syria.

Resources/capabilities: Generates revenue through money-laundering activities and drug trafficking in addition to donations from the Kurdish community and diaspora and left-wing international supporters. The PKK relies on highly mobile units, using guerrilla tactics against Turkish military targets. It is reported to be equipped with counter-drone technology.

(Turkiye-sponsored) Syrian National Army (SNA)

Strength: Approximately 70,000.[2]

Areas of operation: Northern and northwestern Syria.

Leadership: Brig.-Gen. Hassan al-Hamada (defence minister). SNA units are currently deployed alongside Turkish military forces and therefore operate under Turkish leadership.

Structure: A conglomerate of dozens of different militias, ranging vastly in size, affiliation and ideology, composed of Syrian militants, who are trained and equipped by Turkiye.

The SNA is divided into seven main legions, each comprising a wide array of divisions and brigades.

History: Created as a splinter group of the Turkiye-backed Free Syrian Army. The SNA has been trained and equipped by the Turkish government since 2016. In 2019, the Idlib-based and Turkiye-sponsored National Front for Liberation was merged into the SNA.

Objectives: Overthrow the Syrian government and take control of northern Syria.

(Turkiye-sponsored) Syrian National Army (SNA)

Opponents: SDF/YPG.

Affiliates/allies: TSK.

Resources/capabilities: While a handful of formations have received US-sponsored training and equipment, the SNA has relied entirely on Turkish support since its inception. Turkiye has provided small arms as well as light armoured vehicles, and SNA military operations have benefited from Turkish artillery and air support.

Syrian Democratic Forces/People's Protection Units (SDF/YPG)

Strength: 40,000–60,000.[3]

Areas of operation: Northern Syria.

Leadership: Mazloum Kobani Abdi, also known as Sahin Cilo (military commander), and Mahmoud Berkhadan (general commander). Abdi is a former senior PKK member.

Structure: Organised mainly along ethnic and territorial lines. Syrian Kurds lead the YPG and the Women's Protection Units (YPJ); both include a small component of international volunteers grouped into an international battalion. Other ethnic groups are organised under various military formations within the SDF, mainly as military councils.

History: Created in 2015 as a direct response to the advance of the Islamic State (ISIS) into northern Syria, building on various pre-existing alliances. Since then, it has fought against ISIS and the Turkish military.

Objectives: Establish autonomous control over northeastern Syria.

Opponents: SNA and Turkish forces.

Affiliates/allies: PKK.

Resources/capabilities: While it built upon the experience of its militias, since its formal creation the SDF has been equipped, trained and advised by the US. SDF units are equipped with small arms and some light armoured vehicles.

Notes

[1] Bureau of Counterterrorism, US Department of State, 'Country Reports on Terrorism 2021', 2021, p. 300.

[2] IISS, *The Military Balance 2024* (Abingdon: Routledge for the IISS, 2023), p. 388.

[3] EU Agency for Asylum, '1.2. Syrian Democratic Forces and Asayish', September 2020.

4 Sub-Saharan Africa

Regional Analysis	170	Niger	198	Sudan	232	Democratic Republic of the Congo	258
Regional Spotlight	182	Nigeria	204	South Sudan	238	Uganda	266
Country Profiles		Cameroon	212	Ethiopia	244	Mozambique	270
Mali	186	Chad	220	Somalia	252		
Burkina Faso	192	Central African Republic	226				

Sudanese refugees fleeing fighting in Darfur arrive in Adre, Chad, 22 April 2024

Overview

Sub-Saharan Africa is the most conflict-affected region globally, with 14 countries out of a total of 49 engulfed in war. In 2023, the region registered 28 internal conflicts (either with or without external intervention), which is among the highest levels since 1991. Non-state conflicts – that is, armed conflicts between non-state armed groups (NSAGs) without the participation of the state – decreased dramatically from 42 in 2022 to 32 in 2023, which is the lowest level since 2016.[1]

The conflict landscape is largely characterised by internal conflicts featuring multiple coexisting dynamics that impede clear-cut categorisation. Though they are fuelled by diverse drivers, armed conflicts on the continent share some critical features. Over the reporting period, they became conversely both more localised – as jihadist groups increasingly pursued local strategies – and more internationalised, with higher levels of fatalities, forced displacement and humanitarian needs compared to the recent past (e.g., in Burkina Faso, Mali, Nigeria and especially Sudan).

The internationalisation of conflicts continues to be a highly relevant trend due to ongoing geopolitical competition. Third parties' involvement or outright direct intervention in the region complicate conflict-management efforts (e.g., in Sudan) and unravel regional and international alliances (e.g., in the Sahel). Inter-state disputes – for example, between the Democratic Republic of the Congo (DRC) and Rwanda, and between Ethiopia and Somalia – also have negative implications for

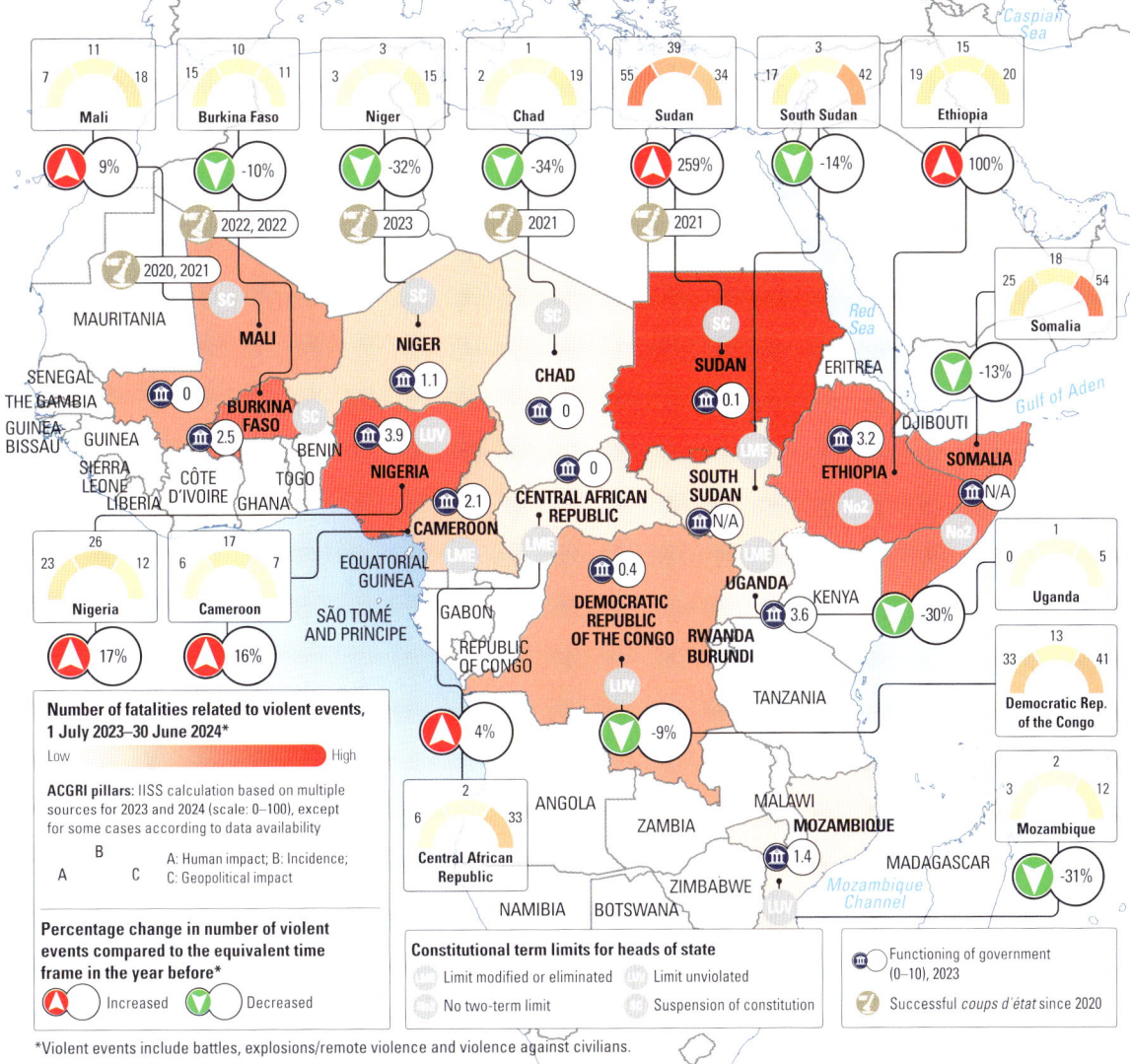

domestic and regional security. Furthermore, the declining respect for international humanitarian law, combined with the demise of multilateral peacekeeping operations (notably in the DRC and Mali), make conflict-affected countries more vulnerable to violence and increase the human impact of conflict.

During the reporting period, armed conflicts in the region evolved in the three main theatres of the Sahel, the Great Lakes Region and the Horn of Africa. In the Sahel, a *coup d'état* in Niger in July 2023 brought to power an anti-Western military junta, which joined forces with juntas in Burkina Faso and Mali. The three countries sent shockwaves through the region when they pulled out of the Economic Community of West African States (ECOWAS) regional grouping and launched a mutual defence pact (the Alliance of Sahel States, AES). The move was the last nail in the coffin for French interests and Western influence in the western and central Sahel. It also completed a diplomatic and geopolitical tectonic shift in the region that witnessed Russia emerging as a leading power in West and Central Africa. Following the death of its leader Yevgeny Prigozhin in August 2023, the private military company Wagner Group transitioned into the Africa Corps under the auspices of Russia's Ministry of Defence and formalised its presence in Burkina Faso, Mali and Niger. Together with stronger bilateral ties between Russia and several countries in the region, this development meant that Moscow's strategic depth in the continent became an official state project.

In the Great Lakes Region, at the intersection of the DRC, Rwanda and Uganda, the rift between Kinshasa and Kigali deepened and risked escalating into direct military confrontation more than once during the reporting period. Rwanda's support for the March 23 Movement (M23) operating in the eastern DRC continued unabated, while M23's military offensive in North Kivu province escalated in the first half of 2024. The threat to the provincial capital of Goma led to mass forced displacement during the reporting period. In controversial presidential elections in the DRC, Félix Tshisekedi won a second term in office. Further, the United Nations Organization Stabilization Mission in the DRC (MONUSCO) was asked to terminate its mission after over 20 years of existence. At the same time, there was a key shift in regional peacekeeping operations in the DRC. The pull-out of the East African Community Regional Force (EACRF) and the invitation to the South African Development Community (SADC) to deploy troops signalled the unstable inter-state relations surrounding regional security in the Great Lakes Region.

In East Africa, the most notable event was the geographic escalation of the civil war in Sudan between the Sudan Armed Forces (SAF) and the paramilitary Rapid Support Forces (RSF). Both forces have acted with impunity and disregard for civilian life and have been held responsible for war crimes. Violence expanded and became concentrated in the west of the country, where North Darfur's capital al-Fashir remained under siege by the RSF as of June 2024. Mass displacement and a humanitarian catastrophe had ensued amid the total collapse of state institutions.

In addition to Sudan, further regional tensions in the Horn of Africa loomed following the January 2024 signing of a memorandum of understanding (MoU) between Ethiopia and the breakaway region of Somaliland. In exchange for supporting Somaliland's quest for independence, landlocked Ethiopia will be granted sea access to the Gulf of Aden. This development was met with dismay in Somalia and has the potential to alter the regional strategic equilibrium.[2]

Several other ongoing armed conflicts continued unabated. Domestically, Ethiopia faced continued instability and violence in Amhara and Oromia regions and an uneasy transition in post-war Tigray Region. Ethiopian Prime Minister Abiy Ahmed has not been able to rein in armed resistance in the two restive regions, nor to forge a comprehensive political settlement and security arrangement. In Mozambique, the Islamist insurgency escalated its activities during the first half of 2024, as the SADC's Standby Force Mission in Mozambique (SAMIM) was scheduled to fully withdraw by July 2024. In Somalia, after some gains against al-Shabaab in 2022–23, the reporting period witnessed the group regain some of its lost territory in Galmadug and Hirshabelle states. Turmoil was observed also in the semi-autonomous regions of Puntland and Somaliland.

Conflict Drivers

Political and institutional
Democracy erosion and military coups
In several of Sub-Saharan Africa's conflict-affected countries, a crisis of legitimacy of the established political order and liberal democracy has been driven by armed violence in recent years. In turn, this crisis exacerbates current conflicts. Since 2020, a string of successful military coups have either interrupted fragile transitions such as in Sudan (2021), or have overthrown democratically elected governments in war-affected countries such as Mali (2020), Burkina Faso (2022) and Niger (2023). Military takeovers have also occurred in Guinea (2021) and Gabon (2023), and an undemocratic transition took place in Chad (2021). These military coups have gone hand in hand with executive branches evading constitutionally set two-term limits. Out of a total of 49 countries in Sub-Saharan Africa, 26 either do not have term limits or have not respected them.[3] The exceptions to this trend of erosion of democratic practices have been Nigeria and Mozambique, where presidents left office voluntarily, and the DRC, where the term limit has not yet been reached but an unsuccessful, amateurish coup attempt took place in May 2024.

Socio-economic
Weak social contracts
Conflict-affected countries in Sub-Saharan Africa suffer from a weak social contract between rulers and citizens. This is manifested through countries' failure to extend basic services to marginalised communities in peripheral regions or to specific groups, which results in the consolidation of parallel informal authorities and local economies. In turn, citizens' feelings of distrust of and disaffection from states' authorities persist. Armed conflicts

exacerbate these dynamics. In some cases, such as in Ethiopia, Mali and South Sudan, intercommunal violence around traditional patterns of competition for scarce resources intersects with lagging state presence. These embedded dynamics provide the bedrock for insurgencies to form and proliferate (including transnational jihadist insurgencies).

Exploitation of natural resources
Competition over high-value commodities further exacerbates conflict and violence. Notable cases include the Central African Republic (CAR), the DRC and Niger, which are rich in minerals (e.g., cobalt and uranium). In these contexts, diverse domestic actors play an important role, including NSAGs (especially violent extremist groups) overseeing a system of local labour exploitation, criminal groups engaging in illicit trafficking, and certain economic and political elites at the national level. Often the boundaries between these actors are blurred. Furthermore, non-Western foreign countries (e.g., China and Russia) increasingly secure commercially advantageous and strategically important mineral concessions in African countries, and often these agreements lack adequate social and environmental safeguards. In conflict-affected countries with high-value minerals, negative impacts on people and the environment are magnified. The confluence of these dynamics makes conflicts more entrenched in local economic systems, and thus more difficult to address.

Security and military
Changes in peacekeeping
The decline of UN peacekeeping in favour of diverse Africa-led operations is also exacerbating armed-conflict dynamics (see Figure 1). During the reporting period, authorities in Mali and the DRC requested that the UN withdraw its peacekeeping missions from their territories. While the UN Multidimensional Integrated Stabilization Mission in Mali had swiftly pulled out by the end of 2023, MONUSCO is expected to leave eastern DRC by December 2024. Arguably, the UN will leave a security and political vacuum in both countries.

The closing of two of the largest UN peacekeeping operations on the continent (and the two longest-serving ones) highlights a larger trend. In the last decade, no new UN peacekeeping operation has been deployed to Sub-Saharan Africa and only four of them remain as of June 2024, which is less than half their number a decade ago. Concomitantly, African-led peace support operations (PSOs) have come to the fore, numbering ten operations in 2023 and including those led by the African Union (AU), regional economic communities (RECs) like ECOWAS and SADC, and ad hoc state-led coalitions.[4] However, the AU currently lacks the legitimacy and capacity of UN actors, and it would require institutional reforms to define RECs' mandates and adopt an overarching approach to peace and security. African PSOs face challenges regarding potential impartiality because of inter-state rivalries and, critically, gaps in financing, among other issues.

Geopolitical
Growing influence by third-party states and Russia's role
Geopolitical instability has increasingly shaped armed conflict and crises in Sub-Saharan Africa over the past five years, as third-party states' involvement in internal conflicts has become one of the most important drivers of insecurity in the region. Third-party states exercise their influence through both direct military intervention and non-military means. From the Sahel to the Great Lakes Region to the Horn of Africa, the role played by great and middle powers (i.e., Western states, Russia, Gulf countries and Turkiye) in making conflicts protracted and intractable is greater than at any time since the end of the Cold War.

There are also inter-state disputes between neighbouring countries or at the level of RECs that reverberate or are played out in internal conflicts. This is true for the Horn of Africa, the Sahel and the Great Lakes Region. For example, tensions between the DRC and Rwanda impact and increasingly drive political violence in the eastern DRC, while other regional states are compelled to take a position. Countries like Kenya and Uganda, among others, are driven by their respective national interests and exercise their influence within RECs, resulting in more regional instability. Uganda is also being accused of supporting the M23. In the Sahel, the unravelling of security partnerships with Western actors has been accompanied (and facilitated) by Russia's increased influence. While Moscow previously operated indirectly in the region through the Wagner Group, it is now doing so openly in Burkina Faso, Mali and Niger, through enhanced diplomatic and commercial ties and through the re-branded Africa Corps.

Conflict Parties

Coalitions and multilateral responses

The reporting period witnessed important changes with respect to coalitions and multilateral responses, including in the Sahel, the eastern DRC and Mozambique. The UN peacekeeping forces' withdrawal from Mali and DRC and the consolidation of regional PSOs were accompanied by continental dilemmas regarding the AU's future approach to peace and security. Calls for reforms to its African Peace and Security Architecture intensified amid ambiguous responses to military coups and the erosion of democracy (e.g., in the Sahel and the CAR), ineffective conflict-management efforts (e.g., in Sudan), and an exclusively military-based approach to peace operations (e.g., in Somalia).

The recent UN Security Council Resolution 2719 (2023) allowing discretionary UN funding for AU peace missions represented an important advancement. Nonetheless, the AU's strategic autonomy regarding the scope, mandate and timeline of peace operations is bound to remain weak as long as funding is externally driven by the UN and Western donors. Thus, African countries' willingness to dispense with UN operations (i.e., Mali and the DRC), diversify security partnerships beyond Western actors (i.e., the CAR, Ethiopia and Sudan), or supplant Western actors altogether (i.e., Burkina Faso, Mali and Niger) also showed frustration with traditional Western modes of security.

One more point of multilateral concern was the flexible relationship between the AU and RECs, which is underpinned by the principle of subsidiarity. In practice, this translates into RECs often being on the front line of crisis management without strong AU backing at the political level or institutional oversight. This approach remained under tremendous strain, as the case of Niger and ECOWAS testifies. Following the July 2023 military takeover in Niger, ECOWAS established swift sanctions and threatened military intervention against Niamey. This was, however, not followed by action nor by the AU's decisive support, and it resulted in a loss of regional legitimacy by ECOWAS and a hopeless fracture that led the military juntas in Burkina Faso, Mali and Niger to pull out from the economic bloc. A similar rift took place between Sudan and the East African REC, the Intergovernmental Authority on Development (IGAD), which has been unable to be influential in brokering a ceasefire. Thus, while RECs have significantly strengthened their PSO footprint, their inability to be effective at the diplomatic level has weakened their political influence.

Additionally, during the reporting period, Burkina Faso, Mali and Niger established the AES with an anti-Western tone, while the G5-Sahel coalition disintegrated. In Mozambique, the SADC opted not to renew its peacekeeping mission in Cabo Delgado (known as SAMIM) and was scheduled to withdraw by July 2024. Likewise, in the DRC, the government terminated the EACRF due to its ineffectiveness and requested the deployment of a SADC mission in December 2023.

Non-state armed groups

Sub-Saharan Africa continued to be the region most impacted by jihadist terrorism and violent extremism in the reporting period. Terrorist fatalities on the continent (including North Africa) nearly doubled from 2021–23.[5] Eight of the 15 countries with the highest terrorism impact are in Sub-Saharan Africa. These include Sahelian Burkina Faso, Mali and Niger; Cameroon and Nigeria in the Lake Chad Basin; and the DRC, Mozambique and Somalia.[6] The Sahel and Somalia witnessed a 43% and a 22% increase from 2022–23 in the number of violent-extremist-linked deaths, respectively.[7]

In 2023, the Sahel notably accounted for almost half of all terrorism fatalities globally and 26% of terrorist attacks. In Burkina Faso alone terrorism fatalities numbered 1,907 (or a quarter of the total number globally) in 2023, a 68% increase from 2022, with the country now suffering from the highest impact of terrorism globally.[8] This is due to the expansion of the al-Qaeda-affiliated Group to Support Islam and Muslims (JNIM) coalition in the Sahel, which perpetrates violence against state forces and local communities and battles other NSAGs.

A number of important dynamics related to NSAGs and jihadist violent extremists also solidified during the reporting period. In 2023, 90% of all terrorist attacks globally took place in conflict-affected countries.[9] Additionally, jihadism on the continent has lost much of its international dimension, with groups instead operating at a more local level. In Mozambique, the Sahel and Somalia, jihadist extremists increasingly pursue local strategies of embedding themselves into communities. This has made uprooting such groups more difficult. Transnational affiliations to the Islamic State (ISIS) and al-Qaeda by local jihadist groups like JNIM, Somalia's al-Shabaab and several ISIS offshoots have substantially weakened over time. This trend responded to a deliberate strategy by jihadist groups in Africa to become more involved in local conflicts either by stirring up pre-existing conflicts or by hijacking local grievances regarding access to and management of natural resources, for example, in areas outside state control.[10]

Third-party involvement

The number of internationalised civil wars in Sub-Saharan Africa (i.e., those internal conflicts that feature the direct military intervention of a third-party state) has increased dramatically year-on-year since 2010, but has slightly decreased since 2020, declining from 18 to 15.[11] Nevertheless, it is the influence and involvement by third-party states in conflict-affected countries that has increased due to heightened geopolitical competition. Alongside major changes in international coalitions and multilateral responses, the reporting period witnessed key shifts in third-party interventions in conflict-affected countries on the continent, especially in the Sahel and the Horn of Africa.

In the former, Russia has consolidated its diplomatic offensive to become an alternative partner to the military juntas in Burkina Faso, Mali and Niger, as well as its dominant position as a security provider. After Mali, both Burkina Faso and Niger formalised their security arrangements with Russia, which sent military trainers and personnel from the Africa Corps to Niger in April. During the reporting period, Moscow's progressive involvement in the Sahel occurred in parallel with the ousting of Western military assistance. The Nigerien junta swiftly denounced its partnership with France, which pulled out in December 2023, and in April 2024 it asked the United States to withdraw its over 1,000-strong contingent and to close Airbase 101 and Airbase 201. This was an important setback for Washington, as Niger represented a key security partner in the surveillance of jihadist terrorist groups in the region, with the set-up of Airbase 201 in Agadez having cost an estimated US$100 million.[12]

The Horn of Africa also continued to experience external involvement and influence by Gulf countries and Turkiye, which consolidated their foreign-policy ambitions in the region. In response to the Ethiopia–Somaliland MoU, Somalia signed a ten-year defence and economic cooperation agreement with Turkiye.[13] Further, in the case of Sudan, the warring parties have strengthened their ties with Iran, Russia and the United Arab Emirates, in addition to Egypt, while resisting pressure from the European Union, Saudi Arabia and the US to initiate a ceasefire.

Regional Humanitarian Trends

Overall, the region has become more violent and deadly as the civil war in Sudan has driven trends in fatalities and events, which increased by 28% and 21%, respectively, compared to the previous 12-month period. In addition to monumental increases in both categories in Sudan, the number of violent events in Ethiopia doubled and the country witnessed a 67% increase in fatalities year-on-year. The number of fatalities in Niger similarly increased nearly twofold, while the number of fatalities in South Sudan, Chad and Mozambique decreased by 54%, 44% and 33%, respectively.[14]

Amid skyrocketing trends in the number of refugees and internally displaced persons (IDPs) globally, Sub-Saharan Africa is home to some of the largest forced-displacement situations and worst humanitarian crises. According to UN High Commissioner for Refugees (UNHCR) official data, at the end of 2023, there were an estimated 9.3m refugees and asylum seekers, nearly 35m IDPs and 1m stateless persons in the region, representing 37% of the total number of forcibly displaced people globally.[15] These escalating numbers and dwindling resources to attend to the immediate needs of displaced people mean that several situations verge on (or are already in) a state of humanitarian catastrophe, including in Burkina Faso, the DRC and Sudan. The scale of food insecurity among displaced people is unprecedented in the twenty-first century, as is the scale of individuals who may soon be facing famine.

Driven by the civil war in Sudan, the Horn of Africa hosts the largest displaced population within

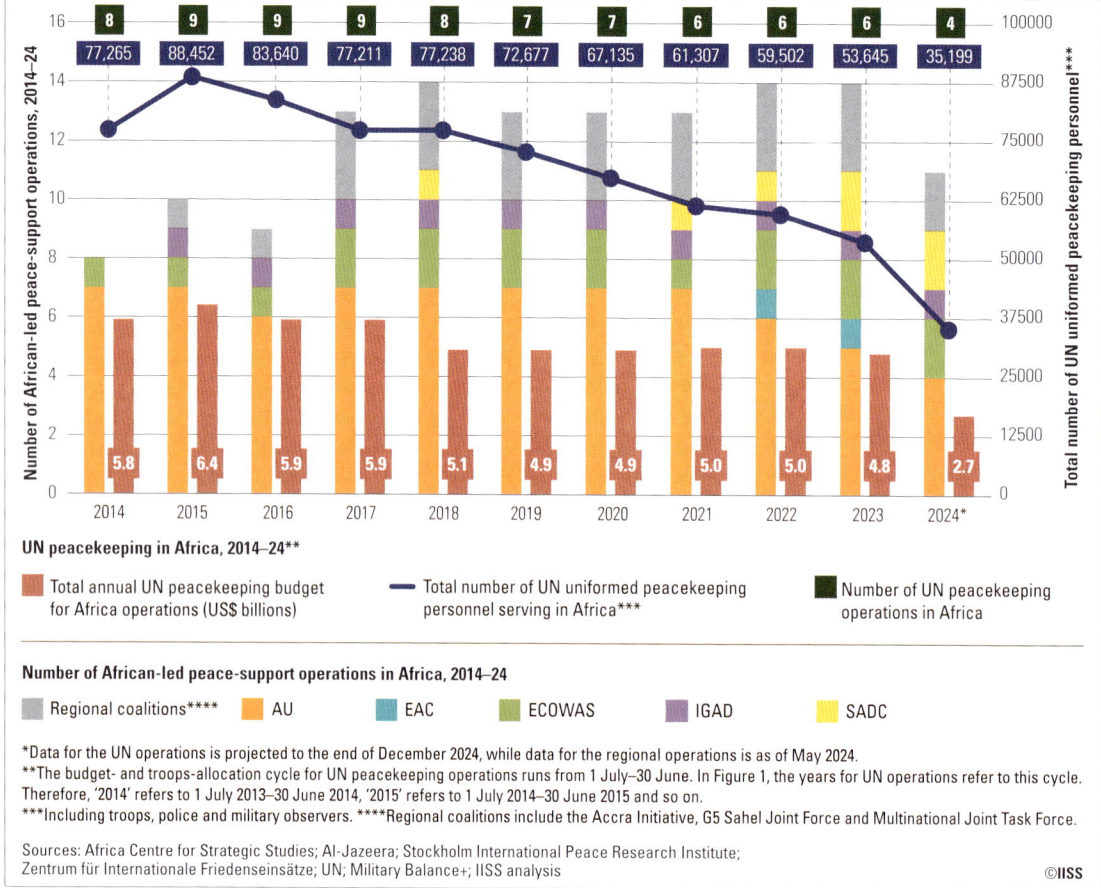

Figure 1: Trends in peacekeeping and peace-support operations in Africa

the continent. By the end of the reporting period, nearly 15 months of fighting in Sudan had produced one of the most horrific impacts on civilians and the largest humanitarian crisis in Sub-Saharan Africa since the end of the Cold War. Since the war started in April 2023, over 10m people have been forcibly displaced from their homes, including 7.7m IDPs and 1.5m refugees as of June 2024.[16] Astonishingly, of the 25m people needing humanitarian assistance, 17.7m suffer from acute food insecurity and nearly 5m people are estimated to be on the brink of famine, as of April 2024.[17] Sudanese refugees in neighbouring countries, especially over 620,000 individuals in Chad as of June 2024, also suffer from catastrophic levels of food insecurity.[18]

The DRC faced unprecedented humanitarian crises during the reporting period as well, driven by increasing violence perpetrated by the M23 in the east of the country. During 2023, 3.8m people were displaced internally, resulting in a total of 6.7m IDPs by December that year. The situation worsened in 2024 as M23's assault on Goma displaced hundreds of thousands more individuals.[19]

Additional relevant hotspots for the reporting period included Somalia and the Sahel. The former suffers not only from displacement due to conflict and insecurity, but also from internal displacement due to climate-related hazards and extreme weather, including disrupted rain patterns, droughts and floods. In 2023, nearly 700,000 individuals were forcibly displaced by al-Shabaab-related violence and an additional 2m were internally displaced by environmental factors.[20] In the Sahel, amid spiralling levels of violence, Burkina Faso has been experiencing the worst humanitarian crisis in its history with one in ten individuals being an IDP. In Burkina Faso's Sahel and Centre-Nord regions, the rate of internal displacement is nearly 25%, driving disruption to services, productive activities and markets.[21]

Outlook

Prospects for peace

With armed conflicts in the region continuing to appear protracted and intractable, prospects for peace in the main Sub-Saharan African conflict theatres remain dim in the short term. There are several ongoing regional trends that explain this outlook. Peace is harder to negotiate when there is security fragmentation, which is underpinned by the proliferation of NSAGs and the increasingly localised nature of several jihadist groups. Because of this trend, negotiated peace agreements in the last decade have been limited in geographic scope and only involved local conflict parties rather than national-level actors. Comprehensive peace agreements like the one that ended the civil war in Ethiopia in November 2022 have become the exception rather than the norm. Further, it is common practice for governments not to negotiate with jihadist extremist groups, which, in turn, have not shown interest in negotiated solutions either.

At the international level, geopolitical tensions do not favour diplomatic solutions in Sub-Saharan African conflict settings, as competing great and middle powers often approach these conflicts as proxy wars. Heightened inter-state tensions in the three main conflict sub-regions likewise discourage potential peace outcomes, including Ethiopia–Somalia tensions in the Horn of Africa, DRC–Rwanda conflict in the Great Lakes Region, and Burkina Faso's, Mali's and Niger's rupture with ECOWAS in West Africa and the Sahel. The progressive loss of legitimacy by multilateral diplomatic institutions (i.e., the UN, the AU and RECs) in several conflict-affected countries (i.e., in the Sahel, the DRC, Somalia and Sudan) represents a key additional obstacle to potential negotiated solutions.

Escalation potential and regional spillovers

Potential for regional escalation exists in all main conflict theatres. In the Sahel, the threat of jihadist extremist groups to the northern provinces of Benin, Côte d'Ivoire, Ghana and Togo persisted in the reporting period and, although small, is likely to continue in the foreseeable future. Benin and Togo are reportedly more exposed to this threat than Ghana and Côte d'Ivoire. So far, the four countries have been resilient and successful at containing insecurity. Meanwhile, jihadist armed groups have not shown significant interest in systematically bringing their insurgencies to these countries, although there are reports that groups have already established operations in northern Benin and Ghana. It is conceivable that the pullout of Burkina Faso, Mali and Niger from ECOWAS will have negative effects on regional security, as cooperation mechanisms unravel and inter-state tensions between the two blocs remain.

The Horn of Africa is also in turmoil. The civil war in Sudan threatens the stability of neighbouring Chad given the influx of over 620,000 refugees, as well as the restive regions in western Ethiopia, which chronically suffer from low-level insurgencies.[22] South Sudan's oil exports are highly dependent on Sudan's pipelines, and Sudan's civil war has slashed oil revenues for Juba, threatening its economic stability and the delicate strategic balance between the country's elites and factions. Regionally, the Ethiopia–Somaliland MoU and the increasing tensions in the Red Sea, due to Ansarullah (the Houthis) disrupting maritime traffic following the outbreak of the Israel–Hamas war, represent potential elements for escalation.

In the Great Lakes Region, the high-level tensions between the DRC and Rwanda have been ongoing for the last three years, but they have abated in a few instances after almost reaching the point of an inter-state conflict. The DRC's and Rwanda's armed forces have allegedly already been confronting one another militarily in the eastern DRC. A recent UN report officially claiming that Uganda has provided support to M23 has raised concerns that Uganda's actions may heighten regional tensions.[23] In the DRC, President Tshisekedi won a controversial second mandate during the reporting period and suffered from a coup attempt, which, though it was amateurish by most accounts, signalled that potential instability in Kinshasa exists.

Strategic prospects

Sub-Saharan Africa routinely features as the upcoming strategic hotspot for great-power competition, although major events in parallel theatres (i.e., the Russia–Ukraine war and Israel–Hamas war) continue to shadow its importance. While most great and middle powers have conducted high-level fora with African states in the last three years (e.g., China, Turkiye and the US as well as, more recently, Italy, Russia and South Korea), these events failed to translate into strategic priorities for the powers involved.[24] This tendency is likely to continue as Africa retains a key strategic role in the production of certain minerals and has significant economic and strategic potential given its young demography and untapped markets.

With respect to conflict-affected countries on the continent, great and middle powers have been strategically competing over the provision of security for the last three to four years – a trend that is likely to continue. A diverse group of non-Western authoritarian states and undemocratic regimes (from Russia to Turkiye to the Gulf states) establish security ties in war-torn countries in a transactional way. These new security partnerships do not adhere to human-rights standards and democratic principles and may exacerbate conflict drivers. While the US and the West have been rightly accused of double standards at times, they do share a commitment to diplomatic conflict-resolution practices and adherence to international norms. On the continent, it is conceivable that the trend of conflict-affected countries relying on security-first solutions and partnering with non-Western states will continue and potentially expand.

REGIONAL KEY EVENTS

POLITICAL EVENTS

 SENEGAL
3 July 2023
President Macky Sall announces he will not run for a third term in Senegal's 2024 elections.

 NIGER
26 July
Nigerien president Mohamed Bazoum is detained by the presidential guard in a *coup d'état* at the presidential palace.

 **ZIMBABWE**
23 August
Zimbabwe's President Emmerson Mnangagwa wins a second term with 52.6% of the vote.

MILITARY/VIOLENT EVENTS

  DEMOCRATIC REPUBLIC OF THE CONGO, RWANDA
27 July 2023
The Congolese army accuses Rwandan forces of crossing its border and attacking the frontier security forces, potentially escalating tensions in Central Africa.

 NIGERIA
19 August
Jama'atu Ahlis Sunna Lidda'awati wal-Jihad (JAS, popularly known as Boko Haram) and the Islamic State West Africa Province (ISWAP) clash after claims of JAS/Boko Haram kidnapping 60 ISWAP fighters in Nigeria.

 MALI
25 August
UN peacekeepers end their first phase of withdrawal from Mali, causing violence between the army and militants to intensify.

 **GABON**
30 August
President Ali Bongo Ondimba is elected to a third term; hours later, Gabonese military officers arrest him in a *coup d'état* at the presidential palace.

 BURKINA FASO, MALI, NIGER
16 September
Burkina Faso, Mali and Niger sign the AES charter, a mutual defence pact aimed at fighting armed rebellions and external aggression.

 ETHIOPIA, SOMALIA
17 September
Ethiopian forces ambush al-Shabaab fighters in western Somalia, resulting in nearly 200 deaths.

 BURKINA FASO
5 November
Unidentified assailants attack Zaongo village in northern Burkina Faso, burning properties and killing at least 70 civilians.

 MADAGASCAR
16 November
Madagascar's President Andry Rajoelina wins a third presidential term with 59% of the vote.

 NIGERIA
3 December
Nigerian military airstrikes accidentally kill at least 85 Nigerian civilians in Tudun Biri village, Kaduna.

 DEMOCRATIC REPUBLIC OF THE CONGO
20 December
Congolese President Tshisekedi wins a second term with 73% of the vote, while the opposition and some civil-society groups demand a rerun.

 SUDAN
21 December
The RSF captures Wad Madani, the capital of Al Jazirah State and Sudan's second-largest city, from the SAF.

 NIGER
22 December
French troops withdraw from Niger, marking the end of the two countries' military cooperation in fighting Islamist insurgencies in the Sahel.

 ETHIOPIA, SOMALIA
1 January 2024
Ethiopia signs an MoU with Somaliland granting Ethiopia access to naval and commercial ports in exchange for recognition of Somaliland's sovereignty.

 SOMALIA
10 January 2024
Al-Shabaab is accused of killing one and abducting six UN workers in Somalia after seizing a UN helicopter.

 **BURKINA FASO, MALI, NIGER**
28 January
Burkina Faso, Mali and Niger announce they will leave ECOWAS after being suspended from the regional bloc.

SUDAN
9–10 March
Sudanese SAF Gen. Yasser al-Atta rejects plans for a ceasefire with the RSF during the month of Ramadan.

 NIGER
16 March
Niger's transitional government ends military cooperation with the US and asks US troops to withdraw.

 SENEGAL
24 March
After postponement and a constitutional crisis, Bassirou Diomaye Faye wins Senegal's presidential elections.

 NIGER
11 April
Russia sends military trainers and air-defence systems to Niger to aid in fighting armed groups in the Sahel.

 CHAD
6 May
Chadian President Mahamat Idriss Déby Itno wins re-election with 61% of the vote in a presidential election that is deemed unfair.

 KENYA
22 May
Kenyan President William Ruto makes a state visit to the US, the first African leader to do so in 15 years.

 SUDAN
24 May
The RSF continues to attack al-Fashir, a strategic SAF stronghold in Sudan, killing 47 people, mostly civilians.

 SOUTH AFRICA
29 May
In South African general elections, the African National Congress loses the majority for the first time since coming to power in 1994.

 BENIN
5 June
Jihadist militants conduct a surprise terrorist attack in northern Benin's Pendjari National Park, killing seven soldiers.

 BURKINA FASO
11 June
Al-Qaeda-affiliated JNIM attacks a military post and allegedly kills 107 soldiers.

Notes

[1] IISS analysis based on data from UCDP/PRIO. See UCDP/PRIO Armed Conflict Dataset Version 24.1 and UCDP Non-State Conflict Dataset Version 24.1. Nils Petter Gleditsch et al., 'Armed Conflict 1946–2001: A New Dataset', *Journal of Peace Research*, vol. 39, no. 5, 2002, pp. 615–37; Shawn Davies et al., 'Organized Violence 1989–2023, and the Prevalence of Organized Crime Groups', *Journal of Peace Research*, vol. 61, no. 4, 2024; and Ralph Sundberg, Kristine Eck and Joakim Kreutz, 'Introducing the UCDP Non-state Conflict Dataset', *Journal of Peace Research*, vol. 49, no. 2, 2012.

[2] For further details, see the Sub-Saharan Africa Regional Spotlight chapter, 'The Ethiopia–Somaliland MoU: A Driver of Regional Instability?'.

3   Africa Center for Strategic Studies, 'Term Limit Evasions and Coups in Africa: Two Sides of the Same Coin', 24 October 2024.
4   Benjamin Petrini and Erica Pepe, 'Peacekeeping in Africa: From UN to Regional Peace Support Operations', IISS, 18 March 2024.
5   Africa Center for Strategic Studies, 'Deaths Linked to Militant Islamist Violence in Africa Continue to Spiral', 29 January 2024.
6   Institute for Economics and Peace, 'Global Terrorism Index 2024: Measuring the Impact of Terrorism', February 2024, p. 6.
7   Africa Center for Strategic Studies, 'Deaths Linked to Militant Islamist Violence in Africa Continue to Spiral'.
8   Ibid., p. 10.
9   Ibid.
10 See 'From Global Jihad to Local Insurgencies: The Changing Nature of Sub-Saharan Jihadism', in IISS, *The Armed Conflict Survey 2023* (Abingdon: Routledge for the IISS, 2023), pp. 160–4.
11 IISS analysis based on data from UCDP/PRIO. See UCDP/PRIO Armed Conflict Dataset Version 24.1. Petter Gleditsch et al., 'Armed Conflict 1946–2001: A New Dataset'; and Davies et al., 'Organized Violence 1989–2023, and the Prevalence of Organized Crime Groups'.
12 Danai Nesta Kupemba and Natasha Booty, 'US Troops to Leave Niger by Mid-September', BBC News, 19 May 2024.
13 Mimi Mefo Takambou, 'Somalia–Turkey Security Deal: How Does It Impact Ethiopia?', Deutsche Welle, 26 February 2024.
14 IISS analysis based on data from the Armed Conflict Location & Event Data Project (ACLED), www.acleddata.com.
15 Aimée-Noël Mbiyozo, 'African Refugees Neglected as Crises Worsen', ISS Today, 20 June 2024; and IISS analysis using UNHCR, 'Refugee Data Finder'.
16 UNHCR, 'Operational Data Portal: Sudan Situation'.
17 UN Office for the Coordination of Humanitarian Affairs, 'Sudan: One Year of Conflict', 15 April 2024.
18 UNHCR, 'Operational Data Portal: Sudan Situation'.
19 Internal Displacement Monitoring Centre, '2024 Global Report on Internal Displacement', 2024, p. 28.
20 Ibid., pp. 23–5
21 UNHCR, 'R4Sahel Coordination Platform: Sahel Crisis: Burkina Faso'.
22 UNHCR, 'Operational Data Portal: Sudan Situation'.
23 See Sonia Rolley, 'Uganda Provided Support to M23 Rebels in Congo, UN Report Says', Reuters, 8 July 2024.
24 During the reporting period, the Russia–Africa Summit in July 2023 featured the presence of 17 heads of state and 49 country delegations. This is a lower number of heads of state or heads of government than those who attended the 2019 summit (43), and critically, a much lower number than the 45 heads of state or heads of government who attended the US–Africa Leaders Summit in December 2022. Moscow announced the existence of cooperation agreements with 40 countries on the continent. See Alex Vines and Tighisti Amare, 'Russia–Africa Summit Fails to Deliver Concrete Results', Chatham House, 2 August 2023; Peace and Security Council Report, 'Russia–Africa Summit: What Was In It for Africa?', Institute for Security Studies, 18 September 2023; and Abubakar Usman, 'Africa Should Push Back Against "One-Plus-Africa" Diplomatic Summits', London School of Economics and Political Science, 16 August 2023.

The Ethiopia–Somaliland MoU: A Driver of Regional Instability?

The signing of a memorandum of understanding (MoU) between Ethiopia and Somaliland on 1 January 2024 surprised countries within the Horn of Africa and risked further destabilising the region. If the MoU is implemented, Ethiopia will have access to the Red Sea via the port of Berbera and a 20-kilometre area along the coastline where it plans to build a military base (see Figure 1). In return, Somaliland expects Ethiopia to recognise its de jure and de facto independence.

Traditionally, the political affairs of countries within the Horn of Africa have been closely intertwined. Multiple transnational interests have fostered a flexible alignment dynamic for any issue that affects two or more regional countries. Tensions between Ethiopia and Somalia as a result of the MoU thus led to the formation of two confronting blocs. Several regional actors, such as Eritrea and Djibouti, and extra-regional actors, such as Egypt, Turkiye and the United Arab Emirates (UAE), felt compelled to take a position on the issue. A strategic convergence between Ethiopia, the UAE and Somaliland caused Djibouti, Egypt and Eritrea to support Somalia unconditionally. Meanwhile, other actors, such as Kenya, South Sudan and Turkiye, have been more neutral in their approach, though they have made some expressions of solidarity with Somalia. These developments will likely significantly affect the political and security dynamics of the region, as evidenced by the signature of an agreement on economic and defence cooperation, including maritime security, between Somalia and Turkiye in early February.

Most indications point to greater regional instability as a result of these shifts, potentially leading to the disruption of political balances in Ethiopia, Somalia and Somaliland. However, the signing of the MoU might also set the stage for greater economic interdependence, thus reducing the likelihood of new inter-state conflicts.

The regional picture
Ethiopia's signing of the MoU came at a time of already shifting domestic balances and regional projections. If implemented, the agreement could accelerate these processes and increase Ethiopian Prime Minister Abiy Ahmed's power. If implementation is delayed, however, it could undermine Abiy's hold on the country.

In October 2023, Abiy put access to the sea at the top of his political agenda. Since Eritrean independence in 1993, Ethiopians have felt the commercial and strategic downside of losing access to its seaports, making it a familiar issue in public debate.[1] When Abiy took office in 2018, one of his rationales for promoting the normalisation of relations with Eritrea was his interest in accessing the ports of Assab and Massawa as alternatives to the port of Djibouti. Currently, Ethiopia relies on Djibouti for 95% of its exports and imports.[2]

After the 2018 Jeddah peace agreement between Ethiopia and Eritrea, it became clear that both Abiy and Eritrean President Isais Afewerki had made a decision that served their countries' domestic interests. Isais's goal was the easing of sanctions and international isolation. Abiy, meanwhile, used normalisation as an opportunity to rebalance domestic politics, concentrating power in the hands of the country's two main ethnic groups, the Amhara and the Oromo, and sidelining the Tigrayans, who were the former power holders. Faced with the rise of Oromo nationalism, Abiy revived the pan-Ethiopian idea behind his Prosperity Party (PP) while presenting himself as the restorer of Ethiopian greatness.

With the outbreak of conflict in Tigray Region in Ethiopia in November 2020, the pragmatic convergence of Abiy's and Isais's interests also became evident. The Eritrean Defence Forces (EDF) intervened by occupying several districts in western Tigray and settled old scores with the Tigray People's Liberation Front (TPLF), under whose rule the two countries had fought a bloody war in 1998–2000. To overcome the Tigrayans, the EDF coordinated with the Ethiopian National Defence Force (ENDF), as well as with the Amhara regional army.

The signing of the November 2022 Pretoria Agreement that put an end to the civil war in

Tigray paved the way for the further transformation of Ethiopia's regional and domestic relations. Ethiopia's position appears weaker than it was a decade ago. Abiy's relationship with Isais cooled following the signing of the agreement, and tensions between the two countries are increasing. Addis Ababa has accused Asmara of supporting Amhara militias in order to destabilise Ethiopia. Likewise, Eritrea did not appreciate Abiy's recent comments on access to the Red Sea being a 'matter of existence' for Ethiopia.[3]

Ethiopia's domestic context

The peace deal with the TPLF also solidified the rift between Abiy's government and Amhara nationalists. The latter, feeling betrayed, began to challenge the central government. The split between the prime minister and the Amhara had two consequences: a reshuffling of political alliances and an increase in inter-ethnic violence, especially between Amhara and Oromo groups.

In Addis Ababa, a process of 'oromisation' of decision-making positions began, with key roles and administrative cadres within the state apparatus awarded to ethnic-Oromo officials. Furthermore, Abiy increased his control over Amhara regional state officials, fuelling the ethnic group's resentment towards central institutions. Consequently, the ranks of Amhara's *fano* militia started to swell, with the armed group expanding its struggle against Oromo groups and symbols of the federal state. Clashes with the Oromo Liberation Army (OLA) in the disputed North Shewa zone resumed amid heightened inter-ethnic tensions. This precarious balance between ethnic groups collapsed in November 2023 with a series of violent attacks by *fano* militias and the OLA against unarmed civilians. The situation escalated further with the intervention of the ENDF.

Meanwhile, not all Tigray Defence Force (TDF) fighters have accepted the Pretoria Agreement's conditions. The agreement effectively froze the western Tigray issue at the status quo, leaving entire districts under Amhara control. This decision has fuelled distrust of the Tigrayan ruling class (especially the TPLF), creating an inter-generational rift among Tigrayans.

This scenario has two main implications. Firstly, it could trigger a local conflict that might quickly escalate into a proxy war between Asmara and Addis Ababa. Secondly, the TPLF, the backbone of Tigrayan and Ethiopian politics for over two decades, risks losing its legitimacy in Tigray itself. These risks come at a time when the country's economic situation is also causing social tensions and political instability, with the population feeling the impact of the war in Tigray and facing rising inflation. Several provinces, not only in the Tigray region, are experiencing recurring cycles of famine. It is within this context of general instability and weakness that Abiy launched his maritime bid with Somaliland.

Somaliland's domestic-politics calculus

The regional context has provided an opportunity for Hargeisa to revive its independence aspirations. Due to its geographic location, Somaliland is a crucial territory for exerting influence in the Red Sea and projecting power into the Indo-Pacific.

From de facto independence in 1991 to the present, the former British Somaliland has been able to foster a rapid and effective state-building process. In a region plagued by constant turmoil, Hargeisa's embryonic institutions have provided stability. Recently, however, there have been several setbacks in consolidating institutions, including the postponement of the 2022 presidential vote until November 2024 – a decision that deepened internal political divisions.

Somaliland faces intense political polarisation, with the populace split between supporters of President Muse Bihi Abdi and supporters of the opposition.[4] Critics of Bihi argue that he has over-centralised power. The news of the signing of the MoU had a rallying effect on Somalilanders for a few weeks, but latent tensions have been subsequently reignited by the failure to publish the text of the agreement. The opposition will likely benefit from any delay in the agreement's implementation.[5]

Somaliland is also experiencing increasing security problems. The MoU has attracted the attention of al-Shabaab to Hargeisa. The terrorist group has had little interest in Somaliland for many years, but it sees Somaliland's potential independence as a threat to Somalia's territorial integrity. Furthermore, it considers an agreement with a non-Muslim state such as Ethiopia to be an open challenge to its authority.

The MoU and the future of Somaliland are thus at the centre of the competition between Mogadishu and al-Shabaab, which wants to legitimise itself

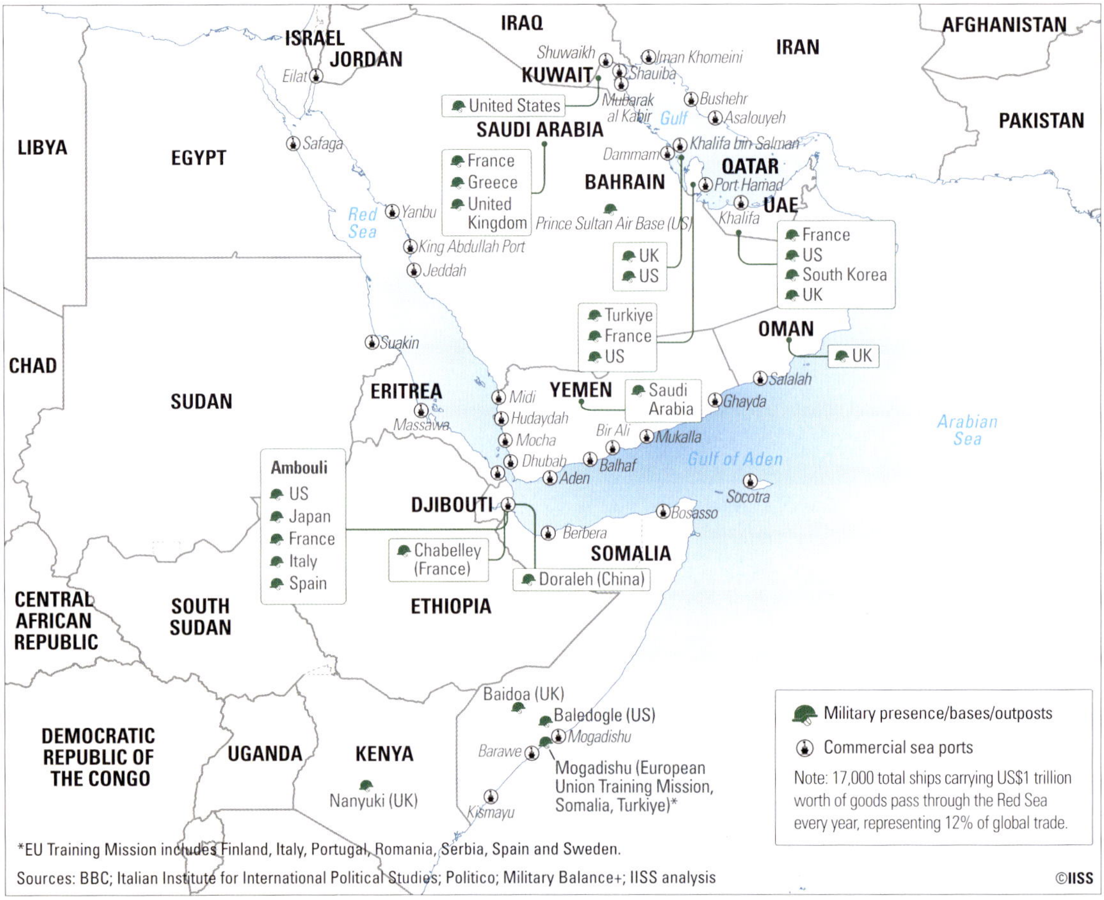

Figure 1: Maritime security in the Horn of Africa and the Gulf region

at the expense of the Somali federal government as a defender of Somalia's borders. As a result, al-Shabaab fighters might look to conduct attacks on infrastructure around Berbera or to reignite the so-called Las Anod conflict. For over a year, unrest in the three Dhulbahante-majority regions of Sool, Sanaag and Cayn (SSC), which seek to establish a new federal state of Khatumo (also known as SSC-Khatumo State), has changed Somaliland's security environment. Since the signing of the MoU, the number of armed groups active in the country has increased, especially around the town of Las Anod. According to authorities in Hargeisa, several militias are being directly supported by Mogadishu to foment unrest and derail Somaliland's ambitions.

Mogadishu's dilemmas

Crucially, the MoU opened a critical new phase in Ethiopia–Somalia relations. Mogadishu sees Addis Ababa's move as an open affront to its sovereignty and territorial integrity. Somalian President Hassan Sheikh Mohamud has therefore launched a diplomatic campaign on two levels: bilaterally and within international organisations. In the name of preserving the principle of territorial integrity, Somalia received prompt support from regional and continental bodies such as the Intergovernmental Authority on Development and the African Union (AU). At the bilateral level, the MoU has triggered a process of realignment, with regional and extra-regional actors taking sides. In particular, Mogadishu has strengthened relations with Ethiopia's main rival, Egypt. At the same time, Hassan Sheikh has exploited inter-clan relations to increase support for Somaliland's political opposition by coordinating with Djiboutian President Ismaïl Omar Guelleh. Eritrea remains in the background, aware of the potential gains to be made from further Ethiopian isolation.

Yet Somaliland and the MoU are not the only issues facing Hassan Sheikh. After some encouraging results in the counter-insurgency operation against al-Shabaab that began in August 2022, the Somali armed forces began to lose ground once again. Al-Shabaab has demonstrated resilience and a continued ability to reorganise itself and regain control of its lost territory. In part, this is because federal authorities have proved incapable of providing alternative governance in liberated areas.

The military stalemate against al-Shabaab has been accompanied by a regression in Somalia's political process. Hassan Sheikh is losing the trust of some of the federal states. Puntland, in particular, has reduced its support for the government. Weakening the president and central authority risks emboldening al-Shabaab and increasing the likelihood of the country's disintegration. The danger of widespread violence has risen with the United Nations Security Council's decision to lift the arms embargo in place since 1992. New local, clan-based militias are forming throughout the country. In this context, Somalia could be plunged back into chaos by the scheduled withdrawal of the AU Transition Mission in Somalia (ATMIS) peacekeeping contingent at the end of 2024.

Turkiye and the UAE's engagement in regional affairs

The implications of the MoU reach beyond just regional actors. The UAE, for instance, played a key role in the conclusion of the agreement. Besides the investments of Emirati company DP World in the port of Berbera and the corridor to the Ethiopian border, the UAE has long supported Abiy financially and politically. At the same time, the UAE also supports Hassan Sheikh and is active in the Somali security sector. The MoU ultimately represents an opportunity for the UAE to be a major player in the Gulf of Aden.

Somalia, meanwhile, is the primary beneficiary of Turkish engagement in the region. Ankara has invested in the country's stabilisation and state-building process for over a decade. From Turkiye's perspective, the MoU poses a threat to the present transition and future stability of Somalia and sets a concerning precedent for Ankara's Kurdish issue. Turkiye also has good relations with Ethiopia and Abiy, including on defence cooperation.

The signing of a security-cooperation agreement between Somalia and Turkiye has renewed concerns about competition between Ankara and the UAE in the region after a recent easing of tensions. However, the scenario is different from five years ago. Rather than competition, there are signs of strategic proximity between Ankara and Abu Dhabi. Their convergence of interests in the region could create suitable conditions for promoting greater stability, which would be a win–win situation for all stakeholders.

Glimmers of hope?

The dynamics prompted by the signing of the MoU could result in contrasting economic and stability outcomes. On the one hand, improved infrastructure and trade could create a virtuous circle for economic development in the Horn of Africa, with a positive spillover at the regional and national levels. To protect their investments, extra-regional players may also have a greater interest in stability in the region. On the other hand, infrastructure development could fuel the grievances of certain groups who may feel excluded from its economic benefits. Moreover, regional actors strengthened by external ties may be more likely to escalate tensions.

Nonetheless, the greatest concerns relate to Somalia. The MoU adds to the uncertainty generated by the end of the ATMIS mission in 2024, the growth of centrifugal forces (i.e., Puntland) and the proliferation of light weapons such as assault rifles due to the lifting of the international ban. Together, these factors may foster a process of implosion and fragmentation into several de facto Somali states in the coming years.

Notes

1. Author interview with Ethiopian politics expert, Addis Ababa, 7 February 2024.
2. Tesfa-Alem Tekle, 'Ethiopia Hopes Somaliland Port Terminal Reduces Dependence on Djibouti', *East African*, 28 June 2021.
3. 'Eritrea Responds to Abiy's Controversial Red Sea Remark', Club of Mozambique, 16 October 2024.
4. Author interview with Somaliland political expert, Hargeisa, 14 February 2024.
5. *Ibid.*

MALI

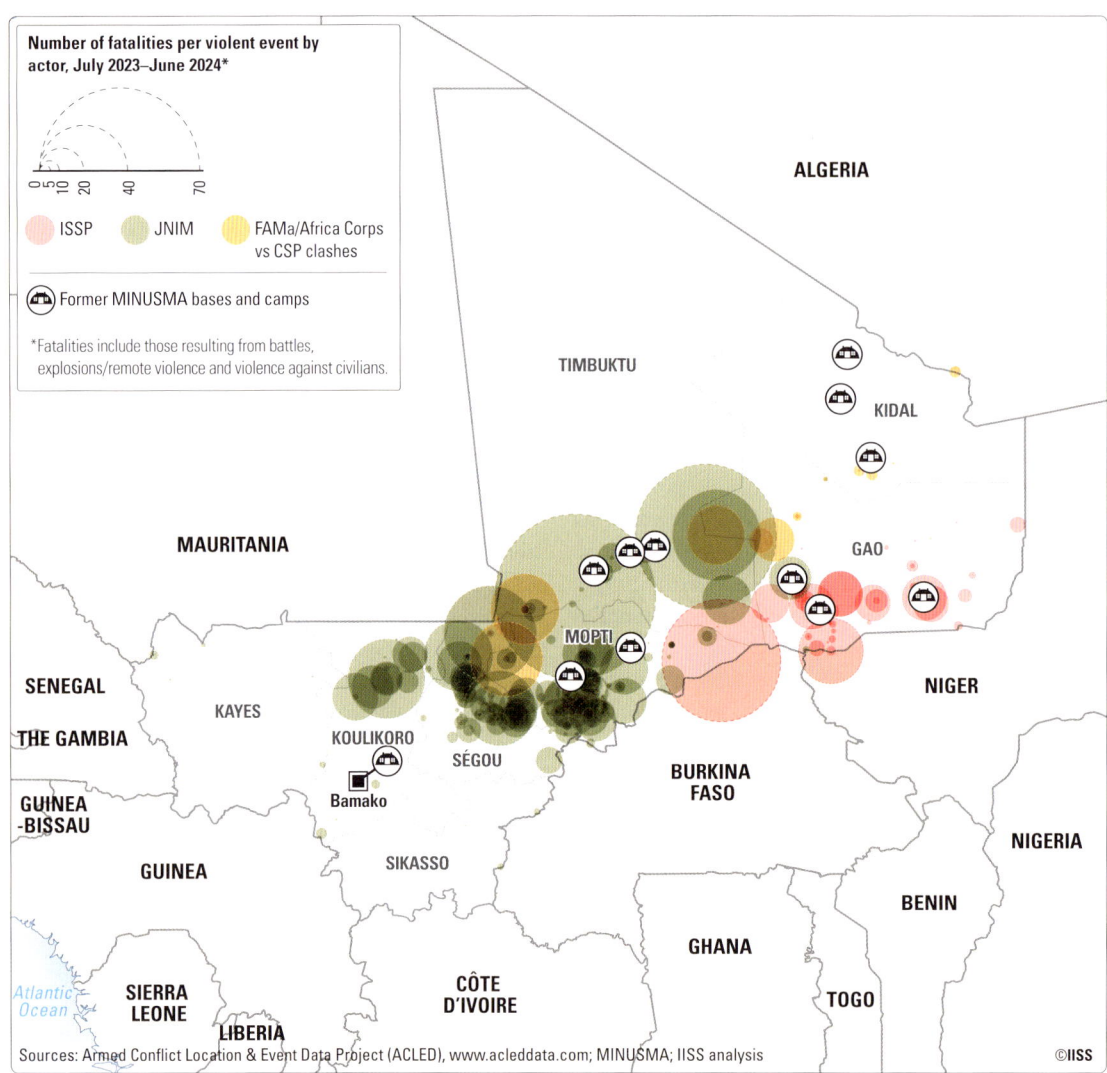

Conflict Overview

Mali is facing a multi-dimensional crisis marked by a long-running Tuareg insurgency, jihadist violence, intercommunal conflicts and political instability. This crisis has been fuelled by grievances over ethnically motivated political exclusion and marginalisation, poor security provision and ineffective governance.

One driver of instability in the country has its roots in the handling of transnational Tuareg aspirations for greater autonomy and recognition. The Tuareg rebellion of the 1960s and subsequent uprisings in the 1990s and early 2000s were precursors to the 2012 rebellion, which led to the collapse of state authority in northern Mali the following year. In response, several foreign interventions took place, including the French-led *Operation Serval* (later rebranded as *Operation Barkhane*) and the deployment of the African-led International Support Mission in Mali, which was later taken over by the United Nations Multidimensional Integrated Stabilization Mission in Mali (MINUSMA). In 2015, a

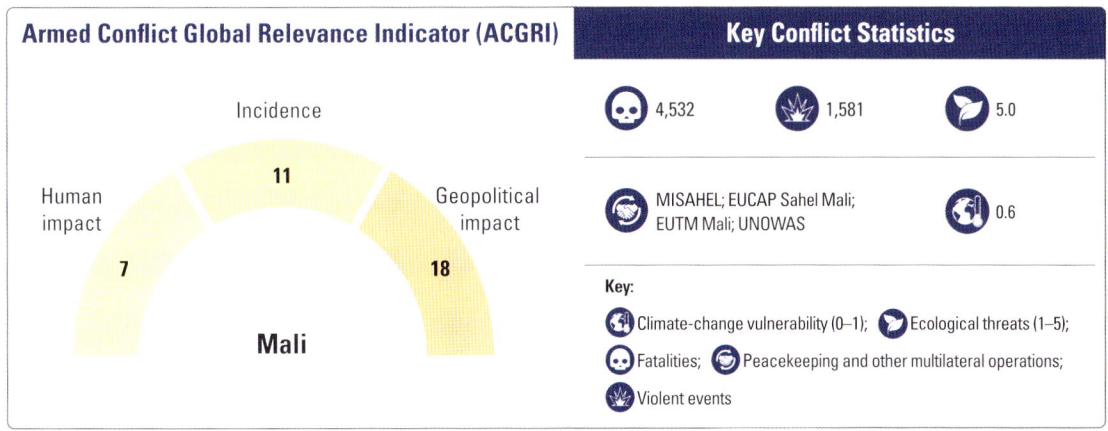

ACGRI pillars: IISS calculation based on multiple sources for 2023 and 2024 (scale: 0–100), except for some cases according to data availability. See Notes on Methodology and Data Appendix for all variables and further details on Key Conflict Statistics.

Conflict(s)	Type	Start date
Tuareg separatist conflict in the north (regions of Gao, Kidal, Timbuktu and northern Mopti)	I LI	2012
Jihadist insurgency (country wide)	II T	2013
Communal conflicts and state violence against the Fulani ethnic-minority groups	I IC	2018, recurrent

Key: **I IC** Internal: intercommunal; **I LI** Internal: localised insurgency; **II** Internationalised internal; **T** Transnational

fragile peace was brokered under the Algiers accord, which aimed to reconcile pro-independence factions like the Coordination of Azawad Movements (CMA) with the state and other Tuareg factions that favoured Malian state authority. The accord temporarily mitigated tensions between signatory groups. Yet, due to continuous delays in the implementation of many of its provisions, by 2023 fighting had resumed once more.

As the 2012 Tuareg uprising was unfolding, jihadist groups exploited the resulting power vacuum to establish themselves in northern Mali. In the years since, the Group to Support Islam and Muslims (JNIM) and the Islamic State Sahel Province (ISSP) have expanded their operations from the north to the southern reaches of the country, launching regular attacks against the state and civilian targets. The response by the state and associated militias and mercenaries has been marked by violence against civilians, notably those of the ethnic Fulani minority, perceived to be associated with jihadist groups.

Political shocks have exacerbated this instability, with successive coups in 2020 and 2021 launched to redress the security crisis. The transitional government, led by Colonel Assimi Goïta, has shifted away from traditional security partners such as Côte d'Ivoire, France, the G5 Sahel and MINUSMA to Russia. However, violence has only intensified, fuelling an ongoing humanitarian and displacement crisis.

Conflict Update

The Malian government's January 2024 termination of the Algiers accord marked a significant shift in Mali's conflict landscape and dimmed prospects for stability in the north. The accord and the presence of MINUSMA had halted hostilities between the government and Tuareg separatists for nearly a decade.

The announcement of the accord's dissolution came after a series of significant escalatory events. The reporting period witnessed a reawakening of a rebellion by Tuareg groups operating under the banner of the Permanent Strategic Framework (CSP), formed in 2021 and comprising members of the CMA and armed groups from the Platform coalition. This reawakening followed years of impasse, with the CSP accusing the military government led by Goïta of neglecting the accord.

Tensions escalated in June 2023 when Malian authorities ordered the departure of MINUSMA, sparking a contest for control over former UN bases in northern Mali. Disagreements arose as MINUSMA began handing over bases to the Malian Armed Forces (FAMa) in areas where former rebel groups were granted control, leading to renewed fighting against the state. In August 2023, clashes erupted between FAMa and CSP fighters at the Ber base, followed by CSP attacks on army outposts across northern and central Mali.[1] In September, the new Azawadian National Army issued its first press release, signalling an escalation in hostilities. Subsequently, several rebel movements, including the pro-government Platform and the Movement for the Salvation of Azawad (MSA), separated from the coalition, refusing to participate in further violence. The FAMa, with the support of the Africa Corps (formerly the Wagner Group), achieved strategic and symbolic victories, culminating in the recapture of the city of Kidal in November 2023.

The army's control over former Tuareg strongholds was not total, however. CSP members sought to deny the FAMa access to important routes and blocked roads leading to Algeria, Mauritania and Niger. By January 2024, the government's announcement that it was dissolving the Algiers accord was met with little surprise. Just months later, in April 2024, rebel groups dissolved the CSP and its former members came together under the Permanent Strategic Framework for the Defence of the People of Azawad (CSP–DPA), with the explicit objective to bring together all armed groups in the north 'at war against the Malian state'.[2]

With respect to the jihadist threat, ISSP militants, emboldened by clashes between signatories of the Algiers accord, consolidated control in Menaka and Gao. ISSP targeted communities perceived to be close to its rivals, leading to violence directed at Songhai, Dawsahak and Tuareg factions. JNIM enforced a blockade of Timbuktu and its surrounding areas, as well as expanded operations near the border with Côte d'Ivoire and Guinea. These developments indicated the growing support that jihadists enjoy and demonstrated their ability to maintain influence.

Counter-insurgency efforts have led to increasing violence perpetrated against civilians. In early 2024, both the FAMa and foreign military personnel faced accusations of human-rights abuses, including the killing of over 25 civilians in Nara on 26 January.[3] Moreover, Fulani and Tuareg ethnic groups bear a disproportionate brunt of the violence. In early March, for instance, Dozo militiamen abducted and killed about 30 Fulani civilians near the city of Ségou.[4] Throughout the reporting period, the resurgence of violence in the north forced thousands to flee and seek refuge in Mauritania or Algeria.

Against this backdrop, the transitional government enhanced its powers and extended its rule by promulgating the country's constitution, banning political parties and delaying elections, which had been planned for February 2024. It doubled down on counter-insurgency efforts, confirming its hardened approach to tackling the country's crises, with intensified military operations, continued cooperation with the Africa Corps, and a shift to air warfare supported by Turkish-made equipment. Bamako has also strengthened its security and diplomatic ties with neighbouring Burkina Faso and Niger through the collective withdrawal from the Economic Community of West African States and the establishment of the Alliance of Sahel States (AES). This initiative has a clear anti-Western tone and signals the deepening geopolitical competition in the region.

The unravelling of the Algiers accord and subsequent volatility underscore the repeated failure by the transitional government to address the grievances that have underpinned Mali's protracted conflict. Ultimately, however, the government maintains widespread popular support and a high degree of confidence in its ability to handle the crisis at hand. Goïta launched a national dialogue in May 2024, suggesting a commitment to conciliation outside the framework of the Algiers accord. This was boycotted by political opposition, however, and tensions among those vying for power remain an obstacle.

Conflict Parties

Malian Armed Forces (FAMa)

Strength: 21,000 active military personnel (air force: 2,000; army: 19,000), as well as 16,000 gendarmerie and national-guard personnel.

Areas of operation: Northern, central and southern Mali, particularly in the tri-border Liptako-Gourma area near Burkina Faso and Niger.

Leadership: Col. Assimi Goïta (interim president and commander-in-chief), Col. Sadio Camara (defence minister) and Maj.-Gen. Oumar Diarra (chief of the general staff).

Structure: Consists of the army, air force, national gendarmerie and national guard.

History: Created at independence in 1960. Following years of underinvestment, the FAMa has been significantly strengthened over the past decade, including through the European Union's military training mission from 2013–22. In June 2024, Goïta met with Burkina Faso's President Ibrahim Traoré in Ouagadougou to reinforce military cooperation within the framework of the AES. Just after the close of the reporting period, in July 2024, Goïta participated in the first joint summit in Niamey as part of this alliance.

Objectives: Ensure national security, maintain territorial integrity and counter jihadist groups.

Opponents: JNIM, CSP and ISSP.

Affiliates/allies: AES members (Burkina Faso and Niger) and Russia.

Resources/capabilities: The defence budget for 2023 was US$1.1 billion, and it is projected to be US$1.2bn for 2024.

Strategic Framework for the Defence of the People of Azawad (CSP–DPA)

Strength: Unclear. The number of CMA fighters was estimated to be 800–4,000 prior to the 2015 Algiers accord.[5]

Areas of operation: Primarily active in northern Mali, including the regions of Gao, Kidal and Tombouctou.

Leadership: The CSP–DPA is led by Bilal Ag Acherif, the head of the National Movement for the Liberation of Azawad (MNLA).

Structure: The CSP–DPA includes all former constituents of the CMA and Platform, which together formed the CSP. These notably include the MNLA, the High Council for the Unity of Azawad, and the Arab Movement of Azawad as well as other smaller factions. The MSA withdrew from the CSP before the dissolution of the coalition and is therefore not a member of the CSP–DPA.

History: Following the collapse of the Muammar Gadhafi regime in Libya and the 2012 Tuareg insurrection, several rebellious factions came together in 2014 to create the CMA. In 2015, the CMA signed the Algiers accord, which put an end to the fighting between former Tuareg rebels and the Malian army. In 2021, the CMA merged with Platform – a coalition comprised of several groups in favour of Malian state authority – to form the CSP to coordinate their actions and reconcile their interests. After the collapse of the Algiers accord and the resurgence of conflict, the CMA established the Azawadian National Army to defend Mali's northern territories against the Malian army. In April 2024, the CMA and Platform were subsequently dissolved, and the CSP was rebranded as the CSP–DPA to focus on military resistance against the Malian state. This resistance is notably carried out through the Azawadian National Army.

Objectives: Defend the people of Azawad against the Malian army and affiliated forces, including the Africa Corps. The debate over the independence of Azawad remains ongoing within the coalition.

Opponents: FAMa, Africa Corps, JNIM and ISSP.

Affiliates/allies: Actors and groups who align with the separatist aspirations of the alliance. The members of the alliance historically had a number of affiliates and allies, and it remains to be seen which of these will be retained under the recently formed CSP–DPA.

Resources/capabilities: Small arms and light weaponry. Former CMA fighters retain remnants of the Libyan military arsenal left behind after the ousting of Gadhafi.

Group to Support Islam and Muslims (JNIM)

Strength: In the central Sahel, the largest military zones – Macina and Burkina Faso – each comprise several thousand fighters. In addition, there are several hundred fighters in nearby sub-regions, including the borderlands.

Areas of operation: Mostly active in northern and central Mali along the border with Burkina Faso. The group is gradually expanding southward towards Bamako.

Leadership: Iyad Ag Ghaly, a long-time Tuareg militant who is also the leader of Ansar Dine, one of the main groups constituting JNIM.

Structure: Created as an alliance of equals.

History: JNIM was created in 2017 as a coalition between al-Qaeda-affiliated groups such as Ansar Dine, al-Mourabitoun, al-Qaeda in the Islamic Maghreb–Sahel, Katibat Macina and other smaller factions.

Objectives: Establish an Islamic caliphate in the Sahel, replacing existing state structures and expelling foreign forces.

Opponents: FAMa, CSP, ISSP and Africa Corps.

Affiliates/allies: Al-Qaeda, al-Qaeda in the Islamic Maghreb–North Africa, Katibat Macina and Katibat Serma. Cooperates with Ansarul Islam, though their relationship is ambiguous.

Resources/capabilities: Small arms, light weapons, uninhabited aerial vehicles and improvised explosive devices (IEDs), including vehicle-borne IEDs and suicide-vehicle-borne IEDs.

Islamic State Sahel Province (ISSP)

Strength: Unclear.

Areas of operation: The group recognises four military zones in the central Sahel: Burkina Faso (specifically around the Sahel and Centre-Nord regions), Liptako-Gourma region (tri-border area), Andéramboukane, and Azawagh (Mali–Niger borderlands). Within Mali specifically, the group largely operates in Gao, Ménaka, Mopti and Tombouctou.

Leadership: Abdul Bara al-Sahrawi (also known as al-Ansari) and a cadre of local commanders.

Structure: Unclear.

History: ISSP emerged from a split within al-Mourabitoun in 2015 and was originally known as the Islamic State in the Greater Sahara (ISGS). ISGS pledged allegiance to the Islamic State (ISIS) in 2015, and in 2019 it became part of the Islamic State West Africa Province (ISWAP). ISIS recognised the group as an independent *wilayat* (province) in March 2022 under the name ISSP.

Objectives: Establish an Islamic caliphate based on strict interpretation of the Koran and adherence to ISIS ideology.

Opponents: JNIM, FAMa, CSP and Russian military contractors.

Affiliates/allies: Katibat Salaheddine, ISIS, ISWAP and other smaller militias.

Resources/capabilities: IEDs and light weaponry.

Africa Corps/Wagner Group

Strength: Around 1,000 personnel.[6] There were at least 25,000 troops in the Wagner Group as of late June 2023 according to its leadership, though the actual number was likely higher.[7]

Areas of operation: Central Mali (Mopti and Ségou), Kidal and Tombouctou. The Wagner Group is also present in Belarus, Ukraine and Russia, while the Africa Corps offshoot is active in Burkina Faso, the Central African Republic, Chad (reports disputed), Libya, Niger and Sudan.

Leadership: Disputed following the deaths of the group's chief, Yevgeny Prigozhin, and commander, Dmitry Utkin, in an aeroplane crash in August 2023. Prigozhin's son, Pavel Prigozhin, has claimed leadership of Wagner, though the group has largely been brought under the control of the Russian Ministry of Defence. Its African operations have been rebranded under the name 'Africa Corps' and are led by Russian Deputy Minister of Defence Col.-Gen. Yunus-bek Yevkurov.

Structure: The company was established by Prigozhin, but its structure has largely been subsumed into the Ministry of Defence following his death.

History: The Wagner Group began as a Kremlin-funded Russian security organisation, with close links to Russian military intelligence and Russia's Ministry of Defence. Wagner was established in 2014 and it and other private military companies proliferated following Russia's involvement in the 2015 war in Syria, where they were often contracted to provide security for extractive operations. The group subsequently took on a similar function in several African countries. Following the aborted mutiny led by Prigozhin on 23–24 June 2023, the group's contracts for soldiers in Russia and Ukraine were largely assumed by the Russian Ministry of Defence. Since late 2023, the African branch of Wagner has been rebranded as the Africa Corps, also in coordination with the Russian Ministry of Defence. The Wagner Group had established ties with Mali's military junta in November 2020 and was involved in the FAMa's counter-insurgency and civilian-protection efforts. The operations of the Africa Corps serve a similar purpose, though now Russia's involvement in Mali is openly recognised as an official state project. In December 2023, Goïta received Yevkurov at Koulouba Palace to discuss the strengthening of cooperation between the two countries. The delegations considered assessing opportunities for the energy, transport, telecommunications and mining sectors. In February 2024, the FAMa and the Africa Corps seized Mali's largest artisanal gold mine in Gao.

Objectives: Support the FAMa's security operations against jihadist groups.

Opponents: JNIM, CSP–DPA and ISSP.

Affiliates/allies: FAMa.

Resources/capabilities: Wagner has been directly armed and supplied by the Armed Forces of the Russian Federation and even received military aircraft during the height of its activity in Ukraine. As it is increasingly brought under the direct control of the Russian Ministry of Defence, it will presumably have access to most of the Russian armed forces' capabilities as well. The group is understood to be paid around US$10 million per month, alongside receiving mining concessions and access to mineral resources, to cover its operational costs.[8]

Notes

[1] Armed Conflict Location & Event Data Project (ACLED), www.acleddata.com.

[2] David Baché, 'Mali: les rebelles du Nord créent le Cadre stratégique pour la défense du peuple de l'Azawad' [Mali: the Northern rebels create the Strategic Framework for the Defense of the People of Azawad], Afriqe, 24 April 2024.

[3] 'UN Rights Chief Decries Death of 50 People in Mali Attacks', Al-Jazeera, 1 February 2024.

[4] Armed Conflict Location & Event Data Project (ACLED), www.acleddata.com.

[5] Baba Ahmed, 'Mali: le business du cantonnement?' [Mali: the cantonment business?], *Jeune Afrique*, 29 April

2016 (updated 5 September 2016); and Baba Ahmed and Christophe Boisbouvier, 'Nord-Mali: guerre à huis clos' [North Mali: war behind closed doors], *Jeune Afrique*, 21 February 2012.

6 'Russian Mercenaries Take Aim at Ethnic Minorities in Mali', *Africa Defense Forum*, 19 March 2024.

7 Torredo, 'Novoe soobshchenie Prigozhina, 25000 idut na Moskvu' Новое сообщение Пригожина, 25000 идут на Москву [Prigozhin's new message, 25,000 go to Moscow], YouTube, 23 June 2023; and Olga Ivshina and Olga Prosvirova, '"Amoralno, no effectivno": kak i kakoi tsenoi ChVK "Wagner" zakhvatyvala Bakhmut' «Аморально, но эффективно»: как и какой ценой ЧВК «Вагнер» захватывала Бахмут ['Amoral, but effective': how and at what cost 'Wagner' seized Bakhmut], BBC News, 10 June 2024.

8 'Russian Mercenaries Take Aim at Ethnic Minorities in Mali'.

BURKINA FASO

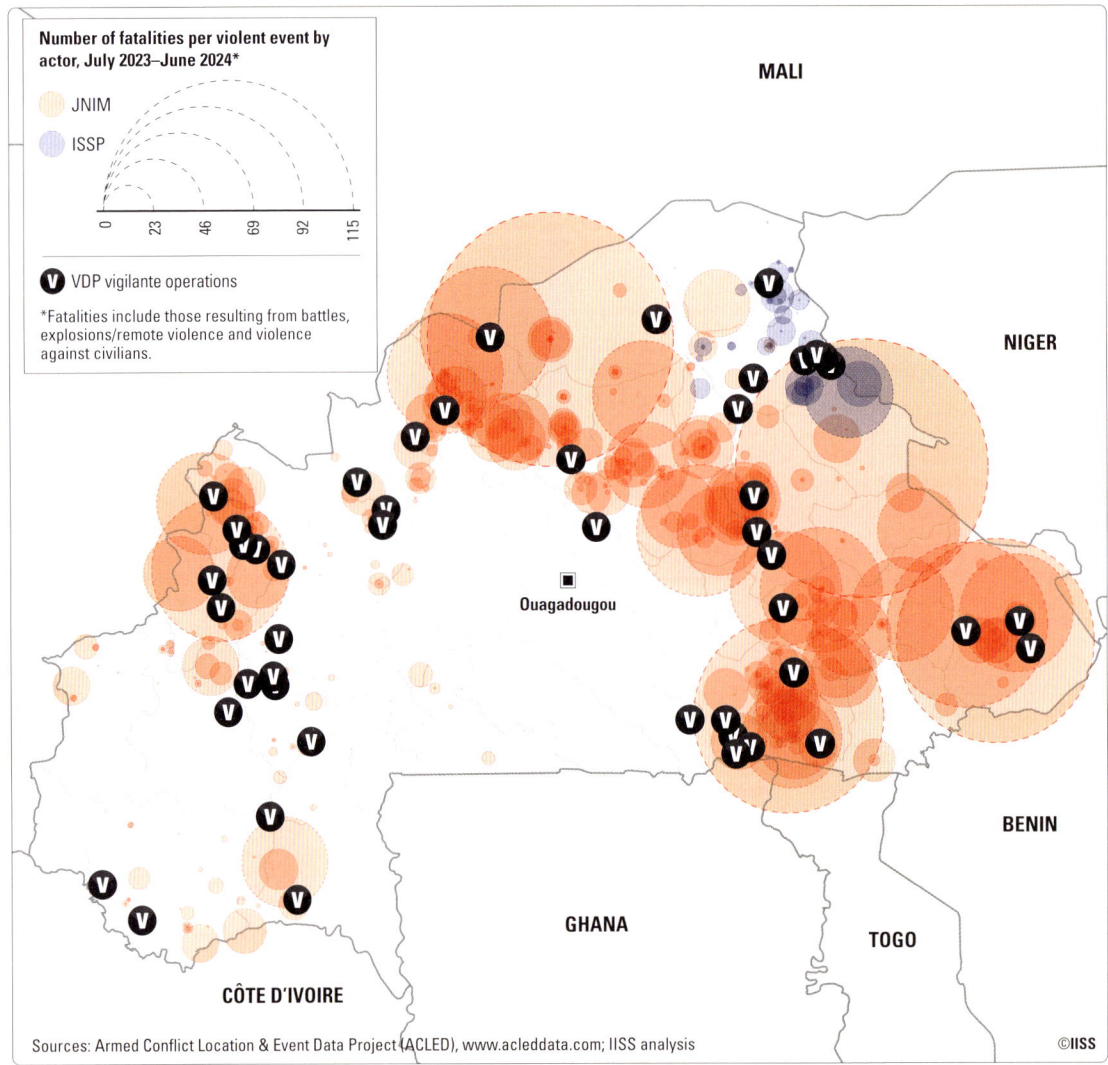

Conflict Overview

The conflicts in Burkina Faso are rooted in long-standing issues of marginalisation, socio-economic disparities and external influences. Significant developments unfolded after October 2014, when a popular uprising ended the authoritarian regime of Blaise Compaoré. The ensuing power vacuum resulted in a surge in violence, exacerbated by the spillover effects of conflicts in Mali and Niger. Porous borders and a lack of state presence in peripheral regions facilitated the spread of transnational organisations such as the al-Qaeda-affiliated Group to Support Islam and Muslims (JNIM) and its rival the Islamic State Sahel Province (ISSP). These groups continue to vie for greater territorial control, intensifying violence nationwide and in neighbouring countries. Furthermore, deep-seated feelings of political exclusion among Fulani herders fuelled the emergence of Ansarul Islam, a local insurgent group operating primarily in the country's north since late 2016. To date, almost 40% of Burkina Faso has fallen

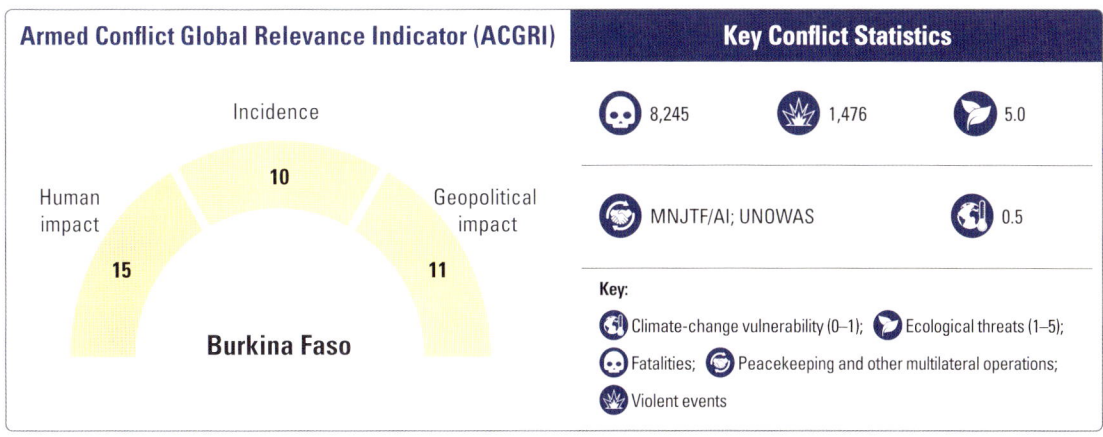

under non-state armed groups' (NSAGs) control.[1] The protracted nature of the jihadist insurgency and the frustration of both civilians and public officials over its handling catalysed two consecutive coups in 2022, precipitating changes in the regional security architecture and leading to the termination of former military partnerships, notably the French-led *Operation Barkhane* and the G5 Sahel Joint Force.

The overlap between transnational jihadist groups and local insurgencies is a defining trait of armed conflict in the country. Extremist groups exploit sentiments of neglect and disenfranchisement to incite local communities against the central government, seen as responsible for their marginalisation. With formal grievance channels lacking, violence becomes a recourse for political expression, exacerbating tensions between communities and state institutions. Two years into current President Ibrahim Traoré's tenure, weak institutions and limited efforts to alleviate tensions cast doubt on the military's capacity to navigate the socio-economic dynamics exacerbating the crisis.

Conflict Update

Burkina Faso faced heightened uncertainty throughout the reporting period, as the country's military junta took steps to scale up its response to the security crisis and entrench its rule. In December 2023, a little over a year after seizing power, President Traoré announced the intensification of war efforts to combat the spread of violent extremism across the country. His 'total war' approach involves raising taxes to finance the expansion of the armed forces and is underpinned by support for the Volunteers for the Defense of the Homeland (VDP), a civilian auxiliary group that the junta relies on for local counter-terrorism operations.[2] Yet these efforts have hardly reduced instability.[3]

The transitional government is not interested in relinquishing power nor in restoring constitutional rule. Instead, it seeks to bolster its domestic capacity by leveraging certain regional and international partnerships. Notably, the reporting period has seen a surge in the army's use of Turkish-made military uninhabited aerial vehicles, and Russian military contractors have appeared as Traoré's personal security. The army also acquired armoured vehicles for the first time from the United Arab Emirates (UAE) and Egypt.[4] In March 2024, Burkina Faso and its fellow Alliance of Sahel States (AES) members, Mali and Niger, announced the creation of a joint task force focused on counter-insurgency in the Liptako-Gourma tri-border area. This new alliance, however, came at the expense of broader regional cooperation, as the members also announced their withdrawal from the Economic Community of West African States.

Despite the country's heightened military capabilities, JNIM has continued to contest state power across the country, unleashing violence from the north to the southeast in response to government initiatives. In November 2023, JNIM killed at least 40 civilians during a raid on the northern town of Djibo, which has been under siege for over two years, and a nearby internally displaced persons camp.[5] As of January 2024, 800,000 people faced restricted movement around 26 cities as a result of ongoing blockades.[6] Furthermore, in the first half of 2024, JNIM significantly strengthened its foothold in the Est and Centre-Est regions through a series of particularly deadly attacks. These assaults targeted civilians and state forces and have triggered a violent state response, as exemplified by the May 2024 killing of 100 civilians in the Est region.[7]

Communal violence surged during the reporting period, particularly targeting Fulani and Gourmantché pastoralist communities, perceived to be overrepresented in jihadist groups. In the face of the VDP's violent reprisals against civilians deemed complicit with such groups, concerns mounted regarding its abuse of power. In September 2023, this was evidenced by the killing of 17 merchants accused of receiving cattle stolen by JNIM militants in the Centre-Est region.[8] In April 2024, Human Rights Watch accused the armed forces of killing 223 civilians in the villages of Nondin and Soro in February. These events, which have been denied by the authorities, are believed to be the army's deadliest abuses since 2015. This misuse of authority has contributed to a dangerous cycle of retaliations by armed groups, further exacerbating tensions and violence. Each passing year in Burkina Faso witnesses an increase in casualty rates; 2023 marked the deadliest year on record with 1,331 terror-related civilian deaths, and this trend continued in the first half of 2024.[9]

The humanitarian crisis in Burkina Faso has worsened as the hold on power in contested areas oscillates between state security actors and NSAGs. There has been a reduction in access for humanitarian agencies in jihadist-controlled areas, while the number of individuals in need of aid has increased. By March 2024, over two million individuals were internally displaced and 6.3m people required humanitarian assistance.[10]

The junta also faced mounting internal pressure during the reporting period. Two purported coup attempts in five months underscored the insecurity of those in power and the fragility of the political situation. Rumours of unrest among the security forces circulated again in June 2024, following JNIM's attack on Mansila, where over 100 soldiers were killed.[11] This marked the highest death toll of Burkinabe soldiers from a single attack yet. Internal criticisms regarding the junta's handling of the security crisis were met with severe repression. Several suspected cases of forced disappearances targeting journalists, human-rights advocates and political opponents were reported. Concurrently, external scrutiny from foreign-media platforms such as Jeune Afrique, the BBC, Voice of America and TV5 resulted in similar crackdowns.[12]

Conflict Parties

Burkina Faso Armed Forces

Strength: 16,600 active military personnel (air force: 600; army: 16,000), as well as an additional 4,200 gendarmerie personnel.

Areas of operation: Active in western, southwestern, northern and eastern Burkina Faso, particularly along the borders with Mali and Niger.

Leadership: Capt. Ibrahim Traoré (chief commander), Brig.-Gen. Kassoum Coulibaly (minister of defence) and Brig.-Gen. Célestin Simporé (chief of the general staff).

Structure: Comprised of the army, air force and gendarmerie.

History: Reached its current form in 1985 with the inauguration of the air force. Burkina Faso joined the AES defence pact in September 2023. In June 2024, Traoré received Mali's President Assimi Goïta in Ouagadougou to reinforce military cooperation within the framework of the AES. Just after the close of the reporting period, in July 2024, Traoré participated in the first joint summit in Niamey as part of this alliance.

Burkina Faso Armed Forces

Objectives: Maintain national security and territorial integrity and counter jihadist groups.

Opponents: Ansarul Islam, ISSP and JNIM.

Affiliates/allies: AES members (Mali and Niger), self-defence groups, VDP, Egypt, Russia, Turkiye and UAE (albeit not always through formal security cooperation).

Resources/capabilities: Burkina Faso's defence budget for 2023 was US$827m (4.1% of GDP), compared to US$1 billion (4.7% of GDP) for 2024. Each new recruit must undergo an initial training of 18 months.[13]

Volunteers for the Defense of the Homeland (VDP)

Strength: A recruitment campaign launched in October 2022 resulted in 90,000 applications. By December 2022, 50,000 volunteers had been selected.[14] In May 2023, Prime Minister Apollinaire Kyélem de Tambèla announced the government's intention to double the number of VDP volunteers to 100,000.[15]

Areas of operation: Mostly in Boucle du Mouhoun, Cascades, Centre-Est, Centre-Nord, Est, Nord and Sahel regions.

Leadership: Col. Boukaré Zoungrana is the de facto commander of the Brigade of Vigilance and Patriotic Defense (BVDP).

Structure: Comprised of volunteers; 35,000 remain in their residential communities and 15,000 are assigned alongside the armed forces across the country.[16] The VDP is a constituent of the BVDP, which also includes the army's reserve forces. It is organised under the regiments present in each of the six regions.

History: President Roch Kaboré (2015–22) created the VDP on the back of existing self-defence groups such as the Koglweogo and the Dozo. The government presented the VDP as an inclusive force for each 'region, ethnicity, political opinion and religious denomination'.[17] Since the VDP's creation in January 2020, however, its fighters have regularly faced accusations of discriminatory attacks against pastoralist Fulani communities.

Objectives: Support the armed forces in fighting armed groups and protecting Burkina Faso's territorial integrity through local security operations.

Opponents: Ansarul Islam, ISSP and JNIM.

Affiliates/allies: Burkina Faso Armed Forces.

Resources/capabilities: Light weaponry. Each volunteer is trained over two weeks to learn to handle weapons and integrate the code of conduct. A Patriotic Support Fund was set up in January 2023 to facilitate the mobilisation of resources.

Islamic State Sahel Province (ISSP)

Strength: Unclear.

Areas of operation: The group recognises four military zones in the central Sahel: Burkina Faso (specifically around the Sahel and Centre-Nord regions), Liptako-Gourma region (tri-border border area), Andéramboukane and Azawagh (Mali–Niger borderlands).

Leadership: Abdul Bara al-Sahrawi (also known as al-Ansari) and a cadre of local commanders.

Structure: Unclear.

History: ISSP emerged from a split within al-Mourabitoun in 2015 and was originally known as the Islamic State in the Greater Sahara (ISGS). ISGS pledged allegiance to the Islamic State (ISIS) in 2015, and in 2019 it became part of the Islamic State West Africa Province (ISWAP). ISIS recognised the group as an independent *wilayat* (province) in March 2022 under the name ISSP.

Objectives: Establish an Islamic caliphate based on strict interpretation of the Koran and adherence to ISIS ideology.

Opponents: Burkina Faso Armed Forces and JNIM.

Affiliates/allies: Katibat Salaheddine, ISIS, ISWAP and other smaller militias.

Resources/capabilities: Improvised explosive devices (IEDs) and light weaponry.

Group to Support Islam and Muslims (JNIM)

Strength: In the central Sahel, the largest military zones – Macina and Burkina Faso – each comprise several thousand fighters. In addition, there are several hundred fighters in nearby sub-regions, including the borderlands.

Areas of operation: Stronghold in the northeast, but activity recorded country wide (with the exception of the Centre region).

Leadership: Iyad Ag Ghaly, a long-time Tuareg militant who is also the leader of Ansar Dine, one of the main groups constituting JNIM.

Structure: Created as an alliance of equals.

History: JNIM was created in 2017 as a coalition between al-Qaeda-affiliated groups such as Ansar Dine, al-Mourabitoun, al-Qaeda in the Islamic Maghreb–Sahel, Katibat Macina and other smaller factions.

Objectives: Establish an Islamic caliphate in the Sahel, replacing existing state structures and expelling foreign forces.

Opponents: Burkina Faso Armed Forces, ISSP and Russian military contractors.

Group to Support Islam and Muslims (JNIM)

Affiliates/allies: Al-Qaeda, al-Qaeda in the Islamic Maghreb–North Africa, Katibat Macina and Katibat Serma. Cooperates with Ansarul Islam, though their relationship is ambiguous.

Resources/capabilities: Heavy weaponry and IEDs, including vehicle-borne IEDs and suicide-vehicle-borne IEDs.

Africa Corps/Wagner Group

Strength: Several hundred personnel in Burkina Faso.[18] There were at least 25,000 troops in the Wagner Group as of late June 2023 according to its leadership, though the actual number was likely higher.[19]

Areas of operation: Ouagadougou in Burkina Faso. The Wagner Group is also present in Belarus, Ukraine and Russia, while the Africa Corps offshoot is active in Burkina Faso, the Central African Republic, Chad (reports disputed), Libya, Mali, Niger and Sudan.

Leadership: Disputed following the deaths of the group's chief, Yevgeny Prigozhin, and commander, Dmitry Utkin, in an aeroplane crash in August 2023. Prigozhin's son, Pavel Prigozhin, has claimed leadership of Wagner, though the group has largely been brought under the control of the Russian Ministry of Defence. Its African operations have been rebranded under the name 'Africa Corps' and are led by Russian Deputy Minister of Defence Col.-Gen. Yunus-bek Yevkurov.

Structure: The company was established by Prigozhin, but its structure has largely been subsumed into the Ministry of Defence following his death.

History: The Wagner Group began as a Kremlin-funded Russian security organisation, with close links to Russian military intelligence and Russia's Ministry of Defence. Wagner was established in 2014 and it and other private military companies proliferated following Russia's involvement in the 2015 war in Syria, where they were often contracted to provide security for extractive operations. The group subsequently took on a similar function in several African countries. Following the aborted mutiny led by Prigozhin on 23–24 June 2023, the group's contracts for soldiers in Russia and Ukraine were largely assumed by the Russian Ministry of Defence. Since late 2023, the African branch of Wagner has been rebranded as the Africa Corps, also in coordination with the Russian Ministry of Defence. From December 2022 onwards, the group has established ties with Traoré's military junta whilst increasing its power and access to resources. Engagement in resource extraction is often done in exchange for security provision. Those forces deployed in Burkina Faso are from the Bear structure, and they largely focus on protecting the regime, for example providing protection to Traoré, rather than military assistance outside the capital. Russia's involvement in Burkina Faso is now openly recognised as an official state project. This was underlined by the symbolic first visit of Russia's foreign minister, Sergey Lavrov, to Burkina Faso in June 2024.

Objectives: Provide protection to President Traoré.

Opponents: JNIM and ISSP.

Affiliates/allies: Burkina Faso Armed Forces and VDP.

Resources/capabilities: Wagner has been directly armed and supplied by the Armed Forces of the Russian Federation and even received military aircraft during the height of its activity in Ukraine. As it is increasingly brought under the direct control of the Russian Ministry of Defence, it will presumably have access to most of the Russian armed forces' capabilities as well. The amount paid to the Africa Corps/Wagner Group by the Burkinabe government is unclear, but the group receives mining concessions and access to mineral resources.

Notes

[1] Maria Gerth-Niculescu, 'Burkina's Faso [sic] Jihadist Conflict Worsens as Military Junta Pursues "Total War"', *New Humanitarian*, 28 November 2023.

[2] 'Burkina Faso: le chef de la junte Ibrahim Traoré annonce intensifier la guerre contre le terrorisme' [Burkina Faso: junta leader Ibrahim Traoré announces intensifying the war against terrorism], Afrique, 11 December 2023.

[3] The country placed first in the Institute for Economics and Peace's Global Terrorism Index 2024. Institute for Economics and Peace, 'Global Terrorism Index 2024: Measuring the Impact of Terrorism', February 2024, p. 6.

[4] Armed Conflict Location & Event Data Project (ACLED), www.acleddata.com.

[5] Ibid.

[6] ACAPS, 'Country Analysis: Burkina Faso'.

[7] European Commission, 'Echo Daily Flash: European Civil Protection and Humanitarian Aid Operations', 21 May 2024.

[8] Armed Conflict Location & Event Data Project (ACLED), www.acleddata.com.

[9] Ibid.

[10] United Nations Office for the Coordination of Humanitarian Affairs, 'Aperçu des besoins humanitaires Burkina Faso' [An overview of humanitarian needs in Burkina Faso], 13 March 2024.

[11] Armed Conflict Location & Event Data Project (ACLED), www.acleddata.com.

[12] Burkina Faso suspended, for various periods of time, Jeune Afrique in September 2023, the BBC and Voice of America in April 2024, and TV5 in June 2024.

[13] 'Pourquoi des activistes sont-ils enrôlés de force comme auxiliaires de l'armée au Burkina Faso?' [Why are activists

forcibly recruited as army auxiliaries in Burkina Faso?], BBC News, 30 March 2023.
14. 'L'armée au Burkina mise sur les civils contre le terrorisme' [The army in Burkina counts on civilians to fight terrorism], DW, 30 December 2022.
15. Rédaction Africanews, 'Burkina PM Vows No Deal With Jihadists, Hints at Election Delay', Africa News, 31 May 2023.
16. 'L'armée au Burkina mise sur les civils contre le terrorisme'.
17. Anna Schmauder and Annabelle Willeme, 'The Volunteers for the Defense of the Homeland', Clingendael Institute, 9 March 2021.
18. John A. Lechner and Sergey Eledinov, 'Is Africa Corps a Rebranded Wagner Group?', *Foreign Policy*, 7 February 2024.
19. Torredo, 'Novoe soobshchenie Prigozhina, 25000 idut na Moskvu' Новое сообщение Пригожина, 25000 идут на Москву [Prigozhin's new message, 25,000 go to Moscow], YouTube, 23 June 2023; and Olga Ivshina and Olga Prosvirova, '"Amoralno, no effectivno": kak i kakoi tsenoi ChVK "Wagner" zakhvatyvala Bakhmut' «Аморально, но эффективно»: как и какой ценой ЧВК «Вагнер» захватывала Бахмут ['Amoral, but effective': how and at what cost 'Wagner' seized Bakhmut], BBC News, 10 June 2024.

NIGER

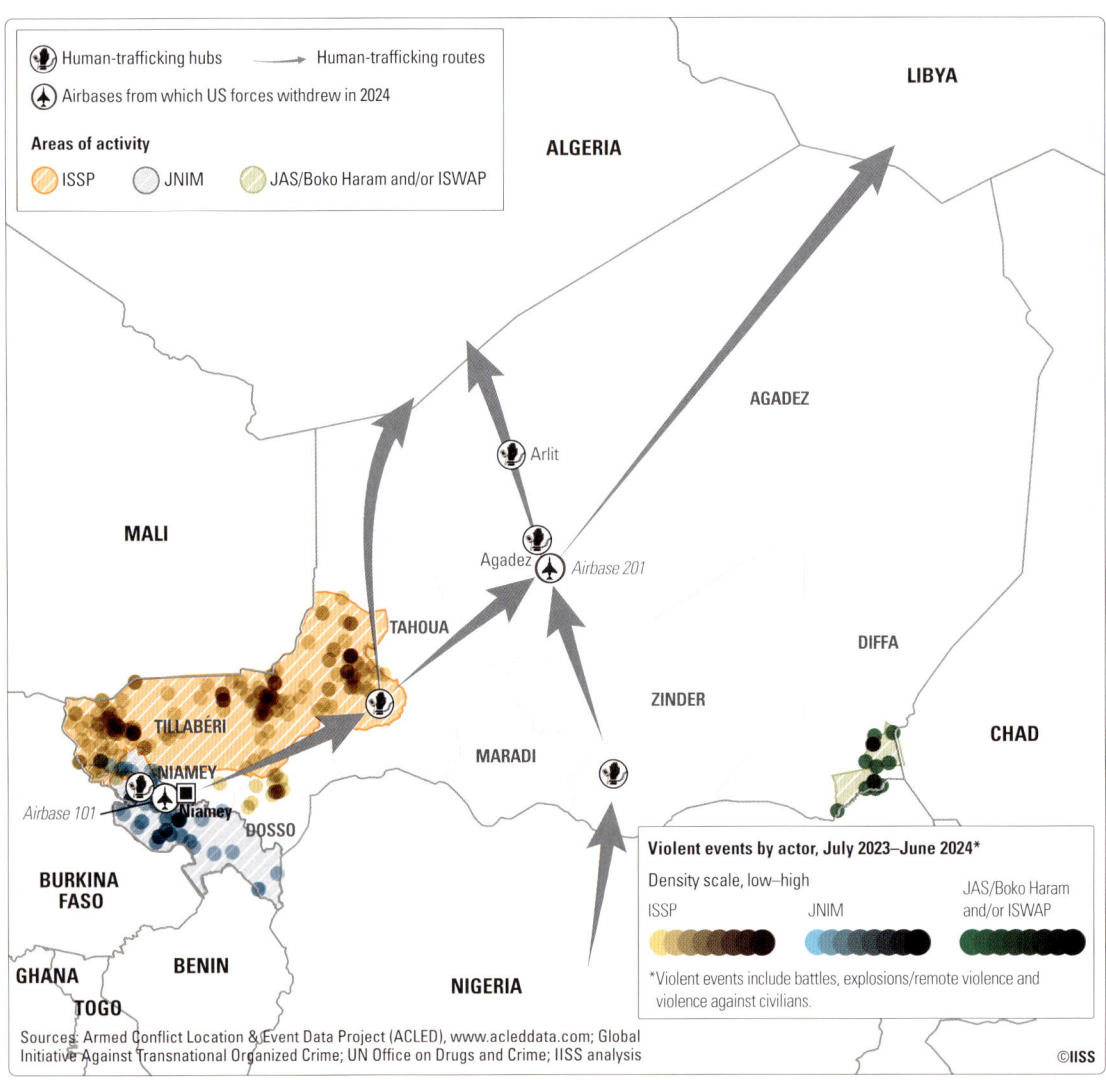

Conflict Overview

Since 2015, Niger has been grappling with insecurity on multiple fronts, driven by long-standing competition for control over land, resources and power. Political and economic marginalisation inform local grievances and result in flare-ups in intercommunal violence and ethnic tensions. Within this mix, a number of actors with vested interests play a destabilising role. This includes non-state actors that operate across permeable borders, such as highly organised armed groups, bandits and jihadist groups.

Over the years, jihadist groups have taken advantage of these localised dynamics, while the escalation of various conflicts in neighbouring countries has also enabled their expansion in Niger. In the southeast, northern Nigeria-based Jama'atu Ahlis Sunna Lidda'awati wal-Jihad (JAS, popularly known as Boko Haram) and its splinter group the Islamic State West Africa Province (ISWAP) have been active for nearly a decade. In the west, insurgencies are driven by two rival factions: the

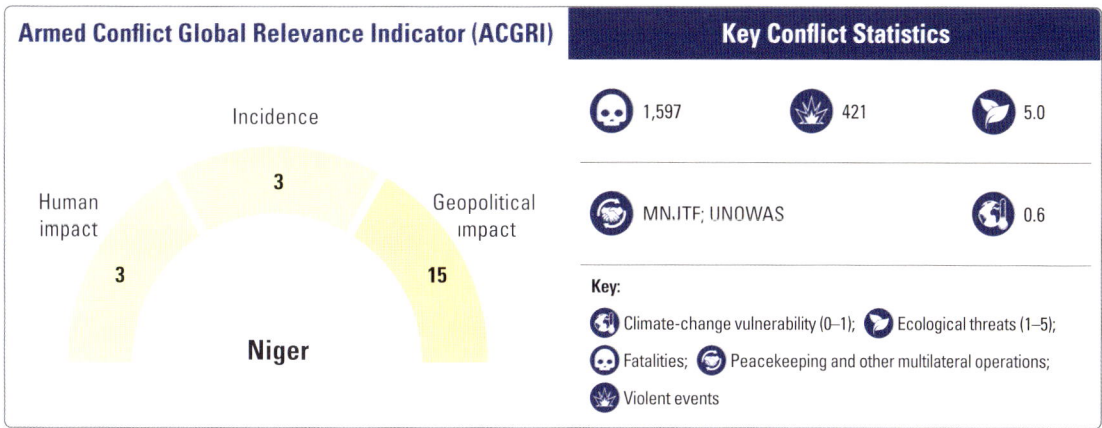

Group to Support Islam and Muslims (JNIM) and the Islamic State Sahel Province (ISSP), which vie for control in the Tahoua and Tillabéri regions. In recent years, jihadist groups have also used the western borderlands as a launch pad for operations in Burkina Faso and Mali.

Niger experienced a surge in violence perpetrated by jihadist groups between 2015 and 2022, after which conflict-related deaths began to decline. This improvement was partially due to coordinated military efforts and the commitment of president Mohamed Bazoum's government (2021–23) to engage in dialogue with non-state armed groups (NSAGs), resulting in the negotiation of peace agreements at the community level. Yet democratic backsliding and harsh living conditions have left many Nigeriens vulnerable and continue to undermine socio-economic progress across the country.

Conflict Update

In July 2023, members of the Nigerien presidential guard deposed president Bazoum on the grounds that the government had failed to address the country's worsening security crisis. This marked the country's fifth successful military takeover since independence in 1960. Brigadier-General Abdourahmane Tchiani appointed himself head of the new military junta, known as the National Council for the Safeguard of the Homeland (CNSP). Within the reporting period, the military government installed itself and took steps to consolidate its power. Despite the Economic Community of West African States (ECOWAS) imposing sanctions on Niger and threatening military intervention, the junta resolutely rejected ECOWAS's conditions that it restore democratic rule and ensure the release of Bazoum, who remained in custody as of June 2024. Instead, it signed the Alliance of Sahel States (AES) defence pact in September 2023 with neighbouring Burkina Faso and Mali, and announced a three-year transition to civilian rule, which garnered recognition from neighbouring Algeria, Burkina

Faso, Chad, Guinea and Mali. ECOWAS eventually repealed its threat to deploy standby forces and lifted its sanctions in February 2024. Yet, in the meantime, all three AES members collectively withdrew from the regional body, making prospects for broader regional cooperation unlikely.

Niger was once celebrated for its commitment to the international order. However, the most recent coup represented its demise as Western partners' lynchpin of democracy and counter-terrorism operations in the region. Since July 2023, there has been a significant deterioration in Niger's relationships with its traditional economic and military allies, particularly France and the United States. French peacekeeping troops fully withdrew from the country in December 2023, and travel restrictions were placed on diplomatic staff. In April 2024, the US government agreed to the junta's demands to withdraw its troops and close its drone base in Agadez (installed in 2013). This move coincided with the public appearances of dozens of Russia's Africa Corps advisers and equipment in the country. Moreover, the junta repealed a 2015 law that had been enacted in exchange for a US$1.3 billion aid package from the European Union, aimed at curbing migration through Niger towards North Africa and, ultimately, Europe's southern flank.[1] This move, widely supported domestically, served as a clear indication of the junta's determination to prioritise the interests of the state and assert autonomy from previous partners.

The dissolution of some security partnerships and re-enforcement of others have not had significant effects on the violence patterns of NSAGs across the country. Although there was an uptick in jihadist activity in the first month following the coup, the situation stabilised thereafter. Throughout the reporting period, the Niger Armed Forces (FAN) and civilians continued to be targeted by ISSP and JNIM militants in the western region of Tillabéri. Clashes between the two groups were rare, with JNIM retaining control over southern Tillabéri along the border with Burkina Faso, while ISSP expanded its influence over northern Tillabéri, northern Dosso and western Tahoua. Meanwhile, JAS/Boko Haram maintained its grip on the Diffa region in the southeast along the border with Nigeria. In the first quarter of 2024, several deadly clashes between JNIM and the FAN in Dosso pointed to the expanding influence of JNIM towards the southwestern border with Benin.[2]

The continued cycles of violence in Niger following the coup also exacerbated communal tensions. The CNSP's failure to adequately protect and support pastoralist communities, particularly the Tuareg and Fulani groups, left them vulnerable to attacks by ethnic militias. Such attacks are frequently backed by agriculturalist communities and often stem from disputes over grazing rights. On 15 August 2023, for instance, Djerma farmers massacred 20 Fulani herders in a series of coordinated attacks in the Tillabéri region.[3]

Furthermore, the CNSP was unable to address several pervasive economic issues that continued to affect the country over the reporting period. Following the coup, sanctions and border closures led to rapid increases in food prices and resulted in acute food shortages for 3.4 million people in Diffa, Tahoua, Tillabéri and Maradi in the south.[4] This economic strain further compounded Niger's ongoing humanitarian and displacement crisis, as over 458,000 people were reported internally displaced as of December 2023.[5]

Since taking power, the military authorities have positioned themselves as the ones that will lead the country out of its security crisis. Strengthened cooperation with Mali and Burkina Faso offers unity against only some of the threats that Niger faces. As porous borders allow violence to spread southwards towards the coastal states of the Gulf of Guinea, drivers of instability will continue to surface, unless collaboration with other neighbouring countries is restored.

Conflict Parties

Niger Armed Forces (FAN)

Strength: 39,100 active military personnel (army: 39,000; air force: 100) and 15,000 gendarmerie.

Areas of operation: Primarily Diffa, Niamey and Tillabéri regions, with limited activity in Agadez, Dosso, Maradi, Tahoua and Zinder regions.

Leadership: Brig.-Gen. Abdourahmane Tchiani (commander-in-chief) and Maj.-Gen. Abdou Sidikou Issa (chief of staff).

Structure: Consists of the army, air force and gendarmerie.

History: Founded upon Niger's independence in 1960 and officered by the French Colonial Forces, the FAN was

Niger Armed Forces (FAN)

reorganised after a 1974 military coup. In 2003, an air-force component was created. The FAN joined the AES defence pact after ECOWAS threatened to intervene militarily to restore civilian rule following the July 2023 coup. Just after the close of the reporting period, in July 2024, the leaders of Burkina Faso, Mali and Niger held their first joint summit in Niamey as part of this alliance.

Objectives: Maintain internal and border security against jihadist groups and protect territorial integrity.

Opponents: Ansarul Islam, ISSP, JNIM, ISWAP and JAS/Boko Haram.

Affiliates/allies: Other AES members (Burkina Faso and Mali), Multinational Joint Task Force (MNJTF) members and Russia.

Resources/capabilities: Niger's defence budget was US$332m (2.0% of GDP) for 2023 and is US$435m (2.3% of GDP) for 2024.

Islamic State Sahel Province (ISSP)

Strength: Unclear.

Areas of operation: The group recognises four military zones in the central Sahel: Burkina Faso (specifically around the Sahel and Centre-Nord regions), Liptako-Gourma region (tri-border area), Andéramboukane, and Azawagh (Mali–Niger borderlands). Within Niger specifically, ISSP largely operates in the west (Dosso, Tahoua and Tillabéri regions).

Leadership: Abdul Bara al-Sahrawi (also known as al-Ansari) and a cadre of local commanders.

Structure: Unclear.

History: ISSP emerged from a split within al-Mourabitoun in 2015 and was originally known as the Islamic State in the Greater Sahara (ISGS). ISGS pledged allegiance to the Islamic State (ISIS) in 2015, and in 2019 it became part of ISWAP. ISIS recognised the group as an independent *wilayat* (province) in March 2022 under the name ISSP.

Objectives: Establish an Islamic caliphate based on strict interpretation of the Koran and adherence to ISIS ideology.

Opponents: JNIM and FAN.

Affiliates/allies: Katibat Salaheddine, ISIS, ISWAP and other smaller militias.

Resources/capabilities: Heavy weaponry and improvised explosive devices (IEDs), including vehicle-borne IEDs.

Group to Support Islam and Muslims (JNIM)

Strength: In the central Sahel, the largest military zones – Macina and Burkina Faso – each comprise several thousand fighters. In Niger and its borderlands, there are several hundred fighters.

Areas of operation: Limited presence in western Niger (Tillabéri region).

Leadership: Iyad Ag Ghaly, a long-time Tuareg militant who is also the leader of Ansar Dine, one of the main groups constituting JNIM.

Structure: Created as an alliance of equals.

History: JNIM was created in 2017 as a coalition between al-Qaeda-affiliated groups such as Ansar Dine, al-Mourabitoun, al-Qaeda in the Islamic Maghreb–Sahel, Katibat Macina and other smaller factions.

Objectives: Establish an Islamic caliphate in the Sahel, replacing existing state structures and expelling foreign forces.

Opponents: FAN and ISSP.

Affiliates/allies: Al-Qaeda, al-Qaeda in the Islamic Maghreb–North Africa, Katibat Macina and Katibat Serma. Cooperates with Ansarul Islam, though their relationship is ambiguous.

Resources/capabilities: Heavy weaponry and IEDs, including vehicle-borne IEDs and suicide-vehicle-borne IEDs.

Multinational Joint Task Force (MNJTF)

Strength: 10,000–13,000 troops from the armed forces of Benin, Cameroon, Chad, Niger and Nigeria.[6]

Areas of operation: Lake Chad Basin.

Leadership: Maj.-Gen. Ibrahim Sallau Ali (force commander since July 2023).

Structure: Headquartered in N'Djamena (Chad), the MNJTF comprises four geographical sectors, with their own headquarters in Monguno (Nigeria), Baga Sola (Chad), Diffa (Niger) and Mora (Cameroon). Each sector is led by a commander with wide autonomy, while the MNJTF force commander has coordination powers.

History: The MNJTF evolved from a Nigerian initiative in 1994 to a multinational force in 1998 to tackle cross-border crimes and banditry affecting the Lake Chad Basin. After years of inactivity, the Peace and Security Council of the African Union (AU) agreed to revive the MNJTF in 2015 to counter JAS/Boko Haram's growing activity. Niger maintained its status as a formal member of the initiative after the coup in July 2023.

Objectives: Coordinate regional counter-insurgency efforts and restore security in areas affected by JAS/Boko Haram, ISWAP and other relevant parties in the Lake Chad Basin. The MNJTF also helps support stabilisation programmes, humanitarian-assistance efforts and the return of forcibly displaced people.

Opponents: JAS/Boko Haram and ISWAP.

Affiliates/allies: The national armies of Cameroon, Chad, Niger and Nigeria, and international partners including the AU, EU,

Multinational Joint Task Force (MNJTF)

United Kingdom and US. There are presently tensions between several regional countries, notably Niger and Nigeria.

Resources/capabilities: Estimated initial operational budget of US$700m. The EU is the force's main contributor, channelling its funds through the AU. Bureaucratic delays and a lack of adequate resources have hampered the MNJTF's ability to fulfil its mandate.

Africa Corps/Wagner Group

Strength: Approximately 100 military advisers arrived in Niger in April 2024.[7] There were at least 25,000 troops in the Wagner Group as of late June 2023 according to its leadership, though the actual number was likely higher.[8]

Areas of operation: In May 2024, Russian military advisers and trainers were stationed alongside American troops, albeit in different compounds, at the Nigerien air-force base, Airbase 101, which is next to Diori Hamani International Airport in Niamey. The Wagner Group is also present in Belarus, Ukraine and Russia, while the Africa Corps offshoot is active in Burkina Faso, the Central African Republic, Chad (reports disputed), Libya, Mali and Sudan.

Leadership: Disputed following the deaths of the group's chief, Yevgeny Prigozhin, and commander, Dmitry Utkin, in an aeroplane crash in August 2023. Prigozhin's son, Pavel Prigozhin, has claimed leadership of Wagner, though the group has largely been brought under the control of the Russian Ministry of Defence. Its African operations have been rebranded under the name 'Africa Corps' and are led by Russian Deputy Minister of Defence Col.-Gen. Yunus-bek Yevkurov.

Structure: The company was established by Prigozhin, but its structure has largely been subsumed into the Ministry of Defence following his death.

History: The Wagner Group began as a Kremlin-funded Russian security organisation, with close links to Russian military intelligence and Russia's Ministry of Defence. Wagner was established in 2014 and it and other private military companies proliferated following Russia's involvement in the 2015 war in Syria, where they were often contracted to provide security for extractive operations. The group subsequently took on a similar function in several African countries. Following the aborted mutiny led by Prigozhin on 23–24 June 2023, the group's contracts for soldiers in Russia and Ukraine were largely assumed by the Russian Ministry of Defence. Since late 2023, the African branch of Wagner has been rebranded as the Africa Corps, also in coordination with the Russian Ministry of Defence. In August 2023, Niger's generals requested the support of Wagner and, in December 2023, a Russian delegation visited the country. The Africa Corps has continued to strengthen its security cooperation with the military junta whilst increasing its power and access to resources. The group has primarily been involved in training FAN personnel to use Niger's new air-defence system.

Objectives: Offer training and military assistance to the FAN in exchange for monetary compensation.

Opponents: JNIM and ISSP.

Affiliates/allies: FAN.

Resources/capabilities: Wagner has been directly armed and supplied by the Armed Forces of the Russian Federation and even received military aircraft during the height of its activity in Ukraine. As it is increasingly brought under the direct control of the Russian Ministry of Defence, it will presumably have access to most of the Russian armed forces' capabilities as well.

Notes

[1] Kate Hairsine, 'Central Niger Celebrates Junta's Repeal of Migration Law', Deutsche Welle, 29 November 2023.

[2] Armed Conflict Location & Event Data Project (ACLED), www.acleddata.com.

[3] Ibid.

[4] European Commission, 'European Civil Protection and Humanitarian Aid Operations: Niger'.

[5] United Nations Office for the Coordination of Humanitarian Affairs, 'Niger: Situation of Population Displacement (as of 31 December 2023)', 8 January 2024.

[6] Freedom Chukwudi Onuoha, Andrew E. Yaw Tchie and Mariana Llorens Zabala, *A Quest to Win the Hearts and Minds: Assessing the Effectiveness of the Multinational Joint Task Force* (Oslo: Norwegian Institute of International Affairs, 2023), p. 37; and Major General Abdul Khalifa Ibrahim, 'Confronting Terrorism in the Lake Chad Basin – The Multinational Joint Task Force in Perspective', Multinational Joint Task Force, 21 November 2022.

[7] Liam Karr, 'Africa File Special Edition: Russia's Africa Corps Arrives in Niger. What's Next?', Institute for the Study of War, 12 April 2024.

[8] Torredo, 'Novoe soobshchenie Prigozhina, 25000 idut na Moskvu' Новое сообщение Пригожина, 25000 идут на Москву [Prigozhin's new message, 25,000 go to Moscow], YouTube, 23 June 2023; and Olga Ivshina and Olga Prosvirova, '"Amoralno, no effectivno": kak i kakoi tsenoi ChVK "Wagner" zakhvatyvala Bakhmut' «Аморально, но эффективно»: как и какой ценой ЧВК «Вагнер» захватывала Бахмут ['Amoral, but effective': how and at what cost 'Wagner' seized Bakhmut], BBC News, 10 June 2024.

NIGERIA

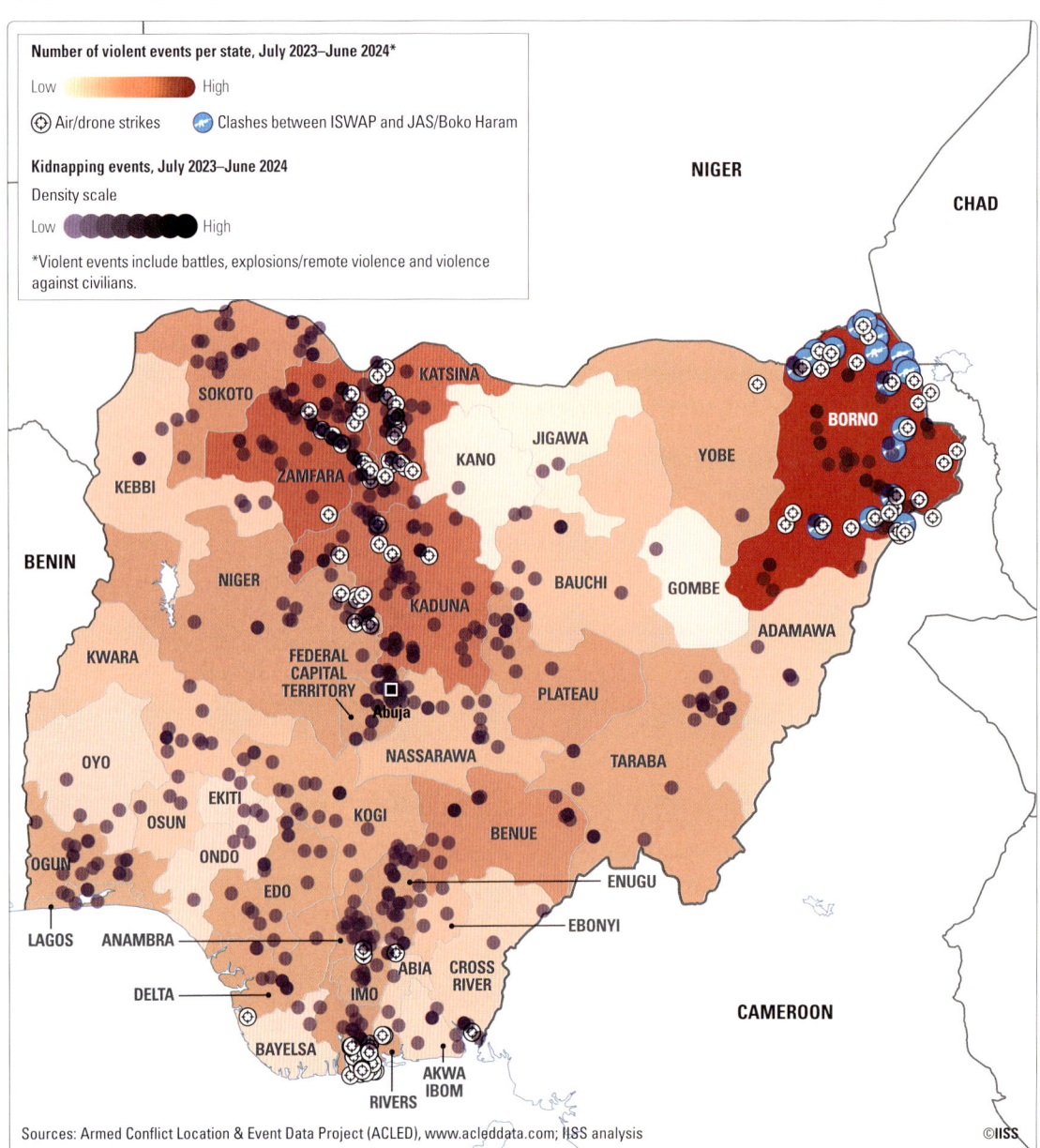

Conflict Overview

Since emerging from military rule in 1999, Nigeria has faced multiple political and security crises, some of which have expanded to imperil parts of the wider region. Although steps have been taken to democratise Nigerian politics, exclusionary, elite politics has persisted, while the tendency of security forces to militarise political and social disputes has similarly endured across the military and civilian eras.

Nigeria's political culture is heavily cartelised, with elites from the country's intertwined

Country Profile: Nigeria

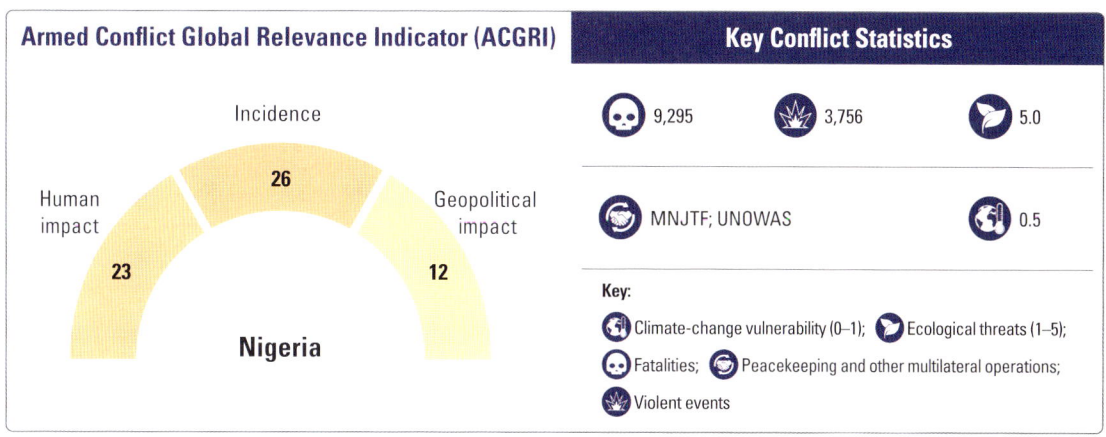

ACGRI pillars: IISS calculation based on multiple sources for 2023 and 2024 (scale: 0–100), except for some cases according to data availability. See Notes on Methodology and Data Appendix for all variables and further details on Key Conflict Statistics.

Conflict(s)	Type	Start date
Jihadist violence in the Lake Chad Basin (North East)	I LI T	2009
Armed 'banditry' (North West)	I IC OC	2011
IPOB ethnic separatist conflict (South East)	I LI	2020
Clashes between Fulani-pastoralist and assorted farmer militias	I IC	Various start dates

Key: **I IC** Internal: intercommunal; **I IC OC** Internal: intercommunal & organised crime; **I LI** Internal: localised insurgency; **T** Transnational

political and business sectors (including the critical oil sector) presiding over an increasingly precarious security and economic situation that has unevenly impacted the country's 36 states. These states are largely dependent on oil revenues dispersed by the government in the federal capital, Abuja. This system is overlaid atop a complex ethnic terrain, characterised by periodic friction between the largely Christian south and Muslim north and mutual suspicion between Nigeria's primary ethnic blocs (the southwestern Yoruba, the southeastern Igbo, and the northern Hausa and Fulani), which have dominated post-colonial politics at the expense of over 200 smaller ethnic groups.

Instability has been driven by discontent coming both from within the political system and from armed groups and unarmed movements outside of the system – with internal and external forms of discontent tending to overlap during election years. The Nigerian electoral cycle has often coincided with the emergence of new security threats, as gangs or armed groups hired by contending politicians become increasingly autonomous and feed into Nigeria's wider security crisis.

Although violence in the oil-producing Niger Delta has declined in recent years, conflict has become entrenched in northern Nigeria. From 2009 onwards, Jama'atu Ahlis Sunna Lidda'awati wal-Jihad (JAS, popularly known as Boko Haram) jihadists expanded their presence from small pockets of Nigeria's North East zone (and adjoining areas of Cameroon) to adjoining parts of Chad and Niger. The ensuing regional security crisis in the Lake Chad Basin saw the revival of the West- and African Union (AU)-backed Multinational Joint Task Force (MNJTF) in 2015, with the Nigerian armed forces making increasing (if qualified) gains against fractious jihadist factions in the North East. More recently, the North West has been beset by nebulous 'bandit' (criminal gang) violence, in which political grievances have become subsumed within economic motivations and warlordism.

Conflict Update

Bola Ahmed Tinubu was elected president of Nigeria during the previous reporting period, on the All Progressives Congress ticket. There were lower levels of violence during the 2023 presidential and state elections compared to 2011, 2015 and 2019, though a period of renewed political polarisation and economic upheaval followed in their wake. A series of (ultimately unsuccessful) legal challenges sought to annul the contentious presidential-election results. Meanwhile, allegations of backroom dealing and patronage politics emerged with regard to ministerial and bureaucratic appointments, despite commitments made during the election to install a technocratic government.[1]

Tensions surrounded President Tinubu's economic-reform agenda – in particular, the removal of Nigeria's substantial fuel subsidies and the unification of multiple exchange rates, both of which have been linked to alleged corruption and fraud.[2] The removal of the fuel subsidy drove inflation and union-led demonstrations, while the currency rapidly depreciated after being floated. These moves compounded an already concerning economic trajectory, raising the possibility of further discontent in restive areas amid reports of looting and food riots.

Tinubu also pledged to prioritise the restoration of security during his campaign. This included expanding on existing security reforms (such as upgrading equipment), while establishing new units to address kidnapping and insecurity in forests, which are often used as hideouts by bandit groups in northwestern areas. The proposed doctrine also emphasised the need to harmonise the security sector to limit inter-agency rivalry while improving conditions for low-ranking security personnel, and to undertake socio-political interventions in conflict-affected areas (including in the Niger Delta and the Lake Chad Basin) to limit recruitment into armed groups. However, the various antagonisms and conflicts of the preceding years continued into the current reporting period. A reshuffle of senior security officials was undertaken in June 2023, though it raised questions about possible overrepresentation of members of Tinubu's Yoruba community.

In the North East zone, conflict among the two largest jihadist factions operating in the Lake Chad Basin – JAS/Boko Haram and the Islamic State West Africa Province (ISWAP) – continued to escalate. Significant gains made by ISWAP since 2021 gradually reversed following a series of JAS/Boko Haram offensives in Borno State, amid internal turbulence within ISWAP and reported defections to JAS/Boko Haram. Although the government retained control of large population centres in the North East, clashes between the military and jihadist groups were reported in Borno, Yobe and Bauchi states during the second half of 2023, as airstrikes on jihadist strongholds continued.

The reporting period also saw a resurgence in mass kidnappings in the North East and North West zones, while kidnapping for ransom further escalated in the capital, Abuja. Bandit activity persisted in parts of the North West, with continued attacks on villages and clashes with the military. In December, a government drone strike inadvertently killed over 120 people in Tudun Biri in Kaduna State after mistaking a ceremony for an armed-group camp.[3] The incident was one of a series of mass-casualty events linked to government drone strikes, and raised concerns regarding the lack of transparency surrounding official investigations into the incident. Meanwhile, volatility continued in Nigeria's Middle Belt, with a series of attacks on villages resulting in hundreds of deaths.[4] The attacks were clustered in Plateau State and were variously attributed to pastoralists or to bandit groups. In the South East zone, tensions and violence linked to Biafran revivalist factions occurred intermittently, including ambushes against a United States diplomatic convoy in May 2023 and the convoy of a former state governor the following month.

These developments came at a time of growing regional discord. President Tinubu's erratic response to the coup in neighbouring Niger created complications for his domestic standing, particularly in northern areas with close cultural and economic ties to Niger. Moreover, turbulence within the Economic Community of West African States (ECOWAS) prompted concerns about its diminishing regional influence, and whether the apparent decline of the bloc may be related to ongoing turmoil within Nigeria.[5]

Conflict Parties

Nigerian armed forces

Strength: 143,000 military personnel, including 100,000 army personnel. Paramilitary forces (known as the Nigeria Security and Civil Defence Corps) number approximately 80,000 troops.

Areas of operation: Across Nigeria.

Leadership: President Bola Ahmed Tinubu (commander-in-chief of the armed forces) and Gen. Christopher Gwabin Musa (chief of defence staff).

Structure: The Nigerian armed forces comprise the army, the air force and the navy. The army is organised into eight divisions, with the 7th Division being responsible for counter-insurgency operations in the North East.

History: Nigeria has the largest army in West Africa, and it has played a dominant role in Nigeria's politics since 1966. Poor performance, morale and equipment have damaged its reputation, while corruption and human-rights abuses have further degraded the institution. There have been multiple reshuffles of senior officers, most recently in June 2023.

Objectives: Establish and maintain security across Nigeria.

Opponents: JAS/Boko Haram, ISWAP, Ansaru, Eastern Security Network (ESN), armed bandits and pastoralist militias.

Affiliates/allies: Vigilante groups, Civilian Joint Task Force (CJTF), MNJTF, United Kingdom and US.

Resources/capabilities: Heavy and light weaponry in the land, air, sea and cyber spheres. Resources and capabilities have significantly improved in recent years, though poor equipment and training remain areas of concern. Despite military spending amounting to US$2.2 billion in 2023, this represents just 0.6% of Nigeria's GDP (one of the lowest rates in West Africa).

Jama'atu Ahlis Sunna Lidda'awati wal-Jihad (JAS)/Boko Haram

Strength: Prior to Abubakar Shekau's death in May 2021, JAS/Boko Haram was estimated to have about 1,500–3,000 fighters in total.[6] However, reportedly a substantial number of fighters have either surrendered to the authorities or defected to ISWAP since then.[7] Recent (unconfirmed) figures indicate the group has 1,500–2,000 fighters, with the majority of these fighters being based in the Lake Chad area, and a smaller number based in the Mandara Mountains along the border between Nigeria and Cameroon.[8] It is not possible to reliably determine what proportion of these forces are based in Nigeria.

Areas of operation: Southern areas of Borno and Yobe states. The breakaway Bakura faction retains a presence on the shores of Lake Chad. A faction under a commander named Sadiku is present in Kaduna State. Ansaru (an al-Qaeda-affiliated splinter group) has expanded its presence in the North Central and North West zones after years of inactivity.

Leadership: Led by Shekau from 2010 until his death in 2021 and now highly factionalised. Notable factional leaders include Bakura Doron (the political leader of the Bakura faction) and Bakura Shalaba Modu (the religious leader of the Bakura faction). Some reports indicate Modu was killed by Doron in 2022.[9]

Structure: Highly decentralised with a weak chain of command, with various offshoots and cells that act independently. Several of these offshoots have been absorbed into ISWAP since 2021, with others (notably the Bakura faction) resisting ISWAP.

History: JAS/Boko Haram was established in 2002 by Mohammed Yusuf. Following Yusuf's death in 2009, Shekau increased the group's territorial control, though predation and indiscriminate violence eroded legitimacy. JAS/Boko Haram pledged allegiance to the Islamic State (ISIS) in 2015, operating under the name of ISWAP. In 2016, Shekau split with ISWAP, and in 2021, Shekau killed himself to avoid capture by ISWAP.

Objectives: Establish an Islamic caliphate in the North East of Nigeria and neighbouring regions.

Opponents: Nigerian armed forces, CJTF, MNJTF and ISWAP.

Affiliates/allies: The Ansaru faction maintains links to al-Qaeda, though elements of the faction may have realigned to ISWAP.

Resources/capabilities: Stolen weaponry from military bases and black-market acquisitions, including rocket-propelled grenades, improvised bombs, mortars, assault rifles, tanks and armoured personnel carriers (APCs). The group has a limited anti-aircraft capability and reportedly has been using uninhabited aerial vehicles since 2018. The group funds itself through looting and kidnapping for ransom.

Islamic State West Africa Province (ISWAP)

Strength: 4,000–7,000 fighters total, though military losses as well as defections may mean actual numbers are lower.[10] It is not possible to reliably determine what proportion of these forces are based in Nigeria.

Areas of operation: Within Nigeria, the core areas of territorial control are the forests of northern Borno State and northeastern Yobe State, extending into Lake Chad and adjoining areas of Cameroon, Chad and Niger.

Leadership: Unclear. Following the death of Abu Musab al-Barnawi (the son of Mohammed Yusuf) in 2021, a succession of ISWAP senior commanders, some of whom were (inconsistently) reported to be the leader of the insurgency, have been killed in military operations and airstrikes.

Structure: ISWAP retains elements of the fragmented leadership structure and volatile factionalism of JAS/Boko Haram, though it has established a more coherent and

Islamic State West Africa Province (ISWAP)

organised approach to governing its territory. The leadership of ISWAP responds to instructions from ISIS and has refined its practices and strategy via this relationship.

History: JAS/Boko Haram became known as ISWAP in 2015, but the two groups split in 2016. ISWAP distinguished itself from JAS/Boko Haram by prioritising military over civilian targets and providing a degree of order in the regions in which it operates. Power struggles among ISWAP commanders have resulted in leadership changes since 2015. In 2021, ISWAP attacked JAS/Boko Haram, and JAS/Boko Haram's Bakura faction retaliated against ISWAP.

Objectives: Establish an Islamic caliphate in northeast Nigeria and neighbouring regions.

Opponents: Nigerian armed forces, CJTF, MNJTF and JAS/Boko Haram.

Affiliates/allies: ISIS and Islamic State in the Greater Sahara. The group has reportedly made inroads in securing support from groups of fighters aligned with the al-Qaeda-affiliated Ansaru faction.

Resources/capabilities: ISWAP has obtained most of its weaponry – including APCs, assault rifles, rocket-propelled grenades and mortars – by raiding military bases and attacking troops. It also used financial assistance from ISIS to acquire looted military equipment from its own fighters. Further income is generated via taxes collected from local populations.

Armed bandits (criminal gangs)

Strength: There are allegedly over 100 bandit gangs in the North West, with the largest groups believed to have around 2,000 members. Estimates for the total number of bandits range from 10,000–30,000.[11]

Areas of operation: North West and North Central zones (particularly Zamfara, Katsina, Kebbi, Kaduna and Niger states, as well as, to a lesser extent, Sokoto State).

Leadership: There are multiple prominent bandit leaders in control of larger bandit groups, though none command widespread allegiance. Major gang leaders include Bello Turji Kachalla and Dogo Gide, while Adamu Aliero Yankuzo was controversially made a customary chief in Zamfara State in 2022 as part of a de facto peace deal.

Structure: Most gangs do not have a formal structure and are prone to splitting (sometimes violently).

History: There has been only limited research into the phenomenon of banditry in northwestern Nigeria, though most accounts suggest that the current iteration of banditry emerged in 2011, with at least some groups being hired by politicians as security during the 2011 general elections. The attacks and abductions have since escalated and spread from Zamfara State to adjoining states. Protection rackets were also established in 2018, targeting Hausa agriculturalist communities. Most gang members are ethnic Fulani, though some gangs are ethnically mixed.

Objectives: Although most groups have a clear criminal motivation, this is interwoven with overt and covert political elements. This includes the reassertion of an 'authentic' Fulani pastoralist identity against ruling elites and security services; grievances surrounding the confiscation of grazing areas; and a reprisal against vigilante actions (often by Hausa vigilantes) that have targeted the bandits or the wider Fulani community.

Opponents: Hausa sedentary farmers, vigilante groups and Nigerian armed forces.

Affiliates/allies: Links with some (though not all) Fulani pastoralist militias, including those in Niger and Mali, and limited tactical cooperation with ISWAP.

Resources/capabilities: Small arms and light weapons. Bandits often use motorcycles to carry out their attacks. There are some indications of bandits receiving training from (former) JAS/Boko Haram members on the use of improvised explosive devises and anti-aircraft guns.

Fulani pastoralist militias

Strength: Unclear.

Areas of operation: Active in Fulani-inhabited areas of northern Nigeria (especially the North West zone) and parts of the Middle Belt. Due to armed bandits, some of whom have engaged in looting or attacks on elements of the Fulani community, there are increased reports of Fulani pastoralists being displaced to southern areas of the country.

Leadership: No formal leadership.

Structure: Fulani groups include both semi-nomadic pastoralists and settled communities in urban and rural areas. Pastoralist communities are highly decentralised, as they are divided into clans (*lenyi*) and sub-clans. Individuals have significant autonomy over whether to fight or retaliate for perceived wrongs; decisions such as these may be made without community leaders' knowledge or approval. For some conflicts, mobilisation occurs along ethnic and kinship lines.

History: Pastoralist–farmer conflicts have a long history in Nigeria, but they have become deadlier in recent years, with the Fulani pastoralist militias acquiring more sophisticated weaponry and cooperating with armed bandits in northern Nigeria.

Objectives: Protect traditional 'cattle culture', secure pasture for grazing, and counter vigilantism and cattle raids.

Opponents: Hausa sedentary farmers, vigilante groups, Nigerian armed forces and ESN in the South East.

Affiliates/allies: Some cooperation with armed bandits.

Resources/capabilities: Small arms, including locally made guns.

Farmer militias and vigilante groups

Strength: Unclear.

Areas of operation: Middle Belt, South West and South East, as well as some Hausa areas of the North West zone.

Leadership: Within several communities in the conflict areas, active mobilisations are primarily driven by traditional community leaders.

Structure: Militias from agriculturalist communities mobilise on an ethnic basis, sometimes leveraging a Christian identity. Militias are recruited predominantly from the Adara, Berom, Tarok and Tiv ethnic groups, while parts of the (Muslim) Hausa have formed vigilante groups against banditry. Larger ethnic groups also maintain self-defence militias with the backing of regional political elites.

History: Pastoralist–farmer conflicts have a long history in Nigeria, though they have become deadlier in recent years. Land encroachment by farmers, disputes over 'indigenous' status and elite meddling have exacerbated conflicts, turning them into ethnic and religious ones. Due to security weaknesses, the Nigerian state has become increasingly reliant on paramilitary and vigilante forces.

Objectives: Protect against raids by Fulani pastoralists and bandits, and prevail in local political disputes.

Opponents: Bandits and Fulani pastoralists.

Affiliates/allies: Nigerian armed forces, CJTF and ESN in the South East.

Resources/capabilities: Small arms, including locally made guns.

Indigenous People of Biafra/Eastern Security Network (IPOB/ESN)

Strength: Unclear.

Areas of operation: South East.

Leadership: Nnamdi Kanu, founder and leader of the IPOB.

Structure: The ESN is the armed wing of the separatist IPOB, though details of its internal structures are unclear. The group is believed to be split into various factions.

History: The IPOB emerged in 2012, promoting an ethnic Igbo separatist agenda. IPOB established the ESN in December 2020 to protect Igbo communities from Fulani pastoralists, some of whom were displaced due to rising insecurity in the North West. A security crisis escalated in January 2021 after the Nigerian armed forces raided the town of Orlu in Imo State in search of ESN militants. Violence, including attacks on security infrastructure, has continued since then.

Objectives: Protect rural communities from armed Fulani pastoralists and achieve the secession of southeastern Nigeria from the rest of the country.

Opponents: Nigerian security forces and Fulani pastoralists.

Affiliates/allies: Ambazonia Governing Council, a Cameroonian separatist group.

Resources/capabilities: Weaponry includes small arms and locally made weapons. There are reports of arms smuggling from Cameroon.

Multinational Joint Task Force (MNJTF)

Strength: 10,000–13,000 troops from the armed forces of Benin, Cameroon, Chad, Niger and Nigeria.[12]

Areas of operation: Lake Chad Basin.

Leadership: Maj.-Gen. Ibrahim Sallau Ali (force commander since July 2023).

Structure: Headquartered in N'Djamena (Chad), the MNJTF comprises four geographical sectors, with their own headquarters in Monguno (Nigeria), Baga Sola (Chad), Diffa (Niger) and Mora (Cameroon). Each sector is led by a commander with wide autonomy, while the MNJTF force commander has coordination powers.

History: The MNJTF evolved from a Nigerian initiative in 1994 to a multinational force in 1998 to tackle cross-border crimes and banditry affecting the Lake Chad Basin area. After years of inactivity, the Peace and Security Council of the AU agreed to revive the MNJTF in 2015 to counter JAS/Boko Haram's growing activity.

Objectives: Coordinate regional counter-insurgency efforts and restore security in areas affected by JAS/Boko Haram, ISWAP and other relevant parties in the Lake Chad Basin. The MNJTF also helps support stabilisation programmes, humanitarian-assistance efforts and the return of forcibly displaced people.

Opponents: JAS/Boko Haram and ISWAP.

Affiliates/allies: The national armies of Cameroon, Chad, Niger and Nigeria, and international partners including the AU, European Union, UK and US. There are presently tensions between several regional countries, notably Niger and Nigeria.

Resources/capabilities: Estimated initial operational budget of US$700 million. The EU is the force's main contributor, channelling its funds through the AU. Bureaucratic delays and a lack of adequate resources have hampered the MNJTF's ability to fulfil its mandate.

Notes

1. 'The End of Tinubu's Beginning', *Africa Confidential*, 2 November 2023; and 'Tinubu: I'll Select Technocrats in First 100 Days in Office, Run Private Sector-driven Economy', *Cable*, 13 January 2023.
2. 'Tinubu Tries Shock Therapy on Sluggish Economy', *Africa Confidential*, 8 June 2023.
3. Amnesty International, 'Nigeria: Victims of Reckless Air Strike Still Awaiting Justice a Year On', 23 January 2024.
4. Bakare Majeed, 'Over 100 Killed in Plateau in 48 Hours — Lawmaker Raises Alarm', *Premium Times*, 17 May 2023; Agence France-Press, 'At Least 160 Dead and 300 Wounded After Attacks by Armed Gangs in Nigeria', 25 December 2023; and Chinedu Asadu, 'At Least 50 Villagers Shot Dead in Latest Violence in Northern Nigerian State of Plateau', AP News, 25 January 2024.
5. Nnamdi Obasi, 'What Turmoil in ECOWAS Means for Nigeria and Regional Stability', International Crisis Group, 29 March 2024.
6. Stig Jarle Hansen, 'The Fractious Future of the Islamic State in West Africa', War on the Rocks, 3 November 2021.
7. International Crisis Group, 'After Shekau: Confronting Jihadists in Nigeria's North East', Briefing no. 180, 29 March 2022. Note that some figures of the numbers of fighters who have surrendered to the government – notably those provided by government authorities – far exceed estimates of the group's size prior to the death of Shekau. These figures are possibly inflated as a result of the difficulties in distinguishing between full-time and part-time fighters as well as civilians (and captives) linked to the group. See International Crisis Group, 'JAS vs. ISWAP: The War of the Boko Haram Splinters', Briefing no. 196, March 2024, fn. 55.
8. UN Security Council (UNSC), 'Letter Dated 23 January 2024 from the Chair of the Security Council Committee Pursuant to Resolutions 1267 (1999), 1989 (2011) and 2253 (2015) Concerning Islamic State in Iraq and the Levant (Da'esh), Al-Qaida and Associated Individuals, Groups, Undertakings and Entities Addressed to the President of the Security Council', S/2024/92, 29 January 2024, p. 9.
9. Maman Inoua Elhadji Mahamadou Amadou and Vincent Foucher, 'Boko Haram in the Lake Chad Basin: The Bakura Faction and Its Resistance to the Rationalisation of Jihad', German Institute for International and Security Affairs (SWP), German Institute of Development and Sustainability, and Kiel Institute for the World Economy, 8 December 2022; and Richard Assheton, 'Boko Haram Chief "Killed for Trying to Defect"', *The Times*, 7 April 2022.
10. UNSC, 'Letter Dated 23 January 2024 from the Chair of the Security Council Committee Pursuant to Resolutions 1267 (1999), 1989 (2011) and 2253 (2015) Concerning Islamic State in Iraq and the Levant (Da'esh), Al-Qaida and Associated Individuals, Groups, Undertakings and Entities Addressed to the President of the Security Council', p. 9.
11. James Barnett and Murtala Rufai, 'The Other Insurgency: Northwest Nigeria's Worsening Bandit Crisis', War on the Rocks, 16 November 2021; 'Matawalle: There Are Over 30,000 Bandits in the North', *Cable*, 2 April 2021; and James Barnett, Murtala Ahmed Rufa'i and Abdulaziz Abdulaziz, 'Northwestern Nigeria: A Jihadization of Banditry, or a "Banditization" of Jihad?', *CTC Sentinel*, vol. 15, no. 1, January 2022, p. 50.
12. Freedom Chukwudi Onuoha, Andrew E. Yaw Tchie and Mariana Llorens Zabala, *A Quest to Win the Hearts and Minds: Assessing the Effectiveness of the Multinational Joint Task Force* (Oslo: Norwegian Institute of International Affairs, 2023), p. 37; and Major General Abdul Khalifa Ibrahim, 'Confronting Terrorism in the Lake Chad Basin – The Multinational Joint Task Force in Perspective', Multinational Joint Task Force, 21 November 2022.

CAMEROON

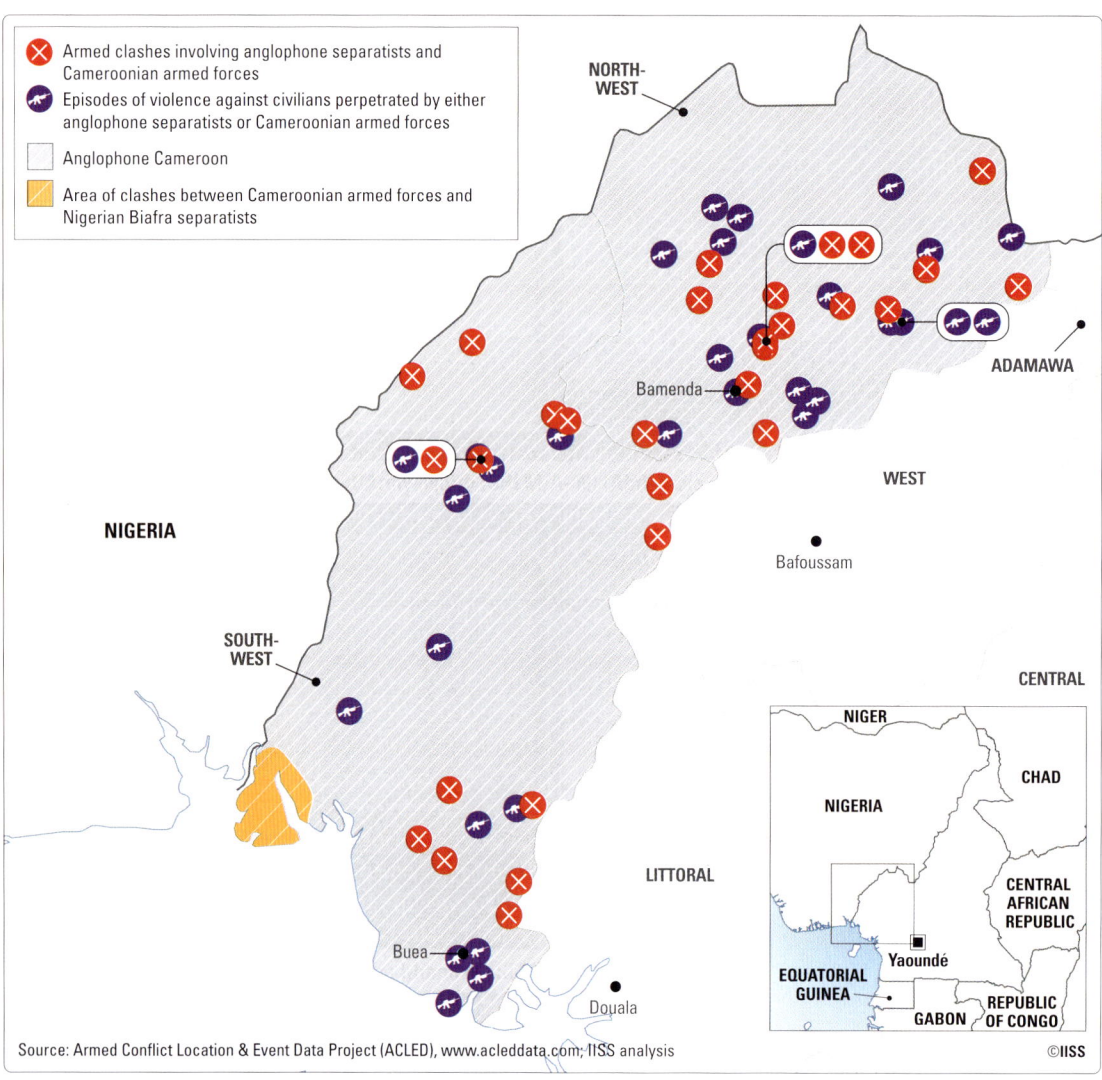

Conflict Overview

Cameroon is grappling with a multitude of complex security issues, compounded by institutional weaknesses and political marginalisation. The primary threat stems from internal strife in Cameroon's Southwest and Northwest regions, where the anglophone minority have long denounced their political and economic exclusion and cultural assimilation by the francophone majority. Historically rooted in colonial dynamics, this conflict began with peaceful demonstrations in 2016, and escalated in 2017 to a full-blown armed struggle marked by separatist aspirations for the creation of 'Ambazonia'. Over time, anglophone politics has undergone significant fragmentation, giving rise to two prominent competing entities: the Interim Government of Ambazonia (IG) and the Ambazonia Governing Council (AGC or AGovC), each backed by its military wing, respectively the Ambazonia Self-Defence Council (ASDC) and the Ambazonia Defence Forces (ADF). The AGC sometimes coordinates with the Southern Cameroons Defence Forces (SOCADEF),

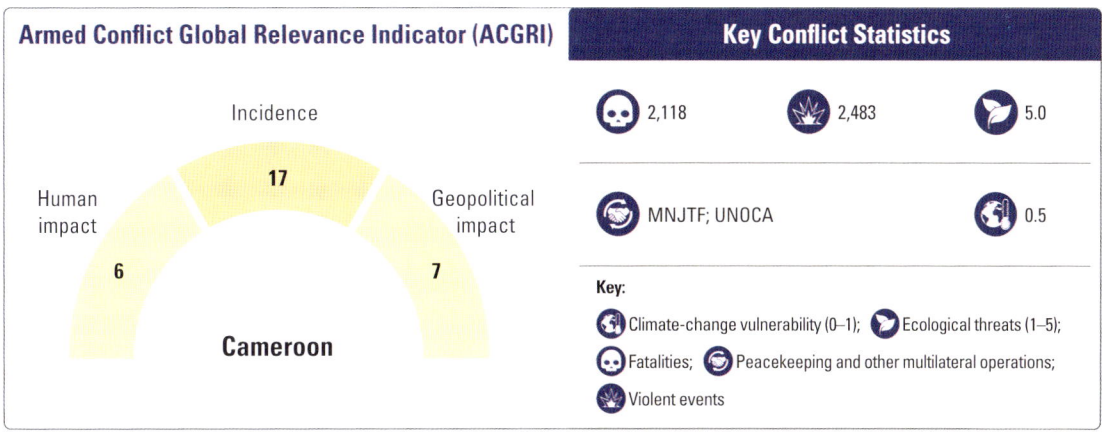

ACGRI pillars: IISS calculation based on multiple sources for 2023 and 2024 (scale: 0–100), except for some cases according to data availability. See Notes on Methodology and Data Appendix for all variables and further details on Key Conflict Statistics.

Conflict(s)	Type	Start date
Anglophone minority separatist conflict	I LI	2017
Jihadist violence in the Lake Chad Basin (North and Far North)	T	2014
Communal conflicts (Northwest and Far North)	I IC	1960s, recurrent

Key: I IC Internal: intercommunal; I LI Internal: localised insurgency; T Transnational

a separatist militia group that grew out of the African People's Liberation Movement (APLM).

In the Northwest region, the anglophone crisis has become progressively linked to the long-standing intercommunal conflicts between Mbororo Fulani herders and indigenous farmer communities. The Mbororo have aligned with the government to gain legitimacy and limit extortion practices, resulting in them quickly becoming targeted by armed anglophone separatists. As the situation has deteriorated, militias mainly composed of Mbororo Fulani – and supported or tolerated by the authorities – have committed abuses against the farming population.[1]

In the Far North and North regions, insurgents of Jama'atu Ahlis Sunna Lidda'awati wal-Jihad (JAS, popularly known as Boko Haram), the Islamic State West Africa Province (ISWAP) and other jihadist groups in the Lake Chad Basin are active in a tri-border area with Nigeria and Chad. The security outlook there is also compounded by intercommunal conflict involving Choa Arab herders and Musgum fishers and farmers. Cameroon's involvement in regional anti-jihadist efforts, notably through its participation in the Multinational Joint Task Force (MNJTF), has strengthened the political position of the ruling elite. This has consequently reduced international pressure for diplomatic solutions to the anglophone crisis, as evidenced by the failure of both the French and the Canadian mediation efforts initiated in 2022.

Conflict Update

The security situation in anglophone regions remained dire between July 2023 and June 2024, characterised by clashes between separatists and Cameroonian armed forces, as well as crimes against civilians. Anglophone separatist militants continued to employ their 'ghost town' strategy – imposing lockdowns aimed at halting economic and social activities to exert pressure on the central government. Separatists violently enforced such lockdowns in several cities in the anglophone Northwest and

Southwest regions, even resorting to lethal force against civilians who defied their orders.

Throughout the reporting period, separatist movements intensified their efforts to garner international support. They sought to build regional alliances, such as the one formed between separatist groups in Ambazonia and Nigeria. In October 2023, the Ambazonia AGC and the Indigenous People of Biafra (IPOB) in Nigeria signed a cooperation agreement in Helsinki, pledging mutual assistance in their respective separatist struggles. The convergence of the two separatist movements resulted in several armed clashes between Nigerian Biafra separatists and Cameroonian soldiers, particularly in the Bakassi Peninsula and Isangele. On the diplomatic front, they collaborated on a joint petition to the chairperson of the African Union (AU), pressing for AU involvement in their quests for independence and calling for mediation efforts and investigations into human-rights violations. Separatists endeavoured to internationalise the struggle also by leveraging the proactive Cameroonian diaspora in the United States. In September 2023, the IG enlisted the services of a US lobbying firm to advocate for the independence of anglophone Cameroon in the US and the United Nations, and in December established an office in Washington DC.

Jihadist violence persisted in Cameroon's Far North and North regions, where factions of JAS/Boko Haram and ISWAP operating in the Lake Chad Basin continued to pose a significant security threat. During the reporting period, these regions experienced 833 violent events resulting in 864 fatalities, indicating an upward trend compared to the previous reporting period.[2] Militants primarily targeted civilians, Cameroonian military personnel and MNJTF forces, with civilian casualties accounting for nearly half of the total fatalities.[3] JAS/Boko Haram made notable advancements in the ongoing conflict among jihadist factions, indicating a shifting landscape in northeastern Nigeria. Over the course of 2023, JAS/Boko Haram effectively seized control of the majority of the Lake Chad islands previously held by ISWAP.[4] This shift in power dynamics suggests a potential escalation in terrorist activities within Cameroon's Far North and North regions, as JAS/Boko Haram extends its influence beyond Nigeria's borders. In the Far North region, the security outlook has been further complicated by intercommunal violence, as land disputes have occasionally escalated into intercommunal clashes. The flow of herders moving from Nigeria to Cameroon as a result of the heightened struggle between ISWAP and JAS/Boko Haram has also contributed to instability in the region.

In the face of mounting domestic security challenges arising from the anglophone conflict and jihadist insurgencies, President Paul Biya pursued an assertive foreign-policy strategy, with the objective of securing vital military-cooperation agreements amidst escalating global geopolitical tensions. This is evidenced by Biya's unwavering support for Israel since the Hamas attacks on 7 October 2023 and by his backing of Russia in the Russia–Ukraine war, as well as the signing of a military agreement between Moscow and Yaoundé shortly after the Russian invasion. This approach reflects the importance of both countries in supplying arms, military equipment and personnel training to Cameroon. Russia's significance was further underscored by Biya's attendance at the Russia–Africa Summit held in August 2023 in St Petersburg, which was particularly noteworthy as the 91-year-old president rarely leaves the country for international engagements.

On the domestic front, Biya, who has been president since 1982, took steps to consolidate his authority, within both the military and the political elite. Against the backdrop of ongoing coups in West Africa and neighbouring Gabon, Biya initiated a reshuffle of the military leadership in August, replacing several colonel-ranked officers. Additionally, in March 2024, the Cameroonian government described two political groups seeking to create opposition coalitions as illegal. This problematic environment is a precursor to the tensions that can be expected to surround Cameroon's presidential elections in 2025, which mark a pivotal moment for the country amidst uncertainties about its future leadership. There are mounting concerns regarding Biya's potential bid for another term due to his advanced age, raising the prospect of a political vacuum that could possibly be filled by Biya's son, Franck Biya.

Conflict Parties

Cameroonian armed forces

Strength: 38,000 military personnel and 10,000 gendarmes. The scale of deployment in anglophone Cameroon is unclear but includes elements of the military police (the gendarmerie) and the elite military force (the Rapid Intervention Battalions, BIRs).

Cameroonian armed forces

Areas of operation: Southwest and Northwest regions, respectively assigned to military regions RMIA 2 (headquarters in Douala) and RMIA 5 (headquarters in Bamenda). The Far North region and the Mayo-Luti department of the North region fall under RMIA 4 (headquarters in Maroua). The rest of the North region is the responsibility of RMIA 3 (headquarters in Garoua). Cameroonian armed forces are also deployed in the Far North region to fight the jihadist insurgency within Sector 1 of the MNJTF (headquarters in Mora).

Leadership: President Paul Biya (commander of the armed forces); RMIA 2 and RMIA 5 are led respectively by Brig.-Gen. Eba Eba Bede Benoît and Brig.-Gen. Bouba Dobekreo. The commanders of RMIA 3 and 4 are respectively Brig.-Gen Agha Robinson and Maj.-Gen. Saly Mohamadou. The MNJTF Sector 1 is commanded by Col. Tiokap Pierre Loti.

Structure: The BIRs are part of the army and are nominally assigned to the various RMIA commands. However, they are recruited separately, along with the Presidential Guard. The gendarmerie is under the authority of the secretary of state in the Ministry of Defence.

History: The BIRs were created in 2001 to combat banditry along Cameroon's frontiers but have been used since then as an elite intervention force. The gendarmerie was created in the early 1960s as a direct descendant of the French colonial-era force.

Objectives: Counter-insurgency against separatist groups in the Northwest and Southwest regions; restoration of the regular flow of commerce disrupted by separatist groups; and combating Boko Haram, ISWAP and other militant organisations operating in the Lake Chad Basin.

Opponents: IG and ASDC; AGC and ADF; various smaller militias; and JAS/Boko Haram, ISWAP and other jihadist groups active in the Lake Chad Basin.

Affiliates/allies: Receives military assistance from France, Israel and the US. Cameroon also has military-cooperation agreements with China and Russia, the latter signed in April 2022.

Resources/capabilities: Much of the equipment inventory is ageing but infantry fighting vehicles and protected patrol vehicles have been acquired from China, France and South Africa and gifted by the US. The armed forces are improving their intelligence, surveillance and reconnaissance capabilities with fixed-wing aircraft and small uninhabited aerial vehicles (UAVs).

Interim Government of Ambazonia (IG)/Ambazonia Self-Defence Council (ASDC)

Strength: The ASDC consists of several local self-defence groups, including the Seven Karta Militia, the Ambazonia Restoration Army (ARA), the Tigers of Ambazonia, SOCADEF, the Manyu Ghost Warriors and possibly the Red Dragons. Collectively the ASDC can draw on an estimated 1,000–1,500 fighters.[5] The largest group is the ARA.

Areas of operation: The ASDC operates throughout the Northwest and Southwest regions. The ARA and SOCADEF operate there too. The Seven Karta is primarily present in Mezam division, the Tigers in Manyu and Meme divisions, the Ghost Warriors in Manyu division and the Red Dragons in Lebialem division.

Leadership: Current elected leader is Iya Marianta Njomia. Before Njomia's appointment, the IG leadership was fractured between Sisiku Julius Ayuk Tabe and Samuel Ikome Sako. The links between the IG and the various groups within the ASDC are often tenuous. Leadership of many of the individual groups is also unclear.

Structure: The IG operates a government structure that includes an executive and a legislative body. The ASDC lacks a centralised command structure. The structure of the several localised self-defence organisations that compose it is unclear, yet many leaders are titled 'general'.

History: The IG emerged from the Southern Cameroons Ambazonia Consortium United Front and declared Ambazonia's independence on 1 October 2017. The ASDC was created in March 2018 as a coordinating mechanism following a call for collective self-defence from the IG.

Objectives: Ambazonia's independence through a strategy of armed insurgency, increased international pressure on the Cameroonian government and disruption of commerce.

Opponents: Cameroonian armed forces.

Affiliates/allies: The IG coordinates with other groups through the Southern Cameroons Liberation Council (SCLC), and at times coordinates with the AGC/ADF.

Resources/capabilities: The IG and ASDC rely on makeshift weaponry and some imports of small arms from neighbouring Nigeria. Financing for the IG comes primarily from donors in the Cameroonian diaspora, while affiliates of the ASDC have been implicated in kidnapping for ransom to fund their operations.

Ambazonia Governing Council (AGC)/Ambazonia Defence Forces (ADF)

Strength: Estimated 200–500 fighters.[6]

Areas of operation: Throughout Northwest and Southwest regions, parts of Littoral region.

Leadership: The AGC is led by Lucas Cho Ayaba (based in Norway), while the chairman of the ADF council is Benedict Kuah.

Structure: The AGC operates a government structure that includes an executive and a legislative branch. Various leaders in the ADF have the title 'general'.

History: The AGC was created in 2013 as a merger of several other self-determination movements and remains outside the IG. In September 2017, the AGC declared a war of independence

Ambazonia Governing Council (AGC)/Ambazonia Defence Forces (ADF)

against the Cameroonian government and the ADF was deployed as its official armed wing.

Objectives: Ambazonia's independence through a strategy of insurgency and disruption of commerce. The AGC's goal is to make the anglophone territory ungovernable and thus compel the Cameroonian government to concede.

Opponents: Cameroonian armed forces.

Affiliates/allies: At times interacts with groups in the ASDC and coordinates with SOCADEF. It has a loose relationship with the IG.

Resources/capabilities: The ADF relies on makeshift weaponry and some imports of small arms from neighbouring Nigeria. Financing for the ADF comes primarily from donors in the Cameroonian diaspora, while some members have been implicated in kidnapping for ransom to fund their operations.

Southern Cameroons Defence Forces (SOCADEF)

Strength: Approximately 400 members.[7]

Areas of operation: Meme division, Southwest region.

Leadership: Led in exile from the US by Ebenezer Derek Mbongo Akwanga.

Structure: While SOCADEF is ostensibly the armed wing of the APLM, the degree of coordination between the two is unclear. SOCADEF's organisation on the ground is also unclear.

History: SOCADEF is an independent armed secessionist group that grew out of the APLM and the Southern Cameroons Youth League.

Objectives: Ambazonia's independence through a strategy of insurgency and disruption of commerce.

Opponents: Cameroonian armed forces.

Affiliates/allies: SOCADEF maintains a loose alliance with the AGC/ADF. In March 2019, its parent organisation, the APLM, joined the SCLC.

Resources/capabilities: Makeshift weaponry and some imports of small arms from neighbouring Nigeria.

Jama'atu Ahlis Sunna Lidda'awati wal-Jihad (JAS)/Boko Haram

Strength: Prior to Abubakar Shekau's death in May 2021, JAS/Boko Haram was estimated to have about 1,500–3,000 fighters in total.[8] However, reportedly a substantial number of fighters have either surrendered to the authorities or defected to ISWAP since then.[9] Recent (unconfirmed) figures indicate the group has 1,500–2,000 fighters, with the majority of these fighters being based in the Lake Chad area, and a smaller number based in the Mandara Mountains along the border between Nigeria and Cameroon.[10] It is not possible to reliably determine what proportion of these forces are based in Cameroon.

Areas of operation: North and Far North regions.

Leadership: Led by Shekau from 2010 until his death in 2021 and now highly factionalised. Notable factional leaders include Bakura Doron (the political leader of the Bakura faction) and Bakura Shalaba Modu (the religious leader of the Bakura faction). Some reports indicate Modu was killed by Doron in 2022.[11] The Boko Haram faction in Cameroon is allegedly led by Aliyu Ngulde.

Structure: Highly decentralised structure with a weak chain of command, various offshoots and cells that act independently.

Several of these offshoots have been absorbed into ISWAP since 2021, with others (notably the Bakura faction) resisting ISWAP.

History: JAS/Boko Haram was established in 2002 by Mohammad Yusuf. Following Yusuf's death in 2009, Shekau increased the group's territorial control, though predation and indiscriminate violence eroded legitimacy. JAS/Boko Haram pledged allegiance to the Islamic State (ISIS) in 2015, operating under the name of ISWAP. In 2016, Shekau split with ISWAP, and in 2021, Shekau killed himself to avoid capture by ISWAP.

Objectives: Establish an Islamic caliphate in northern Cameroon and neighbouring regions.

Opponents: Cameroonian armed forces, MNJTF and ISWAP.

Affiliates/allies: No clear affiliation in Cameroon.

Resources/capabilities: Stolen weaponry from military bases and black-market acquisitions, including rocket-propelled grenades, improvised bombs, mortars, assault rifles, tanks and armoured personnel carriers (APCs). The group has a limited anti-aircraft capability and reportedly has been using UAVs since 2018. The group funds itself through looting and kidnapping for ransom.

Islamic State West Africa Province (ISWAP)

Strength: 4,000–7,000 fighters total, though military losses as well as defections may mean actual numbers are lower.[12] It is not possible to reliably determine what proportion of these forces are based in Cameroon.

Areas of operation: North and Far North regions of Cameroon, extending into adjoining areas of Chad, Niger and Nigeria.

Leadership: Unclear. Following the death of Abu Musab al-Barnawi (the son of Mohammad Yusuf) in 2021, a succession of ISWAP senior commanders, some of whom were (inconsistently) reported to be the leader of the insurgency, have been killed in military operations and airstrikes.

Structure: ISWAP retains elements of the fragmented leadership structure and volatile factionalism of JAS/Boko Haram, though it has established a more coherent and organised approach to governing its territory. The leadership of ISWAP responds to instructions from ISIS and has refined its practices and strategy via this relationship.

Islamic State West Africa Province (ISWAP)

History: JAS/Boko Haram became known as ISWAP in 2015, but the two groups split in 2016. ISWAP distinguished itself from JAS/Boko Haram by prioritising military over civilian targets and providing a degree of order in the regions in which it operates. Power struggles among ISWAP commanders have resulted in leadership changes since 2015. In 2021, ISWAP attacked JAS/Boko Haram, and JAS/Boko Haram's Bakura faction retaliated against ISWAP.

Objectives: Establish an Islamic caliphate in northern Cameroon and neighbouring regions.

Opponents: Cameroonian armed forces, MNJTF and JAS/Boko Haram.

Affiliates/allies: ISIS and Islamic State in the Greater Sahara. The group has reportedly made inroads in securing support from groups of fighters aligned with the al-Qaeda-affiliated Ansaru faction.

Resources/capabilities: ISWAP has obtained most of its weaponry – including APCs, assault rifles, rocket-propelled grenades and mortars – by raiding military bases and attacking troops. It also used financial assistance from ISIS to acquire looted military equipment from its own fighters. Further income is generated via taxes collected from local populations.

Various small militias

Strength: Unclear, but approximately 100–150 members in total across nearly a dozen militias, including the Vipers, often going under the generic term 'Amba Boys'.

Areas of operation: Northwest and Southwest regions.

Leadership: Unclear.

Structure: Unclear.

History: Various small militias emerged following the conflict's beginnings in October 2017; their operations blur the line between insurgency and crime.

Objectives: Ambazonia's independence through insurgency, but many groups also seem to seek short-term material gains from the conflict and are responsible for many of the kidnappings for ransom in the region.

Opponents: Cameroonian armed forces.

Affiliates/allies: The Vipers coordinate with the ADF and SOCADEF on an ad hoc basis.

Resources/capabilities: Makeshift weaponry and small arms imported from Nigeria.

Multinational Joint Task Force (MNJTF)

Strength: 10,000–13,000 troops from the armed forces of Benin, Cameroon, Chad, Niger and Nigeria.[13]

Areas of operation: Lake Chad Basin.

Leadership: Maj.-Gen. Ibrahim Sallau Ali (force commander since July 2023).

Structure: Headquartered in N'Djamena (Chad), the MNJTF comprises four geographical sectors, with their own headquarters in Monguno (Nigeria), Baga Sola (Chad), Diffa (Niger) and Mora (Cameroon). Each sector is led by a commander with wide autonomy, while the MNJTF force commander has coordination powers.

History: The MNJTF evolved from a Nigerian initiative in 1994 to a multinational force in 1998 to tackle cross-border crimes and banditry affecting the Lake Chad Basin. After years of inactivity, the Peace and Security Council of the AU agreed to revive the MNJTF in 2015 to counter JAS/Boko Haram's growing activity.

Objectives: Coordinate regional counter-insurgency efforts and restore security in areas affected by JAS/Boko Haram, ISWAP and other relevant parties in the Lake Chad Basin. The MNJTF also helps support stabilisation programmes, humanitarian-assistance efforts and the return of forcibly displaced people.

Opponents: JAS/Boko Haram and ISWAP.

Affiliates/allies: The national armies of Cameroon, Chad, Niger and Nigeria, and international partners including the AU, European Union, United Kingdom and US. There are presently tensions between several regional countries, notably Niger and Nigeria.

Resources/capabilities: Estimated initial operational budget of US$700 million. The EU is the force's main contributor, channelling its funds through the AU. Bureaucratic delays and a lack of adequate resources have hampered the MNJTF's ability to fulfil its mandate.

Notes

[1] Amnesty International, 'With or Against Us: People of the North-West Region of Cameroon Caught Between the Army, Armed Separatists and Militias', 2023.

[2] Armed Conflict Location & Event Data Project (ACLED), www.acleddata.com. Violent events include battles, explosions/remote violence and violence against civilians.

[3] *Ibid*.

[4] International Crisis Group, 'JAS vs. ISWAP: The War of the Boko Haram Splinters', Africa Briefing no. 196, 28 March 2024.

[5] Institute for Peace and Security Studies, 'Cameroon Conflict Insight', Peace and Security Report, vol. 1, March 2020, p. 9.

6   *Ibid.*, p. 8.

7   *Ibid.*, p. 8.

8   Stig Jarle Hansen, 'The Fractious Future of the Islamic State in West Africa', *War on the Rocks*, 3 November 2021.

9   International Crisis Group, 'After Shekau: Confronting Jihadists in Nigeria's North East', Briefing no. 180, 29 March 2022. Note that some figures of the numbers of fighters who have surrendered to the government – notably those provided by government authorities – far exceed estimates of the group's size prior to the death of Shekau. These figures are possibly inflated as a result of the difficulties in distinguishing between full-time and part-time fighters as well as civilians (and captives) linked to the group. See International Crisis Group, 'JAS vs. ISWAP: The War of the Boko Haram Splinters', Briefing no. 196, March 2024, fn. 55.

10 UN Security Council (UNSC), 'Letter Dated 23 January 2024 From the Chair of the Security Council Committee Pursuant to Resolutions 1267 (1999), 1989 (2011) and 2253 (2015) Concerning Islamic State in Iraq and the Levant (Da'esh), Al-Qaida and Associated Individuals, Groups, Undertakings and Entities Addressed to the President of the Security Council', S/2024/92, 29 January 2024, p. 9.

11 Maman Inoua Elhadji Mahamadou Amadou and Vincent Foucher, 'Boko Haram in the Lake Chad Basin: The Bakura Faction and Its Resistance to the Rationalisation of Jihad', German Institute for International and Security Affairs (SWP), German Institute of Development and Sustainability, and Kiel Institute for the World Economy, 8 December 2022; and Richard Assheton, 'Boko Haram Chief "Killed for Trying to Defect"', *The Times*, 7 April 2022.

12 UNSC, 'Letter Dated 23 January 2024 From the Chair of the Security Council Committee Pursuant to Resolutions 1267 (1999), 1989 (2011) and 2253 (2015) Concerning Islamic State in Iraq and the Levant (Da'esh), Al-Qaida and Associated Individuals, Groups, Undertakings and Entities Addressed to the President of the Security Council', p. 9.

13 Freedom Chukwudi Onuoha, Andrew E. Yaw Tchie and Mariana Llorens Zabala, *A Quest to Win the Hearts and Minds: Assessing the Effectiveness of the Multinational Joint Task Force* (Oslo: Norwegian Institute of International Affairs, 2023), p. 37; and Major General Abdul Khalifa Ibrahim, 'Confronting Terrorism in the Lake Chad Basin – The Multinational Joint Task Force in Perspective', Multinational Joint Task Force, 21 November 2022.

Country Profile: Cameroon 219

Sub-Saharan Africa

CHAD

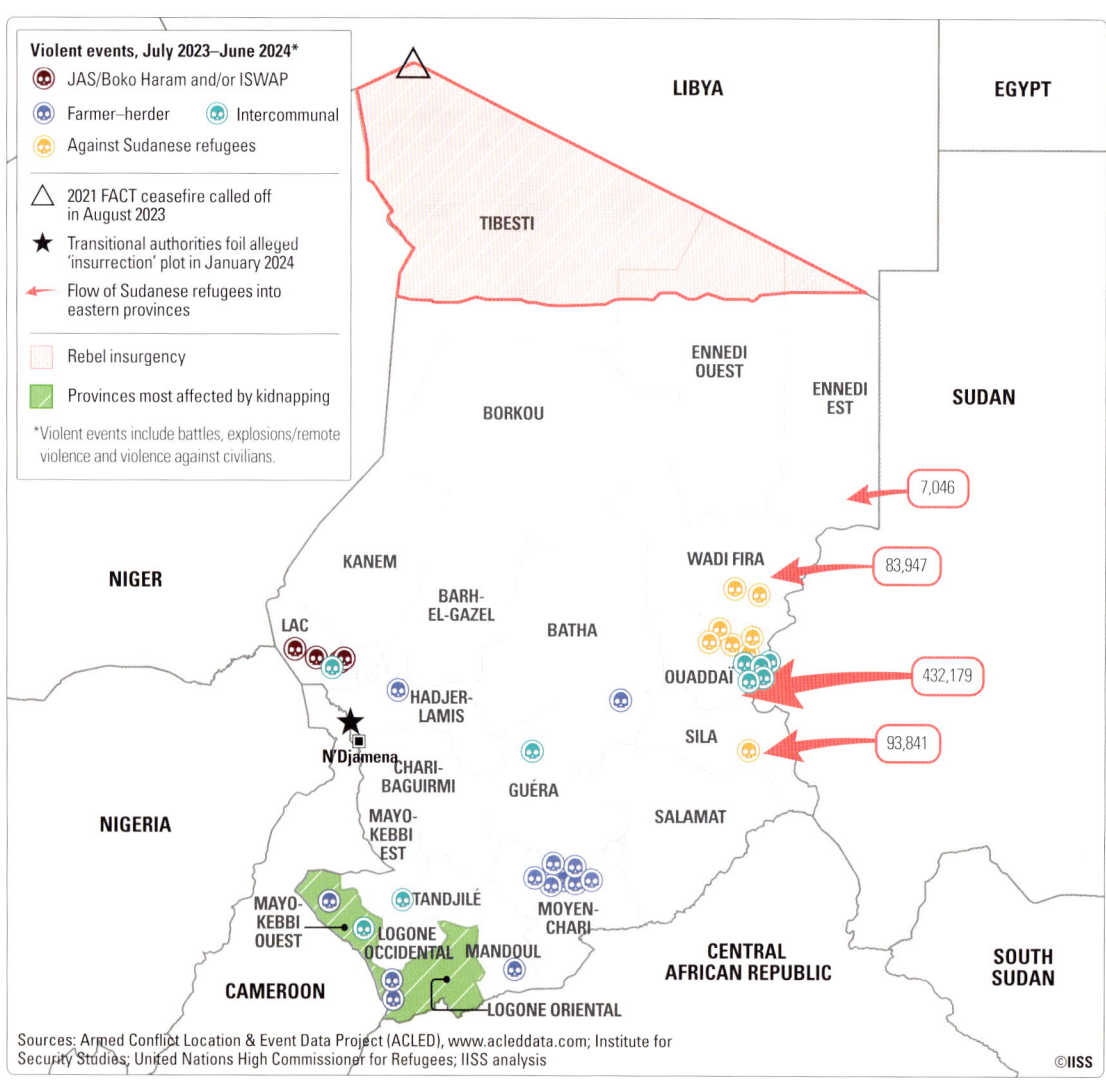

Conflict Overview

Following its independence from France in 1960, Chad witnessed a period of protracted and multifarious civil war (1965–90) that included foreign interventions and military aid by France and Libya and ended with the brutal dictatorship of Hissène Habré. The war was largely driven by grievances related to ethno-religious political exclusion, authoritarianism and poor resource governance. It was followed by a tumultuous three-decade-long authoritarian regime led by late president Idriss Déby Itno, who seized power in 1990.

Throughout Idriss Déby's regime, armed opposition groups fought the state for control of resources and power with the backing of Libya and Sudan. Upon his death in 2021, in a battle against rebels from the Front for Change and Concord in Chad (FACT), his son Mahamat Idriss Déby Itno unconstitutionally seized power and installed a transitional military council (CMT). The new regime, which has

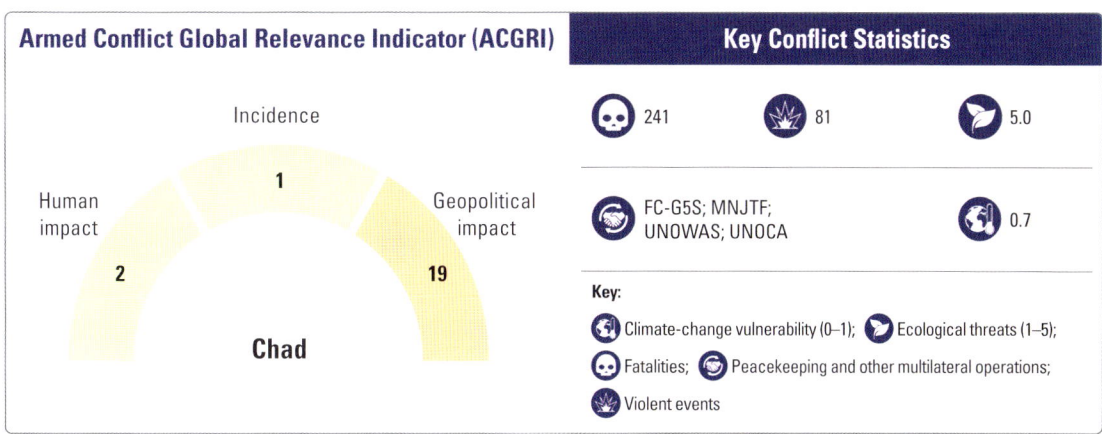

sought to entrench its power by cracking down on non-violent dissent, struck a peace deal with some rebel groups in 2022, but continued to clash with other non-state armed groups (NSAGs) in the country's border areas with Libya and the Central African Republic (CAR).

In parallel, Chad has been plagued by recurrent intercommunal and agropastoral violence for decades, and since 2009, it has faced jihadist violence by Jama'atu Ahlis Sunna Lidda'awati wal-Jihad (JAS, popularly known as Boko Haram) in the Lake Chad Basin. Though Chad has a long history of cooperation with its main military partner and former colonial power France, the interim authorities have recently shown an intent to diversify the country's security partnerships, strengthening ties with other countries such as Saudi Arabia. Chad has also been a member of the Multinational Joint Task Force (MNJTF) combating JAS/Boko Haram and the Islamic State West Africa Province (ISWAP) in the Lake Chad Basin since early 2015.

Conflict Update

Over the reporting period, Mahamat Déby, as interim president, moved to strengthen his grip on power in the face of growing tensions among the country's elite, while armed insurgency and intercommunal violence continued, though the latter at a lower rate than the previous year. At the same time, the transitional authorities sought to navigate the fallout from Sudan's civil war as well as the changing landscape of regional and international security cooperation.

Mahamat Déby's victory in the May 2024 presidential election put an end to the country's three-year transitional period by adding a democratic veneer to his 2021 unconstitutional power grab. In the lead-up to and aftermath of the election, Mahamat Déby quelled peaceful political dissent through co-optation, curtailments and violence.[1] In December 2023, Mahamat Déby also pushed through a controversial constitutional referendum that affirmed the centralised (as opposed to federal) nature of the state in contravention to the recommendations of the 2022 national dialogue, further fuelling armed dissidents' grievances.

Nevertheless, Mahamat Déby faced further challenges to his authority in the form of emerging rifts among the regime's ethnic Zaghawa elite, the army and the former ruling Patriotic Salvation Movement (MPS) party (aligned with Mahamat Déby) over the management of the transition and his position on Sudan's civil war. Notably, despite Mahamat Déby appointing young officers loyal to him to senior postings in July and October 2023, the military announced in January 2024 that it had arrested some 80 officers for plotting an 'insurrection', and in February it detained Déby's uncle Saleh Déby Itno after he defected from the MPS to the opposition.[2]

Meanwhile, rebel insurgency persisted in the country's north. In August 2023, FACT called off its 2021 unilateral ceasefire with the government. Over the next several months, coordinated offensives by Khalifa Haftar's Libyan National Army and Chadian forces, as well as a series of defections in late 2023, left the dissident group weakened and led it to retreat to the northwestern tri-border area. Elsewhere, however, groups signatory to the 2022 Doha agreement continued to disarm and demobilise. Rebel leader Mahamat Abdoul Kadre Oumar (alias 'Baba Laddé'), who reportedly attempted to recruit fighters at the southern border with the CAR in autumn 2023, was also rumoured in March 2024 to be in talks with the government.

In parallel, despite a decrease in casualties compared to the previous reporting period, inter-communal violence between ethnic groups and between herders and farmers continued to plague Chad's south, centre and east, such as in the regions of Guéra, Moyen-Chari and Ouaddaï, forcing thousands to seek refuge in the neighbouring CAR.[3] Criminal activity and cross-border kidnappings also persisted in the tri-border area with Cameroon and the CAR, impacting Chad's Mayo-Kebbi Ouest and Logone Oriental regions.

Chad's eastern regions were affected by a ballooning humanitarian emergency as a result of Sudan's civil war, with an influx as of June 2024 of nearly 620,000 Sudanese refugees, who faced intercommunal violence as increased competition for resources inflamed tensions with host communities.[4] Chad's alleged interference in the conflict soured its relations with the Sudan Armed Forces, after the latter accused N'Djamena in December of facilitating Emirati military support to the paramilitary Rapid Support Forces. This alleged support also fuelled tensions between Mahamat Déby and the ethnic Zaghawa elite, while the threat of inter-ethnic-violence spillover from Sudan continued to loom.

Against this backdrop, Mahamat Déby walked a tightrope managing Chad's relationship with its longstanding security partner France on the one hand, and the newly assertive Russia, which has already replaced France in the central Sahel and the CAR, on the other. Notably, Mahamat Déby appeared to take steps to stamp out growing domestic discontent at France's military presence and alleged Russian interference in Chad by seemingly seeking a security rapprochement with Moscow since January while also cultivating security ties with Hungary. By April, Chad appeared intent on forcing its security partners to increase their offering, after it ordered a halt to United States military activities at the capital's Adji Kosseï Air Base. This prompted Washington to at least temporarily withdraw most of its troops while renegotiating its security-cooperation agreement with N'Djamena.

Finally, Chad reduced its regional security footprint in line with recent political upheaval in the neighbouring Sahel. Following Burkina Faso's and Niger's withdrawal from the G5 Sahel in December 2023, Chad and Mauritania, the only remaining members, moved to dissolve the alliance. Chad also withdrew its peacekeeping contingent from Mali, after the junta in Bamako demanded that the United Nations Multidimensional Integrated Stabilization Mission in Mali cease its activities in June 2023.

Conflict Parties

Chadian armed forces

Strength: 33,250 active military personnel (air force: 350; army: approximately 27,500; state security service: 5,400) and 4,500 gendarmerie.

Areas of operation: Primarily active in counter-insurgency efforts in the Lake Chad Basin and against rebel groups in the country's north, but also involved in nationwide securitisation operations.

Chadian armed forces

Leadership: President Mahamat Idriss Déby Itno, Dago Yacouba (minister of defence) and Gen. Abakar Abdelkerim Daoud (chief of the general staff).

Structure: Comprised of the army, air force, state security service and gendarmerie.

History: Founded in 1960, following the country's independence from France. Throughout the 1960s and 1970s, Chad's military was heavily influenced by France, which continued to provide training, equipment and military advisers. In the 1980s, the armed forces were reorganised and re-equipped with support from the US, which sought to counter Libyan influence in the region. The armed forces have a long history of being politicised, with most presidents since independence coming from a military background.

Objectives: Maintain national security and territorial integrity and counter violent extremism.

Opponents: FACT, Union of Resistance Forces (UFR), Military Command Council for the Salvation of the Republic (CCMSR), other NSAGs, JAS/Boko Haram and ISWAP.

Affiliates/allies: French armed forces and MNJTF.

Resources/capabilities: Chad's defence budget was US$358 million (2.1% of GDP) for 2023 and is projected to be US$563m (3.0% of GDP) for 2024.

Front for Change and Concord in Chad (FACT)

Strength: 1,000–1,500 fighters in 2021 (most recent data available), with reportedly hundreds of defectors in the past year.[5]

Areas of operation: Primarily in northern Chad and southern Libya. Recent security operations by the two countries reportedly forced FACT to abandon at least some of its bases in southern Libya in late 2023.

Leadership: Mahamat Mahadi Ali.

Structure: Unclear.

History: Founded by Mahadi, FACT emerged in 2016 as a splinter group from the Union of Forces for Democracy and Development rebel group. Following Idriss Déby's death in 2021, FACT gained increasing popular support among smaller rebel factions and local ethnic groups such as the Goran (of which Mahadi is a member), Zaghawa and Tebu. However, over the past year, hundreds of fighters have reportedly defected from the group and the once-lenient Libyan authorities have sought to expel the group from its bases in southern Libya.

Objectives: Overthrow the Chadian government, which is deemed illegitimate by FACT.

Opponents: Chadian armed forces.

Affiliates/allies: Unclear.

Resources/capabilities: Light and heavy weaponry, armed vehicles and improvised explosive devices (IEDs).

Union of Resistance Forces (UFR)

Strength: Estimated at 500 fighters in 2019 (most recent data available).[6]

Areas of operation: Northern regions of Chad.

Leadership: Timane Erdimi.

Structure: UFR is an alliance of eight separate Chadian rebel groups, mostly ethnic Zaghawa and Tama.

History: Established in 2009, the main goal of the coalition was initially to overthrow the regime of Idriss Déby. Erdimi, one of Déby's nephews, was allegedly picked to lead the insurgency that same year.

Objectives: Overthrow the Chadian government and 'liberate' the Chadian people.

Opponents: Chadian armed forces and France.

Affiliates/allies: Unclear.

Resources/capabilities: Light weaponry and IEDs.

Military Command Council for the Salvation of the Republic (CCMSR)

Strength: Unclear.

Areas of operation: Operates primarily in the northern Chadian region of Tibesti but originated in southern Libya. The CCMSR is marginally active in eastern Niger and western Sudan.

Leadership: Unclear since the death of former leader Rachid Mahamat Tahir in August 2023.

Structure: Unclear.

History: In 2016, following a dispute among members of the FACT coalition, a faction of primarily Kreda Gorane clansmen decided to split from the group and form the CCMSR.

Objectives: Overthrow the Chadian government.

Opponents: Chadian armed forces.

Affiliates/allies: Unclear.

Resources/capabilities: Light weaponry.

French armed forces

Strength: Approximately 1,000 military personnel in Chad.[7]

Areas of operation: N/A.

Leadership: President Emmanuel Macron (commander-in-chief), Sébastien Lecornu (French minister of defence) and Gen. Thierry Burkhard (chief of the defence staff).

French armed forces

Structure: Consists of French military personnel stationed in Chad, primarily in the N'Djamena French military base and the Chadian military bases of Faya and Abéché.

History: France has provided military assistance to Chadian authorities since Chad's independence in the name of safeguarding the political stability of the region. Between 1986 and 2014, the French military was involved in the Chadian–Libyan conflict through *Operation Épervier*. The Chadian capital of N'Djamena then hosted the headquarters of French-led *Operation Barkhane* (2014–22), which has since been disbanded, along with a major air-force military base still in use today.

Objectives: Assist the Chadian armed forces and the MNJTF in the fight against violent extremism; protect local communities from attacks; and free villages and towns from insurgent control.

Opponents: JAS/Boko Haram, CCMSR, FACT and UFR.

Affiliates/allies: Chadian armed forces and MNJTF.

Resources/capabilities: Heavy weaponry.

Multinational Joint Task Force (MNJTF)

Strength: 10,000–13,000 troops from the armed forces of Benin, Cameroon, Chad, Niger and Nigeria.[8]

Areas of operation: Lake Chad Basin.

Leadership: Maj.-Gen. Ibrahim Sallau Ali (force commander since July 2023).

Structure: Headquartered in N'Djamena (Chad), the MNJTF comprises four geographical sectors, with their own headquarters in Monguno (Nigeria), Baga Sola (Chad), Diffa (Niger) and Mora (Cameroon). Each sector is led by a commander with wide autonomy, while the MNJTF force commander has coordination powers.

History: The MNJTF evolved from a Nigerian initiative in 1994 to a multinational force in 1998 to tackle cross-border crimes and banditry affecting the Lake Chad Basin. After years of inactivity, the Peace and Security Council of the African Union (AU) agreed to revive the MNJTF in 2015 to counter JAS/Boko Haram's growing activity.

Objectives: Coordinate regional counter-insurgency efforts and restore security in areas affected by JAS/Boko Haram, ISWAP and other relevant parties in the Lake Chad Basin. The MNJTF also helps support stabilisation programmes, humanitarian-assistance efforts and the return of forcibly displaced people.

Opponents: JAS/Boko Haram and ISWAP.

Affiliates/allies: The national armies of Cameroon, Chad, Niger and Nigeria, and international partners including the AU, European Union, United Kingdom and US. There are presently tensions between several regional countries, notably Niger and Nigeria.

Resources/capabilities: Estimated initial operational budget of US$700m. The EU is the force's main contributor, channelling its funds through the AU. Bureaucratic delays and a lack of adequate resources have hampered the MNJTF's ability to fulfil its mandate.

Notes

[1] For example, Mahamat Déby appointed prominent opposition leader Succès Masra as prime minister in January, authorities barred two outspoken critics from running in the presidential election, and the security forces killed leading opposition figure Yaya Dillo in February.

[2] James Tasamba, 'Chad Arrests 80 Over Suspected Insurrection', Anadolu Agency, 20 January 2024.

[3] Lalla Sy, 'Thousands of Chadian Asylum Seekers Fleeing Violence Flock to Central African Republic', UN High Commissioner for Refugees, 3 February 2024.

[4] UN High Commissioner for Refugees, 'Tchad: personnes déplacées de force et apatrides: Juin 2024' [Chad: forcibly displaced and stateless people: June 2024], 3 July 2024.

[5] Rose-Marie Bouboutou-Poos, 'FACT: qui sont les rebelles tchadiens et que veulent-ils ?' [FACT: who are these Chadian rebels and what do they want?], BBC News Afrique, 22 April 2021. See, for example, Torbo Soulyemane, 'Tchad: Mahamat Barh Kendji exclu du FACT pour haute trahison' [Chad: Mahamat Barh Kendji ousted from FACT over high treason], *Le N'Djam Post*, 9 November 2023.

[6] 'Raids contre l'UFR au Tchad: l'armée française tire un premier bilan' [Raids against the UFR in Chad: the French army draws a first assessment], Radio France Internationale, 7 February 2019.

[7] Ministère des Armées [Ministry of Armed Forces], 'Tchad – Les forces françaises en soutien médical a la population' [Chad: French forces provide medical support to the population], 13 February 2024.

[8] Freedom Chukwudi Onuoha, Andrew E. Yaw Tchie and Mariana Llorens Zabala, *A Quest to Win the Hearts and Minds: Assessing the Effectiveness of the Multinational Joint Task Force* (Olso: Norwegian Institute of International Affairs, 2023), p. 37; and Major General Abdul Khalifa Ibrahim, 'Confronting Terrorism in the Lake Chad Basin – The Multinational Joint Task Force in Perspective', Multinational Joint Task Force, 21 November 2022.

CENTRAL AFRICAN REPUBLIC

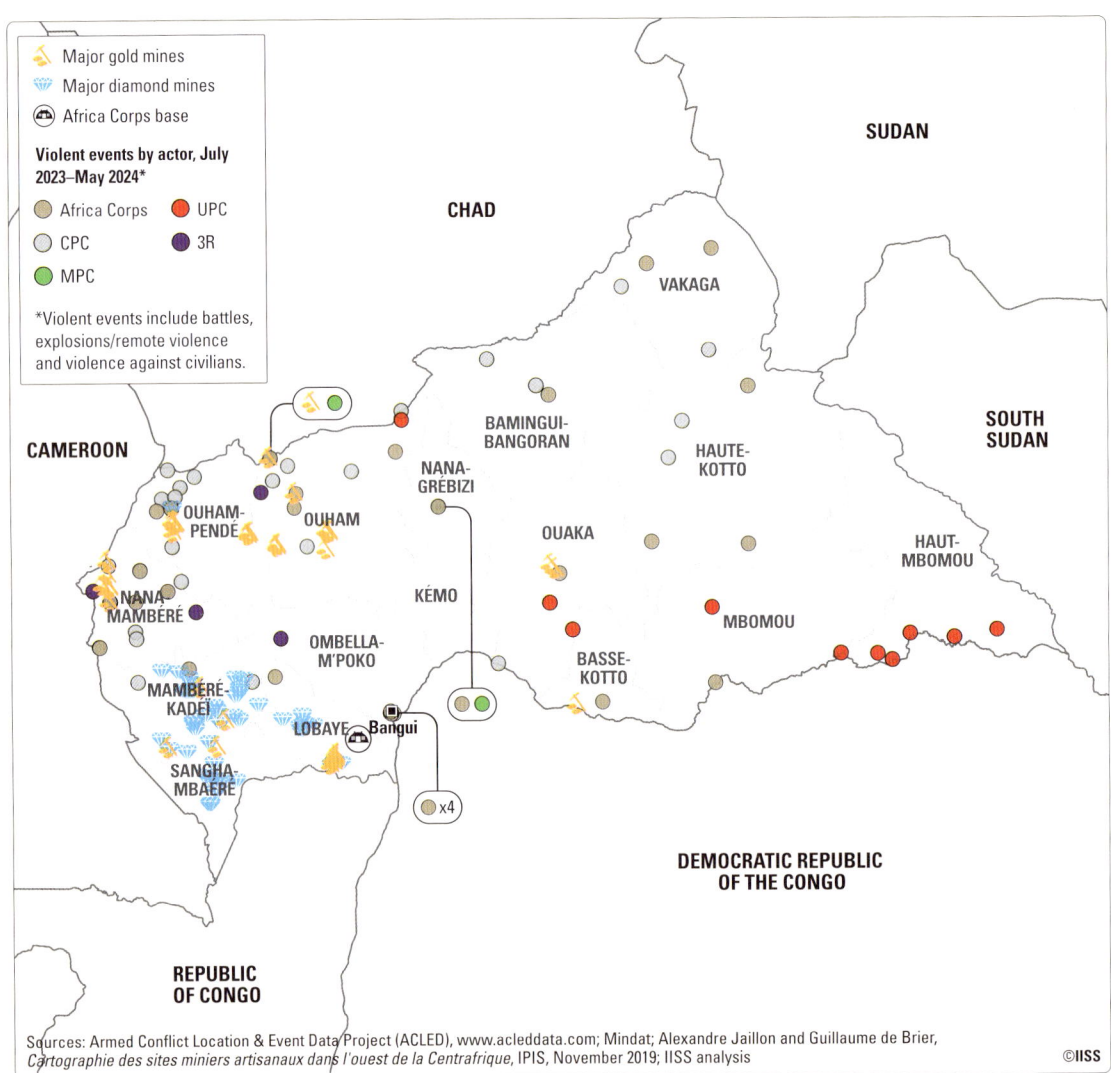

Conflict Overview

The Central African Republic (CAR) has endured decades of conflict marked by recurring cycles of violence, political upheaval and humanitarian crises. At its centre are competing political factions and armed groups vying for power and control over the nation's abundant natural resources. The struggle for political dominance often intersects with ethnic and religious divisions, exacerbating tensions and fuelling violence.

The roots of the current crisis can be traced back to 2012, when a coalition of predominantly Muslim rebel groups known as Séléka launched a coup, overthrowing then-president François Bozizé and installing as president Michel Djotodia. This led to violent reprisals from Christian militias known as 'anti-balaka' groups, resulting in widespread atrocities and the displacement of hundreds of thousands of people. In March 2016, Faustin-Archange Touadéra, Bozizé's former prime minister, was elected president. Several rounds of peace negotiations followed, and in 2019, the CAR authorities and

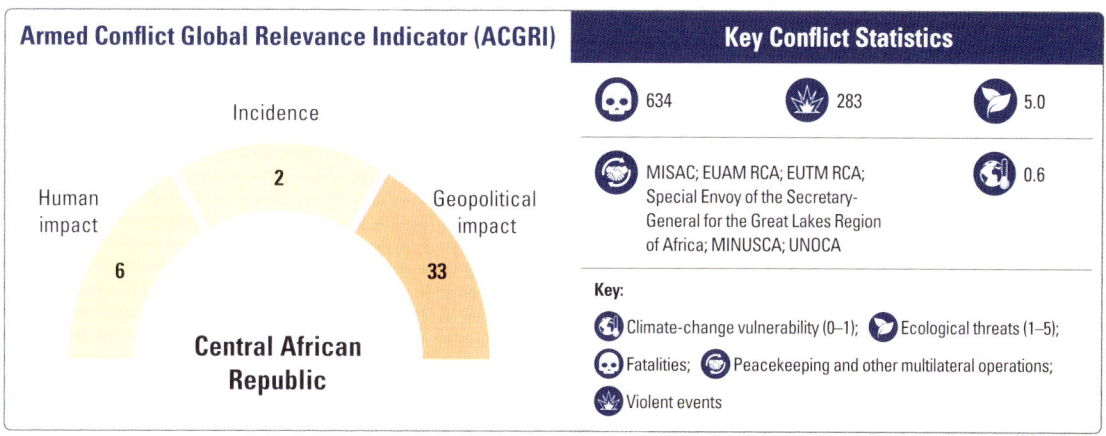

Conflict(s)	Type	Start date
Armed rebellions, including by the CPC coalition	II	2012
Country-wide communal and religious-based violence	I IC	1990s, recurrent

Key: I IC Internal: intercommunal; II Internationalised internal

14 armed groups signed the Political Agreement on Peace and Reconciliation (APPR). Armed confrontations did not stop, however. The political situation further deteriorated in 2020, when the Constitutional Court rejected Bozizé's presidential candidacy. Major rebel groups, allegedly with ties to former president Bozizé, created the Coalition of Patriots for Change (CPC) to disrupt the elections, which were won again by Touadéra. The CPC included the Union for Peace in the Central African Republic (UPC); the Popular Front for the Renaissance of Central Africa (FPRC); Return, Reclamation, Rehabilitation (3R); the Central African Patriotic Movement (MPC); and some anti-balaka groups.

The involvement of external actors – driven by the allure of the CAR's abundant resources – has escalated violence in the country, contributing to a protracted conflict. In 2017, Touadéra turned to the Russian private military company Wagner Group for military and security assistance, allegedly compensating it with control of mining areas. Rwandan troops have been present in the country since December 2020 under a bilateral agreement to support the government, while securing mining concessions and land for agricultural projects. Amid these developments, efforts by France and the United States to regain influence and counteract the expanding Russian presence have intensified, albeit yielding little tangible progress thus far.

Conflict Update

Violence persisted across the country in the reporting period, with deadly confrontations occurring between non-state armed groups – mainly those belonging to the CPC – and the Central African Armed Forces (FACA), supported by the Wagner Group and Rwanda's military. More than half of the recorded violent events specifically targeted civilians, which led to around 280 civilian deaths.[1] A significant development was the restructuring of the Wagner Group, which was rebranded as the Africa Corps and placed under the authority of Russia's Ministry of Defence. This shift was embraced by the CAR, as evidenced by the meeting in September 2023 between Touadéra and the Russian deputy defence minister. The meeting underscored the alignment of the CAR with the newly structured Africa Corps, opening the door for heightened direct influence from Russia.

The peace process remained anchored to the APPR, although its implementation remained elusive, as the CAR authorities, opposition and armed groups appeared reluctant to engage in genuine and constructive dialogue. There was a promising development in November 2023 when the leader of the MPC, Mahamat Al-Khatim, announced the group's withdrawal from the CPC and its return to the 2019 APPR. Just one month later, however, clashes erupted between the Africa Corps and MPC rebels, resulting in the deaths of 30 fighters and two Africa Corps personnel.[2] This showcases that while the revival of the APPR may signify a positive step forward, engaging with warlords without offering credible pathways for the disarmament and reintegration of their militia members is unlikely to yield lasting results. Amid this fragile and rapidly evolving situation, the United Nations Security Council (UNSC) decided to extend the mandate of the Multidimensional Integrated Stabilization Mission in the Central African Republic (MINUSCA) until 15 November 2024, urging all signatories to fully implement the provisions contained in the APPR.

President Touadéra sought to consolidate his grip on power with multiple authoritarian endeavours. The constitutional referendum held on 30 July 2023 abolished the two-term limit, paving the way for Touadéra to pursue a third term in 2025. In September 2023, amid growing apprehension about a potential coup in Bangui – particularly following the military overthrow of president Ali Bongo in Gabon in August 2023 – the presidential guard took pre-emptive action, detaining several army officers. Measures targeting political dissenters also intensified, including the arrest of opposition parliament member Ephrem Dominique Yandocka in December 2023, and of prominent opposition lawyer Crépin Mboli-Goumba in March 2024.

Several events indicated a possible shift in the conflict's geopolitical dynamics, suggesting a potential realignment of the CAR with Western countries. In September 2023 and again in April 2024, Touadéra met with French President Emmanuel Macron, in an effort to pursue diplomatic appeasement with Paris. In December 2023, the government acknowledged that it had engaged in discussions with the US private security company Bancroft concerning possible future activities, including soldier training. These developments reflect Touadéra's intention to diversify the country's security partners in order to reduce overdependence on the Africa Corps. Such a realignment could enable Touadéra to restore the international financial support that had decreased in 2021 as a result of the growing proximity to the Kremlin, while also mitigating frustration within the FACA over the uncontrolled and predominant role of Russian paramilitaries.

It remains to be seen, however, how far Touadéra will push the Africa Corps' tolerance for his diversification strategy. So far, not only have these exploratory attempts largely remained theoretical, but Touadéra has also taken care to keep the Russians constantly assured. Following confirmation of contact with Bancroft, the government announced the opening of a Russian military base in Berengo, where the Africa Corps was already operating a training camp for the CAR army. In February 2024, two months before his second visit to Paris, President Touadéra travelled to Serbia, a close ally of Russia, leading to the signing of three cooperation agreements covering diplomacy, defence and mining. Meanwhile, the Africa Corps has not been waiting passively for Touadéra to decide. In the aftermath of the announcement of Bancroft's potential operations in the CAR, Russia intensified its military support as well as its propaganda campaigns against the US. Alongside the ongoing struggle for influence between the US and Russia, Rwanda's support for the CAR government has remained steadfast. This commitment was highlighted by the assistance provided by Rwandan bilateral troops in training the newly established Rapid Intervention Battalion (BIR).

Conflict Parties

Central African Armed Forces (FACA)

Strength: 14,150 active military, and 1,000 gendarmerie and paramilitary.

Areas of operation: Main cities.

Leadership: Claude Rameaux Bireau (defence minister) and Gen. Zéphirin Mamadou (chief of staff).

Structure: The army is structurally weak, and effective military and security organisation remain largely absent. A lack of financial resources and defence-industrial capacity makes equipment maintenance difficult. The presidential guard is the best trained and equipped unit. The BIR was inaugurated by Touadéra in February 2024, with training conducted by Rwandan forces.

Central African Armed Forces (FACA)

History: Experienced mutinies in 1996 and 1997. Having been involved in many coups since independence, the army evaporated when the Séléka took power in 2013, with many soldiers joining the anti-balaka groups. The army-reconstruction process started gradually in 2014, supported by the European Union, Russia and the UN. Since then, the reconstruction process has been slow.

Objectives: Protect the Touadéra regime and secure CAR territory from external threats and attacks.

Opponents: Non-state armed groups, including UPC, FPRC, 3R, MPC and anti-balaka groups.

Affiliates/allies: MINUSCA, Rwandan deployment and Africa Corps.

Resources/capabilities: Insufficient budget, limited military equipment and mobility. Wages are often unpaid.

Union for Peace in the Central African Republic (UPC)

Strength: Unclear.

Areas of operation: Central and southeastern CAR (Haute-Kotto, Haut-Mbomou, Mbomou and Ouaka provinces).

Leadership: Ali Darassa, a long-standing Fulani rebel and bandit, formerly a commander of the Baba Laddé militia. The UPC leadership is made up of professional bandits and regional mercenaries.

Structure: Unclear.

History: The first group to split from the Séléka coalition in 2014, the UPC has strategically enlarged its territory since then and is widely considered the most powerful armed group currently in the CAR.

Objectives: Officially, the UPC protects Fulani communities, but its main objective is to control natural resources and trade routes between the CAR and some of its neighbours.

Opponents: Government forces and some anti-balaka groups.

Affiliates/allies: 3R and possibly MPC. The UPC is a member of the CPC but has kept a low profile within the coalition. In some locations, the UPC has also been cooperating with the FPRC.

Resources/capabilities: Involved in the cattle and gold trade and weapons trafficking between Chad, the Democratic Republic of the Congo and South Sudan.

Popular Front for the Renaissance of Central Africa (FPRC)

Strength: Unclear.

Areas of operation: Haute-Kotto province.

Leadership: Abdoulaye Hissène (military leader) and Noureddine Adam (political leader).

Structure: Originally composed of Rounga, Goula, Chadian and Sudanese fighters. Most of the Goula elements left the movement in 2017 and 2018, joining the Patriotic Rally for the Renewal of Central Africa.

History: Emerged after the fall of the Séléka coalition in 2014. Leading Séléka members Hissène and Adam created the FPRC to maintain control of the northeast. In 2019, they fought against the Movement of Central African Liberators for Justice (MLCJ) but lost and were pushed out of Birao, the main city in Vakaga province.

Objectives: The FPRC's political agenda focuses on protecting Muslim communities and partitioning the country. In 2015, Adam proclaimed the creation of a short-lived independent state, the Logone Republic, and has subsequently tried unsuccessfully to reunite the former Séléka groups.

Opponents: MLCJ and government forces.

Affiliates/allies: Member of the CPC.

Resources/capabilities: The FPRC controls some of the weapons trafficking, trade and cattle routes between the CAR, Chad and Sudan and thus can count on significant financial resources. It is well connected to the Chadian and Sudanese security services, from which it receives mercenaries as well as military equipment.

Return, Reclamation, Rehabilitation (3R)

Strength: Unclear.

Areas of operation: Ouham-Pendé and Nana-Mambéré provinces, with headquarters in De Gaulle town.

Leadership: Gen. Sembe Bobbo.

Structure: Unclear.

History: 3R emerged in late 2015 at the northwest border between the CAR and Cameroon and was mandated by Fulani cattle owners based in Cameroon to protect their cattle during the transhumance. Its recruitment is Fulani-based.

Objectives: Protect Fulani cattle and economically exploit pastoralists.

Opponents: MINUSCA, government forces and anti-balaka groups.

Affiliates/allies: UPC, and it is a member of the CPC.

Resources/capabilities: 3R's main sources of revenue are the taxation of Fulani pastoralists and gold and weapons smuggling between Chad and Cameroon. Most of its military equipment comes from Chad.

Central African Patriotic Movement (MPC)

Strength: Unclear.

Areas of operation: Mainly Ouham and Nana-Grébizi provinces, with a stronghold in Kaga-Bandoro.

Leadership: Mahamat Al-Khatim, a Chadian whose family has settled in the CAR. He was appointed special adviser to the prime minister after the 2019 Khartoum agreement but resigned in August 2019. Leaders are all Chadian fighters.

Structure: Mostly composed of Chadian fighters from the Salamat region. The Salamat leaders have a strong influence over Khatim.

History: The MPC was initially a splinter group of the FPRC, created by Khatim in mid-2015. The MPC is the strongest armed group in Ouham province. In July 2020, Khatim unsuccessfully attempted to form the 'Markounda coalition' under his leadership.

Objectives: Secure the interests of the Salamat communities in Ouham and Nana-Grebizi provinces (cattle migration, access to land and markets).

Opponents: Anti-balaka groups.

Affiliates/allies: In November 2023, Mahamat Al-Khatim announced the group's withdrawal from the CPC and return to the 2019 APPR; however, many combatants did not adhere to this decision, opting to continue fighting.

Resources/capabilities: The main sources of revenue are weapons smuggling between Chad and the CAR, the taxation of pastoralists from Chad, and the taxation of trade and artisanal gold mining in the CAR provinces under its control.

Anti-balaka groups

Strength: Unclear.

Areas of operation: Activity is sporadic, concentrated in Basse-Kotto, Kémo, Ombella-M'Poko and Ouaka provinces.

Leadership: No central leadership or chain of command but François Bozizé has some political influence over the movement. Two coordination branches (run by Maxime Mokom and Igor Lamaka, respectively) present themselves as interlocutors for the movement and have signed the Khartoum agreement. Igor Lamaka became coordinator of Ngaïssona branch following his arrest by the International Criminal Court (ICC) in 2018. Maximo Mokom, who was arrested in 2021, had all war-crimes charges dropped by the ICC in October 2023.

Structure: No structure.

History: A loose network of anti-Muslim local militias, which initially emerged as a self-defence movement against the Séléka in Bozizé's ethnic stronghold and spread to western CAR in late 2013. In 2017, the movement's territorial reach expanded to southeastern CAR. At present the active anti-balaka groups focus on banditry and extortion.

Objectives: No clear agenda. The initial goal to drive Muslims out of the CAR quickly morphed into violent economic predation (looting and extortion). Despite their initial anti-Séléka motive, some have allied with Muslim armed groups. In December 2020, two anti-balaka factions close to Bozizé (the Ndomaté and Mokom branches) joined the CPC.

Opponents: Competing anti-balaka groups and some Muslim armed groups.

Affiliates/allies: Some anti-balaka groups that are part of the CPC.

Resources/capabilities: Artisanal weaponry, very few automatic weapons. No organised control of natural resources and trade routes.

Rwanda Defence Force (RDF)

Strength: Bilateral deployment estimated to be around 1,000 troops.[3]

Areas of operation: Throughout the CAR.

Leadership: Col. Alphonse Gahima.

Structure: The Rwandan Bilateral Force is based around a single infantry battalion.

History: In December 2020, the Rwandan defence ministry deployed troops to the CAR under a bilateral security agreement with the CAR government. Rwandan forces participated in the protection of Bangui in December 2020 and in the counter-offensive led by Russian contractors and the FACA against the CPC that started in January 2021. Bilateral agreements allow Rwandan troops to operate largely beyond the rules of engagement of MINUSCA, with greater autonomy of action and discretion in the use of force.

Objectives: Support stabilisation and protect the contingent of Rwandan troops within MINUSCA against CPC rebels.

Opponents: CPC forces.

Affiliates/allies: MINUSCA, FACA and Africa Corps.

Resources/capabilities: Unclear.

Africa Corps/Wagner Group

Strength: 1,500 (estimate) in the CAR.[4] There were at least 25,000 troops in the Wagner Group as of late June 2023 according to its leadership, though the actual number was likely higher.[5]

Areas of operation: Central and eastern provinces and Vakaga province in the CAR. The Wagner Group is also present in Belarus, Ukraine and Russia, while the Africa Corps offshoot is active in Burkina Faso, Chad (reports disputed), Libya, Mali, Niger and Sudan.

Africa Corps/Wagner Group

Leadership: Disputed following the deaths of the group's chief, Yevgeny Prigozhin, and commander, Dmitry Utkin, in an aeroplane crash in August 2023. Prigozhin's son, Pavel Prigozhin, has claimed leadership of Wagner, though the group has largely been brought under the control of the Russian Ministry of Defence. Its African operations have been rebranded under the name 'Africa Corps' and are led by Russian Deputy Minister of Defence Col.-Gen. Yunus-bek Yevkurov.

Structure: The company was established by Prigozhin, but its structure has largely been subsumed into the Ministry of Defence following his death.

History: The Wagner Group began as a Kremlin-funded Russian security organisation, with close links to Russian military intelligence and Russia's Ministry of Defence. Wagner was established in 2014 and it and other private military companies proliferated following Russia's involvement in the 2015 war in Syria, where they were often contracted to provide security for extractive operations. The group subsequently took on a similar function in several African countries. It assumed a leading role in the siege of Bakhmut in Ukraine from August 2022–May 2023, which saw its public profile grow significantly in Russia. However, following the aborted mutiny led by Prigozhin on 23–24 June 2023, Wagner agreed to re-base itself in allied Belarus. The group's contracts for soldiers in Russia and Ukraine were thereafter largely assumed by the Russian Ministry of Defence, although there have continued to be (contested) claims to Wagner's leadership, including by Pavel Prigozhin. Since late 2023, the African branch of Wagner has been rebranded as the Africa Corps, also in coordination with the Russian Ministry of Defence. Reports about the presence of the group in the CAR first emerged in 2018, when Russian instructors were sent to train the CAR army at the Berengo base. In February 2024, the CAR authorities announced that an Africa Corps military base will be opened in Berengo.

Objectives: Initially, provide close protection for Touadéra, train the CAR army and set up two bases: Berengo for military training (Lobaye province) and Bria for medical facilities (Haute-Kotto province). Since December 2020 and the CPC attacks, the group's aim has been to protect Bangui and organise a counter-offensive with the FACA and Rwandan troops. Since mid-2021, it has increasingly operated independently from the FACA.

Opponents: CPC forces.

Affiliates/allies: FACA and Rwandan troops.

Resources/capabilities: Wagner has been directly armed and supplied by the Armed Forces of the Russian Federation and even received military aircraft during the height of its activity in Ukraine. As it is increasingly brought under the direct control of the Russian Ministry of Defence, it will presumably have access to most of the Russian armed forces' capabilities as well.

United Nations Multidimensional Integrated Stabilization Mission in the Central African Republic (MINUSCA)

Strength: 18,448 personnel.[6]

Areas of operation: Throughout the CAR.

Leadership: Valentine Rugwabiza (special representative of the secretary-general for the CAR and head of MINUSCA).

Structure: MINUSCA comprises 13,363 military personnel, 2,994 police, 1,230 civilian personnel, 423 staff officers, 150 experts and 288 UN volunteers.[7]

History: MINUSCA was authorised by the UNSC on 10 April 2014. In November 2023, its mandate was extended until 15 November 2024.

Objectives: MINUSCA's highest priority is the protection of civilians. Other tasks include supporting the transition process, facilitating humanitarian assistance, promoting and protecting human rights, supporting justice and the rule of law, and supporting disarmament, demobilisation, reintegration and repatriation.

Opponents: Various armed groups.

Affiliates/allies: CAR government.

Resources/capabilities: Approved budget for 1 July 2023–30 June 2024: approximately US$1.26 billion.[8]

Notes

[1] Armed Conflict Location & Event Data Project (ACLED), www.acleddata.com. Violent events include battles, explosions/remote violence and violence against civilians.

[2] Ibid.

[3] As of November 2023. Rwanda Ministry of Defence, 'Central African Republic Enrols New Soldiers Trained by RDF'.

[4] Author interview with country's analyst, May 2024.

[5] Torredo, 'Novoe soobshchenie Prigozhina, 25000 idut na Moskvu' Новое сообщение Пригожина, 25000 идут на Москву [Prigozhin's new message, 25,000 go to Moscow], YouTube, 23 June 2023; and Olga Ivshina and Olga Prosvirova, '"Amoralno, no effectivno": kak i kakoi tsenoi ChVK "Wagner" zakhvatyvala Bakhmut' «Аморально, но эффективно»: как и какой ценой ЧВК «Вагнер» захватывала Бахмут ['Amoral, but effective': how and at what cost 'Wagner' seized Bakhmut], BBC News, 10 June 2024.

[6] As of February 2024. UN Peacekeeping, 'MINUSCA Fact Sheet'.

[7] Ibid.

[8] UN General Assembly, 'Seventy-seventh Session, Agenda Item 153, Financing of the United Nations Multidimensional Integrated Stabilization Mission in the Central African Republic', A/RES/77/307, 30 June 2023.

SUDAN

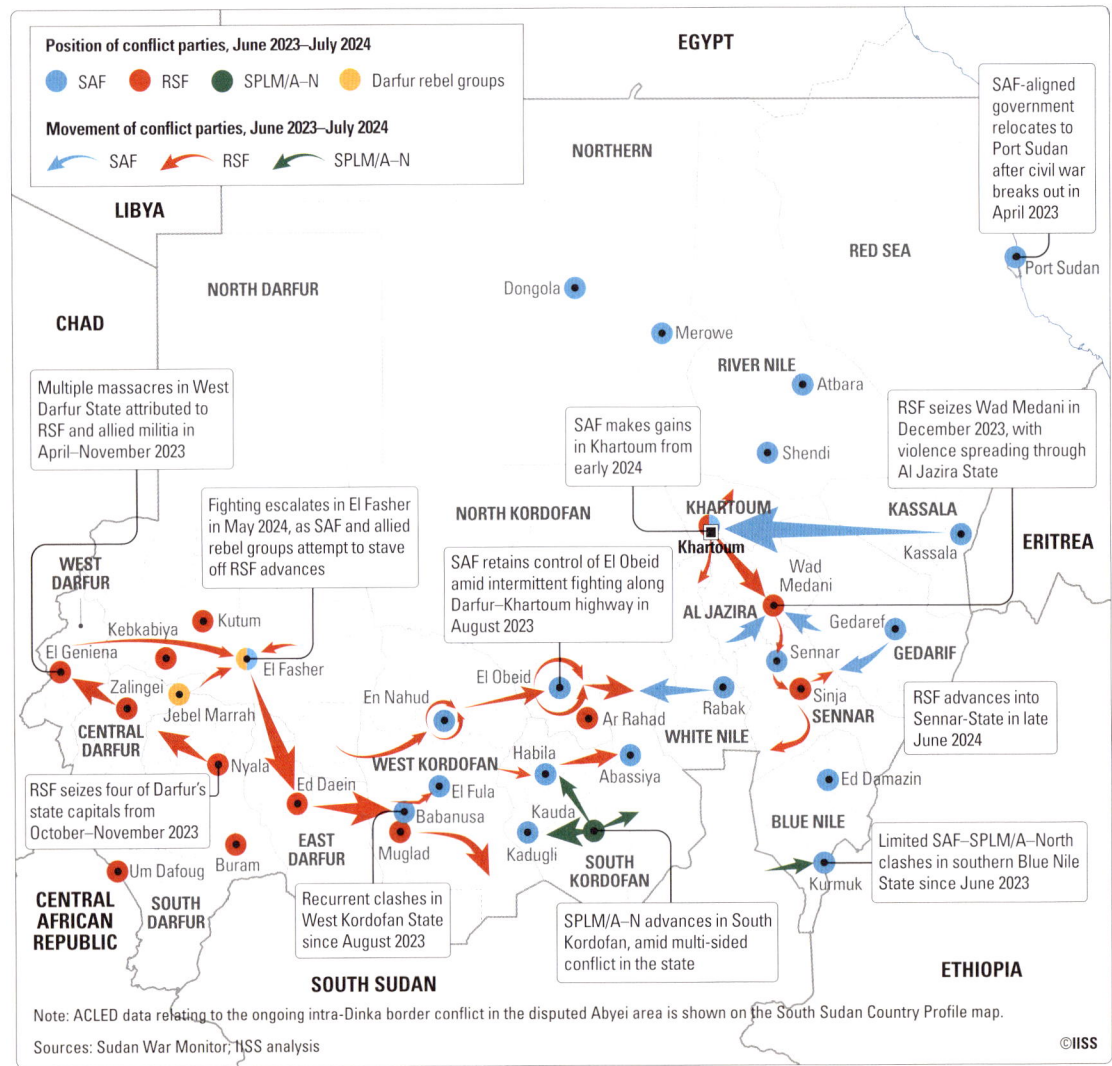

Conflict Overview

Across its multiple wars and military governments, Sudan established a system of rule that embraced perpetual crisis and conflict. Civil wars in southern Sudan (1955–72 and 1983–2005) spread to Blue Nile and South Kordofan states by 1987, with the Sudanese state outsourcing counter-insurgency operations to militias. After Omar al-Bashir seized power in 1989, Sudan's de-institutionalisation accelerated, with tracts of the country abandoned to local power brokers, paramilitaries and rebellions. The remnants of the state clustered around a shadow economy anchored in the capital, Khartoum, as factions of the ruling Islamist party and a burgeoning security cabal competed for resources and influence.

This system was amplified once oil production began in 1999, financing a 2005 peace agreement with the principal southern Sudanese rebel movement, the Sudan People's Liberation Movement/Army (SPLM/A). Meanwhile, a simmering conflict in Darfur escalated in 2003, with the regime's

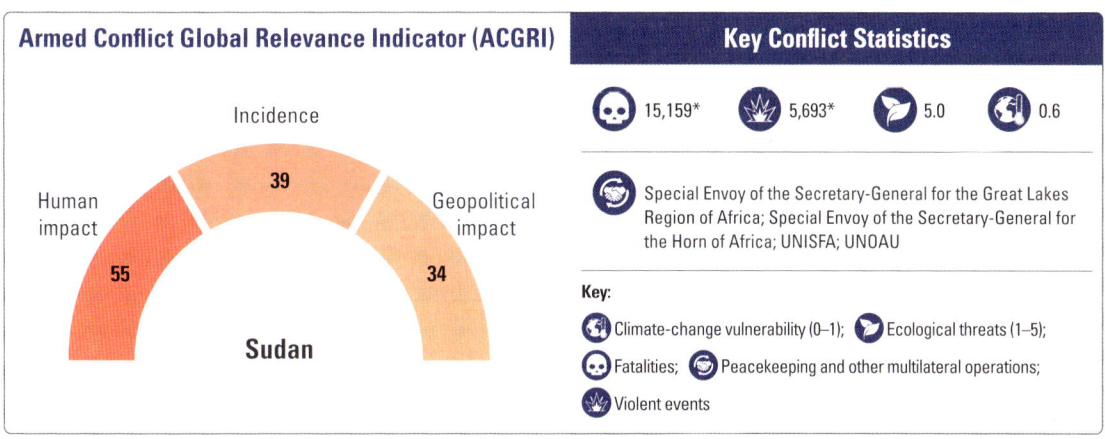

ACGRI pillars: IISS calculation based on multiple sources for 2023 and 2024 (scale: 0–100), except for some cases according to data availability. See Notes on Methodology and Data Appendix for all variables and further details on Key Conflict Statistics. *Includes the Abyei area per source classification.

Conflict(s)	Type	Start date
Civil war between the RSF and SAF	I T	2023
Inter-ethnic clashes in Abyei	I IC	1977
Inter-ethnic conflict and insurgency in Blue Nile, South Kordofan and West Kordofan states	I IC LI	1987
Inter-ethnic conflict and insurgency in Darfur	I IC LI	1987

Key: **I** Internal; **I IC** Internal: intercommunal; **I IC LI** Internal: intercommunal & localised insurgency; **T** Transnational

counter-insurgency strategy catalysing a humanitarian disaster. When South Sudan seceded in 2011, Sudan lost three-quarters of its oil reserves, lighting a long fuse ending in the removal of president Bashir in an April 2019 coup amid widespread demonstrations. In June 2019, the paramilitary Rapid Support Forces (RSF), which emerged from the war in Darfur, violently repressed civilian protesters in Khartoum.

Shortly afterwards, an internationally brokered power-sharing agreement was reached between the military bloc and an unwieldy alliance of civilian groups. However, the transitional period was clouded by mounting political divisions, while the 2020 Juba Peace Agreement (JPA) enlarged the military bloc and exacerbated violence in provincial areas from where most of its signatories hailed. A coup initiated by the military bloc in October 2021 generated further turmoil, paving the way for escalating intra-military tensions.

In April 2023, war between the Sudan Armed Forces (SAF) and the RSF broke out in Khartoum. The violence followed a brewing power struggle between the two dominant military figures: SAF leader General Abdel Fattah al-Burhan and his former deputy, RSF head General Mohamed Hamdan Dagalo, popularly known as 'Hemeti'. The conflict swiftly spread to the Darfur and Kordofan regions as the SAF-backed government largely relocated to Port Sudan. The war has been characterised by looting, mass displacement and a worsening hunger crisis amid multiple reports of atrocities, notably in West Darfur State.

Conflict Update

At the outset of the war between the RSF and the SAF, the former made gains in Khartoum and parts of Darfur as reports materialised detailing ethnic cleansing of the Masalit community in West

Darfur State.¹ Meanwhile, clashes persisted in North Kordofan State, where the RSF surrounded or occupied towns on the highway connecting Khartoum to Darfur. Violence spread to South Kordofan State by late May 2023 and to Blue Nile State shortly after, and it escalated in West Kordofan State the following August, which became a focal point for violence involving an array of actors.

The war has seen surges in the military fortunes of both parties, often accompanied by premature predictions of impending victory that obscure the reality of a conflict that has become progressively more complex and embedded. After a series of botched offensives against RSF positions by the SAF, Burhan escaped the confines of the besieged SAF headquarters in late August 2023, providing a much-needed boost to the army's morale. In October and November, however, the RSF seized four of Darfur region's five state capitals – reportedly with little resistance – and massacred Masalit internally displaced persons (IDPs) in West Darfur State's Ardamata camp.² By December, Wad Medani (the capital of Al Jazirah State and an agricultural and humanitarian hub) unexpectedly fell to the RSF, raising concerns about the circumstances of the loss.³

A series of SAF gains in parts of Khartoum in early 2024 were followed by a counter-offensive against nearby RSF-occupied areas, alongside allegations of looting by SAF soldiers. Despite some progress made by the SAF, the RSF gradually consolidated its control over parts of the Kordofan region over the spring of 2024, while making a surprise incursion into Sennar State in the southeast in the middle of the year. The incursion has pushed the war closer to the strategic states of Blue Nile and Gedaref, increasing the risk of further internationalisation of the conflict as it approaches Ethiopia and South Sudan's unstable Upper Nile State.

Claims by belligerents regarding territorial control, however, have rarely been representative of reality. Actual authority is typically uneven, with localised truces and negotiations between warring parties, their armed affiliates and local elites being commonplace. Other areas nominally under the control of a warring party may be essentially ungoverned or depopulated.

The war sits atop a legacy of prior subnational conflicts and insurgencies, which have re-escalated in provincial areas. In parts of Kordofan, conflict between the SPLM/A–North (SPLM/A–N) and the military has resumed, at times drawing in the RSF. In Darfur, clashes between the RSF and the main non-signatory to the JPA, the Abdel Wahid al-Nur faction of the Sudan Liberation Movement/Army (SLM/A–AW), have been reported near Jebel Marra. The war has also revived existing feuds in parts of South Darfur State, while new configurations of conflict have emerged in parts of North Kordofan State and Port Sudan.

Both the RSF and the SAF increasingly resemble unstable and fragmented military coalitions rather than unified blocs with coherent political agendas. Both groups are enmeshed in tactical political realignments at the national and subnational levels, as ethnicised recruitment creates new (or reinforces existing) ethnic constituencies within each bloc.

Complicating the conflict is a tendency for secondary armed factions – including former rebel groups – to align themselves with the primary belligerents with the expectation of future economic or political opportunities, including positions in a hypothetical post-conflict government. This is compounded by the alleged involvement of Chadian and South Sudanese groups, whose participation may be a temporary measure to build up military capacity for their eventual return across the border.⁴

Moreover, regional and international actors have significantly influenced the conflict by supporting its antagonists, notably the United Arab Emirates (UAE) on the side of the RSF and, to a lesser extent, Egypt on the side of the SAF. Much of the UAE's support is alleged to have been routed via Chad and Libya, with relations between the SAF and the Chadian regime deteriorating as a result of N'Djamena's relationship with the RSF. This relationship risks aggravating conflict along the Chad–Sudan border, given historical tensions between the Darfurian Zaghawa community and the RSF, and divisions within the predominantly Zaghawa leadership of the Chadian regime regarding the conflict in Darfur. The internationalisation of the war has been mirrored in the internationalisation of peacemaking. Multiple, competing peace tracks have fragmented efforts to establish a durable ceasefire, while battlefield successes by either party often result in talks being suspended. Numerous regional initiatives have struggled to maintain momentum, and separate tracks sponsored by the United States and Saudi Arabia on the one hand, and the UAE and Egypt on the other, have complicated diplomatic efforts without meaningfully impacting the conflict.⁵

Conflict Parties

Sudan Armed Forces (SAF)

Strength: About 100,000 active personnel. The SAF is supported by an estimated 60,000 Central Reserve Police (popularly known as Abu Tira) personnel.[6]

Areas of operation: Eastern and northern Sudan, with a presence in parts of Al Jazirah, Khartoum, North Darfur, Sennar and White Nile states, and an uneven presence in parts of Blue Nile State and garrisons in the greater Kordofan region.

Leadership: Gen. Abdel Fattah al-Burhan (commander-in-chief and chairman of the governing Sovereign Council).

Structure: Has a conventional command and ground-force structure supplemented by militias, and a separate military-intelligence branch, which pursues its goals autonomously. The SAF was responsible for overseeing parts of the militia network that proliferated under the Bashir regime. In 2020, the Popular Defence Forces (PDF) militia was disbanded, becoming 'Reservists'.

History: Established in 1925, the military has become a major political player in post-colonial Sudan and has gradually lost its reputation as a professional force. Under presidents Jaafar Nimeiri and Bashir, the SAF's capacity was degraded as part of a coup-proofing strategy, with security outsourced to intelligence agencies and militias.

Objectives: Uphold the territorial integrity of Sudan and check the power of rival state and non-state forces.

Opponents: RSF (and affiliated armed groups), SLM/A–AW and SPLM/A–N (Abdelaziz al-Hilu faction).

Affiliates/allies: Egypt, Eritrea, Iran and Turkiye, with historical connections to South Sudan. The SAF receives additional (limited) support from Ukraine, and it maintains links to militias in eastern Sudan and parts of Blue Nile State, Darfur and Kordofan, and larger JPA signatories. Much of the security sector is aligned with the SAF, including the Central Reserve Police, alongside some ex-PDF militias.

Resources/capabilities: Acquires its military equipment – including ammunition, small arms and armoured vehicles – from a mix of domestic and international manufacturers. This is in addition to Soviet-era tanks, combat and transport aircraft, and Iranian uninhabited aerial vehicles. The SAF also allegedly controls a vast number of commercial companies in several sectors.

Rapid Support Forces (RSF)

Strength: Various estimates. Prior to the RSF–SAF conflict, lower estimates were 40,000 active personnel, with higher estimates in the range of 75,000–100,000.[7] Current upper estimates are in the range of 200,000.[8]

Areas of operation: Concentrated in Darfur, with a presence in parts of Al Jazirah, Khartoum, Sennar and White Nile states, alongside an uneven presence in the greater Kordofan region.

Leadership: Gen. Mohamed Hamdan Dagalo, popularly known as 'Hemeti'. Burhan dismissed him from his role as deputy chairman of the Sovereign Council on 19 May 2023.

Structure: Unclear, though the force likely functions as a hybrid military–militia, with weak formal structures and relatively autonomous commanders who have links to co-ethnic communities and irregular militias. Its geographical command sectors appear to mirror those of the SAF.

History: Established in 2013 from a faction of the Border Guards paramilitary group, the RSF was initially controlled by the intelligence services. The RSF subsequently assumed control of gold mines from rival forces linked to Musa Hilal in 2017, and it has played an increasingly national role after 2019.

Objectives: The RSF's original purpose was to provide security for the Bashir regime, whilst also supporting the SAF in counter-insurgency activities, notably in Darfur, and Blue Nile and South Kordofan states. Since the 2019 coup, it has increasingly served as a platform for Hemeti's personal ambitions and family interests.

Opponents: SAF, SLM/A–AW and SPLM/A–N (Abdelaziz al-Hilu faction).

Affiliates/allies: UAE and Chad, with limited support from Russia. The UAE's supplies are reportedly transited via the Central African Republic, Chad, Kenya, Libya and Uganda, while some fuel supplies are procured via South Sudan. The RSF is supported by several primarily Arab-identifying communities from Darfur and Kordofan, smaller JPA signatories, and Chadian and South Sudanese armed groups.

Resources/capabilities: Financed through Hemeti's extensive involvement in gold production and other business interests, alongside taxation of trade in Darfur, and looting amid the RSF–SAF conflict. In addition to large numbers of land cruisers, the RSF has acquired SAF weapons and vehicles during the conflict, and drones, howitzers and anti-air capabilities via the UAE.

Sudan Liberation Movement/Army–Abdel Wahid al-Nur (SLM/A–AW)

Strength: It is unclear how many fighters the group has in its Jebel Marra Mountains stronghold, though it has recently increased recruitment activity. The group has 200–700 personnel based in South Sudan and had at least 100 based in Libya in 2019.[9]

Areas of operation: Jebel Marra in central Darfur, parts of Libya and South Sudan. The group also has a presence in ethnic Fur IDP camps in Darfur.

Leadership: Abdel Wahid al-Nur (leader), Abdullah Haran (deputy chair) and Youssef Karjakola (chief of staff).

Sudan Liberation Movement/Army–Abdel Wahid al-Nur (SLM/A–AW)

Abdelgadir Abdelrahman Ibrahim (alias 'Gaddura'), the group's long-standing military commander, defected to the RSF during the previous reporting period. Mubarak Aldouk leads the main splinter faction.

Structure: Fragmented structure, with Nur at times bypassing the official chain of command to manage an array of semi-autonomous commanders directly. Several factions have defected to the SAF or the RSF, with some continuing to engage in hostilities and violent competition over gold mines with loyalist factions.

History: Emerged in 2001 as the Darfur Liberation Front out of Fur, Zaghawa and Masalit self-defence militias. The group's insurgency began in 2003 under the SLM/A name, with support from Eritrea, the SPLM/A and the Justice and Equality Movement (JEM). In 2004, it split into two predominantly Fur and Zaghawa factions. The group has experienced further splintering, while Nur refused to sign the JPA.

Objectives: The group's goals have shifted over time, though they have centred on reversing Darfur's subordinate position in Sudan since 2003. With the subsequent fragmentation of the group, these goals have become more parochial and multilayered.

Opponents: SAF, RSF and SLM/A–AW splinter factions.

Affiliates/allies: In recent years the group received support from the UAE (likely suspended) and some qualified support from South Sudan. Splinter factions have often received support from the SAF or the RSF.

Resources/capabilities: Factions of the SLM/A–AW generate income based on opportunities in their geographical area (e.g., gold in Jebel Marra, taxation in IDP camps, smuggling in Libya, and commercial and cross-border trade, as well as limited agricultural activities, in South Sudan).

Sudan People's Liberation Movement/Army–North (SPLM/A–N) (Abdelaziz al-Hilu faction)

Strength: Unclear, likely in the thousands.

Areas of operation: Southern areas of Blue Nile State and the Nuba Mountains of South Kordofan State. The group has expanded operations to the Dilling and Kadugli areas in the current conflict.

Leadership: Abdelaziz al-Hilu (commander) and Joseph Tuka (deputy commander).

Structure: Headquartered in Kauda, the SPLM/A–N has a relatively centralised senior command structure under Hilu, which gives way to a more autonomous tier of commanders at the middle ranks. Tuka commands the Blue Nile division, which mainly comprises non-Ingessana ethnic groups.

History: Emerged from the SPLM/A's campaigns in the Two Areas in 1987. The group's respected former commander, Yousif Kuwa, led forces in the Nuba Mountains until his death in 2001. In 2011, following the secession of South Sudan, SPLA forces marooned in Sudan formed the SPLM/A–N under the leadership of Malik Agar. In 2017, the group split, with the majority of forces siding with Hilu.

Objectives: Restructure power relations in Khartoum, in order to grant autonomy to marginalised or oppressed provinces, and flatten Sudan's ethnic and religious hierarchies.

Opponents: SAF, RSF and SPLM/A–N (Malik Agar faction).

Affiliates/allies: South Sudan.

Resources/capabilities: Unclear, though reportedly heavily financed through gold mining in South Kordofan.

Sudan Liberation Movement/Army–Minni Minnawi (SLM/A–MM)

Strength: Unclear, though recruited heavily in Darfur during the JPA era. Several hundred fighters are reportedly undergoing training in Eritrea as of early 2024.[10]

Areas of operation: North Darfur State and parts of eastern Sudan.

Leadership: Minni Arkou Minnawi (leader).

Structure: Historically unstable structure personalised around Minnawi, with a tendency to undergo periods of fragmentation and reform. The group is currently geographically divided between forces in North Darfur State and eastern Sudan.

History: Emerged from the 2004 SLM/A split amid Fur and Zaghawa tensions and personal rivalries, with Minnawi leading the Zaghawa faction. Minnawi joined the government in 2006, prompting instability in the faction, though he rebelled again in 2010. Following significant RSF-inflicted losses, the faction engaged in mercenary work in Libya before returning to Sudan under the JPA.

Objectives: The group has historically served as a vehicle for the political interests of Minnawi, leading to successive alliances with various more powerful actors. Since the RSF–SAF conflict, Minnawi has pledged to protect civilians in parts of Darfur.

Opponents: RSF and affiliated armed groups.

Affiliates/allies: After initially declaring non-alignment following the outbreak of the current war, Minnawi formally aligned with the SAF in November 2023. Along with some other JPA signatories, parts of the group have been organised into the 'Joint Protection Forces' in North Darfur.

Resources/capabilities: Unclear.

Justice and Equality Movement (JEM)

Strength: Unclear.

Areas of operation: Parts of northwest Darfur and Port Sudan.

Leadership: Jibril Ibrahim (chairman since 2012).

Structure: Unclear. Suleiman Sandal, the long-standing chief of staff, established a breakaway faction in August 2023, building on a series of prior splits.

History: Predominantly Zaghawa rebel group formed in 2003, with links to Chadian Zaghawa elite and Islamist idealogue Hassan al-Turabi. The JEM conducted a Chadian-backed attack on Omdurman in 2008, leading to significant losses. Subsequently, it sought to regroup amid a loss of sponsorship from Chad and Libya and expand its presence in Darfur and Kordofan, whilst engaging in mercenary work in Libya.

Objectives: With a historically Islamist orientation, seeks to reverse the marginalisation of Darfur. Since signing the 2020 JPA, the group has sought to change its brand from an armed group to a political party, with Ibrahim (finance minister since February 2021) implementing a neo-liberal policy agenda.

Opponents: RSF and affiliated armed groups.

Affiliates/allies: The group has connections to Islamists in Khartoum, and it has been formally aligned with the SAF since November 2023. Along with some other JPA signatories, parts of the group have been organised into the 'Joint Protection Forces' in North Darfur. The group has had close links to South Sudan since 2011.

Resources/capabilities: Unclear.

United Nations Interim Security Force for Abyei (UNISFA)

Strength: 3,489 total personnel, including 3,319 troops and staff officers and 46 police.[11]

Areas of operation: Abyei region, primarily in southern areas.

Leadership: Maj.-Gen. Benjamin Olufemi Sawyerr (acting head of mission and force commander).

Structure: UNISFA comprises a sizeable military contingent and smaller police and civilian components.

History: Established in June 2011, UNISFA has been tasked with upholding peace in the contested Abyei area. Ethiopia contributed peacekeepers due to positive relations between Khartoum and Addis Ababa during the mission's inception. However, tensions between the two governments – alongside a request by Tigrayan UNISFA peacekeepers for asylum in Sudan – led to Ethiopian forces being replaced by a multinational force in 2022.

Objectives: Protect civilians, monitor peace and contribute to the demilitarisation of the Abyei area.

Opponents: UNISFA has periodically been engaged in operations against militia groups active in the Abyei area, often from parts of the Misseriya community.

Affiliates/allies: N/A.

Resources/capabilities: Approved budget (July 2023–June 2024): US$294 million.[12]

Notes

[1] UN Security Council (UNSC), 'Letter Dated 15 January 2024 From the Panel of Experts on the Sudan Addressed to the President of the Security Council', S/2024/65, 15 January 2024.

[2] Jérôme Tubiana and Joshua Craze, 'Darfur: The New Massacres', *New York Review*, 10 February 2024; and Mat Nashed, '"Corpses on Streets": Sudan's RSF Kills 1,300 in Darfur, Monitors Say', Al-Jazeera, 10 November 2023.

[3] Abdi Latif Dahir, 'Sudan's Army Faces Scrutiny After Major City Falls to Rival Forces', *New York Times*, 20 December 2023; and 'The Mysterious Fall of Wad Madani', Mada Masr, 20 December 2023.

[4] 'Unending War Deepens Chaos', *Africa Confidential*, vol. 26, no. 20, 5 October 2023; and International Crisis Group, 'On the Horizon: South Sudan, March–August 2024', 21 March 2024.

[5] International Crisis Group, 'Eight Priorities for the African Union in 2024', 14 February 2024; and 'Ceasefire Efforts Resume as Burhan's Forces Go on Offensive', *Africa Confidential*, vol. 65, no. 7, 28 March 2024.

[6] Note that combat losses and reports of SAF soldiers surrendering to the RSF in parts of Darfur, alongside new recruitment in eastern parts of Sudan, mean estimates of the SAF's current size should be approached with caution.

[7] Jérôme Tubiana, 'Darfur After Bashir: Implications for Sudan's Transition and for the Region', United States Institute of Peace, no. 508, 20 April 2022.

[8] Tubiana and Craze, 'Darfur: The New Massacres'.

[9] UNSC, 'Final Report of the Panel of Experts on the Sudan', S/2023/93, 7 February 2023, p. 12; and UNSC, 'Final Report of the Panel of Experts on the Sudan Established Pursuant to Resolution 1591 (2005)', S/2019/34, 10 January 2019, p. 30.

[10] 'Eritrea Military Training Camps Raise Concerns About Security in Eastern Sudan', Radio Dabanga, 26 January 2024.

[11] As of 31 May 2024. UN Peacekeeping, 'Troop and Police Contributors'.

[12] UN General Assembly, 'Budget for the United Nations Interim Security Force for Abyei for the Period From 1 July 2023 to 30 June 2024', A/77/769, 24 February 2023.

SOUTH SUDAN

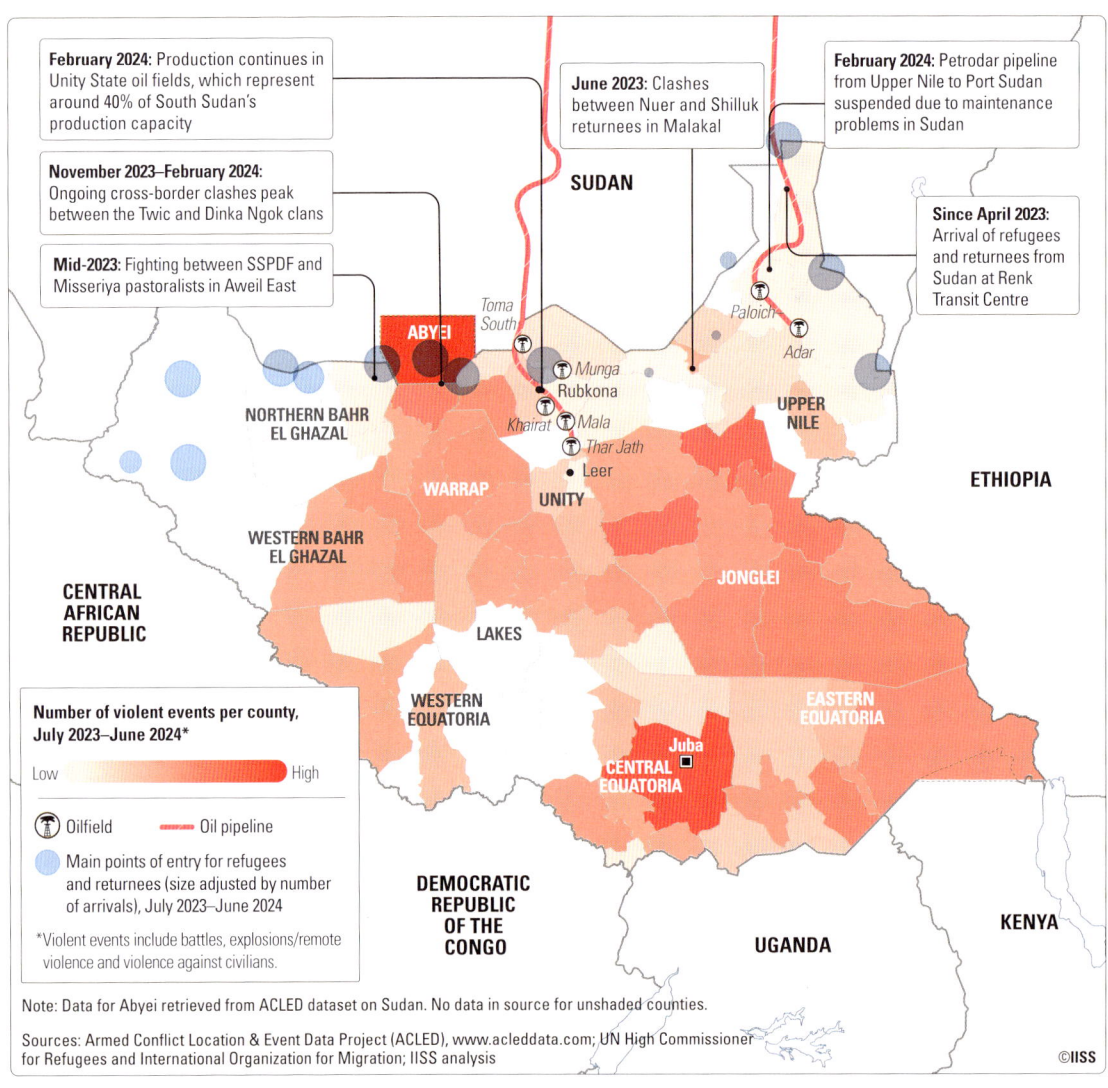

Conflict Overview

Following two lengthy civil wars (1955–72 and 1983–2005), South Sudan formally seceded from Sudan in July 2011, taking three-quarters of Sudan's oil reserves with it. In 2005, the Sudan People's Liberation Movement/Army (SPLM/A), the largest rebel force in the Second Sudanese Civil War, assumed power and initiated its path to statehood with the support of the international community. It nominally separated into political (SPLM) and military (SPLA) wings while absorbing rival factions and militias into the army. The military ruptured in December 2013 amid heightened tensions among South Sudan's fractious elite, instigating a protracted civil war. Military defectors joined forces to form the SPLM/A–In Opposition (SPLM/A–IO) rebellion and initially made gains against the government before government counter-offensives (supported by regional allies) weakened the insurgents.

After the collapse of the 2015 Agreement on the Resolution of the Conflict in the Republic of South

Country Profile: South Sudan

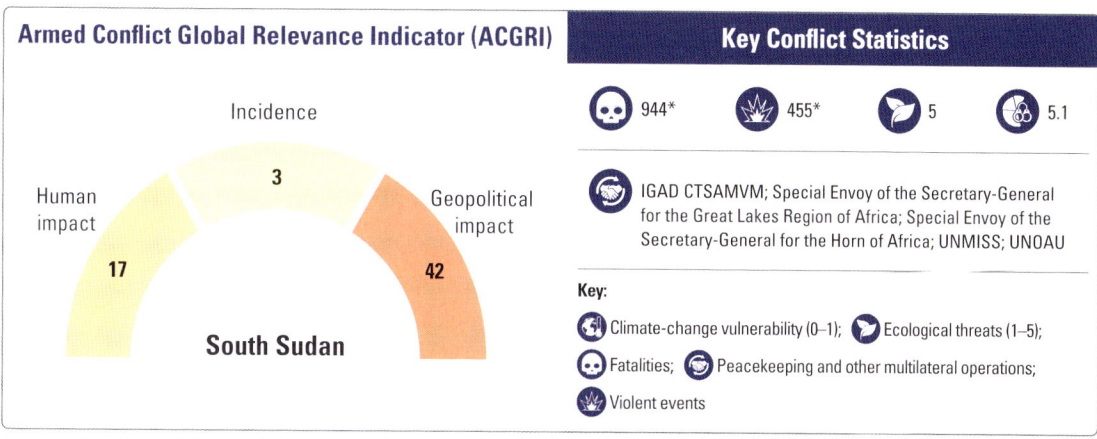

Conflict(s)	Type	Start date
Cross-border conflict involving various Dinka clans in Lakes State, Warrap State and Abyei	I IC	2022; Lakes–Warrap border clashes recurrent since late 1990s
SSPDF vs Anyuak youth conflict	I IC LI	2023; recurrent since 2010s
Misseriya vs SSPDF conflict	I T	2023; recurrent since early 1980s
SPLM/A–IO Kitgwang vs Aguelek conflict in Upper Nile State	I IC LI	2022; dormant since 2023
Dinka Bor and Lou Nuer vs Murle conflict in Jonglei State	I IC	2022; recurrent since mid-1990s

Key: **I** Internal; **I IC** Internal: intercommunal; **I IC LI** Internal: intercommunal & localised insurgency; **T** Transnational

Sudan (ARCSS), conflict spread across the country as the SPLM/A–IO fragmented and new opposition movements emerged. The 2018 Revitalised ARCSS (R-ARCSS) was brokered by Uganda and Sudan and signed by an increasingly confident government and a fraying opposition bloc.

The R-ARCSS era has been characterised by soaring localised violence and defections to the military, both of which are often organised by political and military players and have sometimes fed into one another. Delays and disputes have affected the implementation of critical aspects of the R-ARCSS, raising tensions between the government and SPLM/A–IO while contributing to uncertainty around forthcoming elections. Though scheduled to take place in December 2024, the elections are likely to be postponed, potentially by two years.

Across decades of war, armed conflicts in South Sudan have been defined by factionalism, proliferating numbers of militia groups, and violent resource acquisition. This has culminated in the establishment of a complex military system, financed by diminishing oil revenues. The ability of ruling elites to navigate subnational, national and regional crises while accruing and applying power in a calculated fashion has given the regime in Juba a surprising durability, which may come to be severely tested by the civil war currently under way in Sudan.

Conflict Update

Continuing the pattern of recent years in which multiple subnational conflicts have played out with varying degrees of intensity, South Sudan experienced several ongoing and emerging conflicts during the reporting period, as other episodes of violence dissipated. Increasing national and regional turbulence, however, has put pressure on the Juba regime's survival strategy. This strategy has relied on harnessing localised conflicts or internal disputes to weaken opposition groups, maintaining close relations with neighbouring states (notably Sudan), and preventing rival power centres from emerging within South Sudan's security sector. There are indications that Juba has become increasingly cautious and selective in its engagements with subnational and localised conflicts, adopting a greater focus on supressing insecurity and limiting the spread of certain conflicts while disengaging from others. This has resulted in a reduction in the number of conflicts in which the regime is a direct conflict party. In doing so, the regime is attempting to limit the involvement of opposition groups or rival parts of the security apparatus, which may seek to exploit or enflame these conflicts to instigate instability within the regime.

Political tensions and conflict have begun to shift from eastern parts of South Sudan to its central and especially western areas. Despite indications that serious violence would re-erupt in Jonglei and Upper Nile states to the east, inter-ethnic raiding and violence relating to the 2022 split in the SPLM/A–IO Kitgwang faction declined relative to the previous reporting period. However, latent political and military tensions increased in the remote (predominantly Anyuak) town of Pochalla on the Ethiopian border adjoining Ethiopia's restive Gambella Region, resulting in significant violence and displacement in September 2023.

In central areas, a long-running inter-clan conflict involving parts of the Dinka Agar and Luac-Jang clans reignited along the border of Lakes and Warrap states in early 2024.[1] Meanwhile, limited clashes between government and opposition forces were reported in Unity State to the north. Unity is notably the only state in the country that reported significant military tensions between signatories to the R-ARCSS, representing a decline compared with previous reporting periods which saw more widespread tensions between signatories across various states.

In South Sudan's west, the ongoing conflict involving Dinka Ngok and Twic militias over control of a border town in the disputed Abyei area re-escalated markedly in late 2023 and early 2024, resulting in at least 300 deaths.[2] Additionally, a border dispute between communities from Warrap State's Gogrial East county and Western Bahr el-Ghazal State's Jur River county unexpectedly spiralled in August 2023, resulting in a series of clashes. To the southwest, political antagonisms reportedly increased in Western Equatoria State, which was the site of an intensive conflict in 2021.

These conflicts are unfolding in a precarious strategic context. Concerns have been raised regarding the country's readiness to hold elections, and the potential for elections to catalyse further conflicts at risk of proliferating in peripheral areas of the country.[3] Risks include the politicisation of localised disputes over borders or resources; tensions over the constituencies in which displaced persons will vote; and inter-elite disagreements over the modalities of elections. The issue of election modalities will possibly centre on voter registration, exacerbated by disputed population estimates released in 2023. Rivalries within the regime may re-emerge in the wake of coup-attempt rumours in November 2023.

Political dynamics have also been affected by the Kenyan-mediated Tumaini Initiative, which launched in May 2024 and has revived the stalled peace process between the government and several holdout groups that had previously been facilitated by the Community of Sant'Egidio in Rome. However, the initiative has raised tensions among some signatories to the R-ARCSS, with the SPLM/A–IO seeking to limit the scope of the negotiations to prevent further political marginalisation. Several institutions and election milestones once linked to the R-ARCSS appear to have become subsumed into the Kenyan-mediated process.

South Sudan is also uniquely exposed to the civil war in Sudan. Since 2013, Khartoum and Juba have taken steps to more closely integrate security and economic structures, with a number of South Sudanese elites becoming politically aligned with their Sudanese counterparts. Reports suggest Juba has been increasing oil production in a possible move to accumulate cash reserves to mitigate disruption to the oil pipelines running through Sudan. Spillover violence has been limited to select areas near the border – including clashes among returnees in Malakal – and fighting between Misseriya pastoralists and the military in Aweil East county. Cross-border conflict, however, may escalate as the crisis in Sudan deepens or if damage to oil pipelines induces instability in South Sudan's bloated security sector as finances dwindle.

Conflict Parties

South Sudan People's Defence Forces (SSPDF), formerly Sudan People's Liberation Army (SPLA)/South Sudan armed forces

Strength: The SSPDF's precise size is unclear. Official payroll figures state that over 330,000 people are employed by the defence ministry as a whole, though informal figures suggest the SSPDF comprises at most 90,000 soldiers.[4]

Areas of operation: Uneven presence throughout the country, with control of several areas outsourced to ex-militia commanders. Increased presence along the Sudanese border since the outbreak of war in Sudan.

Leadership: Salva Kiir (commander-in-chief) and Gen. Santino Deng Wol (chief of defence forces).

Structure: 12 divisions, including Presidential Guard (Division 9), Mechanised (Division 10), a Division 11 (based in Warrap State) and a Division 12 (in Lakes State) in breach of the 2018 R-ARCSS. There are three services (ground force, air force and defence, and riverine forces), in addition to military intelligence.

History: The SPLA was founded in 1983 to fight for South Sudan's autonomy. The army fractured at the outset of South Sudan's civil war in 2013. In 2018, the SPLA was renamed the SSPDF, and it has since embarked on a slow integration process with demobilised armed groups that signed the R-ARCSS.

Objectives: Defend the sovereignty and territorial integrity of South Sudan.

Opponents: National Salvation Front–Thomas Cirillo (NAS–TC), and smaller rebel factions including the South Sudan People's Movement/Army and the South Sudan United Front/Army.

Affiliates/allies: National Security Service (NSS) and SPLM/A–IO Aguelek faction in Upper Nile State. SSPDF elements have links to militias in several areas on an ad hoc basis. Regionally, the army has close connections to the Ugandan People's Defence Forces and the Sudan Armed Forces, and it maintains links to several Sudanese rebel groups.

Resources/capabilities: Predominantly an infantry force equipped with small quantities of artillery, tanks and other armoured fighting vehicles and supported by a very small number of attack helicopters, some of which are grounded. Significant off-budget security spending is believed to occur, much of which is routed through the Office of the President.

National Security Service (NSS)

Strength: At least 15,000.

Areas of operation: Nationwide, with a strong presence in Juba.

Leadership: Lt-Gen. Akol Koor (director-general, Internal Security Bureau, ISB) and Lt-Gen. Simon Yien (director-general, General Intelligence Bureau, GIB).

Structure: The ISB is responsible for internal security and maintains a sizeable Operations Division and a Protection Division, which serve as elite military units to secure critical infrastructure. The GIB is tasked with external affairs and has a presence in several neighbouring countries. Both branches appear to maintain small death squads.

History: The NSS was established in 2011, though several prototype intelligence units emerged within the SPLM/A during the 1990s, which were expanded and trained with assistance from Sudan's notorious National Intelligence and Security Service after 2005. Over the course of the 2013–18 civil war, the NSS became increasingly powerful and militarised.

Objectives: Regime security, intelligence and counter-intelligence.

Opponents: Though tasked with protecting the regime, concerns about Koor's growing power led President Kiir to augment SSPDF Military Intelligence as a counterweight to the NSS. This resulted in a proxy war between the two in Warrap State in 2020 that was won by Koor.

Affiliates/allies: The NSS organised pro-government militias during the 2013–18 civil war, though it demonstrates a capacity to subvert the actions of rivals within the government and military through sponsoring militias. Koor revived links with Ethiopian security services in 2021, and he has historical links to a number of rebel groups in Sudan.

Resources/capabilities: Small arms and light weapons. The NSS is better resourced and equipped than other parts of the security sector, possibly due to its significance to regime security, as well as its connections to business – including the oil sector.

Sudan People's Liberation Movement/Army–In Opposition (SPLM/A–IO)

Strength: Unclear. At the outset of the 2013–18 civil war, the SPLM/A– IO had around 40,000 fighters. Following the R-ARCSS, SPLM/A–IO forces likely comprised at most 35,000, but desertions, the 2021 split and recent defections will have reduced this number considerably.

Areas of operation: Following defections beginning in mid-2019, the SPLM/A–IO's territorial scope was reduced to several non-contiguous pockets, including parts of Leer county in Unity State; Maban county in Upper Nile State; parts of Western Bahr el-Ghazal, Jonglei and Western Equatoria states; and limited parts of Central and Eastern Equatoria states (particularly Ikotos county).

Leadership: Riek Machar.

Structure: SPLM/A–IO administrative and geographical structures mostly mirror those of the SPLA at the onset of the 2013–18 civil war. These structures have been undermined by Machar's efforts to personalise power and his rivalries with military commanders, as well as the uneasy integration of new factions into the rebellion after 2015.

Sudan People's Liberation Movement/Army–In Opposition (SPLM/A–IO)

History: The SPLM/A–IO emerged from mass defections in the security sector in 2013. It was initially dominated by ethnic Nuers, who were supplanted by non-Nuer forces after 2015. Since mid-2019, the group has lost several senior commanders and military units, who have defected to or aligned themselves with the government.

Objectives: Prior to the R-ARCSS: remove Kiir from power and govern South Sudan. After the R-ARCSS: secure a favourable position in the new government and the new unified army.

Opponents: SPLM/A–IO Kitgwang (Gatwech faction), SPLM/A–IO Aguelek and NAS–TC. The SPLM/A–IO also experiences periodic tensions with the SSPDF and other security forces.

Affiliates/allies: Nuer militias in parts of Jonglei, Unity and Upper Nile states.

Resources/capabilities: Small arms and light weapons, often taken from government supplies. The SPLM/A–IO has experienced difficulties procuring weapons and ammunition, though it received limited supplies from Sudan during the 2013–18 civil war. The group is likely financed through taxation of trade routes and smuggling.

SPLM/A–IO Kitgwang (Simon Gatwech Dual faction) (also known as Kit-Gwang, Kitgweng)

Strength: Unclear. The core of the force is likely to comprise several hundred soldiers and officers, though the group has been able to deploy alongside large numbers of armed youths during its incursions into Upper Nile.

Areas of operation: Uneven presence in northern Jonglei State and some adjoining areas.

Leadership: Simon Gatwech Dual.

Structure: Hybrid military–militia structure. Dispersed ethnic Nuer SPLM/A–IO Kitgwang forces are under the overall command of Gatwech, though in practice units operate under local commanders who have ties with specific Nuer clan or sectional militia forces and fight alongside these militias.

History: In 2021, senior SPLM/A–IO commanders Gatwech and Johnson Olonyi Thabo signed the Kitgwang Declaration, announcing the removal of Machar. In January 2022, the Kitgwang leadership signed separate peace agreements with the government. In mid-2022, fighting broke out between forces loyal to Gatwech and Olonyi, though the conflict has been largely dormant since 2023.

Objectives: Reverse the political and military marginalisation of senior commanders and secure Nuer interests.

Opponents: SSPDF and SPLM/A–IO Aguelek.

Affiliates/allies: Assorted Nuer militias, particularly from Gawaar, Thiang and Laak clans during fighting with Aguelek forces, alongside some Dinka support from militias based in Canal/Pigi county. Despite previous clashes with SPLM/A–IO, there have been no recent confrontations, and the two forces have cooperated against the Aguelek faction.

Resources/capabilities: Small arms and light weapons.

SPLM/A–IO Aguelek faction (also known as Agwelek)

Strength: Unclear. The core of the force is likely to comprise several hundred soldiers and commanders, periodically supplemented by militia from the Shilluk/Chollo community.

Areas of operation: Northwestern Upper Nile State.

Leadership: Johnson Olonyi Thabo.

Structure: Hybrid military–militia structure. The Aguelek is in effect a personalised Shilluk militia formed around Olonyi, which has entered into a series of partnerships with the government and rebel factions.

History: Several Shilluk commanders (including Olonyi) rebelled following the 2010 elections. Olonyi joined South Sudan's military under a 2013 amnesty but defected in 2015, loosely integrating his forces into the SPLM/A–IO. Olonyi signed the Kitgwang Declaration in 2021 and aligned with the government in 2022. Following lengthy delays, Olonyi arrived in Juba in May 2023 but was put under effective house arrest.

Objectives: Reverse the political and military marginalisation of senior commanders and secure Shilluk interests.

Opponents: SPLM/A–IO and SPLM/A–IO Kitgwang (Gatwech faction).

Affiliates/allies: SSPDF and Shilluk militia.

Resources/capabilities: Small arms and light weapons, with some materiel provided by the government.

National Salvation Front–Thomas Cirillo (NAS–TC)

Strength: Low hundreds.

Areas of operation: Parts of Central and Western Equatoria states, especially around border areas with Uganda and the Democratic Republic of the Congo.

Leadership: Thomas Cirillo Swaka.

Structure: A guerrilla force, which recruits (often forcibly) from southern Equatorian communities. The group was joined initially by some SPLM/A–IO officials who accused Machar of disenfranchising non-Nuers, though several commanders have since established new splinter factions, which are increasingly inactive.

History: Formed in 2017 by Cirillo, who defected from the SPLA in February 2017. After rejecting the R-ARCSS in 2018, the NAS–TC became the main active armed opposition to the government. Since early 2019, intensive counter-insurgency

National Salvation Front–Thomas Cirillo (NAS–TC)

operations by government and SPLM/A–IO forces have weakened the group.

Objectives: Replacement of centralised system of rule under President Kiir with a federal system that allows for greater autonomy of traditionally marginalised groups, particularly in Equatoria.

Opponents: SSPDF and SPLM/A–IO.

Affiliates/allies: Cirillo is chair of the South Sudan Opposition Movements Alliance, and the NAS–TC is the only significant armed group within the alliance. He is based in Addis Ababa, Ethiopia, though Ethiopia does not provide the group with any open support.

Resources/capabilities: Small arms and equipment looted from the SSPDF, mainly during ambushes.

United Nations Mission in the Republic of South Sudan (UNMISS)

Strength: 18,125 total personnel, including 13,258 peacekeepers and 1,539 police.[5]

Areas of operation: Across the country.

Leadership: Nicholas Haysom (special representative of the secretary-general, SRSG, for South Sudan and head of UNMISS).

Structure: UNMISS comprises a sizeable military, a smaller police contingent and civilian components.

History: Established upon South Sudan's independence in 2011. Under SRSG Hilde Johnson, the mission was primarily tasked with preventing and resolving violence and supporting the government's state-building efforts. During the civil war, the mission oversaw Protection of Civilians sites in cities that experienced heavy fighting and ethnic killings.

Objectives: After the war began in 2013, the UNMISS mandate shifted towards civilian protection, human-rights monitoring and supporting humanitarian aid. Since the 2018 R-ARCSS, UNMISS has reoriented its political activities to focus on implementing the agreement, with an emphasis on upcoming elections as of 2022.

Opponents: While neutral, UNMISS has experienced numerous violations of its status-of-forces agreement with the South Sudanese government, including attacks against its personnel and frequent denial-of-access incidents. These incidents have occurred to a lesser extent with SPLM/A–IO rebels.

Affiliates/allies: N/A.

Resources/capabilities: Approved budget (July 2023–June 2024): US$1.2 billion.[6]

Notes

[1] UNSC, 'Situation in South Sudan: Report of the Secretary-General', S/2023/433, 13 June 2023, p. 4; and '20 Killed, 34 Wounded in Rumbek North County Land Dispute', Radio Tamazuj, 1 February 2024.

[2] Joshua Craze, 'Attacked From Both Sides: Abyei's Existential Dilemma', Small Arms Survey, July 2023; UN Interim Security Force for Abyei, 'UNISFA Condemns Continuing Violence That Has Led to the Death of a Second Peacekeeper, Urgently Calls for Calm', 29 January 2024; UN Interim Security Force for Abyei, 'UNISFA Condemns Attacks on Civilians and Peacekeepers, Calls for Immediate End to Violence in Abyei', 5 February 2024; and UN Mission in South Sudan, 'UNMISS Brief on Violence Affecting Civilians (October to December 2023)', 18 March 2024, p. 3.

[3] UN, 'If Not Managed Carefully, South Sudan Elections Could Result in "Disastrous Consequences", Peacekeeping Chief Warns Security Council', SC/15611, 5 March 2024; and Daphne Psaledakis, 'South Sudan Elections Not on Path for Credible Process, US Official Warns', Reuters, 8 March 2024.

[4] Republic of South Sudan Ministry of Finance and Planning, 'Approved Budget Fiscal Year 2022–23', p. 15; and Flora McCrone, 'Hollow Promises: The Risks of Military Integration in Western Equatoria', Small Arms Survey, June 2020.

[5] As of February 2024. UN Peacekeeping, 'UNMISS Fact Sheet'.

[6] UN General Assembly, 'Budget for the United Nations Mission in South Sudan for the Period From 1 July 2023 to 30 June 2024', A/77/752, 16 February 2023.

ETHIOPIA

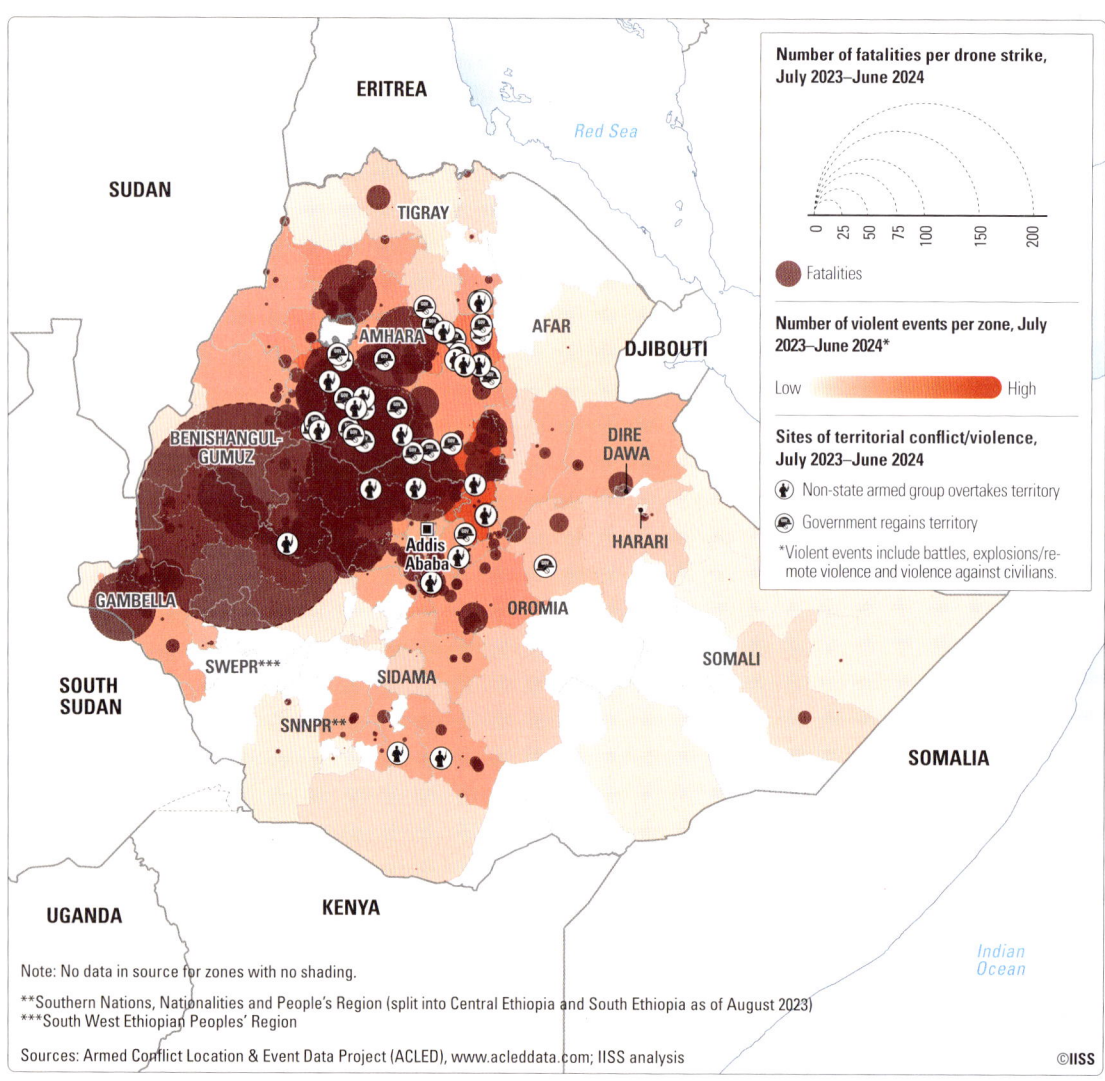

Conflict Overview

Since Emperor Haile Selassie was deposed in 1974, conflicts have proliferated in Ethiopia's peripheral regions and increasingly converged towards the centre. These conflicts take various forms, with localised grievances – some resulting from historical disenfranchisement, others from a selective politicisation of history – escalating into ethnically charged border disputes or insurgencies.[1] In some cases, conflicts have flowed outwards from power struggles in the centre, inflaming provincial disputes, and transforming subnational flashpoints or boundary disputes into national crises.[2] Such conflicts are part of a long-running cycle in which the state experiences phases of fragmentation and (eventual) reunification. Attempts to promote a singular Ethiopian national identity have been hindered by the growth of ethnic identity among marginalised groups.

The current turmoil in Ethiopia stems from the contested transition from the previous government led by the Tigray People's Liberation Front (TPLF) from 1991–2018 to that of Prime Minister Abiy

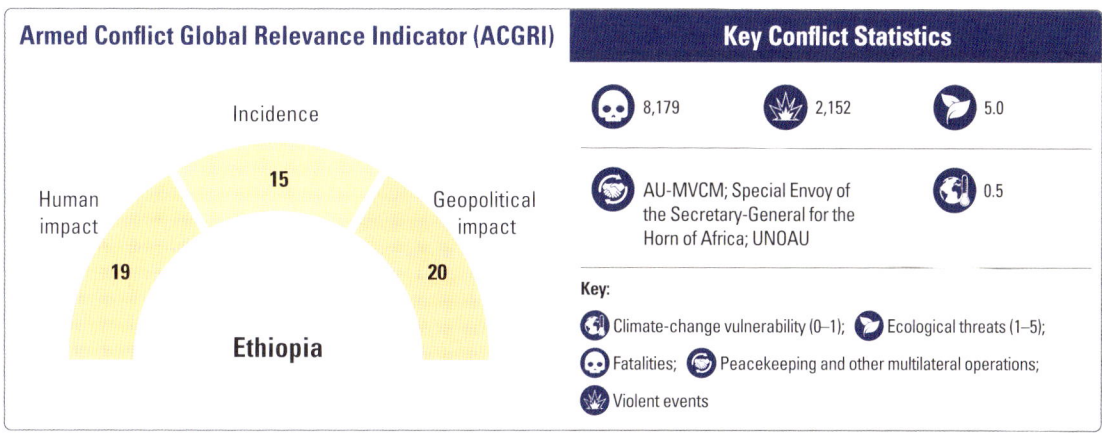

Conflict(s)	Type	Start date
Fano rebellion in Amhara Region	I LI	2023
Insurgency violence in Oromia Region	I IC LI	2019
Post-war tensions in Tigray Region	II	November 2022
Anyuak-Nuer conflict in Gambella Region	I IC	2023; recurrent since 1980s

Key: I IC Internal: intercommunal; I IC LI Internal: intercommunal & localised insurgency; I LI Internal: localised insurgency; II Internationalised internal

Ahmed – an Oromo politician and former military-intelligence officer who came to power as a reformist in 2018. Under Tigrayan prime minister Meles Zenawi (1995–2012), the TPLF oversaw the establishment of a federal system organised around ethnicity, onto which a corresponding party system – the Ethiopian People's Revolutionary Democratic Front (EPRDF) – was grafted. However, the EPRDF system unravelled as antagonisms between Addis Ababa and Ethiopia's two largest regions – Amhara and Oromia – escalated, driving anti-government protests after 2015.

After Abiy became prime minister, tensions with the TPLF increased when he signed a peace agreement with Eritrea in 2018, officially ending the frozen conflict between the two countries. Relations further deteriorated when the EPRDF was dismantled and replaced with the Prosperity Party, signalling Abiy's intention to replace the system of ethnic federalism. In November 2020, conflict erupted in Tigray between the government and the TPLF, drawing in the Eritrean military alongside paramilitary forces from Amhara. A November 2022 ceasefire agreement reached in Pretoria laid the foundation for a *modus vivendi* between the TPLF and Addis Ababa, generating discord within Amhara, partly due to concerns that border areas annexed to Amhara during the war would be returned to Tigray. Insecurity and violence persist in both Amhara and Oromia. While the trend for conflict to be clustered in central and highland regions of Ethiopia has continued, state authority has nonetheless become increasingly fluid in Ethiopia's peripheral lowlands.

Conflict Update

The conflicts and fluctuating power vacuums that have proliferated under the Abiy regime persisted during the reporting period. Ethiopia's fragmentation manifested in the form of large and hastily mobilised armies – comprising members of Ethiopia's security forces, armed groups who have defected from these security forces, and groups who rejoined them following a peace agreement – engaged in intractable struggles along the country's flashpoints. Consequently, political authority increasingly became divided into smaller units distributed among government, insurgent and ex-insurgent forces.

Over the course of 2023, conflict in Amhara Region escalated after the federal government controversially disbanded regional security forces in April. In July and August, tensions between Amhara nationalist forces and the federal government erupted into conflict across much of the region, including the regional capital, Bahir Dar. Nationalist forces consisted of significant numbers of the former Amhara Regional Special Police force, alongside irregular forces of the Amhara nationalist militia known as the *fano*.

After occupying several towns in Amhara, rebelling forces were dislodged from the region's population centres by the military. Increasingly fluid conflict dynamics took hold, playing out under a regional state of emergency and militarised attempts at reimposing order. This included reported executions of civilians by government forces and a growing reliance on drone strikes to compensate for the ineffectiveness of ground forces.[3] Operating in a large area characterised by challenging terrain and multiple internal borders, the *fano* were assisted by the geography of the region, as well as by mounting grievances against the Abiy regime among parts of the local population.

While there was no return to large-scale violence in Tigray, tensions increased in the Interim Regional Administration. Factionalism within the TPLF and disagreements between the TPLF and regional opposition parties clouded political progress, while bitter border disputes with Amhara Region remained unresolved, despite a vague government proposal on a referendum for the disputed areas. While a divided TPLF confers some benefits to Addis Ababa, there are risks that accompany instability within Tigray given the increasingly acrimonious relations between Ethiopia and Eritrea. While Eritrea has been linked to insecurity in parts of Tigray, Tigray acts as a buffer zone for the Abiy regime, limiting direct Eritrean involvement in Ethiopia's other conflicts.

Government peace talks with the Oromo Liberation Army (OLA) restarted in October 2023. Despite initial progress, negotiations broke down in November, prompting renewed fighting. This followed a pattern similar to the first half of the year, when unsuccessful peace negotiations were followed by an escalation of conflict across parts of Oromia. The talks reportedly stalled in part due to disagreements over disarmament and potential government positions that would be offered to the OLA, as well as Addis Ababa's unwillingness to concede to structural reforms favoured by the OLA, including the installation of a transitional government in Oromia.

Progress in consolidating peace in Tigray – and in breaking the deadlock with the OLA – would likely require concessions from Addis Ababa that would risk further alienating important constituencies in Amhara and Oromia, including within the ruling Prosperity Party.[4] Instability in the key regions concerned – Tigray, Amhara and Oromia – is therefore likely to endure until political calculations change for the Abiy regime, when opposition forces in these areas can be brought in to compensate for political weaknesses or to counterbalance rival constituencies.

Alongside these developments, security provision became increasingly uneven across Ethiopia. Notably, there was an increase in reported abductions, including in areas close to the capital. In Gambella Region, recurring violence involving Nuer and Anyuak militias continued to escalate. Violence declined, however, in Benishangul-Gumuz Region, with the exception of attacks east of the regional capital of Asosa in November, allegedly conducted by the OLA. Although security within Somali Region gradually stabilised, conflict re-escalated along the border between the Somali and Afar regions in June 2024, following a period of dormancy. Meanwhile, the Southern Nations, Nationalities and People's Region (SNNPR) was formally dissolved in August 2023 following a referendum earlier in the year. Two new regions – Central Ethiopia and South Ethiopia – emerged from the remnants of the SNNPR, from which the regions of Sidama and South-West had previously separated.

Instability within the regime continued, with discontented elites being removed from the government as new domestic alliances were forged.[5] Turbulence endured at the regional level, notably in the January 2024 announcement by the Somaliland government that it had leased land to Ethiopia for a port – in exchange for Ethiopia's formal recognition of Somaliland – which sent shockwaves through the region (see the Sub-Saharan Africa Regional Spotlight chapter).

Conflict Parties

Ethiopian National Defence Force (ENDF)

Strength: Up to 500,000 active personnel, following a period of rapid mobilisation beginning in 2020. However, this number has likely fluctuated due to significant casualties sustained by the ENDF during the civil war in Tigray from 2020–22.[6]

Areas of operation: Uneven presence across the country.

Leadership: Prime Minister Abiy Ahmed (commander-in-chief) and Field Marshal Berhanu Jula (chief of general staff).

Structure: The ENDF is designed to conduct both conventional war and counter-insurgency missions. It is organised into six regional commands (two of which were established in 2020, reflecting the increasing internal focus and activities of the ENDF), spread across 78 infantry divisions and five mechanised divisions. Additionally, there is a Special Forces and Presidential Guard division.

History: Grew out of a coalition of rebels spearheaded by the TPLF, which removed the Derg regime in 1991. The ENDF underwent a lengthy defence-transformation process following the 1998–2000 war with Eritrea. Once a major contributing country to United Nations peacekeeping missions, numbers of ENDF peacekeepers have declined sharply since 2021.

Objectives: Maintain Ethiopia's territorial integrity and fight armed opposition/secessionist movements inside the country.

Opponents: OLA, *fano*, minor regional separatist movements and al-Shabaab. A permanent cessation-of-hostilities agreement was reached with the Tigray People's Liberation Front/Tigray Defence Force (TPLF/TDF) in November 2022, effectively bringing an end to the two-year civil war. Deteriorating relations between Asmara and Addis Ababa will impact relations with the Eritrean Defence Forces (EDF).

Affiliates/allies: China, Iran, Russia, Somalia, Turkiye and United Arab Emirates (UAE).

Resources/capabilities: Around 220 Soviet-era tanks, 20 attack aircraft, 18 attack helicopters and a small number of uninhabited aerial vehicles. Ethiopia's defence budget more than tripled from US$425 million in 2022 to US$1.5 billion in 2023 as a result of the Tigrayan war and the deteriorating security situation.

Tigray People's Liberation Front/Tigray Defence Force (TPLF/TDF)

Strength: At the outset of the 2020–22 civil war, the TPLF commanded around 30,000 Special Police paramilitaries and was supported by tens of thousands of village-militia members and a small number of ENDF soldiers. In 2023 a figure of 274,000 combatants was put forward to the National Disarmament, Demobilisation and Reintegration Commission by the TPLF, at least 50,000 of which have reportedly been demobilised.[7]

Areas of operation: Central and eastern areas of Tigray Region, with previous incursions into Amhara and Afar regions.

Leadership: Getachew Reda Kahsay (president of the Interim Regional Administration of Tigray) and Gen. Tadesse Werede Tesfay (TDF commander-in-chief).

Structure: The TDF is the armed wing of the TPLF and comprises local militia, ex-regional Special Police (paramilitary units) and Tigrayan ENDF defectors. The post-Pretoria Agreement structure is unclear, with some forces likely to be integrated into the regular security sector.

History: The TDF emerged from the build-up of forces in Tigray prior to the conflict in 2020. After initial losses, the TDF regained control of much of Tigray in 2021, advancing into Amhara and Afar regions. After signing the Pretoria Agreement, the TDF relinquished heavy weaponry in January 2023 and began demobilising in May 2023. The demobilisation process has reportedly stalled.

Objectives: During the conflict, the TPLF/TDF sought to defend the Tigray regional government. Since November 2022, the TPLF has sought to secure Tigray's interests in an agreement with the federal government.

Opponents: ENDF (prior to November 2022), EDF and Amhara nationalist forces, including the *fano*.

Affiliates/allies: Established an office in the Sudanese capital of Khartoum in late February 2021. During the civil war, the TPLF/TDF established links with the OLA and parts of the Qimant ethnic group.

Resources/capabilities: The TDF seized significant amounts of ENDF equipment (including tanks, artillery and long-range rockets) at the outset of the conflict, replenishing military equipment and ammunition through attacks on opposing forces and seizures of weapons caches. Heavy weapons were handed over to the military following the Pretoria Agreement, with some reports indicating some light weapons were also transferred. The TDF is believed to retain its small arms.

Oromo Liberation Army (OLA), previously the Oromo Liberation Front (OLF)

Strength: Over 2,000 estimated OLA fighters in 2020.[8] This number may have increased significantly since then, but new estimates are not official.

Areas of operation: Oromia Region (particularly in the west, as well as parts of the south and centre) and some adjoining

Oromo Liberation Army (OLA), previously the Oromo Liberation Front (OLF)

areas of Amhara Region. OLA activity has also been intermittently reported in parts of Benishangul-Gumuz Region and the former SNNPR.

Leadership: The OLA no longer comes under Dawud Ibsa's political leadership of the OLF and has split into several armed factions under local leadership. The Western Command is led by Kumsa Diriba (also known as Jaal Marroo), the Southern Command by Gemechu Aboye and the Central Command by Sagni Negassa.

Structure: Locally organised into loose groupings of fighters, spread across at least seven commands. An OLF–OLA High Command ostensibly exists to coordinate the commands, though in practice each command is largely autonomous.

History: The OLF was established in 1973 by Oromo nationalists. In mid-2018, the OLF signed a peace agreement with the government. The OLA officially split from the OLF political party in April 2019, amid deteriorating security in Oromia and concerns over demobilisation. The government pejoratively refers to the OLA as OLA Shane/Shene ('the five').

Objectives: Oromo self-determination.

Opponents: ENDF and *fano*.

Affiliates/allies: Until 2018, Eritrea. Following the rapprochement between Eritrea and Ethiopia this support ceased and the OLA in Oromia survived on local support and resources. The OLA entered into a formal alliance with the TPLF (alongside several smaller movements) in late 2021, which is now defunct.

Resources/capabilities: The OLA acts clandestinely and is weak in military terms. It is equipped with small arms. Funding sources are unclear, though allegations of criminal activity – including kidnapping – have surrounded the group.

Fano

Strength: 15,000–20,000 former Amhara Regional Special Police (a disbanded paramilitary force); the number of existing and newly recruited militia is unclear.[9]

Areas of operation: Amhara Region; Metekel zone in Benishangul-Gumuz Region; and Horo Guduru Welega, East Welega and North Shewa zones of Oromia Region. The *fano* is also present in parts of Tigray Region that are disputed with Amhara Region.

Leadership: Multiple leaders across different factions, drawn from a combination of military, political and civil-society backgrounds.

Structure: Dispersed across several emerging factions, some of which are closely linked to specific areas of Amhara Region. Relations between the various factions are uneven, with some cooperative arrangements, and other relations being neutral or antagonistic.

History: Historically, *fano* has referred both to nineteenth-century free peasants and to 1930s-era nationalist forces fighting Italian occupation. The term was revived by Amhara youth during anti-TPLF protests and post-2018 by ethno-nationalist militias. The *fano* supported the government during the 2020–22 Tigray War, though it was the subject of a May 2022 crackdown by authorities.

Objectives: Promote ethnic Amhara interests, including the territorial expansion of Amhara Region and the safety of Amhara settlers across Ethiopia.

Opponents: ENDF, TPLF/TDF, OLA, and Oromo and Gumuz militias.

Affiliates/allies: Unconfirmed claims of Eritrean support.

Resources/capabilities: Arms from defecting Amhara Regional Special Police; financed through diaspora donations and illicit taxation collected from checkpoints.

Gambella Liberation Front (GLF)

Strength: Unclear, though likely to be small.

Areas of operation: Gambella Region.

Leadership: Gatluak Buom Pal.

Structure: Recruited mainly from the ethnic Nuer community of Gambella, with possible links to the co-ethnic eastern Jikany Nuer clan on the South Sudanese side of the common border. Organised into a loose band of young people, whose only major operation has been conducted in conjunction with the OLA.

History: The group emerged following the 2021 Gambella regional elections, citing irregularities, malpractice and grievances against the leadership in Gambella. It also highlighted localised insecurity (specifically regarding ethnic-Murle raids). In June 2022, the group attacked and briefly occupied Gambella town, with assistance from OLA fighters.

Objectives: Replace the Gambella regional leadership and reverse the marginalisation and underdevelopment of the region.

Opponents: ENDF and regional Special Police.

Affiliates/allies: OLA. Gatluak Buom is based in the Sudanese capital of Khartoum, but it is not clear whether this necessarily indicates Sudanese support for the GLF, given that many co-ethnic rebel or militia leaders from the South Sudanese side of the border also reside in Khartoum.

Resources/capabilities: Unclear, though likely small arms, alongside any weapons that may have been captured during the June 2022 raid on Gambella town.

Eritrean Defence Forces (EDF)

Strength: Increased from an estimated 200,000 active personnel in 2021–22 to 301,070 in 2022–23 due to a general mobilisation accompanying the resumption of large-scale hostilities in Tigray in 2022, before the November 2022 peace agreement; 40,000 reportedly remain deployed in Ethiopia.

Areas of operation: Since November 2020, the EDF has been present across Tigray, though it has made partial withdrawals (usually to border areas) at several stages of the conflict. The EDF is reported to still be present in Tigray since the November 2022 Pretoria Agreement, though in smaller numbers.

Leadership: President Isaias Afwerki (commander-in-chief) and Gen. Filipos Woldeyohannes (chief of staff).

Structure: The EDF comprises mostly conscripts. Reservists were called up in 2020 and 2022, during EDF operations in Tigray. The army is made up of approximately 41 divisions (up to 20 of which were present in Tigray during the conflict in northern Ethiopia) and divided between five military zones, largely covering the border with Ethiopia.

History: The EDF was formed after Eritrea's separation from Ethiopia in 1993 but has its roots in the former Eritrean People's Liberation Front rebellion. The EDF has since engaged in two full-scale wars (the 1998–2000 Ethiopian–Eritrean War and the 2020–2022 Tigray War) and various border conflicts.

Objectives: Maintain Eritrea's territorial integrity and fight armed opposition/secessionist movements inside the country.

Opponents: TPLF/TDF. Eritrea has a complex relationship with regional powers. Following a 2018 rapprochement with Ethiopia, relations have deteriorated since 2022. Eritrea is currently providing support to the Sudan Armed Forces and its affiliates in Sudan.

Affiliates/allies: Saudi Arabia, Somalia and UAE. Unconfirmed claims of support to the *fano*.

Resources/capabilities: The scale of the Eritrean defence budget is unclear. Due to prolonged UN sanctions (lifted in November 2018), much of Eritrea's military equipment still comprises outdated Soviet-era systems, which will have resulted in serviceability issues. The navy remains capable of only limited coastal-patrol and interception operations.

Regional Special Police (disbanded in 2023 and integrated into the ENDF)

Strength: Before disbandment, by region: Addis Ababa (numbers unclear; formed in late 2019), Afar (2,000–3,000), Amhara (5,000), Benishangul-Gumuz (3,000–4,000), Dire Dawa (2,000–3,000), Gambella (2,000–3,000), Oromia (9,000–10,000), Sidama (numbers unclear), SNNPR (4,000–5,000), Somali (15,000) and Tigray (27,000–28,000).[10]

Areas of operation: Prior to disbandment, Special Police forces were formed in almost all regions, although the scale of recruitment varied by region.

Leadership: Special Police were under the control of regional presidents.

Structure: Formed into paramilitary units, which at times worked alongside federal or volunteer *kebele* (village) militia. Despite being colloquially referred to as the 'Special Force', the Special Police were not elite commando units (which are instead part of the ENDF). Parts of the Special Police have now been integrated into local ENDF commands.

History: Somali region formed a Special Police force in 2007, with other regions gradually following suit. After 2019, force numbers increased in areas where neighbouring regions posed a threat (specifically Amhara, Oromia and Tigray regions). In April 2023, federal authorities announced the Special Police would be disbanded and absorbed into federal security forces, which fuelled discontent in Amhara Region.

Objectives: Preserve public order and peace within the region, as constitutionally mandated.

Opponents: Armed political opposition, local *shifta* (armed bandits), and neighbouring regional Special Police and militia.

Affiliates/allies: Varied by region.

Resources/capabilities: The Special Police were funded from regional police budgets and equipped with small arms and transport vehicles (and, in some circumstances, riot gear).

Notes

[1] For instance, in Benishangul-Gumuz Region and along the border between Afar and Somali regions.

[2] For instance, in contested areas along the Amhara–Tigray border, and parts of the Amhara–Oromia border, alongside disputes relating to the administration and size of Addis Ababa.

[3] 'Rights Commission Prelim Report Confirms Extrajudicial Killing of Dozens by Security Forces in Amhara State', *Addis Standard*, 13 February 2024; 'Residents Say Ethiopian Soldiers Kill More Than 50 Civilians in Amhara Town', Reuters, 3 February 2024; and Fred Harter, '"Horrific" Civilian Toll as Ethiopia Turns to Combat Drones to Quell Local Insurgencies', *New Humanitarian*, 5 March 2024.

[4] 'Oromo Peace Momentum Falters', *Africa Confidential*, vol. 65, no. 2, 12 January 2024; and International Crisis Group, 'Ethiopia's Ominous New War in Amhara', 16 November 2023.

[5] 'Former State Minister Taye Dendea Arrested Over Alleged Terrorist Ties', *Addis Standard*, 12 December 2023; Laetitia Bader, 'Ethiopia Releases Ex-politician Implicated in Heinous

Crimes', Human Rights Watch, 15 March 2024; and 'Demeke's Exit Points to Deepening Rifts', *Africa Confidential*, vol. 65, no. 4, 5 February 2024.

6   Mulugeta Gebrehiwot Berhe, 'Disarmament, Demobilization and Reintegration in Tigray: An Element in a National DDR/SSR Program or a Compassionate Humanitarian Need for Returning Combatants in Tigray Region?', World Peace Foundation, p. 6.

7   *Ibid.*, p. 10; and Mulugeta Gebrehiwot Berhe, 'Tigray in the Eye of the Storm', World Peace Foundation, 2 January 2024.

8   IISS, *The Armed Conflict Survey 2021* (Abingdon: Routledge for the IISS, 2021), p. 238.

9   '50 Percent of Defunct Amhara Special Force Joined Fano, Says Minister of Peace', Borkena, 15 August 2023; and International Crisis Group, 'Ethiopia's Ominous New War in Amhara', fn. 15.

10   IISS, *The Armed Conflict Survey 2021*, p. 238.

SOMALIA

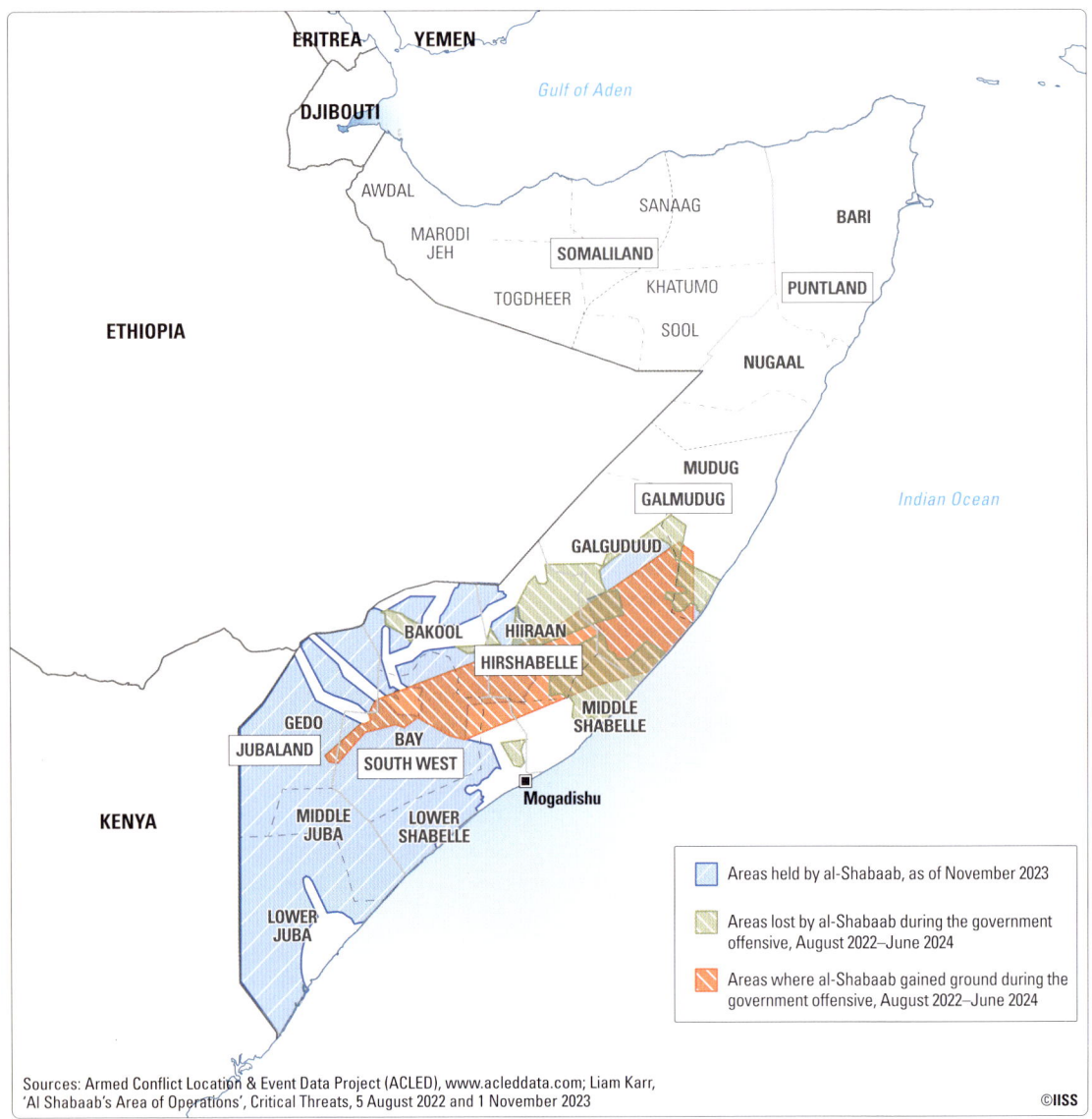

Conflict Overview

Somalia has faced complex patterns of violence involving militias, external militaries and jihadist movements since the collapse of the state in 1991. State collapse was the consequence of a civil war that escalated during the 1980s, ultimately ousting the regime of Mohammed Siad Barre. The northwest was among the most severely affected areas. This region – formerly known as British Somaliland – had been governed separately from Italian-administered Somalia before the two ex-colonies merged in 1960. After the regime disintegrated in 1991, conflict among insurgent groups and splinter factions also plunged southern Somalia into political turmoil, predation and famine, while Somaliland unilaterally declared independence, which was not recognised by the international community. A

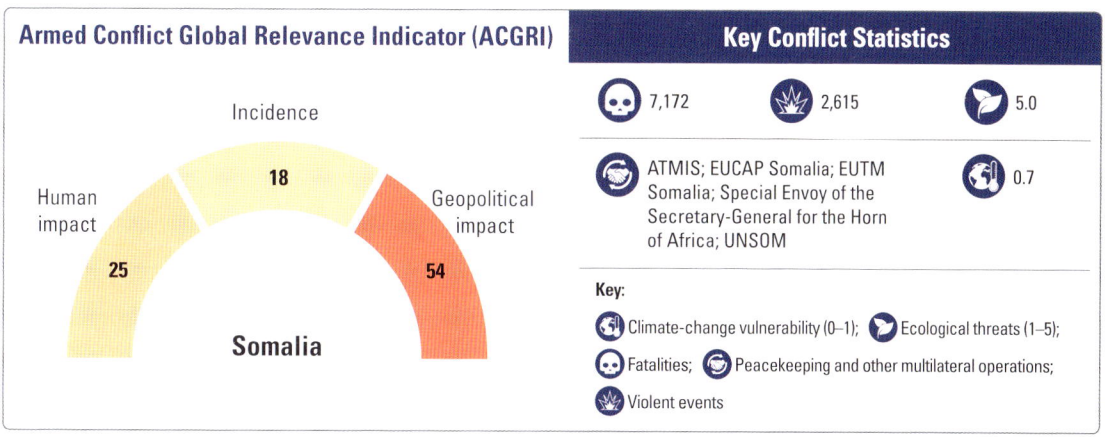

comparatively functional set of institutions developed in Somaliland, despite periodic crises.

A high-profile international intervention in southern and central Somalia in the early 1990s failed to restore order. From the mid-1990s to the mid-2000s, clan-based militias – alongside political and business elites – jostled for positions in hypothetical governments, amid localised insecurity and the emergence of relatively legitimate customary and sharia courts. In 2006, the Islamic Courts Union (ICU), a non-state group that had brought a degree of stability and governance to Mogadishu and nearby areas, was dislodged following an Ethiopian military intervention. This set the stage for a protracted conflict, fought between al-Shabaab ('the youth'; an ICU-linked armed group that later aligned with al-Qaeda) and a multinational United States-led military force, which became enmeshed in internationalised counter-terrorism operations. This force was complemented by the African Union (AU) peacekeeping mission to Somalia (AU Mission in Somalia, AMISOM), which was deployed in 2007 and transitioned into the AU Transition Mission in Somalia (ATMIS) in 2022.

In 2012, the Federal Government of Somalia replaced the Transitional Federal Government. A weak and corrupt transitional government had coalesced into a fragmented federal system heavily reliant on external military support and patronage. The fragmentation in Somalia's political system is often attributed to the primacy of lineage systems and to rivalries within and between the dominant clan families. Historically, the Barre regime manipulated and politicised these clan structures to maintain power, which inadvertently encouraged insurgencies to mobilise along clan lines. As political and social order unravelled from 1991, clan relations further deteriorated. Attempts by external intervenors to incorporate these clan structures into subsequent power-sharing agreements have risked reproducing an inherently unstable system, resulting in dysfunctional governments whose failings have handed al-Shabaab opportunities to expand its influence.[1]

Conflict Update

Multiple regions experienced political and military volatility in the reporting period, with counter-insurgency efforts faltering in central Somalia, amid a widening political crisis in Somaliland. Following years of drought, south-central Somalia was also affected by severe flooding in late 2023.

The first phase of the federal government's military offensive against al-Shabaab – conducted with allied regional forces and clan militias since August 2022 – successfully dislodged the insurgency from several urban centres in central Somalia (particularly Galmadug and Hirshabelle states) and chipped away at its resource base. The second phase began in August 2023, though government forces continued to avoid al-Shabaab's southern strongholds in favour of central regions, reportedly due to a lack of support from external military partners. Despite initial gains, the offensive struggled to uproot al-Shabaab from rural areas, and al-Shabaab swiftly recaptured settlements from the military in Hirshabelle, as well as in Galmadug, where government forces have been more successful at curbing the influence of the Sufi insurgent group Ahlu Sunna wal Jama (ASWJ; a group also hostile to al-Shabaab).[2]

Al-Shabaab operations continued in southern Somalia and around Mogadishu, including an attack on a government base in Daaru Nicma village, northeast of Mogadishu, which resulted in a firefight that reportedly killed 67 militants and soldiers in March 2024.[3] Somalia's fragmented political and security structures – and closer links between al-Shabaab and clan militias in the south – effectively preclude a serious government offensive into the insurgency's southern heartland in the foreseeable future.

During the offensive, the use of clan militias helped the federal government to compensate for its uneven territorial presence and local legitimacy. However, the pressure to simultaneously hold captured territory while coordinating (sometimes unpredictable) militias put the military at risk of overstretch. Al-Shabaab exploited this and engaged in retaliatory attacks on groups and local elites perceived to have sided with the government. For instance, in March 2024, al-Shabaab engineered the defection of clan militias in the strategic town of Xarardheere in Galmadug, while recapturing a series of towns in the state.

In Puntland (a historically autonomous state in the northeast), elections to determine the regional president passed relatively peacefully in January 2024. However, the previous June had seen lethal clashes in Garowe between state forces and a group of opposition-aligned Danab special forces, which compelled the state's leadership to abandon its attempt to introduce direct voting (instead of the established indirect system of voting by representatives appointed by clan elders). Additionally, security forces in Puntland conducted operations against the Islamic State in Somalia (ISS), while the ISS claimed to have made gains against the comparatively more powerful al-Shabaab.

Fighting decreased in Las Anod, which lies in a disputed region claimed by both Somaliland and Puntland. Tensions escalated into heavy fighting between the Somaliland military and Dhulbahante sub-clan militias in February 2023.[4] After months of clashes, Somaliland's military retreated from the town in August 2023, while insecurity persisted in the area. The debacle represents a political embarrassment for Somaliland's president, Muse Bihi Abdi, who will be seeking re-election in (controversially) delayed polls scheduled for November 2024.

The surprise announcement by Hargeisa in January 2024 that Ethiopia would formally recognise Somaliland sparked a diplomatic crisis between Addis Ababa and Mogadishu (see the Sub-Saharan Africa Regional Spotlight chapter). This was amplified after Puntland's regional president, Said Abdullahi Deni, rejected constitutional amendments – including provisions to replace the clan-based selection process with multiparty elections based upon universal suffrage – put forward by the federal president, Hassan Sheikh Mohamud, in late March. The rejection may be linked to personal rivalries and entrenched elite interests, though it revives long-standing questions relating to the relative autonomy of Puntland vis-à-vis Mogadishu. Deni then visited Addis Ababa, which was interpreted as a provocation by Mogadishu, which responded by expelling the Ethiopian ambassador. In early February, a revised defence-cooperation agreement between Somalia and Turkiye was announced, deepening connections between Mogadishu and Ankara and raising concerns that the Ethiopia–Somaliland deal was further polarising geopolitics in the Horn of Africa.

These events have particular implications for counter-insurgency operations against al-Shabaab, given Ethiopia's prominence in the ATMIS. More broadly, the proposed constitutional amendments risk further national discord, given their anticipated effects upon the balance of power between Mogadishu and federal member states, and the reconfiguration of the complex relationship between Somalia's clan and political structures.

Conflict Parties

Somali National Army (SNA)

Strength: 19,000 active military personnel (from a paper strength of 32,000), including 2,000 personnel in the Danab brigade and 4,000 personnel in the two Gorgor brigades.[5]

Areas of operation: Galmudug, Hirshabelle, Jubaland, Puntland and South West states (excluding self-declared independent Somaliland).

Leadership: President Hassan Sheikh Mohamud (commander in chief) and Maj.-Gen. Ibrahim Sheikh Muhyadin Addow (chief of defence forces).

Structure: Comprises five command divisions and a number of independent brigades spread across Somalia's operational sectors. The SNA includes special-forces units such as the US-trained 16th Danab Brigade and the Turkiye-trained 17th and 18th Gorgor brigades.

History: Efforts to build the SNA began in 2008, including new recruitment and the incorporation of existing armed actors, such as clan militias. These efforts were challenged by the lack of coordination among international partners, internecine clan fighting and ongoing insurgency. As a result, the SNA continues to suffer from deep-seated internal cleavages and cohesion problems.

Objectives: Secure the territorial authority of the Federal Government of Somalia, primarily through the defeat of al-Shabaab.

Opponents: Al-Shabaab, ISS, militias and criminal actors.

Affiliates/allies: ATMIS, European Union, Turkiye, United Kingdom and US. The SNA periodically operates alongside external state security forces and – on an ad hoc basis – with clan-based militias. Somalia has become more closely aligned with Eritrea amid deteriorating relations with Ethiopia.

Resources/capabilities: Suffers from severe shortages of resources – particularly of small arms – amid widespread internal corruption. Recent US support has reportedly helped alleviate shortages. Air operations (including drone strikes) are conducted by military partners (notably the US and Turkiye), with Uganda providing helicopter support.

Somaliland National Army (SLNA)

Strength: Approximately 12,500 active military personnel, alongside 600 coastal guards.[6]

Areas of operation: Based in the six administrative regions of the self-declared Republic of Somaliland (Awdal, Maroodi-Jeeh, Sahil, Sanaag, Sool and Togdheer regions), though with a limited presence in the disputed Sanaag and Sool regions.

Leadership: President Muse Bihi Abdi (commander in chief) and Nuh Ismail Tani (chief of staff).

Structure: 14 light infantry brigades, one mechanised infantry brigade and two armoured brigades, organised across five geographical sectors, and headquartered in Hargeisa.

History: The SLNA emerged from the Somali National Movement (SNM) insurgency, which seized control of much of the territory that comprises present-day Somaliland in 1991. Attempts to regularise the SNM into a relatively centralised military in 1992 sparked conflict, though a recognisable military emerged in 1994 following a disarmament and demobilisation programme.

Objectives: Secure the territorial authority of Somaliland, including from territorial claims from Puntland and Somalia.

Opponents: Dhulbahante militia seeking to establish Khatumo State – also referred to as 'Sool, Sanaag and Cayn (SSC)' or sometimes 'SSC-Khatumo' – as a new federal state. The SLNA also experiences periodic tensions with armed forces from Puntland.

Affiliates/allies: Ethiopia.

Resources/capabilities: Soviet-era tanks, alongside some armoured personnel carriers, with small patrol used by the coastguard. The SLNA also has some artillery and air-defence capabilities. Most equipment is reportedly in poor condition, and possibly inoperable.

Harakat al-Shabaab al-Mujahideen ('al-Shabaab')

Strength: Active fighting force of an estimated 7,000–9,000 militants.[7]

Areas of operation: Strongest in southern Somalia (Hirshabelle, Jubaland and South West states). The group's presence is more limited in Galmudug and Puntland.

Leadership: Ahmad Umar Diriye, better known as Abu Ubaidah, is the current leader, or emir.

Structure: A consultative council (*majlis al-shura*) is the group's central decision-making body, although regional political and military authorities enjoy considerable autonomy.

Harakat al-Shabaab al-Mujahideen ('al-Shabaab')

Al-Shabaab's military wing is divided into six regional fighting units. An intelligence wing with a transnational reach (*Amniyat*) oversees a large security apparatus through which the group curtails dissent and maintains internal cohesion.

History: Al-Shabaab emerged in December 2006 after breaking away from the ICU. The group has since evolved into an effective insurgency, often outmatching the federal government while appealing to nationalist sentiments to boost recruitment. Although its power has waned following counter-insurgency campaigns, it has a demonstrable capacity to reconstitute itself.

Objectives: Defeat the federal government, remove foreign military forces and establish Islamist rule in Somalia.

Opponents: Federal government, SNA, ASWJ and ISS.

Affiliates/allies: Aligned with al-Qaeda. Al-Shabaab has forged opportunistic alliances with militias and organised-crime syndicates, alongside long-standing relations with some sub-clans in southern Somalia.

Resources/capabilities: Al-Shabaab has benefited from access to several sources of income, including checkpoint taxation, extortion, kidnappings, illicit trade, revenues from piracy and funding from transnational Islamist groups. Annual revenues reportedly total US$100 million.[8]

Ahlu Sunna wal Jama (ASWJ)

Strength: 5,000 fighters (2017).[9] Subsequent military losses and defections to the Galmadug State government will likely have reduced these numbers.[10]

Areas of operation: Galmadug State and Hiiraan region.

Leadership: Sheikh Mohamed Shakir Ali Hassan (overall leader).

Structure: Unclear. Historically a proportion of ASWJ forces were drawn from local clan and sub-clan militias in central Somalia, likely on an ad hoc basis.

History: Formed in 1991 to resist the Salafist group Al-Itihaad al-Islamiya, though specific information on its methods is limited. The group organised into a highly effective force opposed to al-Shabaab in 2008, while being loosely aligned with the government. Relations with federal and state authorities have since been volatile, with the group temporarily joining Galmadug State in 2018 until fighting resumed in 2020.

Objectives: Resist al-Shabaab and other Salafist movements, and promote and protect Sufism.

Opponents: Al-Shabaab, and currently state and federal forces.

Affiliates/allies: Historically linked to Ethiopia and the US, both of which later distanced themselves from the group. It was previously aligned to state and federal forces.

Resources/capabilities: Small arms and light weapons.

Islamic State in Somalia (ISS)

Strength: 100–280 fighters.[11]

Areas of operation: Based in the Galgala mountain region of Puntland, but periodically conducts targeted attacks in Bosaso and Mogadishu.

Leadership: Abdul al-Qadir Mumin.

Structure: Little is known about its internal structure but given the group's small size and the regular targeting of senior figures by both Somali and US forces, it is likely to be relatively decentralised.

History: Mumin broke away from al-Shabaab with a small group of fighters in October 2015 and pledged allegiance to ISIS. Al-Shabaab has vowed to eliminate the rival group, though ISS has reportedly made gains against al-Shabaab since early 2023.

Objectives: Expand its influence by spreading ISIS's ideology within Somalia and neighbouring countries, such as Ethiopia, and to attract broader support.

Opponents: Al-Shabaab, and Somali and Puntland security forces.

Affiliates/allies: Believed to have connections with other Islamic State affiliates in Yemen and Central Africa.

Resources/capabilities: Small arms.

African Union Transition Mission in Somalia (ATMIS)

Strength: Following two drawdowns in recent years, the current parade strength of ATMIS is approximately 14,000 soldiers.[12] The mission is supported by up to 1,040 police personnel.[13]

Areas of operation: The five troop-contributing countries are Burundi, Djibouti, Ethiopia, Kenya and Uganda. Their forces are each responsible for a sector in central and southern Somalia, including Middle Shabelle (Burundi); Galguduud and Hiiraan (Djibouti); Bay, Bakool and Gedo, with a presence in Galguduud and Hiiraan (Ethiopia); Gedo, Lower Juba, Lower Shabelle and Middle Juba (Kenya); and Mogadishu, Banadir and Lower Shabelle (Uganda).

Leadership: Ambassador Mohamed El-Amine Souef (special representative of the chairperson of the African Union Commission, and head of mission) and Lt-Gen. Sam Kavuma (ATMIS force commander).

Structure: ATMIS comprises a military component (with different troop-contributing countries responsible for specific sectors of south-central Somalia), alongside a police and civilian component.

History: The United Nations authorised the AU to deploy AMISOM in 2007. Amid continued instability, the UN agreed to increase AMISOM troops and extend the mission's mandate

African Union Transition Mission in Somalia (ATMIS)

and scope. In 2022, AMISOM transitioned into ATMIS, with a view to transferring primary responsibility for Somalia's security to the federal government by December 2024.

Objectives: Defeat al-Shabaab, retake its territory and protect the federal government.

Opponents: Al-Shabaab.

Affiliates/allies: Supported by numerous international governments and periodically by military contingents from allied countries that deliver training, including the EU, Turkiye, the UK and the US.

Resources/capabilities: Draws from the military contingents of contributing countries and is occasionally supported by other international partners. The EU has budgeted US$291m for ATMIS in 2024 (representing a significant increase compared to the previous two years), while the AU has made US$5m available.[14]

Notes

1. Alex de Waal, 'Somalia's Disassembled State: Clan Unit Formation and the Political Marketplace', *Conflict, Security & Development*, vol. 20, no. 5, 2020, pp. 561–85.
2. The ASWJ in Somalia is a distinct group from the ASWJ (also known as 'al-Shabaab') in Mozambique.
3. Armed Conflict Location & Event Data Project (ACLED), 'Somalia: Dispute Over Constitutional Amendment and Increased al-Shabaab Attacks', 26 April 2024.
4. The Dhulbahante are part of the Darod clan family (associated with Puntland), though they are seeking to establish a new state within Somalia's federal system (prospectively named 'Khatumo State' or 'Sool, Sanaag and Cayn (SSC)', and sometimes referred to as 'SSC-Khatumo') rather than to merge with Puntland. In November 2023, Mogadishu recognised the self-declared territorial unit, but as a region rather than as a full federal member state.
5. Paul D. Williams, 'The Somali National Army Versus al-Shabaab: A Net Assessment', *CTC Sentinel*, vol. 17, no. 4, April 2024, pp. 35–43; US Embassy in Somalia, 'Somalia and United States Graduate 342 Somali National Army Danab Soldiers', 8 August 2023; and 'Gorgor Forces in Crisis: Desertions and Leadership Failures', *Somali Digest*, 28 March 2024.
6. IISS, *The Military Balance 2024* (Abingdon: Routledge for the IISS, 2024), pp. 516–17.
7. Soufan Center, 'IntelBrief: Somalia Continues to Deteriorate as al-Shabaab Gains Ground', 18 March 2022; and Mapping Militants Project, 'Al Shabaab', Stanford University, 2021.
8. James Barnett, 'Faltering Lion: Analyzing Progress and Setbacks in Somalia's War Against al-Shabaab', Hudson Institute, November 2023.
9. Vanda Felbab-Brown, 'The Problem With Militias in Somalia', in Adam Day (ed.), *Hybrid Conflict, Hybrid Peace: How Militias and Paramilitary Groups Shape Post-conflict Transitions* (New York: UN University, 2020), pp. 112–56.
10. International Crisis Group, 'Avoiding a New Cycle of Conflict in Somalia's Galmudug State', 25 September 2023.
11. UN Security Council (UNSC), 'Letter Dated 11 July 2022 From the Chair of the Security Council Committee Pursuant to Resolutions 1267 (1999), 1989 (2011) and 2253 (2015) Concerning Islamic State in Iraq and the Levant (Da'esh), Al-Qaida and Associated Individuals, Groups, Undertakings and Entities Addressed to the President of the Security Council', S/2022/547, 15 July 2022; and UNSC, 'Letter Dated 23 January 2024 From the Chair of the Security Council Committee Pursuant to Resolutions 1267 (1999), 1989 (2011) and 2253 (2015) Concerning Islamic State in Iraq and the Levant (Da'esh), Al-Qaida and Associated Individuals, Groups, Undertakings and Entities Addressed to the President of the Security Council', S/2024/92, 29 January 2024.
12. International Crisis Group, 'Somalia: Making the Most of the EU–Somalia Joint Roadmap', 30 January 2024.
13. ATMIS, 'Police Component', 2022.
14. International Crisis Group, 'Eight Priorities for the African Union in 2024', 14 February 2024, fn. 67; and Amani Africa, 'One Year of ATMIS Operations: Progress, Challenges and Funding', 28 April 2023.

DEMOCRATIC REPUBLIC OF THE CONGO

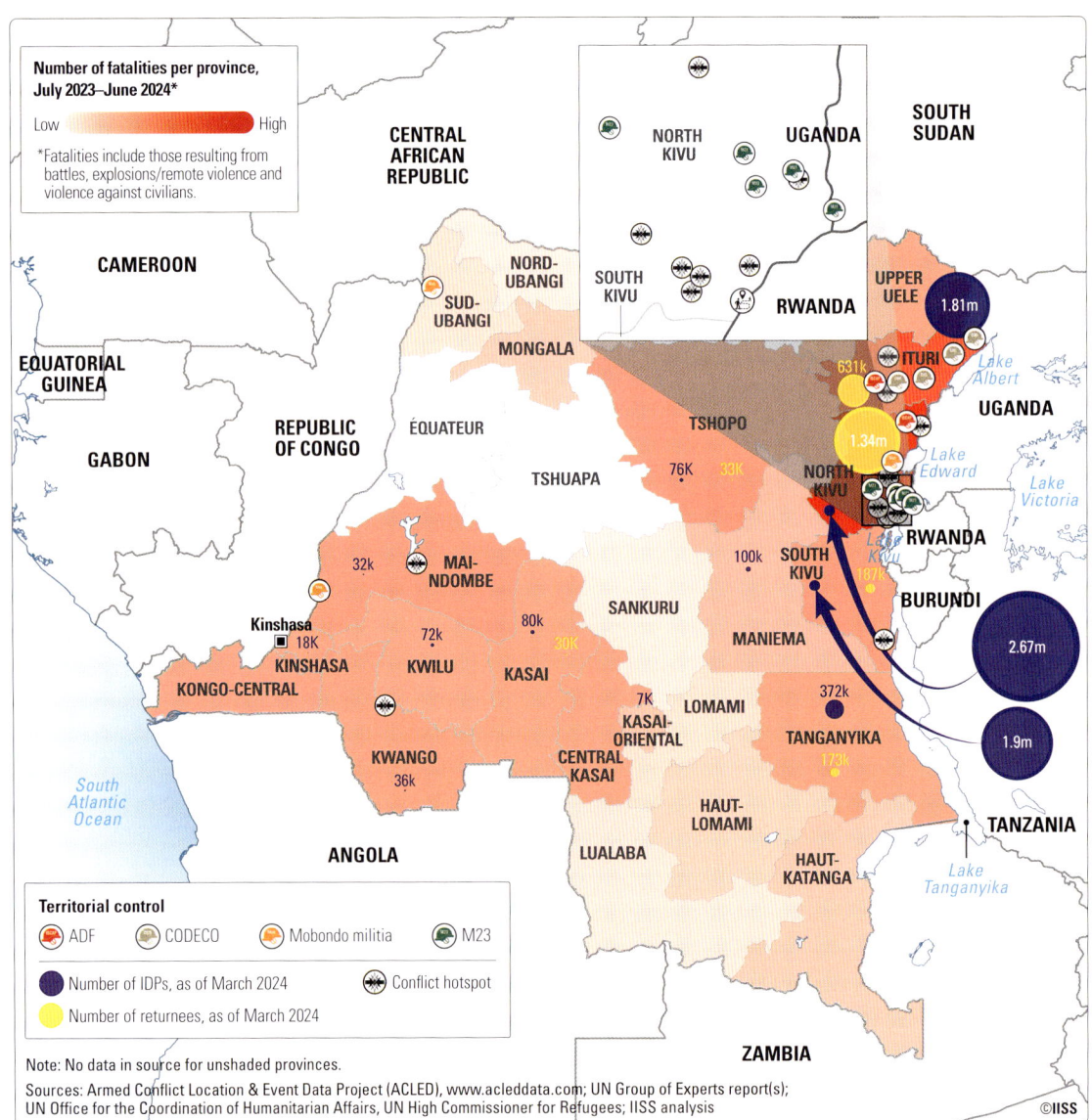

Conflict Overview

Contemporary armed violence in the Democratic Republic of the Congo (DRC) stems from the fallout of the First (1996–97) and Second (1998–2003) Congo wars, which themselves were fuelled by the region's colonial history, long-held intercommunal and anti-governmental grievances, and the 1994 genocide against the Tutsis in Rwanda. Weak governance, corruption, conflict over land and profitable mineral resources, and regional interests remain some of the main drivers of conflict, alongside ethnic tensions and complex discourses around belonging and citizenship in a country comprising over 200 ethnic groups.

Between 120 and 250 local non-state armed groups (NSAGs) and 14 transnational ones currently operate in the country's eastern provinces, namely Ituri,

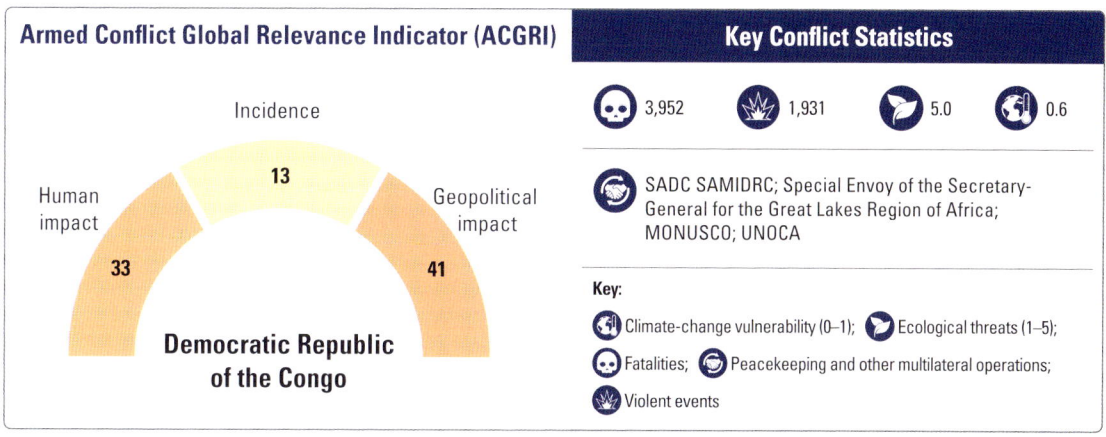

ACGRI pillars: IISS calculation based on multiple sources for 2023 and 2024 (scale: 0–100), except for some cases according to data availability. See Notes on Methodology and Data Appendix for all variables and further details on Key Conflict Statistics.

Conflict(s)	Type	Start date
M23 insurgency supported by Rwanda in the eastern DRC	II T	2021; recurrent since 2012
ADF insurgency in the eastern DRC	II T	1996
Communal conflicts in Ituri, Kwilu, Mai-Ndombe, North Kivu and South Kivu provinces	I IC	1994

Key: **I IC** Internal: intercommunal; **II** Internationalised internal; **T** Transnational

North Kivu and South Kivu, where state authority is weak.¹ Rebel groups from neighbouring countries, such as the Democratic Forces for the Liberation of Rwanda (FDLR), the Ugandan Allied Democratic Forces (ADF, also known as the Islamic State Central Africa Province or ISCAP) and the Resistance for the Rule of Law in Burundi (RED Tabara), have found refuge in the eastern DRC, effectively turning the area into a battleground for external actors. This, in turn, has triggered tensions and enmity between the DRC and some of its neighbours.

Though it faced setbacks in the mid-2010s, the ADF rebounded in 2017 after pledging allegiance to the Islamic State (ISIS) and subsequently rebranding itself as ISCAP. Since 2019, the ADF has extended its operations into Ituri province. In November 2021, Uganda deployed troops in the DRC under *Operation Shujaa* to combat the ADF, following the group's attack in Uganda's capital Kampala. Despite DRC–Uganda joint efforts, however, the ADF remains resilient and has expanded its reach and lethality.

Also in November 2021, the Rwandan-backed, Tutsi-led March 23 Movement (M23) insurgency resurfaced in the eastern DRC after its defeat in 2013. In addition to accusing the Congolese government of not upholding its 2013 peace deal, the revived M23 is primarily driven by claims of belonging in the DRC and pro-Tutsi violent ideology.

Finally, in Mai-Ndombe, a historically peaceful province, violence erupted in 2018 and intensified in 2023 due to long-standing ethnic and communal grievances over land, leadership and colonial-era administrative demarcations.

Conflict Update

In political and security terms, the reporting period witnessed the intersection of four main dynamics: the reignition of M23-related violence; increasing tensions with Rwanda; the termination of the United Nations Organization Stabilization Mission in the DRC (MONUSCO); and the re-election of President Félix Tshisekedi for a second term (with 73% of the vote) in December 2023.[2] The electoral cycle was characterised by political turmoil and some episodes of violence, including the killing of local politicians, curbing of civil liberties and free press, intimidation of opposition figures, and violence against subsets of the electorate. While the opposition rejected the results, citing irregularities and electoral manipulation, Tshisekedi launched a new government in late May 2024. Continued turmoil in domestic politics was highlighted by a swiftly thwarted coup attempt in Kinshasa on 19 May 2024, in which some members of the Congolese diaspora allegedly tried to overthrow the government.

With respect to armed conflict in the east of the country, the collapse of the fragile ceasefire between the Armed Forces of the Democratic Republic of the Congo (FARDC) and M23 in September 2023 followed months of low-profile activities and ignited a new wave of violence from October onwards. An M23 offensive in North Kivu was unsuccessfully counteracted by proliferating self-defence militias (known as 'Wazalendo' or 'patriots'), which significantly exacerbated tensions in the region and in neighbouring South Kivu. These militias emerged in response to Tshisekedi's call to arms in November 2022, urging Congolese youths to support the FARDC in combatting M23, and are now receiving official support from both the government and the army.

In March 2024, M23 managed to isolate Goma, North Kivu's capital, from inland territories of the DRC, cutting off major transport routes leading to Uganda. This disrupted food and conflict-mineral supply chains, and raised fears of a full-blown regional conflict and humanitarian disaster.[3] The violence in February–March resulted in the internal displacement of an estimated 250,000 individuals, with civilians increasingly caught in the middle of fighting as the frontlines move closer to population centres and areas inhabited by internally displaced persons (IDPs).[4] In general, the modus operandi of M23 has undergone significant transformation over the past year, with the group forming alliances with ethnic militias such as the Twirwaneho and expanding into neighbouring South Kivu province.

The expansion of M23 activity in South Kivu coincided with the closure of the MONUSCO Kamanyola base, as part of its agreement to withdraw by December 2024 after more than two decades of operation. In fact, the gradual withdrawal has contributed to an increase in fighting. MONUSCO faced heavy criticism by the government for its inability to stem violence and was the target of a disinformation campaign that resulted in violent protests during the summer of 2023. These culminated in the DRC's request to terminate the mission.

Furthermore, an important shift took place within peace-support operations by regional economic communities. The East African Community Regional Force's (EACRF) failure to uproot M23 and stabilise the region led to its withdrawal in December 2023 after a 13-month deployment. In turn, at the DRC government's request, the South African Development Community (SADC) authorised and deployed troops on 15 December 2023 to restore peace in the eastern DRC. However, these efforts have not yet yielded positive outcomes as not all contributing countries have sent a sufficient number of troops.

In parallel, DRC–Rwanda tensions escalated during the reporting period, at times stoking fears of an inter-state conflict. The FARDC openly accused Rwandan forces of crossing the border and attacking frontier security forces in July 2023 and of crossing the border again in support of M23 in October 2023. Amid rising insecurity in the eastern DRC, Angola has attempted to de-escalate these tensions since the spring of 2024, but the two countries remain at loggerheads.

On other conflict fronts, the FARDC and Uganda Peoples' Defence Forces (UPDF) joint military operation, *Operation Shujaa*, has dealt significant blows to the ADF in Ituri province. Despite these setbacks, however, the ADF has not halted retaliatory attacks against civilians. Ethnic-based militias such as the Cooperative for the Development of the Congo (CODECO) continue to wreak havoc, targeting villages and displacement camps.

Intercommunal conflicts in the DRC also remain persistent. Notably, what began as localised intercommunal conflict in Mai-Ndombe province has spilled over into the neighbouring provinces of Kinshasa and Kwilu, resulting in hundreds of fatalities and the destruction of villages.[5]

Conflict Parties

Armed Forces of the Democratic Republic of the Congo (FARDC)

Strength: 134,250 active personnel.

Areas of operation: Deployed country wide, predominantly in conflict-prone provinces, including North Kivu, South Kivu, Ituri and Mai-Ndombe.

Leadership: President Félix Tshisekedi (commander-in-chief), Guy Kabombo Muadiamvita (defence minister) and Gen. Christian Tshiwewe Songesha (chief of staff).

Structure: Led by the chief of staff, who has authority over all branches (land, navy and air). Other units include the logistics centre, placed under the authority of the chief of staff; the military justice; senior military schools; the directorate general for detection of military anti-patriotic activities; and the military home, which assists the president in designing and developing defence policy and security.

History: Established in 2003 following the signing of the 2002 Pretoria Accord, which brought an end to the Second Congo War (1998–2003) and led to the formation of a transitional government.

Objectives: Safeguard national security, protect the territorial integrity of the country, and maintain peace and stability within the DRC's borders. The FARDC also seeks to contribute to regional stability and participate in peacekeeping efforts.

Opponents: NSAGs, including M23, ADF, RED Tabara, FDLR and various Mai-Mai groups.

Affiliates/allies: SADC Mission in the Democratic Republic of Congo (SAMIDRC) and MONUSCO. Additionally, the FARDC has been supported by the UPDF under *Operation Shujaa* against the ADF since November 2021.

Resources/capabilities: The FARDC remains operationally weak and heterogeneous, with limited availability of heavy weapons and an almost non-existent order of battle due to unsuccessful reforms, including the failed integration of rebel groups.

March 23 Movement (M23)

Strength: The exact number of M23 members is unclear and fluctuates regularly due to various factors such as recruitment, defection and military engagement. M23 is reportedly reinforced in terms of numbers and logistics by the Rwanda Defence Force (RDF).

Areas of operation: The southern area of North Kivu province, particularly Rutshuru, Nyiragongo and Masisi territories, surrounding the strategic border town of Goma.

Leadership: M23 is exclusively made up of Congolese Tutsis. Sultani Makenga is the group's military leader, while Bertrand Bisimwa is its current president. Additionally, Willy Ngoma and Lawrence Kanyuka are the military and political spokespeople, respectively. The group has installed a parallel civil administration in the territory it occupies.

Structure: The group has two factions. The faction that has resumed fighting in the DRC is made up of previously demobilised combatants in Uganda, led by Makenga. The faction of combatants that was demobilised in Rwanda under the leadership of Jean-Marie Runiga Lugerero has remained inactive.

History: Named after the peace agreement signed on 23 March 2009, M23 emerged in 2012 as a proxy of Rwanda claiming that the DRC's government failed to implement the 2009 peace deal with the National Congress for the Defence of the People rebellion, established by Laurent Nkunda in 2006. Defeated in 2013, M23 resurfaced in 2021.

Objectives: Pressure the Congolese government to uphold its commitments to the 2013 peace deal. M23 also presents itself as a guardian of Tutsi rights in the DRC.

Opponents: FARDC, MONUSCO and Hutu militias. The group has also made a point of not clashing with the EACRF.

Affiliates/allies: M23 benefits from the support of the RDF, including the Congo River Alliance.

Resources/capabilities: Receives military support from the RDF.

Allied Democratic Movement (ADF)

Strength: Estimates ranged from 1,000–1,500 in mid-June 2022, but joint FARDC and UPDF operations may have significantly decreased their numbers.[6]

Areas of operation: Active in the border zone between North Kivu and Ituri provinces, especially in Beni, Irumu and Mambasa territories, in an area ranging from Butembo in the south to Komanda in the north.

Leadership: Musa Baluku is the leader of the ADF's biggest (and only active) faction.

Structure: Operates in small, highly mobile groups from camps. The ADF recruits new members from Burundi, the DRC, Kenya, South Africa and Tanzania.

History: Founded in 1995 from a merger between Ugandan rebel factions that aimed to topple the government and expand Salafism in Ugandan society. During the First and Second Congo wars, the group relocated to the eastern DRC, where it was held responsible for civilian massacres and forced recruitment. After a decade of low-level fighting, the ADF re-emerged as a pre-eminent actor in 2013 and pledged allegiance to ISIS in 2017. ISIS started claiming ADF attacks and recognised the group as its Central Africa Province (ISCAP) in 2019.

Objectives: Topple the Ugandan government and establish an Islamic caliphate.

Allied Democratic Movement (ADF)

However, over the past decade, the group's actions have not revealed a clear commitment to this goal beyond utilising it as a narrative to maintain group cohesion. The ADF targets civilians and regularly clashes with the UPDF.

Opponents: FARDC, UPDF, MONUSCO and Wazalendo.

Affiliates/allies: ISIS.

Resources/capabilities: The ADF has been severely weakened by joint FARDC and UPDF operations, particularly in late 2022 and early 2023. However, it has also ramped up its use of improvised explosive devices in urban settings.

Cooperative for the Development of the Congo (CODECO)

Strength: 2,000–2,500.[7]

Areas of operation: Ituri province.

Leadership: Each faction is headed by a different leader.

Structure: CODECO has centralised its communication, with one spokesperson, Basa Zukpa Gerson, issuing communiques. It has seven different factions: Congo Liberation Army, Army of Revolutionaries for the Defence of Congolese People, Bon Temple, Force for the Defence against the Balkanisation of Congo, Gutsi, Islamic, and Union of Revolutionaries for the Defence of the Congolese People. Each faction has its own interests and areas of operations.

History: Rooted in the Lendu ethnolinguistic group, which is traditionally agriculturalist and in conflict with the pastoralist Hema people. Created as an agricultural cooperative in the 1970s, CODECO became an armed group in 2017.

Objectives: Its political and ideological objectives (if any) are unclear. Rooted in the Hema–Lendu conflict, the group seeks to address grievances such as ethnic marginalisation, control over resources, political representation and economic opportunities.

Opponents: FARDC and Hema self-defence groups, especially the Ituri Self-Defense Popular Front Zaire. CODECO members routinely target civilians, especially IDPs, on whom they often inflict sexual violence. CODECO factions periodically clash with one another.

Affiliates/allies: Patriotic and Integrationist Force of Congo (FPIC), a group composed mainly of ethnic Biras who want to 'reclaim' land 'occupied' by the Hema in Irumu territory.

Resources/capabilities: Financial resources derived from the gold mines it controls, especially in the area surrounding Mongbwalu.

Anti-M23 'Wazalendo' coalition

Strength: More than 8,000 Wazalendo (or 'patriots') fighters were established under the new Volunteers for the Defence of the Homeland in late September 2023. However, the coalition has since grown to 28,700 local and foreign fighters, from over 20 armed groups, such as the FDLR.[8]

Areas of operation: North Kivu province, particularly in Masisi, Nyiragongo, Rutshuru and Walikale territories, where M23 is active.

Leadership: Wazalendo is controlled by the main armed groups operating in Petit Nord, primarily the Nduma Defence of Convo–Renovated/Guidon (NDC–R) led by Guidon Shimirayi Mwisa; Coalition of Movements for Change (CMC) led by Dominique Ndarahutse; Patriotic Front for Peace/People's Army led by Fidele Mapenzi and Kabidon Kasanyo; Alliance of Patriots for a Free and Sovereign Congo (APCLS) led by Janvier Karairi Boingo (de facto leader of Wazalendo); and Alliance of Congolese Nationalists for the Defense of Human Rights led by Jean-Marie Bonane (deputy of Wazalendo entrusted with logistics). Jules Mulumba is the spokesperson of both the CMC and Wazalendo.

Structure: The coalition brought together rival armed groups (some of whom were initially self-defence militias), including the FDLR, NDC–R, APCLS, Nyatura Collective of Movements for Change–People's Defence Forces, Nyatura Abazungu, People's Defence Forces (Kabido) and Patriotic Self-Defence Movement.

History: As a coalition of several armed groups, Wazalendo was formed in March 2023 and gained notoriety in North Kivu and South Kivu provinces. It is supported by the FARDC against M23 and the RDF. Since June 2023, the FARDC chief of staff, Gen. Tshiwewe, has coordinated several meetings with Wazalendo leaders in the fight against M23.

Objectives: Liberate territories from the grip of foreign armed groups, particularly M23. However, Wazalendo also seeks to gain legitimacy and position itself to be integrated into the FARDC.

Opponents: M23 and RDF.

Affiliates/allies: A proxy force of the FARDC.

Resources/capabilities: The FARDC provides arms, logistics and cash to Wazalendo leaders and combatants.

Mai-Mai (Mayi-Mayi) groups

Strength: There are estimated to be about 250 Mai-Mai groups, including 136 in South Kivu, 64 in North Kivu, 20 in Ituri, 20 in Maniema and 19 in Tanganyika.[9] The exact number can be difficult to determine due to the groups' fluid nature and the absence of centralised control or coordination.

Areas of operation: Across the eastern DRC, particularly in North Kivu and South Kivu.

Leadership: Mai-Mai groups operate independently, each having its own leadership structure. Some, such as the Raia Mutomboki, are divided into subgroups that each respond to a particular commander.

Structure: Mai-Mai militias primarily function in an informal and decentralised manner, although certain groups have notorious commanders.

Mai-Mai (Mayi-Mayi) groups

History: Mai-Mai groups mostly formed as community-based self-defence militias during the Second Congo War. Thus, they perceive themselves as defenders of their communities in a competition for political or customary power, land resources and access to infrastructure. They are often linked to political elites and are therefore sometimes activated by politicians to achieve political objectives.

Objectives: Officially, community self-defence. In reality, most Mai-Mai militias fight for territorial control and self-enrichment, which they pursue through illegal taxation and looting.

Opponents: Mostly Banyamulenge ethnic militias, such as the Ngumino and Twirwaneho. They have also joined the fight against M23, with some travelling from South Kivu and more distant provinces. Mai-Mai groups regularly clash against the FARDC and each other, and target civilians.

Affiliates/allies: Mai-Mai militias have allied with the FARDC in the fight against M23 in North Kivu. Some militias also form alliances of convenience with each other.

Resources/capabilities: Armed almost exclusively with machetes and other bladed weapons, though some groups have small arms as well.

Rwanda Defence Force (RDF)

Strength: About 33,000 active military personnel. The UN estimated between 3,000 and 4,000 RDF personnel were deployed in the DRC in early 2024.[10]

Areas of operation: Eastern DRC, particularly Masisi, Nyiragongo and Rutshuru territories in North Kivu province.

Leadership: President Paul Kagame (commander-in-chief), Juvenal Marizamunda (defence minister) and Gen. Mubarakh Muganga (chief of defence staff).

Structure: Comprises the army, air force, Reserve Force and special units.

History: The RDF was previously a liberation force known as the Rwanda Patriotic Army in 1994 but was later renamed in 2002.

Objectives: Protect Rwanda's interests, sovereignty and territorial integrity.

Opponents: FARDC–Wazalendo coalition, Rwanda National Congress and FDLR.

Affiliates/allies: M23.

Resources/capabilities: RDF forces in the DRC primarily comprise light infantry units and special forces, supported by small numbers of artillery and mobile air-defence systems.

Uganda Peoples' Defence Forces (UPDF)

Strength: About 40,000–45,000 active military personnel, with an estimated 4,000 deployed under *Operation Shujaa* against the ADF in the DRC.[11]

Areas of operation: Ituri province (Irumu territory).

Leadership: Ugandan President Yoweri Museveni (commander-in-chief) and Gen. Muhoozi Kainerugaba (chief of defence forces as of March 2024).

Structure: Deployed in the DRC as part of the bilateral *Operation Shujaa* against the ADF since November 2021 and as part of the multilateral EACRF from April–December 2023.

History: Originated from the National Resistance Army, a rebel movement led by Museveni that waged a guerrilla war against Milton Obote's regime and took power in 1986.

Objectives: In the DRC, its objective is to defeat the ADF, though there is speculation that it is also largely motivated by economic interests.

Opponents: ADF (in the context of *Operation Shujaa*).

Affiliates/allies: FARDC.

Resources/capabilities: The UPDF is a well-trained, efficient army, which has received support and training from the United States and France, among others, in part due to its involvement in the fight against al-Shabaab in the Horn of Africa. It possesses tanks, other armoured vehicles, artillery and light weapons. It is known to be more effective and better disciplined than the FARDC.

Burundi National Defence Force (FDNB)

Strength: Over 1,000 soldiers deployed in the DRC as part of bilateral agreement between the DRC and Burundi.[12]

Areas of operation: Bilaterally in South Kivu (Fizi, Mwenga and Uvira territories) and as part of the EACRF in North Kivu (mainly in Masisi territory until December 2023).

Leadership: President Evariste Ndayishimiye (commander-in-chief) and Alain Tribert Mutabazi (defence minister).

Structure: Land and air forces. The FDNB forcibly recruits the Imbonerakure (the ruling party's youth wing) to fight in the DRC.

History: Established in 2004, the FDNB resulted from a politico-military accord. After three decades of mono-ethnic military reign, the Arusha Accord signatories embraced the concept of ethnic parity in the national army, stipulating a 50% representation of Hutu and Tutsi.[13] This principle was enshrined in the third protocol. However, the duration of this ethnic equilibrium remains undetermined.

Objectives: Defend Burundi's national integrity and defeat rebel groups.

Opponents: RED Tabara, National Liberation Front and two Burundian rebel groups that operate in South Kivu province.

Burundi National Defence Force (FDNB)

Affiliates/allies: In South Kivu, the FDNB collaborates with the FARDC and local groups such as the Mai-Mai Kijangala, Mai-Mai Kashumba and Gumino to fight against RED Tabara.

Resources/capabilities: Mostly small arms and light weapons. The army is generally considered to lack discipline.

South African Development Community (SADC) Mission in the Democratic Republic of the Congo (SAMIDRC)

Strength: Final mission strength was originally planned to consist in total of 5,000 troops, but in June 2024 a potential increase to approximately 9,000 troops was under discussion.[14]

Areas of operation: North Kivu province.

Leadership: Maj.-Gen. Monwabisi Dyakopu (force commander).

Structure: SAMIDRC's primary contingent is provided by South Africa, with support from smaller contingents deployed by Malawi and Tanzania.

History: SAMIDRC was deployed to help the FARDC fill a security vacuum in the DRC's eastern provinces, following the withdrawal of the EACRF at the end of 2023 and the ongoing drawdown of MONUSCO forces. Full operational capability is expected to be achieved by mid-July according to the UN.

Objectives: Support the DRC in restoring lasting peace and stability, and establish a conducive environment for sustainable development and prosperity.

Opponents: M23 and other NSAGs.

Affiliates/allies: Supports the FARDC with a mandate to combat M23 and other NSAGs.

Resources/capabilities: Since each contingent operates independently, capabilities reflect those of the national army of the troops in question.

United Nations Organization Stabilization Mission in the Democratic Republic of the Congo (MONUSCO)

Strength: 12,814 total personnel, including 11,140 military troops and staff officers, and 1,554 police.[15]

Areas of operation: Ituri and North Kivu provinces. MONUSCO ceased its operations in South Kivu by the end of April 2024. It plans to maintain its presence in North Kivu and Ituri provinces until its final withdrawal in December 2024.

Leadership: Bintou Keita (special representative of the secretary-general in the DRC and head of MONUSCO) and Lt-Gen. Otávio Rodrigues de Miranda Filho (force commander).

Structure: In addition to its military peacekeeping personnel, MONUSCO comprises police, military observers and a Force Intervention Brigade, which is authorised to act offensively against armed actors.

History: The UN Organization Mission in the Democratic Republic of the Congo, which was later renamed MONUSCO, was established in 1999 as part of a broader effort by the African and international communities to end the First and Second Congo wars. It was mandated to monitor various peace processes, including the Pretoria Accord signed in 2002 that ended the Second Congo War. This historic agreement was negotiated alongside another African-led initiative, the Lusaka Ceasefire Agreement, which brought all belligerent groups to the negotiating table. Subsequently, MONUSCO was tasked with facilitating the establishment of the political, security and justice institutions necessary to consolidate the Congolese state.

Objectives: Protect civilians and support efforts towards stabilisation, the strengthening of public institutions and the reform of governance and security.

Opponents: NSAGs.

Affiliates/allies: Periodically conducts joint operations with the FARDC, though relations are often tense.

Resources/capabilities: MONUSCO operates extensive logistical-support networks to sustain its operations. This includes transportation, communications and medical services. It utilises advanced technology such as drones and satellite imagery for gathering intelligence, monitoring the movements of armed groups, and enhancing situational awareness to respond promptly to threats against civilians and peacekeepers. MONUSCO collaborates closely with other UN agencies, non-governmental organisations and local authorities to coordinate efforts in promoting stability, providing humanitarian aid and supporting the rule of law in the DRC.

Other relevant parties

Other armed groups active throughout this reporting period include the Patriotic Resistance Front of Ituri (FRPI), FPIC, and Popular Self-Defense Movement of Ituri in Ituri province; Ngumino (Banyamulenge ethnic militia) in South Kivu province; Nyatura (Hutu ethnic militia), Union of Congolese Patriots and APCLS in North Kivu province; and Mobondo (Yaka ethnic militia) in Mai-Ndombe and Kwilu provinces. In Haut-Uélé and Bas-Uélé provinces, rebel groups from the Central African Republic and South Sudan conducted sporadic attacks or abducted civilians.

Notes

1. James Rupert, 'In Congo, Peace Means a Halt to "Brutal Illegal Mining"', United States Institute of Peace, 7 March 2023; and Global Centre for the Responsibility to Protect, 'Democratic Republic of the Congo', 31 May 2024.
2. *Le Monde* with AFP, 'DR Congo Leader Tshisekedi Wins Second Term in Already Contested Election', *Le Monde*, 31 December 2023.
3. Conflict minerals include tantalum, tin, tungsten and gold, also known as the 3TGs.
4. International Crisis Group, 'CrisisWatch 2024 – March Trends and April Alerts', March 2024.
5. UN Security Council (UNSC), 'Letter Dated 15 December 2023 From the Group of Experts on the Democratic Republic of the Congo Addressed to the President of the Security Council', S/2023/990, 30 December 2023.
6. International Crisis Group, 'A Perilous Free-for-all in the Eastern DR Congo?', Hold Your Fire!, 13 May 2022; and UNSC, 'Final Report of the Group of Experts on the Democratic Republic of the Congo', S/2023/431, 13 June 2023.
7. Adolphe Agenonga Chober and Georges Berghezan, 'La CODECO, au coeur de l'insécurité en Ituri' [CODECO, at the heart of insecurity in Ituri], Group for Research and Information on Peace and Security, 2 June 2021.
8. UNSC, 'Letter Dated 15 December 2023 From the Group of Experts on the Democratic Republic of the Congo Addressed to the President of the Security Council', pp. 11, 68–9.
9. Ivan Kasongo, 'RDC: le P-DDRCS dénombre 252 groupes armes locaux et 14 étrangers actifs dans cinq provinces de l'Est' [DRC: the P-DDRCS (disarmament, demobilisation, and reintegration programme) identifies 252 local armed groups and 14 foreign ones active in five provinces of the east], Actualité, 19 April 2023.
10. UNSC, 'Letter dated 31 May 2024 from the Group of Experts on the Democratic Republic of the Congo Addressed to the President of the Security Council', S/2024/432, 4 June 2024, p. 12.
11. Andrew Bagala and Alex Ashaba, 'Army Calls for Calm Amid Terror Threat', *Monitor*, 19 March 2024.
12. Sonia Rolley, 'Over 1000 Burundian Soldiers Covertly Deploy in Eastern Congo, Internal UN Report Says', Reuters, 30 December 2023.
13. Paul Nantulya, 'Burundi: Why the Arusha Accords Are Central', Africa Center for Strategic Studies, 5 August 2015.
14. Security Council Report, 'In Hindsight: The Escalating Conflict in Eastern DRC and UN Support of Regional Forces', 31 March 2024.
15. As of May 2024. UN Peacekeeping, 'Contribution of Uniformed Personnel to UN by Mission and Personnel Type', 31 May 2024.

UGANDA

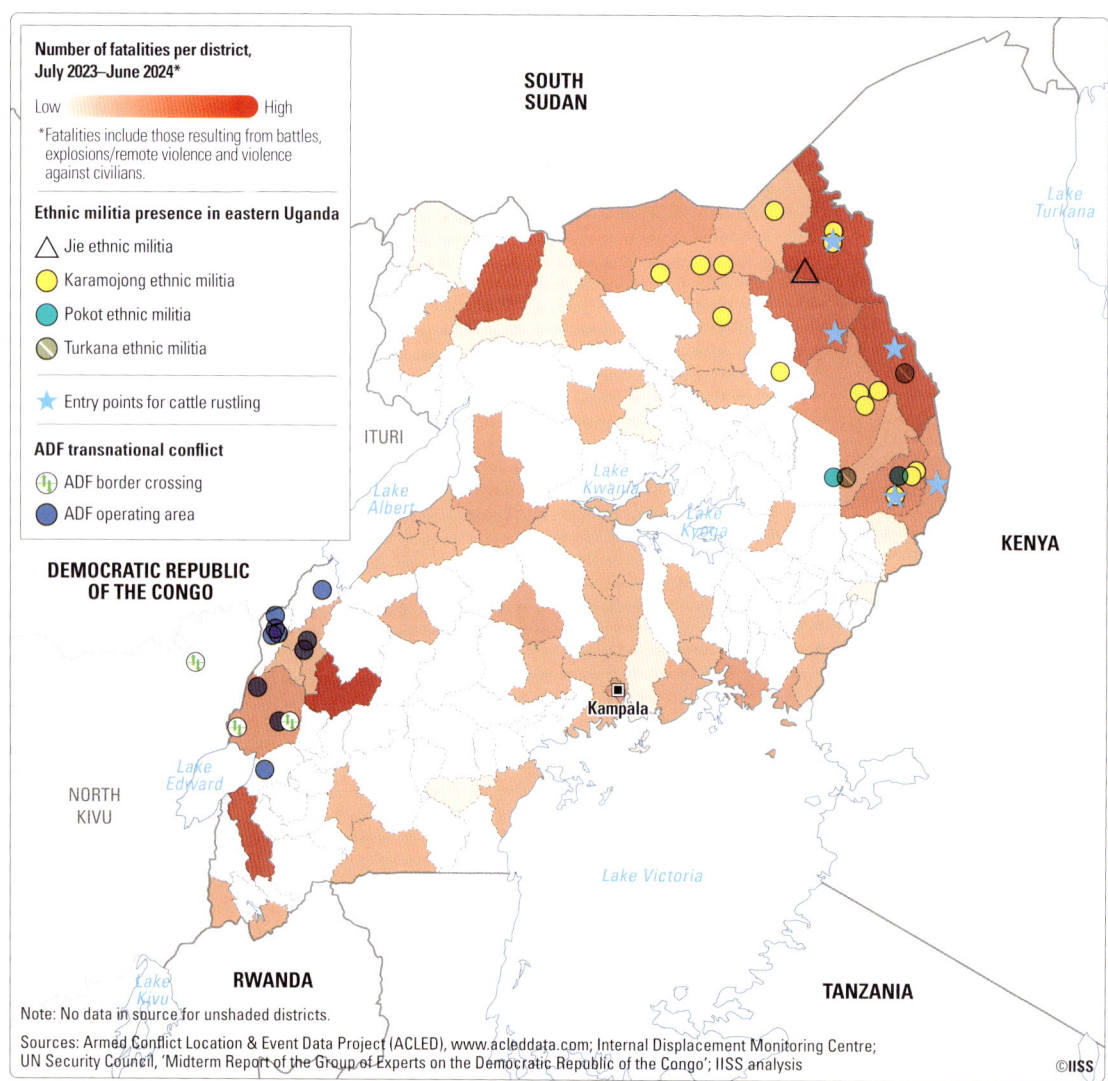

Conflict Overview

In 2017, the Uganda Peoples' Defence Forces (UPDF) ended its military campaign against Joseph Kony's Lord's Resistance Army (LRA), marking a key milestone in the fight against one of Uganda's most notorious rebel groups. However, this did not resolve the country's instability, as threats posed by the Allied Democratic Forces (ADF, also known as the Islamic State Central Africa Province or ISCAP) persist.

The ADF, originally formed in 1995 to topple the Ugandan government, has since morphed into a terrorist group. In 2017, it pledged allegiance to the Islamic State (ISIS) and rebranded itself as the ISCAP. This affiliation brought a new dimension to the group's operations, integrating it into global jihadist networks. In November 2021, the ADF attacked Uganda's capital of Kampala, killing several civilians and marking Uganda's first terrorist incident since 2010.[1]

Since then, the ADF has escalated its activities, exhibiting an increasing ability to execute

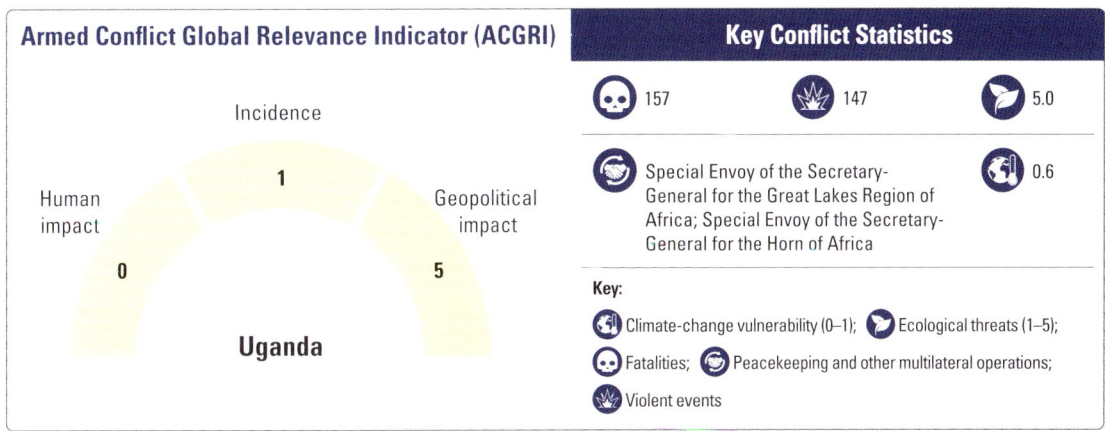

well-coordinated and high-profile attacks. In response, Uganda launched *Operation Shujaa* in November 2021, a joint military campaign with the Democratic Republic of the Congo (DRC) aimed at defeating the ADF. Despite these efforts, the ADF has remained resilient, with it constantly regrouping in its Rwenzori Mountains stronghold, located along the DRC–Uganda border.

While western Uganda grapples with ADF attacks, the northeastern region of Karamoja faces challenges related to cattle rustling, exacerbated by arms trafficking and the region's proximity to conflict-prone areas of Ethiopia, Somalia, South Sudan and Kenya. Despite disarmament efforts, insecurity persists, leading to clashes between Karamoja raiders and the UPDF.

Conflict Update

Since June 2023, Uganda has witnessed a surge in ADF terror attacks, which the group often orchestrates by crossing the DRC–Uganda border from its bases in the eastern DRC. While the UPDF managed to thwart some of these plots during the reporting period, such as the foiled terror attack on a cathedral in Kampala on 3 September 2023, these successes have not drastically diminished the ADF's operational capabilities.[2] The group's ambush of a tourist vehicle in Queen Elizabeth National Park on 17 October 2023, for instance, resulted in the deaths of two foreign tourists and their guide, and it exemplified the ADF's efforts to undermine Uganda's economic interests, particularly the tourism industry.[3] Indeed, this attack, along with bombings in Kampala in December 2023, demonstrated a shift in the ADF's tactics towards more high-profile and symbolic targets.[4] Meanwhile, in western Uganda, two successive ADF raids in Kamwenge district in December 2023, which killed ten and three civilians respectively, illustrated the group's capacity to adapt to UPDF counter-insurgency measures and sustain its terrorist operations.[5]

Alongside the ADF insurgency, the Karamoja region in northeastern Uganda has continued to grapple with rampant incidents of cattle rustling, despite ongoing peacebuilding efforts. The UPDF's apprehension of suspects has yielded limited outcomes, as unrecovered livestock fuels recurring raids and counter-raids in the region.

Given these ongoing security challenges, Uganda's stability remains fragile. Kampala's current security measures appear insufficient to tackle the dual threats posed by ADF terror attacks and local cattle rustlers. Without enhanced counter-insurgency measures, including addressing the deep-seated socio-economic challenges in Karamoja, Uganda risks descending into a more enduring conflict.

Conflict Parties

Uganda Peoples' Defence Forces (UPDF)

Strength: About 40,000–45,000 active military personnel.

Areas of operation: Country wide in Uganda (with extensive deployment in Karamoja). The UPDF is also present in the DRC, with at least 4,000 troops under *Operation Shujaa*, and Somalia, with 3,000 troops as part of the African Union Transition Mission in Somalia (ATMIS) and the United Nations Assistance Mission in Somalia.[6]

Leadership: President Yoweri Museveni (commander-in-chief) and Gen. Muhoozi Kainerugaba (chief of defence forces as of March 2024).

Structure: The UPDF introduced a new organisational structure on 17 February 2024 with centralised command of all its land, naval and air forces, under the chief of defence forces. The chief of joint staff, the third-highest position within the UPDF, manages joint staffs and the Defence Intelligence and Security agency.

History: Originated from the National Resistance Army, a rebel movement led by Museveni that waged a guerrilla war against Milton Obote's regime and took power in 1986.

Objectives: Protect Uganda's interests domestically and abroad, and defend the country's sovereignty and territorial integrity. In the DRC, its objective is to defeat the ADF, though there is speculation that it is also largely motivated by economic interests.

Opponents: Domestically, pastoralist militias in northeast Uganda. In both Uganda and the DRC, the ADF.

Affiliates/allies: Armed Forces of the Democratic Republic of the Congo (FARDC) under *Operation Shujaa*, ATMIS and East African Community Regional Force.

Resources/capabilities: The UPDF is a well-trained, efficient army, which has received support and training from the United States and France, among others, in part due to its involvement in the fight against al-Shabaab in the Horn of Africa. It possesses tanks, other armoured vehicles, artillery and light weapons.

Allied Democratic Forces (ADF)

Strength: Estimates ranged from 1,000–1,500 in mid-June 2022, but joint FARDC and UPDF operations may have significantly decreased their numbers.[7]

Areas of operation: Traditionally present in the Rwenzori Mountains, along the DRC–Uganda border. However, the ADF has also carried out attacks in several metropolitan areas of Kampala.

Leadership: Musa Baluku is the leader of the ADF's biggest (and only active) faction.

Structure: Operates in small, highly mobile groups from camps. The ADF recruits new members from Burundi, the DRC, Kenya, South Africa and Tanzania.

History: Founded in 1995 from a merger between Ugandan rebel factions that aimed to topple the government and expand Salafism in Ugandan society. During the First and Second Congo wars, the group relocated to the eastern DRC, where it was held responsible for civilian massacres and forced recruitment. After a decade of low-level fighting, the ADF re-emerged as a pre-eminent actor in 2013 and pledged allegiance to ISIS in 2017. ISIS started claiming ADF attacks and recognised the group as its Central Africa Province (ISCAP) in 2019.

Objectives: Topple the Ugandan government and establish an Islamic caliphate. However, over the past decade, the group's actions have not revealed a clear commitment to this goal beyond utilising it as a narrative to maintain group cohesion. The ADF targets civilians and regularly clashes with the UPDF.

Opponents: FARDC, UPDF, UN Organization Stabilization Mission in the DRC, and local self-defence militias (Wazalendo).

Affiliates/allies: ISIS.

Resources/capabilities: The ADF has been severely weakened by joint FARDC and UPDF operations, particularly in late 2022 and early 2023. However, it has also ramped up its use of improvised explosive devices in urban settings.

Karamojong ethnic militias

Strength: Unclear, though reportedly thousands of fighters have been arrested.[8]

Areas of operation: Northern region (Abim, Agago, Amudat, Gulu, Kaabong, Karenga, Kitgum, Kotido, Moroto, Nabilatuk,

Karamojong ethnic militias

Nakapiripirit, Napak and Otuke districts) and Eastern region (Bulambuli and Kween districts), with a concentration of activity in Kotido and Moroto districts.

Leadership: No formal leadership.

Structure: 'Karamojong' is a loose term for various ethnic groups living in Karamoja, where the militias are divided along ethnic (predominantly Jie, Karamojong and Pokot) and local lines.

History: Karamojong people have a cultural tradition of cattle rustling (as in other pastoralist societies) as a means of redistributing resources, but traditional weapons (spears, bows and arrows) were replaced with small arms in the 1980s.

Thus, raids in Karamoja became particularly violent between the late 1980s and the early 2000s.

Objectives: Raid cattle and challenge state authority. Traditionally, the Karamojong do not recognise any central government.

Opponents: UPDF and police.

Affiliates/allies: The militias sometimes support each other when clashing with the UPDF.

Resources/capabilities: Small arms and light weapons (often coming from outside Uganda). These weapons are acquired through various means, including illicit arms trafficking, raids on neighbouring communities and occasionally government disarmament programmes.

Turkana ethnic militias

Strength: Unclear, but between hundreds and thousands in Uganda, with higher numbers during the dry season as pastoralists cross over from Kenya into Uganda in search of water and pasture.[9]

Areas of operation: Northwestern Kenya and northeastern Uganda.

Leadership: No formal leadership.

Structure: No formal structure.

History: A memorandum of understanding (MoU) was signed in 2019 between Kenya and Uganda, which allowed the Turkana to graze their cattle in Uganda. However, poor implementation of the MoU has been cited as a reason for the return of the conflict. The Turkana have mostly refused to

disarm, fleeing back to Kenya during disarmament campaigns and crossing back into Uganda with their weapons afterward.

Objectives: Grazing on Karamojong land and cattle rustling.

Opponents: UPDF (in Uganda), Kenya Defence Forces (in Kenya) and other ethnic militias, particularly the Jie (in Uganda).

Affiliates/allies: Turkana raiders from northwestern Kenya have joined forces with local Karamoja raiders from certain communities such as the Matheniko.

Resources/capabilities: Small arms and light weapons, which transformed raiding into a commercialised enterprise leading to the escalation of pastoral conflict.

Notes

[1] Halima Athumani, 'Uganda Police Say Three Killed, 33 Injured in Twin Suicide Bombings', VOA, 16 November 2021.

[2] See Eddie Ddejjoba, 'Uganda Police Recover Three Bombs in Lungujja, Kampala Suburbs', New Vision, 3 September 2023.

[3] Elias Biryabarema, 'Uganda Police Say Suspected Rebels Kill Three in National Park', Reuters, 17 October 2023.

[4] See Kenneth Kazibwe, 'Security Provides More Details About ADF Commander Behind Saturday Twin Blasts', Nile Post, 4 December 2023.

[5] Alex Ashaba, '10 Killed in Kamwenge Attack', *Monitor*, 19 December 2023; and Alex Ashaba, 'Three Dead as Suspected ADF Rebels Raid Another Village in Kamwenge', *Monitor*, 26 December 2023.

[6] Hellen Mukiibi, 'AU Honors Uganda Peacekeepers in Somalia', New Vision, 10 May 2024; and Andrew Bagala and Alex Ashaba, 'Army Calls for Calm Amid Terror Threat', *Monitor*, 19 March 2024.

[7] International Crisis Group, 'A Perilous Free-for-all in the Eastern DR Congo?', Hold Your Fire!, 13 May 2022; and UN Security Council, 'Final Report of the Group of Experts on the Democratic Republic of the Congo', S/2023/431, 13 June 2023.

[8] Liam Taylor, '"Hell Is Coming": The Ugandan Army's Heavyhanded Crackdown in Karamoja', *New Humanitarian*, 1 December 2022.

[9] Hesborn Etyang, 'Governor Wants Turkana Herders Jailed in Uganda for Illegal Weapons Released', *Star*, 14 May 2023; and International Crisis Group, 'CrisisWatch: Tracking Conflict Worldwide', May 2023.

MOZAMBIQUE

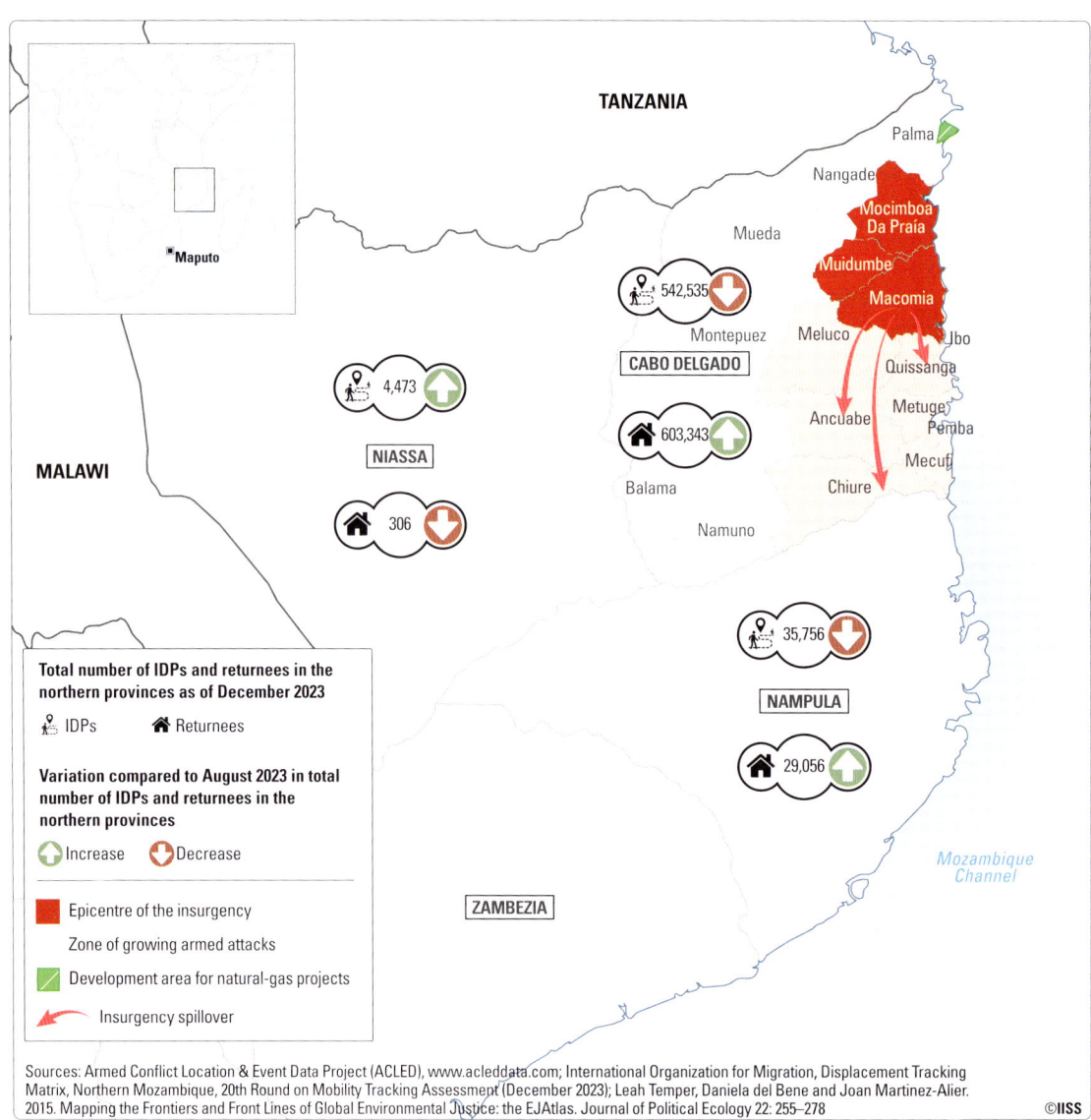

Conflict Overview

The insurgency in Mozambique's northeastern, gas-rich Cabo Delgado province has been ongoing since 2017 and has spread into neighbouring areas, causing a significant humanitarian crisis. The attacks are reportedly associated with the Islamic State (ISIS) in Mozambique, locally known as Ahlu Sunna wal Jama (ASWJ or 'al-Shabaab').[1] The conflict stems from historical disenfranchisement and political marginalisation, exacerbated by widespread poverty, regional disparities and limited job opportunities. Additionally, local communities have not substantially benefited from discoveries of natural gas and rubies, which has strengthened Mozambicans' perception that revenues from natural resources go primarily to the elites, intensifying resentment towards the ruling Frelimo party.[2]

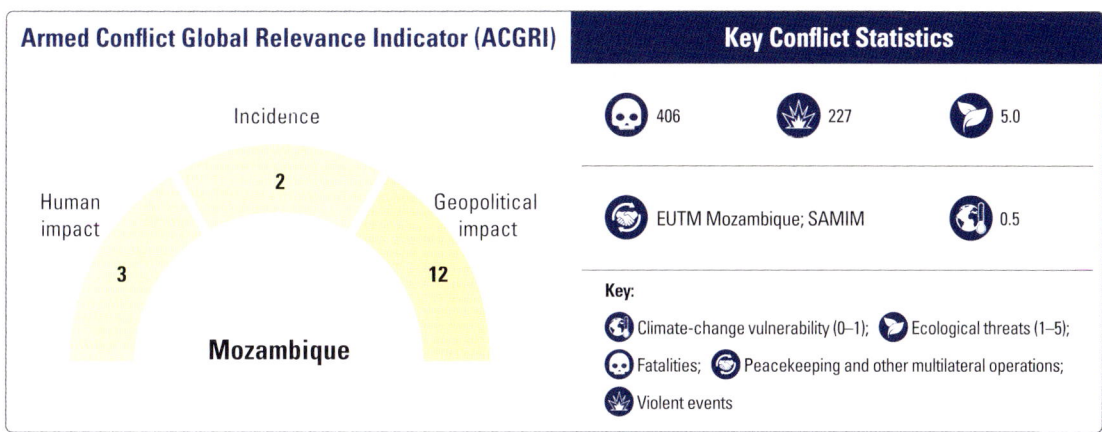

Conflict(s)	Type	Start date
Islamic State insurgency in Cabo Delgado	II	2017

Key: II Internationalised internal

Islamist militants have effectively exploited these grievances to push their propaganda and radicalise youth. Conflict has also been worsened by Mozambique's tight fiscal situation and weak state capacity, especially in peripheral regions.

The insurgents expanded their reach and capabilities between 2019 and early 2021, culminating in an attack on Palma in March 2021, which resulted in many casualties and halted major liquefied natural gas (LNG) projects in the region. In response, the Rwandan military was deployed under a bilateral agreement with Mozambique; the Southern African Development Community (SADC) put in place its Standby Force Mission in Mozambique (SAMIM); and the European Union launched an EU Training Mission (EUTM). Mozambique's armed forces have benefited from the ongoing military support provided by Rwanda and SAMIM, which has helped prevent further violent escalation. Operational coordination has remained limited, however, with Rwandan forces preferring to act unilaterally rather than coordinate with Mozambique's military and police.

Conflict Update

As a result of over three years of foreign-troop deployments in the province, ASWJ and its leadership in Cabo Delgado have suffered significant setbacks, although violence increased again at the end of 2023. From summer 2023 to November 2023, insurgent activity was limited and mainly concentrated in the Macomia, Mocímboa da Praia and Muidumbe districts of Cabo Delgado. Notably, SAMIM forces successfully eliminated ASWJ's operational leader, Ibn Omar, in August 2023. The humanitarian situation remained critical, although more than 600,000 internally displaced persons (IDPs) had returned home by the end of 2023.[3] Mozambique's government sought to leverage these accomplishments to portray a return to normalcy, mainly with the aim of convincing investors to resume LNG projects.

Despite these developments, the security outlook remained highly volatile, as demonstrated by the deterioration that has occurred since the end of 2023. Militants intensified attacks in the aforementioned districts, while expanding their reach towards the southern districts of Meluco, Quissanga, Ancuabe, Chiure, Mecúfi and Metuge. This surge in attacks contradicted the government's narrative that ASWJ no longer poses a threat, and raised concerns about the withdrawal of SAMIM, whose mandate has been extended only until July 2024. Tanzania and South Africa, which were both part of SAMIM, have opted to remain in Cabo Delgado on a bilateral basis. In response to the rising attacks and the withdrawal of SAMIM, Rwanda committed in May 2024 to deploying an additional 2,500 personnel.[4] The EU has also decided to enhance its presence in the country, prolonging the mandate of the EUTM until June 2026, while transitioning it into a Military Assistance Mission as of 1 September 2024.

Conflict dynamics are closely intertwined with local politics. During municipal elections held in October 2023, the surge in conflict was a major topic in the electoral campaign, with the Mozambican National Resistance (Renamo) party blaming Frelimo for inaction and incompetence in tackling the escalating violence. Following Frelimo's victory, accusations of fraud from the opposition sparked violent protests and repression, further aggravating the already precarious security outlook. A similar pattern might emerge with the general elections to be held in October 2024.

Conflict Parties

Mozambican Defence Armed Forces (FADM)

Strength: 12,000 active military personnel (air force: 1,000; army: 10,000; navy: approximately 1,000).

Areas of operation: Northern (Cabo Delgado, Nampula and Niassa) and north-central (Manica, Sofala, Tete and Zambezia) Mozambique.

Leadership: Cristóvão Artur Chume (defence minister) and Joaquim Rivas Mangrasse (chief of staff).

Structure: Consists of infantry forces, a navy and an air force. Together with the Police of the Republic of Mozambique (PRM) they form the Defence and Security Forces (FDS).

History: Created following Mozambique's independence in 1975 but reached its current form after the civil war (1977–92) between Frelimo and Renamo. Former Renamo fighters were integrated into the FADM as part of the 1992 Rome General Peace Accords; this process was then accelerated by a further peace agreement between the government and Renamo in 2019.

Objectives: Protect Mozambique's territory against domestic and foreign enemies, and provide assistance during periods of high insecurity and civil unrest, such as during states of emergency.

Opponents: ASWJ and Renamo Military Junta (RMJ).

Affiliates/allies: SAMIM, Rwanda Defence Force (RDF), EUTM, local self-defence militias and PRM.

Resources/capabilities: Mozambique's defence budget was US$207 million (1.0% of GDP) for 2023 and is US$316m (1.4% of GDP) for 2024.

Police of the Republic of Mozambique (PRM)

Strength: Unclear.

Areas of operation: Nationwide.

Leadership: Bernardino Rafael (commander-general).

Structure: Operates under the Ministry of Interior and consists of multi-level police units, including special-operations units that the government relies on for internal security. Counter-insurgency efforts in Cabo Delgado were initially led by the PRM, with support from foreign-owned private military companies to ensure security. Then, in January 2021, Mozambican President Filipe Nyusi turned counter-insurgency leadership over to the FADM. Together with the FADM they form the FDS.

History: Replaced the People's Police of Mozambique in 1992.

Objectives: Enforce laws and regulations, and ensure public security.

Opponents: ASWJ and RMJ.

Affiliates/allies: FADM, SAMIM, local self-defence militias and RDF.

Resources/capabilities: Unclear.

Ahlu Sunna wal Jama (ASWJ), also known as al-Shabaab

Strength: Estimated around 500 fighters.[5]

Areas of operation: The epicentre of insurgency remains in the districts of Macomia, Mocímboa da Praia and Muidumbe. In early 2024, militants advanced into southeastern districts of Cabo Delgado province, including Pemba, Ancuabe, Chiure, Mecufi, Meluco and Metuge.

Leadership: Farido Selemane Arune is likely to be the successor of Bonomade Machude Omar (alias 'Ibn Omar'), who was killed in August 2023.

Ahlu Sunna wal Jama (ASWJ), also known as al-Shabaab

Structure: Unclear.

History: Formed between 2015 and 2017 and launched its first attack in 2017. ISIS formally recognised it as part of the Islamic State Central Africa Province (ISCAP) in 2019.

Objectives: No specific manifesto, but the group's public statements indicate that it aims to separate Cabo Delgado residents from the Mozambican state and establish a new state in at least part of Cabo Delgado, drawing on its interpretation of Islamic legal structures. The control of mineral-rich areas is also at stake in the conflict.

Opponents: FDS, SAMIM, RDF, local self-defence militias and Mozambican government officials.

Affiliates/allies: ISIS and ISCAP.

Resources/capabilities: Unclear, but weapons and personnel appear to be locally sourced.

Rwanda Defence Force (RDF) and Rwanda National Police (RNP)

Strength: 2,800 (estimated 2,000 RDF and 800 RNP).[6]

Areas of operation: Palma and Mocímboa da Praia districts, as well as segments of Macomia district, in Cabo Delgado. In early 2023, troops were placed in the southern district of Ancuabe.

Leadership: Maj.-Gen. Alex Kagame.

Structure: The Rwandan Security Forces Joint Task Force includes both a military Task Force Battle Group and a police component. It also comprises staff from Rwanda's National Intelligence and Security Service.

History: Deployment began in July 2021, and the commitment scaled up during 2022 and 2023, reaching around 2,800 personnel. In May 2024, Rwanda committed to deploying an additional 2,500 forces to fill the gap left by departing SAMIM troops.[7]

Objectives: Officially, it aims to defeat ASWJ and train Mozambican forces to maintain peace in Cabo Delgado. In practice, it has moved to secure those areas most necessary for work on major natural-gas and mineral projects in Cabo Delgado to resume.

Opponents: ASWJ.

Affiliates/allies: FDS, SAMIM and local self-defence militias.

Resources/capabilities: Funded by the government of Rwanda, according to both the Rwandan and Mozambican governments.

Southern African Development Community Standby Force Mission in Mozambique (SAMIM)

Strength: As of May 2024, SAMIM had effectively completed the withdrawal of its troops ahead of the mission's closure in July 2024. Tanzania and South Africa will maintain a presence in Cabo Delgado on a bilateral basis.

Areas of operation: Macomia, Muidumbe, Mueda, Nangade and Quissanga districts in Cabo Delgado.

Leadership: Maj.-Gen. Patrick Dube.

Structure: National contingents from Angola, Botswana, Democratic Republic of the Congo, Lesotho, Malawi, South Africa, Tanzania and Zambia. Personnel from these states and other SADC members provide logistical support.

History: Established in June 2021 and first deployed the following month. In July 2023, the SAMIM mandate was extended by 12 months, until July 2024, which marks the end of the mission.

Objectives: Officially, it has moved from operating under the SADC's 'Scenario 6' (an intervention to end violent conflict) to 'Scenario 5' (a peacekeeping mission).

Opponents: ASWJ.

Affiliates/allies: FDS, RDF and local self-defence militias.

Resources/capabilities: Funding has been difficult to acquire; the SADC has largely relied on funds and in-kind contributions from member governments.

Notes

[1] The ASWJ in Mozambique is a distinct group from the ASWJ in Somalia.
[2] Emilia Columbo, 'Stabilizing Mozambique', Council on Foreign Relations, 29 August 2022.
[3] International Organization for Migration, Displacement Tracking Matrix, 'Mozambique', December 2023.
[4] Charles Mangwiro, 'Rwanda Deploying Another 2,500 Soldiers to Help Mozambique Fight Cabo Delgado Insurgency', VOA, 20 May 2024.
[5] International Crisis Group, 'CrisisWatch Mozambique', February 2024.
[6] 'Mozambique Takes Aim at Terrorists in Last Stronghold', *Africa Defense Forum*, 23 January 2024; and 'Mozambique, Rwanda: Kigali Puts More Boots on the Ground in Cabo Delgado', *Africa Intelligence*, 27 February 2023.
[7] Mangwiro, 'Rwanda Deploying Another 2,500 Soldiers to Help Mozambique Fight Cabo Delgado Insurgency'.

5 Asia

Regional Analysis	274	Pakistan	298	Thailand	324
Regional Spotlight	286	Kashmir	304	Philippines	328
Country Profiles		Myanmar	310	Indonesia	334
Afghanistan	292	India	318		

Military-junta soldiers in Myanmar parade during a ceremony to mark the country's Armed Forces Day in Naypyidaw, 27 March 2024

Overview

South and Southeast Asia host a number of long-standing armed conflicts. Three of them – armed violence in Afghanistan, Pakistan's struggle with ethnic insurgency and anti-state terrorist groups, and the dispute over Kashmir – affect regional security and have the potential to impact global security. This is primarily due to the transnational actors involved in these conflicts and the possibility that the Kashmir dispute might escalate into a conventional war between nuclear powers India and Pakistan. Meanwhile, the conflict in Myanmar – historically more localised in nature – has become more regionalised as over one million refugees have fled to neighbouring Bangladesh and China's influence on the parties has increased.

The intensity of two of these conflicts – the dispute over Kashmir and armed violence in Afghanistan – has significantly reduced in terms of violence over the last three reporting periods. Tensions along the Line of Control (LoC) between India and Pakistan have abated since a ceasefire took effect in February 2021, leading to a decline in cross-border clashes from 5,133 reported incidents in 2020 to single digits during the current reporting period.[1]

After three years in power, the Afghan Taliban still controls nearly all of Afghanistan's territory. Despite continuing to carry out attacks on Taliban security forces, foreign diplomats and civilians, the Islamic State Khorasan Province (ISKP) has failed to maintain control over territory or meaningfully challenge the Taliban's authority. The Taliban's raids have put significant operational pressure on ISKP, which may partly explain why the group has

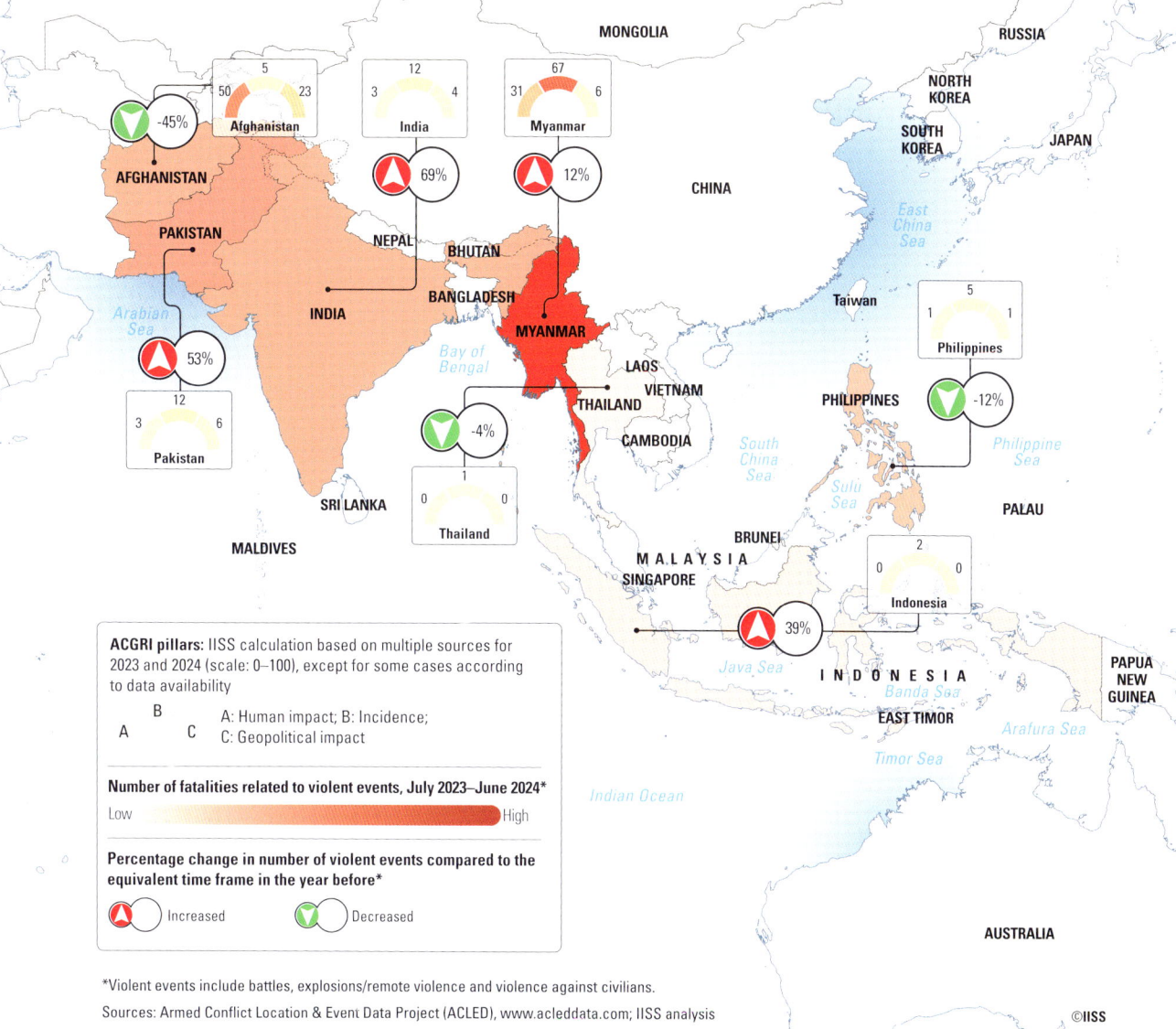

expanded its activities to other countries, such as Russia, where it killed at least 137 people in March 2024.[2] The desire of regional and international powers to maintain stability in Afghanistan so that it does not serve as a staging ground for transnational terrorist groups or produce a mass exodus of refugees has led to sustained diplomacy. Afghanistan is gradually reintegrating into global commerce and connectivity. An example of this was the resumption of flights to Kabul by Turkish Airlines in May 2024.

The Tehrik-e-Taliban Pakistan (TTP), also commonly known as the Pakistani Taliban, continued to take refuge in Afghanistan throughout the reporting period, while escalating its campaign against Pakistan's security forces. Pakistan sent formal and informal envoys to meet with the Afghan Taliban in an attempt to curtail their support for the TTP, with little success. (See the Asia Regional Spotlight chapter for more analysis on this topic.)

Meanwhile, Myanmar's military junta lost significant ground in its war against a loose coalition of pro-democracy forces and ethnic armed organisations (EAOs), which has persisted since the military coup by the State Administration Council (SAC, also known as Myanmar armed forces or the Tatmadaw) in February 2021. Although China had agreed to help maintain a ceasefire between the SAC and the Brotherhood Alliance (BHA), a coalition of three ethnic armed groups, it grew frustrated with the SAC's slow progress on key projects and failure to tackle the cyber-scamming industry originating from SAC-controlled areas that is defrauding victims around the world, particularly Chinese nationals. Given tacit approval by China, the BHA launched *Operation 1027* in October 2023, which expelled regime forces from Rakhine and northern Shan states and resulted in the displacement of an additional 1.2m people between June 2023 and June 2024.[3] The operation ended in January when the Myanmar National Democratic Alliance Army (MNDAA) regained control of the northeastern region bordering China and a negotiated withdrawal of regime forces took place. The SAC has lost influence over much of the border with China, and by the end of the reporting period it was re-routing cross-border trade through Mongla in Bangladesh and northern Thailand and by sea. *Operation 1027* highlighted China's role as the most influential external actor in the conflict, particularly its significant leverage over the SAC compared to Western actors who have imposed sanctions on the military junta, such as the European Union, United Kingdom and United States.

The region's other conflicts, which are more localised and have a lesser impact on regional dynamics, remained relatively stable but registered a slight uptick in violence in the reporting period. This includes the Malay Muslim ethno-nationalist autonomy movement and insurgency in Thailand in which insurgents continued attacks despite ongoing peace talks; the Philippines' Moro insurgency in Mindanao and nationwide Maoist insurgency, which both saw a renewed cycle of retaliatory violence; violent confrontations between the Indonesian military and armed West Papuan factions; and India's Maoist insurgency.

Conflict Drivers

Political and institutional
Post-colonial arrangements
The most active conflicts in the region are rooted in the ethnic, religious, irredentist and centre–province tensions that emerged in newly formed, post-colonial states. The decision of the last Hindu ruler of Jammu and Kashmir (princely state) to join India in 1947, for instance, created a conflict that divided Kashmir between India and Pakistan. In Pakistan, the Baloch insurgency and insecurity in the Pashtun tribal areas are partly fuelled by questions over the legitimacy of the Durand Line as the Afghanistan–Pakistan border, although Islamist extremism increasingly plays a role. The post-colonial order that divided Pakistan into west and east wings, culminating in the secession of East Pakistan to form Bangladesh, also led to ethnic resentment and tensions within the country. The division of the historical Islamic sultanate of Patani by the Anglo-Siamese Treaty in 1909 laid the groundwork for the Malay Muslim autonomy movement and insurgency in southern Thailand. Likewise, in Indonesia, the West Papuan separatist movement began after Jakarta annexed the region from the Netherlands in the early 1960s. In a controversial 1969 referendum, just over one thousand handpicked Papuan representatives, out of an estimated 800,000 residents, unanimously voted to support Indonesian sovereignty over West Papua.[4]

The conflicts in Myanmar, meanwhile, stem from the Bamar majority's attempt to control ethnic-minority groups following the country's independence from British rule in 1948, which triggered struggles for autonomy among these minority groups. Thus, many of Myanmar's internal armed conflicts arise from EAOs vying for autonomy in remote borderlands, which the military junta has responded to with concerted military campaigns and indiscriminate violence, disproportionately affecting civilian populations with affiliations to these groups. More recently, the Bamar-majority National Unity Government (NUG) and its armed wing have partnered with EAOs to fight the military junta.

Socio-economic
Socio-economic divides
Socio-economic inequalities are one of the main causes of the insurgencies in India, Pakistan and the Philippines. Poverty and a lack of economic opportunities in parts of the Philippines continue to provide a fertile terrain for recruitment for both Moro Muslim rebel groups and the New People's Army (NPA). India's Communist Party of India–Maoist has long tapped into sentiments of disenfranchisement in rural, impoverished populations. Similarly, the conflict between Pakistan and Baloch insurgents is partially fuelled by economic disparities, including most recently the distribution of economic benefits derived from natural-resource extraction and the China–Pakistan Economic Corridor (CPEC) traversing Balochistan.

Marginalisation of majority-minority groups
In Myanmar, Pakistan and the Philippines, insurgents have cited internal migration of majority ethnic and religious groups to minority areas or the entry of multinational (especially Chinese) firms as key motivators for continued fighting. These movements are viewed as attempts to subjugate 'majority-minority' groups in their provincial homelands.[5] The Indian government's attempts at loosening residency and voting laws in Indian-administered Jammu and Kashmir (J&K) since the revocation of its special status could heighten ethnic tensions there as well.[6] Projects like the CPEC and the China–Myanmar Economic Corridor simultaneously motivate resistance and incentivise groups to consolidate control over future development zones so that they can engage in rent seeking. In Myanmar, EAOs and the Bamar majority have historically been in conflict; however, pro-democracy Bamar groups have recently formed a tacit alliance with some EAOs.

Illicit economies
Illicit trade and informal taxation are also powerful economic drivers of conflict. The cultivation and export of illicit narcotics play a central role in Afghanistan, while illicit trade in narcotics, gems, timber and people fuels the conflict in Myanmar's periphery. In April 2022, the Taliban banned the cultivation of poppy, which is used to produce opium. By 2023, satellite imagery revealed a 99% decrease in poppy cultivation in Helmand province, the main poppy-growing region of Afghanistan, a development which was met with a rare statement of praise from US Special Representative for Afghanistan Thomas West.[7] This downward trend has continued in year two of the ban. As of 22 July 2023, crop mapping of 14 provinces (which accounted for 92% of the country's poppy cultivation in 2022) showed that cultivation had dropped to less than 4,000 hectares, down from 16,000 hectares in 2023.[8] Badakhshan province, where the ban has not been as effective, is an exception to this trend. While the ban may slightly improve the Taliban's standing with the West, others argue that it risks plunging the economy further into crisis and fuelling migration. If the Afghan Taliban and international community are unable to find alternative streams of income that are resilient to climate change, then communities in southwestern Afghanistan may begin to cultivate poppies again. Moreover, the drop of opium production in Afghanistan has resulted in an increase in Myanmar, which has now become the largest opium producer globally.

Climate vulnerability
Natural disasters, pollution and climate change continue to plague Asia. By some measures, six out of 20 of the countries with the worst air quality globally were located in the region in 2023.[9] Both India and Pakistan faced severe heat waves, while over 70,000 households in Vietnam's Mekong Delta struggled with limited access to fresh water in spring 2024 due to heat-induced saltwater intrusion into the region's primary water sources.[10] East Asia and Southeast Asia reported the highest number of disaster displacements globally from 2010–21, closely followed by South Asia. In the summer of 2022, massive floods submerged one-third of Pakistan, displacing at least 33m people.[11] These floods sparked debates on climate resilience and discussions regarding whether the Global North owed any reparations to the Global South. Conflicts over drinkable water exacerbate tensions in the region, with long-standing disputes over the use of the Indus, Chenab and Jhelum rivers contributing to the conflict between Pakistan and India over Kashmir.

Security and military
Transnational jihadism
Since 2014, various groups in South and Southeast Asia have pledged allegiance to the Islamic State (ISIS). However, this has not yet translated into transnational jihadist campaigns like those during the height of the ISIS caliphate in northern Iraq and Syria, which led to international terrorist attacks, particularly in Western Europe. One reason is that these ISIS offshoots have not achieved the territorial control that ISIS had in Iraq and Syria between 2013 and 2017. Additionally, many of these groups, such as the Bangsamoro Islamic Freedom Fighters in the Philippines, are focused on domestic issues and have simply rebranded themselves as ISIS affiliates. These groups use ISIS's prestige within pan-jihadist networks to enhance their image and for recruitment but do not have the same transnational ambitions or capabilities. Nevertheless,

in March 2024, ISKP executed a major attack at a concert hall in Moscow region, Russia, and attempts by ISIS and its affiliates to hold territory remains a potential driver of conflict.

Geopolitical

International interventions

The conflicts in Afghanistan, Kashmir and Pakistan have strong international drivers that often perpetuate violence by altering power dynamics on the ground. However, India strongly opposes any third-party mediation or involvement in the Kashmir conflict, including by the United Nations. This has been especially true since the 2019 revocation of Articles 370 (1949) and 35A (1954, a provision of Article 370) of the Indian constitution, which had provided special status to J&K, and the division of the region into two separate union territories.

Beijing has shown a moderate but growing level of interest in regional conflicts that impact security on its periphery and its economic interests. It has mostly articulated this through bilateral diplomatic ties, but it has also increasingly spearheaded regional diplomacy regarding Afghanistan. It sees the security of Afghanistan as crucial to ensure Uyghur militants in the East Turkestan Islamic Movement do not find refuge in the country, from which they could then execute terrorist attacks inside China. These interests are evident as well in China's engagement with both Myanmar and Pakistan, which are key recipients of investment through its Belt and Road Initiative. China has also facilitated peace negotiations between Myanmar's military and EAOs and supported both conflict parties at different times according to its strategic interests.

Conflict Parties

Coalitions and multilateral responses

In some regional conflicts, coalitions have been formed between political entities and non-state actors. In Myanmar, EAOs, which are often viewed as independent militias, have also organised themselves into coalitions. During the reporting period, some of these groups collaborated with the Bamar-majority NUG and its nominal armed wing, the People's Defence Force, to wage joint attacks on the military junta. Certain EAOs possess greater strength and autonomy compared to others. This is particularly true for groups situated along the China–Myanmar border, such as the United Wa State Army and the Kachin Independence Army. In contrast, EAOs like the Karen National Union and the Chin National Front have fewer military capabilities and are more likely to rely on coalition dynamics.

The international coalition that once supported the previous Afghan government has been replaced by an international diplomatic effort. Foreign officials are actively engaging with senior Taliban leaders in hopes of softening their strict policies against women and persuading them to rein in groups like the TTP. Acting Minister of Interior Affairs Sirajuddin Haqqani recently participated in Hajj and held meetings with senior Emirati leaders. Special representatives from European countries, Pakistan, Russia, the US and others have continued diplomatic efforts with the Taliban in Kabul, Doha and other regional capitals that are loosely organised with one another. Afghanistan's immediate neighbours, such as China and Pakistan, prioritise security concerns but also see political stability, and to some extent inclusivity, as crucial for maintaining a stable Afghanistan. In contrast, Western European countries and the US emphasise human and women's rights in their engagements with the Taliban. Currently, no foreign powers are seeking direct security or counter-terrorism roles in Afghanistan, and the Taliban has not shown openness to such arrangements.

Non-state armed groups

The vast majority of ongoing conflicts in Asia involve multiple non-state armed groups (NSAGs). These groups are predominantly organised around ethnic or religious affiliations, although some, like the Maoist groups in northeastern India or the NPA in the Philippines, are also driven by secular ideologies. Certain groups, such as militant Kashmiri Muslim groups in J&K or the Patani Malay National Revolutionary Front (Barisan Revolusi Nasional, BRN) in southern Thailand, operate along both ethnic and religious lines. Other groups, like the various EAOs in Myanmar or Baloch separatist movements in Pakistan, are primarily organised along ethnic and subregional divisions.

The majority of the NSAGs active in the region have localised objectives that do not extend beyond the borders of the countries in which they operate, and in some cases, they even remain within specific subregions of those countries. The kinship ties and personal experiences of local or more prominent leaders also matter, as does groups' proximity to criminal practices such as kidnapping for ransom or arms and narcotics smuggling. ISKP and al-Qaeda stand out as exceptions, as their stated goals are above all transnational, and both have a history of carrying out international terrorist attacks. Although the TTP conducts transnational attacks by nature of it being based in Afghanistan while it carries out operations in Pakistan, it has stated that it has no international ambitions beyond Pakistan.

Third-party involvement
Peacekeeping missions and intergovernmental organisations have been largely ineffective at reducing conflict in the region. The UN is primarily playing an observer and monitoring role in the conflicts in Afghanistan and Kashmir. For over 30 years, the UN has been involved in high-level discussions with Myanmar's military junta, beginning in 1990 with the appointment of a Japanese scholar and diplomat as an independent expert for the UN Commission on Human Rights. Despite a succession of special envoys continuing these efforts, no significant progress has been made. Furthermore, the UN Security Council (UNSC) has not taken a decisive stance, and no external nation has demonstrated a strong interest in undertaking a direct peacekeeping role. The Association of Southeast Asian Nations (ASEAN) has similarly been unable to facilitate peace talks in Myanmar.

Regional Humanitarian Trends

Conflict intensity in the region saw some increase in the reporting period year-on-year, with a 13% rise in violent events on average. Related fatalities, on the other hand, decreased by a slight 3%, driven by a major decline in their number in Afghanistan (-57%), alongside a 45% drop in violent events there. However, fatalities rose sharply in India, Indonesia and Pakistan, by 48%, 38% and 33%, respectively, driven by increased intensity of conflict in these countries. Indeed, the number of violent events also rose significantly, by 69% (India), 39% (Indonesia) and 53% (Pakistan). Worsening conflict trends in Indonesia warranted the inclusion of its West Papua separatist conflict in *The Armed Conflict Survey 2024* for the first time. Myanmar saw a 12% uptick in violent events, but a slight decrease in fatalities, likely reflecting a rise in less lethal attacks by resistance groups against the military junta.[12]

The conflicts in Afghanistan and Myanmar, alongside catastrophic climate events, have produced some of the greatest humanitarian consequences in the region. Due to over 40 years of continuous conflict, Afghans make up the third-largest displaced population in the world, after Syrians and Ukrainians. An estimated 6.4m Afghans have been driven out of the country as refugees.[13] The two-decade presence of US and NATO troops in Afghanistan led to widespread awareness of conflict dynamics there as well as the Afghan people's plight. This has translated into a strong emphasis on humanitarian aid to Afghanistan compared to other parts of the world. Concerns over terrorism and the Taliban's flagrant disregard for human rights have also raised interest from the general public, the Afghan diaspora and policymakers in the West. Nevertheless, fears persist that international humanitarian aid will not be maintained. In 2023, the UN World Food Programme stopped food assistance for 10m Afghans due to low funding, and overall humanitarian aid to Afghanistan fell from US$3.8 billion in 2022 to US$1.9bn in 2023, reflecting a global shortage.[14]

As of 2023, there were 1.3m refugees from Myanmar, primarily living in refugee camps in Bangladesh.[15] Additionally, there are over 3.2m internally displaced persons (IDPs) inside Myanmar, and approximately 6,500 Rohingya refugees attempted (via land and sea routes) to go to third countries for greater protection in 2023, resulting in hundreds of deaths at sea.[16] China's Yunnan province, which borders restive parts of Myanmar, has at times hosted tens of thousands of refugees.[17] In 2023, approximately 5,000 Myanmar nationals from Shan State fled into China.[18]

Asia is also the world's most disaster-prone region, partly due to climate change, and this is likely to produce tens of millions of IDPs due to natural disasters by 2050.[19]

Outlook

Prospects for peace

Progress has been made towards peace in certain conflicts in the region, while others have regressed. Along the LoC in Kashmir, a fragile ceasefire reaffirmed in 2021 but still to be formalised between India and Pakistan is likely to remain in place as India focuses on border disputes and competition with China and Pakistan contends with an acute economic crisis and its fight against the TTP. General elections for Pakistan in February 2024 and India in the spring of the same year did not lead to significant provocations nor a warming of relations, although former prime minister Nawaz Sharif, the powerful leader of the ruling Pakistan Muslim League–Nawaz (PML–N) party, has expressed a desire to resume trade (see Figure 1). In India's northeast, the central government signed a peace deal with the United National Liberation Front (UNLF), a Manipur-valley-based insurgent group. Meanwhile, during the first half of 2024, Indian security forces engaged in targeted attacks on Maoist militants to disrupt their annual counter-offensive campaign. Prospects for long-term peace in southern Thailand have slowed with BRN militants engaged in increasingly sophisticated attacks against the Thai government, despite ongoing dialogue. The conflict in the Philippines between separatist movements and the government is likely to remain highly localised and contained.

While Taliban rule has led to worsening economic and human-rights prospects, Afghanistan is now a country at peace by traditional measures, with armed

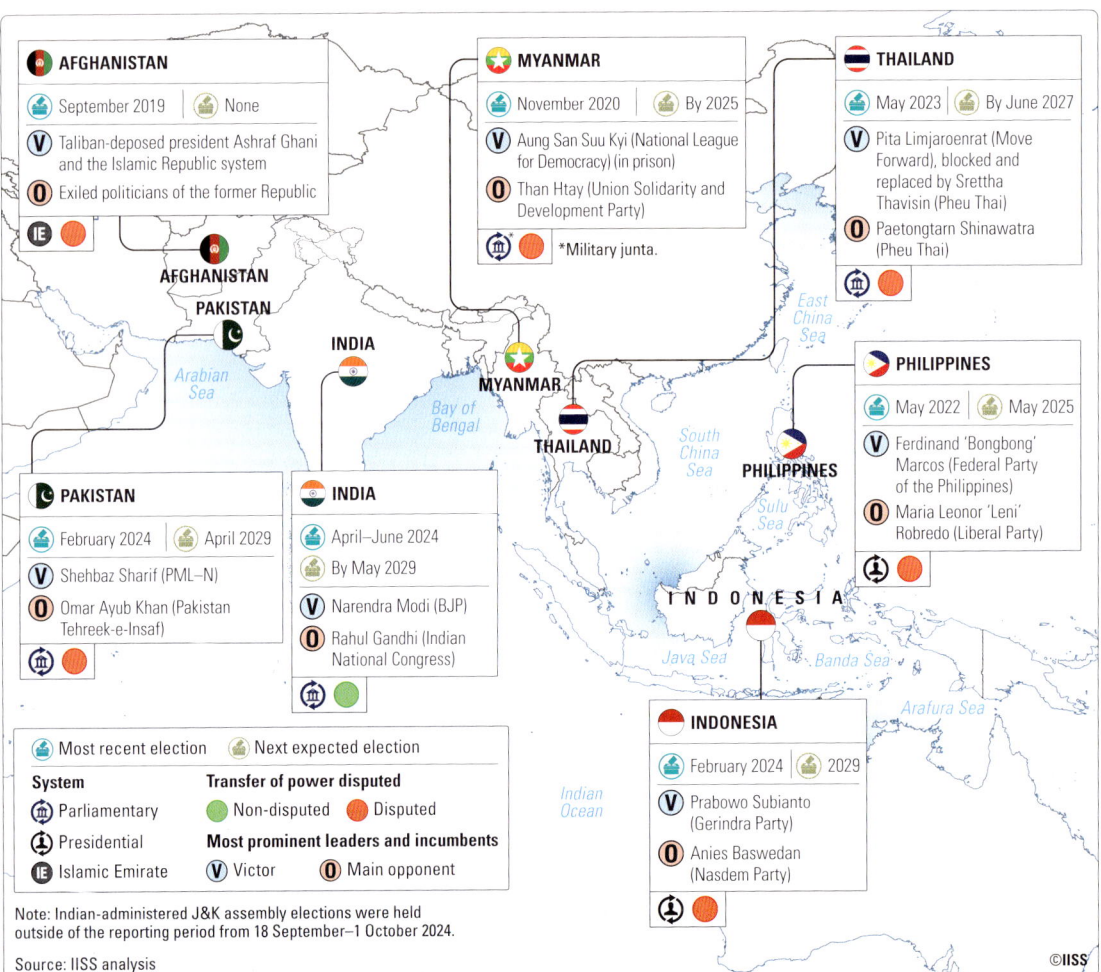

Figure 1: Election dynamics in Asia

resistance and violent deaths having significantly decreased since the Taliban's takeover in August 2021. The Taliban is firmly in control of Afghan territory and outside powers have largely refrained from direct intervention in Afghanistan, apart from occasional border skirmishes between Pakistan and Afghanistan. It remains unlikely that Afghanistan will descend into civil war in the near future.

Escalation potential and regional spillovers

During the reporting period, the conflict between Myanmar's armed forces and the various EAOs intensified. Myanmar's military junta views the tacit cooperation between the NUG and certain EAOs as an elevated threat to its rule since it represents an alliance between elements of the Bamar majority and ethnic minorities. This perception will only be hardened by the territorial control Myanmar's security forces lost along the Myanmar–Chinese border when they were forced to negotiate a withdrawal.

The Taliban's draconian edicts on women have led to diplomatic and economic isolation, which puts a strain on Afghanistan's population and makes it difficult for the Taliban to provide the minimum services expected of a government. This in turn presents a risk for outward migration and refugee flows.

Strategic prospects

Three potential conflicts in the region have the capacity to escalate into major conventional wars with nuclear implications. These include the one between the US and China in the Taiwan Strait; the one between Pakistan and India along the LoC; and the one between China and India along the Line of Actual Control. The first two carry the highest risk of escalation, particularly at the nuclear level. China considers its influence in the Taiwan Strait and eventual reunification with Taiwan to be crucial to its strategic national interests and identity, similar to how both India and Pakistan view Kashmir. By contrast, the strategic implications of the low-intensity insurgencies in India, Indonesia, the Philippines and Thailand are fairly minor for their host states, their regions and the international community. Their effects do not extend outside of the regions in which they are taking place and do not challenge the existing political order of their countries at the federal level. The conflict in Myanmar is more internationalised in that it has attracted international sanctions and Chinese influence over the actions of the belligerent parties. The threat of transnational terrorist groups in Afghanistan and Pakistan, meanwhile, will have greater strategic implications if these groups direct attacks against targets outside of the region. The ISKP attack on the concert hall in Moscow region and intercepted planned attacks in continental Europe demonstrate the seriousness of this risk.

Russia's invasion of Ukraine has raised concerns that China might take similar actions in Taiwan, although some aver that the example of Moscow's troubles could actually deter China. It is unclear how Washington would respond to Chinese military actions against Taiwan. Historically, the US has maintained a position of 'strategic ambiguity', which neither promises nor rejects the defence of Taiwan. The US Congress's increasing hawkishness on China and upcoming presidential elections are likely to bring this ambiguity over Taiwan into question. Relations between Washington and Beijing remained tense during the reporting period, but less so than during the previous one, when then-house speaker Nancy Pelosi travelled to Taiwan on an official visit. In November 2023, President Xi Jinping and President Joe Biden met in San Francisco and agreed to resume military communications, viewed as a necessary stopgap to potential escalation during a crisis.

Regional Key Events

POLITICAL EVENTS

MILITARY/VIOLENT EVENTS

 **PHILIPPINES**
26 July 2023
The Philippine government kills the top leader of the NPA in Northern Mindanao.

MYANMAR
31 July 2023

The SAC military junta extends a state of emergency in Myanmar for the fourth time, further delaying elections.

 PAKISTAN
3 October

Pakistan's caretaker minister for information announces that 'illegal immigrants' have 28 days to leave Pakistan – a move targeting Afghan refugees. Forced round-ups and voluntary deportations begin.

 PAKISTAN
30 July

An ISKP suicide bomber kills at least 44 and wounds nearly 200 people during a political rally in northwest Pakistan.

 PAKISTAN
29 September

Twin suicide bombings result in the death of over 50 people at two mosques in Pakistan, on the day of the Prophet Muhammad's birthday.

 CHINA, PHILIPPINES
22 October

While resupplying the grounded Philippine ship at Second Thomas Shoal, a Philippine supply boat collides with a China Coast Guard vessel that is attempting to block it.

 PAKISTAN
3 November

Heavily armed Baloch Liberation Front rebels ambush a Pakistani military convoy, killing at least 14 soldiers.

 PHILIPPINES
28 November

The government and communist rebels in the Philippines agree to restart peace negotiations after a six-year hiatus.

 INDIA
29 November

India's government signs its first-ever ceasefire with a Manipur-valley-based insurgent group, the UNLF.

 PHILIPPINES
3 December

ISIS claims responsibility for the bombing of a Catholic mass service in Mindanao that kills at least four people.

 INDIA
4 December

Kuki militants kill 13 People's Liberation Army of Manipur militants in India after tensions erupt in May 2023.

 AFGHANISTAN, PAKISTAN
Early January 2024

Fazl-ur-Rehman, leader of the major Islamist party Jamiat Ulema-e-Islam Fazl in Pakistan, becomes one of the few non-Afghan politicians to meet with Afghan Taliban Emir Mullah Hibbatullah Akhundzada.

 MYANMAR
5 January 2024

Over 2,000 military personnel, including six brigadier generals, surrender, resulting in the MNDAA seizing control of Kokang region after the SAC negotiates a withdrawal.

MYANMAR
12 January
The Myanmar military junta reaches a ceasefire agreement with rebel armies, mediated by China.

 PAKISTAN
30 January
Former prime minister of Pakistan Imran Khan is sentenced to ten years in jail for allegedly leaking state secrets.

 MYANMAR
31 January
Myanmar's SAC extends the state of emergency by six months, effectively delaying elections until at least 2025.

 THAILAND
7 February
Malaysian facilitator Zulkifli Zainal Abidin reports that Thailand's government and Muslim separatists have agreed 'in principle' on an updated road map to try to end the conflict through a peace plan.

 PAKISTAN
8 February
Pakistan holds general elections, although the process faces allegations of electoral violence and interference, and Shehbaz Sharif of the PML–N party remains prime minister.

 AFGHANISTAN
18–19 February
National and regional envoys to Afghanistan gather in Doha for a UN meeting to discuss enhancing engagement with Afghanistan. The Taliban chooses not to participate.

 PAKISTAN
Mid-January
Tensions rise along the border between Pakistan's Balochistan province and Iran when the latter launches airstrikes targeting purported militant bases within Pakistan.

  AFGHANISTAN, PAKISTAN
18 March
Pakistan launches airstrikes in Khost and Paktika provinces, Afghanistan, killing civilians.

 INDONESIA
20 March
The West Papua National Liberation Army kills two Indonesian police officers.

AFGHANISTAN
21 March
ISKP suicide bombers kill at least 20 people outside a bank in Afghanistan's second-largest city, Kandahar.

 THAILAND
22 March
Malay Muslim separatists set at least 40 fires throughout southern Thailand, along the border with Malaysia, killing at least one person.

 CHINA, PAKISTAN
26 March
A suicide-bomb blast in northwest Pakistan kills five Chinese workers, who were working on the Dasu Dam project, and their Pakistani driver, targeting Islamabad's close ties with Beijing.

 KASHMIR
19 April–25 May
General elections for the Indian parliament are conducted in J&K, the region's first elections as a union territory since its special status was revoked in 2019.

 INDIA
19 April–1 June
India holds general elections and the National Democratic Alliance, led by the Bharatiya Janata Party (BJP), wins a majority, with Narendra Modi sworn in for a third term as India's prime minister.

 MYANMAR
25 June
The ceasefire brokered by China between the SAC and ethnic-minority insurgents falls apart as fighting resumes in northeast Myanmar.

 PAKISTAN
12 July
The IMF approves a critical US$7bn bailout deal to bolster Pakistan's economic-stabilisation programme.

 BANGLADESH
5 August
Following weeks of protests, Bangladesh's prime minister Sheikh Hasina resigns and flees the country. Nobel laureate Muhammad Yunus is sworn in as interim leader three days later.

Notes

1 'Jammu & Kashmir: Timeline (Terrorist Activities) – 2024', South Asia Terrorism Portal.
2 Amira Jadoon, 'Explaining the Broader Implications of Islamic State–Khorasan's Moscow Attack', Stimson, 16 April 2024.
3 UN Office for the Coordination of Humanitarian Affairs (UNOCHA), 'Myanmar Humanitarian Update No. 39', 1 July 2024, p. 1; and UNOCHA, 'Myanmar Humanitarian Update No. 30', 13 June 2023.
4 John Saltford, *The United Nations and the Indonesian Takeover of West Papua, 1962–1969* (London: Routledge, 2003), p. 3.
5 'Majority-minority' groups refer to ethnic and religious groups

that are a minority relative to the national population but make up the majority in a particular province or area.

6   When referring to developments before 15 August 2019, the acronym 'J&K' refers to the state of Jammu and Kashmir (including Kashmir, Jammu and Ladakh regions, which India controls). For developments after the abrogation of Article 370 and the bifurcation of J&K in 2019, J&K refers to the Union Territory of Jammu and Kashmir (including Jammu and Kashmir regions, which India controls).

7   Alcis, 'Unprecedented Reduction of Opium Production in Afghanistan', 2023.

8   David Mansfield, 'Sowing the Seeds of Division in Badakhshan?', Alcis, 29 July 2024.

9   In descending order, the six countries are Bangladesh, Pakistan, India, Nepal, Indonesia and China. IQAir, '2023 World Air Quality Report', 2023.

10 Save the Children, 'Vietnam's El Niño-induced Drought Leaves About 73,900 Households in Mekong River Delta With Limited Access to Fresh Water', 24 April 2024.

11 Leo Sands, 'Pakistan Floods: One Third of Country Is Under Water – Minister', BBC News, 30 August 2022.

12 IISS analysis based on data from the Armed Conflict Location & Event Data Project (ACLED), www.acleddata.com.

13 UN High Commissioner for Refugees (UNHCR), 'Afghan Refugee Crisis Explained', 29 July 2024.

14 Ayaz Gul, 'UN Sounds Alarm on Shortage of Afghan Humanitarian Aid', VOA, 3 April 2024; and Daniel F. Runde et al., 'The Future of Assistance for Afghanistan: A Dilemma', Center for Strategic and International Studies, 13 June 2024.

15 UNHCR, 'Myanmar Situation', Operational Data Portal; and U.S. Committee for Refugees and Immigrants, 'Myanmar's Human Rights Crisis: In Freefall With Insufficient International Attention', 29 February 2024.

16 UNHCR, 'Myanmar Situation'.

17 United States Institute of Peace China Myanmar Senior Study Group, 'China's Role in Myanmar's Internal Conflicts', 14 September 2018.

18 RFA Burmese, '5,000 Myanmar Nationals Flee Into China, Face Shortages', Radio Free Asia, 11 March 2023.

19 Kwan Soo-Chen and David McCoy, 'Climate Displacement & Migration in South East Asia', Inter press Service News Agency, 28 February 2023.

Towards the Reintegration of Afghanistan into the International Community

Since the Taliban returned to power in Afghanistan in August 2021, no country or international organisation has formally recognised it as the legitimate government of the country. This stance was largely based on an informal international consensus that diplomatic recognition of the Taliban regime would depend on its fulfilment of certain conditions, including mitigating threats posed by terrorists operating from Afghan soil, transitioning to a more inclusive government and ensuring the rights of women and girls. This consensus has frayed, however, as foreign engagement with the Taliban regime has increased. A 'new normal' has emerged, marked by a rise in diplomatic presence in Kabul and the appointment of Taliban officials to key diplomatic missions abroad.

Significant developments have also taken place within Afghanistan. The Taliban regime has improved local security, though it continues to selectively target remnants of former regimes. It has also been relentless in combatting the Islamic State Khorasan Province (ISKP) jihadist group. The country continues to face formidable economic and humanitarian challenges and remains dependent on external financial assistance. Approximately 15.8 million people suffer from acute food insecurity, while two-thirds of households struggle to meet basic needs.[1] From August 2021–January 2024, Afghanistan received at least US$2.9 billion from the United Nations, comprising international-donor contributions to support humanitarian activities of non-governmental and public international organisations and operations of the World Bank and Asian Development Bank.[2]

Against an increasingly complicated geopolitical backdrop and ongoing crises in Ukraine and Gaza, there is little impetus in the West to pursue regime change through force in Afghanistan. Instead, the aim appears to be 'regime transformation'. Regional countries with a diplomatic presence in Afghanistan or hosting Taliban representatives could play a crucial role in achieving this, by pressing the Taliban regime to modify its rigid domestic policies. Given the Taliban's inconsistent participation in large and media-focused international conferences, 'quiet diplomacy' through a series of small, private and strictly confidential 'Track 1.5' dialogues involving the Taliban could help facilitate Afghanistan's reintegration into the international community.

The long road to restored engagement

To date, the Taliban has refused to make compromises on its rigid policies regarding inclusive governance and certain rights of women and girls. This raises questions about the extent to which it genuinely seeks international diplomatic recognition.

The Taliban has interpreted the international community's call for inclusive, representative government as a demand for power-sharing, and specifically for the return of some former political leaders to government. UN Security Council Resolution 2721 endorsed an independent assessment that stated the regime must 'take steps towards an Afghan national dialogue that would establish inclusive governance and ensure sustainable peace and social, cultural and economic development', and made 'pursuing intra-Afghan dialogue to achieve more inclusive governance' one of the conditions for the reintegration of Afghanistan into the international system.[3] This was not, however, a demand for power-sharing, a resurrection of the republic or a Western-style liberal democracy. The assessment stated there were many ways to enable meaningful participation of all Afghans in public affairs, including mechanisms grounded in Afghan traditions of consultation and dialogue.

The Taliban also maintains that its government is inclusive because it comprises members of Afghanistan's various ethnic groups and because it has retained much of the civil service. While several high-level ministers and deputy ministers are indeed Afghan Uzbek, Afghan Tajik or ethnic Hazara, these claims of inclusion are considered insufficient by both non-Taliban Afghan and international stakeholders.[4] The Taliban has also refused to engage in any dialogue with (mostly exiled) political leaders and warlords who were part of the United States-backed Afghan government (2001–21), with a few minor exceptions.[5]

Contrary to expectations, the Taliban did not attend the high-level UN conference on Afghanistan in Doha in February 2024, citing protocol and disagreements over the agenda. The objective of the conference was to delineate a course for international engagement with Afghanistan – including by opening dialogue on inclusive government, human rights and female education – and to appoint a UN special representative to Afghanistan. On 30 June, however, a Taliban delegation attended the third UN-led meeting of special envoys to Afghanistan in Doha. At the request of the Taliban and as a precondition for its participation, no Afghan civil-society representatives attended. UN officials and special representatives met civil-society attendees separately on 2 July, but they were not significant non-Taliban political leaders. In parallel, while the opposition remains fragmented, positive progress is being made as non-Taliban political leaders start to attend other groups' events.

Within the Taliban, there are significant differences of opinion on girls' education. In May 2022, the acting deputy minister of foreign affairs, Sher Mohammad Abbas Stanikzai, voiced support for women's rights and education, noting, 'women make up half of Afghanistan's population' and that 'they are deprived of the right to education'.[6] Some conservative religious scholars, hardline ministers and the supreme leader, Mullah Hibbatullah Akhundzada, oppose any such posture. Acting Minister of Interior Affairs Sirajuddin Haqqani publicly criticised Akhundzada's stance in early 2023, but Akhundzada has since clamped down on dissent. Pluralism and disagreement even within the Taliban are being increasingly suppressed.

Moreover, although the Taliban maintains that it has curtailed the operations of terrorists acting against the US and its allies on Afghan soil, terrorist groups remain active, notably the Tehrik-e-Taliban Pakistan (TTP, also known as the Pakistani Taliban), al-Qaeda, ISKP and the Islamic Movement of Uzbekistan. The US drone strike in July 2022 that killed the leader of al-Qaeda, Ayman al-Zawahiri, in central Kabul – a year after the Taliban takeover – demonstrated that the Taliban had not taken action against al-Qaeda using Afghanistan as a base, and underlined the connections that persist between elements of the Taliban and al-Qaeda. The TTP has also increased attacks across Khyber Pakhtunkhwa in Pakistan's northwest, exacerbating tensions between the Taliban regime and the government of Pakistan. Meanwhile, though the Taliban has largely removed ISKP from rural and urban centres, the group still maintains a presence in the country. Between August 2021 and May 2024, it is estimated that 429 people – 58 Taliban, 220 civilians and 15 others, as well as 136 ISKP cadres – were killed in 73 ISKP-linked incidents.[7] In January 2024, the Afghan Ministry of Interior said that in 2023 it had conducted nearly 3,000 anti-terrorism operations.[8]

Finally, the Taliban has launched effective counter-narcotics operations since it assumed power, with nearly 15,000 operations reported by the Afghan Ministry of Interior in 2023.[9] According to the UN Office on Drugs and Crime (UNODC), opium production was reduced by 95% between 2022 and 2023.[10] How long the Taliban will be able to sustain this is unclear, however, as it has no credible alternative plans for farmers who are reliant on income from poppy cultivation. UNODC also indicates that there has been a major and rapid expansion in the production of methamphetamine.[11]

'New normal'

The absence of formal diplomatic recognition of the regime is in contrast to the Taliban's previous time in power (1996–2001), when it was formally recognised by Pakistan, Saudi Arabia and the United Arab Emirates (UAE). However, the new normal of expanded diplomatic engagement has had the cumulative effect of eroding the 'non-recognition' approach of the international community, and 'creeping normalisation' is taking place as neighbouring countries – especially in Central Asia – need to maintain basic relations with Afghanistan. As of July 2024, 11 countries had appointed ambassadors in Kabul, including China, Iran, Japan, Qatar, Russia, Saudi Arabia, the UAE and Uzbekistan, while several regional countries had chargés d'affaires (CDAs), including India, Kyrgyzstan, Pakistan and Tajikistan. Iran, Pakistan, Tajikistan and Turkiye also had a consular presence in other major cities in Afghanistan; only Iran and Pakistan had a consular presence in Kandahar. India reopened its embassy in Kabul in June 2022, headed by a CDA. One of the Indian mission's priorities is to ensure the development of the Chabahar Port project in Iran, to help boost regional trade.

The US and the United Kingdom engage with Afghanistan through missions in Doha, Qatar, while others, such as Belgium and Sri Lanka, do so through their embassies in Islamabad, Pakistan (see Figure 1). The advantages of having a diplomatic presence in Afghanistan are many, including consistent engagement with the Taliban leadership in Kabul – even as access to the supreme leader in Kandahar is extremely limited – and being able to oversee humanitarian aid and trade relations. The compromise is that re-establishing a permanent diplomatic presence in Kabul would confer legitimacy on the Taliban and would mean effective diplomatic recognition of the regime.

Various foreign governments have held talks with the Taliban. The Chinese foreign minister, Wang Yi, visited Afghanistan and met with his Taliban counterpart, Amir Khan Muttaqi, and the acting deputy prime minister, Mullah Abdul Ghani Baradar, in Kabul on 24 March 2022. Foreign ministers from various other countries (including Uzbekistan and Pakistan) have also visited Kabul since the Taliban's takeover. A top-level Pakistani delegation, led by Defence Minister Khawaja Asif, visited Kabul on 22 February 2023 to discuss security concerns and the TTP threat. A senior Indian official in the Ministry of External Affairs also met the Taliban's acting foreign minister in Kabul in March and June 2024.

US and Taliban representatives in Doha regularly discuss issues related to economic growth, human rights, narco-trafficking and counter-terrorism. The European Union special envoy for Afghanistan has visited Afghanistan several times to meet Taliban officials. In October 2021, Sir Simon Gass, the British prime minister's high representative for the Afghan transition, met the acting foreign minister in Kabul.

While many ambassadors and other diplomatic staff appointed by the previous government remain in post in missions in the region, there is creeping attrition as the Taliban pressures countries to replace them with its own appointees. In July 2024, the Taliban had its representatives in missions in 13 countries. Its first CDA was appointed to Pakistan in October 2021, its first – and, to date, only – ambassador was appointed to China in December 2023, and the first military attaché in Moscow was appointed in March 2024. Its CDAs are also present in Iran, Malaysia, Qatar, Turkiye and the UAE, as well as all five Central Asian states. The Taliban regime also has consular missions in seven countries. Except for Pakistan, it has no official representation in South Asia. The Taliban has attempted to appoint a consul general in Mumbai following the sudden resignation in May 2024 of the officeholder appointed by the previous government, but the Indian government has not yet cleared the appointment.

Gulf Cooperation Council member states have acknowledged the new reality in the region. Qatar has hosted a Taliban office in its territory since 2013. It played an important role in the 2018–20 process that led to the US–Taliban Doha peace agreement and in hosting the pre-August 2021 intra-Afghan negotiations. In May 2023, Qatar's prime minister and foreign minister, Sheikh Mohammed bin Abdulrahman Al Thani, met the Taliban supreme leader in Kandahar. Saudi Arabia and the UAE had initially taken a cautious approach, opting for multilateral rather than bilateral engagement. This has recently begun to change. Saudi Crown Prince Mohammed bin Salman met the Taliban's acting defence minister, Mullah Mohammad Yaqoob, during the Hajj season in 2023. Sheikh Mohamed bin Zayed Al Nahyan, the UAE president and ruler of Abu Dhabi, met with Yaqoob in December 2022 and Sirajuddin Haqqani in June 2024.

In marked contrast to the isolationist posture of its previous rule, the Taliban has highlighted the potential for the private sector to be a catalyst for change and development in Afghanistan. It has stated its commitment to market-led, 'pro-growth' economic policies, indicating a willingness to engage economically with the world. A Taliban trade delegation announced in February 2024 investments worth US$35m in Iran's Chabahar Port aimed at diversifying its regional network and reducing its dependence on Pakistan for transit to international markets.[12]

In early June 2024, Kazakhstan removed the Taliban from its list of terrorist organisations, and Russia is considering doing the same.

Way forward

In light of the new normal of diplomatic engagement with the Taliban, a focus on quiet diplomacy through the convening of private and confidential Track 1.5 dialogues appears to be the most effective way to start the process. Such forums could play a key role in bringing together Taliban officials with non-Taliban Afghans. The objective would be to move from confidence- and trust-building to dialogue and discussion on a road map for the reintegration of Afghanistan into the international community. Such a road map should focus on inclusivity and the elimination of all

Regional Spotlight: Asia 289

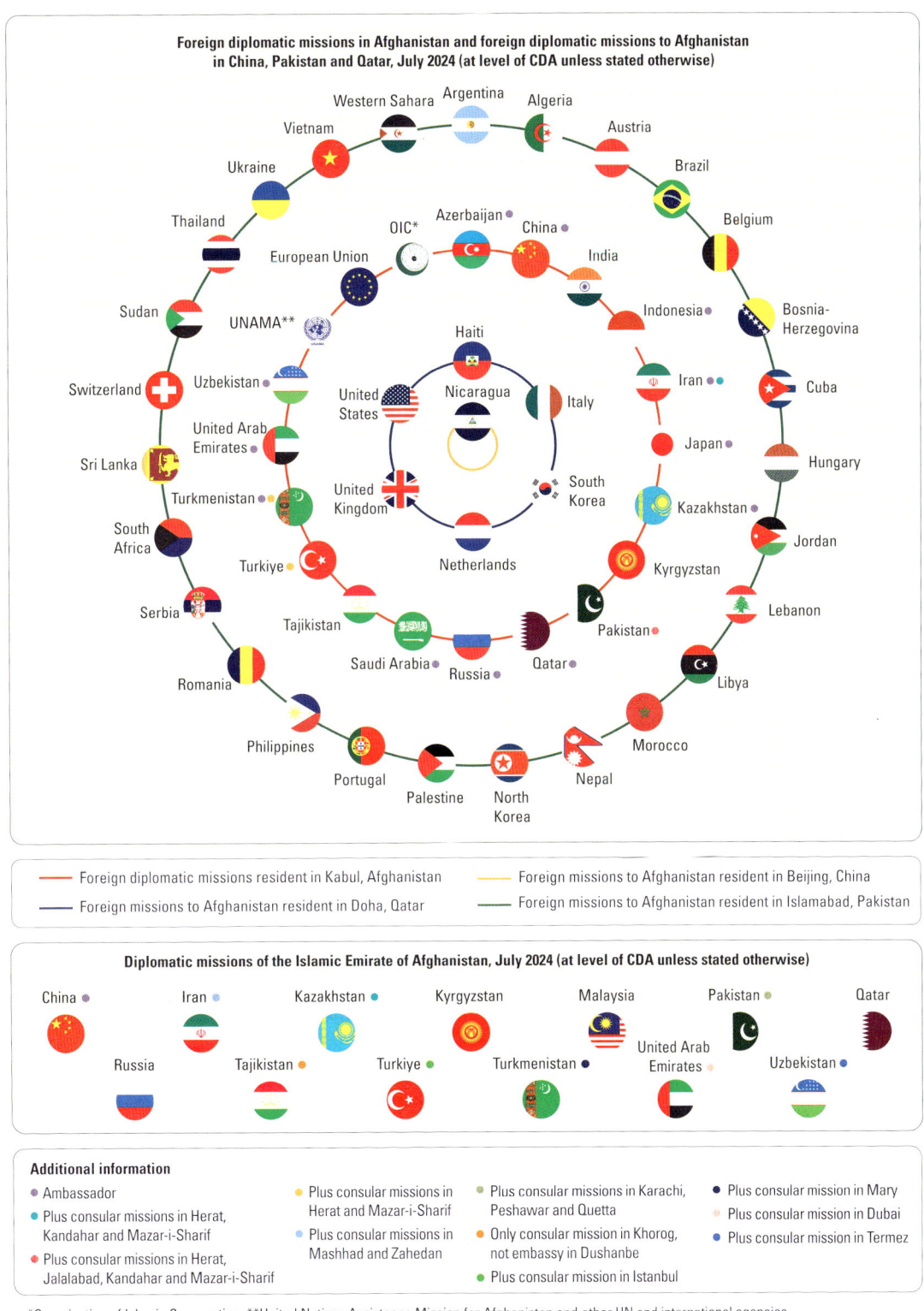

Figure 1: Afghanistan's diplomatic relations

forms of discrimination, with particular reference to women and minorities; identifying mechanisms for ensuring justice, equality and equity, including in the geographical distribution of resources and assets; balancing international and regional security concerns; and identifying an approach towards a larger and public national dialogue and reconciliation process.

To be successful, this approach would require informal outreach to the Taliban leaders based in both Kandahar and Kabul to ensure the participation of Taliban officials and influential representatives. The right mix of non-Taliban Afghans from various ethnic backgrounds including the Pashtuns, Tajiks, Hazara and Uzbeks, as well as women, in such dialogues will need to be sensitively crafted. Influential international independent think tanks may be the most credible entities to facilitate such small, private and strictly confidential dialogues.

Notes

[1] World Food Programme, 'Annual Country Report 2023: Afghanistan', 2023; and World Bank Group, 'World Bank Survey: Living Conditions Remain Dire for the Afghan People', 22 November 2022.

[2] Special Inspector General for Afghanistan Reconstruction, 'Cash Shipments to Afghanistan: The UN Has Purchased and Transported More than $2.9 Billion to Afghanistan to Implement Humanitarian Assistance', January 2024, p. 6.

[3] UN Security Council (UNSC), 'Report of the Independent Assessment Pursuant to Security Council Resolution 2679 (2023)', S/2023/856, 9 November 2023; and UNSC, 'Resolution 2721 (2023) Adopted by the Security Council at Its 9521st Meeting, on 29 December 2023', S/RES/2721, 29 December 2023.

[4] This includes Afghan–Uzbek Abdul Salam Hanafi (acting second deputy prime minister) and Afghan–Tajik Abdul Rahman Rashid (acting minister for agriculture), Qari Fasihuddin (chief of staff of the armed forces), Din Mohammad Hanif (acting minister of economy), Nooruddin Aziz (acting minister of industry and commerce) and two ethnic Hazara acting deputy ministers in the central government in Kabul.

[5] Including talks between a Taliban delegation (led by acting Minister of Foreign Affairs Amir Khan Muttaqi) and Afghan civil-society representatives on 23 January 2022 in Oslo, Norway.

[6] 'Deputy Foreign Minister Calls for Girls' Education', Tolo News, 22 May 2022.

[7] Sanchita Bhattacharya, 'IS-KP: Potent Challenger', *South Asia Intelligence Review*, vol. 22, no. 46, 6 May 2024.

[8] '3,000 Anti-terrorist Operations Conducted in 2023: Islamic Emirate', Tolo News, 6 January 2024.

[9] 'Nearly 15,000 Counter-narcotics Operations in 2023: MoI', Tolo News, 1 January 2024.

[10] From 5,624.5 tonnes produced in 2022 to 302 tn in 2023. UNODC, 'Afghanistan Opium Survey 2023', 2023, p. 3.

[11] UNODC, 'Understanding Illegal Methamphetamine Manufacture in Afghanistan', August 2023, p. 7.

[12] 'Taliban Trade Delegation Announces $35m Investment in Iran', Iran International, 27 February 2024.

Regional Spotlight: Asia

AFGHANISTAN

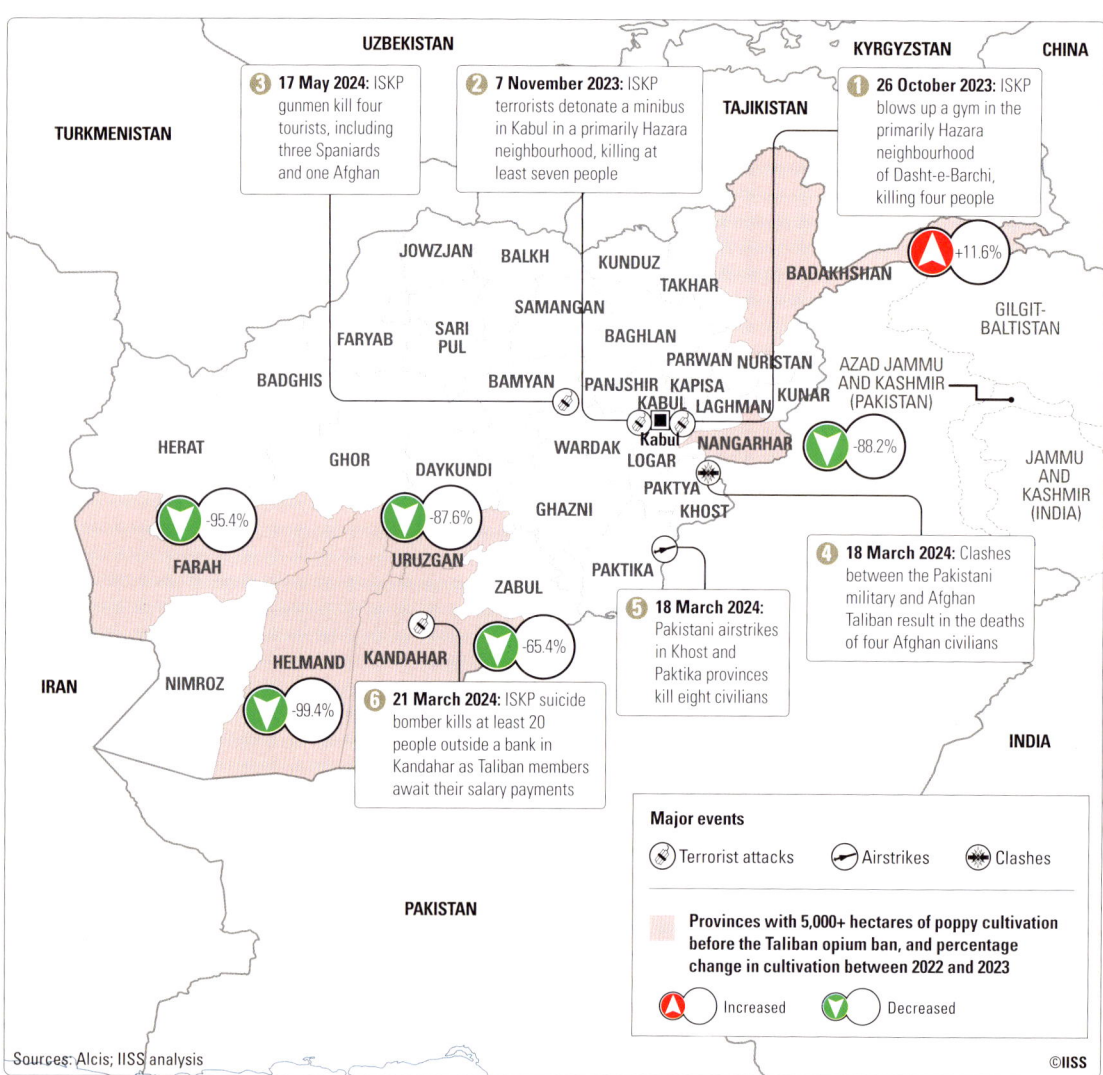

Conflict Overview

Afghanistan has experienced multiple wars across the last four decades, including the 1979–89 Soviet–Afghan War and 1992–96 Afghan Civil War, during which the Taliban consolidated its power. The most recent conflict began with the United States' invasion in October 2001, which initiated two decades of fighting between the Taliban, Afghan security forces and a US-led international coalition.

The original aim of the US invasion was to destroy al-Qaeda, but this later expanded to overthrowing the entire Taliban regime. The Bonn Conference in December 2001 laid the groundwork for a new Afghan government and led to the creation of the International Security Assistance Force to support the newly formed Afghan National Defence and Security Forces (ANDSF). The ensuing US-led counter-insurgency peaked in 2010–11, and in 2014 foreign forces' offensive combat operations ostensibly concluded. The ANDSF took control, but it remained dependent on US air support, funding

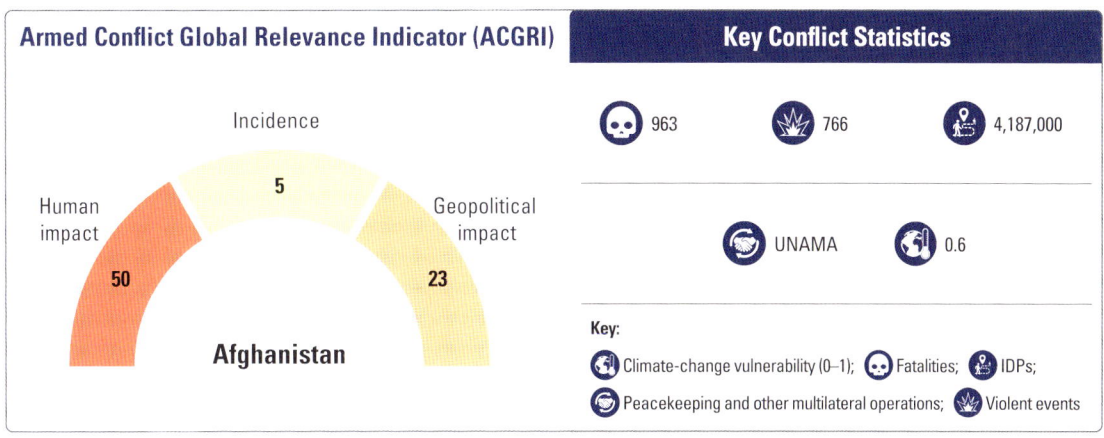

Conflict(s)	Type	Start date
Localised insurgency against the Taliban	I IC LI	2021
Islamist-led armed violence	I T	2021

Key: **I** Internal; **I IC LI** Internal: intercommunal & localised insurgency; **T** Transnational

and technical expertise, and the Taliban gradually contested more districts.

Former US president Donald Trump (2017–21) appointed Zalmay Khalilzad as the US special representative for Afghanistan reconciliation in September 2018 to negotiate an agreement with the Taliban for an acceptable US military withdrawal. The resulting agreement, signed on 29 February 2020, called for a prisoner release, the gradual reduction of US forces and the removal of US and United Nations sanctions. In exchange, the Taliban agreed to participate in intra-Afghan negotiations, work towards a ceasefire, and prevent any group from using Afghanistan to threaten the US or its allies; but the negotiations produced no results. The Taliban made rapid gains throughout the summer as US troops withdrew, and on 15 August 2021, the Taliban entered Kabul without any armed resistance. The last US soldier left Afghanistan on 30 August 2021, after a two-week evacuation effort.

Three years after seizing power in August 2021, the Afghan Taliban maintains firm control over Afghanistan without facing any substantial threats to its rule and territorial control. While it continues to experience attacks by the Islamic State Khorasan Province (ISKP), it has so far prevented the group from holding any territory. Despite this, and although China has accepted a Taliban envoy and sent a Chinese ambassador to Kabul, the Taliban has not received formal recognition from any nation. It now prioritises enhancing trade and connectivity with neighbouring countries and the Middle East over seeking international legitimacy.

Although the country has managed to avert widespread famine and complete economic collapse in the last several years, Afghanistan's long-term economic prospects remain bleak. The Taliban's policies regarding civil liberties and women's rights also continue to be deeply concerning, showing few signs of improvement.

Conflict Update

The reduction in violence that followed the Taliban's assumption of power in 2021 continued throughout the reporting period. The Taliban maintained its control over the government, preventing any competing armed groups from seizing Afghan territory. Despite this stability, ISKP continued to pose a threat in the form of terrorism and targeted attacks against Taliban members and civilians, particularly the Hazara community. On 13 October 2023, an ISKP suicide bombing at a Shia mosque in northern Afghanistan claimed the lives of at least seven individuals and injured 15 others.[1] The threat posed by ISKP also extends beyond Afghanistan. In July 2023, for instance, an ISKP suicide bomber killed over 50 people at a rally of the major Islamist party Jamiat Ulema-e-Islam Fazl (JUI-F) in Pakistan.[2] Several planned attacks were disrupted in continental Europe throughout the reporting period, and there was one successful attack on a concert hall in Russia in March 2024.

The Tehrik-e-Taliban Pakistan (TTP), commonly known as the Pakistani Taliban, also continued to take refuge in Afghanistan, while escalating its campaign against Pakistan's security forces. The Pakistani government holds the Afghan Taliban partly responsible for this increase in violence since 2022, due to the Taliban's ideological influence over the TTP and the sanctuary it has provided. Pakistan therefore continued to send senior diplomatic, military and religious delegations to Afghanistan to persuade the group to adopt more moderate social policies and to curb the TTP. This included Fazl-ur-Rehman, leader of the JUI-F, who became one of the few non-Afghan politicians to meet with Afghan Taliban Emir Mullah Hibbatullah Akhundzada. Significantly, Rehman was educated at the same madrassa in northwestern Pakistan (Darul Uloom Haqqania) as many senior Afghan Taliban leaders and is well regarded by the group. In February 2024, following Rehman's January visit, the Taliban's foreign ministry issued a statement condemning the July 2023 ISKP attack on JUI-F. Despite Pakistan's formal and informal outreach to the Afghan Taliban, however, the group still insists that the TTP is an internal problem of Pakistan and that it is not responsible for curbing the TTP's insurgency.

Meanwhile, Taliban officials continued to engage with the international community, but did not receive formal recognition. The Taliban has especially prioritised engagement with neighbouring countries such as Iran and focused on discussions related to trade and transportation. Mullah Abdul Ghani Baradar, the acting deputy prime minister, is dedicated to developing Afghanistan's economic sustainability without relying on foreign aid. He aims to diversify the country's trade relationships, especially to reduce dependence on Pakistan for trade. On issues of terrorism and women's rights, however, cabinet-level officials are widely viewed as messengers between Akhundzada and the outside world, rather than decision-makers.

The Taliban's poppy ban announced in April 2022 continued to hold and by 2023 satellite imagery showed a 99% decrease in poppy cultivation in Helmand province, Afghanistan's main poppy-growing area.[3] A sharp decline continued into the second year of the ban in the 14 provinces that had accounted for 92% of the country's poppy cultivation in 2022.[4] However, the ban has been less effective in Badakhshan and concerns remain that it could worsen the economy and increase migration, possibly leading communities in southwestern Afghanistan to return to poppy cultivation.

In January 2024, the Taliban rejected United Nations Security Council (UNSC) Resolution 2721, which called for a UN special representative for Afghanistan, claiming it is unnecessary since Afghanistan is not engaged in any conflict. Then, on 17 February 2024, national and regional envoys to Afghanistan gathered in Doha for a UN meeting to discuss enhancing engagement with Afghanistan, but the Taliban chose not to participate. Relations with the international community, especially the West, remain strained due to such actions and the Taliban's strict measures against women. In July 2023, the Taliban banned women's beauty parlours, which had been one of the few remaining public spaces where Afghan women could gather freely. When some women protested this decision, they faced firehoses, tasers and aerial gunfire. The Taliban has also shown no significant signs of movement towards reopening girls' secondary education or permitting women to pursue university studies.

Significantly, in the first week of July 2024, the third instalment of the Doha process, known as Doha III, took place in Doha, Qatar. This meeting involved representatives from the Taliban and special envoys to Afghanistan from various countries. The discussions centred on economic issues, human rights (including women's rights), prisoner exchanges and security. However, it remains uncertain whether the talks will result in any significant progress or breakthroughs on these matters.

Conflict Parties

The Taliban (Islamic Emirate of Afghanistan or de facto government of Afghanistan post-August 2021)

Strength: Reportedly 172,000 active military personnel and 210,000 police. The Taliban has announced plans to expand its regular armed forces to 200,000 personnel in 2025.[5]

Areas of operation: Deployed throughout Afghanistan with activity concentrated in Baghlan, Kabul, Nangarhar, Panjshir and along the border with Pakistan.

Leadership: Mullah Hibbatullah Akhundzada (emir), Mullah Mohammad Yaqoob (defence minister), Mullah Fazal Mazloom (deputy defence minister), Qari Fasihuddin (chief of staff of the armed forces), Haji Mali Khan (deputy chief of staff of the armed forces), Amanuddin Mansour (commander of the air force) and Abdul Haq Wasiq (intelligence director). Sirajuddin Haqqani (interior minister) maintains significant influence over security matters and effectively controls security in Kabul.

Structure: A mix of formal ministries and informal insurgency-era units in the process of shifting towards a formal military structure. The organisation is historically polycentric, but power is increasingly concentrated in the hands of Akhundzada and his inner circle in Kandahar.

History: The Taliban (translated as 'the students') movement began in the Afghan refugee camps of Pakistan following the 1979 Soviet invasion and occupation of Afghanistan. Under Mullah Mohammad Omar, the group entered the Afghan Civil War in 1994 and captured Kandahar city. Taliban fighters quickly conquered other areas of Afghanistan and the group officially ruled as an Islamic emirate from 1996–2001, though it never controlled the whole country. The Taliban seized control over the entire country in August 2021 following the withdrawal of US troops.

Objectives: Maintain territorial control and security; disarm all non-Taliban citizens; stifle any dissent; and fight ISKP.

Opponents: ISKP and various anti-Taliban resistance groups that are typically organised along ethnic lines.

Affiliates/allies: Has connections of varying formality with non-state armed groups in South Asia, including al-Qaeda, the Islamic Movement of Uzbekistan, the Turkistan Islamic Party and the TTP.

Resources/capabilities: Estimated US$2.2 billion annually.[6]

Islamic State Khorasan Province (ISKP)

Strength: 1,000–3,000 primarily in Afghanistan and Pakistan (estimate).[7]

Areas of operation: Primarily confined to Nangarhar province in eastern Afghanistan but able to carry out complex attacks in Kabul and present in nearly all provinces.

Leadership: Led by Sanaullah Ghafari (alias 'Shahab al-Muhajir'). The original leader, Hafiz Saeed Khan (previously head of the TTP Orakzai faction), was killed in a US drone strike in July 2016. Successive leaders were also either killed in US strikes or arrested.

Structure: An Islamist militant organisation, formally affiliated with the larger Islamic State (ISIS), of which it is the Central and South Asia branch.

History: Formed and pledged loyalty to then-ISIS leader Abu Bakr al-Baghdadi in October 2014. The initial membership primarily comprised disgruntled and estranged TTP members.

Objectives: Similar to ISIS, ISKP maintains both local and global ambitions to establish a caliphate in Central and South Asia to be governed under a strict Islamic system, modelled after the group's own interpretation of a caliphate.

Opponents: Mainly focuses on fighting the de facto Taliban government, attacking the Hazara ethnic minority which is also primarily Shia, and targeting foreign diplomats and officials.

Affiliates/allies: ISIS.

Resources/capabilities: Since its founding in 2014, ISIS has invested in improving ISKP's organisation and capabilities. However, with the decline of its territory in Iraq and Syria, ISIS has fewer resources to invest in foreign networks and therefore its investment in the group has declined. ISKP relies on small arms, improvised explosive devices (IEDs) and vehicle-borne IEDs.

Al-Qaeda

Strength: 200 fighters in Afghanistan and the surrounding region.[8]

Areas of operation: The mountainous region between Afghanistan and Pakistan, and potentially Kabul. Al-Qaeda is resident in at least 15 Afghan provinces, primarily in the eastern, southern and southeastern regions.[9]

Leadership: Saif al-Adel assumed leadership of al-Qaeda following the July 2022 drone strike that killed Ayman al-Zawahiri. He is believed to be based in Iran.

Structure: Below Adel and his immediate advisers, the group maintains a *shura* (consultation) council and committees for communications, finance and military operations.

History: Created as a broad alliance structure by Arab fighters who travelled to Afghanistan and Pakistan to fight against the Soviet invasion in the 1980s. The organisation (officially formed in 1988) was initially led by Osama bin Laden, who envisioned it as a base for a global jihadist movement to train operatives and to support other jihadist organisations. The group was responsible for several high-profile terrorist attacks against the US, including the the 9/11 attacks. Bin Laden was killed in a US special-operations raid in Abbottabad, Pakistan, in 2011. Zawahiri, who had led the group since 2011, was killed in an apartment in Kabul by a US drone strike on 31 July 2022.

Al-Qaeda

Objectives: Focus has always been to fight the 'far enemy' (the West), particularly the US, which supports current Middle Eastern regimes, and bring about Islamist governance in the Muslim world. Its affiliate groups often pursue local objectives independent of the goals and strategy of the central organisation.

Opponents: US and other Western and regional countries supporting non-Islamic regimes.

Affiliates/allies: Currently maintains an affiliation with five groups: al-Qaeda in the Islamic Maghreb in North Africa, al-Qaeda in the Arabian Peninsula in Yemen, al-Qaeda in the Indian Subcontinent in South Asia, Jabhat Fateh al-Sham (formerly Jabhat al-Nusra or Al-Nusra Front) in Syria and al-Shabaab in Somalia. As of early 2024, it maintains a strong relationship with the Afghan Taliban but lacks the ability to conduct transnational attacks.

Resources/capabilities: Capable of engaging in complex terrorist attacks on hard and soft targets. It has also provided military advice to the Afghan Taliban.

Anti-Taliban resistance groups

Strength: Unclear.

Areas of operation: Primarily in Panjshir province and Andarab district, Baghlan province. The senior leadership is primarily located outside of Afghanistan.

Leadership: Ahmad Massoud, Amrullah Saleh and others.

Structure: Militia, including former ANDSF soldiers.

History: After the collapse of the ANDSF in August 2021 and the flight of most prominent anti-Taliban warlords, a group of former Afghan commandos retreated to Panjshir to continue fighting. The Taliban ultimately took control of Panjshir, but resistance groups began to coalesce and reorganise inside Afghanistan and abroad, including the National Resistance Front (NRF), organised by Massoud and Saleh, the Afghanistan Freedom Front, the Afghanistan Islamist National and Liberation Movement, and the Unknown Soldiers of Hazaristan. On 11 April 2023, the Taliban reportedly killed eight members of the NRF, including a prominent commander, Akmal Amir.[10]

Objectives: Liberate key areas of Afghanistan and ultimately remove the Taliban from power in Afghanistan.

Opponents: Taliban.

Affiliates/allies: Unclear, but seeking support from the US, European countries and some regional countries.

Resources/capabilities: Unclear.

Other relevant parties

The Pakistan Armed Forces and Pakistan's police force are regularly targeted by the TTP. Pakistan's relationship with the Afghan Taliban has become increasingly strained due to the Taliban's support of the TTP. There were several exchanges of small-arms fire and artillery between the Pakistan Armed Forces and the TTP along the border during the reporting period. Pakistan holds the Afghan Taliban responsible for the TTP's actions, while the Afghan Taliban dismisses such actions as an internal Pakistani matter.

Notes

[1] Mohammad Yunus Yawar, 'Suicide Bombing at Shi'ite Mosque Kills Seven in Northern Afghanistan, Official Says', Reuters, 13 October 2023.

[2] Abid Hussain, 'Attacks in Pakistan Buttressed by Region's "Militant" Landscape: Analysts', Al-Jazeera, 2 August 2023.

[3] Alcis, 'Unprecedented Reduction of Opium Production in Afghanistan', 2023.

[4] David Mansfield, 'Sowing the Seeds of Division in Badakhshan?', Alcis, 29 July 2024.

[5] These figures are speculative and largely based on Taliban statements. Special Inspector General for Afghanistan Reconstruction (SIGAR), 'Quarterly Report to the United States Congress', 30 April 2024, p. 59; and SIGAR (@SIGARHQ), post on X, 16 May 2024.

[6] BTI Transformation Index, 'Afghanistan's Outlook: Under Taliban Rule, the Economy Slumps as Taxation Income Rises', 15 August 2023; and World Bank Group, 'The World Bank in Afghanistan', 18 April 2024.

[7] UNSC, 'Sixteenth Report of the Secretary-General on the Threat Posed by ISIL (Da'esh) to International Peace and Security and the Range of United Nations Efforts in Support of Member States in Countering the Threat', S/2023/76, 1 February 2023, p. 8.

[8] US Department of Defense, 'Lead Inspector General Report to the United States Congress: Operation Enduring Sentinel and Other U.S. Government Activities Related to Afghanistan: January 1, 2024–March 31, 2024', May 2024, p. 9.

[9] UNSC, 'Twelfth Report of the Analytical Support and Sanctions Monitoring Team Submitted Pursuant to Resolution 2557 (2020) Concerning the Taliban and Other Associated Individuals and Entities Constituting a Threat to the Peace Stability and Security of Afghanistan', S/2021/486, 1 June 2021, p. 12.

[10] Ayaz Gul, 'Taliban Raid Kills 8 Afghan Opposition Fighters', VOA, 11 April 2023.

PAKISTAN

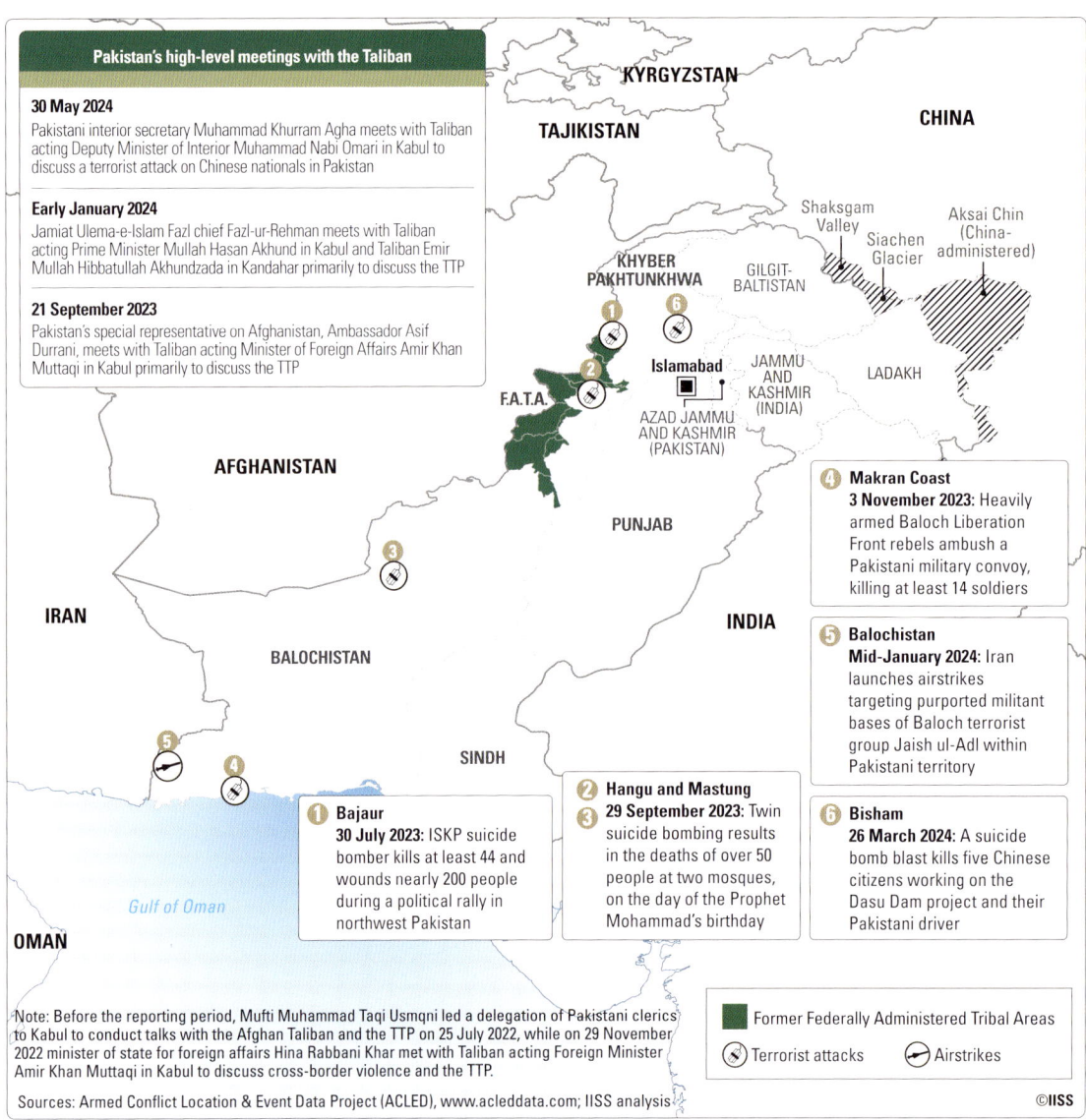

Conflict Overview

Pakistan has experienced ethnic and centre–province tensions resulting from the perceived marginalisation of the Baloch, Pashtuns and Sindhis by the Punjabi majority since gaining independence in 1947. The 1971 secession of East Pakistan to form Bangladesh made Punjab the country's majority province in terms of population and increased these tensions.[1] The mass migrations that followed British India's partition also enflamed ethnic unrest as Urdu-speaking migrants, or Mohajirs, emigrated from contemporary northern India to Sindh province in Pakistan. This means that conflicts in Pakistan sometimes conflate demands for increased civil liberties and provincial autonomy with violent separatist insurgent movements, primarily in Balochistan and Khyber Pakhtunkhwa (KP). Terrorist groups and violent separatist and insurgent

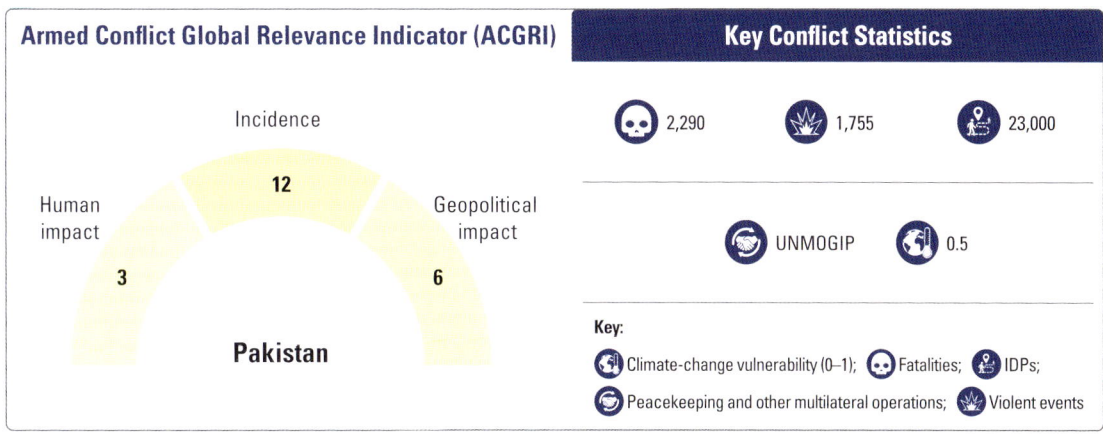

ACGRI pillars: IISS calculation based on multiple sources for 2023 and 2024 (scale: 0–100), except for some cases according to data availability. See Notes on Methodology and Data Appendix for all variables and further details on Key Conflict Statistics.

Conflict(s)	Type	Start date
Baloch insurgency in Balochistan and Karachi	I LI T	Restarted in 2003
Militant Islamist insurgency in KP and the former FATA	I IC LI T	2001

Key: **I IC LI** Internal: intercommunal & localised insurgency; **I LI** Internal: localised insurgency; **T** Transnational

movements capitalise on underlying ethnic and economic agitation to stoke tensions.

The Baloch insurgency has fought the state for greater autonomy or the secession of Balochistan by waging campaigns in 1948, 1958, 1962 and 1973. The return to violence in 2003 launched the phase of the insurgency that continues today. Baloch armed groups have fragmented on numerous occasions and some splinter organisations have demobilised. Several of these groups set aside some of their differences in 2018 to form a coalition under the banner of the Baloch Raaji Ajoi Sangar (BRAS). The BRAS began to splinter in late April 2023, but one of its members, the Baloch Liberation Army (BLA), continues to pose the most significant threat to the Pakistani state in Balochistan and Karachi. The BLA also threatens Pakistan's key relationship with China as it targets Chinese nationals.

Groups originating in KP and Pashtun tribal areas (formerly known as the Federally Administered Tribal Areas, or FATA) have also fought against the state and the Shia religious minority since 2001. Increased Pakistani incursions into the then FATA targeting al-Qaeda members raised tensions following the 9/11 terrorist attacks. Militant groups coalesced to form the Tehrik-e-Taliban Pakistan (TTP), also commonly known as the Pakistani Taliban. The TTP's attack on the Army Public School in Peshawar in December 2014 led the government to formulate the National Action Plan, its first counter-terrorism policy. Subsequent operations in 2014 and 2017 led to a noticeable decline in TTP attacks, but these have steadily increased again since 2021. Pakistan's efforts to engage diplomatically with the Afghan Taliban, which is believed to provide support to and influence the TTP, have been unsuccessful in curtailing the group. Additionally, neither Pakistani airstrikes within Afghanistan nor ground military operations in northwestern Pakistan have proven effective in eradicating the threat.

Conflict Update

Pakistan's security situation continued to deteriorate throughout the reporting period, with the TTP inflicting significant casualties on Pakistani security forces. Despite reportedly providing ongoing support and sanctuary to the TTP, the Afghan Taliban persisted in downplaying TTP violence as an internal Pakistani issue. In October 2023, the Pakistani government announced a plan to expel undocumented foreigners, including an estimated 1.7 million Afghan refugees, starting that November.[2] The move was intended to appease anti-refugee sentiment and force the Afghan Taliban to pressurise the TTP by curtailing the remittances sent by Afghans living in Pakistan.

In the first week of July 2024, the third instalment of the Doha process took place in Doha, Qatar. Pakistan's special representative on Afghanistan, Asif Durrani, met with Taliban officials, and both sides expressed hopes for positive relations. Around the same time, Pakistan announced a new counter-terrorism campaign, *Operation Azm-e-Istehkam* (Resolve for Stability), aimed at combating the TTP, and Pakistani Defence Minister Khawaja Asif pledged to continue attacks inside Afghanistan.

Meanwhile, throughout the reporting period, Baloch separatist groups and the Islamic State Khorasan Province (ISKP) continued to carry out acts of terrorism and fuel tensions between Iran and Pakistan. On 26 March 2024, an unclaimed suicide-bomb blast in northwest Pakistan killed five Chinese workers (and their Pakistani driver) who were working on the Dasu Dam project, targeting Islamabad's close ties with Beijing.[3] In mid-January, tensions rose along the border between Pakistan's Balochistan province and Iran when the latter launched airstrikes targeting purported militant bases within Pakistan. Islamabad retaliated with airstrikes on alleged military hideouts in Iran, but diplomatic exchanges managed to de-escalate the situation. Then, on 4 April 2024, the Baloch terrorist group Jaish ul-Adl conducted a large-scale attack on the Chabahar seaport in Iran.

On 12 July 2023, the IMF approved an essential US$3 billion bailout deal to bolster Pakistan's economic-stabilisation programme and prevent Pakistan from defaulting on its debt repayments.[4] One year later, on 12 July 2024, Pakistan and the IMF reached a staff-level agreement on a comprehensive US$7bn bailout, set to last for 37 months.[5] However, without significant reforms to Pakistan's tax structure, enforcement of tax collection, and management of government salaries and pensions, as well as improvements in productivity and increases in foreign direct investment, Pakistan will likely require further assistance, which it is not guaranteed to receive.

Economic troubles and violence perpetrated by non-state armed groups took place against a backdrop of political turmoil. From August 2023–February 2024, former prime minister Imran Khan (2018–22) was charged with multiple criminal offences for which he is currently serving concurrent sentences. Khan's supporters claim that his arrest and sentencings were politically motivated, aimed at preventing his return to power.

The Pakistan Muslim League–Nawaz (PML–N) party and its leader, former prime minister Nawaz Sharif, have capitalised on Khan's rift with Pakistan's military establishment and his legal troubles. On 21 October, Sharif returned to Pakistan after four years in self-imposed exile, announcing his readiness to lead his party in the upcoming elections. In January 2024, Pakistan's Supreme Court denied an attempt by Khan's Pakistan Tehreek-e-Insaf (PTI) party to keep its electoral symbol, a cricket bat, which posed another setback in a country with high illiteracy rates and where voters often rely on symbols to identify candidates on the ballot. The PTI responded by employing innovative tactics like online political rallies to mobilise voters.

Voting for a new parliament began on 8 February 2024 amid strict security measures, though the process faced allegations of electoral violence and interference. Initially, the PTI seemed to lead nationwide by a significant margin, but as the official public reporting of final results was withheld and margins diminished, the PML–N emerged with a majority of seats. Shehbaz Sharif, the brother of the PML–N's leader and former prime minister Nawaz Sharif, was declared prime minister amid both domestic and international accusations of election interference by the country's powerful military.

Tensions along the Line of Control (LoC) with India, meanwhile, remained relatively calm, largely due to a ceasefire that went into effect in February 2021. The PML–N even expressed a willingness to resume dialogue over trading with India. This move was likely aimed at satisfying merchants in Pakistan's Punjab province, who stand to benefit from increased trade, and at addressing Pakistan's economic challenges. India, however, is unlikely to agree to this.

Conflict Parties

Pakistan Armed Forces

Strength: 660,000 active military.

Areas of operation: Deployed throughout Pakistan (particularly along the LoC with India) and in Balochistan and KP, including the former FATA, along the border with Afghanistan.

Leadership: President Asif Ali Zardari (commander-in-chief), Gen. Sahir Shamshad Mirza (chairman of the joint chiefs of staff committee), Gen. Syed Asim Munir (chief of army staff), Adm. Naveed Ashraf (chief of naval staff), Air Chief Marshal Zaheer Ahmed Baber Sidhu (chief of air staff) and Lt-Gen. Nadeem Anjum (director general, Inter-Services Intelligence, or ISI). ISI falls outside the military command structure, but its leaders are drawn from the military and have significant oversight over some operations.

Structure: Two (XI and XII) of the army's nine corps are stationed in KP and Balochistan respectively. *Operation Raad-ul-Fasaad* involves an array of military units that support the police and the paramilitary Civil Armed Forces (CAF) in counter-terrorism operations. *Operation Azm-e-Istehkam* was announced in June 2024.

History: The ongoing *Operation Raad-ul-Fasaad* succeeded the 2014–17 *Operation Zarb-e-Azb*. It was launched in response to a resurgence in attacks by TTP splinter group Jamaat-ul-Ahrar. *Operation Khyber-4* was launched in 2017 under *Operation Raad-ul-Fasaad* to eliminate terrorists in what is now Rajgal valley, Khyber district.

Objectives: Eliminate insurgent groups that threaten the Pakistani state; control or eliminate the TTP; ensure border security with Afghanistan; and guard the LoC and the China–Pakistan Economic Corridor.

Opponents: TTP, ISKP, BLA and other Baloch separatist groups, and Indian Armed Forces. The Pakistan Armed Forces' relationship with the Afghan Taliban is increasingly strained due to the group's support for the TTP.

Affiliates/allies: CAF, Pakistani police and anti-India armed groups based in Pakistani-administered Azad Jammu and Kashmir.

Resources/capabilities: Well resourced with an array of weapons systems and equipment. The defence budget for 2023 was US$7.9bn, and it is US$8.5bn for 2024.

Civil Armed Forces (CAF)

Strength: Estimated 180,000 paramilitary personnel (85,000 Frontier Corps, 50,000 Pakistan Rangers, 30,000 Frontier Constabulary and 15,000 Coast Guard and Gilgit-Baltistan Scouts).

Areas of operation: Throughout Pakistan, but most active fighting is against insurgent groups in Balochistan and KP.

Leadership: Various. Founded by the Interior Ministry, although most divisions are commanded by officers seconded from the Pakistan Armed Forces.

Structure: The main divisions of the CAF involved in conflict with insurgent groups and participating in the military-led *Operation Raad-ul-Fasaad* are the four Frontier Corps (Frontier Corps KP North, KP South, Balochistan North and Balochistan South), the Frontier Constabulary, the Sindh Rangers and the Punjab Rangers. Each group's authority is limited to its respective geographic area.

History: Contributed to *Operation Raad-ul-Fasaad* since its commencement in 2017 and to the army's 34th Light Infantry Division (Special Security Division) since 2016.

Objectives: Eliminate insurgent groups that threaten the Pakistani state, and provide additional security in tribal areas and major urban areas.

Opponents: TTP, ISKP, and BLA and other Baloch separatist groups.

Affiliates/allies: Pakistan Armed Forces and Pakistani police.

Resources/capabilities: Primarily equipped with small arms and light weapons, with some shorter-range artillery and mortars.

Tehrik-e-Taliban Pakistan (TTP)

Strength: Circa 4,000–6,000 in Afghanistan, where the majority of TTP fighters are currently based.[6] The TTP's strength in Pakistan is unclear, although recent analysis suggests there may be several thousand fighters in the country.

Areas of operation: Balochistan and KP.

Leadership: Mufti Noor Wali Mehsud (emir and overarching leader), supported by a central *shura* (consultation) council.

Structure: Divided by locality into factions, or constituencies, each of which is led by a local emir and supported by a local *shura* council, which reports to the central *shura* council. Each faction has a *qazi* (judge) to adjudicate local disputes.

History: In 2007, some factions of militant groups in Pakistan's tribal areas unified as the TTP under the leadership of Baitullah Mehsud, who was killed in a US airstrike in 2009. A TTP *shura* council elected Hakimullah Mehsud as the organisation's second emir, but internal divisions grew under his leadership over legitimate targets for attacks and peace talks with the government. The divisions later worsened under Fazal Hayat (Mullah Fazlullah) and caused several factions to break away, including leaders who formed ISKP in 2014. The 2014 TTP attack on the Army Public School in Peshawar triggered a debilitating Pakistan Armed Forces counter-offensive. Following Hayat's death in 2018, the leadership reverted to the Mehsud clan under Mufti Noor Wali Mehsud, who sought to reunite and rebuild the group. Noor Wali Mehsud reiterated his allegiance to the Afghan Taliban's leadership following the latter's takeover of Afghanistan and began to target Pakistan soldiers and police.

Tehrik-e-Taliban Pakistan (TTP)

Objectives: Defend and promote a rigid Islamist ideology in KP, including in the former FATA.

Opponents: Pakistan Armed Forces and CAF.

Affiliates/allies: Afghan Taliban, al-Qaeda and occasionally ISKP.

Resources/capabilities: Has access to small arms and improvised explosive devices (IEDs).

Baloch Raaji Ajoi Sangar (BRAS, an alliance that includes the Balochistan Liberation Army, BLA; the Baloch Republican Army, BRA; and the Baloch Liberation Front, BLF)

Strength: Unclear.

Areas of operation: Balochistan and Karachi.

Leadership: BLA: leadership contested between Hyrbyair Marri and Bashar Zaib. BRA: Brahumdagh Bugti. BLF: Allah Nazar Baloch.

Structure: The BRAS is an alliance of the BLA, BRA and BLF. Pakistan's government alleges that several factions of the BLA exist and are led by different individuals. The insurgency is deeply divided, with different groups, infighting and fragmentation. The BRAS reportedly began to splinter in April 2023 due to the arrest of Baloch Nationalist Army senior leader Gulzar Imam Shambay.

History: The alliance was formed in 2018. The BLA is the largest group and was formed in 2000 under the leadership of Afghanistan-based Balach Marri, who was subsequently killed in an airstrike in Helmand in 2007. Its leadership since then has been subject to additional deaths and significant internal contestation. In July 2019, the United States Department of State listed the BLA as a Specially Designated Global Terrorist.

Objectives: Seeks independence for the region of Balochistan as a solution to perceived discrimination against the Baloch people. The alliance opposes the extraction of natural resources in Balochistan by Pakistani and foreign actors, especially China, due to the implications of the China–Pakistan Economic Corridor for Baloch aspirations.

Opponents: Pakistan Armed Forces and CAF.

Affiliates/allies: None formally, but the Pakistani state has accused it of periodically working with Indian intelligence and the TTP.

Resources/capabilities: Attacks by BRAS members have involved small arms and IEDs, including suicide vests and car bombs.

Islamic State Khorasan Province (ISKP)

Strength: 1,000–3,000 primarily in Afghanistan and Pakistan (estimate).[7]

Areas of operation: Balochistan, KP and Afghanistan.

Leadership: Led by Sanaullah Ghafari (alias 'Shahab al-Muhajir'). The original leader, Hafiz Saeed Khan (previously head of the TTP Orakzai faction), was killed in a US drone strike in July 2016. Successive leaders were also either killed in US strikes or arrested.

Structure: An Islamist militant organisation, formally affiliated with the larger Islamic State (ISIS), of which it is the Central and South Asia branch.

History: Formed and pledged loyalty to then-ISIS leader Abu Bakr al-Baghdadi in October 2014. The initial membership primarily comprised disgruntled and estranged TTP members.

Objectives: Similar to ISIS, ISKP maintains both local and global ambitions to establish a caliphate in Central and South Asia to be governed under a strict Islamic system, modelled after the group's own interpretation of a caliphate.

Opponents: Mainly focuses on fighting the Pakistan Armed Forces and CAF in Pakistan, but also targets Shia religious sites.

Affiliates/allies: ISIS.

Resources/capabilities: Since its founding in 2014, ISIS has invested in improving ISKP's organisation and capabilities. However, with the decline of its territory in Iraq and Syria, ISIS has fewer resources to invest in foreign networks and therefore its investment in the group has declined. ISKP relies on small arms, IEDs and vehicle-borne IEDs.

Al-Qaeda

Strength: 200 fighters in Afghanistan and the surrounding region.[8]

Areas of operation: The mountainous region between Afghanistan and Pakistan, and potentially Kabul. Al-Qaeda is resident in at least 15 Afghan provinces, primarily in the eastern, southern and southeastern regions.[9] Some al-Qaeda cells are believed to be present in Pakistan and the group may attempt to use its refuge in Afghanistan to plan attacks on soft targets inside Pakistan, including Western embassies.

Leadership: Saif al-Adel assumed leadership of al-Qaeda following the July 2022 drone strike that killed Ayman al-Zawahiri. He is believed to be based in Iran.

Structure: Below Adel and his immediate advisers, the group maintains a *shura* council and committees for communications, finance and military operations.

History: Created as a broad alliance structure by Arab fighters who travelled to Afghanistan and Pakistan to fight against the Soviet invasion in the 1980s. The organisation (officially formed in 1988) was initially led by Osama bin Laden, who envisioned it as a base for a global jihadist movement to train operatives and to support other jihadist organisations. The group was responsible for several high-profile terrorist attacks against the US, including the 9/11 attacks. Bin Laden was killed in a US special-operations raid in Abbottabad, Pakistan, in 2011.

Al-Qaeda

Zawahiri, who had led the group since 2011, was killed in an apartment in Kabul by a US drone strike on 31 July 2022.

Objectives: Focus has always been to fight the 'far enemy' (the West), particularly the US, which supports current Middle Eastern regimes, and bring about Islamist governance in the Muslim world. Its affiliate groups often pursue local objectives independent of the goals and strategy of the central organisation.

Opponents: US and other Western and regional countries supporting non-Islamic regimes.

Affiliates/allies: Currently maintains an affiliation with five groups: al-Qaeda in the Islamic Maghreb in North Africa, al-Qaeda in the Arabian Peninsula in Yemen, al-Qaeda in the Indian Subcontinent in South Asia, Jabhat Fateh al-Sham (formerly Jabhat al-Nusra or Al-Nusra Front) in Syria and al-Shabaab in Somalia. As of early 2024, it maintains a strong relationship with the Afghan Taliban but lacks the ability to conduct transnational attacks.

Resources/capabilities: Capable of engaging in complex terrorist attacks on hard and soft targets. It has also provided military advice to the Afghan Taliban.

Other relevant parties

Occasional instances of artillery and small-arms fire occurred between the Afghan Taliban and Pakistani troops during the reporting period. The TTP has pledged allegiance to the Afghan Taliban's emir and has links to the group through ideology, family ties and resources. Some analysts view the TTP as an extension of the Afghan Taliban. Although there are differences in objectives between the Afghan Taliban and the TTP, the latter is undoubtedly supported and protected by the Afghan Taliban.

Notes

[1] Michael Kugelman and Adam Weinstein, 'In Pakistan, a Tale of Two Very Different Political Movements', *Lawfare*, 4 January 2021.

[2] Munir Ahmed and Riaz Khan, 'Pakistan Announces Big Crackdown on Migrants in the Country Illegally, Including 1.7 Million Afghans', AP News, 4 October 2023.

[3] Sophia Saifi and Nectar Gan, 'Chinese Workers Killed in Suicide Bomb Blast as Pakistan Grapples With Attacks on Beijing's Interests', CNN, 27 March 2024.

[4] Munir Ahmed, 'IMF Approves Much-awaited $3 Billion Bailout for Pakistan, Saving It From Defaulting on Debt', AP News, 12 July 2023.

[5] IMF, 'Pakistan: IMF Reaches Staff-Level Agreement on Economic Policies With Pakistan for 37-month Extended Fund Facility', 12 July 2024.

[6] United Nations Security Council (UNSC), 'Fourteenth Report of the Analytical Support and Sanctions Monitoring Team Submitted Pursuant to Resolution 2665 (2022) Concerning the Taliban and Other Associated Individuals and Entities Constituting a Threat to the Peace Stability and Security of Afghanistan', S/2023/370, 1 June 2023, p. 17; Asfandyar Mir, 'Afghanistan's Terrorism Challenge: The Political Trajectories of al-Qaeda, the Afghan Taliban, and the Islamic State', Middle East Institute, 20 October 2020; US Department of Defense Office of Inspector General, 'Operation Freedom's Sentinel: Lead Inspector General Report to the United States Congress', 21 May 2019, p. 25; and Daud Khattak, 'The Pakistan Taliban Is Back', *Diplomat*, 9 March 2021.

[7] UNSC, 'Sixteenth Report of the Secretary-General on the Threat Posed by ISIL (Da'esh) to International Peace and Security and the Range of United Nations Efforts in Support of Member States in Countering the Threat', S/2023/76, 1 February 2023, p. 8.

[8] US Department of Defense, 'Lead Inspector General Report to the United States Congress: Operation Enduring Sentinel and Other U.S. Government Activities Related to Afghanistan: January 1, 2024–March 31, 2024', May 2024, p. 9.

[9] UNSC, 'Twelfth Report of the Analytical Support and Sanctions Monitoring Team Submitted Pursuant to Resolution 2557 (2020) Concerning the Taliban and Other Associated Individuals and Entities Constituting a Threat to the Peace Stability and Security of Afghanistan', S/2021/486, 1 June 2021, p. 12.

KASHMIR

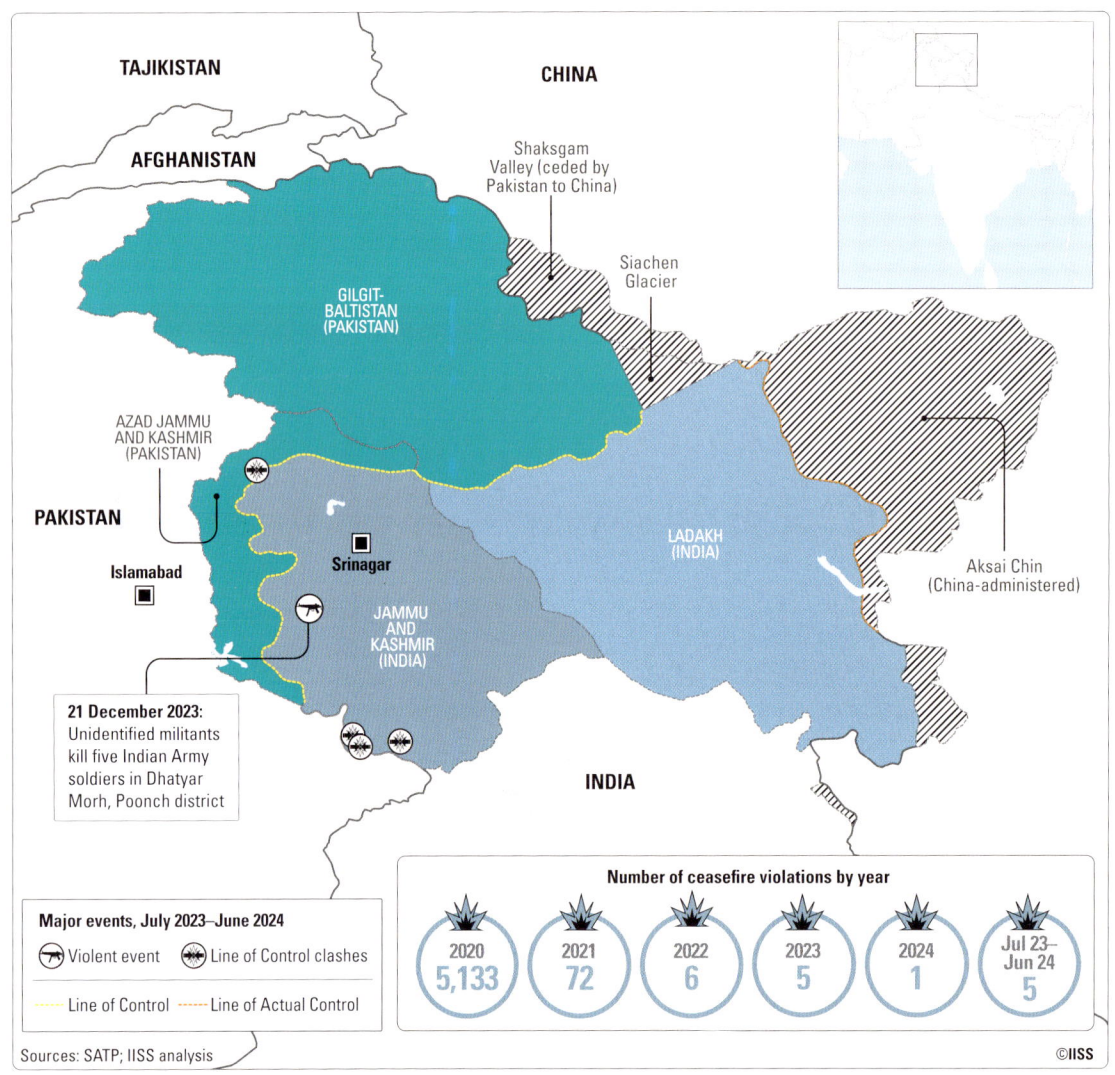

Conflict Overview

The conflict in the former Muslim-majority princely state of Jammu and Kashmir erupted following the partition of India in August 1947. Immediately after, Muslim rebels seized Poonch in Jammu province and declared an 'Azad' (free) government, while thousands of militants crossed the border from Pakistan in an attempt to remove Jammu and Kashmir's Hindu Maharaja. Amid this growing crisis, the Maharaja provisionally acceded to the Indian Union, resulting in the Indo-Pakistani War of 1947–48 over Kashmir. A United Nations-brokered ceasefire in January 1949 divided Jammu and Kashmir into Indian-administered Jammu and Kashmir (J&K) and Pakistani-administered Azad Jammu and Kashmir (AJ&K). The conflict was effectively frozen until the Indo-Pakistani War of 1965, which resulted in a stalemate.

In 1987, widespread perceptions that the Jammu and Kashmir legislative-assembly elections were rigged sparked a mass mobilisation against the Indian government. The initially indigenous,

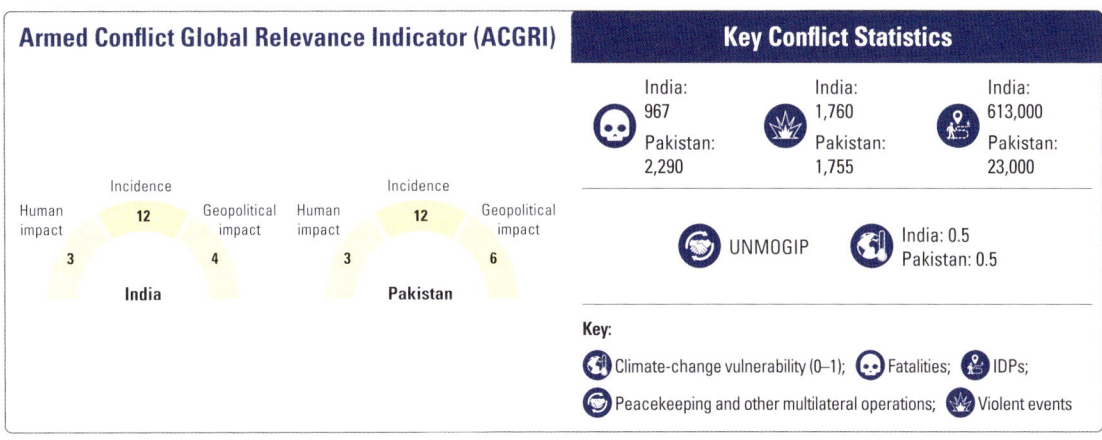

ACGRI pillars: IISS calculation based on multiple sources for 2023 and 2024 (scale: 0–100), except for some cases according to data availability. See Notes on Methodology and Data Appendix for all variables and further details on Key Conflict Statistics.

Conflict(s)	Type	Start date
Bilateral tensions between India and Pakistan over disputed territory	I-S	1947
Localised insurgency against Indian rule	II	1947

Key: II Internationalised internal; I-S Inter-state

pro-independence movement was led by the Jammu Kashmir Liberation Front (JKLF), but it was gradually supplanted by pro-Pakistani factions seeking incorporation into Pakistan, such as the Hizbul Mujahideen (HM), which absorbed large numbers of foreign fighters into the insurgency. In 1990, the Indian state imposed direct rule over J&K, deployed large numbers of security forces and introduced the Armed Forces Special Powers Act, leading to aggressive counter-insurgency operations against Kashmiri militants throughout the following decade. Talks between India and Pakistan from 1997–2008 reduced violence levels within Indian-administered Kashmir and along the Line of Control (LoC) separating the Indian and Pakistani regions, but they did not result in any substantive peace agreements. Between 2008 and 2016, three large uprisings took place in the Kashmir Valley, partly fuelled by social media and combining elements of civil unrest and low-level insurgency. In August 2019, India's ruling Bharatiya Janata Party (BJP) revoked Article 370 of the Indian constitution, which guaranteed J&K's special autonomous status.[1] This split the region into two centrally controlled 'Union Territories': Jammu and Kashmir, and Ladakh. Since 2020, the BJP has started to loosen residency, employment and voting restrictions that previously favoured indigenous Kashmiris. Following increased violence across the LoC in 2019–20, India and Pakistan signed a ceasefire agreement in February 2021.

Conflict Update

On 11 December 2023, the Supreme Court of India upheld the government's decision to withdraw Article 370 of the Indian constitution. Despite this politically sensitive decision, internal insurgency-related violence within J&K itself decreased during the reporting period, with fatalities dropping from 135 to 123 year-on-year.[2] A number of serious incidents did occur; on 21 December, for example, unidentified militants killed five army soldiers in Poonch district, and on 9 June 2024, militants from The Resistance Front (TRF), an offshoot of Lashkar-e-Taiba (LeT), fired on a bus of Hindu pilgrims, resulting in the deaths of nine civilians.[3] However, these incidents were not widespread. This was likely a reflection of the relatively small number of militants active within the state itself, with only about 100 militants suspected to be active as of June 2024.[4] These low levels of insurgent violence are closely linked to the largely enduring ceasefire along the LoC between India and Pakistan. There were only five cross-border clashes during the reporting period, marking a significant reduction from the 5,133 incidents reported during 2020 and indeed even from the 27 reported in 2022.[5]

The continued quiet likely also reflects Pakistan's current position of weakness vis-à-vis India. In April 2023, a senior Pakistani journalist quoted former Pakistan Army chief Qamar Javed Bajwa as having said that the Pakistan Army is not in a position to fight India and thus should seek peace and a deal regarding Kashmir. His replacement, General Syed Asim Munir, did take a firmer stance in January 2024, stating that 'India has not reconciled with the concept of Pakistan [as a state; therefore,] how can we reconcile with it'.[6]

Despite this harsher tone, there were no real escalations or major violations of the ceasefire arrangements following Munir's statement. Instead, Pakistan continued to grapple with serious internal conflicts, particularly those with Balochistan separatists and Tehrik-e-Taliban Pakistan militants. This forced its attention away from Kashmir towards its western borders with Iran and Afghanistan, where militants from these conflicts have sought sanctuary. During 2023, there were 1,533 terrorism- and counter-terrorism-related fatalities in Pakistan, with the majority of these fatalities occurring in Khyber Pakhtunkhwa and Balochistan.[7] Indeed, domestic political pressures and a deepening economic crisis have forced the new Pakistani government to convey its 'serious intent' to rejuvenate trade relations with India – another factor that is likely to keep ceasefire violations and support for cross-border militant incursions at a low level.[8]

For much of the reporting period, India had little reason to intensify its operations beyond the core task of containing local insurgents. Holding the G20 presidency throughout much of 2023, the country sought to bolster Kashmir's image as an emerging site of normalcy by hosting a May 2023 working group there, while also focusing on military build-ups vis-à-vis China on its northern border. That being said, J&K held one general election during the period 19 April–20 May 2024. The polling took place without any major escalations in violence; conflict-related fatalities during April (seven) and May (seven) remained below the 2023 monthly average (11), and no major boycotts were issued by Kashmiri armed groups.[9] Reflecting this improved situation, J&K registered a higher local turnout of 39% in districts such as Srinagar in the Kashmir Valley, which had previously boycotted the elections.[10] While the BJP claimed this was a vindication of its policy of abrogating Article 370, others have suggested that the increased turnout may reflect intensified opposition to the BJP in the Kashmir Valley since 2019. Indeed, the BJP did not contest the two Kashmir Valley seats, which were won by the Jammu and Kashmir National Conference (a member of the wider, Indian National Congress-led Indian National Developmental Inclusive Alliance), although it won the two seats in Jammu.

A series of armed clashes then took place after the elections in June 2024, resulting in the deaths of nine civilians, 11 militants and one member of the security forces.[11] This revived level of insurgent activity took place in the Jammu region, reflecting a strategic shift away from the well-defended Kashmir Valley to capitalise on the Indian government's redeployment of troops from Jammu to Ladakh. As of June 2024, the Indian government had started to intensify its counter-insurgency efforts in Jammu in response to this trend. The upcoming state-assembly elections (to be held by 30 September 2024) will probably see increased political mobilisation in the Kashmir Valley, which militants may attempt to exploit alongside seeking to disrupt the elections themselves.

Conflict Parties

Indian Armed Forces

Strength: At least 318,000 Indian security personnel in J&K. This includes approximately 130,000 army soldiers; 45,000 infantry troops within the Rashtriya Rifles (RR), the special counter-insurgency unit; 60,000 paramilitary personnel of the Central Reserve Police Force (CRPF), as well as battalions of the Border Security Force, Indo-Tibetan Border Police, Sashastra Seema Bal and Central Industrial Security Force; and around 83,000 personnel from the J&K Police (JKP).[12]

Indian Armed Forces

Areas of operation: All districts of J&K and along the LoC. The CRPF's Jammu and Kashmir Zone Srinagar Sector covers Budgam, Ganderbal and Srinagar districts; its Kashmir Operations Sector covers Anantnag, Awantipora and Baramulla districts; and its Jammu Sector covers the Jammu region.

Leadership: Indian troops in the region are primarily under the Northern Command based in Udhampur (J&K) and led by Lt-Gen. M.V. Suchindra Kumar. The CRPF, the primary paramilitary force, is under the Ministry of Home Affairs. A special director general has overall command of the CRPF in J&K, while inspectors general command the respective sectors.

Structure: The Northern Command has four assigned corps headquarters, controlling nine infantry divisions and several independent brigades. The XV Corps, with its headquarters in Srinagar, has operational command of the Kashmir Valley. The RR is organised into five division-sized counter-insurgency forces, with four deployed in J&K and one deployed in Ladakh.

History: A heavy troop presence has been maintained along the LoC since 1949. Thousands of troops were used to crush an anti-India armed rebellion in the late 1980s. Initially, paramilitary and regular army troops fought the Pakistan-backed insurgents. The RR was introduced in 1994 and coordinates with other security agencies including the Special Operations Group, a JKP counter-insurgency unit.

Objectives: Border defence and counter-insurgency.

Opponents: HM, LeT, Jaysh-e-Mohammad (JeM), TRF, Ansar Ghazwat-ul-Hind, Al-Badr and Pakistan Armed Forces.

Affiliates/allies: Village Defence Guards, volunteer state-armed groups concentrated in hilly and border areas with sizeable Hindu populations (Doda, Kathua, Kishtwar, Poonch, Rajouri, Ramban and Reasi districts).

Resources/capabilities: Ministry of Defence and Ministry of Home Affairs budgetary funds; voluntary donations through the National Defence Fund, the Army Central Welfare Fund and the Armed Forces Battle Casualties Welfare Fund; voluntary web-based public donations through portals such as 'Bharat Ke Veer' (India's Bravehearts); and government contracts under *Operation Sadbhavana*.

Pakistan Armed Forces

Strength: In total, 660,000 active military personnel. Elements of the Rawalpindi-based X Corps as well as paramilitary and local forces are deployed in AJ&K; their strength is believed to be approximately 125,000.

Areas of operation: All districts of AJ&K and along the LoC.

Leadership: Pakistani troops in the region are under the I and X Corps of the Pakistan Army. The I Corps headquarters is based in Mangla Cantonment (Pakistan) and the X Corps headquarters is based in Rawalpindi (Pakistan). The Mujahid Force, a paramilitary unit, is headquartered in Bhimber (AJ&K) and works under the National Guard of Pakistan, which is controlled and commanded by the chief of army staff based in General Headquarters in Rawalpindi.

Structure: The X Corps consists of four infantry divisions, attached independent brigades and the division-sized Force Command Northern Areas, which operates in the Gilgit-Baltistan area. The I Corps is composed of two infantry divisions, an armoured division and attached independent brigades.

History: Pakistan has maintained a heavy troop presence along the LoC since 1949. The Azad Army, an anti-Maharaja militia composed of ex-servicemen of the British Indian Army, captured the main districts of Muzaffarabad and Mirpur before the Pakistan Army officially entered Jammu and Kashmir in May 1948 to take control and consolidate the territorial gains. The Pakistan Army has not faced any insurgency within AJ&K. Its operations are directed at Indian forces and the LoC.

Objectives: Guard the LoC and China–Pakistan Economic Corridor.

Opponents: Indian Armed Forces.

Affiliates/allies: Anti-India armed groups based in AJ&K.

Resources/capabilities: Ministry of Defence budgetary funds, arms exports, government contracts and commercial ventures under army-controlled charitable foundations, such as the Fauji Foundation, Army Welfare Trust, Shaheen Foundation and Bahria Foundation.

Hizbul Mujahideen (HM)

Strength: The number of members in J&K and AJ&K is unclear. A broader network of supporters and sympathisers also support the main organisation on both sides of the LoC.

Areas of operation: Concentrated in Anantnag, Kulgam, Pulwama and Shopian districts, with a marginal presence in northern Kashmir districts.

Leadership: Mohammad Yusuf Shah (alias 'Syed Salahuddin').

Structure: Headquarters in Muzaffarabad, AJ&K. Cadres comprise mostly local Kashmiris who receive rudimentary arms training from senior members. Divisional commanders work under a semi-autonomous structure but also receive instructions on both sides of the LoC via satellite communication and encrypted messaging apps.

History: An indigenous armed group with a pro-Pakistan ideology, HM was founded in September 1989 by Mohammad Ahsan Dar, a former member of the pro-independence organisation JKLF. (The JKLF was an affiliate of Jamaat-e-Islami, a pro-Pakistan religio-political organisation in J&K). Many JKLF members joined HM after 1994, when the former suffered heavy losses and voluntarily quit the armed conflict to pursue non-violent means. HM recruitment of local

Hizbul Mujahideen (HM)

Kashmiri youth also surged after the death of its young commander Burhan Muzaffar Wani in July 2016. Despite suffering heavy losses between 2017 and 2020, HM survived by procuring funds and weapons locally.

Objectives: Dislodge Indian rule in Kashmir and merge the region with Pakistan through a war of attrition. The group has stated that it would support a negotiated settlement through dialogue under certain circumstances.

Opponents: Indian government and security forces.

Affiliates/allies: LeT, JeM and TRF.

Resources/capabilities: Resources, including weapons and improvised explosive devices, are procured locally by associates and sympathisers. Funding is provided by charities, mosque-based donations across Pakistan and the Pakistani military establishment.

Lashkar-e-Taiba (LeT)

Strength: Unclear.

Areas of operation: Across the Kashmir Valley, mostly active in the northern districts of Baramulla, Bandipora and Kupwara.

Leadership: Hafiz Muhammad Saeed. Overall command is in the hands of a divisional commander, who is often a non-Kashmiri. Mohammad Yusuf Dar (alias 'Yusuf Kantroo'), killed in 2022, was the last 'operational head' of the group in the Kashmir Valley.

Structure: Headquarters in Muridke, Punjab province, Pakistan. Valley-based cadres are mostly Pakistani nationals working under district commanders and trained in camps.

History: Pakistan-based cleric Saeed, who also heads the missionary organisation Jamaat-ud-Dawa (JuD), founded LeT in the late 1980s. Since LeT entered Kashmir in the early 1990s, it has carried out several deadly attacks against the Indian Armed Forces and political workers. Despite losing its commanders in quick succession since the 2017 launch of the Indian Army's *Operation All Out*, the group has survived and has recruited increasing numbers of local youth, particularly in the last four years.

Objectives: Merge Kashmir with Pakistan.

Opponents: Indian government.

Affiliates/allies: HM, JeM, TRF and Al-Badr. Though banned by the Pakistani government in 2002, LeT is believed to maintain connections to Pakistani intelligence agencies.

Resources/capabilities: Fundraising through charities in Pakistan (e.g., JuD and Falah-e-Insaniyat), which receive government and public contributions, and social networks in Pakistan and Afghanistan. Funds are also raised through the collection and selling of sacrificial-animal skins on Eid.

Jaysh-e-Mohammad (JeM)

Strength: Unclear.

Areas of operation: Southern Kashmir.

Leadership: Maulana Mohammad Masood Azhar Alvi is the group's founder and leader.

Structure: Headquartered in Bahawalpur, Punjab province, Pakistan, the group's members are mostly Pakistanis. Divisional commanders work under the chief operational commander based in Kashmir.

History: Founded by Pakistani Masood Azhar in 2000, JeM entered Kashmir in the early 2000s and introduced suicide attacks. The Pakistani government banned the group in 2002. After a period of dormancy, JeM re-emerged in 2017 with an attack on a paramilitary camp in Pulwama.

Objectives: Merge Kashmir with Pakistan.

Opponents: Indian government.

Affiliates/allies: HM and LeT. The group is believed to have ties to the Taliban in Afghanistan.

Resources/capabilities: The most powerful insurgent group in Kashmir, with highly trained cadres and better resources than other groups. Fundraising is done through seminaries, mosques (e.g., Binori Town Mosque) and charities in Pakistan (e.g., Al Rashid Trust) and donation appeals published in magazines and pamphlets. Money is also raised through legal businesses operating in Pakistan and funds allegedly received from political (e.g., Jamiat Ulema-e-Islam) and other militant organisations in Pakistan.

The Resistance Front (TRF)

Strength: Unclear.

Areas of operation: Has carried out attacks in northern, central and southern districts of Kashmir Valley.

Leadership: No central leadership. Mohammad Abbas Sheikh, who was killed in August 2021, was the last known leader of the group.

Structure: Composite organisation without a defined structure. The JKP claims that TRF is a hybrid militant outfit composed of cadres from existing armed groups such as LeT and HM. TRF militants killed by Indian security forces and arrested TRF sympathisers have been identified as native Kashmiris.

History: Founded after the abrogation of Article 370 in August 2019, TRF started by lobbing grenades in Srinagar in late 2019. The group has used social media to publish statements and claim attacks. The Indian government declared it a terrorist organisation in January 2023.

The Resistance Front (TRF)

Objectives: Dislodge Indian rule in Kashmir and violently deter settlers from mainland India.

Opponents: Indian government.

Affiliates/allies: India in January 2023 declared it a 'proxy' of LeT and banned it along with LeT.

Resources/capabilities: The JKP claims that TRF uses a broader network of supporters and sympathisers who are not formally part of the group – and do not feature in police records – to carry out some targeted killings. These are called 'hybrid militants' in Indian security forces parlance.

United Nations Military Observer Group in India and Pakistan (UNMOGIP)

Strength: 40 experts on mission from countries including the Philippines, South Korea, Croatia, Thailand, Argentine, Mexico, Switzerland, Italy, Romania and Sweden (in descending order of troop numbers), as well as 68 civilian staff.[13]

Areas of operation: UN field stations: six based in AJ&K and four based in J&K. The Sialkot field station in Pakistan monitors the working boundary, which is the international border between Punjab province, Pakistan, and the disputed territory of Jammu and Kashmir.

Leadership: Rear Admiral Guillermo Pablo Ríos (chief military observer and head of mission) and George E. Scheibner (chief of mission support).

Structure: UNMOGIP is mandated by UN Security Council (UNSC) Resolution 91. Headquarters alternates between Islamabad in November–April and Srinagar in May–October.

History: The UN Commission for India and Pakistan (UNCIP) was created under UNSC Resolution 39 in 1948. In January 1949, the first team of unarmed military observers arrived to supervise the ceasefire between India and Pakistan. UNMOGIP replaced UNCIP under Resolution 91 of March 1951. After Resolution 307 in 1971, India and Pakistan made minor adjustments to the ceasefire line and in 1972 established the LoC to be supervised by UN military observers.

Objectives: Monitor, investigate and report ceasefire violations as a neutral observer along the 770-kilometre LoC and working boundary between India and Pakistan. It also receives petitions from political groups within Kashmir on the situation at the LoC and submits findings to India, Pakistan and the UN secretary-general.

Opponents: N/A.

Affiliates/allies: N/A.

Resources/capabilities: Funding through UN regular budget: estimated US$10.52 million.[14]

Notes

[1] When referring to developments before 15 August 2019, the acronym 'J&K' refers to the state of Jammu and Kashmir (including Kashmir, Jammu and Ladakh regions, which India controls). For developments after the abrogation of Article 370 and the bifurcation of J&K in 2019, J&K refers to the Union Territory of Jammu and Kashmir (including Jammu and Kashmir regions, which India controls).

[2] 'Yearly Fatalities', Datasheet – Jammu & Kashmir, South Asia Terrorism Portal (SATP).

[3] Wire Staff, 'Five Army Soldiers Killed in Anti-militancy Operation in J&K's Poonch', Wire, 22 December 2023; and 'Why the Terror Attack in J&K's Reasi That Killed 9 Pilgrims Poses New Security Concerns', Firstpost, 10 June 2024.

[4] Hakeem Irfan Rashid and Rahul Tripathi, 'Jammu Region Witnesses 29 Terrorist Attacks Since 2021', Economic Times, 17 June 2024.

[5] 'Jammu & Kashmir: Timeline (Terrorist Activities) – 2024', SATP.

[6] 'COAS Sets Out Foreign Policy Redlines', Express Tribune, 25 January 2024.

[7] Center for Research & Security Studies, 'Annual Security Report 2023 | Pakistan', February 2024.

[8] 'Why Pakistan's New Government Wants to Reopen Trade Routes with India Now?', Economic Times, 25 March 2024.

[9] 'Yearly Fatalities', Datasheet – Jammu & Kashmir, SATP.

[10] 'LS Polls: 39% Voting Recorded by Displaced Kashmiri Pandits in Srinagar', Business Standard, 14 May 2024.

[11] 'Amit Shah Chairs High-level Meeting, Directs Agencies to Implement Area Domination, Zero-terror Plans in Jammu', Economic Times, 17 June 2024; and 'Yearly Fatalities', Datasheet – Jammu & Kashmir, SATP.

[12] Anushka Vats, 'Centre Plans to Replace Indian Army with CRPF in Kashmir Valley; Withdrawal to Be Done in Phased Manner', English Jagran, 20 February 2023; and Zulfikar Majid, 'No Final Call by Centre on Removal of Army from Kashmir Valley', Deccan Herald, 23 February 2023.

[13] Numbers as of February 2024. UN Peacekeeping, 'UNMOGIP Fact Sheet'.

[14] Estimated from the January 2021–December 2021 approved budget. Ibid.

MYANMAR

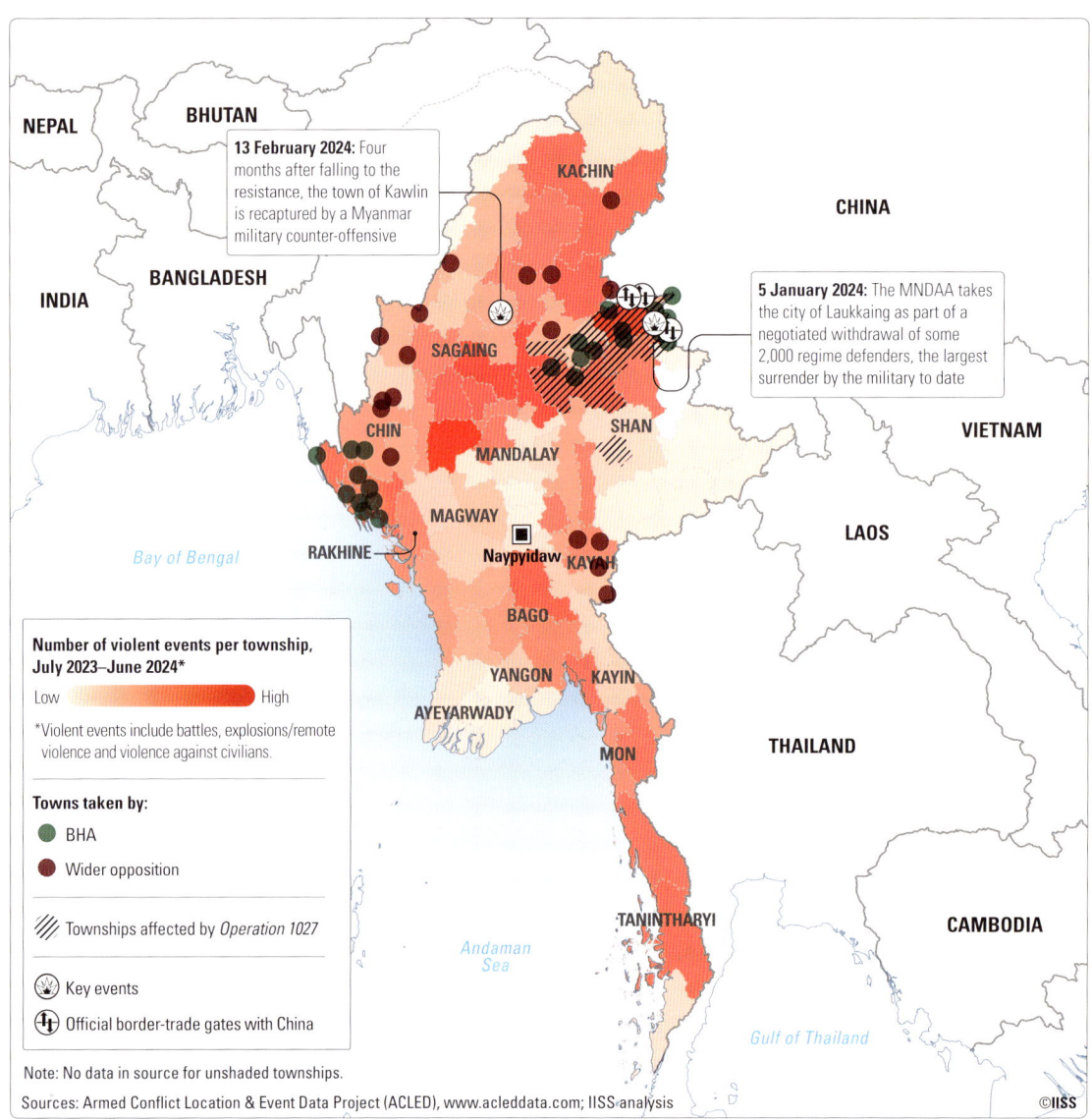

Conflict Overview

Myanmar has suffered from persistent ethnic and political conflicts since gaining independence from Britain in 1948. In the borderlands, where ethnic minorities reside, various non-state armed groups have fought for greater autonomy against central regimes dominated by the Bamar majority. Between 1948 and 1989, the Communist Party of Burma (CPB) waged a potent insurgency against the central government, but the conflict ended when the party fractured along ethnic lines.

In addition to conflicts between the centre and periphery, Myanmar's history has been marked by a struggle between opposing Bamar elites over the role of the military in national politics. This led to severe political infighting in the immediate post-independence period, which took a turn in 1962, when

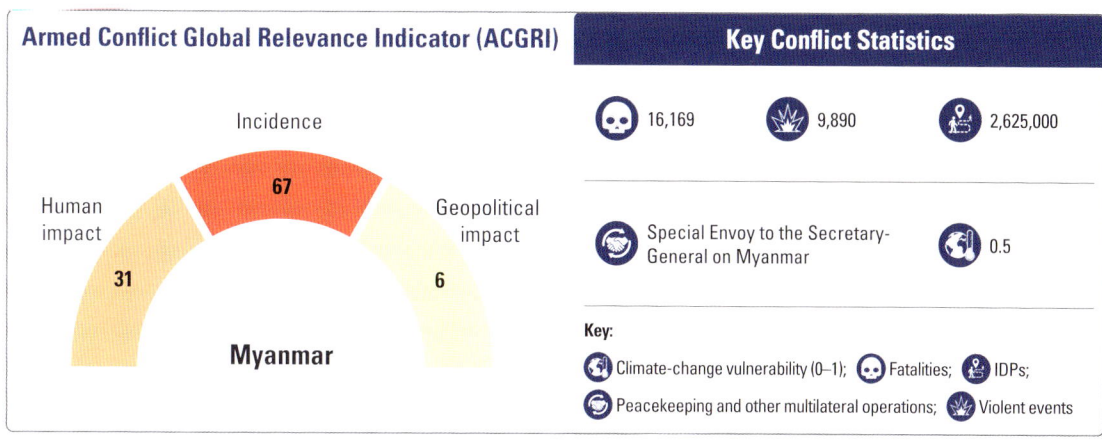

Conflict(s)	Type	Start date
Anti-junta uprising	I	2021
Ethnic insurgency for self-determination	I LI	1948

Key: I Internal; I LI Internal: localised insurgency

the Myanmar armed forces under General Ne Win staged a *coup d'état*. A popular uprising in 1988 gave rise to Aung San Suu Kyi and her National League for Democracy (NLD), which led a non-violent opposition movement over the next two decades.

Seeking to shake its status as an international pariah and modernise its army, the then-ruling military junta enacted a new constitution in 2008, setting the country on a transition path towards a quasi-democracy. It also began a peace process, which culminated in the signing of the Nationwide Ceasefire Agreement (NCA) in 2015. That same year, the NLD won elections by a landslide and entered into a power-sharing agreement with the military, which had retained 25% of the seats in parliament for itself.[1] The next five years, however, were marked by a deadlock in the peace process, escalating conflicts in the northeast and west, and fraught civil–military relations.

Unnerved by the NLD's growing power, the army manufactured a crisis over the 2020 elections, which the NLD had won, and staged a *coup d'état* on 1 February 2021, taking power as the State Administration Council (SAC). The widespread protests that followed were violently suppressed, leading to the emergence of a new generation of resistance groups, which came to be known as the People's Defence Force (PDF). Outraged by the military's behaviour, several key ethnic armies abandoned their ceasefires to renew armed struggle, leading to the worst violence seen in the country since the Second World War.

Conflict Update

After nearly three years of stalemate, the trajectory of the conflict between Myanmar's military junta and resistance forces shifted suddenly in October 2023 when the Brotherhood Alliance (BHA), a powerful tripartite alliance of ethnic armed organisations (EAOs), abandoned an informal ceasefire and launched a major coordinated offensive dubbed *Operation 1027*. By June 2024, the campaign had expelled regime forces from swathes of territory in Rakhine and northern Shan states. The sudden escalation resulted in an additional 1.2 million people being displaced between June 2023 and June 2024.[2]

Inspired by the success of *Operation 1027*, other opposition groups stepped up attacks throughout the country and began to challenge the regime from the periphery. The rebel offensives – albeit uncoordinated – resulted in the regime losing control in parts of Chin, Kachin, Kayah and Kayin states. These humiliating losses generated significant dissatisfaction within the army, raising the possibility of an internal schism. Though weakened, the regime has managed to halt opposition advances in the centre of the country, and it continues to control the state apparatus, major population centres, ports, industrial bases and supply chains. It remains the most powerful actor in the conflict, possessing considerable reserves of firepower and the support of numerous militias, which have helped it maintain, or in some cases even reverse, its losses. Significantly, in February 2024, the regime began enforcing a controversial conscription law to draft an additional 60,000 soldiers.[3]

The reporting period saw increased diplomatic involvement from China, which mediated at least six rounds of talks between the BHA and the SAC (Tatmadaw), the third of which led to a ceasefire announced on 12 January 2024, although this largely broke down on 25 June 2024. It is believed that the BHA's initial attacks to eliminate the growing cyber-scam industry originating from northeast Myanmar targeting Chinese civilians had been tacitly supported by China in a move against the SAC, which had been unwilling to crack down on the industry. Although China's peacemaking efforts have failed to fully contain the fighting, its ability to influence an array of conflict actors in Myanmar illustrates its capacity to shape the trajectory of the wider war. This contrasts sharply with Western nations' reluctance to provide substantial support beyond aid and diplomatic gestures to the insurgency. In March 2024, for instance, the United States appropriated US$121m in non-lethal aid to the resistance movement under the Burma Unified through Rigorous Military Accountability Act for the first time since the act's passage in December 2022.[4]

Meanwhile, the Association of Southeast Asian Nations (ASEAN) has remained committed to its Five Point Consensus. During its 2023 tenure as chair, Indonesia conducted 'quiet diplomacy', engaging with relevant stakeholders over 180 times, although it admitted to making no progress.[5] Under Laos's chairmanship in 2024, the junta finally agreed to send 'non-political' representatives to ASEAN events.[6] It had previously declined this invitation after taking offence at the exclusion of the SAC chair and senior government officials from ASEAN events in 2021. Thailand has also increased its engagement in Myanmar since the start of 2024, unveiling plans to set up a humanitarian corridor along their shared border.

While elections planned by the SAC have been viewed as a potential resolution by some regional actors, they now appear unlikely. Many initial promises by the regime to ensure speedy and fair elections – for instance, to hold polls by August 2023 and for coverage to extend nationwide – have been largely abandoned. In January 2024, the SAC relaxed several participation requirements for political parties, and in February 2024, the regime again extended the state of emergency by six months, effectively delaying potential elections until at least 2025. Some military leaders have even suggested holding a 'by-election' instead.

Conflict Parties

State Administration Council (SAC) (Myanmar armed forces or Tatmadaw)

Strength: 100,000–300,000 active military personnel (estimate). Combat operations are supported by a host of paramilitary and auxiliary forces, estimated at 100,000 personnel (numbers are disputed). The SAC has begun a conscription drive and is slated to draft 60,000 new personnel by mid-2025.[7]

Areas of operation: Operates nationwide, with headquarters in Naypyidaw.

Leadership: Senior-General Min Aung Hlaing (commander-in-chief of defence services and SAC chairperson) and Vice Senior-General Soe Win (vice commander-in-chief of defence services and SAC vice chairperson).

Structure: The armed forces comprise three service branches: the army, navy and air force. The army is divided into six Bureaus of Special Operations controlling 14 regional military commands. These are complemented by ten light infantry divisions, which conduct most kinetic operations.

History: The military seized power in 1962 and ruled via several successive regimes for the next five decades. It then rewrote the constitution in 2008 to initiate a partial democratic transition, retaining 25% of the seats in parliament for itself. In 2016, it entered into a power-sharing agreement with the NLD before seizing back state power in another coup on 1 February 2021 amid growing tensions around allegations of electoral fraud.

State Administration Council (SAC) (Myanmar armed forces or Tatmadaw)

Objectives: Preserve the union; combat various insurgency movements; contain political and ethnic dissent; conduct Bamar-centric state-building; modernise the military; and regain international legitimacy.

Opponents: Over 20 EAOs, PDF/National Unity Government (NUG), potentially hundreds of localised resistance groups, and sizeable portions of the general population.

Affiliates/allies: A host of People's Militia Forces and several Border Guard Forces (BGFs), whose numbers range from a few dozen to several thousand armed fighters.[8] The SAC has exponentially grown its number of locally organised militias in many majority-Bamar areas. Though largely isolated internationally, it also still enjoys political and military support from both China and Russia.

Resources/capabilities: Through over a dozen arms factories, the SAC can locally produce small arms, light weapons, ammunition, and even aerial munitions and artillery rounds. It has invested heavily in the navy to domestically produce patrol boats, corvettes, frigates and landing craft, and has been expanding its abilities in surveillance and intelligence. Though its inventory mainly comprises legacy equipment, the air force also has an assortment of more modern fixed- and rotary-wing aircraft.

People's Defence Force/National Unity Government (PDF/NUG)

Strength: 300 PDF battalions of 200–500 troops each, estimated at over 65,000 personnel, as well as several hundred Local People's Defence Forces (LPDFs). Estimates of the number of resistance fighters vary widely from 100,000–200,000, though over half of these fighters are either unarmed or poorly equipped due to financial and equipment shortages.[9]

Areas of operation: Almost nationwide. PDF units and LPDFs are mostly located in Sagaing and Magway regions, with some presence in Kayin and Kayah states and Tanintharyi and Bago regions. They also have a growing presence in Mandalay Region and in and around Shan State. Most of the leadership is based abroad, while several key figures are based in the border areas in EAO territories.

Leadership: Aung San Suu Kyi (state counsellor), U Win Myint (president), Duwa Lashi La (acting president), Mahn Win Khaing Thann (prime minister), U Yee Mon (defence minister) and Zin Mar Aung (foreign minister).

Structure: The NUG operates 17 ministries, with the Ministry of Defence responsible for the PDF. It provides basic education, healthcare and humanitarian aid in certain areas of the country. It does not exercise full control over the wider insurgency, with its authority mainly limited to those actors subordinated under its three semi-autonomous Military Division Commands (MDCs), in collaboration with EAO war leaders, as well as two other joint commands with EAOs.

History: The NUG was formed in April 2021 and officially unveiled the PDF in May 2021, though armed resistance had begun before then. PDF units began to proliferate in September 2021 after the NUG called for a nationwide 'defensive war'.[10]

Objectives: Restore democracy by overthrowing the SAC and form a federal democratic union.

Opponents: SAC and its proxy militias.

Affiliates/allies: K3C coalition of the Karen National Union (KNU), Kachin Independence Army (KIA), Karenni Army (KA) and Chin National Front (CNF). The NUG also has growing ties with the BHA, which supplies some PDF groups with arms and training. Political coordination is undertaken through the National Unity Consultative Council (NUCC), which includes a diverse range of ethnic stakeholders, political parties, pro-democracy advocates and civil-society organisations.

Resources/capabilities: The NUG initially funded itself almost entirely with voluntary online donations, amassing over US$150m.[11] It is projected to spend US$5m a month on the PDF and LPDFs.[12] However, most PDF units and LPDFs also fund themselves independently either through donations or by extracting fees from businesses and travellers in their areas. The NUG claims that it now collects taxes in nearly 50 townships.[13] Only about 20% of PDF fighters carry automatic rifles, while almost all LPDF fighters rely on home-made weapons.[14] PDF units operating under joint EAO commands are better equipped and have greater access to automatic rifles, mortars, unguided 107-millimetre rockets and limited quantities of other light weapons.

Karen National Liberation Army/Karen National Union (KNLA/KNU)

Strength: Approximately 7,000 regular fighters and 2,000 home-guard fighters (estimate) organised as the Karen National Defence Organisation (KNDO). The KNLA controls nearly a dozen PDF 'columns', which operate as mobile units in certain KNLA territories.

Areas of operation: Military operations in Bago and Tanintharyi regions and Mon and Kayin states. Several KNLA elements also operate in Kayah State. Political elements are active in and along the border with Thailand.

Leadership: Gen. Saw Kwe Htoo Win (chairperson), Padoh Saw Hser Gay (vice chairperson) and Padoh Saw Tahdoh Moo (general secretary).

Structure: The KNLA comprises seven brigades and a few specialised regiments that operate with varying degrees of autonomy. Its political wing, the KNU, administers 14 departments and oversees self-administration in its areas of control.

History: The KNU was established in 1947 and, that same year, it formed the KNDO, a collection of local armed units that later evolved into the KNLA. It is one of the most influential armed groups in Myanmar. It fought fierce battles with the military in the 1950s and 1960s, reaching the peak of its power in the early 1990s, after which it suffered numerous splits. It agreed to a ceasefire in 2012 before signing the NCA in 2015. Some brigades, but not all, resumed heavy fighting after the 2021 coup.

Karen National Liberation Army/Karen National Union (KNLA/KNU)

Objectives: Achieve Karen self-determination within a federal democratic union and reunite splinter groups. Various factions support either peaceful or violent opposition against the military, with the latter camp having slowly gained greater traction.

Opponents: SAC and its proxy militias.

Affiliates/allies: Allied with the NUG via the Joint Command and Coordination structure. It is also a participant in the NUCC and other dialogue platforms.

Resources/capabilities: Primarily fields small arms and light weapons including mortars and rocket-propelled grenade launchers. Some older-generation man-portable air-defence systems (MANPADs), with three identified as the HN-5A, have been found in the hands of KNLA fighters, though they have not been used in combat thus far. The KNLA is capable of overrunning fixed positions and interdicting major roads. It is funded through business ventures, taxation and fundraising among the Karen diaspora. It has a dedicated department to interface with foreign organisations.

Karenni Army (KA) and Karenni Nationalities Democratic Force (KNDF)

Strength: Up to 3,000 fighters from the KA and 7,000 from the KNDF, though equipment constraints mean that the actual fighting strength of the latter comprises only about 2,000–3,000 fighters.[15]

Areas of operation: Kayah State and its borders with southern Shan State, especially around Pekon and Pinlaung townships.

Leadership: The KNDF was initially formed under the tutelage of the KA but has since become increasingly independent. The KA is led by Khu Oo Reh (chairperson), Abel Tweed (vice chairperson) and Khu Plureh (general secretary). The KNDF is led by Khun Bedu (chief of staff) and Mar Wi (deputy commander).

Structure: The KA is organised into five battalions. The KNDF was initially formed as an umbrella network of Karenni PDF units but now fields 22 well-integrated and organised battalions.

History: The KA was founded in 1957. It signed a state- and union-level ceasefire in 2012 but never signed the NCA despite encouragement from the military and fellow EAOs. The KNDF was formed in May 2021 to organise and consolidate the various resistance groups in Kayah State.

Objectives: Overthrow the SAC and expand the current Kayah State to a more autonomous Karenni state corresponding roughly with its larger pre-independence borders.

Opponents: SAC and various Pa-O militias, notably Pa-O National Army (PNA).

Affiliates/allies: The KA and KNDF fight with PDF units under the Central Command and Coordination Committee (C3C) of the NUG. Political decisions are made by the Karenni State Interim Executive Council (IEC) – a transitional government comprising senior members of the Karenni National Progressive Party and KNDF. Though their exact links are unclear, the IEC is said to regularly engage with the NUG, which has backed its endeavour.

Resources/capabilities: Capable of interdicting major roads, overrunning fixed positions and waging protracted urban combat. Both groups utilise automatic rifles, launchers, mines and home-made weapons and have teams dedicated to operating commercial off-the-shelf (COTS) uninhabited aerial vehicles to drop explosives. The group has become increasingly well armed after establishing links with members of the BHA, from which it sources most of its materiel.

Chinland Council (CC)

Strength: 8,000–9,000 (estimate) fighters across Chin State.

Areas of operation: Chin State and along its foothills, which border Sagaing and Magway regions.

Leadership: Leading figures from the Chin National Front (CNF) occupy several top seats in the CC and the Government of Chinland, including Pu Zing Cung (chairperson of both the CNF and CC), Sui Khar (foreign minister of the Government of Chinland and vice chairperson two of the CNF) and Pu Thawng Za Lian (defence minister of the Government of Chinland and chairperson of the military affairs committee for the CNF).

Structure: Comprises 112 members from the CNF, local administrative organisations and resistance groups and members of parliament elected in 2020.[16] It dissolved the Chinland Joint Defence Committee in December 2023 and took over its alliance structure.

History: The CC was formed on 6 December 2023 after the ratification of the Chinland Constitution.[17] The CC acts as the legislature of the self-governing State of Chinland and it appointed the first Government of Chinland on 1 February 2024.

Objectives: Achieve greater Chin self-determination; build a system of governance based on federal democracy; and cooperate with other EAOs, PDF units and pro-democracy organisations.

Opponents: SAC and Chin Brotherhood, a coalition of three armed outfits which oppose what they say is the 'domination' of Chin politics by the CNF.

Affiliates/allies: The CNF, which occupies critical defence roles in the CC, is part of the K3C coalition and the C3C chain of command with the NUG. The CNF severed ties with the Interim Chin National Consultative Council in March 2023, and it is unclear if it is still participating in the NUCC, which has yet to publicly back the endeavour.

Resources/capabilities: The Chin resistance comprises very competent guerrilla fighters who have adapted to fight in the rugged, mountainous terrain of the state and are capable of interdicting major roads. Although the Chin resistance fighters are still unable to contest the nine township capitals, they have been able to overrun minor fixed positions and have captured seven sub-towns.

Kachin Independence Army/Kachin Independence Organisation (KIA/KIO)

Strength: 10,000–15,000 (estimate) armed fighters, with over 4,000 PDF fighters under its command.[18]

Areas of operation: Operates mainly in and around Kachin populations in Kachin and Shan states, alongside some stretches of the border with China. It expanded its operations to Sagaing and Mandalay regions following the 2021 coup.

Leadership: Gen. Gam Shawng (KIO chairperson) and Lt-Gen. Khaung Lun (KIA commander-in-chief and chief of staff).

Structure: Divided into ten brigades (seven of them in Kachin State and three in northern Shan State), with control over multiple subordinate PDF units.

History: Formed in 1961 and signed a ceasefire agreement in 1994 that broke down in 2011. The KIA/KIO founded the Northern Alliance in 2016 before launching a major joint offensive against the SAC. A new, de facto ceasefire lasted from 2018 to the 2021 coup, after which the group launched renewed offensives.

Objectives: Seek greater autonomy for the Kachin, establish a federal democracy as outlined in the 1947 Panglong Agreement, and overthrow the military regime.

Opponents: SAC, Shanni Nationalities Army (SNA) and some local ethnic militias allied to the SAC.

Affiliates/allies: The KIA/KIO is a member of the Federal Political Negotiation and Consultative Committee (FPNCC). The KIA is militarily allied to the NUG via the C3C, with its commander-in-chief leading MDC 1. It coordinates with the NUCC through the Kachin National Consultative Assembly.

Resources/capabilities: Generates revenue through taxation and various activities including mining and hydropower. The KIA/KIO enjoys widespread support from the Kachin diaspora. It manufactures and assembles small arms and ammunition in its areas of control and possesses light weapons and some heavy machine guns. It can hold and contest territory and is capable of shooting down helicopters.

Brotherhood Alliance (BHA): Ta'ang National Liberation Army/Palaung State Liberation Front (TNLA/PSLF)

Strength: 10,000–15,000 troops (estimate), including irregulars and reservists.[19]

Areas of operation: Operates in and around Ta'ang enclaves across northern Shan State. *Operation 1027* saw it expel junta forces from seven towns as part of its 'Ta'ang State', a quasi-nation-building project.[20]

Leadership: Gen. Tar Aik Bong (general chairperson), Lt-Gen. Tar Jok Jar (first vice chairperson), Maj.-Gen. Tar Khu Lang (second vice chairperson) and Maj.-Gen. Tar Hol Plarng (commander-in-chief of the TNLA).

Structure: The TNLA is organised into seven brigades, totalling around 35 battalions.[21]

History: The PSLF was founded in 1991 when the former Palaung State Liberation Organisation (PSLO) surrendered to the government. The group began rearming in 2009 with the help of the KIO/KIA and clashed with the Myanmar military from 2012 onward. Following the 2021 coup, it only sporadically clashed with the junta, focusing instead on expanding its area of control. It increased its attacks in the lead-up to *Operation 1027*.

Objectives: Formation of a Ta'ang State within a federal democratic union, with equality and protection of rights for the Ta'ang people.

Opponents: SAC and several local ethnic militias.

Affiliates/allies: The TNLA/PSLF is a member of the FPNCC and the BHA. It maintains a level of political coordination with the NUCC through the Ta'ang Political Consultative Committee.

Resources/capabilities: Derives much of its income from taxation, mainly levied on businesses and commercial trucking along the main highway from Mandalay to China, as well as on tea cultivation. The TNLA fields fighters well armed with automatic rifles and light weapons and has gained several towed artillery and anti-aircraft flak guns from junta forces since *Operation 1027*. The PSLF has been improving its delivery of public services since 2018 and has opened courts, schools and health facilities.

Brotherhood Alliance (BHA): Myanmar National Democratic Alliance Army/Myanmar National Truth and Justice Party (MNDAA/MNTJP)

Strength: Up to 6,000 regular troops, with over 1,000 PDF fighters under its command.[22]

Areas of operation: Kokang Region, which it fully seized alongside several adjacent areas during *Operation 1027*, in northern Shan State.

Leadership: Peng Daxun (MNDAA/MNTJP chairperson).

Structure: Four brigades, including a 'multi-ethnic' formation comprising around 1,200 PDF fighters.[23]

History: The MNDAA/MNTJP was formed in 1989 and gained control of Kokang Region in a ceasefire. In 2009, the SAC expelled the MNDAA/MNTJP from Kokang. It attempted to re-enter the region several times, and only succeeded after *Operation 1027*.

Objectives: Continued self-administration of Kokang and economic development.

Opponents: SAC, remnants of Kokang BGF and several local ethnic militias.

Affiliates/allies: The MNDAA/MNTJP is a member of the FPNCC and the BHA.

Brotherhood Alliance (BHA): Myanmar National Democratic Alliance Army/Myanmar National Truth and Justice Party (MNDAA/MNTJP)

Resources/capabilities: The MNDAA/MNTJP is regarded as among the most affluent armed groups in Myanmar, possibly due to its historic links to the illicit drugs trade. Its fighters are well armed with automatic rifles and light weapons, and it has demonstrated proficiency in attacking with multiple synchronised COTS drones to drop explosives. The group seized over a dozen armoured vehicles, towed artillery and even some truck-mounted multiple-launch rocket systems from junta forces after *Operation 1027*.

Brotherhood Alliance (BHA): Arakan Army/United League of Arakan (AA/ULA)

Strength: The AA claims to have 30,000 fighters, though independent sources estimate its strength to be 16,500.[24]

Areas of operation: Historically, the ULA/AA has operated in Rakhine State and Paletwa township in adjacent Chin State, with a fraction of its troops apportioned to fight alongside its allies in Kachin and Shan states. After the 2021 coup, it began operating in Sagaing and Magway regions, adjacent to Kachin and Rakhine states respectively. It gained control of most of northern Rakhine after a major offensive beginning in November 2023, during the height of *Operation 1027*.

Leadership: Maj.-Gen. Twan Mrat Naing (chairperson of the ULA and commander-in-chief of the AA) and Brig.-Gen. Nyo Twan Aung (vice-chairperson of the ULA and vice commander-in-chief of the AA).

Structure: The ULA is in charge of the Arakan People's Authority, which comprises a police force and a judiciary and has recently made forays into education and healthcare. The AA claims to possess 100 combat battalions grouped into an unspecified number of larger formations known as 'military regions'.[25]

History: The AA/ULA was founded in 2009 in Kachin State with the help of the KIA. The group began re-entering Rakhine State in 2014 and started clashing with the SAC occasionally the following year. It fought two wars with the Myanmar military in 2018–20 and for four months in 2022.

Objectives: Creation of an autonomous state for the Rakhine people, as part of a 'confederation'.[26]

Opponents: SAC, Arakan Liberation Army/Arakan Liberation Party (ALA/ALP), Arakan Rohingya Salvation Army (ARSA) and Rohingya Solidarity Organisation.

Affiliates/allies: The AA/ULA is a member of the FPNCC and the BHA.

Resources/capabilities: The AA is regarded as one of the most competent ethnic armies in Myanmar and can field sizeable combat formations for extended periods to assault fixed positions. Fighters are well equipped with automatic rifles, light weapons and 107-mm surface-to-surface rockets; the group also fields dedicated drone teams.

United Wa State Army/United Wa State Party (UWSA/UWSP)

Strength: 20,000–30,000 regular fighters.[27]

Areas of operation: Wa State, a de facto autonomous enclave with two non-contiguous territories in eastern Shan State.

Leadership: Currently undergoing a generational leadership change, with Bao Youxiang (chairperson) expected to hand power to his son, Bao Ai Kham.

Structure: Nine brigades deployed across two separate regions.[28]

History: Arose from the CPB in 1989 and immediately signed a ceasefire with the government, which it maintains today. The UWSA/UWSP captured additional territory along the Thai border in the 1990s and built a large drugs empire to fund its operations. Its status as the most powerful EAO and greatest potential source of weapons for anti-junta groups gives it substantial influence over the nation's conflicts. It operates an autonomous statelet with a fully functioning administration and local economy.

Objectives: Preserve autonomy over Wa State, boost economic development, and maintain buffer zones with the SAC with the help of allies and proxies.

Opponents: SAC.

Affiliates/allies: The UWSA/UWSP leads the FPNCC. It is allied to the National Democratic Alliance Army (NDAA), a fellow CPB splinter, and the Shan State Progress Party (SSPP), and it also has significant influence over the BHA. It maintains close economic and political ties with the Yunnan provincial government.

Resources/capabilities: Possesses Chinese-made drones, armoured vehicles, towed artillery, anti-aircraft guns and FN-6 MANPADs. It also manufactures small arms, most notably its own version of the Type-81 assault rifle.

Other relevant parties

All Burma Students' Democratic Front, ALP, Burma People's Liberation Army, Democratic Karen Benevolent Army, KNU–Peace Council, Kawthoolei Army, NDAA, New Mon State Party, PNA, Pa-O National Liberation Army, ARSA, Restoration Council of Shan State, SNA, SSPP, various urban guerrilla groups and independent local resistance outfits.

Notes

1. 'Myanmar Election: Suu Kyi's NLD Wins Landslide Victory', BBC News, 13 November 2015.
2. United Nations Office for the Coordination of Humanitarian Affairs (UNOCHA), 'Myanmar Humanitarian Update No. 39', 1 July 2024, p. 1; and UNOCHA, 'Myanmar Humanitarian Update No. 30', 13 June 2023.
3. Grant Peck, 'Myanmar Will Start Drafting 5,000 People a Month Into the Military Soon. Some Think of Fleeing', AP News, 15 February 2024.
4. Zo Tum Hmung, 'Analysis of Fiscal Year 2024 Draft Appropriations for Burma', Baltimore Council on Foreign Affairs, 21 March 2024.
5. Ministry of Foreign Affairs of the Republic of Indonesia, 'Office of the Special Envoy Engagements with Myanmar Stakeholders Jakarta, 20–22 November 2023', 24 November 2023.
6. Moe Thuzar and Sharon Seah, 'What Is Laos' Game Plan for the Myanmar Crisis?', Fulcrum, 31 January 2024.
7. Peck, 'Myanmar Will Start Drafting 5,000 People a Month Into the Military Soon. Some Think of Fleeing'.
8. See John Buchanan, 'Militias in Myanmar', Asia Foundation, July 2016, p. 29.
9. See, for example, Naw Theresa, '2 Years of Turmoil: Myanmar's Grinding Stalemate', *Diplomat*, 14 April 2023.
10. Tommy Walker, 'Myanmar's Shadow Government Announces "Defensive War"', VOA, 8 September 2021.
11. Zachary Abuza, 'The National Unity Government's Revenue Denial Strategy', Stimson, 20 September 2023.
12. Altaf Parvez, 'How Are Guerillas in Myanmar Raising Their Funds?', Daily Star, 24 February 2024.
13. Ibid.
14. Ye Myo Hein, 'Understanding the People's Defence Forces in Myanmar', United States Institute of Peace, 3 November 2023.
15. See Morgan Michaels, 'Battle for Kayah Is Key for Myanmar Junta and Its Opponents', IISS, June 2023.
16. June N.S., 'The First Chin-written Constitution: A New Template for Self-determination?', *Irrawaddy*, 26 December 2023.
17. Zo Tum Hmung and Jon Indergaard, 'Chinland Council Established in Myanmar', Stimson, 11 January 2024.
18. See, for example, Hein I Itoo Zan, 'Kachin Independence Leader Steps Down', *Irrawaddy*, 4 January 2023.
19. International Crisis Group, 'Treading a Rocky Path: The Ta'ang Army Expands in Myanmar's Shan State', 4 September 2023.
20. Kachin News Group, 'TNLA ထိန်းချုပ်ထားတဲ့ မြို့နယ် ၇ မြို့ညမထွက်ရအမိန့်ရုတ်သိမ်း' [TNLA revokes junta-imposed curfews in seven of its controlled towns], 6 March 2024.
21. 'TNLA Reveals Conscription System for Towns Under Their Control', Shan News, 9 February 2024.
22. Kyaw Hsan Hlaing and Naing Lin, '"Operation 1027": A Turning-point for Myanmar's Resistance Struggle?', *Diplomat*, 30 October 2023.
23. Sai Wansai, 'MNDAA: Beating a Bold Revolutionary Path to Fulfill the People's Aspirations?', Shan News, 10 January 2023.
24. Anthony Davis, 'Myanmar Junta in a Make-or-break Rakhine Fight', *Asia Times*, 1 February 2024.
25. 'Arakan Army Grows Up Quickly', Burma News International, 19 April 2022.
26. Nan Lwin Hnin Pwint, 'Confederation the Only Option for Arakanese People, AA Chief Says', *Irrawaddy*, 11 January 2019.
27. Bertil Lintner, 'Silence on Coup Makes Strategic Sense for Myanmar's Wa', *Irrawaddy*, 12 July 2021.
28. Anthony Davis, 'Wa an Early Winner of Myanmar's Post-coup War', *Asia Times*, 22 February 2022.

INDIA

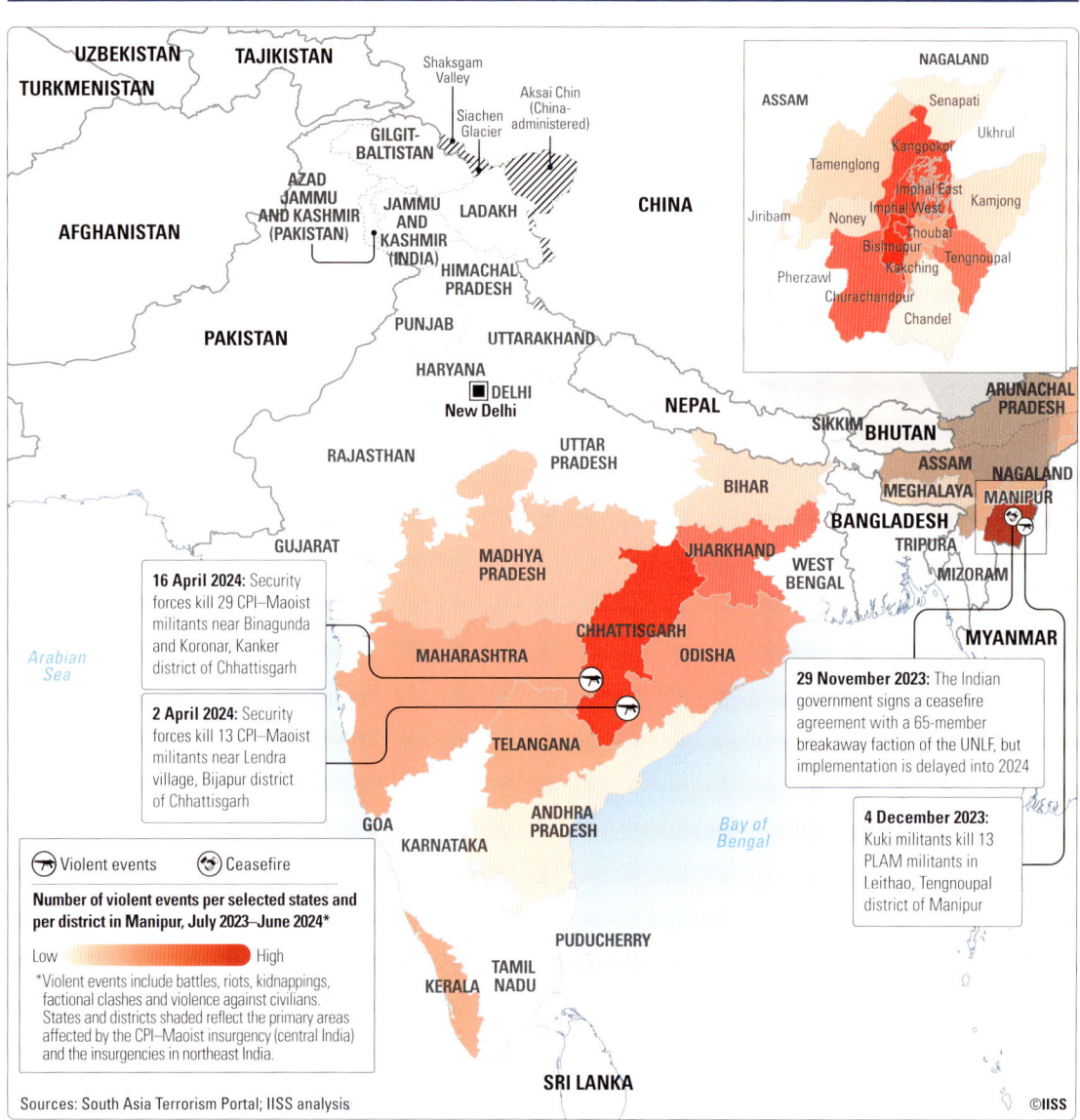

Conflict Overview

The conflicts in India's central heartlands and northeastern peripheries are a lower priority for New Delhi than the politically and strategically more important Kashmir conflict. Thus, both conflicts have simmered for several decades, with the Indian state's approach being characterised by containment rather than a concerted effort to crush insurgencies. Both conflicts also stem from perceived neglect or a fear of assimilation or exploitation, either by the 'mainland' or by a class-based or ethnic 'other'.

Conflict in these regions began in the northeast in the 1950s, when the Naga National Council mobilised, fearing that the Nagas would be assimilated into India. A series of failed peace agreements led to the emergence of numerous Naga armed factions. Many of these armed groups have coexisted with

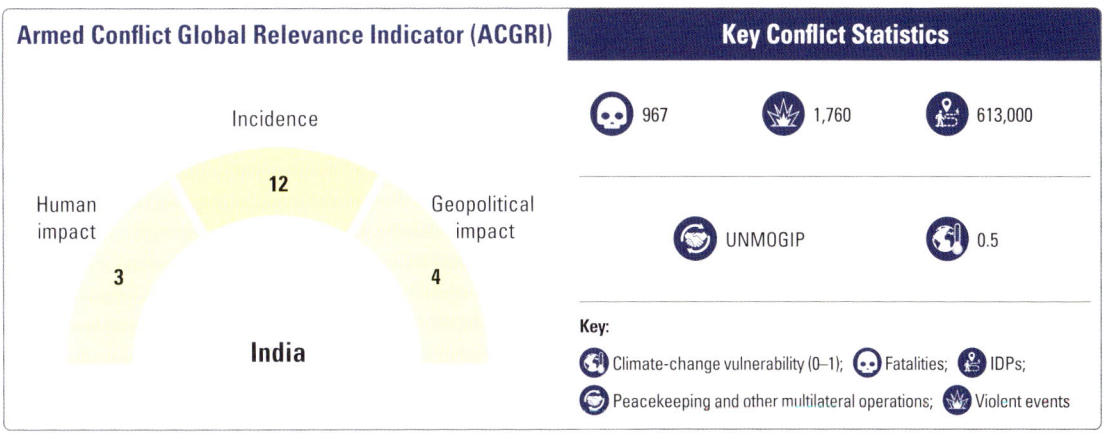

Conflict(s)	Type	Start date
Ethnic conflicts in the northeast	I IC LI	1955
Maoist insurgency in central India	I LI	1967

Key: I IC LI Internal: intercommunal & localised insurgency; I LI Internal: localised insurgency

New Delhi through a series of prolonged ceasefires since 1997. However, peace negotiations remain gridlocked over issues such as the proposed degree of autonomy and the territorial extent of a post-peace-accord Naga state within India. New Delhi signed a peace agreement with Mizoram-based insurgents in 1986, while a host of other ethno-separatist conflicts in Assam, Manipur, Meghalaya and Tripura, driven by a fusion of anti-Delhi sentiments, local ethnic rivalries and extremely porous international borders, peaked in the 1990s and have steadily declined since.

Central India's Maoist insurgency is relatively insulated from geopolitical dynamics compared with the northeast. A peasant revolt at Naxalbari in 1967 gave rise to the 'Naxalite' movement, which sought to overthrow feudal landlords and impose a socialist economic order. The insurgency peaked in 2009–10 when the Communist Party of India–Maoist (CPI–Maoist) operated across a 'Red Corridor' spanning much of Bihar, Chhattisgarh, Jharkhand, Maharashtra and West Bengal states. Since 2014, security forces' successes have gradually eroded CPI–Maoist influence.

Conflict Update

Large-scale communal violence in Manipur accounted for almost all conflict-related fatalities (152 out of 161) in the northeast during the reporting period.[1] In May 2023, tensions between the state's majority Meitei and minority Kuki communities escalated, resulting in clashes between armed groups hailing from both communities. On 4 December 2023, for example, Kuki militants killed 13 People's Liberation Army of Manipur (PLAM) militants in a clash in Tengnoupal district.[2]

On 29 November 2023, the Indian government signed its first-ever ceasefire with a Manipur-valley-based insurgent group – a pro-talks faction of the United National Liberation Front (UNLF). However, this faction was made up of only 65 militants, far smaller than the 300-strong anti-talks faction known as the UNLF–Koireng.[3] As a result, violence perpetrated by both valley-based Meitei insurgents and the Kuki insurgents in the hills remained a significant challenge.

The number of fatalities related to the Maoist conflict in July 2023–June 2024 almost doubled compared to the equivalent 2022–23 period, increasing from 140 to 279.[4] This largely reflected growing pressure from security forces on CPI–Maoist militants, particularly in strongholds around the Bastar region of Chhattisgarh State. During the first four months of 2024 – around the same time that the Maoists typically launch their annual tactical counter-offensive campaign (TCOC) – security forces killed 105 CPI–Maoist militants, significantly surpassing the total of 56 insurgents killed throughout 2023.[5] This reflected concerted efforts by the newly elected Bharatiya Janata Party state government in Chhattisgarh to disrupt the Maoists' TCOC. On 16 April 2024, security forces killed 29 Maoists in Kanker district in Chhattisgarh – the largest Maoist loss in a single incident in the history of the state.[6]

Conflict Parties

Indian Armed Forces

Strength: 1,475,750 active military personnel.

Areas of operation: Northeast (III and IV Corps). The army does not play a direct role in anti-CPI–Maoist operations in central India.

Leadership: Lt-Gen. H.S. Sahi (III Corps commander) and Lt-Gen. Manish Erry (IV Corps commander).

Structure: Zonal command structure subdivided into corps commands.

History: The Indian Army was formed as a direct successor to the British Indian Army after independence in 1947. The army, navy and air force are primarily responsible for external defence, but the army and air force have played a pivotal role in Indian counter-insurgency operations since the 1950s.

Objectives: Counter-insurgency and border defence.

Opponents: Non-state armed groups (NSAGs).

Affiliates/allies: Other state forces, although coordination challenges persist.

Resources/capabilities: Most suitably equipped and trained to operate in the difficult, rugged terrain of northeast India, drawing upon logistics and airpower to supply distant outposts. Heavy weaponry is rarely deployed to counter-insurgency operations, though there have been exceptions.

Assam Rifles

Strength: 66,411.[7]

Areas of operation: Northeast India (Nagaland and Manipur).

Leadership: Lt-Gen. Pradeep Chandran Nair (director general).

Structure: Organised into 47 battalions officered by army personnel.[8] It is under the jurisdiction of the Ministry of Defence, but as a central paramilitary force it is answerable to the Ministry of Home Affairs.

History: Originally formed as the Cachar Levy in 1835, the Assam Rifles plays a central role in counter-insurgency operations in northeast India.

Objectives: Counter-insurgency and border defence.

Opponents: Naga armed groups, Manipur valley-based insurgent groups and other armed groups in the hills of Manipur.

Affiliates/allies: Cooperates with other state forces, although challenges exist around intelligence sharing, overlapping jurisdictions and operational coordination.

Resources/capabilities: Battalions are typically equipped to the same standard as an Indian Army infantry battalion, with small-arms and mortar capabilities.

Central Reserve Police Force (CRPF)

Strength: 324,654.[9]

Areas of operation: Northeastern, central and eastern India. It takes a leading role in central India, in states such as Andhra Pradesh, Bihar, Chhattisgarh, Jharkhand, Maharashtra and Odisha.

Leadership: Anish Dayal Singh (director general).

Structure: CRPF battalions are central-government forces but are deployed to specific states to assist in law-and-order activities. CRPF forces are designed to augment existing state police forces to combat CPI–Maoist insurgents across the Red Corridor. The central government is responsible for deploying CRPF forces and for coordinating with individual state governments.

History: Originally founded as the Crown Representative Police Force in 1939 before being rechristened after independence. The force has evolved into one of the largest of the central police forces and has the broadest remit of supporting state governments in law-and-order duties, as well as a limited counter-insurgency remit.

Objectives: Support state-level law enforcement in counter-insurgency duties.

Opponents: CPI–Maoist in central India and an array of armed groups in northeastern India.

Affiliates/allies: Cooperates with other state forces, although challenges exist around intelligence sharing, overlapping jurisdictions and operational coordination.

Central Reserve Police Force (CRPF)

Resources/capabilities: CRPF battalions vary in degrees of modernisation. While special units such as the CRPF's 'Commando Battalions for Resolute Action' are equipped with modern INSAS rifles and AK-series rifles, this varies across units. Some units have anti-mine vehicles; however, these are rare and CRPF units are thus often vulnerable to improvised-explosive-device (IED) attacks.

State Police Forces

Strength: 450,000.

Areas of operation: Varied.

Leadership: Led by a state-level director general of the police, answerable to state government political leadership.

Structure: Typically organised into zones and ranges, with supplementary armed police battalions for counter-insurgency support.

History: Varied according to the formation of individual states.

Objectives: Law-and-order and counter-insurgency duties.

Opponents: NSAGs.

Affiliates/allies: Cooperates with other state forces, although challenges exist around intelligence sharing, overlapping jurisdictions and operational coordination.

Resources/capabilities: While special armed police units are better equipped and have undergone modernisation, the bulk of state police forces face logistical challenges in navigating treacherous terrain and fair-weather roads, as well as deficiencies in firearms, including reliance on old, colonial-era rifles.

National Socialist Council of Nagalim–Isak Muivah (NSCN–IM)

Strength: Over 4,000.[10]

Areas of operation: Naga-inhabited northeast India (Arunachal Pradesh, Assam, Manipur and Nagaland).

Leadership: Thuingaleng Muivah (general secretary).

Structure: The group is organised centrally but is demographically dominated by the Tangkhul tribe of Manipur.

History: After splitting from the original NSCN in 1988, the NSCN–IM has since emerged as one of the most powerful NSAGs in northeast India. Observing a ceasefire limited to the territorial jurisdiction of Nagaland with the Indian government since 1997, the group continues to recruit; clashes with rivals and occasionally Indian security forces in non-ceasefire areas; and runs its own parallel government from its 'capital' in Camp Hebron, on the outskirts of Dimapur. In 2015 it signed a Framework Agreement with the government of India with a view to concluding a comprehensive settlement, but the group's ethnic composition remains a bone of contention.

Objectives: Gain hybrid 'sovereignty' over Nagaland, incorporating Nagas under one territorial entity with a separate flag and constitution.

Opponents: State forces, National Socialist Council of Nagaland–Khaplang, Zeliangrong United Front and Kuki armed groups.

Affiliates/allies: Naga civil society.

Resources/capabilities: The NSCN–IM is the best equipped of northeast India-based insurgents with connections to the Southeast Asia regional arms market.

Kuki armed groups under Suspension of Operations (SoO) agreements

Strength: 25 Kuki militant groups, most of which are broadly organised under two umbrella fronts, the Kuki National Organisation (KNO) and the United People's Front (UPF). There are approximately 2,000 KNO militants and 2,000 UPF militants. The KNO is comprised of 23 armed groups, and the UPF is comprised of nine.[11]

Areas of operation: Kuki-inhabited areas of Manipur and Assam.

Leadership: In the February 2023 renewal of the SoO ceasefire agreements, the UPF was represented by Ketheos Zomi and Joshua Thadou and the KNO was represented by Seilen Haokip.

Structure: Loosely organised umbrella organisations.

History: SoO agreements were initially signed by the central government, the Manipur government and Kuki groups in 2008 and had been renewed annually. While the Manipur Legislative Assembly voted in February 2024 to abrogate the agreements and refused to send a representative to renew them, Ministry of Home Affairs sources claimed that the 'status quo' of ceasefire nonetheless held.

Objectives: Gain statehood for Kuki-inhabited areas of Manipur.

Opponents: State forces, NSCN–IM and Meitei activists. There are numerous rivalries between Kuki factions which have led to inter-factional violence.

Affiliates/allies: Member groups within respective umbrella organisations and elements of Kuki civil society.

Resources/capabilities: Weapons are stored in KNO and UPF designated camps.

United National Liberation Front–Pambei (UNLF–Pambei)

Strength: 65.[12]

Areas of operation: Moved into Manipur from Myanmar after May 2023.

Leadership: Khungongbam Pambei (chairman).

Structure: Unclear.

History: Formed after UNLF chairman Khungongbam Pambei began ceasefire negotiations in 2020 with the Indian government, leading to his expulsion and creation of a separate faction in 2021.

Objectives: Gain sovereignty over Manipur and secure a ceasefire with the Indian government.

Opponents: UNLF–Koireng.

Affiliates/allies: Unclear.

Resources/capabilities: Unclear.

United National Liberation Front–Koireng (UNLF–Koireng)

Strength: 300.[13]

Areas of operation: Manipur valley, based in Myanmar.

Leadership: R.K. Achou Singh (alias 'Koireng').

Structure: The UNLF is led by a central committee and has armed and political wings. The armed component of the organisation is divided by district, while the civilian component includes a publicity wing, a women's wing and a developmental component. In 1990, a faction led by Namoijan Oken split from the parent organisation to form the UNLF–Oken, which later joined splinter movements from other organisations to form the Kanglei Yawol Kanna Lup (KYKL). In 2020, the UNLF–Pambei split from the group to pursue peace negotiations.

History: Formed in 1964 by Rajkumar Meghen, a descendant of the royal family of the former Manipuri kingdom. The UNLF began armed operations in 1991.

Objectives: Gain sovereignty over Manipur through armed struggle.

Opponents: UNLF–Pambei.

Affiliates/allies: National Socialist Council of Nagaland–Khaplang/Yung Aung, United Liberation Front of Asom–Independent (ULFA–Independent) and Coordination Committee (CorCom) of Manipuri armed groups.

Resources/capabilities: Capable of conducting attacks against Indian security forces but predominantly strikes civilians.

Coordination Committee (CorCom)

Strength: Umbrella organisation of six anti-talk armed groups.[14]

Areas of operation: Arunachal Pradesh, Manipur and Myanmar.

Leadership: Formed by the leader of the PLAM.

Structure: CorCom's organisational structure is best described as a framework for cooperation between its member armed groups.

History: When formed in 2011, CorCom included a seventh armed group, the United People's Party of Kangleipak (UPPK). However, the UPPK was expelled from the group in 2013 after it began responding to peace overtures from the Indian government.

Objectives: Gain sovereignty over Manipur.

Opponents: State forces and rival anti- and pro-talks Manipuri armed groups.

Affiliates/allies: Some of its constituent organisations have aligned with the Myanmar military as of 2021.

Resources/capabilities: Significant variation in capabilities. Whereas the PLAM and the UNLF are well-trained and disciplined outfits, the Kangleipak Communist Party (KCP) is comprised of a series of small, fragmented factions.

Communist Party of India–Maoist (CPI–Maoist)

Strength: In December 2023, police estimated the CPI–Maoist's strength at 800–900 in Chhattisgarh, 242 in Odisha and 120 in Andhra Pradesh.[15] Operational strength in other important states such as Jharkhand is unclear, but Chhattisgarh is thought to remain the group's base of operations.

Areas of operation: Andhra Pradesh, Bihar, Chhattisgarh, Jharkhand, Kerala, Madhya Pradesh, Maharashtra, Odisha, Telangana and West Bengal. There is a hotspot of CPI–Maoist activity in the Bastar region of Chhattisgarh.

Leadership: Comprised of a central committee made up of representatives from the various states. The committee is led by Nambala Keshava Rao (general secretary, alias 'Basavraj').

Structure: Local command structures include 'zonal' commanders (zones roughly correspond to Indian districts) and local 'area' commanders under sub-committees.

History: Formed in 2004 following the merger of the Communist Party of India (Marxist–Leninist), People's War (People's War Group) and the Maoist Communist Centre of India. The organisation peaked in its control of territory in approximately 2009, leading then-prime minister Manmohan Singh to label the insurgency the country's single-largest security challenge. Since 2014, counter-insurgency operations and organisational splits have led to the group's gradual decline.

Objectives: Overthrow Indian parliamentary democracy in favour of a communist regime through rural insurgency, and mobilise a power base by tapping into marginalised communities in India's hinterlands. The CPI–Maoist deploys hit-and-run attacks against Indian security forces.

Communist Party of India–Maoist (CPI–Maoist)

Opponents: Indian security forces, civilians suspected of collaboration and smaller splinter factions such as the People's Liberation Front of India.

Affiliates/allies: Seeks to cultivate alliances with disempowered local civilians.

Resources/capabilities: Primarily arms itself with home-made firearms, although its elite fighting units wield AK-47s and semi-automatic weapons seized from police. The group also makes frequent use of IEDs.

Other relevant parties

Other relevant parties include the Working Committee, an umbrella organisation of seven pro-talks armed groups that signed a Framework Agreement with the Indian government in 2017, and the ULFA–Pro Talks Faction (ULFA–PTF), which was formed when it split from the ULFA in 2009. While it had largely demobilised since then, the ULFA–PTF signed a peace agreement with the Indian government in December 2023.

Notes

[1] See 'Yearly Fatalities', Datasheet – Insurgency North East, South Asia Terrorism Portal.

[2] '13 Killed in Gunfight Between Two Groups of Militants in Manipur Village', *Business Standard*, 4 December 2023.

[3] Sangeeta Barooah Pisharoty, 'Optics Aside, the Truth Behind Manipur's Ceasefire Agreement', Wire, 2 December 2023.

[4] See 'Yearly Fatalities', Datasheet – Maoist Insurgency, South Asia Terrorism Portal.

[5] *Ibid.*

[6] Jatindra Dash, 'Indian Security Forces Kill at Least 29 Maoists in Gunbattle', Reuters, 16 April 2024.

[7] Ministry of Home Affairs, 'Annual Report: 2022–23', Government of India, 2023, p. 97.

[8] *Ibid.*, p. 73.

[9] *Ibid.*, p. 96.

[10] Rajeev Bhattacharyya, 'Manipur: Making Sense of the UNLF's "Peace Agreement" With the Government', Quint, 6 December 2023.

[11] Afrida Hussain, 'Manipur Crisis: What Is Suspension of Operations Agreement?', *India Today*, 7 June 2023.

[12] '13 Killed in Gunfight Between Two Groups of Militants in Manipur Village'.

[13] *Ibid.*

[14] Including the PLAM, People's Revolutionary Party of Kangleipak (PREPAK), PREPAK–Progressive, UNLF, KYKL and KCP.

[15] PTI, '3,000 CAPF Troops to Move From Odisha to Chhattisgarh as Part of Plan to End Naxalism', *Deccan Herald*, 31 December 2023; Deepak Kumar Nayak, 'Andhra Pradesh: Residual Vexations', *Sri Lanka Guardian*, 9 January 2024; and SATP and Deepak Kumar Nayak, 'India: Residual Vexations in Andhra Pradesh – Analysis', *Eurasia Review*, 9 January 2024.

THAILAND

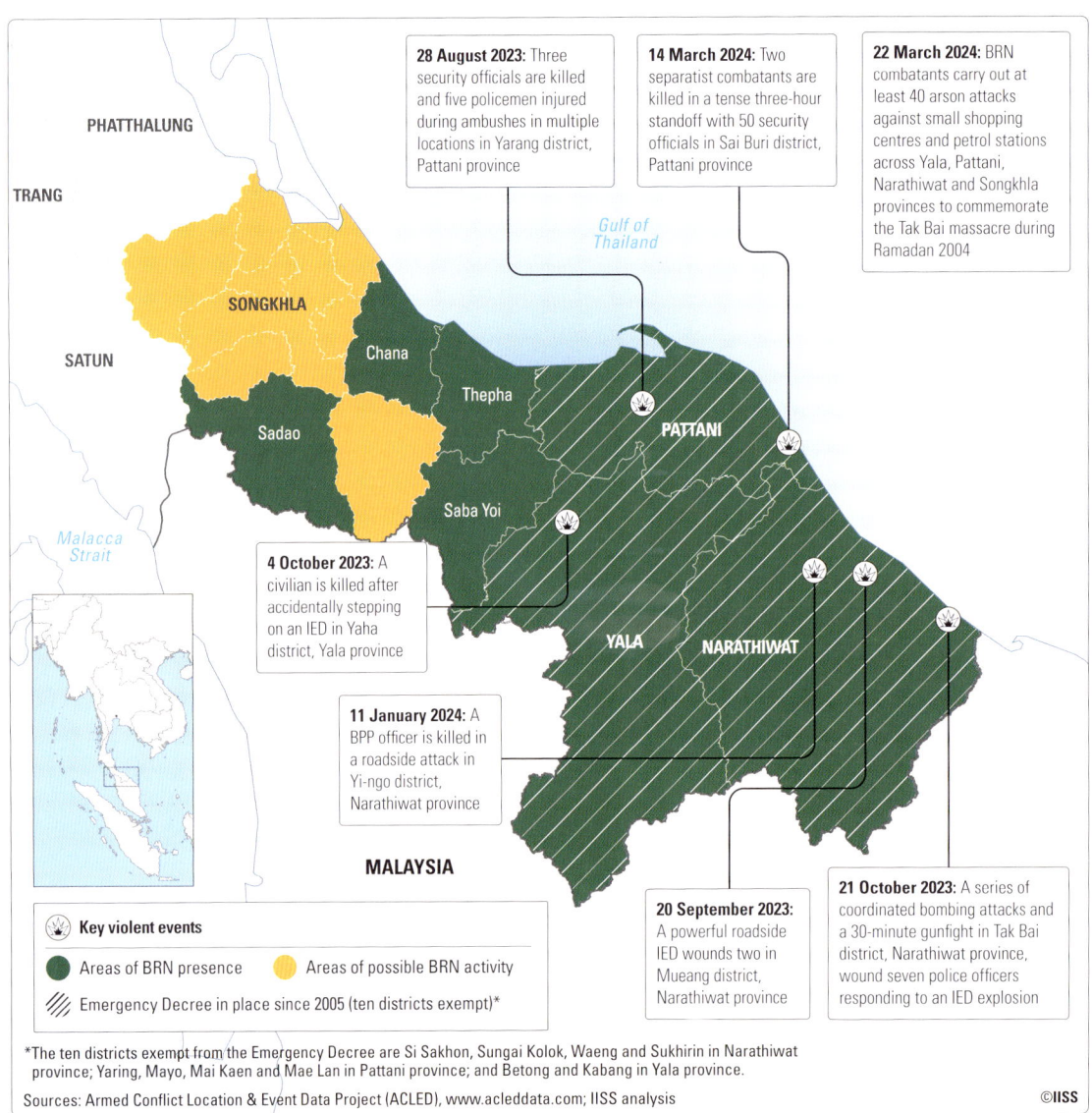

Conflict Overview

Armed conflict in Thailand's southernmost border provinces erupted in the late 1950s, 50 years after the region came under Bangkok's direct rule following the 1909 Anglo-Siamese Treaty that established the modern-day political border between Malaysia and Thailand. The struggle was a reaction to Thailand's policy of assimilation, which came at the expense of the cultural history and ethno-religious identity of the Malays of the former Islamic sultanate of Patani. Several armed separatist groups, which received financial support and military training from various Middle Eastern and North African countries (such as Libya and Syria), emerged in the late 1960s and the following decade. Armed conflict subsided in the 1990s and resurfaced again in 2001 under the leadership of the Patani Malay National

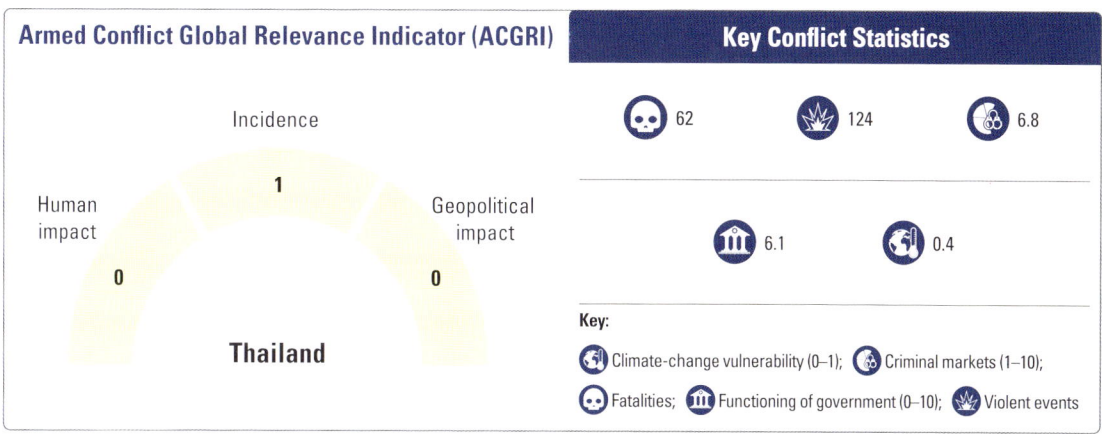

ACGRI pillars: IISS calculation based on multiple sources for 2023 and 2024 (scale: 0–100), except for some cases according to data availability. See Notes on Methodology and Data Appendix for all variables and further details on Key Conflict Statistics.

Conflict(s)	Type	Start date
Southern Thailand separatist conflict	I LI	2001

Key: I LI Internal: localised insurgency

Revolutionary Front (or Barisan Revolusi Nasional, BRN). However, it was not until 4 January 2004, when BRN combatants raided a Royal Thai Army battalion and made off with about 350 weapons, that the Thai government acknowledged the return of separatist insurgency in Thailand's Muslim-majority south.[1] The following year, the region was placed under an Emergency Decree (still ongoing), which permits the detention of suspected insurgents for up to 30 days without formal charges. Since the 2004 arms raid, more than 7,500 people have been killed by insurgency-related violence.[2]

In January 2020, the BRN and the Thai government finally agreed to negotiate, though Thai army and BRN combatants on the ground were not fully supportive of a formal peace process. After a year-long pause from February 2023–February 2024, peace talks resumed, but the two sides have struggled to move the process beyond confidence-building measures.[3]

Conflict Update

There is now a renewed opportunity for a peace settlement, as the new government in Thailand has indicated that it is willing to make serious concessions to the separatist insurgents, while the rebels themselves have suggested that they might be prepared to settle for something less than complete independence. BRN combatants on the ground, however, have not given up on their campaign of violence against the Thai security forces. Many are not convinced that formal negotiation is in the best interest of the movement. Increasingly, violence, including the choice of targets and the timing of attacks, has become an essential part of the rebels' political messaging. The uptick in violent events in 2023 and the intense nature of some of these high-profile attacks, which usually involved up to 15 operatives and lasted up to 30 minutes before BRN militants retreated, was a significant escalation from the three-minute gunfights that previously followed the use of roadside improvised explosive devices (IEDs). While the overall number of violent incidents has dropped significantly since 2013, the intensity and psychological impact of recent attacks represent a cause for concern. Furthermore, insurgents' commitment to resistance has seemed to grow only firmer. Only one BRN militant has surrendered during repeated stand-offs – resulting in the deaths of over 70 combatants – with government security forces over the past three years.[4]

Conflict Parties

Royal Thai Army

Strength: 245,000 active military personnel.

Areas of operation: The Fourth Army Area, headquartered in Nakhon Si Thammarat, oversees day-to-day security in the three insurgency-affected southernmost border provinces of Narathiwat, Pattani and Yala and the four Malay-speaking districts of Songkhla province.

Leadership: Lt-Gen. Santi Sakuntanark commands the Fourth Army Area as well as Internal Security Operations Command (ISOC) Region 4, operating under the Royal Thai Army Commander-in-Chief Gen. Charoenchai Hinthao.

Structure: The Royal Thai Army has ten infantry divisions, three (mechanised) cavalry divisions, an artillery division and a division-sized special-operations command. Two of the infantry divisions, along with supporting elements, are assigned to the Fourth Army Area to oversee security operations in the provinces of Narathiwat, Pattani, Songkhla and Yala.

History: Formed in 1874 in response to Western colonial power expanding into Southeast Asia, and shaped by nationwide counter-insurgency campaigns in the 1960s, the Royal Thai Army was instrumental in ending Thailand's absolute monarchy in 1932 and shifting the country towards a constitutional monarchy. Since then, the army has carried out 13 successful coups (most recently in 2014).

Objectives: Defend the monarchy and protect the political order enshrined in the 2017 military-backed constitution introduced by the National Council for Peace and Order, the junta behind the 2014 coup. The Royal Thai Army leads the country's counter-insurgency operations in the far south, utilising a two-pronged strategy that involves both development initiatives and military operations.

Opponents: BRN, crime syndicates and smugglers.

Affiliates/allies: Thai monarchy, Palang Pracharath Party and United Thai Nation Party. The Royal Thai Army also commands the paramilitary light infantry force, the Thai Rangers (Thahan Phran). The army coordinates its operations with the Royal Thai Police and the Volunteer Defense Corps (VDC) – locally hired security personnel who fall under the jurisdiction of the Ministry of Interior's provincial governor.

Resources/capabilities: The Fourth Army Area is primarily equipped with small arms, light weapons and field artillery. The divisional cavalry squadrons operate some older armoured vehicles. The Royal Thai Army also possesses tanks, modern armoured vehicles, self-propelled artillery and attack helicopters. Equipment is purchased primarily from China, the United States, a number of European countries and Israel.

Thai paramilitary and militia forces

Strength: Approximately 28,800 security officials and volunteers from the Border Patrol Police (BPP), Thai rangers and VDC across the southern provinces of Narathiwat, Pattani, Songkhla and Yala.[5]

Areas of operation: Paramilitary forces provide security along the border with Malaysia, while local recruits serve in their communities and at road checkpoints across the four southern provinces. Rangers are posted in remote villages in platoon-sized units as part of a security grid to shorten response time when insurgency violence erupts in their area of responsibility.

Leadership: Paramilitary forces are coordinated by the ISOC, Royal Thai Army, Royal Thai Marine Corps, Royal Thai Police and Ministry of the Interior.

Structure: Paramilitary forces active across the south include the Rangers, the BPP and the VDC. At the local level, Village Defence Volunteers (*Chor ror bor*) and Village Protection Volunteers (*Or ror bor*) defend communities.

History: The Rangers paramilitary force was created in 1978 to aid the Royal Thai Army in counter-insurgency operations and border protection. A marine-corps component of the Rangers was also established. The BPP and the VDC were initially formed in 1951 and 1954, respectively, to fight communist rebels.

Objectives: Rangers are trained for combat and join regular army soldiers on long-range reconnaissance patrols. Meanwhile, the VDC carries out basic security tasks for provincial officials, district chiefs and governors, all of whom fall under the jurisdiction of the Ministry of Interior. Village Defence Volunteers carry out evening guard duty in their respective villages and provide local surveillance and intelligence support to the military.

Opponents: BRN, Patani United Liberation Organisation (PULO) and crime syndicates in the region.

Affiliates/allies: The Rangers is an auxiliary corps to the Royal Thai Army and Royal Thai Marine Corps. The two forces often work alongside each other in long-range reconnaissance patrols and military operations.

Resources/capabilities: Rangers are lightly armed to allow for greater mobility on the ground. The VDC and Village Defence Volunteers are provided with rifles and shotguns, 15 days of training and a small monthly stipend.

Patani Malay National Revolutionary Front (Barisan Revolusi Nasional, BRN)

Strength: Approximately 3,000 fighters.[6]

Areas of operation: Narathiwat, Pattani and Yala provinces and the four Malay-speaking districts in Songkhla province (Chana, Saba Yoi, Sadao and Thepha). The BRN has carried out attacks in Bangkok, Koh Samui and tourist spots in Thailand's upper south, though it has no firm presence there.

Patani Malay National Revolutionary Front (Barisan Revolusi Nasional, BRN)

Leadership: Led by the Dewan Pimpinan Parti, a secretive decision-making body made up of elders with strong religious credentials. Anas Abdulrahman has served as the lead negotiator in peace talks with the Thai government since January 2020.

Structure: The BRN has never made its structure known, but it is believed that its organisational units cover politics, economic and financial affairs, women's affairs, youth, and armed forces. BRN fighters operate in a loose, cell-like structure, coordinating with other cells only when it is necessary for a particular operation.

History: Founded in the 1960s by religious teacher Haji Abdul Karim Hassan, the BRN had split into three branches by 1984: BRN-Congress, BRN-Ulama and BRN-Coordinate. The movement went underground in the 1990s alongside other long-standing separatist movements that had emerged between the early 1960s and 1980s. Many of these groups were funded by countries in the Middle East, which also provided political and military training. Support from the Middle East ended in the early 1990s as countries repositioned themselves for a post-Cold War world. After a ten-year pause, the BRN was the only movement to return to the battlefield in the early 2000s.

Objectives: Initially established to fight for independence in the former territory of the historical Patani sultanate, which existed from the 1400s until it was conquered by the kingdom of Siam in 1786 and later absorbed into the Thai state. The BRN is now open to negotiating for autonomy or self-rule, while continuing attacks aimed at making the region ungovernable in the short term.

Opponents: Royal Thai Army, Royal Thai Police and paramilitary forces in the far south. Targets include local informants – mostly local villagers who received payments from authorities for information leading to the location or arrest of known cell members and operatives. Collateral damage and the deliberate targeting of civilians, including teachers and Buddhist monks, were common in the early years of the current wave of insurgency (beginning in 2001).

Affiliates/allies: Residents in remote villages provide logistical support to the group, functioning as informants and providing temporary shelter for combatants. Ideologically, the BRN is allied to other long-standing movements, such as the PULO, the Pattani Islamic Mujahideen Movement and the Islamic Liberation Front of Patani.

Resources/capabilities: Firearms, grenade launchers and IEDs using basic materials. The group depends largely on local support and donations from the Malay diaspora.

Notes

[1] Paul Chambers, Srisompob Jitpiromsri and Napisa Waitoolkiat, 'Introduction: Conflict in the Deep South of Thailand: Never-ending Stalemate?', *Asian International Studies Review*, vol. 20, June 2019, p. 5.

[2] Deep South Watch, Facebook post 16 April 2024. The data covers January 2004–March 2024.

[3] Don Pathan, 'A New Round of Negotiations in Thailand's Far South', *Kyoto Review of Southeast Asia*, no. 28, September 2020.

[4] See, for example, Don Pathan, 'What to Make of Thailand's Ramadan-time "Truce" Offer to BRN Rebels', Benar News, 10 April 2023.

[5] Paul Chambers and Srisompob Jitpiromsri, 'Frontline Informality: Paramilitary Forces and Pro-government Militias in Thailand's Deep South Counter-insurgency', in *Pathways for Irregular Forces in Southeast Asia* (London: Routledge, 2022), pp. 152–3.

[6] Srisompob Jitpiromsri, Napisa Waitoolkiat and Paul Chambers, 'Special Issue: Quagmire of Violence in Thailand's Southern Borderlands Chapter 1: Introduction', *Asian Affairs: An American Review*, vol. 45, no. 2, 28 April 2019.

PHILIPPINES

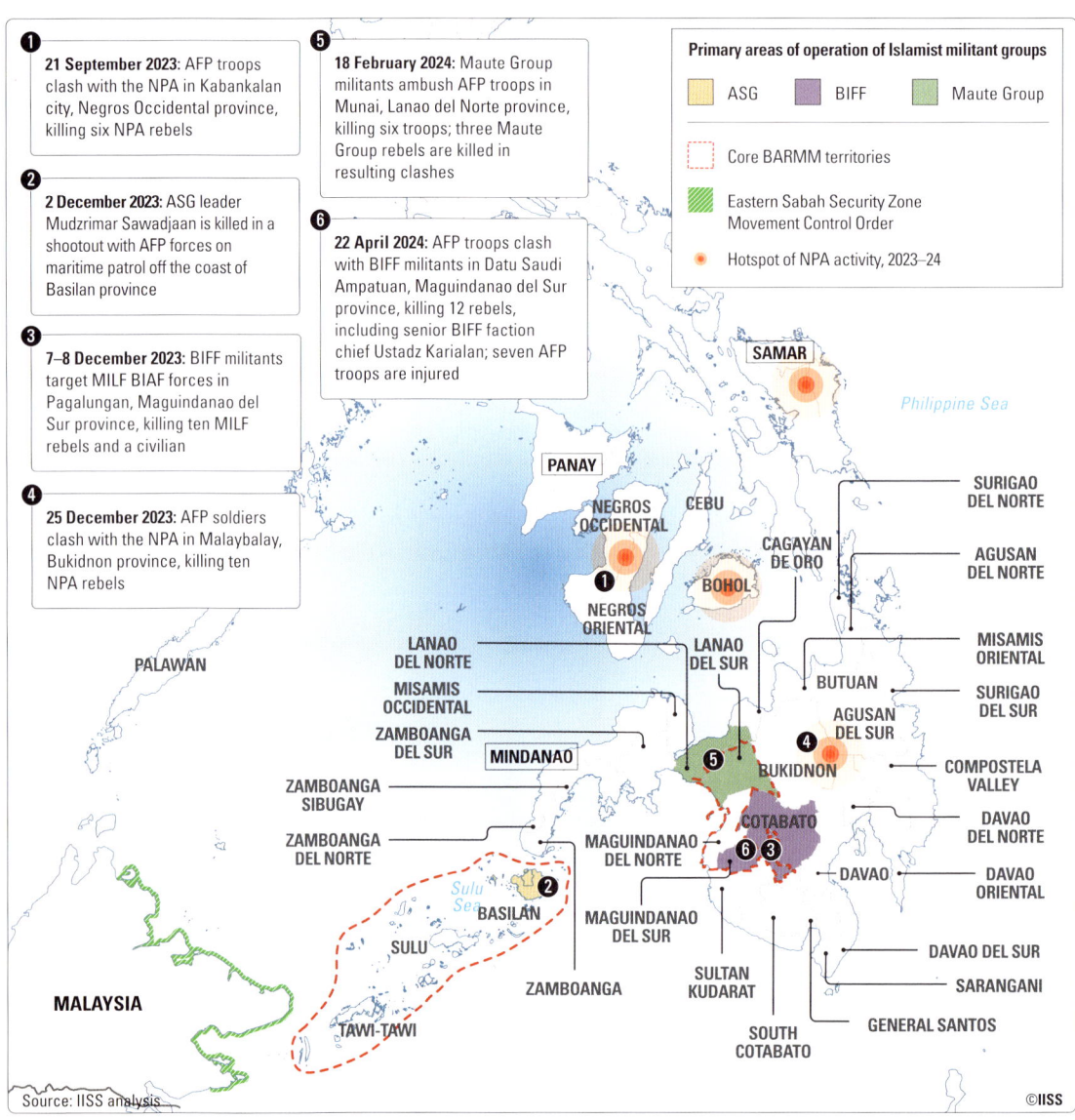

Conflict Overview

The Philippine government has fought Moro separatists in western Mindanao since 1972. After earlier uprisings against colonial authorities, the March 1968 Jabidah massacre of Moro army recruits by Philippine soldiers ignited revived secessionism. Driven by the political, cultural and religious oppression of Moro Muslims, the Moro National Liberation Front (MNLF) and later the Moro Islamic Liberation Front (MILF) waged an armed campaign for independence. Both groups eventually signed final peace deals with Manila (the MNLF in 1996 and the MILF in 2014), which included provisions for disarmament and self-rule.

Since 2019, MILF chairperson Al Haj Murad Ebrahim has led a transitional authority in the Bangsamoro Autonomous Region in Muslim

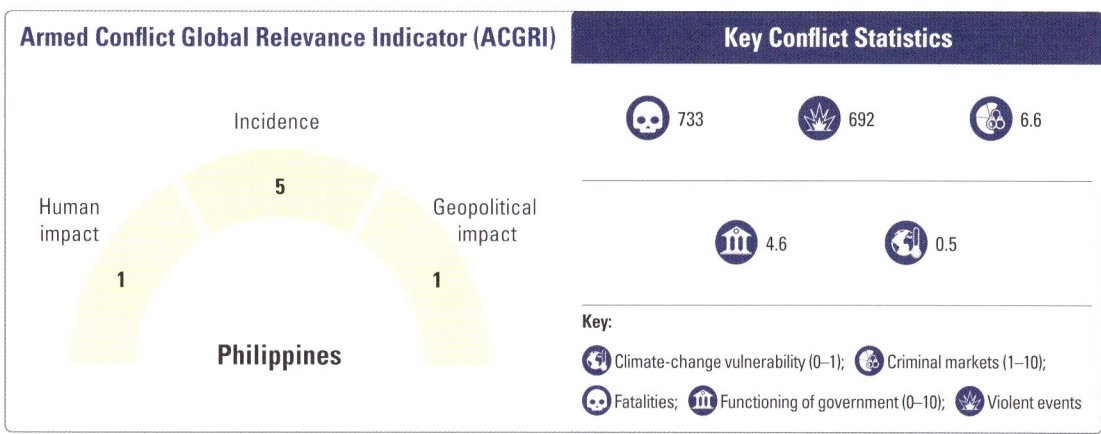

Mindanao (BARMM), which will govern until planned elections in May 2025. However, several militant extremist groups aligned with the Islamic State (ISIS) remain active. The Abu Sayyaf Group (ASG), the Bangsamoro Islamic Freedom Fighters (BIFF) and the Maute Group joined forces in 2017 in an attempt to forge a regional caliphate centred on Marawi city but were defeated by Philippine troops in a five-month urban war.[1] Militants have since executed several high-profile bombings but are now largely restricted to remote areas. Alongside ideology, high rates of poverty and joblessness in the BARMM have long driven rebel recruitment.

Similar factors have fuelled a nationwide Maoist insurgency by the New People's Army (NPA) since 1969. Fighting spiked during the dictatorship of Ferdinand Marcos Sr before receding in recent decades, yet the NPA retains a foothold in rural parts of eastern Mindanao and the Visayas. Peace talks with the NPA's political wing, the Communist Party of the Philippines (CPP), have repeatedly failed in the post-1986 democratic era, most recently under president Rodrigo Duterte in 2017. The mountainous and forested terrain on which both Maoist rebels and Islamist militants strategically operate has hindered attempts by the military to defeat them.

Conflict Update

The MILF-led political transition and disarmament of MILF rebels in the BARMM continued throughout the reporting period, as lawmakers approved the boundaries of parliamentary districts for the May 2025 elections. Though about 14,000 of the MILF's 40,000-strong fighting force have yet to demobilise, the administration of President Ferdinand Marcos Jr has insisted that there will be no further extension to the transition, after the elections were previously delayed from 2022.[2]

Violence between Islamist militant groups and the Armed Forces of the Philippines (AFP) entered a retaliatory cycle in December 2023–April 2024. The killing of ASG figurehead Mudzrimar Sawadjaan in Basilan province was soon followed by the bombing of a Catholic mass in Marawi city by the Maute Group. An intensified military crackdown targeting the BIFF and the Maute Group ensued over the next months, drawing attacks on AFP forces in response.

Though Islamist groups have been weakened, there is potential for them to rebound. MILF rebels frustrated with the limited socio-economic gains of the peace process could constitute a recruitment pool for jihadists, while Islamist groups angered by the MILF's acceptance of autonomy rather than independence might seek to launch attacks aimed at destabilisation as the 2025 elections draw closer. Powerful political clans and private armed groups could also come into conflict with the MILF as it seeks to establish itself as an electoral force.[3]

The NPA still poses a threat in eastern Mindanao, the Visayas and northern Luzon. Despite agreeing to restart peace talks with the Philippine government in November 2023, dialogue had not resumed as of June 2024, and fighting with the AFP had intensified.[4] Manila's refusal to release imprisoned members of the CPP's peace negotiation panel, the National Democratic Front of the Philippines (NDFP), has complicated efforts to restart dialogue. The AFP has used this impasse to degrade the NPA on the battlefield as it aims to reorient its forces towards external defence.

Conflict Parties

Armed Forces of the Philippines (AFP)

Strength: 146,250 active personnel across the army, navy and air force. Reserve force of 131,000, as well as 50,000 reservists in Citizen Armed Force Geographical Units.

Areas of operation: Operates nationwide. Its headquarters, Camp Aguinaldo, is in Quezon city, Metro Manila.

Leadership: Led by Gen. Romeo Brawner Jr (chief of staff of the AFP), appointed in July 2023. The Western Mindanao Command, operating in the BARMM, is led by Lt-Gen. William Gonzales.

Structure: Divided into seven unified commands and one combatant command. The Western Mindanao Command, with three assigned infantry divisions, is tasked with combatting Islamist groups, while the Eastern Mindanao Command, with two assigned infantry divisions, is primarily tasked with combatting the NPA. AFP infantry battalions are comprised of 300–500 soldiers.[5]

History: Established by the 1935 National Defense Act under the United States' colonial rule. The AFP passed to Philippine control upon the country's independence in 1946.

Objectives: Defeat the NPA nationwide and defeat Islamist militant groups active in western Mindanao. To this effect, the AFP launches targeted raids and air/ground offensives and conducts routine patrols in areas of militant activity, often over difficult terrain.

Opponents: ASG, BIFF, Maute Group and NPA.

Affiliates/allies: MILF and MNLF, which provide intelligence support in operations against Islamist militants. The AFP is supported by the Philippine National Police (PNP) in active shoot-outs and law-enforcement raids.

Resources/capabilities: The army primarily uses small arms and artillery in operations against rebels and is assisted by air-force light-attack aircraft and helicopters. Naval assets are deployed in the Sulu Sea to prevent the transit of militants.

Moro Islamic Liberation Front (MILF)

Strength: 13,868 active fighters serving in the MILF's Bangsamoro Islamic Armed Forces (BIAF), down from 40,000 in 2019 as 26,132 have since been demobilised.[6] The remainder of the BIAF force is set to be decommissioned under the terms of the 2014 Comprehensive Agreement on the Bangsamoro (CAB) by mid-2025.

Areas of operation: Most fighters remain encamped in a network of MILF bases in the BARMM and no longer fight the AFP. Up to 3,000 demobilised MILF rebels will serve alongside the AFP and PNP in Joint Peace and Security Teams, while several hundred ex-rebels will become PNP officers.[7] The MILF's headquarters, Camp Darapanan, is in Maguindanao del Norte province.

Leadership: Led by chairperson Al Haj Murad Ebrahim. He also serves as interim chief minister of the BARMM pending regional elections in May 2025.

Structure: Operates similarly to a regular army, with battalions and a centralised leadership body. The MILF is in the process of decommissioning and has formed a political party – the United Bangsamoro Justice Party – to contest future BARMM elections.

History: Founded in 1977 by Hashim Salamat after breaking away from the MNLF. The MILF fought a separatist guerrilla war against the AFP for decades in western Mindanao.

Objectives: Initially advocated for an independent state for Moro Muslims and targeted the AFP in ambushes and bomb attacks. In the late 1990s the MILF began peace talks with Manila, seeking autonomy. After signing the CAB in 2014, the MILF committed to peace. It has led the transitional BARMM government since 2019 and aims to retain power in the May 2025 elections.

Opponents: ASG, BIFF and Maute Group. MILF fighters still clash intermittently with MNLF forces at the local level, where fighting is often tied to land disputes and long-standing clan rivalries.

Moro Islamic Liberation Front (MILF)

Affiliates/allies: Formally allied to the AFP. Both main factions of the MNLF, under Muslimin Sema and Nur Misuari, have expressed support for MILF-led governance of the BARMM.

Resources/capabilities: Access to small arms, grenade launchers and other conventional weapons. These are all set to be decommissioned under the CAB, with the process expected to be complete by mid-2025. As of August 2023, MILF forces had surrendered 4,625 firearms.[8]

Moro National Liberation Front (MNLF)

Strength: Fewer than 10,000 active fighters. The MNLF's strength has declined since the 1970s, when it had around 30,000 members.

Areas of operation: Western Mindanao and the Sulu archipelago. Most fighters are encamped and rarely engage in combat, aside from local inter-factional and clan disputes with the MILF or other MNLF members.

Leadership: Led by chairperson Muslimin Sema. MNLF founder Nur Misuari remains influential and leads a 3,000-strong faction in Sulu. Misuari's son, Abdulkarim Tan Misuari (MNLF vice chair and deputy speaker of the BARMM parliament), is an increasingly prominent figure.

Structure: Initially a centralised organisation, the MNLF splintered into two after signing a peace deal with the government in 1996. In September 2023, the factions signed an agreement to form a Joint MNLF Executive Committee and pledged to cooperate to implement the 1996 peace accord.

History: Formed as a splinter of the now-defunct Muslim Independence Movement in 1972 and fought the AFP with the aim of forging an independent Moro state in western Mindanao.

Objectives: No longer advocates for Moro independence. To contest the BARMM elections in 2025, the Sema faction has formed a political party, the Bangsamoro Party, and the Misuari faction has formed the Mahardika Party. The Sema faction has consistently supported the peace process between the MILF and the Philippine government. The Misuari faction had previously been critical of the process, but in 2022 it publicly backed the MILF-led interim authority and has since maintained its support.

Opponents: BIFF and Maute Group. The Sema faction is opposed to the ASG, while the Misuari faction is rhetorically opposed but retains kinship ties to the group. The MILF is a historical rival of the MNLF, but the two sides rarely resort to violence (aside from clashes related to localised clan disputes).

Affiliates/allies: The AFP since a 1996 peace deal, but violence has occasionally broken out – most notoriously in the 20-day siege of Zamboanga city in September 2013, led by Misuari.

Resources/capabilities: The MNLF no longer fights the AFP but retains access to rebel bases and small arms. The Misuari-led faction remains a powerful but dormant actor in Mindanao, and fears over it adopting an armed spoiler role in the MILF peace process have receded.

Bangsamoro Islamic Freedom Fighters (BIFF)

Strength: 100–200 active fighters (estimate).

Areas of operation: Active in Maguindanao del Sur province, primarily in Liguasan Marsh and an area known as the 'SPMS box' (encompassing the towns of Shariff Aguak, Pagatin, Mamasapano and Datu Salibo). The BIFF is also present in Maguindanao del Norte and Cotabato provinces.

Leadership: Divided into three main factions. Esmael Abdulmalik (alias 'Abu Toraife') and Ismael Abubakar (alias 'Imam Bongos') are factional leaders. Ustadz Karialan (alias 'Imam Minimbang'), leader of the third faction, was killed by AFP troops in Datu Saudi Ampatuan in April 2024.

Structure: No centralised leadership, though its factions and sub-factions cooperate in an ad hoc manner. In March 2024, the Bongos and Minimbang factions joined forces to attack AFP soldiers.

History: Formed as a splinter of the MILF in 2010 when its founder, Ameril Umbra Kato, grew frustrated with the MILF's decision to drop demands for independence in favour of autonomy and self-governance. The BIFF fought in the 2017 Marawi siege alongside the ASG and Maute Group.

Objectives: Establish an independent homeland for the Moro people. The BIFF pledged allegiance to ISIS in 2014 and fought to establish a regional caliphate. The Toraife faction still holds this ambition, while the other two factions act in a more retaliatory and defensive manner against the AFP and their allegiance to ISIS is unclear. The BIFF is known to extort local businesses to sustain itself financially.

Opponents: AFP and MILF. Despite being the BIFF's parent group, the MILF has cooperated with the AFP in offensives against the BIFF in recent years. In retaliation, the BIFF has attacked MILF rebels and their family members. The BIFF is also opposed to the MNLF but has not engaged in direct confrontation with the group.

Affiliates/allies: Nominally allied to the ASG and the Maute Group but has no operational ties.

Resources/capabilities: Uses small arms in shoot-outs with AFP troops and retains the ability to construct improvised explosive devices (IEDs), targeting AFP checkpoints and military vehicles in roadside ambushes. Civilians have also been targeted in bomb attacks on public buses.

Maute Group

Strength: 40 active fighters (AFP estimate).[9] The Maute Group previously comprised up to 1,000 members but most were killed by AFP troops during the 2017 siege of Marawi.

Areas of operation: Active in Lanao del Norte and Lanao del Sur provinces. The group operates primarily in remote mountainous and forested areas, moving between temporary camps.

Leadership: Nasser Daud (alias 'Mahater') replaced Khadafi Mimbesa (known as 'the Engineer' for his role in bomb-making) as leader after he was killed in an encounter with AFP troops in Piagapo in January 2024. His predecessor, Faharudin Hadji Satar (alias 'Abu Zacaria'), who was also the 'emir' of the Islamic State in Southeast Asia, was killed by AFP forces in June 2023.

Structure: Fighters operate in small units. Since founders Abdullah Maute and Omar Maute were killed during the 2017 Marawi siege, the group has lacked a defined structure or hierarchy.

History: Founded in 2010–11 and espouses an extreme form of Salafi-Wahhabi ideology more often associated with jihadist groups in the Middle East. The Maute Group led the 2017 Marawi siege, in which its senior leaders were killed and capabilities damaged, alongside the ASG and BIFF.

Objectives: Through seizing and holding territory in Marawi, the Maute Group aimed to forge a regional Islamic caliphate in Southeast Asia centred on Mindanao. Despite its defeat in Marawi in 2017, the group still claims to represent the East Asian wilayat (province) of the Islamic State.

Opponents: AFP, MILF and MNLF.

Affiliates/allies: Ideologically and rhetorically aligned with ISIS, though any operational ties with affiliated groups abroad are uncertain. It is nominally allied to the ASG and the BIFF faction led by Toraife.

Resources/capabilities: Possesses a limited cache of small arms and retains the ability to construct low-grade, remotely detonated explosive devices, using improvised grenades and mortars.

Abu Sayyaf Group (ASG)

Strength: 20 active members (AFP estimate).[10]

Areas of operation: Active presence in the maritime province of Basilan. Remnants of the group also exist in Sulu province. The ASG is no longer operational in Tawi-Tawi, the Zamboanga peninsula or Malaysia's Sabah State, which it previously used as a hideout. Its presence in the Sulu and Celebes seas is restricted by naval patrols.

Leadership: Unclear. ASG leader Mudzrimar Sawadjaan (alias 'Mundi') was killed by AFP forces in December 2023. His uncle, former ASG leader Hatib Hajan Sawadjaan, was killed by AFP troops in July 2020.

Structure: Operates as a loose network of affiliated factions and sub-factions arranged along clan and family lines. Little of the group remains.

History: Formed in 1991 by radical Islamist preacher Abdurajak Abubakar Janjalani. In the 2000s, the group became notorious for hostage-taking in the Sulu Sea. The ASG temporarily joined forces with the BIFF and the Maute Group in 2017 to lay siege to Marawi city. It has since retreated to outlying islands.

Objectives: Sustain itself through criminal enterprise and re-establish an Islamic sultanate in the Sulu archipelago. In 2014, then-leader Isnilon Hapilon (now deceased) declared allegiance to the Islamic State and sought the creation of a regional caliphate in Southeast Asia.

Opponents: AFP, MILF and an MNLF faction led by Muslimin Sema. MNLF fighters based in Sulu under Nur Misuari have traditionally been tolerant of the ASG, but in 2022 the MNLF vowed to assist the AFP in anti-ASG operations.

Affiliates/allies: Allied ideologically with ISIS, the BIFF and the Maute Group but has no known operational ties.

Resources/capabilities: Uses small arms and IEDs to attack AFP troops. The group retains bomb-making skills, but its capacity to conduct suicide bombings (as it did from 2018–20) and carry out maritime kidnappings has reduced substantially in recent years.

New People's Army (NPA)

Strength: 1,500 fighters (AFP estimate) across 11 'weakened' guerrilla fronts nationwide.[11] The NPA's estimated strength has fallen from its historical 3,000–4,000 fighters (consistent over the past decade) due to sustained military operations and a high surrender rate.

Areas of operation: Active in its traditional strongholds of eastern Mindanao, the Visayas (particularly in Negros Occidental and Northern Samar) and northern Luzon. The NPA operates primarily in rural and forested areas, with fighters moving frequently between makeshift bases.

Leadership: NPA founder and CPP chairperson Jose Maria Sison died in self-imposed exile in the Netherlands in 2022, aged 83. No replacement has been named as overall CPP/NPA leader. Sison's widow, Julie de Lima, serves as interim chairperson of the NDFP peace-negotiation panel, with Luis Jalandoni as another key figure. Fighting on the ground is overseen by local NPA commanders.

Structure: Rebels operate in small, closely knit units in the countryside, while hit squads operate in Special Partisan Units in urban areas to carry out assassinations. The NPA is the armed wing of the CPP, which is represented in peace talks by the NDFP.

History: The NPA was formed in 1969 by the CPP, which was established in 1968. It has battled government troops for more than 50 years, with fighting centred on rural areas. NDFP-led peace talks have failed under six Philippine presidents in the post-1986 democratic era.

New People's Army (NPA)

Objectives: Ideology has remained unchanged since the 1960s. The NPA is fighting what it labels a 'protracted people's war' to overthrow the Philippine government and replace it with a socialist system.[12] It does not seize territory but exercises de facto control in rural areas via extortion and intimidation. It also launches ambushes targeting AFP troops, with the aim of weakening AFP morale.

Opponents: AFP and PNP. The NPA does not engage in conflict with Moro or Islamist rebel groups based in western Mindanao and largely avoids operating in the BARMM provinces. The NPA does, however, operate on the Zamboanga peninsula to the north.

Affiliates/allies: Has no known affiliates, though in its early years the NPA received funds and weapons from China and like-minded Maoist rebel groups based abroad.

Resources/capabilities: Small arms looted from AFP and PNP bases, and other firearms seized from private security guards during armed raids on businesses. The NPA also deploys IEDs and rudimentary explosives.

Other relevant parties

Philippine authorities often use the term Dawlah Islamiyah (Islamic State) to refer to the ASG, the BIFF and the Maute Group, drawing little distinction. This term also included a smaller Islamist group linked to the BIFF, Ansar Khalifah Philippines (AKP), which in recent years had engaged in criminal activities and carried out IED attacks in the southern Mindanao provinces of Sarangani and South Cotabato. AKP (also referred to as the Hassan or Maguid factions of the BIFF) is now inactive as a separate entity and its remnants have effectively been subsumed into or are indistinguishable from the BIFF, though they may retain a presence in their former areas of operation. Al-Khobar, an extortion group with ties to the BIFF, is also sometimes considered part of the broader Dawlah Islamiyah network.

Notes

[1] Amnesty International, 'Philippines: "Battle of Marawi" Leaves Trail of Death and Destruction', 17 November 2017.

[2] Necva Tastan, 'Decommissioning of Combatants in Southern Philippines to Be Completed by 2025: IDB', *Anadolu Agency*, 8 September 2023; and Rommel Rebollido, 'Marcos Not in Favor of Another Extension for Bangsamoro Transition Authority – Galvez', Rappler, 4 April 2024.

[3] International Crisis Group, 'The Philippines: Keeping the Bangsamoro Peace Process on Track', 30 January 2024.

[4] Presidential Communications Office, 'Oslo Joint Communique', 28 November 2023.

[5] Julie S. Alipala, 'AFP Reduces Troop Presence in Sulu; Improved Security Status Cited', *Inquirer*, 3 September 2022.

[6] Wilnard Bacelonia, 'MILF Decommissioning on Track, Galvez Tells Senators', Philippine News Agency, 6 February 2024.

[7] Priam Nepomuceno, 'Joint Peace Security Team Activated in Lanao Norte Town', Philippine News Agency, 12 December 2022; and Jiselle Anne C. Casucian, 'Nearly 300 MILF, MNLF Members Sworn In as PNP Personnel', GMA News, 29 December 2023.

[8] Office of the Presidential Adviser on Peace, Reconciliation and Unity, 'Galvez: PH Gov't Has Solid Plan to Complete MILF Decommissioning Process', 12 October 2023.

[9] Froilan Gallardo, 'Brawner: Militants Caught Soldiers Off Guard During Deadly Lanao del Norte Strike', Rappler, 22 February 2024.

[10] John Eric Mendoza, 'Abu Sayyaf Now "Dismantled" After Over 30 Years – Westmincom Chief', *Inquirer*, 22 March 2024.

[11] Michael Punongbayan, '1,500 Reds, 11 Weakened Guerrilla Fronts Left – AFP', *Philippine Star*, 17 January 2024.

[12] Stanford University, Center for International Security and Cooperation, 'Communist Party of the Philippines – New People's Army'.

INDONESIA

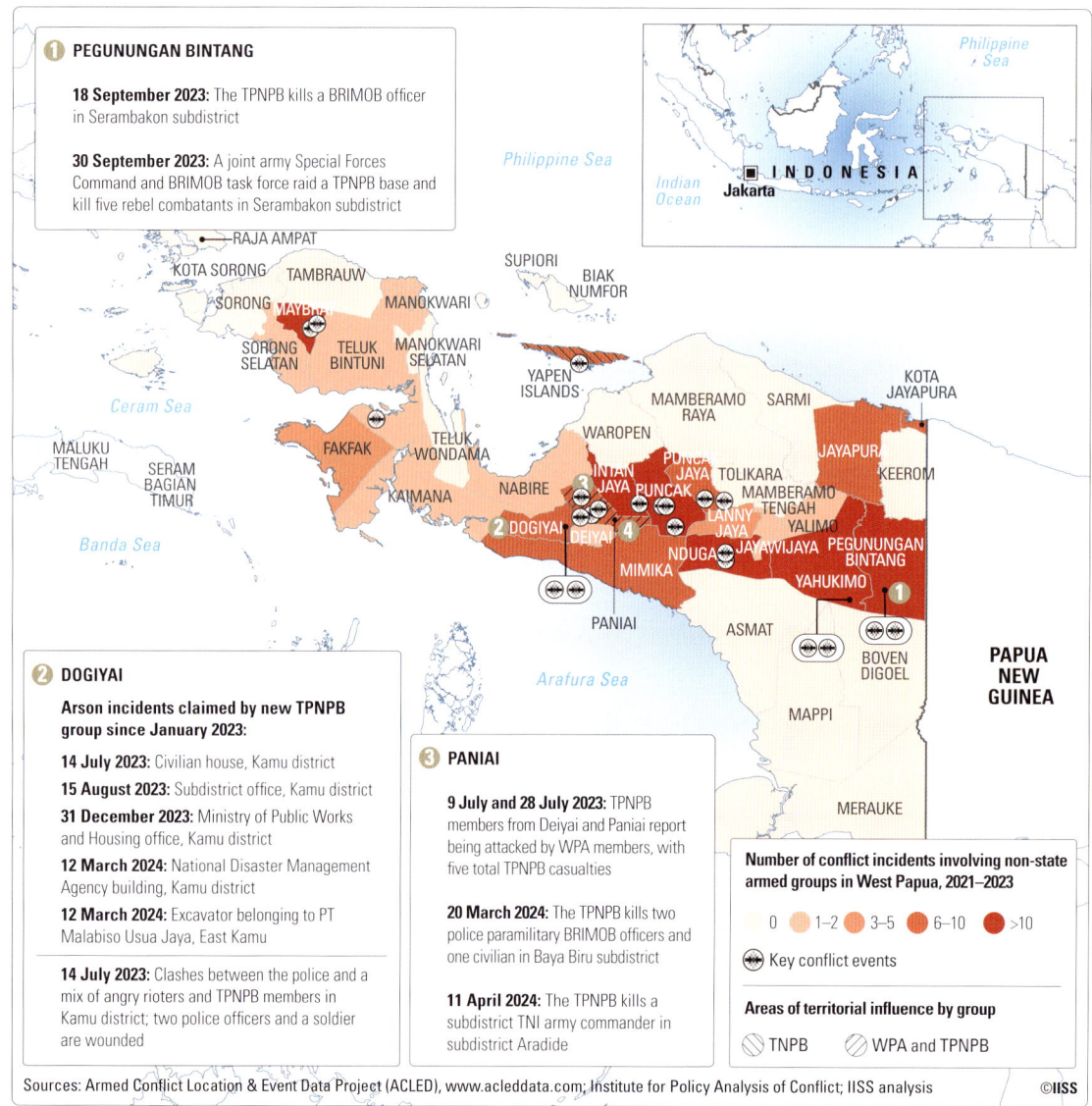

Conflict Overview

The West Papuan separatist movement started after the Indonesian government annexed the region from the Netherlands colonial administration in the early 1960s. The integration was formalised by a referendum called the Act of Free Choice in 1969, which many Papuans considered neither free nor a choice. Out of an estimated 800,000 residents in the region, the Indonesian military handpicked 1,022 Papuan representatives who then voted unanimously to support Indonesia's sovereignty over West Papua.[1] Since then, grievances over the disputed referendum, as well as widespread state repression, neglect, perceived racism, resource exploitation and an influx of people from the rest of Indonesia, have fuelled the separatist movement and triggered violent conflict.

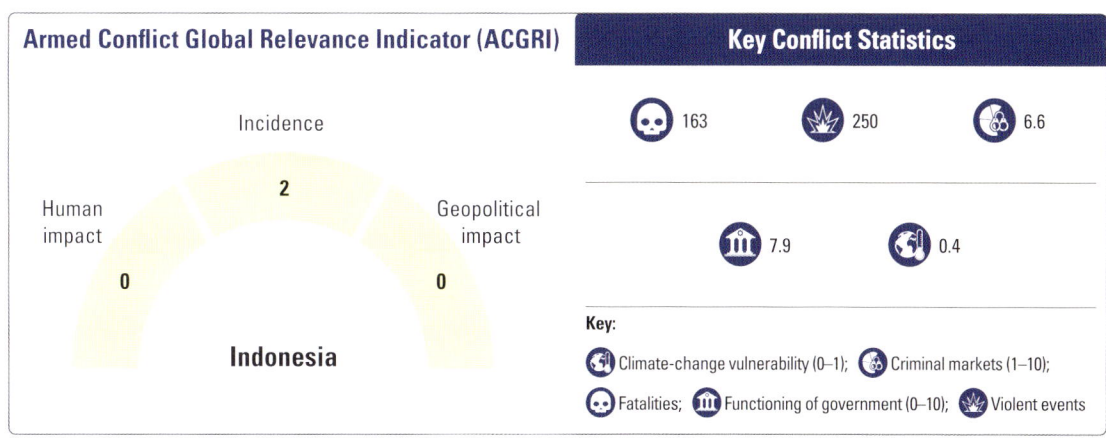

Conflict(s)	Type	Start date
West Papua separatist conflict	I LI	1961

Key: I LI Internal: localised insurgency

The Free Papua Organisation (OPM) initially led the insurgency, but leadership disputes in the 1970s left the group fragmented politically and militarily. Without clear leadership and centralised command, the armed factions began operating independently, in geographical isolation from each other; became divided along ethnic lines; and no longer possessed a shared strategy or political agenda.[2] From 1980–2010, insurgent activity was marked by low-intensity violence in highland regions surrounding the Freeport mining sites in Mimika regency and along the Papua New Guinea border.[3] Violence escalated significantly after one of the armed factions of the OPM, the West Papua National Liberation Army (TPNPB), issued a declaration of war in January 2018. Since then, attacks on security apparatus and non-Papuans have become more frequent and widespread.[4] The assassination of the Papua chief of intelligence, Brigadier-General I Gusti Putu Danny Karya Nugraha, in April 2021 prompted the government to label the TPNPB as a terrorist organisation.

Conflict Update

Security operations have failed to reduce the TPNPB's sporadic, but widespread, attacks. Operations to rescue a New Zealand pilot abducted by the TPNPB in early 2023, for instance, have been fruitless and have resulted in multiple fatalities sustained by the Indonesian military. Meanwhile, attempts to negotiate have been largely unsuccessful. In February 2024, the kidnapper, TPNPB commander Egianus Kogoya, refused ransom payment and demanded the United Nations' involvement in negotiations with the Indonesian government as a condition of the hostage's release.

Throughout the reporting period, the TPNPB continued to expand its operations to other regencies in West Papua. In Pegunungan Bintang, a new TPNPB local group that had formed in December 2022 launched several attacks until the military tracked it down and killed five of its combatants in September 2023. In Dogiyai, another new TPNPB group was responsible for a series of arson attacks targeting public facilities from July 2023–March 2024. Finally, in Paniai, TPNPB members ambushed and killed two police officers on 20 March 2024 and a military subdistrict commander on 11 April.[5]

Following the violent events in Paniai, the military decided to refer to the insurgents by their organisation's name, the OPM, rather than as 'armed criminals' or 'separatist-terrorists'.[6] This relabelling indicates that the Indonesian National Armed Forces (TNI) is planning to confront the OPM militarily, without regard to the law-enforcement efforts carried out by the police or human-rights protections for civilians. TNI commander Agus Subiyanto has proposed a 'smart power' approach, which involves employing drones to improve penetration in the highlands and reduce the number of military casualties.[7]

President-elect Prabowo Subianto, a former Indonesian Army general known for his involvement in operations in Papua in the 1990s and currently serving as defence minister, is expected to endorse a military-dominated approach to quelling insurgencies in West Papua when he takes office in October 2024. However, he has also promised amnesty for any armed groups that wish to surrender.

Conflict Parties

Indonesian National Armed Forces (TNI)

Strength: 404,500 active personnel across the army, navy and air force, as well as 8,574 civilian reservists.[8] Between 20,000 and 25,000 active personnel are estimated to be stationed in West Papua.[9]

Areas of operation: Nationwide. The TNI's headquarters, Mabes TNI, is in Cilangkap, Jakarta.

Leadership: Gen. Agus Subiyanto (commander), appointed in November 2023.

Structure: Two military regional commands (KODAM) oversee the provinces of West Papua: KODAM XVII/Cenderawasih based in Papua province and KODAM XVIII/Kasuari based in West Papua province. Each command has an organic infantry brigade, lower-level military resort commands and support units. One of the TNI's three Joint Regional Defence Commands is also in Mimika, Central Papua.

History: Founded in 1945 during the nationalist struggle against Dutch colonial power. The armed forces included the police from 1960 onwards, until the legislature (the People's Consultative Assembly) separated the two in 2000, with the military made responsible for security and defence and the police made responsible for law enforcement and public order. A civilian reservist force (commonly known as KOMCAD) was created in 2021.

Objectives: Defeat the West Papuan insurgents, safeguard infrastructure development, conduct community outreach and assist development in rural areas. The TNI regularly deploys infantry battalions and special-forces units for counter-insurgency operations. The TNI also sends army engineering detachments to carry out construction projects in conflict zones.

Opponents: TPNPB and other West Papuan insurgents, which the TNI broadly identifies as 'armed criminal' or 'separatist-terrorist' groups.

Affiliates/allies: Often collaborates with the State Intelligence Agency for intelligence gathering, and the Indonesian National Police (POLRI) to conduct law-enforcement operations against suspected rebels, to safeguard national vital objects such as public infrastructure and the property of key private companies, and for riot control.

Resources/capabilities: The TNI primarily uses small arms and light artillery such as mortars, as well as helicopters to provide troop transport and combat air support. West Papua's mountainous and forested terrains restrict the TNI's use of armoured vehicles in the highland region.

Indonesian National Police (POLRI)

Strength: Approximately 440,000 personnel, including 45,108 officers from the police paramilitary unit, the Mobile Brigade Corps (BRIMOB).[10] There are an estimated 22,419 personnel stationed in the West Papuan provinces.[11]

Areas of operation: Nationwide. The POLRI's headquarters, Mabes Polri, is in Jakarta.

Leadership: Pol. Gen. Listyo Sigit Prabowo (chief).

Structure: Police regional stations are present from province to district levels. The POLRI is also involved in counter-insurgency led by the *Operation Cartenz's* Peace task force, a joint police–military unit formed in 2022.

History: Founded in 1946, the POLRI was integrated into the armed forces in 1960 with a limited role in security. However, after Indonesia's democratic reforms in 1998, the TNI ceded much of its role in domestic security affairs to the POLRI.

Objectives: Law enforcement, counter-terrorism, maintaining public order, and counter-insurgency and anti-terrorist financing.

Opponents: West Papua pro-independence movement, including armed combatants, members of political organisations and student activists.

Affiliates/allies: TNI.

Resources/capabilities: The BRIMOB unit is equipped with small arms and uses modified commercial uninhabited aerial vehicles (UAVs) for surveillance and rotary-wing UAVs to drop explosive shells on rebel camps.

West Papua National Liberation Army (TPNPB)

Strength: 500–1,000 fighters.[12]

Areas of operation: The TPNPB claims to have 34 local groups in all six provinces in West Papua.[13] However, its operations have been concentrated in only 13 regencies over the past five years: Paniai, Deiyai, Dogiyai, Puncak Jaya, Puncak, Mimika, Intan Jaya, Lanny Jaya, Nduga, Pegunungan Bintang, Yahukimo, Teluk Bintuni and Maybrat.[14]

Leadership: Goliat Tabuni (supreme commander).

Structure: TPNPB central command serves as an information hub rather than a military headquarters. Insurgency activities are carried out by local TPNPB groups, referred to as Regional Defence Commands or *Kodaps*, which operate autonomously with a limited degree of coordination between one another.

History: The TPNPB is one of the OPM's most prominent armed factions. Its formation was the result of the 2012 OPM conference on Biak island, where several OPM militant factions joined together and rebranded themselves under a new name.

Objectives: Total revolutionary war to expel Indonesian security forces, foreign companies, and non-Papuan migrant workers and civil servants from West Papua. The TPNPB demands political negotiation with the Indonesian government through mediation involving the UN.

Opponents: TNI, POLRI, non-Papuan migrants and West Papua Army (WPA).

Affiliates/allies: OPM and other political factions such as the National Committee for West Papua.

Resources/capabilities: Small arms (mostly standardised weapons used by TNI and POLRI personnel), homemade arms, and traditional weapons such as bows and arrows and machetes.

West Papua Army (WPA)

Strength: 50–100 fighters.[15]

Areas of operation: Paniai regency, Central Papua province.

Leadership: Demianus Yogi (supreme commander).

Structure: Several camps in Paniai. A few TPNPB local commanders who joined the WPA had a history of operating around the Freeport mining sites in Mimika.

History: The United Liberation Movement for West Papua (ULMWP) facilitated the establishment of the WPA in August 2021 as an attempt to unify and control the armed movement commander.[16] The TPNPB sees the WPA as an enemy trying to divide the armed movement.

Objectives: West Papua independence through political negotiation or a referendum.

Opponents: TPNPB, TNI and POLRI. The WPA had several deadly clashes against TPNPB members in Puncak and Paniai in 2023.[17] However, there have been no reports of the WPA clashing with TNI or POLRI personnel.

Affiliates/allies: ULMWP.

Resources/capabilities: Small arms used by security apparatus and homemade weapons.

West Papua National Army (TNPB) (also known as the National Liberation Army of the OPM, TPN–OPM)

Strength: 20–50 fighters.[18]

Areas of operation: Yapen Islands regency and the northern coastal regions of West Papua.

Leadership: Fernando Worabay (regional commander).

Structure: The TNPB's most active members are based in Sasawa village, Yapen Islands.

History: The TNPB is part of the OPM military wing TPN–OPM. The TPN–OPM used to be active in the coastal areas of West Papua and the Papua New Guinea border, but most local units have been dormant or disbanded since the security forces cracked down on them in the 1970s and 1980s. Currently, the TNPB is the only active armed faction still operating in the coastal areas.

Objectives: West Papua independence and gaining international recognition of the TNPB's 'belligerent' status as an armed separatist organisation. Like the TPNPB, the TNPB opposed the 2022 humanitarian pause and demanded that the Indonesian government negotiate directly with the armed groups instead of with West Papuan political organisations.

Opponents: TNI and POLRI.

Affiliates/allies: OPM and TPNPB. Despite having different leadership, the relationship between these groups has been amicable. TNPB members report their insurgency activities to the TPNPB's spokesperson, Sebby Sambom, who is based in Papua New Guinea.

Resources/capabilities: Small arms, mostly homemade weapons and Molotov cocktails. The TNPB engages in sporadic ambushes targeting the military and police patrol units in the Yapen Islands regency.

Notes

1. John Saltford, *The United Nations and the Indonesian Takeover of West Papua, 1962–1969* (London: Routledge, 2003), p. 3.
2. Institute for Policy Analysis of Conflict, 'The Current Status of the Papuan Pro-Independence Movement', Report no. 21, 24 August 2015.
3. The Indonesian government refers to the sub-provincial

4. administrative units as 'regencies' (*kabupaten* in Indonesian). 'Districts' refer to the sub-regency administrative units (*kecamatan*).
4. Institute for Policy Analysis of Conflict, 'Escalating Armed Conflict and a New Security Approach in Papua', Report no. 77, 13 July 2022; and Sindy Ajara, Laura Sorica and Elliott Bynum, 'Papuan Independence and Political Disorder in Indonesia', Armed Conflict Location & Event Data Project (ACLED), 5 October 2022.
5. Armed Conflict Location & Event Data Project (ACLED), www.acleddata.com.
6. 'Violence in Papua Is Increasing, OPM Labelling Needs to Be Clarified', Kompas, 12 April 2024.
7. 'TNI Embraces "Smart Power" Approach to Counter KKB Attacks', *Antara*, 1 December 2023.
8. Indonesia Ministry of Defence, 'Menhan Prabowo Wakili Presiden Jokowi Tetapkan 2.497 Komcad TNI TA. 2023' [Defence minister Prabowo representing President Jokowi appoints 2,497 Komcad TNI year 2023], 11 August 2023.
9. Latest estimations are from 2013. The TNI has never disclosed the total number of soldiers in West Papua or how many combat-ready units are deployed annually for counter-insurgency operations. See Antonius Made Tony Supriatma, 'TNI/Polri in West Papua: How Security Reforms Work in the Conflict Region', *Indonesia*, no. 95, April 2013, p. 98.
10. Markas Besar Kepolisian Negara Republik Indonesia Staf Sumber Daya Manusia [Headquarters of the National Police of the Republic of Indonesia Human Resources Staff], 'Rencana Kerja Staf Sumber Daya Manusia POLRI Tahun Anggaran 2023' [Work plan of the National Police human resources staff for the 2023 fiscal year], POLRI, 12 August 2022; and 'Brimob Bakal Tempatkan 36 Ribu Personel di 3 Wilayah Tugas Baru', [Brimob will deploy 36 thousand personnel in three new assignment areas], CNN Indonesia, 14 June 2022.
11. The Papua province regional police headquarters reported in 2022 that it has 14,218 personnel and the West Papua province regional police headquarters reported in 2023 that it has 8,201 personnel. See Bumi Papua, 'Polda Papua Masih Butuh 14 Ribuan Personel, Berminat?' [Papua Polda needs 14 thousand personnel, interested?], Kumparan, 28 December 2022; and Fransiskus Salu Weking, 'Polda Papua Barat pecat 38 personel selama 2023' [West Papua Polda fired 38 personnel in 2023], *Antara*, 2 January 2024.
12. Author's sources.
13. Ria Rizki Nirmala Sari, 'Jubir Umumkan 34 Kodap TPNPB-OPM Bakal Gelar Upcara Kemerdekaan Papua Pada 1 Juli mendatang' [Spokesperson announced 34 TPNPB-OPM Kodaps will hold independence rally on 1 July], suara.com, 29 June 2022.
14. Armed Conflict Location & Event Data Project (ACLED), www.acleddata.com.
15. Author's estimate based on field research in Nabire regency (neighbouring Paniai) in October 2023.
16. 'Komnas TPNPB-OPM Tuding Demianus Magay Yogi Lakukan Kudeta Militer Revolusi' [TPNPB-OPM national command accuses Demianus Magay Yogi of committing a revolutionary military coup], Suara Papua, 17 August 2021.
17. A TPNPB commander, Undius Kogoya, ambushed and killed four TPNPB members from Mimika regency who had entered his territory in Beoga, Puncak regency, on 20 April 2023. Kogoya justified his actions by claiming that the Mimika group and its leader, Joni 'Botak' Beanal, had defected and joined the WPA. See Alfons Nedabang, 'Komandan Sorong Samarai Gussby Waker Bantah Joni Botak Cs Pengkianat KKB Papua,' [Sorong Samarai Commander Gussby Waker denies Joni Botak was a traitor to Papua armed criminal group], *Pos Kupang*, 26 April 2023.
18. Author interview with Frits Ramandey, Papuan representative for the National Commission on Human Rights, October 2023.

Data Appendix

Number of violent events, by country, 1 July 2023–30 June 2024

Number of violent events (defined by the Armed Conflict Location & Event Data Project (ACLED) as battles, explosions/remote violence or violence against civilians) from 1 July 2023–30 June 2024. Data collected on 23 July 2024.

Source: IISS calculation based on data from the Armed Conflict Location & Event Data Project (ACLED), www.acleddata.com.

	Number of violent events
Russia–Ukraine*	42,788
Israel–Palestinian Territories**	14,676
Syria	11,385
Myanmar	9,890
Brazil	7,743
Mexico	6,486
Lebanon	6,350
Iraq	6,037
Sudan***	5,693
Nigeria	3,756
Somalia	2,615
Cameroon	2,483
Yemen	2,395
Colombia	2,302
Ethiopia	2,152
Democratic Republic of the Congo	1,931
India	1,760
Pakistan	1,755
Mali	1,581
Burkina Faso	1,476
Afghanistan	766
Haiti	758

	Number of violent events
Philippines	692
South Sudan****	455
Nagorno-Karabakh**	439
Niger	421
Honduras	413
Central African Republic	283
Indonesia	250
Mozambique	227
Turkiye	206
Uganda	147
Thailand	124
Libya	114
Chad	81
El Salvador	39
Egypt	23

*Refers to Ukraine data only.

**The figure represents the sum of events for the two parties involved in the conflict. For the Nagorno-Karabakh conflict, it represents the sum of events for Armenia and Azerbaijan.

***Includes the Abyei area per the source classification.

****Does not include the Abyei area per the source classification.

Number of fatalities due to violent events, by country, 1 July 2023–30 June 2024

Number of reported fatalities due to violent events (defined by ACLED as battles, explosions/remote violence or violence against civilians) from 1 July 2023–30 June 2024. Data collected on 23 July 2024.

Source: IISS calculation based on data from the Armed Conflict Location & Event Data Project (ACLED), www.acleddata.com.

	Number of fatalities
Israel–Palestinian Territories*	41,318
Russia–Ukraine**	37,014
Myanmar	16,169
Sudan***	15,159
Nigeria	9,295
Burkina Faso	8,245
Ethiopia	8,179
Mexico	7,396
Somalia	7,172
Brazil	6,640
Syria	6,545
Mali	4,532
Democratic Republic of the Congo	3,952
Yemen	2,372
Pakistan	2,290
Cameroon	2,118
Colombia	1,807
Niger	1,597
Haiti	1,490
Iraq	1,061
India	967
Afghanistan	963

	Number of fatalities
South Sudan****	944
Philippines	733
Lebanon	640
Central African Republic	634
Nagorno-Karabakh*	565
Honduras	476
Mozambique	406
Chad	241
Indonesia	163
Uganda	157
Libya	131
Turkiye	76
Thailand	62
El Salvador	36
Egypt	21

*The figure represents the sum of fatalities for the two parties involved in the conflict. For the Nagorno-Karabakh conflict, it represents the sum of fatalities for Armenia and Azerbaijan.
**Refers to Ukraine data only.
***Includes the Abyei area per the source classification.
****Does not include the Abyei area per the source classification.

Number of refugees (total), counted by country of origin, as of 31 December 2023

Number of refugees, not including asylum seekers, under the mandate of the United Nations High Commissioner for Refugees (UNHCR), and Palestinian refugees recorded by the UN Relief and Works Agency for Palestine Refugees in the Near East (UNRWA).

A refugee is someone who is unable or unwilling to return to their country of origin owing to a well-founded fear of being persecuted for reasons of race, religion, nationality, membership of a particular social group or political opinion (as per the UNHCR 1951 Refugee Convention). In the case of Palestinian refugees, these are persons whose normal place of residence was Palestine during the period 1 June 1946–15 May 1948, and who lost both their home and means of livelihood as a result of the 1948 conflict.

Data from UNHCR and UNRWA is updated to 31 December 2023 and was collected on 16 June 2024.

Sources: UNHCR, www.unhcr.org/refugee-statistics/download; and UNRWA, 'Refugee Data Finder', www.unhcr.org/refugee-statistics/download/?url=p7aBkY.

	Number of refugees
Afghanistan	6,403,144
Syria	6,355,788
Israel–Palestinian Territories*	5,968,636
Russia–Ukraine**	5,960,362
South Sudan	2,292,482
Sudan	1,496,923
Myanmar	1,283,426
Democratic Republic of the Congo	978,209
Somalia	842,044
Central African Republic	759,187
Nigeria	410,308
Iraq	329,032
Mali	249,046
Nagorno-Karabakh***	173,170
Ethiopia	158,344
Turkiye	127,738
Haiti	122,139
Colombia	115,513
Cameroon	110,715
Pakistan	94,481
Honduras	84,363
El Salvador	68,633
Burkina Faso	54,869
Yemen	48,044
India	25,319
Niger	24,794
Egypt	23,160
Mexico	21,869
Libya	17,958
Indonesia	11,756
Chad	10,196
Uganda	8,376
Lebanon	7,392
Brazil	3,798
Philippines	645
Thailand	222
Mozambique	117

*Refers to Palestinian Territories data only.
**Refers to Ukraine data only.
***The figure represents the sum of refugees for Armenia and Azerbaijan.

Number of internally displaced persons (total), by country, as of 31 December 2023

Total number of internally displaced persons (IDPs) due to conflict and violence recorded by the Internal Displacement Monitoring Centre (IDMC).

IDPs are persons or groups of persons who have been forced or obliged to flee or to leave their homes or places of habitual residence, in particular as a result of or in order to avoid the effects of armed conflict, situations of generalised violence, violations of human rights or natural or human-made disasters, and who have not crossed an internationally recognised state border (as per the 1998 UN Guiding Principles on Internal Displacement).

Data from the IDMC is as of 31 December 2023 for all countries except Egypt, for which the data is as of 31 December 2020, collected on 27 July 2024.
Source: IDMC, www.internal-displacement.org/database/displacement-data.

	Number of IDPs (conflict and violence)
Sudan*	9,053,000
Syria	7,248,000
Democratic Republic of the Congo	6,734,000
Colombia	5,077,000
Yemen	4,516,000
Afghanistan	4,187,000
Somalia	3,862,000
Russia–Ukraine**	3,689,000
Nigeria	3,340,000
Ethiopia	2,852,000
Myanmar	2,625,000
Burkina Faso	2,063,000
Israel–Palestinian Territories***	1,910,000
Iraq	1,124,000
South Sudan*	1,121,000
Turkiye	1,099,000
Cameroon	1,044,000
Nagorno-Karabakh***	665,600
India	613,000
Mozambique	592,000
Central African Republic	512,000
Chad	452,000
Mexico	392,000
Niger	347,000
Mali	344,000
Haiti	311,000
Libya	119,000
Philippines	113,000
Honduras	101,000
Lebanon	74,000
Indonesia	55,000
El Salvador	49,000
Thailand	41,000
Pakistan	23,000
Brazil	16,000
Uganda	4,800
Egypt	3,200

*Does not include 42,000 IDPs in the Abyei area.
**Refers to Ukraine data only.
***The figure represents the sum of IDPs for the two parties involved in the conflict. For the Nagorno-Karabakh conflict, it represents the sum of IDPs for Armenia and Azerbaijan. For the conflict in Israel–Palestinian Territories, it only includes Palestinian IDPs since there is no data available for Israel.

Number of foreign countries 'involved' in the conflict, by country, as of 30 June 2024

Number of foreign countries deemed to be involved in the conflict.

For *internal conflicts*, foreign countries are considered 'involved' if they are either present through the deployment of military capabilities (outside of a multilateral mission as defined in the Armed Conflict Global Relevance Indicator (ACGRI)) or if they meet all the following criteria: presence of intelligence assets; provision of military financial support; role in an advisory or operational command-and-control capacity; and sale or transfer of military equipment.

For *inter-state conflicts*, foreign countries are considered 'involved' if they are either present through the deployment of military capabilities (outside of a multilateral mission as defined in the ACGRI) or if they meet two or more of the following criteria: presence of intelligence assets; provision of military financial support; role in an advisory or operational command-and-control capacity; and sale or transfer of military equipment. The numbers indicated in the table refer to the scores used for the purpose of the ACGRI calculation.*

Data collected on 26 June 2024 from the Military Balance+. Military-aid data for Ukraine is from 30 April 2024, collected on 28 June 2024 from the Ukraine Support Tracker by the Kiel Institute for the World Economy, and covers the time period from 1 February 2022–30 April 2024.

Sources: IISS calculation based on data from the Military Balance+, milbalplus.iiss.org; and Christoph Trebesch et al., 'The Ukraine Support Tracker: Which Countries Help Ukraine and How?', Kiel *Working Paper*, no. 2218, 2024, pp. 1–75.

	Foreign countries 'involved'	Number of foreign countries
Russia–Ukraine**	Belarus Denmark France Germany Netherlands Poland Sweden United Kingdom United States	9
Syria	Iran Israel Russia Turkiye United States	5
Yemen	Iran Saudi Arabia United Arab Emirates United States (*Operation Poseidon Archer*)***	5
Iraq	Iran Turkiye United States (*Operation Inherent Resolve*)***	4
Democratic Republic of the Congo	Burundi Rwanda Uganda	3
Lebanon	Iran Israel United States	3

	Foreign countries 'involved'	Number of foreign countries
Somalia	Turkiye United Kingdom United States	3
Central African Republic	Russia Rwanda	2
Israel–Palestinian Territories	Iran United States	2
Libya	Russia Turkiye	2
Nagorno-Karabakh	Russia Turkiye	2
Niger	Russia United States	2
Burkina Faso	Russia	1
Chad	France	1
Ethiopia	Eritrea	1
Mali	Russia	1
Mozambique	Rwanda	1
Nigeria	United Kingdom	1
Afghanistan	None	0
Brazil	None	0
Cameroon	None	0

	Foreign countries 'involved'	Number of foreign countries
Colombia	None	0
Egypt	None	0
El Salvador	None	0
Haiti	None	0
Honduras	None	0
India	None	0
Indonesia	None	0
Mexico	None	0
Myanmar	None	0
Pakistan	None	0
Philippines	None	0
South Sudan	None	0
Sudan	None	0
Thailand	None	0
Turkiye	None	0
Uganda	None	0

*For the purpose of the ACGRI calculation, any involvement of the Russian paramilitary Wagner Group (or Africa Corps) is counted as Russia's involvement given that the group's structure has largely been subsumed into the Russian Ministry of Defence following the death of its chief Yevgeny Prigozhin in August 2023.
**Refers to Ukraine data only. Support includes the provision of weapons, equipment and financial aid with military purposes as per the Ukraine Support Tracker by the Kiel Institute for the World Economy.
***In the case of involvement of coalitions of countries, the name of the coalition and the country leading it are displayed. Each coalition is assigned a score of two for the purposes of the ACGRI calculation.

Number of UNSC resolutions concerning conflicts under review, by country, 1 July 2023–30 June 2024 Number of resolutions announced by the UN Security Council (UNSC) between 1 July 2023 and 30 June 2024 concerning the country and conflict under review. Countries for which no resolution was announced receive a value of 0.
Source: IISS calculation based on data from UNSC, www.un.org/securitycouncil/content/resolutions-0.

	Number of resolutions
Somalia	7
Sudan	5
Israel–Palestinian Territories	4
Libya	4
South Sudan	4
Yemen	4
Afghanistan	3
Haiti	3
Central African Republic	2
Colombia	2
Democratic Republic of the Congo	2
Iraq	2
Lebanon	1
Brazil	0
Burkina Faso	0
Cameroon	0
Chad	0
Egypt	0

	Number of resolutions
El Salvador	0
Ethiopia	0
Honduras	0
India	0
Indonesia	0
Mali	0
Mexico	0
Mozambique	0
Myanmar	0
Nagorno-Karabakh	0
Niger	0
Nigeria	0
Pakistan	0
Philippines	0
Russia–Ukraine	0
Syria	0
Thailand	0
Turkiye	0
Uganda	0

Number of military personnel deployed by major geopolitical powers in conflict-affected countries, by country, as of 30 June 2024*

Total number of military personnel deployed into conflict-affected countries by geopolitical powers within the G20 group (including unilaterally, as part of a combat coalition or a mission under the aegis of an international organisation and excluding deployments which are not conflict related). Data collected on 26 June 2024, except for the data for Ukraine, which was collected on 1 September 2024.

Source: IISS calculation based on data from the Military Balance+, milbalplus.iiss.org.

	Number of personnel deployed
Russia–Ukraine**	425,000
Syria	8,140
Iraq	7,437
Nagorno-Karabakh***	5,130
Democratic Republic of the Congo	4,650
Lebanon	4,579
South Sudan	3,802
Yemen	2,500
Chad	1,500
Niger	1,100
Sudan	734
Libya	661
Egypt	625
Somalia	548
Honduras	400
Philippines	300
Central African Republic	271
Israel–Palestinian Territories***	100
Nigeria	80
Colombia	70
Mozambique	13
India****	12
Pakistan****	12
Afghanistan	0
Brazil	0
Burkina Faso	0
Cameroon	0
El Salvador	0
Ethiopia	0
Haiti	0
Indonesia	0
Mali	0
Mexico	0
Myanmar	0
Thailand	0
Turkiye	0
Uganda	0

*The variable covers only deployments related to the specific conflict. This means that either the deployed military forces are conflict parties or that the deployment has an explicit mandate to assist the conflict parties with training and capability building.
**Refers to Russian deployments in Ukraine.
***The figure represents the sum of deployments in the two parties involved in the conflict. For the Nagorno-Karabakh conflict, it represents the sum of deployments in Armenia and Azerbaijan.
****The personnel deployed as part of the UN Military Observer Group in India and Pakistan are attributed to both India and Pakistan.

Number of operational peacekeeping, special political and military missions, and other multilateral missions concerning conflicts in countries under review, as of 30 June 2024

Number of multilateral peacekeeping operations, special political and military missions, and other multilateral presences under the aegis of international organisations present in a country. These include missions undertaken by the UN, regional organisations or ad hoc groups related to UN sanctions/UNSC resolutions or endorsed by the UN and other international organisations.

Data refers to active missions as of 30 June 2024 that fulfil the two following criteria: 1) objective (relating to multidimensional peace and conflict resolution) and 2) geographical scope (relating to the number of multilateral peacekeeping operations, special political and military missions, and other multilateral presences under the aegis of international organisations present in a country). The numbers indicated in the table refer to the scores used for the purpose of the ACGRI calculation.

Data collected on 26 June 2024 from the Military Balance+, Stockholm International Peace Research Institute's (SIPRI) Map of Multilateral Peace Operations 2024 published in May 2024 and the UN Special Political Missions and Other Political Presences 2024 published in April 2024.

Sources: IISS calculations based on data from the Military Balance+, milbalplus.iiss.org; SIPRI, www.sipri.org/publications/2024/other-publications/sipri-map-multilateral-peace-operations-2024; UN Political and Peacebuilding Affairs, www.dppa.un.org/en/dppa-around-world; and the official websites of the UN, European Union, regional organisations and ad hoc coalitions.

	Names of missions	Number of missions
Central African Republic*	African Union (AU) Mission for the Central African Republic and Central Africa (MISAC)	5
	EU Advisory Mission in the Central African Republic (EUAM RCA)	
	EU Training Mission in the Central African Republic (EUTM RCA)	
	Special Envoy of the Secretary-General for the Great Lakes Region of Africa	
	UN Multidimensional Integrated Stabilization Mission in the Central African Republic (MINUSCA)	
	UN Regional Office for Central Africa (UNOCA)	
Somalia*	AU Transition Mission in Somalia (ATMIS)	4.5
	EU Capacity Building Mission in Somalia (EUCAP Somalia)	
	EU Training Mission Somalia (EUTM Somalia)	
	Special Envoy of the Secretary-General for the Horn of Africa	
	UN Assistance Mission in Somalia (UNSOM)	
Israel–Palestinian Territories	EU Border Assistance Mission for the Rafah Crossing Point (EUBAM Rafah)	4
	EU Police and Rule of Law Mission for the Palestinian Territory, EU Coordinating Office for Palestinian Police Support (EUPOL COPPS)	
	UN Special Coordinator for the Middle East Peace Process (UNSCO)	
	UN Truce Supervision Organization (UNTSO)	
Mali*	AU Mission for Mali and the Sahel (MISAHEL)	3.5
	EU Capacity Building Mission Sahel Mali (EUCAP Sahel Mali)	
	EU Training Mission Mali (EUTM Mali)	
	UN Office for West Africa and the Sahel (UNOWAS)	

	Names of missions	**Number of missions**
South Sudan*	Intergovernmental Authority on Development (IGAD) Ceasefire and Transitional Security Arrangements Monitoring and Verification Mechanism (CTSAMVM) Special Envoy of the Secretary-General for the Great Lakes Region of Africa Special Envoy of the Secretary-General for the Horn of Africa UN Mission in the Republic of South Sudan (UNMISS) UN Office to the AU (UNOAU)	3.5
Democratic Republic of the Congo*	Southern African Development Community (SADC) Mission in the Democratic Republic of Congo (SAMIDRC) Special Envoy of the Secretary-General for the Great Lakes Region of Africa UN Organization Stabilization Mission in the Democratic Republic of the Congo (MONUSCO) UN Regional Office for Central Africa (UNOCA)	3
Iraq	EU Advisory Mission in support of Security Sector Reform in Iraq (EUAM Iraq) NATO Mission Iraq (NMI) UN Assistance Mission for Iraq (UNAMI)	3
Lebanon	Special Envoy for Implementation of Security Council Resolution 1559 UN Interim Force in Lebanon (UNIFIL) UN Special Coordinator for Lebanon (UNSCOL)	3
Libya	AU Mission in Libya EU Border Assistance Mission in Libya (EUBAM Libya) UN Support Mission in Libya (UNSMIL)	3
Chad*	G5 Sahel Joint Force (FC-G5S) Multinational Joint Task Force (MNJTF) UN Office for West Africa and the Sahel (UNOWAS) UN Regional Office for Central Africa (UNOCA)	2.5
Sudan*	Special Envoy of the Secretary-General for the Great Lakes Region of Africa Special Envoy of the Secretary-General for the Horn of Africa UN Interim Security Force for Abyei (UNISFA) UN Office to the AU (UNOAU)	2.5
Colombia	Organization of American States (OAS) Mission to Support the Peace Process in Colombia (MAPP/OEA) UN Verification Mission in Colombia (UNVMC)	2
Ethiopia*	AU Monitoring, Verification and Compliance Mission (AU-MVCM) Special Envoy of the Secretary-General for the Horn of Africa UN Office to the AU (UNOAU)	2
Haiti	Multinational Security Support Mission (MSSM) to Haiti UN Integrated Office in Haiti (BINUH)	2
Mozambique	EU Training Mission in Mozambique (EUTM Mozambique) Southern African Development Community Mission in Mozambique (SAMIM)	2
Nagorno-Karabakh	EU Mission in Armenia (EUMA) Personal Representative of the Chairperson-in-Office on the conflict dealt with by the Organization for Security and Co-operation in Europe (OSCE) Minsk Conference	2
Russia–Ukraine**	EU Advisory Mission Ukraine (EUAM Ukraine) EU Military Assistance Mission in support of Ukraine (EUMAM Ukraine)	2
Yemen	Special Envoy of the Secretary-General for Yemen UN Mission to Support the Hudaydah Agreement (UNMHA)	2

	Names of missions	Number of missions
Burkina Faso*	Multinational Joint Task Force/Accra Initiative (MNJTF/AI) UN Office for West Africa and the Sahel (UNOWAS)	1.5
Cameroon*	Multinational Joint Task Force (MNJTF) UN Regional Office for Central Africa (UNOCA)	1.5
Niger*	Multinational Joint Task Force (MNJTF) UN Office for West Africa and the Sahel (UNOWAS)	1.5
Nigeria*	Multinational Joint Task Force (MNJTF) UN Office for West Africa and the Sahel (UNOWAS)	1.5
Afghanistan	UN Assistance Mission in Afghanistan (UNAMA)	1
India***	UN Military Observer Group in India and Pakistan (UNMOGIP)	1
Myanmar	Special Envoy to the Secretary-General on Myanmar	1
Pakistan***	UN Military Observer Group in India and Pakistan (UNMOGIP)	1
Syria	Special Envoy of the Secretary-General for Syria	1
Uganda*	Special Envoy of the Secretary-General for the Great Lakes Region of Africa Special Envoy of the Secretary-General for the Horn of Africa	1
Brazil	None	0
Egypt	None	0
El Salvador	None	0
Honduras	None	0
Indonesia	None	0
Mexico	None	0
Philippines	None	0
Thailand	None	0
Turkiye	None	0

*Multi-country political missions are assigned a score of 0.5 for the purposes of the ACGRI calculation.
**Refers to Ukraine data only as it is the theatre of the conflict.
***UNMOGIP is attributed a score of one for both India and Pakistan for the purposes of the ACGRI calculation.

Humanitarian funding (in US$), by recipient country, as of 31 December 2023

Total reported incoming funding from governments and multilateral organisations, by recipient country, in 2023. This includes financial funding received by local governments, multilateral organisations, non-governmental organisations, pooled funds, private organisations and Red Cross and Red Crescent organisations operating in the country under review. Data collected in July 2024.

Source: UN Office for the Coordination of Humanitarian Affairs, Financial Tracking Service, fts.unocha.org.

	Total funding (US$ millions)
Russia–Ukraine*	3,249.7
Syria	2,489.1
Yemen	2,033.4
Afghanistan	1,663.2
Israel–Palestinian Territories*	1,562.9
Ethiopia	1,556.7
Sudan	1,297.4
Somalia	1,231.6
South Sudan	1,177.2
Turkiye	1,095.0
Democratic Republic of the Congo	986.0
Lebanon	661.7
Nigeria	595.9
Chad	494.0
Myanmar	406.1
Burkina Faso	372.0
Colombia	348.3
Central African Republic	337.3
Haiti	319.0
Pakistan	317.3
Niger	310.7
Mozambique	263.8
Mali	248.5
Uganda	226.9
Cameroon	151.5
Iraq	149.5
Honduras	104.7
Egypt	98.0
Libya	88.9
Nagorno-Karabakh**	55.7
Mexico	38.7
El Salvador	30.9
Philippines	27.6
Brazil	22.8
Thailand	14.8
Indonesia	11.6
India	1.3

*Refers to Ukraine and Palestinian Territories data only.
**Represents the sum of funding for Armenia and Azerbaijan.

Gini index, by country, latest available data

The Gini index measures the extent to which the distribution of income (or, in some cases, consumption expenditure) among individuals or households within an economy deviates from a perfectly equal distribution. A Lorenz curve plots the cumulative percentages of total income received against the cumulative number of recipients, starting with the poorest individual or household. The Gini index measures the area between the Lorenz curve and a hypothetical line of absolute equality, expressed as a percentage of the maximum area under the line. Thus, a Gini index of 0 represents perfect equality, whilst an index of 100 implies perfect inequality.

Source: World Bank, data.worldbank.org/indicator/SI.POV.GINI?most_recent_year_desc=true.

	Gini index	Year
Colombia	54.8	2022
Brazil	52.0	2022
Mozambique	50.5	2019
Honduras	48.2	2019
Democratic Republic of the Congo	44.7	2020
Turkiye	44.4	2021
South Sudan	44.1	2016
Mexico	43.5	2022
Central African Republic	43.0	2021
Uganda	42.7	2019
Cameroon	42.2	2021
Haiti	41.1	2012
Philippines	40.7	2021
El Salvador	38.8	2022
Indonesia	38.3	2023
Israel	37.9	2021
Burkina Faso	37.4	2021
Chad	37.4	2022
Yemen	36.7	2014
Mali	35.7	2021

	Gini index	Year
Nigeria	35.1	2018
Ethiopia	35.0	2015
Thailand	34.9	2021
Sudan	34.2	2014
Palestinian Territories*	33.7	2016
Niger	32.9	2021
India	32.8	2021
Egypt	31.9	2019
Lebanon	31.8	2011
Myanmar	30.7	2017
Pakistan	29.6	2018
Iraq	29.5	2012
Armenia	27.9	2022
Azerbaijan	26.6	2005
Syria	26.6	2022
Ukraine	25.6	2020
Afghanistan	N/A	N/A
Libya	N/A	N/A
Somalia	N/A	N/A

*Refers to the West Bank and Gaza as per the source classification.

GDP per capita, constant prices, purchasing power parity (international dollars), per country, 2023

GDP per capita represents the constant price purchasing-power-parity terms of final goods and services produced within a country during a specified time period divided by the total population. It is expressed in 2017 international dollars. Data collected on 30 July 2024 from the World Economic Outlook (April 2024) by the International Monetary Fund (IMF).

Source: IMF, www.imf.org/en/Publications/WEO/weo-database/2024/April.

	GDP per capita
Israel	44,335
Turkiye	33,284
Mexico	19,247
Thailand	17,915
Libya	17,242
Colombia	15,890
Brazil	15,192
Armenia	15,071
Azerbaijan	14,963
Egypt	13,619
Indonesia	12,945
Ukraine	10,722
Iraq	10,436
Lebanon*	9,988
El Salvador	9,307
Philippines	8,890
India	7,054
Honduras	5,786
Pakistan	5,662
Palestinian Territories**	5,393
Nigeria	5,004
Myanmar	4,105

	GDP per capita
Cameroon	3,739
Sudan	3,698
Ethiopia	2,909
Haiti	2,677
Uganda	2,563
Afghanistan***	2,329
Burkina Faso	2,180
Mali	2,130
Yemen	1,712
Chad	1,449
Niger	1,277
Mozambique	1,243
Democratic Republic of the Congo	1,168
Somalia	1,121
Central African Republic	915
South Sudan	410
Syria	N/A

*As of 2022.
**Refers to the West Bank and Gaza as per the source classification.
***As of 2020.

Functioning of government, by country, 2023

The functioning of government, a pillar of the Economist Intelligence Unit (EIU) Democracy Index, assesses the effectiveness of the system of checks and balances on the exercise of government authority as well as elements such as openness and transparency of government, public access to information, government accountability, pervasiveness of corruption, and public confidence in government and political parties. The functioning of government is scored on a 0–10 scale (higher is better). Data collected on 30 June 2024 from the EIU Democracy Index 2023. **Source:** EIU, www.eiu.com/n/campaigns/democracy-index-2023/.

	Functioning of government
India	7.9
Indonesia	7.9
Israel	7.5
Colombia	6.1
Thailand	6.1
Brazil	5.4
Turkiye	5.0
Armenia	4.6
Mexico	4.6
Philippines	4.6
Pakistan	4.3
Honduras	3.9
Nigeria	3.9
Uganda	3.6
Egypt	3.2
El Salvador	3.2
Ethiopia	3.2
Ukraine	3.1
Azerbaijan	2.5
Burkina Faso	2.5
Cameroon	2.1
Mozambique	1.4
Niger	1.1
Lebanon	0.8
Democratic Republic of the Congo	0.4
Afghanistan	0.1
Palestinian Territories	0.1
Sudan	0.1
Central African Republic	0
Chad	0
Haiti	0
Iraq	0
Libya	0
Mali	0
Myanmar	0
Syria	0
Yemen	0
Somalia	N/A
South Sudan	N/A

Climate-change vulnerability score, by country, 2022
The Notre Dame Global Adaptation Initiative (ND-GAIN) vulnerability score summarises a country's exposure, sensitivity and capacity to adapt to the negative externalities of climate change across six sectors: food, water, health, ecosystems, habitats and infrastructure. It is scored on a 0–1 scale (higher is better). Data collected on 26 July 2024.
Source: ND-GAIN, www.gain.nd.edu/our-work/country-index/.

	ND-GAIN vulnerability score
Chad	0.7
Somalia	0.7
Afghanistan	0.6
Central African Republic	0.6
Democratic Republic of the Congo	0.6
Mali	0.6
Niger	0.6
Sudan	0.6
Uganda	0.6
Burkina Faso	0.5
Cameroon	0.5
Ethiopia	0.5
Haiti	0.5
Honduras	0.5
India	0.5
Mozambique	0.5
Myanmar	0.5
Nigeria	0.5
Pakistan	0.5
Philippines	0.5
Syria	0.5
Yemen	0.5
Armenia	0.4
Azerbaijan	0.4
Brazil	0.4
Colombia	0.4
Egypt	0.4
El Salvador	0.4
Indonesia	0.4
Iraq	0.4
Lebanon	0.4
Libya	0.4
Mexico	0.4
Thailand	0.4
Turkiye	0.4
Ukraine	0.4
Israel	0.3
Palestinian Territories	N/A
South Sudan	N/A

Criminal markets, by country, 2023

Criminal markets, a sub-pillar of the criminality component of the Global Initiative Against Transnational Organized Crime (GI-TOC)'s Global Organized Crime Index, assesses political, social and economic systems surrounding all stages of the illicit trade in or exploitation of commodities or people.

In the latest iteration of the index, 15 criminal markets are included. Both the value and reach of each market are assessed. The 'value' refers to the entire value chain (e.g., from income generated from the production of the commodity to profits earned selling the finished product). Meanwhile, 'reach' may be thought of as the non-monetary impact of a criminal market – in other words, the level of pervasiveness that a particular illicit market has achieved in a society. The 'reach' of a market may be determined by a number of factors, including the number of people affected; the number or kinds of victims; the extent of illicit flows; the degree of violence involved in the market; and whether the commodity is in decline or renewable. The assessment of both the value and reach of each criminal market is based on expert assessments and supplemented with information gathered during the data-collection period.

Criminal markets are scored on a 1–10 scale (lower is better). Data collected on 30 June 2024 from the GI-TOC Global Organized Crime Index 2023.
Source: GI-TOC, www.ocindex.net/.

	Criminal markets
Mexico	8.1
Myanmar	7.7
Nigeria	7.4
Colombia	7.3
Afghanistan	7.0
Brazil	6.9
Russia	6.8
Thailand	6.8
Turkiye	6.8
India	6.7
Indonesia	6.6
Libya	6.6
Philippines	6.6
Mali	6.5
Syria	6.4
Uganda	6.4
Iraq	6.3
Lebanon	6.3
Pakistan	6.3
Ukraine	6.3
Cameroon	6.2
Democratic Republic of the Congo	6.2
Ethiopia	6.1
Honduras	6.0
Mozambique	5.9
Burkina Faso	5.8
Haiti	5.8
Niger	5.7
Central African Republic	5.6
Yemen	5.6
El Salvador	5.4
Somalia	5.3
Sudan	5.2
Chad	5.1
Egypt	5.1
South Sudan	5.1
Israel	5.0
Azerbaijan	4.1
Armenia	2.9
Palestinian Territories	N/A

Ecological threats, by country, 2023

The Institute for Economics and Peace (IEP)'s Ecological Threat Report (ETR) assesses four categories of threats directly related to drivers of conflict, including food insecurity, natural disaster, water risk and demographic pressures. The resulting composite indicator is scored on a 1 (very low)–5 (severe) scale, depending on the severity of the risks. A country's overall ETR score is the maximum score of any of its categories. Thus, if a country has at least one indicator score of 'severe', its overall ETR score will be rated as severe, or 5. Data collected on 30 June 2024 from the IEP ETR.

Source: ETR 2023, www.economicsandpeace.org/wp-content/uploads/2023/12/ETR-2023-web.pdf.

	ETR
Afghanistan	5.0
Burkina Faso	5.0
Cameroon	5.0
Central African Republic	5.0
Chad	5.0
Democratic Republic of the Congo	5.0
Ethiopia	5.0
Haiti	5.0
Iraq	5.0
Mali	5.0
Mozambique	5.0
Myanmar	5.0
Niger	5.0
Nigeria	5.0
Palestinian Territories	5.0
Somalia	5.0
South Sudan	5.0
Sudan	5.0
Syria	5.0
Uganda	5.0

	ETR
Yemen	5.0
Thailand	4.6
Indonesia	4.5
Philippines	4.5
Honduras	4.3
Azerbaijan	4.2
Colombia	4.1
India	4.1
Pakistan	4.1
El Salvador	4.0
Brazil	3.9
Armenia	3.2
Egypt	3.2
Israel	3.2
Lebanon	3.0
Libya	3.0
Mexico	3.0
Russia	2.9
Ukraine	2.3
Turkiye	2.0

Total mineral production as a percentage of GDP, by country, 2022

Total mineral raw-materials production in millions of US dollars as a percentage of GDP. Data collected on 30 June 2024.

Sources: IISS calculation based on data from World Mining, www.world-mining-data.info/?World_Mining_Data___Data_Section; and IMF, www.imf.org/en/Publications/WEO/weo-database/2024/April.

	Total mineral production (% GDP)
Libya	96.9
South Sudan	64.0
Iraq	63.5
Democratic Republic of the Congo	50.3
Mozambique	45.9
Azerbaijan	41.2
Russia	31.7
Chad	27.8
Mali	22.3
Indonesia	18.8
Burkina Faso	18.3
Colombia	14.4
Nigeria	13.1
Sudan	12.9
Myanmar	11.1
Yemen	10.2
Brazil	9.1
India	8.9
Egypt	8.1
Mexico	7.4

	Total mineral production (% GDP)
Cameroon	7.2
Armenia	7.1
Niger	6.7
Ukraine	6.7
Philippines	4.2
Pakistan	4.1
Turkiye	3.6
Central African Republic	3.5
Afghanistan	3.4
Thailand	2.5
Israel	1.7
Honduras	0.8
Ethiopia	0.3
El Salvador	0.0
Lebanon	0.0
Uganda	0.0
Haiti	N/A
Palestinian Territories	N/A
Somalia	N/A
Syria	N/A

Armed groups, by region, as of 30 July 2024*

Number of armed groups by region. This data is drawn from the International Committee of the Red Cross's (ICRC) annual survey on armed groups completed by all ICRC delegations in July 2024.

Source: Matthew Bamber-Zryd, 'ICRC Engagement with Armed Groups in 2024', ICRC Humanitarian Law & Policy, 31 October 2024, blogs.icrc.org/law-and-policy/2024/10/31/icrc-engagement-with-armed-groups-in-2024/.

Region**	Number of armed groups
Sub-Saharan Africa***	195
Middle East and North Africa	89
Americas	84
Asia	76
Europe and Eurasia	11

*The ICRC uses the generic term 'armed group' for a group that is not a state but has the capacity to cause violence that is of humanitarian concern. Armed groups also include those groups that qualify as conflict parties to a non-international armed conflict according to the Geneva Conventions, which the ICRC defines as 'non-state armed groups'.

**The regional figure refers to the sum of armed groups active in the countries covered by the ICRC survey in each region. The survey was completed by the following ICRC offices (as listed by the ICRC): Brazil, Colombia, El Salvador, Guatemala, Haiti, Honduras, Mexico, Nicaragua, Paraguay, Peru and Venezuela for the Americas; Egypt, Iraq, Islamic Republic of Iran, Israel and the Occupied Territories, Jordan, Kuwait (regional), Lebanon, Libya, Syrian Arab Republic, Turkiye and Yemen for the Middle East and North Africa; Abidjan (regional), African Union, Algeria, Burkina Faso, Central African Republic, Chad, Dakar (regional), Democratic Republic of the Congo, Eritrea, Ethiopia, Kampala (regional), Mali, Mauritania, Mozambique, Nairobi (regional), Niger, Nigeria, Pretoria (regional), Somalia, South Sudan, Sudan, Tunis (regional) and Yaoundé (regional) for Sub-Saharan Africa; Armenia, Azerbaijan, Balkans (regional), Brussels, Budapest (regional), Georgia, Greece, London (regional), Moscow (regional), Paris (regional), Republic of Moldova Tashkent (regional) and Ukraine for Europe and Eurasia; and Afghanistan, Bangkok (regional), Bangladesh, Beijing (regional), Jakarta (regional), Kuala Lumpur (regional), Myanmar, New Delhi (regional), Pakistan, Philippines, Sri Lanka and Suva (regional) for Asia.

***Includes Algeria as per the source classification for Africa.

Population living under either the full or contested control of armed groups, in millions, by region, as of 30 July 2024*

People living in areas under the full or contested control of armed groups, in millions. This data is drawn from the International Committee of the Red Cross's (ICRC) annual survey on armed groups completed by all ICRC delegations in July 2024.

Source: Matthew Bamber-Zryd, 'ICRC Engagement with Armed Groups in 2024', ICRC Humanitarian Law & Policy, 31 October 2024, blogs.icrc.org/law-and-policy/2024/10/31/icrc-engagement-with-armed-groups-in-2024/.

Region**	Population under the full or contested control of armed groups (millions)
Sub-Saharan Africa***	102
Americas	41
Middle East and North Africa	40
Asia	26
Europe and Eurasia	0.7

*The ICRC uses the generic term 'armed group' for a group that is not a state but has the capacity to cause violence that is of humanitarian concern. Armed groups also include those groups that qualify as conflict parties to a non-international armed conflict according to the Geneva Conventions, which the ICRC defines as 'non-state armed groups'.

**The regional figure refers to the sum of armed groups active in the countries covered by the ICRC survey in each region. The survey was completed by the following ICRC offices (as listed by the ICRC): Brazil, Colombia, El Salvador, Guatemala, Haiti, Honduras, Mexico, Nicaragua, Paraguay, Peru and Venezuela for the Americas; Egypt, Iraq, Islamic Republic of Iran, Israel and the Occupied Territories, Jordan, Kuwait (regional), Lebanon, Libya, Syrian Arab Republic, Turkiye and Yemen for the Middle East and North Africa; Abidjan (regional), African Union, Algeria, Burkina Faso, Central African Republic, Chad, Dakar (regional), Democratic Republic of the Congo, Eritrea, Ethiopia, Kampala (regional), Mali, Mauritania, Mozambique, Nairobi (regional), Niger, Nigeria, Pretoria (regional), Somalia, South Sudan, Sudan, Tunis (regional) and Yaoundé (regional) for Sub-Saharan Africa; Armenia, Azerbaijan, Balkans (regional), Brussels, Budapest (regional), Georgia, Greece, London (regional), Moscow (regional), Paris (regional), Republic of Moldova Tashkent (regional) and Ukraine for Europe and Eurasia; and Afghanistan, Bangkok (regional), Bangladesh, Beijing (regional), Jakarta (regional), Kuala Lumpur (regional), Myanmar, New Delhi (regional), Pakistan, Philippines, Sri Lanka and Suva (regional) for Asia.

***Includes Algeria as per the source classification for Africa.

Number of armed groups providing public services or extracting taxes, by region, as of 30 July 2024*

Number of armed groups providing public services to or extracting taxes from the population under their full or contested control, by region. This data is drawn from the ICRC's annual survey on armed groups completed by all ICRC delegations in July 2024.

Source: Matthew Bamber-Zryd, 'ICRC Engagement with Armed Groups in 2024', ICRC Humanitarian Law & Policy, 31 October 2024, blogs.icrc.org/law-and-policy/2024/10/31/icrc-engagement-with-armed-groups-in-2024/.

Region**	Number of armed groups providing public services or extracting taxes
Sub-Saharan Africa***	157
Americas	81
Middle East and North Africa	65
Asia	51
Europe and Eurasia	11

*The ICRC uses the generic term 'armed group' for a group that is not a state but has the capacity to cause violence that is of humanitarian concern. Armed groups also include those groups that qualify as conflict parties to a non-international armed conflict according to the Geneva Conventions, which the ICRC defines as 'non-state armed groups'.

**The regional figure refers to the sum of armed groups active in the countries covered by the ICRC survey in each region. The survey was completed by the following ICRC offices (as listed by the ICRC): Brazil, Colombia, El Salvador, Guatemala, Haiti, Honduras, Mexico, Nicaragua, Paraguay, Peru and Venezuela for the Americas; Egypt, Iraq, Islamic Republic of Iran, Israel and the Occupied Territories, Jordan, Kuwait (regional), Lebanon, Libya, Syrian Arab Republic, Turkiye and Yemen for the Middle East and North Africa; Abidjan (regional), African Union, Algeria, Burkina Faso, Central African Republic, Chad, Dakar (regional), Democratic Republic of the Congo, Eritrea, Ethiopia, Kampala (regional), Mali, Mauritania, Mozambique, Nairobi (regional), Niger, Nigeria, Pretoria (regional), Somalia, South Sudan, Sudan, Tunis (regional) and Yaoundé (regional) for Sub-Saharan Africa; Armenia, Azerbaijan, Balkans (regional), Brussels, Budapest (regional), Georgia, Greece, London (regional), Moscow (regional), Paris (regional), Republic of Moldova Tashkent (regional) and Ukraine for Europe and Eurasia; and Afghanistan, Bangkok (regional), Bangladesh, Beijing (regional), Jakarta (regional), Kuala Lumpur (regional), Myanmar, New Delhi (regional), Pakistan, Philippines, Sri Lanka and Suva (regional) for Asia.

***Includes Algeria as per the source classification for Africa.

Index

A

Abraham Accords 110, 112, 139, 140, 158
Afewerki, Isais 182
Afghanistan 11, 274–275, *275*, 277–279, *280*, 281–284, *289*, 290, *292*, 296, 300–302, 306
    Afghan Civil War (1992–96) 292, 295
    Afghan National Defence and Security Forces (ANDSF) 292, 296
    anti-Taliban resistance groups 286, 296
    chargés d'affaires (CDAs) in 287–288
    Doha process 287–288, 294, 300
    Hazaras 286, 290, 294–295
    Taliban 11, 275, 277–278, 281–282, 290, 295–296, 299, 301, 303, 308
    women's rights in 278, 281, 286–287, 290, 293–294
Afghanistan War (2001–2021) 293, 295
Africa Corps (formerly Wagner Group) 7, 97, 82, 85, 99–100, 158–160, 171, 173, 175, 188, 190, 196, 200, 202, 227–228, 231
African Union (AU) 173–174, 177, 184, 205, 209, 214, 253, 255
    Transition Mission in Somalia (ATMIS) 185, 268
    Mission in Somalia (AMISOM) 253, 255, 257
Ahmed, Abiy 172, 183, 244–246
Akhundzada, Hibbatullah 282, 287, 294–295
al-Dulaimi, Laith 134
Algeria 158, 199
Al Haj Murad Ebrahim 328
al-Halbousi, Mohammed 117, 134
Alliance of Sahel States (AES) 10, 171, 174, 188, 194–195, 199, 201
al-Qaeda 112, 129, 132, 163–164, 175, 207–208, 253, 256, 279, 287, 292, 295–296, 299, 303
    al-Qaeda in the Arabian Peninsula (AQAP) 152–154
    Group to Support Islam and Muslims (JNIM) 174–175, 180, 187–189, 192, 194, 196, 199–201
    Jund al-Islam 164
al-Sadr, Muqtada 134
al-Sudani, Mohammed Shia' 134
Angola 55, 260, 273
Ansar Beit al-Maqdis (ABM) 163–164
Arab–Israeli War (1973) 139, 144
Arab League 128
Arab Spring 110–111
Argentina 9, 21, 28, 34, 37, 57
Aristide, Jean-Bertrand 60, 62
Armenia 10, 78–79, 82–85, 106
    Armenian armed forces 105
Assad, Bashar al- 115, 122, 126–131, 160
Assimi, Goïta 189
Association of Southeast Asian Nations (ASEAN) 279, 312
Aung San Suu Kyi 311, 313
Australia 23, 41, 99
Azerbaijan 5, 10, 78–79, 82–85, 106, 115
    Azerbaijani armed forces 105

B

Bahrain 110, 115, *123*, 139–140, *184*
Bancroft (private security company) 228
Bangladesh 274, 276, 284
Barak, Ehud 145
Barre, Mohammed Siad 252–253
Barrio 18 67–69, 72, 75
    Revolucionarios 66, 69
    Sureños 66, 69
Bashagha, Fathi 158
Bashir, Omar al- 232–233, 235
Bathily, Abdoulaye 158

Bazoum, Mohamed 178, 199
Belarus 82–83, 85–86, 99, 160
Benin 177, 180, 209
Biden, Joe 85, 98, 115, 118, 140, 281
Bihi, Muse Abdi 183
Bin Laden, Osama 295
Biya, Franck 214
Biya, Paul 214
Black Sea Grain Initiative 98
Boko Haram *see* Jama'atu Ahlis Sunna Lidda'awati wal-Jihad (JAS) (Boko Haram)
Bolivia 28–29, *35*, 37, 57
Bolsonaro, Jair 30
Borrell, Josep 91–92
Bosnia-Herzegovina 10, 78, 90, *91*, 92–93
    Republika Srpska (RS) 90, 92–93
Botswana 273
Bozizé, François 226–227, 230
Brazil 21–22, *21*, 24, 26, 29–30, 34, *35*, 37, *54*, 59
    Amazon 55–56, 58
    Crime Syndicate (Rio Grande do Norte State) 55
    Family of the North (FDN) 54, 58
    First Capital Command (PCC) 26, 31, 34, 37, 51–52, 54–58
    Friends of Friends (ADA) 57–58
    Guardians of the State (Ceará State) 55
    homicide rate 56
    Military Police of Rio de Janeiro (PMERJ/PM) 56
    militias 58
    Pure Third Command (TCP) 58
    Red Command (CV) 26, 51–52, 54, 57
BRICS 92
Bukele, Nayib 24, 27, 30, 67–68
Bulgaria 78
Burhan, Abdel Fattah al- 233
Burkina Faso 7, 10–11, 160, 171, *171*, 173–177, 179–180, 188–189, *192*, 196, 199–201, 222
    2022 coup 172, 193
    Ansarul Islam 192
    Burkina Faso Armed Forces 195
    Group to Support Islam and Muslims (JNIM) 194
    Volunteers for the Defense of the Homeland (VDP) 193–195
Burundi 256
    Burundi National Defence Force (FDNB) 264
    Resistance for the Rule of Law (RED Tabara) 259

C

Cabo Verde 55
Calderón, Felipe 40–41, 43
Cameroon *171*, 174, 209, *212*, 217, 222, 229
    Ambazonia Governing Council (AGC) 209, 212, 214, 216
    anglophone separatism 213–214, 216–217
    Cameroonian armed forces 215
    Interim Government of Ambazonia (IG) 212, 214–215
    Southern Cameroons Defence Forces (SOCADEF) 212, 215–216
Camp David Accords (1978) 162, 164
Canada 213
Castro, Xiomara 73
Central African Republic 160, *171*, 173, 221, 222, *226*, 231, 235
    anti-balaka groups 226–227, 229–230
    Central African Armed Forces (FACA) 227–230
    Central African Patriotic Movement (MPC) 227–228, 230
    Patriots for Change (CPC) 227, 230
    Political Agreement on Peace and Reconciliation (APPR) (2019)

227–228, 230
Popular Front for the Renaissance of Central Africa (FPRC) 227, 229–230
Rapid Intervention Battalion (BIR) 228
Return, Reclamation, Rehabilitation (3R) 227, 229
Séléka 226, 229–230
Union for Peace in the Central African Republic (UPC) 227, 229
Chad 159, 160, *171*, 172, 175–177, 180, 200, 205, 209, 213, *220*, 224, 229–230, 234–235, 237
2024 election 221
Chadian armed forces 223
civil war (1965–90) 220
Front for Change and Concord in Chad (FACT) 220, 222–223
Military Command Council for the Salvation of the Republic (CCMSR) 223
Patriotic Salvation Movement (MPS) 222
transitional military council (CMT) 220
Union of Resistance Forces (UFR) 223
Chérizier, Jimmy 62, 63
Chile 9, 21, 28, 30, *35*, 37
China 7, 11, 28, 34, *35*, 37, 41, 82, 85, 90–91, 93, 110, 112–113, 115, 168, 215, 275, 277–278, 282, 284, 287–288, 293, 300, 302, 312–313, 315, 326
Belt and Road Initiative (BRI) 93
Collective Security Treaty Organisation (CSTO) 105
Colombia 9, *21*, 22, *23*, 24–27, 29, 31, 34, *35*, 36, *48*, 57–58, 73
Central General Staff (EMC) 26–27, 31, 49–50, 52
Colombian armed forces 49, 51
Gulf Clan 26–27, 50–51
National Liberation Army (ELN) 26–27, 29, 34, 49, 50–51
Operation Orion 25
Plan Colombia 25, 49–50
Revolutionary Armed Forces of Colombia (FARC) 26, 36, 49–50, 52
Second Marquetalia 27, 49
'total peace' initiative 50
United Self-Defense Forces of Colombia (AUC) 49, 51
Vida Colombia Strategy 50
Combined Joint Task Force–*Operation Inherent Resolve* (CJTF–OIR) 110–112, 126, 128, 131, 135–136
Compaoré, Blaise 192
Conville, Garry 62
Costa Rica *23*, 28
Côte d'Ivoire 177
Croatia 92
Cuba 24, 28
Czech Republic 84

D

Dbeibah, Abdul Hamid 157
Déby Itno, Idriss 220, 223
Déby Itno, Mahamat Idriss 180, 220, 222
Democratic Republic of the Congo 7, 10–11, 13, 170–179, *171*, 229, 242, *258*, 264, 267–268, 273
2023 election 260
2024 coup attempt 172, 177, 260
2024 elections 172
Anti-M23 'Wazalendo' coalition 260, 262
Armed Forces of the Democratic Republic of the Congo (FARDC) 260–262, 264
Cooperative for the Development of the Congo (CODECO) 260, 262
Mai-Mai (Mayi-Mayi) groups 263
March 23 Movement (M23) 10, 172–173, 176–177, 259–263
Deni, Said Abdullahi 254
Djibouti 182, 184, *184*, 256
Djotodia, Michel 226
Dodik, Milorad 92
Dominican Republic *23*, 29
drug trafficking 22, 24, 26, 28, 37, 46, 55, 57–58, 67–68, 72–73, 75, 316
Caipira Route 55
cocaine 21–22, 24–26, 29, 37, 44–46, 48, 50–52, 55, 57–58, 68–69, 73, 75
heroin 45
opium 277, 287–288, 294
synthetic drugs 9, 21–22, 25–26, 28–29, 34–37, 41, 44–46, 75, 128, 287
Durrani, Asif 300
Duterte, Rodrigo 329

E

East African Community Regional Force (EACRF) 172, 174, 260, 264
Economic Community of West African States (ECOWAS) 7, 171, 173–174, 177, 179, 194, 199, 201, 206
Ecuador 9, 21–22, *23*, 25, 27–31, 34, *35*, 36
2024 state of exception 36
homicide rate 36
Los Choneros 36
Los Lobos 22, 31, 36
Egypt 11, *109*, 110, 112, 117, 140, 156–157, 159, *162*, 165, 175, 182, *184*, 194–195, 234–235
2011 revolution 162
2013 military coup 156, 162
Belal Mosque attaack (2017) 164
Egyptian Armed Forces (EAF) 163, 164
Military Intelligence and Reconnaissance Department 164
Operation Sinai 163
Philadelphi Corridor 164
Sinai Tribes Union (STU) 163, 165
El Salvador 24–25, 27–28, 30–31, *66*, 69, 74–75
2022 state of exception 24, 67–69, 73
Centre for the Confinement of Terrorism (CECOT) 67–68
civil war (1979–92) 66, 68–69
El Salvador armed forces 68
homicide rate 67
National Civil Police (PNC) 68
environmental crime 9, 22, 26, 28, 34, 36–37, 42, 46, 48, 51–52, 55, 173
Erdoğan, Recep Tayyip 128, 160
Eritrea 182–183, *184*, 235–236, 245–248, 255
Eritrean Defence Forces (EDF) 182, 247, 249
Ethiopia 7, 170, *171*, 172, 175, 177, 179, 185, 234, 237, 240–241, 243, *244*, 249, 254–256, 267
2024 memorandum of understanding with Somaliland 172, 175, 177, 179, 185
Amhara Region 172, 183, 246–249
Anyuaks 240, 246
Ethiopian National Defence Force (ENDF) 182–183, 247
Ethiopian People's Revolutionary Democratic Front (EPRDF) 245
fano 246–249
Gambella Liberation Front (GLF) 248
Oromo Liberation Army (OLA) 183, 246, 248
Prosperity Party 182, 245, 246 *see also* Ethiopian People's Revolutionary Democratic Front (EPRDF)
Regional Special Police 246, 248–249
Tigray Defence Force (TDF) 183
Tigray People's Liberation Front (TPLF) 182–183, 245–248
Tigray War (2020–22) 172, 177, 183, 245, 247–249 *see also* Pretoria Agreement
European Union 25, 28, 78, 87, 93, 99, 104, 110, 152, 154, 166, 175, 189, 200, 209, 229, 255, 257, 271, 288
EU Training Mission (EUTM) (Mozambique) 271, 272

F

FARC *see* Revolutionary Armed Forces of Colombia (FARC)
Faye, Bassirou Diomaye 180
Finland 81
France 11, 82, 105, 109, 113, 140, 147, 164, 171, 175, 179, 186, 200, 213, 215, 220–223, 227–228, 268
French armed forces 224
Operation Barkhane 186, 193, 224
Fulani 187–188, 192, 194–195, 200, 205–206, 208–209, 213, 229
Funes, Mauricio 67

G

G5 174, 193
G5 Sahel 222
G20 306
Gabon 172, 214, 228
Gadhafi, Muammar 156, 189
Gantz, Benny 140
García Luna, Genaro 41
Gatwech, Simon Dual 242
Georgia 79, 81–84
Germany *23*, 82, 84, 98, 113, 147, 164
Ghana 177

Goïta, Assimi 187–188, 190, 194
Greece 78
Guatemala 25–26, 69, 74
Guinea 172, 200

H

Habré, Hisène 220
Haftar, Belqasim 158
Haftar, Khalifa 156–160, 222
Haftar, Saddam 158
Haiti 9, 13, *21*, 22, 26–31, *60*
  5 Segond 63
  G9 30, 61–63
  G-Pèp 30, 61–62, 64
  Grand Ravine 63
  Haitian National Police (PNH) 63
  La Saline massacre (2018) 60
  Multinational Security Support Mission (MSS) 9, 26, 28, 31, 62, 63
  Transitional Presidential Council (TPC) 62
  Viv Ansanm coalition 62–63
Hammad, Osama 158
Haniyyeh, Ismail 114, 141
Harris, Kamala 115
Hasina, Sheikh 284
Hassan Sheikh Mohamud 184–185
Hausa 205, 208–209
Hemeti (Mohamed Hamdan Dagalo) 233, 235
Henry, Ariel 31, 61–62, 64
herder–farmer violence 194, 200, 209, 213–214, 221–222, 262
Hernández, Juan Orlando 31, 73
Honduras *21*, 24–27, 31, *35*, 69, *72*, 75
  2022 state of exception 73
  coca cultivation 74
  homicide rate 73
  International Commission against Impunity in Honduras (CICIH) 73
  Military Police of Public Order (PMOP) 74
  National Police 74
Hungary 92, 222
Hussein, Saddam 132

I

IMF 284, 300
India 7, 11, 15, 34, *35*, 105, 116, 274, *275*, 276, 277–282, *280*, 284, 287–288, 300, 302, 309, *318*, 323
  Assam Rifles 320
  Bharatiya Janata Party (BJP) 284, 305–306
  Central Reserve Police Force (CRPF) 307, 321
  Chhattisgarh 320
  Communist Party of India–Maoist (CPI-Maoist) 276, 319, 320, 323
  Coordination Committee (CorCom) 322
  Indian Armed Forces 307–308, 320
  Kuki separatism 282, 319, 321
  Line of Control (LoC) 300–301
  Manipur 280, 282, 319, 320, 322
  Naga separatism 319, 321
  National Socialist Council of Nagalim–Isak Muivah (NSCN–IM) 321
  People's Liberation Army of Manipur (PLAM) 282, 319, 322
  State Police Forces 321
  United National Liberation Front (UNLF) 280, 319, 322
  Working Committee 323
Indonesia 13, *275*, 279, *280*, 281, 283, 312, *334*, 337
  assassination of I Gusti Putu Danny Karya Nugraha 335
  Free Papua Organisation (OPM) 335, 337
  Indonesian National Armed Forces (TNI) 336
  Nduga hostage crisis (2023) 335
  West Papua Army (WPA) 337
  West Papua National Army (TNPB) 337
  West Papua National Liberation Army (TPNPB) 283, 335, 337
International Criminal Court (ICC) 118, 140, 230
Iran 7, 10, 22, 28, 82, 108–113, 115–116, 118, *123*, 126–128, 131, 133–134, 144, 146–147, 151–152, 163, 168, 175, *184*, 235, 283, 287–288, 294–295, 300, 306
  Iranian armed forces 130
  Iranian Revolution 120–122, 142, 147
  Islamic Revolutionary Guard Corps (IRGC) 109, 111, 118, 120–121, 124, 130, 134, 140–141, 143, 145–147
  Quds Force 120, 122, 130, 142
Iraq 7, *109*, 110–113, 115–118, 120–121, *123*, 124, 128, *132*, 136, 167
  2023 elections 134
  Badr Brigades 132
  Counter Terrorism Service (CTS) 135
  de-Ba'athification 132
  Iraqi Armed Forces 134–135
  Islamic Resistance in Iraq 121, 134
  Kurdish Peshmerga 111, 136
  Kurdistan Democratic Party (KDP) 134, 136
  Kurdistan Regional Government (KRG) 133–134, 136
  Kurdistan Workers' Party (PKK) 117, 133, 136
  Mahdi Army 132
  Patriotic Union of Kurdistan (PUK) 134, 136
  Popular Mobilisation Units (PMU) 111, 120, 133, 135–136
  Shi'ite Coordination Framework (SCF) 133–134
Iraq war (2003–11) 132
Islamic State (ISIS) 110, 112–113, 115–116, 120, 126–131, 133–136, 147, 153, 154, 175, 217, 270, 278, 282, 329, 331–333
  Ahlu Sunna wal Jama (ASWJ) 270–271, 273
  Allied Democratic Forces (ADF) (Islamic State Central Africa Province) (ISCAP) 259–260, 262–263, 268
  ISIS–Libya 112–113, 159
  Islamic State Central Africa Province (ISCAP) 273
  Islamic State in Somalia (ISS) 254, 256
  Islamic State Khorasan Province (ISKP) 10–11, 79, 83, 87, 274, 278–279, 281–282, 284, 286–287, 293–295, 300, 302
  Islamic State Sahel Province (ISSP) 187–188, 190, 192, 195, 199–201
  Islamic State West Africa Province (ISWAP) 178, 198, 206, 208, 213–217, 221, 223
  Sinai Province (Wilayat Sinai) 110, 163, 164
Israel 5, 7, 10, 31, 50, 104, *109*, 115–118, 120–122, 124, 127, 131, 133, *138*, 143, 148, 152, 153, 158, 162–164, 214–215, 326
  Israel Defense Forces (IDF) 10, 108, 112, 114, 118, 140–141, 147
Israel–Hamas war (2023–present) 5, 7–8, 10, 14–15, 28, 31, 50, 118, 120–122, 128, 133–134, 140, 142, 146, 152, 154, 158, 164, 177, 214, 286
  7 October attacks 10, 108, 113, 116, 121–122, 127, 139, 145–146, 163
  genocide case against Israel 117, 140
  Israeli hostages 108, 140
Italy *35*, 57, 105, 113, 147
  'Ndrangheta 34, 57

J

Jabhat Fateh al-Sham (formerly Jabhat al-Nusra) 147
Jama'atu Ahlis Sunna Lidda'awati wal-Jihad (JAS) (Boko Haram) 178, 198, 200, 205–207, 209, 213 217, 221, 223
Japan 99, 287
Johnson, Hilde 243
Jordan 108–109, 113, 116–117, 128, 134, 140

K

Kashmir 11, 14–15, 274, 276–280, *304*, 309, 318
  2019 changes to India's constitution 278, 305–306
  2021 India–Pakistan ceasefire 11, 305–306
  2024 Jammu and Kashmir election 284, 306
  Azad Jammu and Kashmir (AJ&K) 304, 307, 309
  Hizbul Mujahideen (HM) 305, 308
  Jammu and Kashmir (J&K) 277, 304–307, 309
  Jammu and Kashmir Police (JKP) 306–309
  Jammu Kashmir Liberation Front (JKLF) 305, 307
  Jaysh-e-Mohammad (JeM) 308
  Lashkar-e-Taiba (LeT) 305, 308
  Line of Control (LoC) 7, 11, 274, 280–281, 305–307, 309
  The Resistance Front (TRF) 309
Kazakhstan 85, 288
Kenya 26, 28, 31, 62, 64, 173, 180, 182, *184*, 235, 240, 256, 267, 269
Khamenei, Sayyid Ali 147
Khan, Imran 283, 300
Kiir, Salva 241–243
Koor, Akol 241
Kosovo 10, 78, 85, 90, *91*, 92–93
Kosovo war (1998–99) 90, 93
Kurti, Albin 91–92
Kyrgyzstan 79, 81, 85–87, 287

L

Lake Chad Basin 174, 205–206, 209, 213–216, 221–222
Laos 312
Lebanon 5, 13, 108, *109*, 111, 113, 115, 117, 120–122, *123*, *144*, 148
   2019 financial crisis 146
   Hizbullah 7, 108, 111–112, 114–115, 121–122, 124, 131, 140–142, 146–147, 150
   Lebanese Armed Forces (LAF) 145, 147
Lesotho 273
Libya *109*, 110, 112–115, 140, *156*, 160, 164, 220–221, 223–224, 234–237
   444 Brigade 157
   2011 revolution 156–157
   2020 ceasefire 157–158
   Government of National Accord *see* Government of National Unity (GNU)
   Government of National Stability (GNS) 157–158
   Government of National Unity (GNU) 157–160
   High Council of State (HCS) 158
   House of Representatives (HoR) 158–159
   Libyan Armed Forces (LAF) 159–160
   Libyan National Army (LNA) 157–160, 164, 222
   Operation Dignity 159
   Special Deterrence Force (SDF) 157
liquefied natural gas (LNG) 271
Lithuania 85
López Obrador, Andrés Manuel 42–43
Lula (Luiz Inácio Lula da Silva) 56

M

Machar, Riek 241–242
Macron, Emmanuel 228
Maduro, Nicolás 9, 22, 24, 27, 30–31, 34
Malawi 273
Malaysia 288, 324, 326–327
Mali 7, 10–11, 160, 171, *171*, 173–175, 177–179, *186*, 190, 192, 194, 199–222
   2020 coup 172, 187
   2021 coup 187
   Algiers accord 187–189
   Coordination of Azawad Movements (CMA) 187–189
   Malian Armed Forces (FAMa) 188–190
   Strategic Framework for the Defence of the People of Azawad (CSP-DPA) 188–189
   Tuareg separatism 187–189
Mara Salvatrucha (MS-13) 26–27, 37, 67–69, 72, 75
Marcos, Ferdinand Jr 329
Marcos, Ferdinand Sr 329
Marcos Willians Herbas Camacho ('Marcola') 56–57
Mauritania 222
Mexico 20, *21*, 22, *23*, 24–26, 28–31, *40*, 46, 69
   2024 elections 9, 22, 42
   Beltrán Leyva Organisation (BLO) 45
   Cartel Jalisco New Generation (CJNG) 9, 21, 26, 41–42, 44, 51–52
   Gulf Cartel 45
   homicide rate 42
   Los Zetas 34, 42, 45
   Mérida Initiative 25, 40, 43
   Mexico–US Bicentennial Framework for Security, Public Health, and Safe Communities 25, 41, 43
   Michoacán Family/Knights Templar (Cárteles Unidos) 30, 42, 44–46
   National Guard (GN) 42–43
   Secretariat of National Defence (SEDENA) 43
   Secretariat of the Navy (SEMAR) 43, 45
   Sinaloa Cartel 9, 21, 26, 36–37, 41–42, 44–46, 51–52
   Tijuana Cartel 46
Mnangagwa, Emmerson 178
Modi, Narendra 114, 284
Mohamed Al Senussi 158
Mohamed bin Zayed Al Nahyan 288
Moïse, Jovenel 30, 60–61
Moldova 87
Montenegro 90–91, *91*, 93
Mordisco, Ivan (Néstor Gregorio Vera Fernández) 31, 50
Morocco 110, 139–140
Morsi, Muhammad 162

Mozambique 55, 57, *171*, 172, 174–175, *270*, 273
   2023 elections 272
   2024 elections 272
   Frelimo 270, 272
   Mozambican Defence Armed Forces (FADM) 272
   Mozambican National Resistance (Renamo) 272
   Palma attack (2021) 271
   Police of the Republic of Mozambique (PRM) 272
   Renamo 272
Mubarak, Hosni 162
Mudzrimar, Sawadjaan 329, 332
Muhammad bin Salman Al Saud 288
Multinational Joint Task Force (MNJTF) 202, 205, 207, 209, 213–214, 217, 221, 223–224
Munir, Syed Asim 306
Muslim Brotherhood 141, 154, 159, 164
Myanmar 11, *275*, *280*, 284, *310*, 316
   1962 coup 311
   2021 coup 311–313, 315
   2024 conscription law 312
   Brotherhood Alliance (BHA) 276, 311–314, 316
   Chinland Council (CC) 314
   Communist Party of Burma (CPB) 310
   ethnic armed organisations (EAOs) 275–278, 281, 284, 311, 313–314
   Kachin Independence Army (KIA)/Kachin Independence Organisation (KIO) 315
   Karen National Liberation Army/Karen National Union (KNLA/KNU) 313–314
   Karenni Army (KA)/Karenni Nationalities Democratic Force (KNDF) 314
   Local People's Defence Forces (LPDFs) 313
   National League for Democracy (NLD) 311–312
   National Unity Consultative Council (NUCC) 313–314
   National Unity Government (NUG) 276, 278, 281, 313
   Nationwide Ceasefire Agreement (NCA) (2015) 311, 313–314
   Operation 1027 276, 311, 315–316
   People's Defence Force (PDF) 311, 313–314
   State Administration Council (SAC) 11, 276, 279, 282–284, 311–313, 315
   Tatmadaw *see* State Administration Council (SAC)
   United Wa State Army/United Wa State Party (UWSA/UWSP) 316

N

Nagorno-Karabakh 9–10, 14–15, 78–79, 85–86, *102*, 106
   2020 ceasefire agreement 103, 105–106
   depopulation of Armenians 10, 83, 85, 103–104
   First Nagorno-Karabakh War (1988–94) 83, 102, 104–105
   Nagorno-Karabakh Defence Army (NKDA) (disbanded) 10, 103, 105
   Republic of Artsakh 86, 103–105
   Second Nagorno-Karabakh War (2020) 102–103, 105
   Third Nagorno-Karabakh War (2023) 83, 85, 104
NATO 81, 84, 90, 92–93, 99, 156, 160, 168
Navalny, Alexei 86
Netanyahu, Benjamin 114, 140
Netherlands *23*, 57
Ne Win 311
Niger 5, 7, 11, 160, 171, *171*, 173–175, 177, 179–180, 188, 192, 194–195, *198*, 202, 205–206, 209, 222
   2023 coup 10, 171–172, 174–175, 178, 199, 201
   National Council for the Safeguard of the Homeland (CNSP) (junta) 200
   Niger Armed Forces (FAN) 200–202
Niger Delta 205–206
Nigeria 7, *171*, 174, 178–179, *204*, 209, 213–216
   2023 elections 172, 206
   armed bandits 205–206, 208
   farmer militias 209 *see also* Hausa
   Indigenous People of Biafra (IPOB) 209, 214
   Nigerian armed forces 205, 207, 209
Noboa, Daniel 36
North Korea 82
North Macedonia 78, 90–91, *91*, 93

O

Öcalan, Abdullah 166–167, 168
Olonyi, Johnson Thabo 242
Oman 115, *123*, *184*

P

Pakistan 7, 11, 15, 104, *275*, *280*, 284, 287–288, 294–296, *298*, 303, 309
  2024 elections 280, 283, 300
  Army Public School (TPP) (Pakistani Taliban) 299–300, 302
  Baloch Raaji Ajoi Sangar (BRAS) 282, 299, 302
  Baloch separatism 276, 299–300, 302, 306
  China–Pakistan Economic Corridor 301–302, 307
  Civil Armed Forces (CAF) 301
  Federally Administered Tribal Areas (FATA) 299, 301–302
  Jaish ul-Adl 300, 306
  Jamiat Ulema-e-Islam Fazl (JUI-F) 282, 294
  Khyber Pakhtunkhwa (KP) 298–299, 301–302, 306
  Operation Azm-e-Istehkam 300–301
  Operation Raad-ul-Fasaad 301
  Pakistan Armed Forces 301, 306–307
  Pakistan Muslim League–Nawaz 283, 300
  Tehreek-e-Insaf (PTI) 300
  Tehrik-e-Taliban Pakistan (TTP) (Pakistani Taliban) 275, 278–280, 287–288, 294–296, 300–303, 306
Palestinian Territories 5, 10, *109*, 110–111, 118, 120, *123*, *138*, 143, 152, 164
  Gaza Strip 113, 139–141
  Hamas 110–112, 115, 118, 121–122, 127, 133, 139–141, 143, 145, 163
  Palestinian Authority (PA) 114–115, 139
  Palestinian Islamic Jihad (PIJ) 108, 141, 143, 145
  West Bank 10, 108, 115, 139, 140, 143
Panama 23, 25, 27
Papua New Guinea 335, 337 *see also* Indonesia: Free Papua Organisation (OPM)
Paraguay 23, 28, 31, 34, *35*, 37, 57
Pashinyan, Nikol 104
Pelosi, Nancy 281
Peru 29, 57–58
Petro, Gustavo 22, 26–28, 49–50
Pezeshkian, Masoud 118
Philippe, Guy 62–63
Philippines *275*, 276, 280–282, *280*, *328*, 333
  2014 Comprehensive Agreement on the Bangsamoro (CAB) 330–331
  2025 elections 329, 330–331
  Abu Sayyaf Group (ASG) 329, 331–333
  Al-Khobar 333
  Ansar Khalifah Philippines (AKP) 333
  Armed Forces of the Philippines (AFP) 329–331, 333
  Bangsamoro Autonomous Region in Muslim Mindanao (BARMM) 329–331
  Bangsamoro Islamic Freedom Fighters (BIFF) 277, 329, 331–333
  Communist Party of the Philippines (CPP) 329
  Marawi 329, 331–332
  Maute Group 329, 331–333
  Moro Islamic Liberation Front (MILF) 328–331
  Moro National Liberation Front (MNLF) 328, 330–331
  New People's Army (NPA) 276, 281, 329–330, 333
  Philippine National Police (PNP) 330
  Sulu 330–332
Portugal 23, 57
Prabowo Subianto 336
Pretoria Agreement 177, 182–183, 245, 247, 249
Prigozhin, Pavel 160
Prigozhin, Yevgeny 7, 82, 97, 158, 160, 171 *see also* Africa Corps (formerly Wagner Group)
Putin, Vladimir 9, 78–79, 96, 98–99

Q

Qatar 112–113, 117, *123*, *184*, 287–288

R

Raisi, Ebrahim 118
Rehman, Fazl-ur- 282, 294
Russia 7, 11, 22, 28, 78, 83, 90, 92–93, 100, 102, 104–105, 112–113, 120, 126–128, 158–160, 164, 171, 173, 175, 180, 187, 193, 195–196, 214–215, 222, 227–229, 235, 278, 287–288, 313
  Armed Forces of the Russian Federation 99, 106, 130, 160
  Ministry of Defence 160
  Northern Fleet 160
Rwanda 7, 10, 13, 170–173, 177–178, 227–228, 258–261, 271, 272
  Democratic Forces for the Liberation of Rwanda (FDLR) 259
  Rwanda Defence Force (RDF) 230, 261, 263, 273
  Rwanda National Police (RNP) 273

S

Sall, Macky 178
Sánchez Cérén, Salvador 67
Saudi Arabia 109–111, 113, 115, 120–122, *123*, 140, 150–153, 175, *184*, 221, 234, 287–288
  Saudi Arabian armed forces 154
Schmidt, Christian 92
Senegal *23*, 180
  2024 election 180
Serbia 10, 78, 85, 90, *91*, 92–93, 228
Sharif, Nawaz 280, 300
Sharif, Shehbaz 283
Sheinbaum, Claudia 31, 42
Shekau, Abdukar 216
Sisi, Abdel Fattah al- 164
Six-Day War (1967) 139, 144
Soleimani, Qasem 120
Somalia 7, 117, 170, *171*, 172, 174–177, 179, 182, *184*, *252*, 257, 267
  Ahlu Sunna wal Jama (ASWJ) 254, 256
  al-Shabaab 172, 175–176, 179, 183–185, 247, 253–256
  clan militias 253–256
  Federal Government of Somalia 253–254
  Islamic Courts Union (ICI) 253, 256
  Somali National Army (SNA) 255
Somaliland 172, 175, 177, 179, 185, 246, 252, 254–255
  Las Anod conflict 184
  Somaliland National Army (SLNA) 255
  Somali National Movement (SNM) 255
South Africa 57, 117, 140, 215, 272–273
South African Development Community (SADC) 172–174, 271
  Mission in the Democratic Republic of the Congo (SAMIDRC) 260–261, 264
  Standby Force Mission in Mozambique (SAMIM) 172, 174, 271–273
South Korea 99
South Sudan *171*, 175, 177, 182, 229, 233–237, *238*, 243, 248, 267
  2015 Agreement on the Resolution of the Conflict in the Republic of South Sudan (ARCSS) 238, 240–242
  2018 Revitalised Agreement on the Resolution of the Conflict in the Republic of South Sudan (ARCSS) 239–243
  civil war (2013–18) 238, 241–243
  Kitgwang Declaration 242
  National Salvation Front–Thomas Cirillo (NAS–TC) 243
  National Security Service (NSS) 241
  Nuers 242, 246, 248
  South Sudan People's Defence Forces (SSPDF) 241
  Sudan People's Liberation Movement/Army–In Opposition (SPLM/A–IO) 238–243
  Sudan People's Liberation Movement/Army (SPLM/A) 232, 236, 238, 241
Spain *23*, 84
Storm Daniel (2023) 158
Sudan 5, 110, 139, 158–160, *171*, 172, 174–175, *184*, 220, 229, *232*, 237, 239–242, 248
  2019 coup 233, 235
  2021 coup 172, 233
  civil war (1983–2005) 232, 238
  civil war (2023–present) 8, 10–11, 120, 172, 175–177, 179–180, 221–222, 237, 239–241
  Juba Peace Agreement (JPA) 233–237
  Justice and Equality Movement (JEM) 236–237
  Rapid Support Forces (RSF) 10–11, 158–159, 172, 222, 233–236
  Sudan Armed Forces (SAF) 10–11, 158, 172, 179, 180, 222, 234–236, 241
  Sudan Liberation Movement/Army–Minni Minnawi (SLM/A–MM) 236
  Sudan Liberation Movement/Army–Abdel Wahid al-Nur (SLM/A–AW) 234, 236

Sudan People's Liberation Movement/Army–North (SPLM/A–N) 234, 236
Sweden 81
Syria 7, 81, *109*, 110–113, 115–116, 118, 120–122, *123*, *126*, 131, 145–146, 160, 164, 167–169
    ceasefire agreement (March 2020) 128
    Deir ez-Zor Military Council 128
    Hayat Tahrir al-Sham (HTS) 126, 128–129
    Homs Military Academy attack (5 October 2023) 128
    Occupied Golan Heights 111, 128, 139, 145–146
    Sweida protests 128
    Syrian Armed Forces (SAF) 110, 113, 126, 128–129, 130, 160
    Syrian Democratic Forces/People's Protection Units (SDF/YPG) 110, 113, 126, 128, 130, 167, 169
    Syrian National Army (SNA) 126, 128–129, 168, 169

T

Taiwan 7, 11, 281
Tajikistan 79, 81, 83, 85–86, 287
Tanzania 272–273
Tchiani, Abdourahmane 199
Thailand *275*, 276, 280–281, *280*, 283–284, 312, *324*
    2004 arms raid 325
    2014 coup 326
    2017 constitution 326
    Barisan Revolusi Nasional (BRN) 280, 325, 327
    Emergency Decree (2005) 325
    Internal Security Operations Command (ISOC) 326
    paramilitary and militia forces 326
    Patani Malay National Revolutionary Front *see* Barisan Revolusi Nasional (BRN)
    Patani United Liberation Organisation (PULO) 326–327
    Royal Thai Army 325–326
    Volunteer Defense Corps (VDC) 326
Tinuba, Bola Ahmed 206
Togo 177
Touadéra, Faustin-Archange 226–228, 231
Traoré, Ibrahim 189, 193–194, 196
Trump, Donald 28–29, 84, 92, 115, 293
Tshisekedi, Félix 172, 177, 179, 260
Turkiye 34, *35*, 82, 104, *109*, 110–113, 115, 117–118, 126–129, 133, 140, 156, 158–159, *166*, 169, 175, 182, 185, 188, 193, 195, 235, 254–255, 257, 275, 287–288
    Kurdistan Workers' Party (PKK) 111, 127, 168
    Newroz arrests (2024) 167
    Operation Claw-Lock 167
    Operation Euphrates Shield 131
    Operation Olive Branch 131
    Operation Peace Spring 131
    Turkish Armed Forces (TSK) 127, 131, 136, 160, 168
Turkmenistan 83, 85

U

Uganda 171, *171*, 177, 235, 239, 242, 255–256, 259–261, *266*, 269
    cattle rustling 267–269
    Karamojong ethnic militias 267, 269
    Lord's Resistance Army (LRA) 266
    Operation Shujaa 259, 260–261, 263, 267–268
    Turkana ethnic militias 269
    Uganda Peoples' Defence Forces (UPDF) 241, 260–261, 263, 266–268
Ukraine 5, *79*, *80*, *96*, 100, 160, 235
    Armed Forces of Ukraine 99
    Orange Revolution 96
    Revolution of Dignity 96
    Ukraine war (2022–present) 5, 9–10, 14–15, 28, 90–91, 93, 100, 105, 112, 160, 177, 214, 281, 286
    2014 annexation of Crimea and Donbas 81, 96, 99
    2015 Minsk II agreement 96
    2023 Ukranian counter-offensive 97
    2024 Kursk offensive 80, 84, 87, 98
    2024 Russian offensive 97–98
    2024 US aid package 84–85, 98
    UAV use 80, 84–87, 97–99
United Arab Emirates 11, 109–110, 122, *123*, 139–140, 152–153, 159–160, 164, 175, 182, *184*, 185, 194–195, 222, 234–236, 287–288
    United Arab Emirates armed forces 154
United Kingdom 81–82, 84, 92, 109–110, 113, 117, 140, 147, 152–154, 164, 207, 209, 255, 257, 287–288
United Nations 11, 24, 26, 35, 37, 73, 113, 127, 151, 158, 173, *176*, 177, 214, 229, 247, 249, 256, 268, 278–279, 283, 286–287, 293–294
    Multidimensional Integrated Stabilization Mission in Mali (MINUSMA) 11, 173–174, 178, 186–187, 222
    Multidimensional Integrated Stabilization Mission in the Central African Republic (MINUSCA) 228, 230–231
    Multinational Security Support Mission in Haiti (MSS) 26, 28, 31, 62–64
    Interim Force in Lebanon (UNIFIL) 148
    Interim Security Force for Abyei (UNISFA) 237
    Military Observer Group in India and Pakistan (UNMOGIP) 309
    Mission in the Republic of South Sudan (UNMISS) 243
    Organization Stabilization Mission in the DRC (MONUSCO) 11, 172–173, 259–261, 264
    Relief and Works Agency (UNRWA) 113
    United Nations Security Council (UNSC) 7, 15–16, 145, 151, 174, 185, 228, 286, 294
United States 7–8, 11, 21, *23*, 24–26, 29, 31, 34, 40–41, 44, 46, 49–50, 53, 69, 73, 81–82, 85, 90–93, 98–99, 104, 110–113, 115–117, 120–121, 126–128, 130, 132–134, 139–141, 146–147, 152–154, 156, 162–164, 166, 169, 175, 178, 180, 200, 207, 209, 214–215, 222–223, 227–228, 234, 253, 255–257, 268, 278, 281, 286–288, 293, 295–296, 312, 326, 330
    Department of Defense 130
    Drug Enforcement Administration (DEA) 34–36
    United States Army 130
Uruguay 9, 21, 28, *35*, 37
Utkin, Dmitry 160
Uzbekistan 81, 85, 87, 287–288

V

Venezuela 7, 9, 22, 24, 27–31, 34, *35*, 51–52, 57, 73
Vietnam 277
Villavicencio, Fernando 22, 29, 36
Vučić, Aleksandar 90–93

W

Wagner Group *see* Africa Corps (formerly Wagner Group)
Wang Yi 288

X

Xi Jinping 281

Y

Yeltsin, Boris 90
Yemen *109*, 110–111, 120, *123*, *150*, 154, 163, *184*
    2018 Stockholm Agreement 151
    al-Islah 154
    Hadrami Elite Forces 153
    Houthi movement (Ansarullah) 7, 110–112, 115, 117, 120–122, 140, 142, 154, 163, 177
    Joint Forces 153
    peace process 122, 152
    Presidential Leadership Council (PLC) 151–153
    Saudi-led coalition 122, 151–152, 154
    Southern Transitional Council (STC) 151–154

Z

Zambia 273
Zawahiri, Ayman al- 287, 295
Zelenskyy, Volodymyr 86–87
Zenawi, Meles 245

SUBSCRIPTION INFORMATION

The Armed Conflict Survey (Print ISSN 2374-0973, Online ISSN 2374-0981) is published annually for a total of one issue per year by Taylor & Francis Group, 4 Park Square, Milton Park, Abingdon, Oxon, OX14 4RN, UK.

Send address changes to Taylor & Francis Customer Services, Informa UK Ltd., Sheepen Place, Colchester, Essex CO3 3LP, UK.

Subscription records are maintained at Taylor & Francis Group, 4 Park Square, Milton Park, Abingdon, OX14 4RN, UK.

Subscription information:
For more information and subscription rates, please see tandfonline.com/pricing/journal/tarm. Taylor & Francis journals are available in a range of different packages, designed to suit every library's needs and budget. This journal is available for institutional subscriptions with online only or print & online options. This journal may also be available as part of our libraries, subject collections, or archives. For more information on our sales packages, please visit: librarianresources.taylorandfrancis.com.

For support with any institutional subscription, please visit help.tandfonline.com or email our dedicated team at subscriptions@tandf.co.uk.

Subscriptions purchased at the personal rate are strictly for personal, non-commercial use only. The reselling of personal subscriptions is prohibited. Personal subscriptions must be purchased with a personal check, credit card, or BAC/wire transfer. Proof of personal status may be requested.

Back issues:
Please visit https://taylorandfrancis.com/journals/customer-services/ for more information on how to purchase back issues.

Ordering information:
To subscribe to the Journal, please contact: T&F Customer Services, Informa UK Ltd, Sheepen Place, Colchester, Essex, CO3 3LP, United Kingdom. Tel: +44 (0) 20 8052 2030; email: subscriptions@tandf.co.uk.

Taylor & Francis journals are priced in USD, GBP and EUR (as well as AUD and CAD for a limited number of journals). All subscriptions are charged depending on where the end customer is based. If you are unsure which rate applies to you, please contact Customer Services. All subscriptions are payable in advance and all rates include postage. We are required to charge applicable VAT/GST on all print and online combination subscriptions, in addition to our online only journals. Subscriptions are entered on an annual basis, i.e., January to December. Payment may be made by sterling check, dollar check, euro check, international money order, National Giro or credit cards (Amex, Visa and Mastercard).

Disclaimer: The International Institute for Strategic Studies and our publisher Taylor & Francis make every effort to ensure the accuracy of all the information (the "Content") contained in our publications. However, The International Institute for Strategic Studies and our publisher Taylor & Francis, our agents (including the editor, any member of the editorial team or editorial board, and any guest editors), and our licensors make no representations or warranties whatsoever as to the accuracy, completeness, or suitability for any purpose of the Content. Any opinions and views expressed in this publication are the opinions and views of the authors, and are not the views of or endorsed by The International Institute for Strategic Studies and our publisher Taylor & Francis. The accuracy of the Content should not be relied upon and should be independently verified with primary sources of information. The International Institute for Strategic Studies and our publisher Taylor & Francis shall not be liable for any losses, actions, claims, proceedings, demands, costs, expenses, damages, and other liabilities whatsoever or howsoever caused arising directly or indirectly in connection with, in relation to, or arising out of the use of the Content. Terms & Conditions of access and use can be found at http://www.tandfonline.com/page/terms-and-conditions.

All Taylor & Francis Group journals are printed on paper from renewable sources by accredited partners.